Date Due

FE 17 '71			
AP 1 '71			
DE 1 '74			
NO 3 1975			

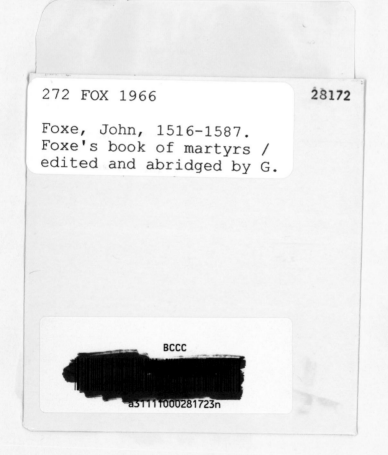

FOXE'S BOOK OF MARTYRS

FOXE'S BOOK OF MARTYRS

Edited and Abridged by

G. A. WILLIAMSON

LITTLE, BROWN AND COMPANY
Boston *Toronto*

Library of Congress Catalog Card No. 66–11277

First American Edition

Printed in Great Britain

CONTENTS

ILLUSTRATIONS

ACKNOWLEDGMENTS

I gratefully acknowledge the assistance which I have received from Mr R. H. Harries, Mr R. H. Mottram, Mr J. Hampden Jackson, and Miss Rachel Young, who have given expert help in the solving of historical, topographical and linguistic difficulties; and from my wife, who has patiently collaborated throughout in the making of this book.

G. W. A.

INTRODUCTION

In reviewing for *The Observer* Professor Haller's book, *Foxe's Book of Martyrs and the Elect Nation*, Mr Philip Toynbee wrote of the original work, 'Here is one of the most influential books both of our religious and of our literary history. It is also, alas, one of the most unreadable in its available forms; and it seems a pity that no modern publisher has thought of giving us a shortened and (perhaps) popular edition.' Mr Toynbee is right. In all its forms, available and unavailable, Foxe's vast work would try both the patience and the eyesight of present-day readers. The most recent edition was published nearly a century ago; and though it may be found lurking in the recesses of libraries here and there, like all its predecessors and all the fairly numerous abridgments, it is out of print. He would be a bold publisher who would risk reprinting the entire work at present-day costs; and as the mid-Victorian edition extended to eight bulky volumes, six thousand pages, and over four million words, no modern reader, unless a dedicated scholar, would face the gigantic task of reading it through. Yet the book is of immense historical value and much of it is of absorbing interest. It would be a sad loss to Englishmen whose hearts are stirred by the record of what their ancestors thought and did, what they believed in and were ready to die for, what sufferings they endured and what spirit they displayed, if they should be denied access to this unique source of information, and if one of the most famous and influential works in their language should be neglected and forgotten.

There is therefore a real need for the 'shortened and (perhaps) popular edition' which Mr Toynbee suggests. As another recent writer remarked, 'the present age demands above all brevity and conciseness.' We have already seen that not only the original work but all existing abridgments are out of print. Nor would these abridgments be to the taste of modern readers; for they were written, not to put those who lacked the means to buy huge expensive books or the time and patience to read them in a position to acquaint themselves with the gist of Foxe's book and to get a fair idea of its contents, but to do propaganda for the Protestant cause and to extract the last ounce out of the theme of martyrdom. Much of what Foxe had written—and his matter was very varied indeed—was omitted, new martyrdom-stories were added, and new illustrations, lurid and unauthentic, provided. Moreover his simple, outspoken, and sometimes colloquial language was bowdlerised and 'improved' in accordance with the elegant tastes of the eighteenth and early nineteenth centuries, one abridger even having the impudence to alter Tindall's memorable last utterance. It is to supply the needs of present-day readers that I have ventured to compose this book. Like all abridgments, it will fail to satisfy those who know and love the original work; but I trust that at least it will prove readable, and will give a true impression of what Foxe had to say. I have tried to keep the right proportion between political history, martyr-stories, arguments, the author's views, anecdotes, and jests; for our author did not lack a sense of humour. When John Wesley made an abridgment for the edification of his disciples, he omitted 'all the trash which that honest, injudicious writer has heaped together, and mingled with those venerable records which are worthy to be had in everlasting remembrance.' Perhaps this great man was justified, but I have not followed his example. I have kept the most trustworthy historical narratives: I have kept also stories which have been attacked as fictitious, and stories which even an uncritical reader will be unlikely to swallow. When arranging a small exhibition of a prolific artist's work, should one display only the best, or make the selection truly representative, including a due proportion of 'trash'?

Before going into any detailed explanation of the principles followed in the present abridgment let us consider how the original work came to be out of print. It would have surprised our ancestors if they had been told that this great book, which was a best-seller from the start, would one day pass out of circulation and become a vague memory to most people. When published it was an instant success; it went through four editions in its author's lifetime and through many more after his death, generation after generation for three hundred years. Its huge size, its great cost, and in at least the early days the fewness of what Foxe calls 'the learned' failed to prevent it from being from the publisher's point of view an unbroken and unqualified success. But in the last century two things happened. First, persecution was a thing of the past, and the fear which long after Mary Tudor was in her grave still hung over men's heads was forgotten. Forgotten too were the bitter controversies which had divided and inflamed the people of England so disastrously. Other things besides religion had begun to occupy men's minds, and life was full of new interests. Secondly, Foxe, whose reputation had long stood so high, surviving all attacks from his natural enemies, was now being criticised, and criticised very bitterly indeed, by scholars who were not 'Papists', and whom no one seemed able to refute. Foxe had once been esteemed next to the Bible; now the veracity of both was being impugned. It was not until this present generation that there was any attempt to restore Foxe to favour.

In 1940 appeared a work by J. F. Mozley entitled *John Foxe and His Book*. Mozley had made a meticulous study both of the book itself and of the criticisms which had been published a century before and had remained unanswered. He was able to vindicate both the integrity of Foxe and the remarkable accuracy of most of his statements, in addition to writing a most interesting account of the author, his strenuous life and voluminous works, and the subsequent fortunes of the one great book for which he is still remembered. Mozley's highly readable book was received with enthusiasm by the press, and as far as I am aware, his conclusions have not been challenged. In 1963 the book to which I referred in my first sentence, the work of Professor Haller, was published. It is on quite different lines from Mozley's, but equally interesting, equally well informed, equally fair and balanced, and equally convincing as proof that a study of Foxe is amply worth while. I hope that when readers of the present work have come to the end of the passages which I have selected from Foxe's book, they will go to bookshop or library and obtain both these excellent (and quite short) works.

Is the time opportune now for the republication of Foxe's book, if not as a whole, at least in some small part? I think it is. The huge sales of historical works, both learned and popular, are proof of a great and increasing thirst for knowledge about the life of our people in byegone times, the achievements of great men, the deeds—or 'facts', as Foxe would say—of both the famous and the infamous, and the conditions in which our humble ancestors passed their troubled days. And it would be hard to find a period so stimulating to twentieth-century imaginations as the century of the Tudor monarchs, above all the lifetime of the first Elizabeth, in whom we neo-Elizabethans take a very special interest—a lifetime the first twenty-five years of which provide the material for half of Foxe's book. The fact that life in the first Elizabethan age was very different from that in the second, so far from lessening the interest greatly increases it; and particularly so, in that while in our own age life is more secure than it has been at any time in our island story, for those who held strong and controversial opinions the earlier age was one of extreme danger, and the better a man was, the less likely he was to reach old age. Then a man must believe, or profess to believe, the accepted things, or the vengeance of potentate or prelate would descend upon him and destroy him. Now a man need believe nothing: so far from having to be the 'right' sort of Christian he need not be a Christian at all—he can openly repudiate and ridicule Christianity. Positive disbelief is growing, and half-hearted belief, indifference, and life without religion are to be seen on every side. To these things no dangers, humanly speaking, are attached, and the religious are more likely to be scorned by the irreligious than the irreligious by the religious—witness the letters in our best Sunday newspapers. It is hard for our generation to imagine a time when men, and women too, could be tortured and burnt at the stake for denying the metaphysical doctrine of transubstantiation, for possessing a New Testament, for saying the Lord's Prayer in English, for inscribing a text on a tavern wall, for inattendance at church, for eating flesh on a Friday. It is true that these things, though we naturally put them down to narrow-minded intolerance, did at least originate in religious ardour, and that such ardour is conspicuously lacking today; but at least we have discovered how to live together without treating each other in ways that would make angels weep. In those days Papists and Protestants were bitterly opposed. In later generations Protestantism was itself fissiparous, and until late in the last century sects were constantly multiplying. In some parts of the world this is happening still, but on the whole the movement now is increasingly towards unity—in this country dissenting bodies are uniting with each other, Nonconformists and Anglicans are coming ever closer together, and collaboration with Roman Catholics is proceeding at a rapidly increasing pace which augurs well for the future. There are still formidable obstacles to be surmounted before we can hope for the reunion of Christendom, but there is an unquestionable slackening of tension, and differences of doctrine and practice, at least between Canterbury and Rome, are being narrowed down.

Much more might be said on this subject, but for the moment I ask whether this extraordinary contrast between the two Elizabethan ages, the one so tempestuous, the other so placid, makes the documents to which the first gave birth less or more significant for us who live in the second. It is my belief that all who are prepared to study the writings of Foxe, even as compressed in this volume, will unhesitatingly answer 'more'.

Compression or abridgment involves many problems. Foxe's book is enormously long and very loosely constructed. Anything in the nature of a précis can be ruled out: we want Foxe's own words. Opinions will differ as to how the necessary shortening should be done, and it is well that I should save misunderstanding by explaining the method which I have followed in cutting the book down to about an eighteenth of its real length. I have combined a number of methods. In the first place, with the exception of the opening paragraph, I have omitted the whole of the first fifth of the book. Foxe originally started with Wickliffe; but when he found that his readers wanted as much as possible, he went back not only to the early days of Christianity in this realm but to the very beginning of Church history. He retold the stories which he had found in ancient writers, particularly Eusebius. Few of the reading public in Foxe's time had access to such a work as *The History of the Church*; but in our own time it is easy to obtain in modern English translations both this and the other works drawn upon, and no one will wish to read these thrilling and heart-warming stories as retold by an Elizabethan compiler. As for the history of *Ecclesia Anglicana* in its earlier phases, I felt that this could be more easily spared than the later history for which Foxe had better sources of information; and if we make Wickliffe our starting-point we have a unified work on the Reformation and its consequences.

In the second place, it would be a pity to keep Foxe's numerous and very lengthy accounts of events abroad at the cost of omitting many stories of events at home; so without any disrespect to his many valuable pages concerning Luther and Hus, and without implying that martyrdoms on the Continent mattered any less than martyrdoms in our own land, I have cut out almost every narrative of events abroad except the story of William Tindall, which could on no account be spared.

There being still far too much material left, the third step was to remove much that would only weary a modern reader not engaged in special research: bulls, decrees, sermons, and letters have almost all been omitted, though these are still of historical value, while some of the sermons are of great interest and many of the letters full of charm. Above all, the theological disputations which Foxe recorded at such enormous length, and which meant so much to those involved in, or on the fringe of, the conflicts that raged, particularly in Mary's time, would mean very little to a generation unacquainted with the formal logic of the Schoolmen, and unaware of the overwhelming importance of *Barbara, Celarent, Darii . . . Fesapo, Fresison.* So these disputations have been swept away, leaving only enough to show what charges were brought by the accusers, and what rebuttals were put forward by the 'answerers'.

The fourth necessity was to eliminate many of the stories which form the meat of the book. Some of these are told twice, and many are painfully alike, especially the stories of martyrdoms. Selection was necessary, and although I have retained many, perhaps too many, I have tried to include only those which differ in some way from each other, and which combine to give a complete and detailed picture of the terrible plight of those who came into collision with the authorities of the day. I have also given preference to stories that are interrelated by means of forward or backward references, and have omitted such as break the continuity of the narrative. This has made it unnecessary to insert any summaries of the passages omitted; indeed, it is my hope that while intruding no words of my own and allowing no voice but Foxe's to be heard I have managed to make the story much less desultory than it is in its original form.

Still further shortening was necessary, and after reducing the matter of the book in the four ways described, still further cutting down was possible by taking liberties with the author's language—not by altering a single word from beginning to end, but by careful omissions. The language could be simplified by leaving out words, phrases, or whole clauses. The Elizabethans loved a torrent of words, and there was little tautness in their language. Foxe himself was no stylist. His paragraphs, unless I am sadly mistaken, are improved by these omissions. He was no Gibbon, whose brilliant writing could never be treated in this way. Quite apart from irrelevant details and unwanted comments Foxe's writing is full of tautologies and pleonasms. It was a habit of the time. There are very many in the English Prayer Book. Here are a few specimens from Foxe—weighty and ponderous, bishops and prelates, smothered and stifled, false and untrue; speech or talk, tongue or language, peril or danger; dead corpse, secular layman, menacing threats, first protomartyr, superfluous excesses, to advance forward, she replying answered again.

In fairness to Foxe it must be stated that his prolixity did not equal that of some of his fellow countrymen. The full version of 'A Mandate of Thomas Arundell, directed to the Bishop of London, to warn men to worship the Holy Mother of God at the ringing of the morning bell as at the ringing of Curfew' has to be seen to be believed. The 'Writ or Mandate of Boner, Bishop of London, set up at Charing Cross, on Paul's Church door, and at St Martin's in the Field, for the citing and requiring out of the case of John Tooley' was over a thousand words long, where a hundred would more than suffice. Foxe, indeed, was anxious not to be prolix. Though it did not occur to him to avoid the use of superfluous words and to quicken his pace, he at least was chary of introducing any more matter. 'Considering how this present volume is grown already very large, I thought not to pester the same with any more superfluity than needs must.' And again, 'Because my purpose is to abridge and make short, I will here stay.' Moreover his readers, who could not have enough, begged him to make his giant of a book still bigger, but he refused to do so; nor did he ever write a further volume devoted to the reign of Elizabeth, though, as readers will note when they reach my last chapter, it was at one time his intention to do so. I have already mentioned that later editors and abridgers found the direct and simple English which he employed too direct and simple for them and tried to improve it. No such thing has been done in this abridgment: every word is Foxe's own, except the eleven brief chapter headings and a few clearly marked footnotes. The many headings printed in italics are all Foxe's own, though occasionally shortened. Where Foxe failed to provide a heading, I have left a space.

I have, as I say, changed no word that Foxe wrote. It follows that I have not corrected any of his grammatical peculiarities or inserted any missing words. He had a disconcerting habit of omitting the subjects of his verbs—or perhaps it was one of his collaborators, for this occurs in particular stretches of the book. Readers must mentally insert the missing pronouns—'he', 'she', 'it', or 'they', as the case may be. I have not followed the 1877 editors in altering dates suspected of being wrong. Are we certain that they are wrong? And if we once start correcting doubtful statements of fact, where are we to stop? Will the book still be Foxe's? A certain amount of modernisation, however, seems desirable. There is surely no point in inflicting on present-day readers the Old English type in which the bulk of the book was printed, or in arranging the print in fancy patterns where this was done by the first printers. Modern print and layout were substituted within a century of Foxe's death. Nor is there any virtue in retaining the original punctuation, with its multiplicity of commas, its colons introduced disconcertingly where no stop of any kind is required, its total lack of certain stops that we find useful today—the dash, the exclamation-mark, and above all the quotation marks in which we invariably enclose direct speech. These modifications, which are merely printers' devices, will make the book much easier to read. One further point. The old printers were extremely erratic and inconsistent in the use of capital and small letters, often beginning a common noun with a capital letter and a proper noun with a small letter: in one stretch of the book even God is denied a capital G. There would be no advantage in preserving these aberrations.

This brings us to the difficult question of Foxe's spelling, which varies from page to page and from line to line without apparent reason, but becomes more regular and more like ours in his later editions. It probably varied with the whim of the printer, and cannot be regarded as sacred. So incalculable is it that there is no distinction between strait and straight, between counsel and council, between travel and travail. To keep such spellings would be an unnecessary infliction on both compositor and reader. In this abridgment the spelling is standardised throughout, but genuinely different *forms* of words are retained, for example milner, sumner, amner, register, bare, spake, shronk. Retained also are completely obsolete words such as unneth, harborous, nott, postil, forbar, refricate. All these are of course explained in the Glossary.

And here let me digress from spelling to interject a warning which will be repeated later. The reader who finds a word which is wholly unfamiliar will no doubt readily turn to the Glossary, which is much easier than consulting a many-volumed dictionary, the only alternative where Foxe's rare words are concerned. It is a heavy task to dig these out, and a still heavier task to light upon the peculiar meanings with which he uses words still common. The danger is that the unwary reader will look up the unfamiliar words, but will pass over the everyday words, hundreds of which have unusual meanings in Tudor literature. Some of these words look so innocent that they are almost sure to be misunderstood if reading is rapid or careless. Some twenty-five words that appear in this abridgment are particularly dangerous, for instance 'while' in the sense still surviving in Yorkshire but not in

London or East Anglia, and 'namely' in the sense surviving nowhere, as far as I am aware. Misunderstanding of these words would be disastrous; so to assist the reader they are printed in the Glossary in capital letters; and though the other words may best be looked up as they appear in the text, I do urge every reader to look at the words printed in capitals before he starts to read *Acts and Monuments*, and to look at them again and again.

As I have digressed to issue one warning, I may as well add two more at this point. First, beware of misunderstanding adverbs and long adverbial phrases which are placed Latin fashion before infinitives and past participles in Foxe, but would follow them in modern English. Foxe, of course, never descends to the splitting of an infinitive. It is only too easy to misinterpret a phrase like 'a sitting of the chancellor appointed,' or a sentence like 'He hath promised at one time or another to clear his servants.' Secondly, it is a rule of modern English that the antecedent must immediately precede the relative pronoun. Not so in Foxe, who can write, 'The godly saint was then sentenced by the bishop, who next day was burnt in Smithfield.'

To return to the question of spelling. Proper names present a special problem. They vary in different editions, in different stretches of the same edition, in different paragraphs, and even within the same line. Often again there is a difference of spelling between text and margin. Of course the Elizabethans preferred not to standardise the spelling of their names, and Shakespeare was not the only one to avoid dull uniformity in his signature. Stephen Gardiner's name appears in Foxe almost equally often as Steven Gardener, a spelling which enables our author to pun on the bishop's surname. Variations between stretches of Foxe's narrative may perhaps be due to a different source, a different translator of the original Latin, or a different compositor. In the first half of the story of Thomas Tomkins the name of his tormentor is spelt Bonner; elsewhere—and the name occurs hundreds of times—it is consistently spelt Boner. If this was not sufficient reason for using the shorter spelling, the matter should surely be settled by the form Bonerus which appears in the Latin verses to be found on page 418 of this book. Readers with the most elementary knowledge of classical prosody will have no difficulty in deciding that the doubling of the consonant is impossible.

How should these variations of spelling be dealt with in a modern edition of the book? It is surely more convenient that proper names like ordinary words should be regularly spelt the same way, and that is what I have normally done, choosing the spelling that is commonest in the Foxian editions. I see no reason for substituting modern spellings unknown in Foxe's time. A man's name is his own property, which he is entitled to spell as he likes. Our forebears surely knew how they wished their names to be spelt, and there can be no justification for imposing on them spellings which, to judge by Foxe's scholarly pages, they never employed. To do this would mean changing the author's own name to Fox, as was in fact done in the edition of 1684. For that reason I have rejected forms commonly used nowadays, but never in Foxe's book. Such are Catherine or Katharine, Humphrey, Grey, Howard, Huss, Seymour, and Wriothesley. Place names too I have standardised, adopting the modern spelling if it was occasionally used by Foxe, even if he preferred an older form, for example Northfolke for Norfolk. Where justified in this way I have removed a superfluous final -e, as from Bathe and Yorke, and I have preferred final -y to -ie, as in Canturbury. It should be noted that Canterbury never appears; nor do Eton, Bristol, and Calais. In the case of the last, Calis is used in some passages, Calice in others, both representing the pronunciation current in this island until the Victorian age, as is made clear by rhymes. As neither of these two forms prevails I have retained both, as I have done with Lennam and Linne (King's Lynn), and with Bullein and Bullonois (Boulogne). Often Foxe's spelling correctly represents the pronunciation still in use, though longer and perhaps fanciful spellings have superseded the old forms. We may instance Ciceter, Deram, Windam, Pomfret, and Wisbich. Notice too that the old spelling of place names survives in some present-day surnames, such as Carlile and Gascoigne. In both indexes as in the text I have retained the Foxian spelling, in the case of place names which have undergone changes adding (in the index) the modern spelling in brackets. But modern spelling of the names of persons long dead I have disregarded altogether. As regards titles, Foxe writes D. for Doctor and M. for Master: I have substituted Dr and Mr, and have put Mrs for Mistress. All these forms were in use in Shakespearian times.

The question of spelling does not exhaust the problems of modernisation. How should the book be organised and divided? If the whole of *Acts and Monuments* were to be reprinted there would be no need to depart in any way from the shape in which Foxe left it; but in a short abridgment other methods are inevitable. Foxe's work appeared first in one volume, then two, then three, finally eight. That is a matter of convenience. The essential division is not into volumes but into books, and Foxe divided the work into twelve books which vary enormously in length and cover very different periods of time. This division could perhaps be retained in an abridgment that preserved the proportions of the original work. That, for reasons already explained, is far from being the case with the abridgment that is now being introduced: Foxe's structure is quite unsuited to my purpose. What I have done is to divide the material selected into eleven chapters, and as these chapters are not Foxe's (there are no chapters in the original) to provide my own headings. These, I am afraid, give only a rough clue to the contents of the chapters that follow them, since Foxe's mainly chronological arrangement of his material prevents full continuity of thought. This had been the case also in Eusebius, the predecessor to whom, as we shall see, he owed so much.

It may well be that some who read these fragments of a great book will wish to turn to the original in order to study some particular story or discussion in its full form. That would have been much easier had I been able to give page references to the complete text; but this would have been an impossibly complicated task, since no two of the full editions agree in their pagination, and readers cannot hope to find any particular edition in the library they frequent, and few will be in a position to buy a copy of any edition at all. All editions from Elizabethan times are provided with indexes, but as the names of important places and persons appear on so many different pages it is by no means easy to locate a wanted passage. Those who have access to one edition or another may find the following table of use.

This abridgment	*Acts and Monuments*
To the Reader	Book I
Chapter 1	V
2	V–VII
3	VII–VIII
4	VIII
5	IX
6	X
7–9	XI
10–11	XII
Conclusion	Conclusion

'What is the use of a book, thought Alice, without pictures or conversations?' Foxe anticipated the young lady's question by three hundred years. He gave ample space to conversation, some of it infuriating, some deeply moving, and some highly entertaining. But it was surely a remarkable achievement to illuminate his story with woodcuts, very costly to produce, to the number of some one hundred and seventy. These vary in quality and character. Some are conventionalised and impersonal, and so far from being true portraits that a number of them are used more than once, to symbolise the martyrdom or penance of quite different persons. A few are allegorical, and are the direct ancestors of the modern cartoon. One example is the remarkable representation of Henry VIII placing his foot on the neck of the Pope, while a gathering of supporters and opponents register their contrary reactions; another is the last picture of all, which shows a figure of Justice, blindfolded and holding in one hand an uplifted sword, in the other a huge pair of scales in which the word of God, silently watched by Christ and his apostles, is weighing down one end of the beam while volumes of decrees, images, chalices, bells, censers, and everything else that the Pope can pour into the pan, aided by the devil himself and by a muscular monk, are powerless to hold down the other end. The third and largest group of illustrations is much the most valuable, consisting of skilfully drawn and very vivid representations of real people and incidents, each picture being realistic and individual, illustrating the story with all the accuracy possible. It is from this group that I have chosen the eight illustrations scattered through the chapters that follow. The editors of the eighteenth- and nineteenth-century editions had to trace or redraw the original woodcuts, and the results were not very good: in the 1684 edition some of the pictures are the wrong way round. Thanks to the photographer's art I can provide the reader with exact reproductions of the woodcuts as they were presented to Foxe's own generation, and unlike my immediate predecessors I have not replaced the original captions by modern substitutes.

The main outlines of John Foxe's life are known with sufficient accuracy, our chief source of information being the memoir included in the 1641 edition of his book. This, in spite of Maitland's arguments to the contrary, was almost certainly written by Foxe's younger son Simeon, and Mozley has established its reliability. Simeon informs us that when his father died (18 April 1587) he had not quite completed his seventieth year. This statement is confirmed by the portrait in the

National Portrait Gallery, which bears the date 1587 and affirms that the sitter was *aetatis suae 70*—not seventy years old but in his seventieth year. He must therefore have been born about the middle of 1517, not in 1516, as stated in the *Dictionary of National Biography*. His birthplace was Boston, whence the studious boy proceeded to Oxford, becoming a student at Brasenose College. From there he moved to Magdalen, where he was elected fellow; but seven years later, in 1545, he was suspected of Protestant sympathies and compelled to resign. Following the custom of the time he became a tutor in a private house—that of the Lucys at Charlecote in Warwickshire. Matrimony came very soon after this, his bride being Agnes Randall of Coventry. His next move was to London, where he became tutor to the Duke of Norfolk's grandchildren, with whom he was long to maintain his connexion.

If he was devoted to learning, he was still more devoted to religion and the gospel; in 1550 he was ordained deacon by Nicholas Ridley, and from that moment gave himself to the cause of Protestantism. He had already produced some translations and short tracts; but from then on his pen was never idle and his output of books was immense. His greatest work was begun when he embarked on a Latin history of persecution in England *a Wiclevi temporibus ad hanc usque aetatem*. This was not yet finished when in 1554 he fled from the Marian persecution, pursued by the minions of Stephen Gardiner, whom perhaps for that and certainly for much greater reasons he was to execrate till his dying day. Safely across the water he settled with his wife at Strasbourg, where the first part of his book was soon published. Then came a year in Frankfurt, where he, always a hater of sectarian disputes, became involved in the arguments then raging among the exiles concerning the use of the English Prayer Book. His next move was to Basel, where he engaged in various literary activities and greatly extended his Latin history, which was printed and issued in folio in 1559.

Mary was now dead and Foxe brought his wife and family back to London, where he lived for most of his remaining years. Persuaded by friends that his history would reach a far wider public if it was reissued in English, he had his Latin volume translated by collaborators—in places not too accurately—and by extracting a wealth of additional information, both from official documents and from the written or oral testimony of witnesses sought out by him with the most commendable industry, he was enabled to produce a much longer and better work in his native language. This saw the light in 1563: it was the first edition of

Acts and Monuments, the work which made him famous and but for which, in spite of his endless labours with tongue and pen, he might have long ago been forgotten. For the moment we will turn our backs on this, his greatest achievement, and look briefly at the other activities which, combined with the constant correction and enlargement, and the frequent republication of this major work, kept him endlessly toiling for twenty-four more years.

In 1560, ten years after his ordination by Ridley, he was ordained priest by another Bishop of London, Edmund Grindal, to whom he was indebted for much important matter incorporated in his book. He was offered various preferments; but Foxe had strong views on absentee clergymen, and he knew that his main work must be writing in London; so he refused them all except prebends at Salisbury and Durham. He did his best to fulfil all his clerical obligations and preached frequently; but Durham was a long way from London, and after one year his scruples made him resign his prebend there. It was not that he did not need the money; he received no royalties from his books and was always on the verge of penury. His massive volume sold in surprising numbers despite its great cost, and there was a brisk demand also for his famous sermon, 'Of Christ Crucified', preached at Paul's Cross in 1570. Unlike ourselves, our ancestors were avid for sermons; they gathered in great crowds to hear them, and they parted with their money in their eagerness to read them. But neither preaching, writing, nor acting as editor for Archbishop Parker could exhaust his seemingly limitless energy. In the year when his masterpiece was published London was swept by a plague, and he toiled to assist or comfort the victims. He was at all times in demand for spiritual advice, which he gave both freely and frankly. Indeed, he spoke freely and frankly at all times, even to the greatest in the land, whether they wanted his advice or not. He showed no little courage when in 1575 he wrote to his imperious and formidable monarch, demanding that she and her Privy Councillors should reprieve the Anabaptists who had been sentenced to death, courage surpassed six years later when he even tried to save a number of Jesuits likewise condemned. This courage and warm human sympathy appealed to many, and among the friends that he won at many levels of society he numbered Lord Burleigh and Sir Francis Drake. No doubt these two appreciated also the devotion of Foxe to his motherland, and his conviction of her great destiny under the hand of God. How wonderful it would have been for Foxe had he lived but a year longer, and had heard the news flashed from end to end of England that Drake and his fellow admirals had overwhelmed the Invincible Armada, sent against her shores by that same Philip who had once been consort of the terrible Queen Mary, and acknowledged as King of England!

But at sixty-nine Foxe had lived far beyond the average lifetime of men in those days, and into those years he had packed the labours of many lifetimes. On 18 April 1587 the aged toiler passed away, and on the 20th he was buried in the chancel of St Giles, Cripplegate, where the somewhat disappointing inscription set up by his elder son Samuel is still to be seen. Foxe left a widow, two sons, and at least one daughter.

Much might be said about this man's character. Readers of his book, or of even a short abridgment, will find plenty of material to form their own judgments. His animosity against Gardiner, Boner, Tyrrell, and others is so evident that he may be deemed vindictive, though he never wrote anything so vicious and cruel as Harding, who described the Protestant martyrs as 'detestable heretics, thieves, church-robbers, murderers, rebels, and traitors', nor as More had done when he wrote on Wickliffe, Fish, Tindall, and 'the bare, ugly, gargoyle faces of their abominable heresy'. No less evident is Foxe's tenderness, his compassion, his hatred of tyranny and cruelty. From this sprang the opposition to counter-persecution mentioned above; and because of this he began his literary life by writing, as his first original work, a tract protesting against the infliction of the death penalty for adultery, a sin whose heinousness he would have been the last to minimise. 'We judge wrongdoers too harshly and forget the charity of the gospel. Though we hate the vice we should not hate the men.' Again, because of this he lavished praise on Edward and Elizabeth, both so much more merciful than the other Tudor monarchs. Nor can any reader fail to notice his unending condemnation of 'cruel' persecutors, or his innumerable expressions of sympathy for their 'poor' victims.

Perhaps his praises of Edward and Elizabeth may seem excessive. Was he guilty of flattery? Indeed no. He did of course write a good deal of nonsense about Elizabeth's loss of liberty, discomforts, and potentially wet feet. But much sillier stuff is written about royalty today, when the future of our people no longer depends, as it did then, on the survival of one prince or princess. I do not think any impartial reader will question the whole-hearted and genuine admiration felt by Foxe for the child king and his majestic sister. He had seen the terrible change that had occurred when his hopes of a bright future for England were dashed by the premature death of Edward; he had seen the wonderful change brought about when Mary was replaced by her sister; he knew that the next change might bring back all the horror of the elder sister's domination. Two of Henry's children had died before their time; the third had suffered from dangerous illnesses and her real toughness was unsuspected. She might die at any time, and then? Was it not for this reason that Foxe ended so many of the later martyrdom-stories with prayers? 'Thus these two martyrs ended their lives with great triumph: the Lord grant we may do the like.' 'These good men yielded their lives gloriously and joyfully: which constancy the Lord grant we may imitate and follow to the end, whether it be death or life.' 'Richard George and his wife were laid in prison, where they remained till the death of Queen Mary, and were delivered by our most gracious sovereign Lady Queen Elizabeth, whom the Lord grant long to reign among us for his mercy's sake.'

Let us turn from the man to his book—the book which is best known as *Foxe's Book of Martyrs*, as it has been ever since the printer added these words at the end of the first volume. Foxe used many titles, lengthy and varying from edition to edition. The later ones start with the words *Ecclesiastical History*, the title which he sometimes gives to his model, the great work of Eusebius, though elsewhere he calls it *The Story of the Church*. But the key phrase in his long titles is *Acts and Monuments*, a phrase which he introduces from time to time in the course of his work, using as occasional variants 'acts and records', and 'acts and memory', which serve to show what he meant by 'monuments'. *Acts and Monuments of matters most special and memorable happening in the Church* fairly describes the contents of the book: *Book of Martyrs* does not, for there are many things in the book besides stories of martyrdoms. That Foxe gave various titles to his own book as the years went on is not surprising: within a few pages he calls the tiny pamphlet of Simon Fish by no fewer than four! Titles in those days were as flexible as the spelling of proper names.

The purpose of the book is unmistakable: the historiographer (his own description of himself) wrote it to make his fellow countrymen aware of the history of their country from early times to their own day, and interlaced with it the history of the Christian Church, 'especially in this realm of England'; Foxe the prophet wrote it to warn them of the peril in which they stood, in the event of a not improbable reversion to the conditions of the previous reign; Foxe the preacher wrote it to hold up before their eyes the glorious martyrs as shining examples for them to follow if ever the call should come, assuring them that God would never fail to strengthen those who believed in Him and strove to follow the supreme example of His Son. Such a purpose necessitated the change from Latin to English, which was used in every edition published in this country.

As we have seen, the first English edition appeared in 1563, four years after Foxe's return to his native land. It was printed by John Daye, and was a folio volume nearly one thousand eight hundred pages long. A second edition followed seven years later, when Foxe had collected a great deal of additional information, much of it official. Moreover he had decided to include English history before Wickliffe, and also the stories of foreign Protestants such as Luther. Many new woodcuts were added. The book now extended to two volumes and two thousand three hundred pages. Even so Foxe had to omit much that had been in its predecessor, though he considered some of the omitted passages important enough to justify occasional references to them in later editions. Some of these references are included in this present abridgment; but I am satisfied that Foxe knew his business, and have not followed the example of the last edition, which the Victorian editor enlarged to eight volumes partly by restoring many of these passages amidst a medley of asterisks, thereby producing a monster of a book which corresponds to none of the author's own editions.

The second edition, like the first, was rapturously received. The Convocation of Canterbury ordered a copy to be placed alongside the *Bishop's Bible* (published three years before) in every cathedral. But the delight which the book caused to Protestant readers was nothing to the fury which it aroused in 'bapistical' bosoms. Thomas Harding had called the first edition 'a huge dunghill of stinking martyrs', and a much more formidable critic, Nicholas Harpsfield, had written six dialogues in the Fleet prison, one of them directed against Foxe. The dialogues had been published in Antwerp under the name of the printer, Alanus Copus, and Foxe, after spending much time in the collection of new information which would enable him to meet Harpsfield's attack, made a brief reply in his second edition. But now admirers and critics alike made sure that this edition too was speedily sold out, and Foxe set to work to produce a third. This was ready in 1576, six years after the second. Little need be said about it, except that slightly more words were printed on smaller pages in smaller type, and the paper, as a candid friend remarked, was foul, so that the result was unsatisfactory. Foxe was urged to produce a more handsome—and still longer—book.

And so we come to Foxe's fourth and last edition, only a little longer than the third, but a much better specimen of the printer's art. It was published in October 1583, and new information still continued to arrive, so that Foxe began making preparations for yet another edition, though he did not expect to live long enough to produce it. The time between the earlier editions had been six or seven years; only half that time elapsed after the appearance of the fourth before Foxe was dead. Before the end of the century there was a fifth edition. Published in 1596–7 it was to all intents and purposes a reprint of the fourth, for the additions, which probably came from his notes, were trifling. This may fairly be regarded as Foxe's work, and as his last word. It is from this edition that my extracts have been taken. Further editions, for which he was in no way responsible, followed in 1610, 1632, 1641, and 1684, all in folio; for the popularity of the work lasted without diminution throughout the period of the Stuarts, and like the bishops of 1571 the tinker of Bedford placed it second only to the Bible. Last of all came the Victorian editions to which I have referred so often, the last of which bears the date 1877. And there we will leave the history of the book, only adding that its circulation has not been confined to this country, nor to the English-speaking peoples.

Though no fault can be found with Foxe's manner of life, many things can be said against his book and against some of his ideas. Many of his faults stem from his close adherence to the pattern set by Eusebius, the model whom he admired so greatly that he borrowed from him the title *Ecclesiastical History*. Both men were clerics, learned, studious, readers of every chronicle they could buy or borrow, indefatigable writers, enthusiasts for Christ, for orthodoxy as they saw it, for the Scriptures, for the Church. Both lived in times of terrible persecution and suffered, but neither unto death. Both were passionately interested in history, which they saw as the working out of God's plan for men and nations: both wrote history from an ecclesiastical point of view, but were interested enough in secular affairs to find space from time to time for the doings of monarchs, statesmen, and soldiers, which they introduced sporadically into their narrative. This is inevitable in view of their excessive adherence to chronological order. In Foxe's case the dates of the martyrdoms are the pegs on which much of the story hangs. Arrangement on a basis of subject matter seems to have been beyond them both. Both were given to overmuch quotation from earlier writers, whose works were in many cases available to those who wished to read them. Both were apt to modify the wording of their sources without actually rewriting or summarising the passages quoted. Both were extravagant in distributing praise and blame, seeing men always as either black or white. Some would find fault with both for an overgreat interest in the details of martyrdoms, and matter-of-fact readers may be irritated by the seriousness with which both dwell on the fulfilment of visions and prophetic dreams. They did not, of course, make up these stories, and Foxe makes it clear that he is only repeating what he has been told by reputable witnesses, adding the sage comment that it is a logical fallacy to suggest that 'visions be not true in some, ergo they be true in none'. Many will dismiss all such stories as pure fancy: those of us who have had similar experiences ourselves *know* that visions and prophetic dreams can be both true and purposeful.

The one dangerous delusion that Foxe shared with Eusebius was the belief that everything that happened was directly caused by either God or the devil. Thus Foxe writes of Julins Palmer, 'Satan envying his success would not suffer him long to be quiet. He stirred up against him certain double-faced hypocrites.' On the other hand it was God who in His justice sent Mary to punish the English people, and in His mercy sent Elizabeth to rescue them. This notion that God punishes the wicked and rewards the righteous, and does it here and now, is an obsession with both Eusebius and Foxe. They are constantly and delightedly telling us of the assortment of horrible deaths meted out to the 'enemies of the truth'. This leads both authors into extravagance and absurdity, so filled were they with the notion of poetic justice. The belief, of course, was universal. It pervades the Old Testament and is found in the New; neither the arguments of Job nor the plain speaking of Our Lord could shake it. All Englishmen, both Protestant and Catholic, took it for granted, and Foxe was no more absurd than More had been. Foxe's conviction of divine retribution, based though it was on wishful thinking, is not surprising in view of the long list (drastically shortened in this abridgment) of persecutors who came to astonishing and terrible ends. He hopes that the tales, all of which came from trusted informants, will serve as warnings to every class of what will happen to them if they behave likewise—lawyers, gentlemen, and courtiers; atheists, epicures, belly-gods, mockers, blasphemers, swearers. 'Let all young maids, boys, and young men, take example by this silly young wench'—Dennis Benfield, a girl of twelve who had died suddenly after 'casting out impious words of horrible blasphemy'; in other words, after calling her teacher's husband 'an old doting fool'. Evidently the children of Walthamstow resembled those who taunted Elisha and met with a similar fate. Foxe thinks that the story will warn off other children. This hardly accords with our methods of imparting morals to the young; but did not the enlightened Dickens unblushingly take poor little Oliver into the prison to see Fagin the day before his execution, in order to ensure that he did not follow Fagin's example?

At least it can be said for Foxe, that with his conviction of God as the immediate cause of all that happened went a strong sense of gratitude even in the worst circumstances. We in this generation take good things for granted, not as divine mercies, but as if they came of themselves or by our own unaided efforts: in prosperity we congratulate ourselves, and in adversity we repine. Foxe would have appreciated the words written two or three years after his death by a very different writer:

> Poor soul! God's goodness hath been great to thee:
> Let never day nor night unhallowed pass,
> But still remember what the Lord hath done.

There is one further notion for which both Eusebius and Foxe may be criticised—their blind optimism, which made them feel certain that the Golden Age had arrived, in the one case because Constantine had vanquished all his enemies, in the other because Elizabeth was safely on the throne. But neither was really blind. Eusebius knew well the dangers in which the Church stood through the heresies and schisms by which it was torn; Foxe was equally distressed by the divisions, not only between Papists and Protestants but between Protestants themselves. With Paul's adjuration to the Corinthians in mind he writes, 'Would God that all things in all places were so free from all dissension that there were no mention made among Christians of Zuinglians and Luther, when neither Zuinglius nor Luther died for us, but that we might be all one in Christ. Neither do I think that anything more grievous could happen unto those worthy men than their names to be abused to sects and factions, who so greatly strove against all factions. Neither do I detract anything from either part, but rather wish I might join either part unto the other. But now, forsomuch as we entreat of

John Frith, I must needs embrace the moderation which was in that man, who maintaining this quarrel of the sacrament, did it so moderately, without contention, that he would never seem to strive against the Papists except he had been driven to it.'

Foxe's book has many obvious faults. We all feel its prolixity, desultoriness, and imbalance. We would prefer to be without the frequent subjective judgments, the comments in parentheses and margin, the labelling of people as godly, faithful saints, or as wicked enemies of Christ. These judgments, comments, and labels are all evidence of bias, and the charge of bias can be very damaging to a historian. Foxe could hardly be other than biased, writing about such emotion-charged events, events that seemed to him so meaningful and portentous, for readers who shared his opinions and feelings. His beliefs were so genuine and so strong that they could not be left out of the picture in the name of impartiality. But beware of impartiality! Partisan writing is far less dangerous; it need not be misleading, and partiality does not destroy objectivity. Who can write of Catholics and Protestants without being one or the other? A man who is neither can understand neither; he is no Christian, something is missing from his experience, and he cannot understand how Christians feel and what moves them to act as they do. Either he is opposed to Christianity—a plague o' both your houses!—or he is indifferent. If the former, then he is biased; if the latter, then he is not equipped for his task. Bias, after all, is very different from unreliability, and writing coloured by personal feelings bears no resemblance to falsification or dishonesty. If we read a writer whose bias is evident, we shall not be deceived; if we read one whose impartiality is only bias disguised, we shall be led far astray. It may unhesitatingly be asserted that Foxe was an entirely honest man who made every effort to collect reliable information from all possible sources, and to record facts. At times he accepted too readily stories that were not properly authenticated, such as the legend of the murder by Jews of St William of Norwich. But who in his day thought of questioning such legends? Is not historical criticism a science of much later development? At least it must be admitted that when any of his stories was questioned he made every endeavour to obtain further information, in the light of which he either substantiated the story, modified it, or withdrew it altogether.

Falsification is of course one of the numerous vices of which Foxe has been accused, and many people have opened their mouths wide to swallow the largely unsupported allegations brought by a series of antagonists from Harpsfield to Maitland, who in publication after publication pursued his vendetta against Foxe, doing his utmost to destroy his reputation for truthfulness. The first counterblow was struck as recently as 1940, when Mozley published his admirable book, in which he not only rehabilitated Foxe's character and writings generally, but showed the insubstantiality of the evidence brought against them. In particular he discussed the notorious story of the Guernsey martyrdoms with the most scholarly thoroughness, and disposed—I trust for ever—of the arguments of Foxe's vilifiers.

Leaving controversy aside let us take a look at the sources which Foxe collected and consulted so assiduously. For ecclesiastical history of the first millennium he used such written records as were available, from Eusebius onwards. For English history he had the records of abbeys and priories and the episcopal registers of four or five dioceses, supplemented by the chronicles of such individuals as Walden, Walsingham, and Edward Hall, the polemical writings of More and Polydor Virgil, pamphlets such as Fish's *Book of Beggars*, the letters which the martyrs wrote, often in prison, the sermons and oaths of Gardiner and Boner. He had also the records of trials and disputations, penned sometimes by the notaries, sometimes by unofficial observers. These were not always biased in favour of the accused: the record of Cranmer's trial was from a Papist's hand. Other sources were the statements of those who had survived martyrdom by recanting, by escaping from prison or from the country, or by being condemned but not yet executed at the time of Mary's death. There were also statements from brothers, friends, or men such as Matthew Parker, the future archbishop, who witnessed the death of Thomas Bilney in the Lollard's Pit. Some of the martyrs Foxe had known personally, especially the saintly Bishop Hooper. Finally there are sources hinted at by the introduction of apparently irrelevant names, such as Harbottell in the story of Bishop Farrar's purloined cattle. Perhaps Foxe had learnt this little device from St Luke, its first exponent. We may add that, like Eusebius, when Foxe depends on hearsay he does not hesitate to admit the fact, and that he is equally ready to confess his ignorance. He gives us a very full account of the horrible methods employed to undermine Cranmer's resistance by indulgence, flattery, threats, lying promises, and scientific brainwashing; but he makes no attempt to say with any certainty what went on in the unfortunate victim's mind, how he came to recant, to what extent he practised deception, or whether the documents he was alleged to have signed were all genuine or in part fraudulent.

Of the value of the book there can be no serious question. It provides an immense amount of material, mostly documented, for the political and ecclesiastical history of England, and to some extent of Europe. Valuable sources are incorporated and preserved. Much light is shed also on the customs of the day, on the manner of life of different classes, on economic problems, on the conduct of trials, in which accuser and judge were too often the same person and the result a foregone conclusion, and the horrible punishments inflicted—the foul dungeons, the stocks, the pillory, the rack, the whip, starvation. We read of Vincent Gosset, who for the theft of sixpence was whipped, set in the pillory with her ear nailed to the wood, and finally banished. Light is shed too on the games that people played, the books they read, the clothes they wore (see illustrations); on family life, education in homes, schools, and universities, the interests, habits, and character of the people. How stoical they could be, but how freely they expressed their emotions! No shame at shedding tears in those days! The book is not entirely given up to martyrdoms, but they do fill many, many pages, and open our eyes to much that otherwise we should never have guessed. Foxe's determination to record them in such detail was not surprising, after all that he had seen and endured. He had too much respect for royalty to apply his favourite epithet 'bloody' to Mary. But bloody her reign was, and the deaths of more than three hundred must be laid at the door of the queen 'in the heat of whose flames', as Weaver tells us, 'were burnt five bishops, one and twenty divines, eight gentlemen, eighty-four artificers, an hundred husbandmen, servants, and labourers, twenty-six wives, twenty widows, nine virgins, two boys, and two infants. . . . Sixty-four more were persecuted for their profession of faith; whereof seven were whipped, sixteen perished in prison, twelve were buried in dunghills. Many lay in captivity condemned, but were released and saved by the auspicious entrance of peaceable Elizabeth.'

For those interested in theology and Church history Foxe makes perfectly clear what the reformers stood for. They wanted to go back to the beliefs and practices of the Early Church 'before corruption came in'; they wanted to go back from Scotus and Aquinas to Augustine and Chrysostom, and above all to the Bible, especially to the gospels and the epistles of St Paul. Their devotion to the Apostle we see in their insistence on faith, not works; in their reverence for princes (Cranmer's attitude was quite different from that of Gardiner and Boner); and in the repeated use of the name Christ Jesus, which, as students of the New Testament will have noticed, is used constantly by Paul and by none else. They rejected any doctrine or practice not laid down in Scripture. 'I cannot find the mass', declared Latimer after reading the whole New Testament seven times. 'I cannot find in the Scriptures', protested Laverock, 'that the priests should lift up over their head a cake of bread.' It was the same with images and pilgrimages. We must beware of thinking that Roman opposition to the English New Testament was simply a protest against Tindall's prefaces and marginal comments: Foxe makes it abundantly clear that they would have no truck with vernacular translations, and were opposed to any Bible reading by the laity. The story of Latimer and the friar speaks for itself.

Above all the reformers wished to go back from Antichrist to Christ. What were they to think of the divine who said to Tindall, 'We were better to be without God's laws than the Pope's'? Catholics and Protestants had quite different points of view, as is shown by the dialogue between Boner and Taylor. 'The bishop said, "Mr Doctor, I would you would turn to your Mother, Holy Church." Taylor answered, "I would you and your fellows would turn to Christ."' To go back from Antichrist to Christ was at the same time to go back from wickedness to righteousness, and the reformers, horrified by what they saw on every side, were constantly protesting against corruption, vice, and wickedness of every sort. Puritans in the best sense, they were zealous for Christian standards of conduct. Taylor, amidst the merriment in which he continually indulged, even on the road to the stake, did not forget to preach against evil. 'All the way Taylor was merry, as one going to a banquet or bridal. He spake many notable things to the sheriff and yeomen, and often moved them to weep through his calling on them to amend their wicked living.' Specially strong disgust was felt for vice at the Court and in the clergy.

They were anxious also to purify doctrine, which they believed to have been corrupted. They repudiated transubstantiation, which caused the priests to regard themselves as workers of miracles. They objected to the elevation of the sacrament, which led ignorant worshippers into idolatry. They would not acknowledge that the mass was an atoning sacrifice. They protested vehemently against masses for the dead, solemnised by the priests for money as often as their customers could afford to pay for them. If this last abuse did not shock the followers of the Pope then, it shocks some of them now. I quote from a recent issue of *The Tablet*. 'The reformers were turning Scripture against the Church, proclaiming the Bible the sole rule of faith. They were particularly concerned to oppose a lopsided development of the mediaeval Church. It was no heretic but Rosmini who observed that in the later Middle Ages those doctrines had been developed which were most to the advantage of the clergy, like indulgences specially linked to Purgatory, an arithmetical notion of the Mass as though two were twice as efficacious as one, which encouraged monarchs and nobles to endow chantries so that they should have far more masses said for their souls than were within the range of anybody else.'

In the reformers' eyes the priesthood was full of abuses. They rightly saw that it was detrimental to pastoral work for bishops to hold political power as Lord Chancellors, ambassadors, and royal advisers. They deemed it utterly wrong that they should have the right to summon men before them and condemn them to imprisonment, torture, and death, and that mayors, sheriffs and bailiffs should be forced against their will to carry out these sentences. They objected to monetary exactions, to Peter's Pence and tithes, still more to pardons and indulgences. In the *Supplication of Beggars* which he sent to Henry VIII, and of which that Catholic monarch seems to have approved, Simon Fish had some pungent things to say about 'strong, puissant, and counterfeit holy and idle beggars'. 'There are', he said, 'ravenous wolves going in sheep's clothing, devouring the flock: bishops, abbots, priors, deacons, archdeacons, suffragans, priests, monks, canons, friars, pardoners, and sumners. Who is able to number this idle, ravenous sort, that setting all labour aside have begged so importunately that they have gotten into their hands more than the third part of all your realm? The goodliest lordships, manors, lands, and territories are theirs. They have the tenth part of all the corn, meadows, pasture, grass, woods, colts, calves, lambs, pigs, geese, and chickens. Over and besides, the tenth part of every servant's wages, the tenth part of wool, milk, honey, wax, cheese, and butter; yea, the poor wives must be countable to them of every tenth egg, or else she shall be taken as an heretic. What money pull they in by probates of testaments, privy-tithes, and by men's offerings to their pilgrimages and at their first masses! Every man and child that is buried must pay for masses and diriges to be sung for him, or else they will accuse their executors of heresy. What money they get by mortuaries, by hearing of confessions, by hallowing of churches, altars, superaltars, chapels, and bells, by cursing of men and absolving them again for money! What a multitude of money gather the pardoners in a year! How much money get the sumners by extortion, by asciting the people to the commissary's court and afterwards releasing the appearance for money! Finally, the infinite number of begging friars, what get they in a year!' And now, four hundred and thirty-three years later, this from Archbishop Roberts, S.J.: 'I never feel quite comfortable in St Peter's; I keep remembering that it was built on the sale of indulgences.'

Another charge was that of idleness. Foxe complains of priests who did not preach and incumbents who did not even visit their parishes, contrasting them with Latimer. 'Being weary of the Court, having a benefice offered by the king at the suit of Cromwell and Buts, contrary to the mind of Buts he would needs depart and be resident of the same.' At a later date Foxe showed his adherence to the same principle himself. But if they did not work the priests sometimes accumulated great wealth, and if they could not serve both God and mammon were content to serve the latter. An extreme case was that of Cardinal Beaufort, Bishop of Winchester in the reign of Henry V, who on his death-bed brazenly admitted that he had increased his treasure in hope to wear the triple crown—treasure so great that he was able to sustain the king's armies in war without any taxing of the commons. With wealth went pomp and luxury, most conspicuously in the case of another cardinal, the arrogant Wolsey. When his love of display was attacked by Dr Barnes, Wolsey exclaimed, 'What, Mr Doctor, had you not sufficient scope in the Scriptures to teach the people, but that my golden shoes, pole-axes, pillars, golden cushions, crosses did so sore offend you? Do you think it more necessary that I should have all this royalty because I represent the king's person, or to sell all these things and give it to the poor?' The reformer retorted, 'I think it necessary to be given to the poor. For the King's Majesty is not sustained by your pomp and pole-axes, but by God.'

Again, the priests were condemned for their ignorance and lack of learning. Tindall spoke scornfully of 'a sort of unlearned priests, rude and ignorant, who have seen no more Latin than that which they read in their portueses and missals, which many of them can scarcely read.' Cranmer, when he was an examiner at Cambridge, refused to pass a number of candidates for a degree in Divinity until they knew something of the Bible. This accusation of ignorance is confirmed by other authorities. We read how a test in King Henry's time revealed that many priests could not recite the Paternoster, and Erasmus tells us of a Continental examiner who refused to accept ordination candidates because they were so ignorant, but was forced to relent by the officials who stood to lose the gratuities customarily bestowed upon them by the successful candidates.

But if they did not study, the priests knew how to enjoy themselves. Fat-paunched Boner was much given to banqueting, and in the story of Tindall's early years we read that 'blind priests, flocking to the alehouse (for that was their preaching-place) raged against him'. Hence the Ecclesiastical Injunctions of King Edward. 'Ecclesiastical persons shall in no wise for any other cause than for their honest necessity resort to any taverns or alehouses; and after their dinner or supper they shall not give themselves to drinking and riot, dice, cards, tables-playing, or any other unlawful games.'

These were not the most disreputable forms of self-indulgence. The priests were accused of widespread sexual depravity, and much evidence was forthcoming. The root of the trouble was the assumption that continence was impossible, except to the specially gifted, an assumption responsible for the preface to the marriage service in the 1662 Prayer Book, so embarrassing to chaste bridegrooms and modest brides. 'Because I would not be a whoremonger', declared Thomas Benet the godly schoolmaster, 'I married a wife.' Or as Rowland Taylor said in reply to Gardiner's question, 'Thou art married?', 'I thank God I am, and have had nine children, all in lawful matrimony. Blessed be God that ordained matrimony and commanded that every man that hath not the gift of continency should marry a wife and not live in adultery or whoredom.'

The prevalence of priestly immorality is made plain enough by the 'Act against Fornication of Priests' passed when Foxe was a young man. 'Besides these Six Articles there was another constitution annexed withal which was this: that priests and ministers of the Church, seeing they would be bound from all matrimony, should therefore by law be likewise bound to such honesty and continency of life that carnally they should use and accustom no manner of woman, married or single, by way of adultery or fornication.' Penalties were laid down for first and second offences. But 'Gardiner with his fellow bishops so basted this article with their accustomed shifts' that the penalties were lightened and it was not till the third offence that the punishment would be more than a heavy fine. When the bishops showed thus how lightly they regarded licentiousness in clerics, it is not surprising that the act did little to cleanse these Augean stables; and when in the early months of Edward's reign the king's commissioners visited St Paul's, where Boner still occupied the bishop's throne, 'the commissioners being set, and the canons and priests appearing before them and being examined upon oath for their doctrine and conversation, first John Painter, one of the canons, openly confessed that he viciously and carnally had often the company of a certain man's wife; in which crime divers other canons and priests confessed in like manner,' Boner was not in the least shocked.

What kind of society was it where William Swinderby, himself a priest, could be alleged to have said that parishioners ought to withhold their tithes 'if they know their curate to be a lecher incontinent and an evil man', and that 'no priest entereth any house but to evil-entreat the wife, daughter, or maid'? If Swinderby did not say this, Simon Fish certainly did. 'Yea, and what do they more? Truly nothing but apply themselves, by all the sleights they may, to have to do with every man's wife, every man's daughter, and every man's maid, that licentiousness should reign over all among your subjects, that no man should know his own child; that their bastards should inherit the possessions of every man.' Specially bad cases reported by Foxe were those of 'John Averth, parson of Aldam, an open advouterer and whoremonger', and Berry, parson of Aylsham. 'To write how many concubines and whores he had none would believe it but such as knew him in the country where he dwelt. He was altogether given to women.' Moreover Tindall, after experience of the Gloucestershire clergy, tells us of priests who apart from portueses and missals only read 'Albertus, *De Secretis Mulierum*, in which they pore day and night and make notes therein, and all to teach the midwives as they say.'

If in England the reputation of the priests was unsavoury, on the Continent it was just as bad. Witness the argument between Gardiner and Rogers, whose allegations are confirmed by at least two independent authorities. 'My Lord, I pray you grant me one thing.' 'What is that?' 'That my poor wife, being a stranger, may come and speak with me. For she hath ten children that are hers and mine, and somewhat I would counsel her, what were best for her to do.' 'No, she is not thy wife.' 'Yes, my Lord, and hath been these eighteen years.' 'She shall not come at thee.' 'Then I have tried out all your charity. Ye make yourself highly displeased with the matrimony of priests, but ye maintain their open whoredom; as in Wales, where every priest hath his whore openly dwelling with him and lying by him; even as your Holy Father suffereth all the priests in Dutchland and France to do the like.' And according to a named printed source, at the Council of Trent only one year before Foxe's book was published, there were 'two filthy adulterous bishops to the said Council belonging, of whom the one, haunting to an honest man's wife, was slain with a boar-spear. The other, whose haunt was to creep through a window, in the same window was subtly taken, and hanged in a gin laid for him of purpose; and so conveyed that in the morning he was seen openly in the street hanging out of the window, to the wonderment of all that passed by.'

For such allegations we do not depend only on Foxe. Ample evidence is available about the insolent depravity of clerics high and low. There was strong objection to marriage, but none to paternity. The priests, it was commonly said, were busy producing bastards, and such habits did not prevent a man from reaching the highest position of all. Rodrigo Lenzuoli fathered five children on Rosa Vanozza; these included Cesare and Lucrezia Borgia. He was cruel, cunning and grasping, a perjurer and a poisoner. This did not prevent him from becoming (through the nepotism of his uncle) a cardinal, and (through his own bribery) Pope Alexander VI. Eneo Silvio Piccolomini was a lecher from his earliest years, and author of licentious poems, at least one novel after the pattern of Boccaccio, and an obscene drama. At forty he was ordained, and announced that he intended to reform 'forsaking Venus for Bacchus'. Soon he was bishop, then cardinal, finally Pope Pius II (*pius Aeneas*?). Described as 'a most decorous Pope', he openly and shamelessly declared himself the father of children, and justified in being so. To return to our own shores and the ranks of the parish priests, let us glance at John Skelton, Rector of Diss. Many stories were current of his irregular life in Norfolk and elsewhere. In his rectory he kept a concubine who bore him many children. So unashamed was he that as proof of God's approval he displayed one fine specimen naked before his congregation. He was called before Bishop Nix, but no penalty was imposed. Later he said that he had been married at the time, but had been too cowardly to confess it. Evidently the bishop thought concubinage preferable to marriage, which he would have been prepared to punish. Breach of God's law was a venial offence, breach of the Church's tradition a mortal sin.

But whoredom was not the deepest degradation alleged, especially against the friars. Of the references to sodomy I quote only one. As early as 1395 a *Book of Conclusions* was exhibited to parliament. 'The law of chastity enjoined unto priesthood, the which was first ordained to the prejudice of women, induceth sodomy into the Church . . . forsomuch as the delicate feeding and fare of the clergy will have either a natural purgation or some worse.'

Today we have the strange anomaly that Roman Catholic priests must be unmarried, Orthodox married, and Anglicans whichever they like. There are of course non-Romans who prefer celibacy on principle, and there is much to be said for it, if the choice is between divided responsibilities and total devotion to evangelical or pastoral duty. But in those days it was not self-indulgent, cosy domestic life *versus* dedicated self-denying chastity; the reformers, at least, saw it as God's institution of holy marriage *versus* devilish, filthy lechery. The reformers, obviously, were devoted to their wives, and there are many touching stories of mutual affection. These men would gladly die, rather than that the bishops, defying both their Master's teaching on divorce and a ruling from the highest ecclesiastical authority, should put them asunder.

There was much, then, in the life of the Church to justify the protests of the reformers. Were they also right in attacking its doctrines? This is a most involved problem, of which I can only skim the surface. Anglo-Catholics who feel that the reformers rejected beliefs and ceremonies that they themselves hold precious must try to understand what it was in current preaching and practice that they condemned so strongly and, if you will, extravagantly. They must study what was meant when they denied the 'real' presence of Christ in the sacrament. It is plain enough in the teaching of Wickliffe and Redman. They must observe that to condemn pilgrimages, organised fraudulently to confer magic benefits on the pilgrims and to bring money to the priests, was a very different thing from condemning the pilgrimages of devotion that we know today. If they do not see why the cult of our Lady was condemned, they should study not only the decree of Arundell which in a compressed form appears later in this book, but the Primer for children issued in Queen Mary's time, and Our Lady's Psalter composed by Bonaventura, a shocking parody of Scripture which transfers to the Virgin all the attributes of God, His works, and the honour due to His name. It is too blasphemous to quote.

Cynics and sceptics, reading of the quarrels between Christians, of the miseries that one group brought upon the other, and of the crimes committed in the name of the Holy Catholic and Apostolic Church, may be inclined to echo the words of Lucretius, '*Tantum religio potuit suadere malorum.*' They would be wrong. It was not the teaching of Christ or the religion of Christ that produced the crimes; it was the neglect of that teaching, the perversion of that religion, the substitution of the traditions of sinful men, that produced them. But it was faith in Christ and whole-hearted acceptance of His gospel, persistence in prayer which over and over again was so unmistakably answered, that gave the martyrs such wonderful fervour and such inward calm, patience under insults, strength to endure torments of body and mind, strength to resist threats, promises, and cajolements, strength to put Christ and the truth above home and possessions, above their beloved wives and children, above life itself, and finally grace to follow the example of their dying Master and from their hearts forgive their slayers. There is nothing here to turn us from religion.

But what a change has come over the Church! Gone is the fear of persecution; gone are the hatred and bitterness, the charges and countercharges, the moral corruption, the frauds, the service of mammon. Much is still wrong with us, but we have learnt much. Christian churches that once scorned and fought each other have become tolerant and friendly. 'We are reaching out towards the Church of Rome', says the Archbishop of Canterbury. Can this be the same Rome whose bishop was once denounced as Antichrist? And in the eyes of the present Bishop of Rome Anglicans are no longer heretics, damned body and soul, but 'separated brethren' and members of a 'great Christian Church'. Romans and non-Romans alike may read the Bible in their own tongues; soon they may be using the same translations. Romans agree with Protestants that doctrine must be tested by Scripture, and that there is no objection to services in the vernacular. They are speaking from the same platform, joining in worship together, and singing each other's hymns. We have a long way to go yet and there are many obstacles to surmount, but we have come a long way since Foxe's time, and we are on the right road. We look forward to a united Church, or at least to Churches unitedly striving against their common enemies, darkness and ignorance, sin and self-destruction. May no more wounds be inflicted on the body of Christ!

REMINDER

Before beginning to read the following chapters, it will be wise to turn to the Glossary and study the words printed in small capitals, which may otherwise be sadly misunderstood.

In Io. Foxum theologum celeberrimum cum Christo exultantem

In quiet peace thou sleepest now at rest,
O learned Foxe, the phoenix of our age,
Most happy thou with crown of glory blest,
For ever freed from persecuting rage:
  With comfort great thou gained hast the shore,
  And stormy tempests now needst fear no more.

Thy life not stained with spots of foul defame,
Thy learning great, who dare the same deny?
Thy worthy works abroad do sound thy name,
And shall for ever to posterity.
  So long as learning and the learned live,
  Thy works to thee immortal praise will give.

Thy hand was always stretched out to give,
Thy eye from poor was never turned aside,
What one of thee might not have learned to live,
Who in thy life so many ways wast tried?
  And yet the same didst always still endure,
  No change thy heart to change could once procure.

The afflicted soul by thee did comfort find,
The conscience weak by thee did strength attain,
Thy sermons sweet raised up the feeble mind,
And many a soul from hell to Christ did gain:
  Such care thou hadst God's mercies still to preach,
  Such grace thou hadst the truth of Christ to teach.

Thy tongue and pen the truth did still defend,
Thou banishment for Christ didst gladly bide,
In him thou liv'st, in him thou mad'st thy end,
Most happy thou that hadst so good a guide.
  Most happy thou while life thou didst retain,
  Most happy now that dost with Christ remain.

Io. Hopkins

ACTS AND MONUMENTS

OF MATTERS MOST SPECIAL AND MEMORABLE

HAPPENING IN THE CHURCH,

ESPECIALLY IN THE REALM OF ENGLAND

TO THE READER

Christ our Saviour, in the gospel of St Matthew ch. 16, hearing the confession of Simon Peter, who first of all other openly acknowledged him to be the Son of God, and perceiving the secret hand of his Father therein, called him a rock, upon which he would build his church so strong that the gates of hell should not prevail against it. In which words three things are to be noted: first, that Christ will have a church in this world; secondly, that the same church should mightily be impugned, not only by the world but also by the uttermost powers of all hell; and thirdly, that the same church, notwithstanding the uttermost of the devil and all his malice, should continue: which prophecy of Christ we see wonderfully to be verified, insomuch that the whole course of the Church unto this day may seem nothing else but a verifying of the said prophecy. First, that Christ hath set up a church needeth no declaration. Secondly, what force, what sides and sorts of men, of princes, kings, monarchs, governors, and rulers of this world, with their subjects, publicly and privately, with all their strength and cunning, have bent themselves against this church! And thirdly, how the said church, all this notwithstanding, hath yet endured and holden its own! What storms and tempests it hath overpast, wondrous it is to behold; for the more evident declaration whereof I have addressed this present history, intending, by the favourable aid of Christ our Lord, not so much to delight the ears of my country in reading of news, as most specially to profit the hearts of the godly in perusing antiquities; to the end that the wonderful works of God in his church might appear to his glory; also that the continuance and proceedings of the Church being set forth in these Acts and Monuments, more knowledge and experience may redound thereby, to the profit of the reader and edification of Christian faith.

CHAPTER I

WICKLIFFE AND HIS FRIENDS

KING EDWARD III

We will begin our history with the story of John Wickliffe our countryman, and other moe of his time and country, whom the Lord (with the like zeal and power of spirit) raised up here in England, to detect more fully the poison of the Pope's doctrine and false religion set up by the friars. In whose opinions and assertions albeit some blemishes may be noted, yet such they be which rather declare him to be a man that might err, than one who directly did fight against Christ our Saviour, as the Popes and the friars did. What learned man hath been from the prime age of the Church so perfect, in whom no opinion hath sometime swerved awry? and yet be the said articles of his neither so many nor so gross and cardinal as those cardinal enemies of Christ give them out to be.

This is certain, that he, being the public Reader of Divinity in the University of Oxford, was for the rude time wherein he lived reputed for a great clerk, a deep schoolman, expert in all kinds of philosophy; the which doth not only appear by his own learned writings and monuments, but also by the confession of Walden, his most cruel and bitter enemy, who in an epistle to Pope Martin V saith that he was astonished at his strong arguments, with the places of authority which he had gathered, with the force of his reasons, etc.

Wickliffe flourished about 1371, Edward III reigning in England; for thus we find in the Chronicles of Caxton: 'In the year of our Lord 1371 Edward III was against the Pope's clergy; he willingly hearkened to the voices and tales of heretics, with certain of his Council conceiving sinister opinions against the clergy; wherefore afterwards he suffered much adversity. Not long after, in the year 1372, he wrote unto the Bishop of Rome that he should not meddle any more within his kingdom.' Thus much writeth Caxton. This is out of all doubt, that in what time the world was in most desperate and vile estate and lamentable ignorance of God's truth had overwhelmed the whole earth, this man stepped forth like a valiant champion.

Thus doth Almighty God continually succour when all things are in despair; which thing never more plainly appeared than in these latter days and extreme age of the Church, when the whole state, not only of worldly things but also of religion, was depraved and corrupted beyond all man's remedy. The name only of Christ remained among Christians: his true and lively doctrine was unknown unto the most part. Touching faith, consolation, the end of the law, the office of Christ, our impotency, the Holy Ghost, the strength of sin, justification by faith, the liberty of a Christian man, there was no mention, nor any word almost spoken of Scripture; learning and divinity was known but to a few, and that in the schools only; there also they turned almost all into sophistry. Instead of Peter and Paul men occupied their time in studying Aquinas and Scotus. The world, forsaking the power of God's spiritual word, was blinded with outward ceremonies and human traditions. In these was the hope of salvation fully fixed, insomuch that scarcely any other thing was seen in churches, taught in sermons, or intended in their whole life, but only heaping up of ceremonies on ceremonies.

Wickliffe, after he had now a long time professed divinity in the University of Oxford, and perceiving the true doctrine of Christ's gospel to be adulterate with so many filthy inventions of bishops and monks, and that he, after long deliberating with himself, could no longer abide the same, at last determined to remedy such things as he saw to be wide of the way. But forsomuch as he saw that this dangerous meddling could not be attempted without great trouble, neither that these things, which had been so long rooted in men's minds, could be suddenly plucked up, he thought that this matter should be done by little and little. Wherefore he, taking his original at small occasions, first assailed his adversaries in logical and metaphysical questions, disputing with them of *the increase of time* and of *the intelligible substance of a creature* with other suchlike sophisms of no great effect; notwithstanding, it did not a little help him, who minded to dispute of greater matters. At length he came to touch the matters of the sacraments, and other abuses of the Church; touching which things this holy man took great pains, protesting openly that it was his principal purpose to call back the Church from her idolatry, especially in the matter of the body and blood of Christ. But this sore could not be touched without the great grief and pain of the whole world; for first the whole glut of monks and begging friars was set in a rage, who ever as hornets with their sharp stings did assail this good man on every side, fighting, as is said, for their altars and bellies. After this the priests and bishops, and then the archbishop, took the matter in hand, being then S. Sudbury, who deprived him of his benefice in Oxford. Notwithstanding, he being somewhat friended by the king bore the malice of the friars and the archbishop till about 1377; after which I must fetch a little compass to infer some mention of John of Gaunt, Duke of Lancaster, the king's son, and Lord Henry Percy, which were his special maintainers.

As years grew on, King Edward III, who had now reigned about 51 years, after the decease of Prince Edward his son was strucken in great age, and in such feebleness that he was unwieldy to govern the realm. Wherefore a parliament being called the year before his death, it was there put up by the knights and burgesses that twelve discreet lords free from note of all avarice should be placed as tutors about the king, to have the disposing under him of matters pertaining to the public regiment. Here I omit to speak of Alice Perris, the wicked harlot who as the story reporteth had bewitched the king's heart, and governed all through the devilish help of a friar Dominic: who by the Duke of Lancaster was taken and convicted, and would have suffered for the same had not the Archbishop of Canturbury and the friars, more regarding the liberty of their church than the punishment of vice, reclaimed him for their own prisoner. Alice Perris, notwithstanding she was banished by parliament from the king, afterwards came again, and left him not till at his death she took all his rings and other jewels from him, and so fled away like an harlot.

These 12 governors, being appointed to have the tuition of the king, remained for a space about him; afterwards it so fell out that they being again removed, all the regiment of the realm was committed to the Duke of Lancaster; for Richard the son of Prince Edward was under age. This duke had long conceived displeasure against the popish clergy; whether for corrupt doctrine joined with abominable excess of life, or for what other cause, is not precisely expressed: the cause may be guessed to rise by William Wickham, Bishop of Winchester. The matter is this. *Ex Chron. Monasterii Albani.*

The bishop was reported to affirm that John of Gaunt was not the son of King Edward nor of the queen; who being in travail at Gaunt had no son, he said, but a daughter, which by lying upon of the mother in bed was smothered. The queen, fearing the king's displeasure, caused a man-child of a woman of Flanders, born the same time, to be brought unto her instead of her daughter; and so brought up the child whom she bare not, who now is called Duke of Lancaster. This, said the bishop, did the queen tell him lying on her death-bed, under seal of confession, charging him that if the duke should aspire to the crown or if the kingdom should fall unto him, he should declare to the world that the duke was no part of the king's blood but a false heir. This slanderous report of the wicked bishop, as it savoureth of a contumelious lie, so seemeth it to proceed of a subtle zeal towards the Pope's religion; for the duke by favouring Wickliffe declared himself an enemy against the Pope's profession; which thing was not unmarked of the bishops then in England. The sequel of the story thus followed.

This slanderous report being blazed abroad and coming to the duke's ear, he sought by what means he could to be revenged. Having now all the government of the realm, under his father, in his hands, he so pursued the bishop that by act of parliament he was condemned and deprived of all his goods; which goods were assigned to Prince Richard of Burdeux, the next inheritor of the crown; furthermore he inhibited the bishop not to approach near to the Court by twenty miles. In 1377 a parliament was called by the duke upon certain causes; in which parliament request was made by the clergy for the deliverance of the bishop. When a subsidy was asked in the king's name of the clergy, and request made for speedy expedition to be made for dissolving parliament, the archbishop convented the bishops for the tractation thereof. The bishops complained for lack of their brother the Bishop of Winchester, whose injury, said they, did derogate from the liberties of the Church; therefore they refused to join in tractation of such matters before all the members were united with the head. They seemed moreover to be moved against the archbishop, because he suffered himself so to be cited of the duke.

The archbishop, although having sufficient cause wherefore not to send for him, because of the perils which might ensue, yet being forced by the importunity of the bishops directed letters to the Bishop of Winchester, willing him to resort unto the convocation of the clergy; who being glad to obey was received with great joy by the other bishops; and at length by means of Alice Perris, the king's paramour, having given her a good quantity of money, Winchester was restored to his temporalities again.

The duke in the meantime had sent for John Wickliffe, who had been deprived of his benefice, as hath been afore touched. The opinions wherefore he was deprived were these: that the Pope had no more power to excommunicate any man than hath another; that if it be given to the Pope to excommunicate, to absolve is as much in the power of another priest as in his; that neither the king nor any temporal lord could give any perpetuity to the Church or to any ecclesiastical person; for when such persons do sin *habitualiter*, the temporal powers ought to take away from them what before hath been bestowed upon them. This he proved to have been practised in England by William Rufus; 'which thing,' said he, 'if he did lawfully, why may not the same be practised now? If unlawfully, then doth the Church err in praying for him.'

Besides these opinions he began to touch the matter of the sacrament, proving that the accidents of bread remained not without the substance, and this both by the Holy Scriptures and by the authority of the doctors, especially such as were most ancient. As for the later writers, such as have written under the thousand years since Christ's time, he refused them, saying that after these years Satan was set at liberty, and that since that time man hath been most in danger of errors; the plain truth to appear in the Scriptures, whereunto all human traditions must be referred, especially such as are published of late years. This was the cause why he refused the later writers, stoutly affirming that the body of Christ is not present without the bread, as the common sort of priests did dream. Herein the truth, as the poet speaketh, had gotten John Wickliffe hatred at many men's hands, specially of the monks and richest priests.

Albeit through the favour of the Duke of Lancaster and Lord Henry Percy he persisted, till at last, about 1376, the bishops, urging their archbishop Simon Sudbury, who before had deprived him and prohibited him to stir any more in those matters, had obtained by process of citation to have him brought before them; whereunto both place and time was to him assigned. The duke, fearing that he being but one was too weak against such a multitude, calleth to him out of the orders of friars four Bachelors of Divinity, out of every order one, to join them with Wickliffe for more surety. When the day was come (Thursday the 19th of February) John Wickliffe, accompanied with the four friars, the duke, and Lord Henry Percy, Lord Marshal of England, was coming to the place where the bishops sat; whom by the way they exhorted not to shrink a whit at the company of the bishops present, who were all unlearned in respect of him, neither dread the concourse of the people; whom they would themselves assist in such sort as he should take no harm. Wickliffe, in heart encouraged, approached the Church of St Paul in London, where a press of people was gathered to hear what should be said and done. Such was the throng that the lords, for all the puissance of the High Marshal, unneth with great difficulty could get through; insomuch that the Bishop of London, William Courtney, seeing the stir that the Lord Marshal kept in the church among the people, said that if he had known what masteries he would have kept in the church, he would have stopped him from coming there; at which words the duke answered that he would keep such mastery there, though he said Nay.

At last after much wrestling they pierced through and came to Our Lady's Chapel, where the dukes and barons were sitting together with the archbishops and bishops; before whom Wickliffe stood to know what should be laid unto him. To whom first spake Lord Percy, bidding him sit down. But the Bishop of London, cast into a fumish chafe by those words, said he should not sit there. Neither was it according to law or reason that he who was cited to appear before his ordinary should sit down during the time of his answer. Upon these words a fire began to kindle between them: they began so to revile one the other that the whole multitude began to be set on a hurry. Then the duke, taking Lord Percy's part, with hasty words began to take up the bishop. The bishop again, nothing inferior in reproachful checks and rebukes, did render not only to him as good as he brought, but also did so far excel him in this art of scolding that, to use the words of mine author, *erubuit dux, quod non potuit praevalere litigio*; i.e. the duke blushed, because he could not overpass the bishop in brawling; and therefore he fell to plain threatening, menacing the bishop that he would bring down the pride not only of him but of all the prelacy of England. 'Thou,' said he, 'bearest thyself so brag upon thy parents, which shall not be able to help thee; they shall have enough to do to help themselves'; for his parents were the Earl and Countess of Devonshire. The bishop answered that his confidence was not in his parents nor in any man else, but only in God. Then the duke, whispering in the ear of him next by him, said that he would rather pluck the bishop by the hair of his head out of the church than take this at his hand. This was not spoken so secretly but that the Londoners overheard him. Whereupon being set in a rage they cried out that they would not suffer their bishop to be abused. Rather they would lose their lives than that he should be drawn out by the hair. Thus that council, broken with scolding and brawling for that day, was dissolved before nine o'clock, and the duke with Lord Percy went to parliament; where the same day before dinner a bill was put up in the name of the king by Lord Thomas Wostock and Lord Henry Percy that the City of London should no more be governed by a mayor, but by a captain as in time before; and that the Marshal of England should have all the ado in taking the arrests within the City as in other cities, with other petitions tending to the derogation of the liberties of London.

The same year upon the 12th of June died the worthy and victorious prince, King Edward III, after he had reigned 51 years; a prince no more aged in years than renowned for many singular virtues, but principally noted for his meekness and clemency towards his subjects and inferiors, ruling them without all rigour and severity. Among other noble ornaments of his nature thus he is described of some, which may suffice for the comprehension of the rest: 'To the orphans he was a father, compatient to the afflicted, mourning with the miserable, relieving the oppressed, and to all them that wanted an helper in time of need.' But above all other things in this prince to be commemorate, in my mind, is this, that he, above all other kings of this realm unto the time of Henry VIII, was the greatest bridler of the Pope's usurped power and outrageous oppressions: during all the time of which king neither the Pope could greatly prevail in this realm, and also John Wickliffe was maintained with favour and aid sufficient.

KING RICHARD II

After King Edward III succeeded his son's son, Richard II, of the age of eleven years; who in the same year with great pomp and solemnity was crowned at Westminster: who was no great disfavourer of the doctrine of Wickliffe: albeit at the first beginning, partly through the iniquity of time and partly through the Pope's letters, he could not do that he would. Notwithstanding something he did in that behalf; more than in the end he had thank for of the Papists, as shall appear. But as times do change, so changeth commonly the cause and state of men. The bishops now seeing the aged king to be taken away, during the time of whose old age all the government of the realm depended upon the Duke of Lancaster, and seeing the duke with Lord Percy, the Lord Marshal, give over their office and remain in their private houses without intermeddling, thought now the time to have some vantage over John Wickliffe; who hitherto under the protection of the duke and

Lord Marshal had some rest and quiet. Concerning the story of which Wickliffe I trust, gentle reader, it is not out of thy memory how, he being brought before the bishops, by the means of the duke and Lord Henry Percy, the council was interrupted and brake before nine o'clock, by reason whereof Wickliffe at that time escaped without any further trouble. Who notwithstanding being by the bishops forbid to deal in that doctrine any more, continued with his fellows going barefoot and in long frieze gowns, preaching diligently unto the people.

The year following, Pope Gregory, taking his time, after the death of King Edward sendeth his bull unto the University of Oxford, rebuking them sharply, imperiously, and like a Pope, for suffering so long the doctrine of John Wycliffe to take root, and not plucking it up with the crooked sickle of their catholic doctrine. Which bull when it came to be exhibited unto their hands, the proctors and masters of the university stood long in doubt, deliberating whether to receive the Pope's bull with honour or to reject it with shame. Beside this bull sent to Oxford the Pope directed letters to the Archbishop of Canturbury and the Bishop of London, with the Conclusions of John Wickliffe enclosed, commanding them by virtue of those his letters apostolical to cause the said John Wickliffe to be apprehended and cast into prison.

The day of examination being come, a certain personage of the prince's Court named Lewes Clifford, entering in among the bishops, commanded them that they should not proceed with any definitive sentence against John Wickliffe. With which words all they were so amazed and their combs so cut that they became speechless. Thus by God's providence escaped Wickliffe the second time out of the bishops' hands, and was by them dismissed upon his declaration made of his articles. The story addeth these words: 'Not only the citizens of London but also the vile abjects of the city presumed to be so bold in the same chapel at Lambeth where the bishops were sitting on Wickliffe, both to entreat for him and also to let and stop the same matter; trusting, I suppose, upon the negligence which they saw before in the bishops.'

Thus Wickliffe through the favour and diligence of the Londoners either shifted off the bishops or else satisfied them, so that for that time he was dismissed and scaped clearly away, only being charged by the bishops that he should not teach any such doctrine any more. This good man notwithstanding ceased not to proceed in his godly purpose, labouring still in the Church as he had begun; unto whom this was a great help, that in the same year Pope Gregory XI, the stirrer up of all this trouble against him, turned up his heels and died. After whom ensued a schism in Rome between two Popes and other succeeding them, one striving against another. The schism endured thirty-nine years until the Council of Constance. The occasioner of which schism was Urban VI, who in the beginning of his Popedom was so insolent to his cardinals, and to dukes, princes, and queens, and so set to advance his nephew and kindred, that his cardinals and courtiers by little and little shrunk from him, and set up a French Pope against him, named Clement.

As touching this pestilent and miserable schism, it would require another Iliad to comprehend all the circumstances thereof; what trouble in the whole Church, what parts-taking in every country, what imprisoning of priests and prelates, what shedding of blood did follow thereof; how Ottho, Duke of Brunsewicke and Prince of Tarentum, was murdered; how Joan, Queen of Hierusalem and Sicillia, his wife, who before had sent to Pope Urban, besides other gifts, 40,000 ducats in pure gold, after by the said Urban was committed to prison and strangled; what cardinals were racked and without all mercy tormented on gibbets to death; what battles were fought between the two Popes, whereof 5000 on the one side were slain, beside the number of them which were taken prisoners; of the beheading of five cardinals together after long torments; and how the Bishop Aquilonensis, being suspected of Urban for not riding faster with the Pope, his horse being not good, was slain by the Pope's commandment, sending his soldiers to slay him and cut him in pieces. All which things with divers moe acts of horrible cruelty, because they are discoursed at full by Theodoricke Niem, who was near to Pope Urban and present at all his doings, I here pretermit.

About three years after there fell a cruel dissension in England between the common people and the nobility, the which did not a little disturb the commonwealth. In this tumult Simon of Sudbury, Archbishop of Canturbury, was taken by the rustical people and beheaded; in whose place succeeded William Courtney, which was no less diligent than his predecessor to root out heretics. Notwithstanding Wickliffe's sect daily grew to greater force until William Barton, Vice-chancellor of Oxford, about 1380 had the rule of that university: who calling together eight monastical doctors and four other set forth an edict declaring unto every man, and threatening them under a grievous penalty, that no man should be so hardy hereafter to associate with any of Wickliffe's fautors; and unto Wickliffe himself he threatened excommunication and imprisonment, and to all his fautors, unless they after three days' warning did amend. Which when Wickliffe understood, forsaking the Pope and all the clergy he thought to appeal unto the king's Majesty; but the Duke of Lancaster forbade him, that he should not attempt any such matters but submit himself unto the judgment of his ordinary. Whereby Wickliffe, beset with vexations as it were in the midst of the waves, was forced once again to make confession of his doctrine, qualifying his assertions after such a sort that he did assuage the rigour of his enemies.

The next year, by the commandment of William Archbishop of Canturbury, there was a convocation holden at London, where John Wickliffe was commanded to be present; but whether he appeared or not I find it not certainly affirmed. Here is not to be passed over the great miracle of God's divine admonition; for when the archbishop and suffragans, with Doctors of Divinity, lawyers, and a great company of babbling friars, were gathered together at the Grey Friars in London to consult as touching Wickliffe's books and that whole sect, the very hour that they should go forward with their business a terrible earthquake fell throughout England; whereupon divers of the suffragans, feared by the strange demonstration, thought it good to leave off from their purpose. But the archbishop, more bold than wise, interpreting the chance which had happened clear contrary to another meaning, did confirm their minds to proceed in their enterprise; who then discoursing Wickliffe's articles, not according unto the sacred canons of Holy Scripture but unto their private affections, gave sentence that some of them were plainly heretical, othersome half erroneous, other irreligious, some seditious.

THE ARTICLES OF JOHN WICKLIFFE CONDEMNED AS HERETICAL

1. The substance of material bread and wine doth remain after consecration.
2. The accidents do not remain without the subject.
3. Christ is not in the sacrament truly and really, in his corporal person.
4. If a bishop or priest be in deadly sin, he doth not order, consecrate, nor baptize.
5. If a man be truly contrite, all exterior confession is superfluous.
6. It is not stablished by the gospel that Christ did ordain the mass.

7. If the Pope be a reprobate, he hath no power over faithful Christians, except peradventure it be given him from the emperor.
8. Since the time of Urban VI there is none to be received for Pope, but to live every man under his own law.
9. To be against the Scripture that ecclesiastical ministers should have temporal possessions.

The vice-chancellor in Oxford was Mr Robert Rigges; the proctors were John Huntsman and Walter Dish; who as far as they durst favoured the cause of Wickliffe. The same year 1382, when certain public sermons should be appointed at the feast of the Ascension and of *Corpus Christi* to be preached in the cloister of St Frideswide (now called Christ's Church) by the vice-chancellor and proctors, the doings thereof the vice-chancellor and proctors had committed to Philip Repington and Nicholas Herford. First Herford beginning was noted to defend John Wickliffe openly to be a faithful, good, and innocent man; for the which no small ado with outcries was among the friars. Herford grew first in suspicion among the enemies of the truth; for as soon as he began to utter anything which tended to the defence of Wickliffe, by and by the Carmelites and all the orders of religion were in his top, and laid not a few heresies unto his charge, the which they had strained out of his sermons and compiled through the industry of one Peter Stokes, a Carmelite, a kind of people prone to all kind of mischief, uproars, and dissension. After this the feast of *Corpus Christi* drew near, upon which it was looked for that Repington should preach. This man was a canon of Leicester, who preaching at Brodgates became suspected and hated of the Pharisaical brood of the friars; but through the dexterity of his wit, accompanied with modesty and honesty, he did so assuage this cruelty and persecution towards him that shortly after, by consent of the whole fellowship, he was admitted Doctor; as soon as he had taken it upon him, he stepped forth in the schools and began to show forth that which he had long hidden, protesting openly that in all moral matters he would defend Wickliffe; but as touching the sacrament he would hold his peace 'until the Lord shall otherwise illuminate the minds of the clergy'.

Now the day of *Corpus Christi* approaching, when the friars understood that this man should preach, fearing that he would rub the galls of their religion, they convented with the Archbishop of Canturbury that a little before Philip should preach, Wickliffe's *Conclusions* should be openly defamed in the presence of the whole university; the doing of which matter was committed unto Peter Stokes, standard-bearer and chief champion against Wickliffe. There were also letters sent unto the commissary that he should help in publishing the *Conclusions*. These things done, Repington at the hour appointed proceeded to his sermon; in which among other things he was reported to have uttered these sayings: that Popes or bishops ought not to be recommended above temporal lords; also that in moral matters he would defend Wickliffe as a true catholic doctor.

The sermon done, Repington entered St Frideswide's church accompanied with many friends who, the enemies surmised, were privily weaponed under their garments. Friar Stokes, suspecting this to be against him, kept himself within the Sanctuary of the church, not daring to put out his head. The vice-chancellor and Repington, friendly saluting one another in the church porch, sent away the poeple, and so departed every man to his own home. There was joy throughout the university for that sermon; but the unquiet Carmelite slipt not his matter. For by his letters he declared the whole order of the matter unto the archbishop, exaggerating the perils that he was in, desiring his help, pretermitting nothing whereby to move the archbishop's mind, which of his own nature was as hot as a toast, and ready enough to prosecute the matter of his own accord though no man had pricked him thereunto.

Three days after, the friar took the way unto the schools, minding there to prove that the Pope and the bishops ought to be prayed for before the lords temporal. Whiles this friar was thus occupied he was derided of all men, and shortly after he was sent for by the archbishop; whom the vice-chancellor and Brightwell followed up, to clear themselves from the accusations of Friar Peter. At length, being examined upon Wickliffe's *Conclusions*, they did all consent that they were worthily condemned. The vice-chancellor being afterward accused for contempt of the archbishop's letters, when he saw that no excuse would prevail, to avoid that danger, humbling himself upon his knees he desired pardon; which when he had obtained by the help of the Bishop of Winchester, he was sent away with commandments to seek out all the favourers of John Wickliffe, Herford, and Repington. This commandment being received, Herford and Repington, being privily warned by the vice-chancellor, fled to the Duke of Lancaster for help; but the duke, whether for fear or for what cause else I cannot say, forsook his miserable clients.

The eighteenth day of June, in the chamber of the preaching friars before the archbishop, in the presence of divers Doctors and Bachelors of Divinity, appeared Mr Nicholas Herford and Philip Repington, Bachelors of Divinity; who were examined severally before the archbishop, and who required day and place to deliberate upon the *Conclusions*, and to give their answer in writing. In the twentieth day of the said month, before the archbishop, in the presence of divers Doctors of Divinity and lawyers both civil and canon, appeared Mr Nicholas Herford and Philip Repington. Nicholas and Philip, being required to say fully and plainly their judgment upon the *Conclusions*, did exhibit to the archbishop certain answers in writing.

The Friday following, that is to say the 28th day of June, Nicholas and Philip appeared before the archbishop in the chapel of his manor of Otford. To whom the bishop said that, because he had not the assistance of the doctors, he continued the business touching Nicholas and Philip till Tuesday next, the first of July; and prefixed unto Nicholas and Philip to appear before him, wheresoever he should then chance to be. Tuesday being come the archbishop, in the chief house of his church at Canturbury, with the doctors and other clerks, expected Nicholas and Philip, long time by the beadle calling them, who nevertheless appeared not. Then the archbishop, pronouncing Masters Nicholas and Philip guilty of contumacy and disobedience, excommunicated them. Against this blind excommunication the parties excommunicate exhibited their appeal unto the Bishop of Rome; which appeal, as insufficient, or rather to him unpleasant, the archbishop utterly rejected, proceeding in his excommunication against them, and writing to him that should preach next at Paul's Cross to denounce openly Nicholas Herford and Philip Repington to be excommunicate. Which archbishop moreover sent another letter to Mr Rigge, Commissary of Oxford, charging him not only to denounce the sentence of excommunication and to give out public citation against them, but also to make diligent search through all Oxford for them, to have them apprehended and sent to him. In the meantime Nicholas Herford and Repington being repulsed of the duke and destitute of his supportation, whether they were sent or of their own accord went to the archbishop it was uncertain. This I find in a letter of the archbishop contained in his register, that Repington the 23rd of October the same year 1382 was reconciled to the archbishop, released, and admitted to his scholastical acts in the university. Of Nicholas Herford I find no special relation.

In the meantime, about the 23rd of September, the king sent his mandate to the archbishop for collecting of a subsidy, and to have a convocation of the clergy summoned against the next parliament, which should begin the 18th of November. The archbishop on the 15th of October directed his letters monitory to Richard Braybroke, Bishop of London, to give the same admonition to all his suffragans and other of the clergy within his province, for the assembling of the convocation. Parliament begun being holden at Oxford the 18th of November, where convocation was kept in the monastery of Frideswide. On the 24th November, in the presence of the prelates and the clergy, came in Philip Repington (otherwise called Rampington) who there abjured the conclusions aforesaid. Thus Rampington was discharged, who afterward was made Bishop of Lincoln and became the most bitter persecutor of all the bishops within the realm, as hereafter may appear.

As touching Nicholas Herford, during the time of this convocation he did not appear; and therefore had the sentence of excommunication, against which he put his appeal from the archbishop to the king and his Council. The archbishop would not admit it, but caused him to be apprehended and enclosed in prison. Notwithstanding he escaped out of prison, returning to his former exercise and preaching as before, albeit in as secret manner as he could. Whereupon the archbishop, thundering out his bolts of excommunication against him, sendeth to all pastors and ministers, willing them in all churches to divulge the excommunication to all men: he writeth moreover and sendeth charge to all the laity to beware that their simplicity be not deceived by his doctrine, but that they like catholic children will avoid him. Not contented with this he addresseth his letters unto the king, requiring the aid of his temporal sword to chop off his neck whom he had already cast down. Note, reader, the seraphical charity of these priestly prelates towards the poor redeemed flock of Christ. Yet these be they which, washing their hands with Pilate, say *Nobis non licet interficere quemquam*: 'It is not our parts to kill any man'.

Meanwhile what became of John Wickliffe is not certainly known: so far as may be gathered out of Walden, it appeareth that he was driven to exile. He was alive wheresoever he was, as by his letter may appear, which he about this time wrote to Pope Urban VI, declaring a brief confession of his faith. But this Urban, otherwise termed Turbanus, was so hot in his wars against Clement, the French Pope, that he had no leisure and less list to attend unto Wickliffe's matters; by which schism God so provided for poor Wickliffe that he was in some more rest and quietness. Concerning which schismatical wars it shall not be impertinent from the order of our story to touch something of the tragical doings of these two holy Popes striving for the triple crown; to the intent that the Christian reader, judging by their fruits and proceedings, may see what difference is between these Popes and Christ and his apostles. For though in the gospel it is read that certain of the disciples did strive which should be the greater, yet neither do we read that one of them took ever weapon against the other; moreover they, in striving as they did, were sharply rebuked of our Saviour Christ.

About the beginning of the year following, 1383, Pope Urban, setting all his study how to conquer the contrary Pope, being then at Avinion, seeing all his other means to fail and that his cross-keys could do no good, took the sword of Romulus and set upon him with open war. First devising whom he might best choose for his chief champion, he thought none meeter than Henry Spenser, Bishop of Norwich, a young and stout prelate, fitter for the camping cure than for the peaceable Church of Christ, as might appear by his acts done at Lennam in striving for the mayor's mace. Unto this bishop the Pope had sent his bulls to croysy whosoever would go with him into France to destroy the Antipope and to make war against all that took his part. Which bulls, for that they gave him so great authority, he caused to be published in the parliament house, and copies to be sent all about and fastened upon church doors and monastery gates, that all might read them.

This courageous or rather outrageous bishop, armed with the Pope's authority, about the time of Lent came to the parliament, where great contention and almost no less schism was about the voyage of this popish bishop than was between the Popes themselves. Many thought it not safe to commit the king's subjects unto an unskilful priest. So great was the diversity of judgments that the voyage of the bishop was protracted unto the Saturday afore Passion Sunday. In the which Sunday was sung the anthem *Ecce crucem Domini, fugite partes adversae:* 'Behold the cross of the Lord, fly away you adversaries.' After which the parties agreed amongst themselves by common decree that the bishop should set forward in his voyage, having to him given the

Fifteenth. Which things concluded, this warlike bishop set forward in his Pope-holy journey; who about May being come to Canturbury, and there tarrying for a wind in the monastery of St Augustine, received a writ that he should return to the king to know further of his pleasure. The bishop, fearing that his journey should be stayed and all his labour lost with great derision unto him, thought better to commit himself to fortune with that little army he had than by tarrying to be made a ridicule unto his adversaries. He sent word to the king that he was now prepared and well forward on his journey, and that it was not expedient to protract the time for any kind of talk; and that it was more convenient for him to hasten his journey to God's glory and also to the honour of the king. Thus he, calling his men unto him, entered forthwith the seas and went to Calis; where he waiting a few days for the rest of his army, on its arrival took his journey to Gravenidge, which he besieged so desperately, without any engines of war or counsel of men skilful in such affairs, that he seemed rather to fly upon them than to invade them. At length through the superstition of our men, trusting upon the Pope's absolution, he so harishly approached the walls and invaded the enemies that a great number of them were piteously slain with shot and wild-fire; till at the end, the inhabiters being vanquished, our men entered the town with their bishop, where they at his commandment destroying man, woman, and child, left not one alive of all them which remained in the town. 'And so it came to pass by the virtue of the cross that our men so prevailed against the enemies of the cross that not one of them remained alive.' *Ex Chron. Mon. D. Albani.*

From Gravenidge this warlike bishop set forward to Dunkyrke, where not long after the Frenchmen joined with them in battle; in which battle, if the story be true, 12,000 of the Frenchmen were slain in the chase, and of our men but seven missing. It would require a long tractation to discourse of all things done in these Popish wars; but certes lamentable it is to see the pitiful slaughter of Christ's people by means of these pitiless Popes during these wars in France; as when the bishop coming from Dunkyrke to the siege of Ypres, a great number of Englishmen there were lost and much money consumed, and yet nothing done effectually, to the ignominy of the bishop. Again, after the siege of Ypres thus with shame broke up, the bishop, proceeding with a small power to fight with the French king's camp contrary to the counsel of his captains, was fain to break company with them; whereby part of the army went unto Burburgh, and the bishop with his part returned to Gravenidge; which both towns shortly after were besieged by the French army, to the great loss both of the English and French. In fine, when the bishop could keep Gravenidge no longer, the said bishop with his croysies came home again as wise as he went. And thus making an end of this pontifical war, we will return from whence we digressed to the story of John Wickliffe.

Wickliffe returning within short space either from banishment or from some other place where he was secretly kept, repaired to his parish of Lutterworth where he was parson, and there quietly departing this mortal life slept in peace in the Lord in the year 1384, upon Silvester's Day.[1] Wickliffe albeit in his lifetime had many grievous enemies, yet there was none so cruel unto him as the clergy. Notwithstanding he had many good friends, not only of the meanest sort but also nobility, amongst whom are to be numbered John Clenbon, Lewes Clifford, Richard Sturius, Thomas Latimer, William Nevill, John Mountegew. Besides all these there was the Earl of Salisbury, who for contempt towards the sacrament in carrying it home was enjoined by Radulf Ergom, Bishop of Salisbury, to make a cross of stone in which all the story of the matter should be written; and every Friday during his life to come to the cross barefoot and bareheaded in his shirt, and there upon his knees to do penance.

Let us adjoin the testimonial of the University of Oxford of John Wickliffe:

'Forsomuch as it is not commonly seen that the acts and monuments of valiant men, nor the praise and merits of good men, should be hidden with perpetual silence, but that true report and fame should continually spread abroad the same in strange and distant places; forsomuch also as the provident discretion of man's nature, being recompensed with cruelty, hath devised this buckler and defence against such as slander other men's doings, that whensoever witness by word of mouth cannot be present, the pen may supply the same: it followeth that the special good will and tender care which we bear unto J. Wickliffe, sometime child of this our university and Professor of Divinity, moving and stirring our minds, with one voice and testimony we witness his whole life to have been most sincere and commendable; whose honest manners, profoundness of learning, and most redolent renown, we desire the more earnestly to be known unto all faithful, for that we understand the ripeness of his conversation, his diligent labours and

[1] 31st December.—Ed.

travails, to tend to the praise of God, the safeguard of others, and the profit of the Church.

'Wherefore we signify that his conversation from his youth unto his death was so praiseworthy that never at any time was there any note of suspicion noised of him. In his answering, reading, preaching, and determining, he behaved himself laudably and as a stout champion of the Faith, vanquishing by the force of the Scriptures all such who by their wilful beggary blasphemed Christ's religion. Neither was this doctor convict of any heresy. God forbid that our prelates should have condemned a man of such honesty for an heretic; who had written in logic, philosophy, divinity, morality, and the speculative art without peer. The knowledge of which all and singular things we desire to testify to the intent that the renown of this doctor may be the more evident and had in reputation. In witness whereof we have caused these our letters testimonial to be sealed with our common seal.

'Dated the 5th day of October 1406.'

As we have declared the testimony of the University of Oxford, it followeth likewise that we set forth the contrary judgments of his enemies, blinded with malicious hatred against him; especially of the Pope's Council gathered at Constance, proceeding first in condemning his books, then his articles, and afterward burning his bones, commanding them to be taken up forty-one years after he was buried, as appeareth by the decree of the said synod, the form whereof we thought hereunto to annex.

'Forsomuch as by the decree of the Council of Rome and by the commandment of the Apostolical See, after due delays being given they proceeded unto the condemnation of Wickliffe and his memory; having made proclamation to call forth whosoever would defend the said Wickliffe if there were any such, but there did none appear; and witnesses being examined by commissioners appointed by Pope John and this Council upon the impenitency and obstinacy of the said John Wickliffe, as the order of the law requireth; and his impenitency and obstinacy being proved by evident signs and tokens: wherefore the Sacred Synod declareth and giveth sentence that John Wickliffe was a notorious heretic and died in his heresy; cursing and condemning both him and his memory.

'This Synod also decreeth that the body and bones of the said John Wickliffe, if they might be discerned from the bodies of other, faithful people, be taken out of the ground and thrown away far

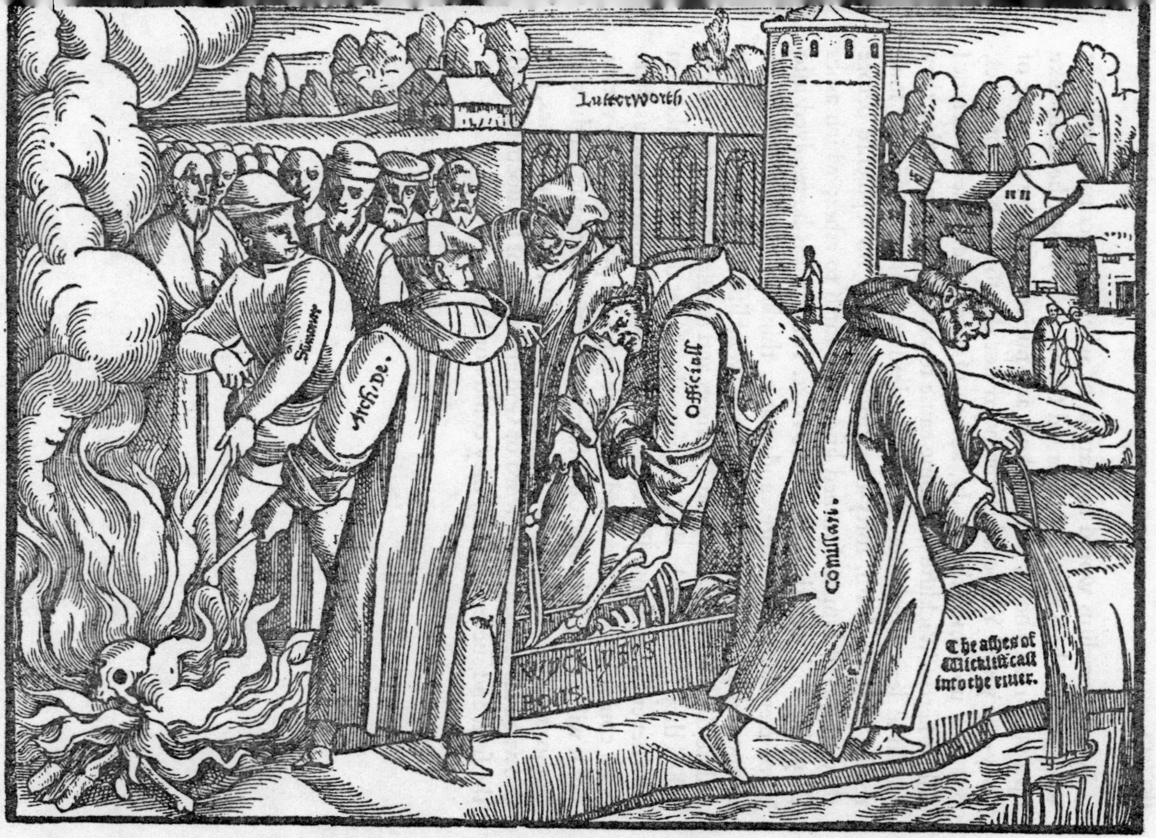

'The order and maner of taking up the body of John Wickcliffe, and burning his bones 41 yeares after his death.'

from the burial of any church, according unto the canon laws and decrees.'

What Heraclitus would not laugh, or what Democritus would not weep, to see these sage and reverend Catos occupy their heads to take up a poor man's body, so long dead, and buried before by the space of forty-one years? Yet peradventure were not able to find his right bones, but took up some other body, and so of a catholic made an heretic! Albeit herein Wickliffe had some cause to give them thanks, that they would at least spare him till he was dead and also give him so long respite after his death, forty-one years to rest in his sepulchre before they ungraved him and turned him from earth to ashes; which ashes they also took and threw into the river. And so was he resolved into three elements, earth, fire, and water, thinking thereby utterly to extinct both the name and doctrine of Wickliffe for ever. Not much unlike the example of the old Pharisees and sepulchre-knights, which, when they had brought the Lord unto the grave, thought to make him sure never to rise again. But these and all other must know that as there is no counsel against the Lord, so there is no keeping down of verity, but it will spring and come out of dust and ashes, as appeared right well in this man. For though they digged up his body, burnt his bones, and drowned his ashes, yet the word of God and truth of his doctrine, with the fruit and success thereof, they could not burn.

CHAPTER 2

THE LOLLARDS

These things thus accomplished which pertain to the story of Wickliffe, let us now proceed to entreat of the rest which, springing out of the same university and raised up out of his ashes, were partakers of the same persecution: of whom Thomas Walden, in his book *De Sacramentis & Sacramentalibus*, saith that many suffered most cruel death and many did forsake the realm; in the number of whom was William Swinderby, Walter Brute, John Purvey, Richard White, William Thorpe, and Raynold Pecocke, Bishop of Chichester. To this catalogue also pertaineth Laurence Redman, Master of Art; David Sautre, divine; John Ashwarby, vicar of St Mary Church at Oxford; William James, an excellent young man; Rafe Greenhurst, John Scut, and Philip Norice; which being excommunicated by Pope Eugenius IV in 1446 appealed unto a General Council; Peter Paine, who flying from Oxford unto Bohemia did stoutly contend against the sophisters as touching both kinds of the sacrament; who afterward was sent unto the Council of Basil, where he disputed upon the fourth article, touching the civil dominion of the clergy, *an.* 1438; also Lord Cobham. To these and other favourers of Wickliffe we may add also the Bohemians; forsomuch as the doctrine of Wickliffe in that country also took root, coming from England as here followeth.

There chanced at that time a student of Bohemia to be at Oxford, one of a wealthy house and a noble stock; who returning from Oxford to the University of Prage carried with him certain books of Wickliffe. It chanced the same time a nobleman of Prage had built a great church of Mathias and Mathew, giving it great lands and finding it two preachers every day to preach to the people. John Hus was one; a man of great knowledge and of a pregnant wit. Hus, having familiarity with this young man in perusing these books of Wickliffe, took such pleasure and fruit in reading thereof that not only he began to defend this author openly in the schools but also in his sermons, commending him for a good, holy, and heavenly man, wishing himself, when he should die, to be placed where the soul of Wickliffe should be.

Thus much concerning the adherents of Wickliffe in general. Now particularly and in order let us prosecute the stories of the parties aforenamed, beginning with William Swinderby and Walter Brute.

The history of William Swinderby

In the year 1389 William Swinderby, priest within the diocese of Lincoln, was presented before John, Bishop of Lincoln, and examined upon certain articles: his denouncers were Friar Frisby, Observant; Friar Hincely, Augustine; and Thomas Blaxton, Dominican. The articles in form of words might seem somewhat strange; yet that all may see the spiteful malice of these spider-friars in sucking all things to poison and forging that is not true, I thought good to notify the same:

'Men may in no manner for debt imprison any man; if parishioners know their curate to be a lecher incontinent and an evil man, they ought to withdraw from him their tithes, or else they be fautors of his sins; no prelate may curse a man except he know beforehand that he is cursed of God; any priest may absolve any sinner, being contrite; any priest being in deadly sin, if he give himself to consecrate the body of the Lord, committeth idolatry; no priest entereth any house but to evil-entreat the wife, daughter, or maid; a child is not truly baptized if the priest, godfather, or godmother be in deadly sin.'

These articles, untruly collected, were cruelly exhibited against him in the bishop's court. Although he never taught or defended them, the friars declared him to be convict, bringing also dry wood with them to burn him; and would not leave him before he swore for fear of death never to hold or teach them, under pain of relapse; and that he should go to certain churches to revoke the foresaid conclusions, which he never affirmed; which penance he did obediently accomplish. Whereby it may be conjectured what credit is to be given to the conclusions which these cavilling friars, wresting all things to the worst, have imputed to Wickliffe and all others of that sort, whom they so falsely belie and so maliciously persecute. After these things done in the diocese of Lincoln, Swinderby removed to the diocese of Herford, where he was molested by the friars again and by John Trefnant, Bishop of Herford. On the 16th day of August, the bishop in the parish church of Whithorn sitting in judgment gave sentence against William as followeth:

'The name of Christ being invocated, we John, by permission of God Bishop of Herford, weighing and considering the articles by faithful

Christians put up against Swinderby, pretending himself to be priest, with mature deliberation had before with Masters and Doctors of Divinity and other faculties, with their consent do pronounce and declare the said William an heretic, schismatic, and false informer of the people, and such as is to be avoided of faithful Christians. Wherefore we admonish under pain of the law all Christians of what condition soever, that neither they nor any of them within our diocese or any other do believe, defend, or favour the said William, till he deserve fully to be reconciled to the bosom of Holy Church.'

What afterward became upon him I have not certainly to affirm; whether he in prison died, or escaped their hands, or was burned, there is no certain relation made. During the time of Richard II no great harm was done unto him. Richard being wrongfully deposed, Henry IV invaded the kingdom of England; about the beginning of whose reign we read of a certain parliament mentioned also of Thomas Walden, in which it was decreed that favourers of Wickliffe should be apprehended, who at that time were called Lollards: if they did obstinately persever in that doctrine they should be delivered unto the bishop of the diocese, and from him should be committed to the secular magistrate. This law brought a certain priest unto punishment the same year, who was burned at Smithfield. It doth not appear by the story what the priest's name was: by divers conjectures it appeareth unto me that his name was Swinderby. If he were burned, the bishops, friars, and priests who were the causes thereof have a great thing to answer to the Lord, when he shall come to judge the quick and the dead, *et seculum per ignem*.

The process against Walter Brute

After the story of William Swinderby I thought good to adjoin the doings of Walter Brute, his companion, being a layman and learned, brought up in the University of Oxford; the tractation of whose discourse as it is something long, so therein may appear things worthy to be read—the mighty operation of God's Spirit in him, his ripe knowledge, modest simplicity, valiant constancy, and manifold conflicts against God's enemies. The chiefest occasion that seemed to stir up the zeal of this Walter against the Pope was the impudent pardons and indulgences of Urban granted to Henry Spenser Bishop of Norwich, to fight against Clement; secondly the wrongful condemnation of the articles of William Swinderby. The order whereof in the process here following more plainly may appear:

'To all faithful people that shall hear this our process John Bishop of Herford sendeth greeting. We would that you all should know that of late by many zealous followers of the Catholic Faith it was lamentably done us to understand that a son of ours going out of kind, named Walter Brute, of our diocese, hath under a cloaked show of holiness damnably seduced the people; and setting behind him the fear of God doth seduce them as much as he can, teaching as well the nobles as the commons in conclusions heretical, schismatical, erroneous, and heretofore condemned.'

The bishop appointed to Walter the 3rd of October to hear his opinion: which day now at hand, being Friday in the year 1393, Walter appeared before him sitting in the cathedral church at Herford, having for his assistants divers prelates and abbots and twenty Bachelors of Divinity and two Doctors of the Law. Amongst these was Nicholas Herford. Now was Walter apposed of his writings. Earnest were they in picking out his heresies, schisms, errors, and divers other things. After they had continued all that day and the two days following in their examinations, Brute submitted himself to the determination of the Church and to the correction of the bishop, as appeareth in a scroll written in English, the tenor of which is as followeth:

'I Walter Brute submit myself principally to the evangely of Jesus Christ and to the determination of Holy Kirk, to the General Councils of Holy Kirk, and to the sentence and determination of the Four Doctors of Holy Writ, that is, Augustine, Ambrose, Hierome, and Gregory. And I meekly submit me to your correction, as a subject ought to his bishop.'

Which scroll Brute read with a loud voice at the cross in the churchyard, in presence of the bishop and other above written and a great multitude of people. After which Thomas Crawlay, Bachelor of Divinity, made the sermon unto the people, and took for his theme the words of the Apostle to the Romans: 'Be not over-wise in your own conceits, but stand in fear.'

What became to Walter Brute, or what end he had, I find it not registered; but like it is that he for this time escaped.

Unto the narration of these abovesaid we will adjoin the story of Peter Pateshull, an Austin friar, who obtaining by the Pope's privilege liberty to change his coat and religion, and hearing the doctrine of John Wickliffe and others of the same sort, began to preach openly and to detect the vices of his order, in such sort as all men wondered to hear the horrible reciting thereof. This being brought to the ears of his order, they to the number of twelve, coming to the place where he was preaching, thought to have withstood him perforce: among whom one stood up openly in his preaching and contraried that which he said, who then was preaching in the Church of St Christopher in London. This when the Londoners did see, were moved with great ire against the friar, thrusting him with his brethren out of the church, whom they not only had beaten and wounded but followed home, minding to have destroyed their mansion with fire; and so would have done had not one of the sheriffs with gentle words mitigated their rage. After this Pateshull was desired by the Londoners to put in writing that which he had said, and other things more that he knew by the friars; who then writing the same accused the friars of murder committed against divers of their brethren. To make the matter more credible he declared the names of them that were murdered, with the names of their tormentors, where and when they were murdered, and where they were buried. He affirmed further that they were Sodomites, and traitors to the king and the realm, with many other crimes which mine author for tediousness leaveth off to recite. For the confutation of the friars the Londoners caused the bill to be set up at St Paul's Church door, which was there read and copied out by many. This was in the year of our Lord 1387, the tenth year of King Richard II.

Thus it may appear how the gospel of Christ, preached by John Wickliffe and others, began to spread and fructify in London and other places of the realm; and more would have done, no doubt, had not William Courtney the archbishop, and other prelates with the king, set them with might and main to gainstand the course thereof; albeit, as is said before, I find none which were put to death therefore during the reign of King Richard II: although he cannot be utterly excused for molesting the godly preachers of that time, yet neither was he so cruel against them as others that came after him; and that which he did seemed to proceed by the instigation of the Pope and other bishops rather than by the consent of his parliament or advice of his Council, or by his own nature. For as the decrees of parliament in all his time were constant in stopping out the Pope's provisions and bridling his authority, as we shall see anon, so the nature of the king was not so fiercely set if he had not stood so much in fear of the Bishop of Rome and his prelates, by whose importune letters he was continually urged to do contrary to that which both right required and will perhaps in him desired. But howsoever the doings of this king are to be excused or not, undoubted it is that Queen Anne his wife deserveth singular commendation; who living with the king had the gospels of Christ in English. Anne was a Bohemian born, and sister to Wincelaus, King of Bohemia, before; who was married to King Richard about the fifth year of his reign and continued with him eleven years. It may seem not unprobable that the Bohemians resorting into this realm after her perused here the books of John Wickliffe, which afterwards they conveyed into Bohemia.

Queen Anne, after she had lived with King Richard about eleven years, changed this mortal life and was buried at Westminster; at whose funeral Thomas Arundell, then Archbishop of York and Lord Chancellor, made the sermon; in which, as remaineth in the library of Worcester recorded, he said that it was more joy of her than of any woman that ever he knew; for notwithstanding that she was an alien born, she had in English all four gospels, with the doctors upon them; and he said they were good and true. And further did greatly commend her in that she, being so great a lady, would study so lowly so virtuous books; and he blamed sharply the negligence of the prelates and other men; insomuch that some said he would on the morrow leave the office of Chancellor, forsake the world, and give him to fulfil his pastoral office for that he had read in those books; and then it had been the best sermon that ever they heard. Notwithstanding the same Thomas Arundell after this sermon and promise made became the most cruel enemy that might be against English books and the authors thereof.

Drawing now towards the latter end of King Richard's reign, it remaineth that we show forth a summary recapitulation of such parliamentary notes and proceedings as were practised in this king's time against the jurisdiction of the Bishop of Rome; to the intent that such that think the receiving of the Pope's double authority to be such an ancient thing within this realm may diminish their opinion, as evidently may appear by divers arguments concerning the election of bishops by the king. Innumerable examples of the sort are to be seen in ancient histories of this our realm, as also out of the parliament rolls in the time of King Edward III; whereunto may be added the notes of parliaments holden in the reign of King Richard II, the collection whereof in part here followeth:

'In the first year of King Richard II, in the parliament holden at Westminster, it was requested and granted that the Pope's collector be willed no longer to gather the first fruits of benefices within this realm, being a very novelty, and that no person do any longer pay them; that no man do procure any benefice by provision from Rome; that no Englishman do take to farm of any alien any benefice or prebend; that remedy might be had against the Pope's reservations to dignities elective.

'In the second year of the said king it was requested that order might be taken touching aliens, having the greatest part of the church dignities in their hands. It was enacted that all the benefices of cardinals and other rebels to Pope Urban shall be seized into the king's hands.

'In the fourth year it was requested that all priors, aliens, might be removed out of their houses, and Englishmen placed in their livings.

'In the 11th year it was put up by the petitions of the Commons that impositions gathered by the Pope's bulls *Volumus* and *Imponimus* might be employed on the king's wars against the schismatics of Scotland, and that such as bring into the realm the like bulls may be reputed traitors.

'In the 15th year it was accorded, for that Sir William Brian had purchased from Rome a bull directed to the Archbishops of Canturbury and York, to excommunicate such as had broken up his house and taken away divers letters and charters: the same bull, being read in parliament, was adjudged prejudicial to the Crown and in derogation of the laws; for which he was by the king, and assent of the Lords, committed to the Tower.

'In the 17th year it was desired that remedy might be had against such religious persons as caused their underlings to marry free women inheritable, whereby the lands came to those religious men's hands by collusion.

'In the year of the same king's reign 21 the Commons accused Thomas Arundell, Archbishop of Canturbury, for that he procured the Duke of Gloucester and the Earls of Arundell and Warwick to encroach to themselves royal power, and to judge to death Simon de Burley and Sir John Berners without the king's assent. The archbishop submitted himself to the king's mercy; wherefore the king, lords, and Sir Thomas Percy, proctor for the clergy, adjudged the fact of the archbishop to be treason, and ordered that the archbishop should be banished, his temporalities seized, his lands and goods forfeited. The king further prescribed that the said archbishop should take his passage within six weeks at Dover, toward France.'

We come now to the twenty-second year of King Richard's reign, 1399. In which year happened the lamentable deposing of Richard from his kingly sceptre. The king, upon certain affairs to be done, took his voyage into Ireland. Meanwhile Henry of Bolingbroke, Duke of Herford, and with him Thomas Arundell, which before were both exiled, returning out of France to Calice came into England, challenging the dukedom of Lancaster after the death of his father. With them also came the son and heir of the Earl of Arundell, being yet but young. These together arrived at Ravenspur in the north; at the knowledge whereof much people gathered unto them. As the duke was hovering on the sea to enter the land, Edmund Duke of York, the king's uncle, to whom the king committed the custody of the realm, having intelligence thereof called to him the Bishop of Chichester, Edmund Stafford, Chancellor of the realm; W. Scroupe, Earl of Wiltshire, Lord Treasurer, with divers other, consulting with them what was to be done; who gave their advice—very unfruitful—that he should go to St Albon's, there to wait for more strength, able to encounter with the duke. But as the people out of divers quarters resorted thither, many protested that they would do nothing to the prejudice of the Duke of Lancaster, who, they said, was unjustly expulsed. The rest of the council (J. Busshey, W. Bagot, Henry Grene, W. Scroupe), hearing how the commons were minded to join with the Duke of Herford, left the Duke of York and the Lord Chancellor and fled to the castle of Bristow. These four were they to whom the common fame ran that the king had let out his realm to farm; and were so hated that for hatred of them more than for the king this commotion was among the people.

As this broil was in England, the noise thereof sounding to the king's ears being then in Ireland, for speed of returning left both his business and most of his ordnance behind; and passing the seas landed at Milford Haven, not daring to come to London.

On the contrary side, unto Henry Duke of Herford came the Earl of Northumberland and Henry his son, Lord Radulph Nevill, Earl of Westmorland, and other lords to a great number, so that the multitude rose to 60,000 able soldiers; who first making toward the castle of Bristow took Busshey, Grene, Scroupe, and Bagot; of whom three incontinent were beheaded: Bagot escaped and fled to Ireland.

The king meanwhile, lying about Wales without comfort or counsel, and perceiving the commons that were up in such power against him would rather die than give up that they had begun, for fear of themselves, seeing no other remedy called to him Lord T. Percy, Earl of Worcester, and steward of his household, willing him with other of his family to provide for themselves in time; who then openly in the hall brake his white rod before them all, commanding every man to shift for himself; although Fabian and some other say that he did this of his own accord, contrary to his allegiance. The king, compassed on every side with miseries, shifted from place to place, the duke still following him; till at length at the castle of Conewey the king desired to talk with Thomas Arundell and the Earl of Northumberland; to whom he declared that he would resign his crown in condition that an honourable living might be for him provided, and life promised to eight persons, such as he would name. Which being granted and ratified but not performed, he came to the castle of Flint, where after talk had with the Duke of Lancaster he was brought the same night to Chester, and from thence conveyed secretly into the Tower, there to be kept till the next parliament. As he came near to London divers evil-disposed men of the city gathered themselves, thinking to have slain him for the cruelty he had used before toward the city; but by the policies of the mayor and rulers of the city the madness of the people was stayed. Not long after followed the duke, and also began the parliament; in which the Earl of Northumberland with many other lords were sent to the king in the Tower, to take of him a full resignation according to his promise. This done, accusations were laid and engrossed against the king to the number of thirty-three, some say thirty-eight; and the next year was had to Pomfret Castle, and there famished to death.

KING HENRY IV

King Richard by common assent being deposed from his rightful crown, the Duke of Lancaster was led by the archbishop to the seat royal; who there standing up and crossing himself on forehead and breast spake as followeth:

'In the name of God, Amen. I Henry of Lancaster claim the realm of England, and the crown with all the appurtenances, as I that am descended by right line of blood coming from King Henry III, and through the right that God of his grace hath sent to me, with the help of my kin and of my friends to recover the same, etc.'

After which words the archbishop asking the assent of the people, being joyful of their new king, took the duke by the hand and placed him in the kingly throne, *an.* 1399; and shortly after by the foresaid archbishop he was crowned King of England. *Ex Chron. De Alban.*

The next year followed a parliament holden at Westminster, in which one William Sautre, a good man and a faithful priest, inflamed with zeal of true religion, required he might be heard for the commodity of the whole realm. But the matter being smelt before by the bishops, they obtained that the matter should be referred to the convocation, where Sautre being brought before the bishops the convocation was deferred to the Saturday ensuing. When Saturday was come, the 12th of February, Thomas Arundell Archbishop of Canturbury, in the presence of his council provincial, objected that the said Sir William before the Bishop of Norwich had once abjured sundry conclusions heretical and erroneous; and that after such abjuration made he publicly preached the same conclusions, disagreeing to the Catholic Faith, and to the great peril and pernicious example of others. After this he caused suchlike conclusions, holden and preached by Sir William, to be read unto the archbishop by Mr Robert Haull, chancellor to the said bishop.

Then the archbishop demanded whether he would stand to the determination of the Holy Church or not. To this Sir William said that he would stand to the determination of the Church, where such determination was not contrary to the will of God. This done, he demanded what his judgment was concerning the sacrament of the altar; who affirmed that after the words of consecration by the priest duly pronounced remained very bread, the same bread which was before the words spoken. This examination about the sacrament lasted from eight o'clock until eleven: during all this time William would no otherwise answer. Wherefore Canturbury by the consent of his whole covent there present did promulgate and give sentence against Sir William Sautre. Sentence being read, the archbishop continued the council till the 23rd of the same month of February.

The 23rd of February aforesaid, in the chapter house of St Paul in London, the archbishop objected against Sir William that after he had before the Bishop of Norwich abjured divers errors and heresies, he affirmed that in the sacrament of the altar after the consecration made by the priest there remained material bread. Hereunto William answered in mocking wise, denying that he knew of the premises. Notwithstanding he affirmed that he held and taught the aforesaid things after the date of the process made by the Bishop of Norwich, and that in the council also he held the same. Whereupon the archbishop by the assent of the whole Council determined to proceed to the degradation and deposing of William Sautre, as refallen into heresy and incorrigible.

Thus Sautre, the servant of Christ, thrust out of the Pope's kingdom and metamorphosed from a clerk to a layman, was committed unto the secular power; which done, the bishops, yet not contented, cease not to call upon the king to cause him to be brought forth for speedy execution. Whereupon the king, ready enough and too much to gratify the clergy and to retain their favours, directeth a terrible decree against William Sautre, and sent it to the Mayor and Sheriffs of London to be put in execution; the tenor whereof ensueth:

'Whereas the Reverend Father Thomas Archbishop of Canturbury hath pronounced William Sautre, sometime chaplain, to be a manifest heretic, and hath degraded him from all prerogative of the clergy, decreeing to leave him to the secular power; we therefore being lovers of the Catholic Faith command you straitly, enjoining you that you cause the said William, in some public place within your city, to be put into the fire and there really to be burned, to the manifest example of other Christians. Fail not in the execution hereof, upon the peril that will fall thereupon.'

Thus it may appear how kings have been blinded by false prelates, insomuch that they have been their slaves and butchers to slay Christ's poor innocent members. See therefore what danger it is for princes not to have understanding themselves but to be led by other men's eyes, trusting to such guides who through hypocrisy deceive them, and through cruelty devour the people.

As Henry IV, the deposer of King Richard, was the first of English kings that began the unmerciful burning of Christ's saints for standing against the Pope; so was William Sautre, the faithful martyr of Christ, the first to be burned in the reign of the foresaid king, which was the year of our Lord 1400. After the martyrdom of this man the rest of the same company began to keep themselves more closely for fear of the king, who was altogether bent to hold with the Pope's prelacy. To the godly he was terrible, in his actions immeasurable, to few men heartily beloved; but princes never lack flatterers about them. Neither was his reign very quiet, but full of trouble, of blood and misery. Such was their desire of King Richard again that many years after he was rumoured to be alive (of them which desired that to be true which they knew to be false), for which divers were executed. For six or seven years together almost no year passed without some conspiracy against the king. Long were it to recite the blood of all such nobles and other which was spilt in the reign of this king, as the Earls of Kent, Salisbury, Huntington, Surrey, Exeter, and Gloucester. *Ex lib. cui tit. Calendarium Bruti.*

The year following Sir John Clarendon with two of his servants, and the Prior of Laund with eight friars, were hanged and quartered. After these Henry Percy the younger; the Earl of Worcester, his uncle; the Lord of Kinderton and Lord Richard de Vernoun. The Earl of Northumberland scarce escaped with his pardon, *an.* 1403; in which year the prison in Cornhill called the Tun was turned into the Conduit there now standing. To let pass others hanged and quartered the same time, as Blunt, knight, Benet Kely, knight, and Thomas Wintersell, esquire, the same year was taken and executed Sir Bernard Brokes, Sir John Shilley, Sir John Mandelin, and William Frierby. After all these Lord Henry, Earl of Northumberland, and Lord Bardolfe, conspiring the king's death, were taken in the north and beheaded, which was in the 8th year of this King Henry.

This rebellion of so many nobles and other declared what grudging hearts the people bore against this king, among whom I cannot pretermit the Archbishop of York, Richard Scrope, who with Lord Moubrey, Marshal of England, gathered a great company in the north country, to whom was adjoined the help of Lord Bardolfe and Henry Percy, Earl of Northumberland. To stir up the people to take their parts they collected certain articles against the king and fastened them upon the doors of churches and monasteries, to be read of all men in English. These being seen and read, much concourse of people daily resorted more and more to the archbishop. The Earl of Westmorland, hearing of this, mustered his soldiers and bent towards the archbishop; but seeing his part too weak to encounter with him, useth policy where strength would not serve. Coming to him under cover of friendship, laboureth to seek out the causes of this great stir; to whom the archbishop answering no hurt to be intended, but profit rather to the king and commonwealth, and maintenance of public peace, withal showed him the articles aforesaid; which when the earl had read, seemed highly to commend the purpose of the bishop, promising moreover that he would help forward in that quarrel to the uttermost of his power; and required a day to be set when they might meet in some place appointed to have further talk. The archbishop was content, although much against the counsel of the Earl Marshal, and came; where the articles being openly published, the Earl of Westmorland with his company pretended well to like the same. Which done, he exhorted the archbishop that, forsomuch as his garrison had been long in armour and from home, he would discharge his soldiers and dismiss them to their business, and they would drink and join hands in the presence of the whole company. Thus they shaking hands together, the archbishop sendeth away his soldiers, not knowing himself to be circumvented before he was arrested by the earl. Shortly after, the king coming with his power to York, was there beheaded, and with him Thomas Moubrey, Marshal, with divers other of the City of York which had taken their parts; after whose slaughter the king proceedeth farther to prosecute the Earl of Northumberland and Lord Bardolfe, who then did fly to Barwicke. Two years after were slain in the field, *an.* 1408; in which year divers other were condemned by the king and put to death; among whom the Abbot of Hales was hanged.

The king, after shedding so much blood seeing himself so hardly beloved of his subjects, thought to keep in with the clergy and with the Bishop of Rome; and therefore was compelled in all things to serve their humour, as did appear as well in condemning William Sautre before as in other, which we have now to intreat of; in the number of whom cometh now to write of J. Badby, a layman, who by the cruelty of Thomas Arundell and other prelates was brought to his condemnation in this king's reign, *an.* 1409, as by their own registers appeareth.

John Badby, artificer

In the year 1409, on the first of March, the examination of John Badby, tailor, was made in a hall within the precinct of the preaching friars of London, upon the crime of heresy, before Thomas Arundell Archbishop of Canturbury, the Archbishop of York, of London, Winchester, Oxford, Norwich, Salisbury, Bath, Bangor; Edmund Duke of York, Thomas Bewford, Chancellor of England; Lord de Roos, Clerk of the Rolls, and a great number of lords, both spiritual and temporal, being present. Whilst they were in his examination, the archbishop, weighing that he would in no wise be altered, and seeing his countenance stout and heart confirmed, so that he began to persuade other in the same; when he saw that it was not in his power by exhortations nor arguments to bring Badby from his constant truth to his catholic faith, proceeded to ratify the sentence given before by the Bishop of Worcester against the said John Badby, pronouncing him an open heretic. Thus shifting their hands of him they delivered him to the secular power, and desired the temporal lords there present that they would not put John Badby to death nor deliver him to be punished in the presence of the lords above recited.

These things thus concluded by the bishops, the king's writ was not far behind; by the force whereof John Badby, still persevering in his constancy unto the death, was brought into Smithfield, and there being put into an empty barrel, was bound with iron chains fastened to a stake, having dry wood put about him. As he was standing in the tun, it happened that the king's eldest son was present, who, showing some part of the Good Samaritan, began to endeavour to save the life of him whom the Levites and Pharisees sought to put to death. He counselled him that he should withdraw himself out of these dangerous labyrinths of opinions, adding threatenings which might have daunted any man's stomach. Also Courtney, Chancellor of Oxford, preached unto him the Faith of Holy Church.

In the mean season the prior of St Bartlemew's in Smithfield brought with all solemnity the sacrament of God's body with twelve torches borne before, and showed the sacrament to the poor man at the stake. Then they demanding how he believed in it, he answered that it was hallowed bread, not God's body. Then was the tun put over him and fire put unto him. When he felt the fire he cried 'Mercy!' calling upon the Lord; so the prince commanded them to take away the tun and quench the fire. His commandment done, the prince asked him if he would forsake heresy to take him to the Faith of Holy Church; which if he would do, he should have goods enough; promising him also a yearly stipend out of the king's treasury. But this valiant champion of Christ, neglecting the prince's fair words, as also contemning all men's devices, refused worldly promises, being more vehemently inflamed with the Spirit of God than with any earthly desire. When he continued unmovable, the prince commanded him straight to be put again into the tun; and that he should not afterward look for any favour. But as he could be allured by no rewards, so was he nothing abashed at their torments, but persevered invincible to the end; not without a great and cruel battle, but with much greater triumph of victory; the Spirit of Christ having always the upper hand in his members, maugre the fury and power of the whole world.

Thus the poor Christians were oppressed in every place, but especially here in England, because the king went whole with the Pope against the Gospellers; by reason whereof the kingdom of the Pope and his members in this realm began to be so strong that none durst stir or once mute against them. The bishops, having the king on their side, armed moreover with statutes, imprisonments, sword, and faggot, ruled as they listed, as kings themselves. So strong were they that no force was able to stand against them; so exalted in pride that they thought all things subject to their Reverend Majesties. Whatsoever they decreed must of all men be obeyed. Whatsoever toy came in their fantasy was straightways stablished for a law, were it never so frivolous or superstitious; as well appeareth by Thomas Arundell and other, who having now a little leisure from killing innocent people, and having brought their enemies (as they thought) under feet, began to invent new customs, as the guise is of the Pope's church ever to intrude into the Church of God some ceremony of their own making. So this Arundell bringeth in a new-found gaud called the Tolling of Aves, in honour of our Lady, with certain Aves to be said and days of pardon to be given for the same; for the ratification whereof he directed his mandate to the Bishop of London in form as followeth:

'When we behold how the Word that was in the beginning with God chose a holy and immaculate virgin of kingly stock, in whose womb he took true flesh by inspiral inspiration, we sing to God our Saviour with great joy, thinking that though all people of the Christian religion did extol so worthy a virgin, we, the servants of her own inheritance and her peculiar dower, ought more than others to show our devotion in praising her, who being merciful to us would that our power, defended with the buckler of her protection, did subdue unto our victorious standards nations both near at hand and far off. Likewise our happy estate since the beginning of our lives may be attributed only to her medicine; to whom also we may ascribe, under our most Christian king, our diliverance from the ravening wolves which had prepared against our banquets a mess of meat full of gall. Wherefore that she being on high, sitting before the throne of the heavenly Majesty, the patroness of us all, being magnified with all men's praises may more plentifully exhibit to us, the sons of adoption, the teats of her grace; we command your brotherhood that you command the subjects of your diocese to worship our Lady, the Mother of God, with such prayer and ringing as the devotion of Christ's faithful people is wont to worship her at the ringing of curfew. We therefore grant to every man that shall say the Lord's Prayer and the Salutation of the Angel five times at the meaning peal, how oft soever, forty days of pardon.'

In the 13th year of his reign King Henry IV, keeping Christmas at Eltham, fell grievously sick. He was conveyed to London, where he began to call a parliament but tarried not the end. The infirmity of the king more and more increasing, he was brought into a fair chamber at Westminster; and as he lay in his bed he asked how they called the chamber: they answered, Jerusalem. Then he said it was his prophecy that he should make his end in Jerusalem. And so disposing himself toward his end, in the aforesaid chamber he died; whether of leprosy or of some other sharp disease I have not to affirm. *Ex vetust. Chron. Anglico.* The like prophecy we read of Pope Silvester II; to whom being inquisitive for the place where he should die, it was answered that he should die in Jerusalem. Who then saying mass in a chapel called likewise Jerusalem, perceived his end to be near, and died. Thus King Henry IV, successor to the lawful King Richard II, finished his life at Westminster, and was buried at Canturbury by the tomb of Thomas Becket, *an.* 1413.

KING HENRY V

After this Henry IV reigned Henry V his son, born at Monmouth in Wales, of whose other virtues and great victories gotten in France I have not greatly to intermeddle; especially seeing the memory of his prowess, sufficiently described in other writers, may both content the reader and unburden my labour herein: these latter perturbations of the Church offer me so much that unneth any leisure shall be left to intermeddle with matters profane.

The persecution of Lord Cobham

After the coronation then of this new king, the ninth day of April, Passion Sunday, a day so tempestuous that many did wonder at the portent, a parliament began to be called, and to be holden after Easter at Westminster, *an.* 1413. At which time the Archbishop of Canturbury collected in Paul's Church a synod of all the bishops and clergy of England. Among other weighty matters was determined that the day of St George, and also of St Dunstan, should be a double feast in holy kitchen—in Holy Church, I would say. The principal cause of the assembling thereof, as recordeth the Chronicle of St Albon's, was to repress the spreading of the gospel, and especially to withstand the noble and worthy Lord Cobham, a principal favourer and maintainer of them whom the bishop misnamed Lollards, setting them up whom the bishops had not licensed and sending them about to preach, which was against the constitution provincial, holding also and teaching opinions of the sacrament, of images, of pilgrimage, of the Keys and Church of Rome, repugnant to the determination of the Romish Church.

The articles being brought in, they proceeded in their communication, concluding among themselves that it was not possible for them to make whole Christ's coat without seam (meaning their patched Popish synagogue) unless certain great men were brought out of the way; among whom Sir John Oldcastle, Lord Cobham, was complained of by the proctors to be the chief. Him they accused first for a mighty maintainer of suspected preachers in the diocese of London, Rochester, and Herford. Not only they affirmed him to have sent thither the said preachers, but also to have assisted them by force of arms. Last of all they accused him that he was far otherwise in belief of the sacrament of the altar, of penance, of pilgrimage, of image-worshipping, and of the ecclesiastical power, than the Holy Church of Rome had taught. In the end it was concluded among them that without further delay process should be awarded out against him as a most pernicious heretic.

Some which were of more crafty experience than the other thought it not best to have the matter so rashly handled: considering Lord Cobham was a man of great birth and in favour with the king, their counsel was to know first the king's mind. This counsel was accepted, and Arundell with his bishops and a great part of the clergy went straightways unto the king, then at Keningston, and there laid most grievous complaints against Lord Cobham, to his great infamy and blemish, being a man right godly. The king gently heard those blood-thirsty prelates, and far otherwise than became his princely dignity; notwithstanding instantly desiring them that in respect of his noble stock and knighthood they should favourably deal with him; and if it were possible, without extreme handling reduce him again to the Church's unity. He promised them also that his self would seriously commune the matter with him.

Anon the king sent for Lord Cobham. As he was come he called him secretly, admonishing him betwixt him and him to submit himself to Mother Church and as an obedient child acknowledge himself culpable. The Christian knight made answer: 'You, most worthy prince, I am always willing to obey, forsomuch as I know you a Christian king and the appointed minister of God, bearing the sword to the punishment of evildoers and for safeguard of them that be virtuous. Unto you, next my God, owe I my whole obedience, and submit, as I have ever done, all that I have, ready at all times to fulfil whatsoever ye shall in the Lord command me. But touching the Pope and his spiritualty, I owe them neither suit nor service, forsomuch as I know him by the Scriptures to be the great Antichrist, the Son of Perdition, the Adversary of God, and the Abomination standing in the Holy Place.'

When the king heard this, he would talk no longer with him; and as the archbishop resorted unto him for an answer, he gave him full authority to cite, examine, and punish him, according to their devilish decrees which they called the Laws of Holy Church. Then the archbishop appointed to call before him Sir John Oldcastle, Lord Cobham, to answer to such articles as they should lay against him: so he sent his chief summoner with a very short citation unto the Castle of Cowling, where he at that time dwelt; and as the summoner was come thither, he durst in no case enter the gates of so noble a man without his licence, and returned home his message not done.

Then called the archbishop one John Butler unto him, the doorkeeper of the king's privy chamber, and with him covenanted through promises and rewards to have this matter craftily brought to pass under the king's name. Whereupon Butler took the sumner with him and went unto Lord Cobham, showing him that it was the king's pleasure that he should obey that citation; and so cited him fraudulently. Then said he to them that he in no case would consent to those devilish practices of the priests. As they informed the archbishop of that answer, he decreed by and by to have him cited by public process; and upon the Wednesday before the Nativity of our Lady, in September, he commanded letters citatory to be set upon the gates of the Cathedral Church of Rochester, three miles from thence, charging him to appear before him at Ledis the eleventh day of the same month. Those letters were taken down anon by such as bare favour unto Lord Cobham. After that caused the archbishop new letters to be set up, which also were rent down and consumed.

As he did not appear at the day appointed at Ledis, where he sat in consistory, as cruel as Cayphas, he judged him, denounced him, and condemned him of deep contumacy. After that, when he had been falsely informed by his hired spies and other glozing glaverers that Lord Cobham had laughed him to scorn, disdained all his doings, maintained his old opinions, contemned the Church's power, the dignity of a bishop, and the order of priesthood, in his moody madness without proof did he excommunicate him. Yet was not with all this his fierce tyranny satisfied, but commanded him to be cited afresh, to appear before him the Saturday before the feast of St Mathew: if he did not obey at that day he would more extremely handle him. And he compelled the lay power by terrible menacings of cursings and interdictions to assist him against that seditious apostate, schismatic, and heretic, the troubler of the public peace, enemy of the realm, and adversary of Holy Church; for all these names did he give him.

Lord Cobham, beholding the unpeaceable fury of Antichrist thus kindled against him, perceiving himself also compassed on every side with deadly dangers, took paper and pen in hand and wrote a confession of his faith, signing and sealing it with his own hand; wherein he also answered the chiefest articles laid against him. That done, he took the copy with him and went to the king, trusting to find mercy and favour at his hand. None other was that confession than the common belief or sum of the Church's Faith, the Apostles' Creed, with a brief declaration upon the same. The king would in no case receive it, but commanded it to be delivered unto his judges. Then desired he in the king's presence that an hundred knights and esquires might be suffered to come in, which would clear him of all heresies. Moreover he offered after the law of arms to fight for life or death with any man living, Christian or heathen, in the quarrel of his faith; the king and the lords of his Council excepted. Finally with all gentleness he protested before all present that he would refuse no manner of correction that should, after the laws of God, be ministered unto him. Notwithstanding all this the king suffered him to be summoned personally in his own privy chamber. Then said Lord Cobham to the king that he had appealed from the archbishop to the Pope of Rome, and therefore he ought in no case to be his judge. And having his appeal ready written he showed it with all reverence to the king; the king was then much more displeased than afore, and said angerly unto him that he should not pursue his appeal, but should tarry in hold till such time as it were of the Pope allowed. Then would he or nild he the archbishop should be his judge. Thus was there nothing allowed that Lord Cobham had lawfully required; but as he would not be sworn in all things to submit himself to the Church and take what penance the archbishop would enjoin him, he was arrested again at the king's commandment and led to the Tower of London, to keep his day that the archbishop had appointed him.

The 23rd of September, the archbishop sitting in the chapterhouse of Paul's with Richard Clifford, Bishop of London, and Henry Bolingbroke, Bishop of Winchester, Sir Robert Morley, Lieutenant of the Tower, brought before him Lord Cobham; unto whom the archbishop said, 'Sir John, in the last convocation of the clergy of this our province ye were detected of certain heresies and by sufficient witnesses found culpable: whereupon ye were by form of spiritual law cited, and would in no case appear. In conclusion upon your rebellious contumacy ye were excommunicated. Notwithstanding we neither showed ourselves unready to have given you absolution, nor do not to this hour, would ye have asked it.'

Unto this Lord Cobham showed as though he had given no ear; but said he would gladly before him and his brethren make rehearsal of that faith which he held and intended always to stand to. Then he took out of his bosom a certain writing concerning the articles whereof he was accused, and read it before them, giving it unto the archbishop as he had made thereof an end. Then counselled the archbishop with the other bishops and with the doctors what was to be done, commanding him to stand aside. In conclusion by their assent he said unto him, 'Come hither, Sir John: in this writing are many good things and catholic also; but ye must consider that this day was appointed for you to answer to other points whereof no mention is made in this bill: and therefore ye must declare us your mind more plainly: thus, whether ye believe that in the sacrament of the altar, after the consecration rightly done by a priest, remaineth material bread or not; moreover whether ye believe that concerning the sacrament of penance every man is bound to be confessed of his sins to a priest or not.'

This was the answer of good Lord Cobham, that none otherwise would he answer unto his articles than was expressly there contained. Then said the archbishop, 'Beware what ye do; for if ye answer not clearly to those things that are here objected against you, the law of Holy Church is that we may proclaim ye an heretic.' Unto whom he gave this answer: 'Do as ye think best, for I am at a point.' Whatever he or the other bishops did ask him after that, he bade them resort to his bill; for thereby would he stand to the death. Other answer would he not give that day, wherewith the prelates were amazed and wonderfully disquieted.

When the 25th of September was come, the archbishop commanded his judicial seat to be removed from the chapterhouse of Paul's to the Dominic Friars within Ludgate. As he was there set with Richard Bishop of London, Henry Bishop of Winchester, and Bennet Bishop of Bangor, Sir Robert Morley brought Lord Cobham, there leaving him as a lamb among wolves to his examination and answer. Then said the archbishop, 'Lord Cobham, we once again require you to have none other opinion than the universal belief of the Holy Church of Rome. So like an obedient child return to the unity of your mother. See to it in time, for anon it will be too late.' Lord Cobham said expressly before them all, 'I will none otherwise believe in these points than I told you afore. Do with me what ye will.' Finally the archbishop said, 'Well, then I see we must needs do the law; we must proceed to the sentence definitive and condemn you for an heretic.'

With that the archbishop stood up and read a bill of his condemnation, all the clergy and laity vailing their bonnets. After he had read the bill, Lord Cobham said with a most cheerful countenance: 'Though ye judge my body, which is but a wretched thing, yet am I certain that ye can do no harm to my soul. He that created that will of his infinite mercy save it; I have therein no manner of doubt. Concerning these articles, I will stand to them to the very death by the grace of my God.' Therewith he turned him unto the people, casting his hands abroad and saying with a very loud voice, 'Good Christian people, for God's love be well ware of these men, for they will else beguile you and lead you blindling into hell with themselves. For Christ saith plainly unto you, "If one blind man leadeth another, they are like both to fall into the ditch."' After this he fell down upon his knees, and before them all prayed for his enemies, holding up his hands and his eyes towards heaven and saying, 'Lord God Eternal, I beseech thee of thy great mercy's sake to forgive my pursuers, if it be thy blessed will.'

After all this, the 10th of October 1413, the sentence of death being given, Lord Cobham was sent away, Sir Robert Morley carrying him again unto the Tower, where after he had remained a certain space, in the night season—it is not known by what means—he escaped, and fled into Wales, where he continued four years. In the meantime this may seem strange, that Thomas Arundell, who a little before sitting upon judgment against Lord Cobham pronounced sentence of death upon him, did himself feel the stroke of death, and the sentence of God executed upon him, before the other. Who would have thought that Lord Cobham, being condemned definitively by the archbishop's sentence, but that he should have died long before the archbishop? But such be the works of God's almighty hand, who so turned the wheel that this condemned lord survived his condemner three or four years.

In the meantime a great sum of money was proclaimed by the king to him that could take Sir John Oldcastle, quick or dead. About the end of which four years Lord Powes, whether for love of the money or for hatred of true doctrine of Christ, seeking all ways how to play the part of Judas and outwardly pretending him great amity, at length obtained his bloody purpose and brought Lord Cobham bound to London, about the year 1417 and about December; at which time there was a parliament assembled in London for the relief of money to be sent to the king, whom the bishops had sent to fight in France. The records of which parliament say that on the 14th of December Sir John Oldcastle, being outlawed in the King's Bench, and excommunicated before by the Archbishop of Canturbury for heresy, was brought before the Lords. Upon which process it was adjudged that he should be taken as a traitor to the king and the realm; that he should be carried to the Tower of London, and from there drawn through London unto the new gallows in St Giles without Temple Bar, there to be hanged, and burned hanging.

As touching the pretensed treason of Lord Cobham falsely ascribed unto him in his indictment, it is to be noted that he was never executed by force of the indictment, because he should then have been brought to the bar in the King's Bench, and the judges should have given the judgment of treason. Besides, that he was not executed upon the indictment the manner of his execution proveth, because it was neither the execution of a traitor nor was the whole punishment thereof pronounced by the judge. His religion first brought him in hatred of the bishops; the bishops brought him in hatred of the king; the hatred of

‘The description of the cruell Martyrdome of Sir John Oldcastle, Lord Cobham.’

the king brought him to his martyrdom. Moreover in the records above mentioned it followeth how in the said parliament motion was made that Lord Powes might 'be thanked and rewarded for his great travail taken in the apprehension of Sir John Oldcastle, heretic,' Thus stand the words of the record; where two things are to be noted: first, how Sir John is called not traitor but heretic; secondly, mark how this brother of Judas craveth his reward for betraying innocent blood. It is not to be doubted but that his light fee and *Quid vultis mihi dare?* in this world will have an heavy reward in the world to come, unless he repented.

KING HENRY VI

An. 1422 King Henry V, fighting in France, fell sick at Boys and died, after he had reigned nine years, five months, three weeks, and odd days from his coronation. This king in his life and in all his doings was so serviceable to the Pope and his chaplains that he was called the Prince of Priests: who left behind him a son, nine months and fifteen days of age, whom he had by Queen Katherine, daughter to the French king, married to him two or three years before; the name of which prince, succeeding his father, was Henry VI, who was left under the protection of his uncle, Humfrey Duke of Gloucester. This young prince in the eighth year was crowned at Westminster; and the second year after was crowned also at Paris, and reigned thirty-eight years; and then was deposed by Edward IV, as hereafter shall be declared.

In the first year of his reign was burned the constant witness-bearer of Christ's doctrine, William Taylor, priest, under Henry Chichesley, Archbishop of Canturbury. Of this William I read that in the days of Arundell he was apprehended and abjured. Afterwards in the days of Chichesley William appeared again before the archbishop, being complained of to have taught at Bristol these articles: that whosoever hangeth any Scripture about his neck taketh away the honour due only to God; that no human person is to be worshipped as regardeth his manhood; that the saints in heaven are not to be worshipped or invocated. Upon these articles Taylor being examined in conclusion was contented to revoke the same, and for his penance was condemned to perpetual prison. Notwithstanding through favour they were contented that he should be released from his carceral indurance, in case he would swear that he shall never hold such opinions hereafter. Thus Taylor, appointed to appear at Lambeth before the archbishop, to take his absolution from his long excommunication during the time of Thomas Arundell, appeared again before him, where he, laying aside his *armilausa*, that is his cloak, his cap, and stripped unto his doublet, kneeled at the feet of the archbishop. Who then, standing up and having a rod in his hand, began the psalm *Miserere etc.*, his chaplains answering the second verse. After that was said the collect *Deus cui proprium etc.*, with certain other prayers. And so taking an oath of him the archbishop committed him to the custody of the Bishop of Worcester.

In the meantime there passed certain writings between him and one Thomas Smith, priest at Bristow, in which William replied against Thomas concerning the worshipping of saints. Which reply being brought to the bishop, Taylor began anew to be troubled and was brought again before the convocation of the clergy to answer unto his writings. This was *an.* 1422, the 11th of February. The tenor of whose writing only tended to prove that every prayer for any supernatural gift ought to be directed to God alone. He did not utterly deny that it was not lawful in no respects to pray to saints: he seemeth little or nothing to differ from the Papists. Notwithstanding, the same writing being delivered to the four orders of friars to be examined was found erroneous and heretical. To make up a number every order of friars thought to find some matter to offer up to the archbishop against him, lest one order should seem more cunning than another. When Saturday was come, the 20th of February, first appeareth Friar John Tille for the Black Friars; then Friar Winchelsey for the Friars Minor; then Friar Lowe for the Augustines; after Friar Ashwell for the Carmelites; each severally bringing his heresy. The verdict of these four orders being given to the archbishop, hereupon cometh down a writ from the king directed to the Lord Mayor and Sheriffs of London *De haeretico comburendo*, beginning thus: *Rex Majori et Vicecomitibus.* Whereupon Taylor condemned as a relapse first was degraded and after to be burned, and was committed to the secular power; who then being had to Smithfield, the 1st of March after long imprisonment there did consummate his martyrdom, 1422.

In 1428 King Henry VI sent down most cruel letters of commission unto John Exeter and Jacolet Germaine, keeper of the Castle of Colchester, for the apprehending of Sir William White, priest, and others suspected of heresies. By virtue of which commission we find in old monuments that John Exeter attached six persons in the town of

Bungay in the diocese of Norwich, and committed them to William Day and William Roe, constables, to be sent within ten days under safe custody unto the Castle of Norwich; whose names, through the antiquity of the monument, were so defaced that we could not attain to perfect knowledge of them all; only three names remained to be read—John Waddon of Tenterden in Kent; Bartlemew, monk of Ersham in Norfolk; Corneleader, a married man. Besides these we also find in the old monuments within the diocese of Norfolk and Suffolk, specially in Beckles, Ersham, and Ludney, a great number both of men and women to have been cast into prison, and after their abjuration brought to open shame in churches and markets by the bishop of the diocese called William and his chancellor William Bernham, John Exeter being the register; so that within three or four years (from 1428 to 1431) about 120 men and women were examined and sustained great vexation for the profession of the Christian Faith; of whom some were taken upon suspicion only for eating of meats prohibited upon vigil days, who escaped with less punishment. The other were more cruelly handled, and some of them were put to death and burned; among whom we specially find mention of these three: Father Abraham of Colchester; William White, priest; John Waddon, priest. The residue were forced to abjure, sustaining such cruel penance as pleased the bishop and his chancellor to lay upon them.

William White gave over his priesthood and benefice and took unto him a godly young woman to wife; notwithstanding he did not cease from his duty, but continually laboured to the glory of his spouse Christ by reading, writing, and preaching. He, being attached at Canturbury under Archbishop Chichesley, for a space manfully witnessed the truth which he had preached. But like as there he lost his courage and strength, so afterward he became much more stout and strong in Christ, and confessed his own offence. For going into Norfolk with his wife and there occupying himself in converting the people unto the true doctrine of Christ, at last, by means of the king's letters sent down for that purpose, he was brought before William Bishop of Norwich, by whom he was convict and condemned, and burned in Norwich in September 1424; whose wife Joan, following her husband's footsteps according to her power, confirmed many in God's truth; wherefore she suffered much punishment the same year at the hands of the bishop. About the same time also was burned Father Abraham of Colchester and John Waddon, priest.

John Beverley, alias *Battild*

John Beverley, *alias* Battild, a labourer, was attached by the vicar of Southcreke and delivered unto William Barnam, the bishop's commissary, who sent him to the Castle of Norwich, there to be kept in irons: where having nothing proved against him he took an oath that he should confess his sins once a year to his curate and receive the sacrament at Easter; and for his offence was enjoined that the Friday and Saturday next he should fast bread and water, and upon the Saturday be whipped from the Palace at Norwich, going round about by Tomelandes and St Michael's Church, by Cattlerew, and about the Market, having in his hand a wax candle of two pence to offer to the image of the Trinity after he had done his penance. And as he confessed that he had eaten flesh upon Easter Day, and was not shriven in all Lent, nor received upon Easter Day, the judge enjoined him that he should fast Tuesday, Wednesday, and Friday in Whitsunweek, having but one meal a day of fish and other white meats; and after his penance he should depart out of the diocese and never come there any more.

John Skilley of Flixton, miller

John Skilley of Flixton, miller, being brought before the Bishop of Norwich the 14th of March 1428, was convict and forced to abjure, and after this abjuration had a most sharp sentence pronounced against him: that as the said Skilley was convict by his own confession for receiving certain godly men into his house, as Sir William White and John Waddon, whom they called notorious and damnable heretics, he was enjoined for penance seven years' imprisonment in the monastery of Langley. And forsomuch as in times past he used upon Fridays to eat flesh, he was enjoined to fast bread and water every Friday by the space of seven years; and that by the space of two years next after the seven every Wednesday in the beginning of Lent and every Maundy Thursday he should appear before the bishop in the Cathedral Church of Norwich to do open penance for his offences.

Besides these there were other which were forced to like abjuration and penance. The next year, 1429, there ensueth a great number in the same register which were examined and did penance, to the number of sixteen or seventeen; in the number of whom was John Baker, otherwise called Usher Tunstall, who for having a book with the

Paternoster, the Ave, and the Creed, in English, was caused to abjure and sustain such penance as the other had done.

Ex Regist. Norw. The year following, which was 1430, the like happened unto John Finch of Colchester, who albeit he was of the diocese of London, being suspected of heresy, was attached in Ipswich in the diocese of Norwich and brought before the bishop there, before whom he being convict was enjoined penance, three disciplinings in solemn procession about the Cathedral Church of Norwich three several Sundays, and three disciplinings about the market place three principal market-days, his head, neck, and feet bare and his body covered only with a short shirt, having in his hands a taper of wax of a pound weight, which the Sunday after his penance he should offer to the Trinity; and that for three years after, every Ash Wednesday and Maundy Thursday, he should appear in the Cathedral Church before the bishop to do open penance.

To proceed in our story of Norfolk and Suffolk, we find that in 1431 Nicholas Canon of Eye was brought before the Bishop of Norwich for suspicion of heresy, and the bishop's commissary pronounced the said Nicholas to be an heretic, and enjoined penance for this offences: three disciplinings about the cloister of the Cathedral Church, bare-headed and bare-foot, carrying a taper of half a pound; which penance should be respited until the coming of the bishop into his diocese, and that in the meantime he should be kept in prison, to the end that he should not infect the flock with his venom and poison.

Thus have we briefly discoursed unto you the great afflictions which happened in Norfolk and Suffolk by the space of those four years, having drawn out briefly for every year certain notable examples sufficient for the declaration of all the rest, forsomuch as their opinions being nothing different their punishment did also nothing differ, otherwise than may be plainly seen.

Proceeding now to the year wherein suffered Humfrey, that good Duke of Gloucester, which was 1447, we will begin in few words to intreat of his life and conversation; then of the manner and cause of his death. He was the son of Henry IV, brother to Henry V, and uncle to Henry VI, assigned to be governor and protector of his person. He seemed meek and gentle, loving the commonwealth, a supporter of the poor commons, of wit and wisdom, discreet and studious, well affected to religion and a friend to verity, and no less enemy to pride and ambition, especially in haughty prelates; which was his undoing. And, which is rare in princes, he was both learned himself and given to study, as also a singular patron to them which were studious and learned. Furthermore as the learning of this prince was rare and memorable, so was the wisdom and prudence in him no less to be considered; as for more manifest proof I thought here good, amongst many other his godly doings, to recite one example, reported as well by Sir Thomas More as by Mr William Tindall, the apostle of these latter days, to the intent to note not only the crafty working of false miracles in the clergy, but also that the prudent discretion of this high and mighty prince may give us the better to understand what man he was.

In the young days of King Henry VI, being yet under the governance of Duke Humfrey, there came to St Albon's a beggar with his wife, and was walking about the town begging five or six days before the king's coming thither, saying that he was born blind, and was warned in his dream that he should come out of Barwicke, where he had ever dwelled, to seek St Albon; and that he had been at his shrine and had not been holpen, and therefore he would go and seek him at some other place; for he had heard some say that St Albons' body should be at Colen; and indeed such a contention hath there been. But as I am surely informed, he lieth here at St Albon's, saving some relics of him which they there show shrined. But to tell you forth my tale, when the king was come and the town full, suddenly this blind man at St Albon's shrine had his sight again, and a miracle solemnly rung, and *Te Deum* sung; so that nothing was talked of in all the town but this miracle. Duke Humfrey having great joy to see such a miracle called the poor man unto him; and first showing himself joyous of God's glory showed in the getting of his sight, and exhorting him to meekness, nor to be proud of the people's praise, which would call him a good and godly man thereby, at last he looked well upon his eyne and asked whether he could see nothing at all before. When as well his wife as himself affirmed fastly No, then he looked advisedly upon his eyne again and said, 'I believe you very well, for methinketh ye cannot see well yet.' 'Yes, sir,' quoth he, 'I thank God and his holy martyr, I can see now as well as any man.' 'Yea, can?' quoth the duke, 'What colour is my gown?' Anon the beggar told him. 'What colour is this man's gown?' He told him also, and without any sticking he told him the names of all the colours that could be showed him. When the duke saw that, he bade him 'Walk, traitor!' and made him to be set in the stocks: for though he could have seen suddenly by miracle the difference between divers colours, yet could he not by the sight so suddenly tell the names of all these colours, except he had known them before, no more than the names of all the men that he should suddenly see.

By this may it be seen how Duke Humfrey had not only an head to dissever truth from hypocrisy; but study also and diligence was in him to reform that which was amiss.

Thus much for the virtues and prowess shining in this princely duke: for which as he was loved of the poor commons and well spoken of all men, being called the good Duke of Gloucester; so yet neither wanted he his enemies, privy enviers, and secret maligners. Of whom specially was Henry Bewford, cardinal, Bishop of Winchester and Chancellor of England; who, long envying the authority of the duke, first had appointed himself to remove the king's person from Eltham unto Windsor out of the duke's hands, and there to put in such governors as him listed. After that, intending the duke's death, he set men of arms at the end of London Bridge, and forbarring the highway with a draw-chain set men in chambers, cellars, and windows, with bows and arrows and other weapons, to the purposed destruction of the duke and his retinue, if God had not disposed to turn his journey another way. Beside other injuries and molestations the ambitious cardinal, seeking by all means to be Pope, procured such trouble against him that great division was thereby in the whole realm; insomuch that all the shops within the City of London were shut for fear of the favourers of these two great personages. For the pacifying whereof the Archbishop of Canturbury and the Duke of Quinber, the Prince of Portugal, rode seven times in one day between those two adversaries.

Beside this cardinal another capital enemy to the duke was William de la Pole, Duke of Suffolk, a man very ill reported of, to be not only the instrument of this good man's death but also the ruin of the realm. For by him only was concluded the unprofitable marriage between the king and Lady Margaret of Angeow; whereas the king had contracted a marriage before with the daughter of the Earl of Arminik, upon conditions so much more profitable as more convenient it is for a prince to marry a wife with riches and friends than to take a maid with nothing and disinherit himself and his realm of old rights and ancient inheritance; which so came to pass. All this the good duke did well foresee, and declared no less; but his counsel would not be taken.

Whereupon followed the giving away the Duchy of Angeow and the whole country of Maine to Reiner, Duke of Angeow and father of the damsel, having thereof no penny profit.

Another sore enemy and mortal plague to the duke was the queen herself, lately married to the king; who, being of haughty stomach and set upon glory, of wiliness lacked nothing, and perceiving her husband to be simple of wit and easy to be ruled, took upon her to govern both king and kingdom. And because the counsel of Humfrey Duke of Gloucester was somewhat a stay that her regiment could not so fully proceed, and because the duke before did disagree from that marriage, this manly woman ceased not by all practices possible to set forward his destruction, having for her helper the Duke of Buckingham.

These being his mortal foes, fearing lest some commotion might arise if such a prince, so near the king's blood and so dear to the people, should be openly put to death, devised how to trap him: a parliament was summoned at Bury, *anno* 1447, far from the citizens of London, as Tindall in his *Book of Practice* writeth; where resorted all the peers of the realm, amongst them the Duke of Gloucester, thinking no harm to himself. Who on the second day of the session was by Lord Beamond, High Constable of England, accompanied with the Duke of Buckingham, apprehended and put in ward, and all his servants put from him; of whom thirty-two of the principal were dispersed into divers prisons, to the great murmuring of the people. The duke put into ward, the night after saith Hall, six nights after saith Fabian and Polychron., he was found dead in bed, and his body showed to the Lords and Commons as though he had been taken naturally with some sudden disease. Although no wound could be seen, it might well be judged that he died of no natural pang but of some violent hand. Some suspected him to be strangled, some that a whole spit was privily forced into his body; some affirm that he was stifled between two featherbeds. His body being interred at St Albon's, after he had politicly by the space of twenty-five years governed this realm, five of his household, to wit one knight, three esquires, and a yeoman, were arraigned and convict to be hanged, drawn, and quartered. Who being hanged and cut down half alive, the Marquis of Suffolk showed the charter of the king's pardon and they were delivered. Notwithstanding all this could not appease the people, saying that the saving of the servants was no amends for the murdering of the master.

In this cruel fact of these persons which did so conspire and consent to the death of this noble man, the marvellous work of God's judgment appeareth herein to be noted, who turned all their policies clean contrary; so that where the queen thought most to preserve her husband in honour and herself in state, thereby she lost her husband, her husband lost his realm, the realm lost Angeow, Normandy, Aquitaine, with all her parts beyond the sea, Calice only except; as whoso will read the stories shall well understand.

The next year the cardinal, the principal artificer of all this mischief, was suffered of God no longer to live. Of whose wicked conditions, being more largely set forth in Edward Hall, I omit to speak. What he himself spake on his deathbed I thought not best to pretermit; who hearing that he should die and that there was no remedy, murmured wherefore he should die having so much riches, saying that if the whole realm would save his life he was able either by policy to get it or by riches to buy it; adding moreover 'Fie, will not death be hired? will money do nothing? When my nephew of Bedford died I thought myself half up the wheel, but when I saw my other nephew of Gloucester deceased, then I thought myself equal with kings, and so thought to increase my treasure in hope to have worn the triple crown.' *Ex Edwar. Hallo.* Thus is the Bishop of Winchester with all his pomp and riches gone; with which riches he was able not only to build schools and universities, but also to sustain the king's armies in war without any taxing of the commons. In whose seat succeeded William Wanflet; who though he had less substance yet having a mind more godly disposed did found and erect the College of Mary Magdalen in Oxford; for which foundation as there be many students bound to yield thanks unto God, so I must needs confess myself to be one.

Among the other mischievous adversaries which wrought the death of Humfrey, was William de la Pole, Marquis of Suffolk, who also lived not long after nor long escaped unpunished. For although he was highly exalted by the queen unto the favour of the king and was made duke, and bear the whole sway in the realm; yet God's judgment still hanging over him he enjoyed not long this triumphant victory: for within three years after the death and ruin of the cardinal the voices of the whole commons of England were utterly turned against him, accusing him in parliament for delivery of Angeow and Maine, also for the death of the noble Prince Humfrey. They imputed moreover to him the loss of all Normandy, laying unto him that he was a swallower-up of the king's treasure, the expeller of all good counsellors from the king and advancer of vicious persons, apparent adversaries to the public wealth; so that he was called in every mouth a traitor, murderer, and robber of the king's treasure.

The queen, albeit she tenderly loved the duke, yet to appease the commons was forced to commit him to the Tower; where he with as much pleasure and liberty as could be remained for a month; which being expired, he was delivered and restored unto his old place and former favour with the king; whereat the people more grudged than before. It happened by occasion of a commotion then beginning amongst the rude people, by one whom they called Bluebeard, that parliament was adjourned to Leicester, thinking to the queen by rigour of law to repress the evil will conceived against the duke. But at that place few of the nobility would appear: wherefore it was again re-journed unto London and kept at Westminster, where was a whole company and a full appearance with the king and queen, and with them the Duke of Suffolk as chief counsellor. The Commons renewed their accusations against the duke, the Bishop of Salisbury, Sir James Finies, Lord Say, and other. When the king perceived that no glozing nor dissimulation would appease the continual clamour of the Commons, to make some pacification he sequestered from him Lord Say, Treasurer of England, and other the duke's adherents from their offices. Then he put in exile the Duke of Suffolk for five years, supposing by that space the rage of the people would assuage. But God would not suffer the blood of Humfrey to be unrevenged, or that flagitious person to continue. For when he shipped in Suffolk, intending to be transported into France, he was encountered with a ship of war belonging to the Tower, whereby he was taken and brought into Dover Road, and there on the side of a ship boat one strake off his head; which was about 1450.

Thus have ye heard the full story of Duke Humfrey and of his adversaries; also of God's condign punishment for their bloody cruelty. After the death of the duke mischiefs came in by heaps upon the king and his realm. For after the giving away of Angeow and Maine to the Frenchmen by the unfortunate marriage of Queen Margaret, the Frenchmen, perceiving now by the death of the duke the pillar of this commonwealth to be decayed, and seeing moreover the nobility to be divided, forslacked no time, having such an open way into Normandy that in short time they recovered the same and also got Gascoigne, so that no more now remained to England beyond the sea, but only Calice. Neither did the calamity of the realm only rest in this: for the king having lost his friendly uncle, the stay and staff of his age which had brought him up so faithfully from his youth, was now more open to his enemies, and they more emboldened to set upon him; as appeared first by Jack Cade the Kentish captain, who encamping first on Black Heath afterward aspired to London and had the spoil thereof, the king being driven into Warwickshire. After the suppressing of Cade ensued the Duke of York, who with three earls set upon the king near St Albon's, where the king was taken captive, and the duke was by parliament declared protector, which was in 1453. After this followed mortal war between the houses of Lancaster and York, continuing many years. At length about 1459 the Duke of York was slain in battle by the queen near Wakefield, and with him his son the Earl of Rutland; by which queen shortly after were discomfited the Earl of Warwick and the Duke of Norfolk, to whom the keeping of the king was committed by the Duke of York; and so the queen again delivered her husband.

After this victory the northern men, advanced not a little in pride, began to take upon them great attempts, not only to rob churches, religious houses, and villages, but also were fully intended, partly by themselves, partly by the inducement of their captains, to sack the City of London and take the spoil thereof; and no doubt, saith my history, would have proceeded in their intent had not the favour of God provided a speedy remedy. For as these mischiefs were in brewing, suddenly cometh Prince Edward unto London with a mighty army the 27th of February, who was the son and heir to the Duke of York, accompanied with the Earl of Warwick and divers more. King Henry in the meantime went to York, when Edward, being at London, caused there to be proclaimed certain articles concerning his title to the crown. The next day the Lords being assembled, the articles were approved. The 4th of March 1461 after a solemn procession the Bishop of Exeter made a sermon at Paul's Cross, wherein he proved by manifest evidences the title of Prince Edward to be just and lawful, answering all objections which might be made. This matter thus discussed, Prince Edward with the Lords spiritual and temporal and much concourse of people rode to Westminster Hall, and there, by full consent of the Lords as also by the voice of all the Commons, took possession of the crown and was called King Edward IV.

These things thus accomplished, and money sufficiently being ministered of the Commons with most willing minds for the furniture of his wars, he with the Duke of Norfolk and Earl of Warwick and Lord Fauconbridge in speedy wise took his journey toward King Henry, who being now at York and forsaken of the Londoners had all his refuge only reposed in the northern men. When King Edward with his army had passed over the River Trent and was come near to Ferebrig, where the host of King Henry was not far off, upon Palm Sunday between Ferebrig and Tadcaster the southern and northern men joined battle. And although at the beginning divers horsemen of King Edward's side turned their backs and spoiled the king of carriage and victuals, yet the courageous prince with his captains, little discouraged, manfully set on their adversaries: which battle on both sides was so cruelly fought that in the conflict were slain, as is reported, beside men of name 30,000 of the poor commons. The conquest fell on King Edward's part, so that King Henry having lost all was forced to flee into Scotland, where he gave up to the Scots the town of Barwicke, after he had reigned thirty-eight years and a half.

Thus much for the reign of King Henry VI, who now lacked his uncle and protector about him. But commonly the lack of such friends is never felt before they be missed.

In the time of this king was builded the house in London called Leaden Hall, founded by Symon Eyre *an.* 1445. Also the Standard in Cheap, builded by John Wells *an.* 1442; the conduit in Fleet Street, by William Eastfield *an.* 1438; item, Newgate, builded by goods of Richard Whittington *an.* 1422. Moreover Henry VI founded the College of Eaton, and another house having then the title of Nicholas in Cambridge, now called the King's College.

KING EDWARD IV

King Edward after his victory returned to London, where upon the vigil of St Peter and Paul, being Sunday, he was crowned King of England, and reigned twenty-two years, albeit not without much perturbation.

Queen Margaret hearing how her husband was fled into Scotland was also fain to fly the land, and went to her father, Duke of Angeow: from whence the year following she returned to renew war against King Edward, with small succour and less luck. For being encountered by the Earl of Warwick, about November she was driven to the seas again, and by tempest driven into Scotland.

In this year we read that King Edward, in the cause of a certain widow for rape, sat his own person in Westminster Hall, upon his own bench, discussing her cause.

The year following, *an.* 1463, King Henry, issuing out of Scotland with a sufficient power of Scots and Frenchmen, came into the north country to recover his crown, unto whom Lord Radulph Percy and Lord Radulph Gray, flying from King Edward, did adjoin themselves; but the Lord so disposing, King Henry was repulsed at Exham by Lord Mountacute, having then the rule of the north; where the Duke of Somerset, Lord Hungerford, Lord Rosse, with certain other were taken. Lord Radulph Percy was slain, the residue fled. Albeit the history *Scala Mundi* referreth this battle to the year 1464, the 15th of May; in which month were beheaded the Duke of Somerset, Lord Hungerford, Lord Rosse, Lord Philip Wentworth, Lord Thomas Hussy, Lord Thomas Findern, besides twenty-one other belonging to the household of King Henry VI. Queen Margaret finding no resting-place here took her progress again from whence she came, learning in her own country to drink that drink which she herself had brewed in England.

The next year, *an.* 1465, on the day of St Peter and Paul, King Henry being found in a wood by one Cantlow was arrested by the Earl of Warwick and of a king made prisoner in the Tower of London. *An.* 1471 upon Ascension Even King Henry departed, after he had reigned in all thirty-eight years and six months. Polydore and Hall affirm that he was slain with a dagger by Richard Duke of Gloucester for the safeguard of the king his brother.

Touching the affairs of King Edward, how he through the incitement of Charles Duke of Burgoyne ventured into France with a puissant army and how the duke failed him; how peace was at length concluded; of the marriage promised between the Dolphin and King Edward's eldest daughter, but afterward broken off on the French king's part; furthermore as touching the expedition of King Edward into Scotland, and how the matter was composed, and of the recovery of Barwicke; of these and other things I omit to speak. Two things I find specially to be remembered.

The first is concerning John Goose, which was unjustly condemned and burnt at Tower Hill *an.* 1473. Thus had England his John Hus as well as Bohemia. The said John being delivered to one of the sheriffs to see him burnt, the sheriff like a charitable man had him home to his house and there exhorted him to deny his errors. But the godly man after long exhortation heard desired the sheriff to be content, for he was satisfied in his conscience. Notwithstanding he desired the sheriff to give him some meat, saying that he was very sore hungered. The sheriff commanded him meat; whereof he did eat as he had been toward no manner of danger, and said to such as stood about him, 'I eat now a good dinner, for I shall pass a little sharp shower ere I go to supper.' When he had dined he gave thanks, and required that he might shortly be led to the place where he should yield up his spirit unto God. *Ex Polychron.*

The second thing to be noted is the death of George Duke of Clarence, the king's second brother. He assisted King Edward against the Earl of Warwick at Barnet Field and helped him to the crown; and now after all these benefits was apprehended and cast into the Tower, where he being adjudged a traitor was privily drowned in a butt of Malmsey. What the true cause was of his death cannot certainly be affirmed. Some imputed to the queen's displeasure.

King Edward IV ceased his life *an.* 1483, after he had reigned twenty and two years. In the time of which king this also is not to be forgotten, that one Burdet, a merchant dwelling in Cheapside at the sign of the Crown (now the Flower de luce), merrily speaking to his son said that he would make him inheritor of the Crown, meaning his own house; which words when King Edward interpreted as though he had meant the crown of the realm, within four hours he was apprehended, judged, drawn, and quartered, in Cheapside.

KING EDWARD V

King Edward left behind him by his wife Elizabeth two sons and two daughters; which two sons, Edward and Richard, as they were under age, a consultation was called among the peers, to debate whether the young prince and king should be under the government of his mother, or Richard Duke of Gloucester, brother to King Edward and uncle to the child, should be governor of the king and protector of the realm. The Duke of Buckingham, a man of great authority, had married King Edward's wife's sister. Because the duke had been unkindly, as he thought, of the king entreated, having no advancement according to his expectation, took part with Richard Duke of Gloucester to make the duke governor and protector. Which being brought to pass by the aid of the Duke of Buckingham, the ambitious protector and unnatural uncle, having possession of his two nephews and innocent babes, thought himself almost up the wheel where he would climb; although he could not walk in such mists but his purposes began to be espied; which caused him more covertly to go about to blind the people's eyes. But before he could accomplish his execrable enterprise, some there were whom he thought first must be rid out of the way, namely Lord Hastings and Lord Stanley. The Protector approaching Lord Hastings arrested him as a traitor. Another let fly at Lord Stanley; who to avoid the blow shrunk under the table, or else his head had been cleft asunder; notwithstanding he received such a wound that the blood ran about his ears. At the same time the Archbishop of York and Dr Morton, Bishop of Ely (Archbishop after that of Canturbury) were bestowed in divers chambers. Lord Hastings was commanded to shrive him apace, for before dinner the Protector sware that he should die. Incontinently without further judgment his head was stricken off: the queen's kindred were the same day beheaded at Pomfret.

After this murder the mischievous Protector, aspiring to the crown, through gifts and fair promises did subordinate Dr Shaw, a famous preacher then in London, to insinuate to the people that neither King Edward nor the Duke of Clarence were lawfully begotten nor the children of the Duke of York, but begotten in adultery on their mother, and that he alone was the lawful heir of the Duke of York. When this sermon would take no effect with the people, the Protector rested not thus, but few days after excited the Duke of Buckingham first to break the matter in covert talk to the mayor and certain heads of the City; that done to come to the Guild Hall, to move the people by all lying persuasions to the same which Shaw had preached at Paul's Cross. Which the Duke being both learned and well spoken endeavoured to accomplish, making a long and articial oration, supposing that the people would cry 'King Richard!' But there was no King Richard in their mouths, less in their hearts. Whereupon the Duke, looking to the Lord Mayor, asking what this silence meant, it was answered of the Mayor that the people peradventure understood him not; wherefore the duke reiterating his narration in other words, declared again that he had done before. Likewise the third time he repeated his oration. Then the commons, which before stood mute, began to mutter softly among themselves, yet no King Richard could sound in their lips, save only that in the nether end of the hall certain of the duke's servants, with other belonging to the Protector, thrusting into the hall began suddenly at men's backs to cry 'King Richard!' throwing up their caps: whereat the citizens turning their heads marvelled but said nothing.

KING RICHARD III, USURPER

Thus Richard Duke of Gloucester took upon him to be proclaimed King of England, *an.* 1483, in June; who coming to the Tower by water first made his son, a child ten years old, Prince of Wales, and John Haward he advanced to be Duke of Norfolk, and Thomas his son he ordained Earl of Surrey. His coronation was solemnized the sixth of July. His usurped coronation being finished, this unquiet tyrant yet could not think himself safe so long as young Edward, the right king, and his brother were alive; wherefore the next enterprise which he set upon was this—how to rid those innocent babes out of the way.

While this ruffling was in hand, what dread and sorrow the tender hearts of these fatherless and friendless children were in, it is not hard to understand. As the younger brother lingered in thought and heaviness, so the prince, who was 11 years old, was so out of heart and fraught with fear that he never tied his points nor enjoyed good day, till the traitorous impiety of their cruel uncle had delivered them of their wretchedness; which was not long in dispatching. For after King Richard first attempting to compass his devilish device by Robert Brakenbury, Constable of the Tower, and could not win him to such a cruel fact, he got one James Tyrell, with John Dighton and Miles Forrest, to perpetrate this heinous murder. Which Dighton and Forrest about midnight entering their chamber so entangled them amongst the clothes, keeping down the featherbed and pillows hard unto their mouths, that they smothered and stifled them in their bed.

Thus ended these young princes their lives through the cruelty of these tormentors, who for their detestable murder escaped not long unpunished by the just hand of God. First Miles Forrest at St Martin's *le Graund* by piecemeal miserably rotted away: John Dighton lived at Calis long after, so hated that he was pointed at of all men and there died in great misery. Sir James Tyrell was beheaded at Tower Hill for treason. Richard himself within a year and a half was slain in the field, hacked and hewed of his enemies' hands, torn and tugged like a cur-dog. Furthermore the justice of God's hand let not the Duke of Buckingham escape free, which was a great setter-up of this butcherly usurper; for less than a year after he was himself beheaded for treason by the king whom he so unjustly had set up.

Mention was made a little before of Dr Morton, by whose means the device was broached for the conjoining of the houses of York and Lancaster. This device was broken to the Duke of Buckingham, which cost him his life. Notwithstanding the device took such effect that message was sent over the sea to Henry Earl of Richmond by his mother and by the queen, mother to Lady Elizabeth, that if he would return and promise to marry Lady Elizabeth, King Edward's daughter, he should be received. After Earl Henry had intelligence how it was purposed by his friends, he with all diligence advanced his journey, helped and furnished by Francis Duke of Britaine, and shipped his men. His first voyage sped not; for by force of weather his ships were dispersed and repulsed back into France. His second voyage was more prosperous, who taking the seas at Harflet in August 1485, with only two thousand men and a small number of ships, arrived at Milford Haven and came to Haverfordwest, where he was joyfully received, and by the coming of the Pembroke men was in power increased. Thence he removed by Cardigan to Shrewsbury, then to Newport and so to Stafford, from thence to Lichfield, his army still augmented. Like as a great flood by coming in of many small rivers gathereth more abundance of water, so to this earl divers noble captains and men of power adjoined themselves. At last the earl hearing of the king's coming conducted his whole army to Tamworth.

King Richard, hearing of the arrival of Earl Henry in Wales after such a slender sort, did give little or no regard unto it. But after, understanding that he was come to Lichfield without resistance, he was sore moved and exceedingly took on, cursing those who had deceived him; and in all speed sent for John Duke of Norfolk, Henry Earl of Northumberland, Thomas Earl of Surrey, with other friends of special trust. Robert Brakenbury also was sent for with certain knights and esquires, of whom he partly misdoubted. Thus King Richard, well fortified and accompanied, leaving nothing undone that diligence could require, set forward toward his enemies. The earl by this time was come to Tamworth, to whom secretly resorted Sir John Savage and many other, forsaking King Richard, whom all good men hated as he deserved. The king, having perfect knowledge the earl to be encamped at Tamworth, embattled himself near a village called Bosworth, not far from Leicester. Here the matter lay in great suspense concerning Lord Stanley (which was the earl's father-in-law and had married his mother), to what part he would incline. For although his heart went with the earl, and had secret conference with him the night before, yet because of his son and heir, George Lord Strange, being in the hands of King Richard, lest the king should attempt any prejudicial thing against him, durst not be seen openly to go that way where in heart he favoured, and therefore kept himself between both till the push came, that his help might serve at a pinch.

When time and place was appointed where the two battles should encounter, great blows were given on both sides and many slain. If number might govern the success of battle, King Richard had double to the earl. But God is he that giveth victory, by what means it seemeth to his divine providence best. By what occasion this field was won and lost, the certain intelligence we have not certainly expressed, but only the history of Polydore Virgil, whom Sir Thomas More doth follow word for word. In which history it doth appear that as these two armies were coupling together, Richard, understanding by his espials where Richmond was, and how he was but slenderly accompanied, and seeing him approach, set spurs to his horse, and ranging out of the compass of his ranks, pressed towards the earl, setting upon him so sharply that first he killed Sir William Brandon, the earl's standard-bearer, then overthrew Sir John Cheinie, thinking likewise to oppress the earl. But as the earl, being overmatched, began to despair of victory, suddenly and opportunely came Sir William Stanley with three thousand well appointed men, whereby King Richard's men were driven back, and he himself, fighting in the thick of his enemies, was slain. Meantime the Earl of Oxford discomfited the forefront of King Richard's host and put them to flight, in which chase many were slain, of noblemen especially John Duke of Norfolk, Lord Ferrers, Sir Richard Radcliff, and Robert Brakenbury. Lord Thomas Haward submitted himself, and although he was not received at first to grace but long remained in the Tower, yet at length was delivered and advanced to his dignity again.

King Richard had but one son, who shortly after the murder of King Edward's sons was taken with sickness and died. The wife of King Richard, whether by poison or by sickness, died also a little before the field of Bosworth, after whose decease the story of Polydore and Sir Thomas More affirmeth that he intended himself to marry Elizabeth, his own brother's daughter, and so prevent the Earl of Richmond.

As touching Lord Stanley thus reporteth the story, that King Richard being in Bosworth Field sent for Lord Stanley by a pursuivant, to advance with his company and come to his presence: otherwise he sware by Christ's passion that he would strike off his son's head before dinner. Lord Stanley sent word again that if he did he had more sons alive. The king immediately commanded Lord Strange to be beheaded; which was the very time when the armies were ready to join together. The king's counsellors persuaded the king that it was now time to fight, not to do execution, advising him to delay the matter till the battle were ended. So as God would Richard breaking his oath, or rather keeping his oath, for he himself was slain before dinner, Lord Strange was committed to be kept prisoner within the king's tent; who after the victory was brought to his joyful father. Thus have ye the tragical life and end of this wretched king.

The Earl of Richmond after hearty thanks given to Almighty God for his glorious victory proceeded to Leicester, where was brought to him by Lord Strange the crown, and put on the earl's head. Meantime the corpse of King Richard was shamefully carried to Leicester, naked and despoiled to the skin; and being trussed behind a pursuivant of arms was carried like a hog or a dog, having his head and arms hanging on one side of the horse and the legs on the other, all sprinkled with mire and blood. Thus ended the usurped reign of King Richard, who reigned two years and two months.

KING HENRY VII

When King Henry by the providence of God had obtained this triumphant victory and diadem of the realm, first sending for Edward Plantagenet, Earl of Warwick, son to George Duke of Clarence, and committing him to the Tower, from Leicester removed to London; and not long after according to his promise espoused Elizabeth, heir of the house of York; whereby both houses were conjoined, to the rejoicing of all English hearts and quiet unto the realm, *an.* 1485. This king reigned twenty-three years and eight months, and being a prince of great policy, justice, and temperance, kept his realm in good, tolerable order.

In the year 1494, the ninth year of King Henry VII, the 28th of April, was burned a very old woman named Joan Boughton, widow, mother to Lady Young. Her mother was fourscore years of age or more, and held eight of Wickliffe's opinions, for which she was burnt in Smithfield. My author saith she was a disciple of Wickliffe, whom she accounted for a saint, and held so firmly eight of his ten opinions that all the doctors of London could not turn her from one of them. When it was told her that she should be burnt for her obstinacy, she set nothing by their menacing words but defied them; for she said she was so beloved of God and his holy angels that she passed not for the fire; and in the midst thereof she cried to God to take her soul into his holy hands.

Shortly after the martyrdom of this godly mother, in 1497 and the 17th of January, two men, Richard Milderale and James Sturdy, bare faggots before the procession of Paul's and after stood before the preacher in the time of his sermon. The Sunday following stood other two men at Paul's Cross all the sermon time; the one garnished with painted and written papers, the other having a faggot on his neck. Upon Passion Sunday Hugh Glover bare a faggot before the procession at Paul's, and after with the faggot stood before the preacher all the sermon. On the Sunday following four men did open penance at Paul's, and many of their books were burnt. The next year, 1498, in May, the king being at Canturbury, was a priest burnt which was so strong in his opinion that all the clerks and doctors could not remove him from his faith; whereof the king being informed caused the priest to be brought before his presence, who by his persuasion caused him to revoke; so he was burnt immediately. In the same year after the beheading of Edward Plantagenet, the king and queen being removed to Calis, a man named Babram, in Norfolk, was burnt in July, as is in Fabian recorded. About which year or the year following was an old man burnt in Smithfield.

William Tilsworth, martyr

Forsomuch as the world is come to such peevish insensibility in these contentious days of ours that nothing can be so circumspectly written but shall lie in danger of one sycophant or another, which never will credit there where they list not to like; neither will they ever like that which seemeth prejudicial to their faction: therefore to stop the mouths of such carping cavillers be it known to all such persons who by evidence and witness will be satisfied, that in Amersham be yet alive both men and women which bear witness of this that I shall declare. There is William Page, an aged father and yet alive, witness to the same. Also Agnes Wetherley, widow, about the age of an hundred years, yet living and witness hereof; that in the days of King Henry

VII, *an.* 1506, in the diocese of Lincoln, in Buckinghamshire, William Tilsworth was burned in Amersham, about sixty years ago; at which time Joan Clerke, the only daughter of William Tilsworth and a faithful woman, was compelled with her own hands to set fire to her dear father; and at the same time her husband John did penance and bare a faggot, as did other twenty-two. All these bare faggots and afterwards were compelled to wear badges. Divers of these men were afterward burned in the cheek, as William Page, who bare a faggot with the aforesaid. Furthermore Agnes Wetherley testifieth that at the burning of Tilsworth sixty and above were put to bear faggots. In which number was Robert Bartlet, a rich man, who was put out of his farm and goods and condemned to be kept in the monastery of Ashridge seven years together.

It followeth in the testimony of the forenamed that about the same time was one Father Roberts burned at Buckingham. He was a miller and dwelled at Missenden; and at his burning there were above twenty persons that were compelled to do such penance as the wicked Pharisees did compel them. After that by the space of two or three years was burned at Amersham Thomas Bernard, husbandman, and James Mordon, labourer; and there was William Littlepage, who is yet alive, burned in the right cheek, and Father Rogers, and Father Rever, which after was burned. Father Rogers was in the bishop's prison fourteen weeks, where he was so cruelly handled with cold, hunger, and irons, that after his coming out of prison he was so lame in his back that he could never go upright as long as he lived, as can testify divers honest men that be now living. There were thirty burned in the right cheek, and bare faggots. The cause was that they would talk against superstition and idolatry and were desirous to hear and read the Holy Scriptures. The manner of their burning was this: their necks were tied fast to a post and their hands holden that they might not stir, and so the iron being hot was put to their cheeks; and thus bare they the prints and marks of the Lord Jesus.

The cruel handling of Thomas Chase of Amersham

Thomas Chase of Amersham, one of them that was thus cruelly handled, was a man of godly and honest behaviour and could not abide idolatry and supersitition, but many times would speak against it. Wherefore the wicked did the more hate him, and brought him before the blind bishop, being at that time at Woburne in the county of

Buckingham. He had Thomas Chase before him, asking him many questions with many taunts and rebukes. What answer Chase made is unknown: howbeit it is to be supposed that his answers were most zealous; for Thomas was commanded to be put in the bishop's prison called Little Ease, in the bishop's house. There Thomas lay bound most painfully with chains, gyves, manacles, and irons, sore pined with hunger, where the bishop's alms was daily brought unto him by his chaplains; which alms was nothing else but rebukes and threatenings, floutings and mockings. All which cruelty the martyr took most patiently, remembering Christ's promises: 'Blessed are they which suffer persecution for righteousness' sake, for theirs is the Kingdom of Heaven': and 'Blessed are ye when men revile you and persecute you.' When the bishop with his band of shavelings perceived that by their cruelty they could not prevail against him, but rather that he was the more fervent in professing Christ's true religion, they imagined how they might put him to death, lest there should be a tumult among the people. And as Richard Hun shortly after was strangled in Lollards' Tower, so these blood-suppers strangled Thomas Chase in prison, which called upon God to receive his spirit; as witnesseth a woman that kept him in prison.

After these stinging vipers had impiously murdered this faithful Christian, they were at their wits' end to cloke their shameful murder: at last to blind silly people these bloody butchers caused it to be bruited abroad that Chase had hanged himself in prison—an abominable lie; for the prison was such that a man could not stand upright, as they report that did know it. Besides, this man had so many irons upon him, that he could not well move hand nor foot, as the women did declare that saw him dead; insomuch that they confessed that his blood-bulk was broken by reason they had so vilely beaten him. Yet these holy Catholics had not made an end of their wicked act in both killing and slandering this martyr: to put out the remembrance of him they caused him to be buried in Norland Wood, to the intent he should not be taken up again to be seen. But He that is effectually true hath promised at one time or another to clear His true servants by his own true word. 'No secret,' saith He, 'is so close but once shall be opened, neither is anything so hid that shall not at the last be known clearly.'

Thomas Harding, being one of this company thus molested in Amersham for the truth of the gospel, after his abjuration and penance done was again sought for and brought to the fire in the days of King

Henry VIII: whose martyrdom we shall record when we come to the year of his suffering.

After the martyrdom of these two I read also of one Thomas Norice, who for the same cause was burnt at Norwich *an.* 1507. In the next year in the consistory of London was convented Elizabeth Sampson of the parish of Aldermanbury, for speaking against pilgrimage and adoration of images, and for that she had spoken these or like words, that our Lady of Wilsdon was but a burnt arse stock; and that if she might have holpen men and women which go to her on pilgrimage, she would not have suffered her tail to have been burnt; and better it were for people to give their alms at home to poor people than to go on pilgrimage. For these and other articles she was compelled to abjure before Mr William Horsey, chancellor.

Laurence Ghest

Lamentable it is to remember the names of all them that have been slain by the rigour of the Pope's clergy for the true maintaining of Christ's cause; whose memory being registered in the Book of Life, albeit it need not the commemoration of our stories, yet for the confirmation of the Church I thought it not unprofitable the suffering of them to be notified which have given their blood to be shed in Christ's quarrel. In the catalogue of whom next cometh the memorial of Laurence Ghest, burned in Salisbury in the days of King Henry VII. He was of a comely and tall personage, and not unfriended; for which the bishop and the close were loth to burn him, but kept him in prison two years. Laurence had a wife and seven children. Wherefore they thinking to persuade his mind by stirring his fatherly affection, as he was at the stake they brought him his wife and seven children; at the sight whereof, although nature is wont to work in other, yet in him religion overcoming nature made his constancy unmovable. When his wife began to exhort him to favour himself, he desired her to be content and not to be a block in his way, for he was in a good course, running toward the mark of his salvation. And so fire being put to him he finished his life, renouncing not only wife and children but also himself, to follow Christ. As he was burning, one of the bishop's men threw a firebrand at his face; whereat the brother of Laurence ran at him with his dagger, and would have slain him had he not been stayed.

Testified by William Russell, who was present at the burning of Laurence and was himself burned in the cheek, whose daughter is yet living. Confirmed also with the testimony of Richard Web, who sojourning in the house of William Russell heard him many times declare the same.

A faithful woman burned

Amongst all the examples of them whereof so many have suffered for Christ, I cannot tell if ever were any martyrdom wherein God's judgment hath been more evident against the persecutors of his flock than at the burning of the godly woman put to death in Cheapingsadbery about the same time. The constancy of which blessed woman, as it is glorious to behold, so the example of the bishop's chancellor which cruelly condemned the innocent may offer a terrible spectacle to the eyes of all papistical persecutors to consider. The name of the woman is not yet come to my knowledge; the name of the chancellor was Whittington. After this godly woman and manly martyr was condemned by the wretched chancellor for profession of the truth which the Papists called heresy, a great concourse, as the manner is in such times, was gathered to behold her end; among whom was Whittington. Thus this faithful woman, committing her cause to the Lord, gave over her life to the fire, refusing no torments to keep her conscience unreprovable in the day of the Lord. The sacrifice ended, the people began to return homeward. It happened in the meantime that as the catholic executioners were busy slaying this silly lamb at the town's side, a certain butcher within the town was as busy slaying a bull which he had fast bound in ropes, ready to knock him on the head. But the butcher, not so skilful in his art of killing beasts as the Papists be in murdering Christians, as he was lifting his axe to strike the bull, failed in his stroke and smit a little too low. The bull, somewhat grieved at the stroke but not strucken down, put his strength to the ropes and brake loose into the street, the very same time as the people were coming in great press from the burning. Who seeing the bull coming toward them and supposing him to be wild, gave way for the beast, every man shifting for himself. Thus the people making a lane for the bull, he passed through the throng, touching neither man nor child till he came where the chancellor was: against whom the bull, as pricked with a sudden vehemency, ran full butt with his horns; and taking him upon the paunch gored him through and through, and so killed him immediately, carrying his guts and trailing them with his horns all the street over, to the wonder of all that saw it.

For the credit of this story, lest I be said upon mine own head to commit to story things rashly which I cannot justify, I will discharge myself with authority, I trust, sufficient; that is, with the witness of a Papist present at the burning of the woman, whose name was Rowland Web; which Rowland had a son named Richard, servant sometime to Mr Latimer, who enduring with him in time of his trouble six years together was himself persecuted for the same cause. Unto which Richard, being then young, Rowland his father, to exhort him from heresy as he called it, recited to him many times the burning of this woman, and added the story of the bull which he himself did see and testify. Richard Web is yet living, a witness of his own father's testimony, which I trust may satisfy all readers except such as think no truth to be believed but that only which is in their portues.

Thus much concerning the state of the Church; wherein is to be understood what storms and persecutions have been raised up against the congregation of Christ by the Bishop of Rome and his retinue. Where also is to be noted, in the reign of King Henry VIII, how mightily the working of God's gospel hath increased, and what great numbers of men and women have suffered for the same.

THE REIGN OF KING HENRY VIII

Touching the state of the Commonwealth and of the Church under the reign of King Henry VII; how he entered into possession of the crown; how the two houses were in him conjoined through marriage with Elizabeth; how long the king reigned, and what persecution was in his time for lack of knowledge of God's word; and further what punishment God sendeth upon realms public for neglecting the safety of his flock, hath been already specified: many more things might have been added incident to the reign of this prince, which we have for brevity pretermitted. Otherwise I might have inferred mention of the seditious tumult of Perkin Werbecke *an.* 1494; also of Black Heath Field *an.* 1496. I might have recited the commendation of Georgius Lilius in his Latin Chronicle, testifying of King Henry VII how he sent three orators to Pope Julius II, to yield his obedience to the See of Rome *an.* 1506; and how Pope Alexander IX, Pius III, and Julius II sent to the king three sundry ambassadors, electing him to be the chief Defender of the Faith; the commendation of which, how glorious it is in the eyes of Lilius and Fabian, I leave to them. This I suppose, that when King Henry sent to Pope Julius three orators with obedience, if he had sent him three thousand harquebussiers to furnish his field against the French king at Ravenna, it had pleased Pope Julius much better.

As we are fallen into mention of Georgius Lilius, this in him is not unworthy noting, how after the burning of Thomas Norice at Norwich, the same year followed such a fire in Norwich that the whole city well near was consumed. As also after the burning of the aged father in Smithfield, the same year 1500 we read in the Chronicle of Fabian that a great plague fell upon London, to the great destruction of the inhabitants; wherein again is to be noted that according to the state of the Church the disposition of the Commonwealth commonly is guided, either to be afflicted or to flourish. But after these notes of King Henry VII, now to the story of King Henry VIII.

Henry VII, finishing his course in 1509, had by Elizabeth four men children and of women children as many, of whom three only survived, Henry, Margaret, and Mary: Henry VIII after his father succeeded; Margaret was married to James IV, King of Scots; Mary was affied to Charles King of Castile.

Not long before the death of King Henry, Arthur his eldest son had espoused Katherine, daughter to Ferdinandus, being of the age of fifteen years and she about seventeen; and shortly after his marriage departed and was buried at Worcester. The succession fell next to Henry, who being of the age of eighteen entered his reign *an.* 1509, and shortly after married Katherine, his late brother's wife, to the end that her dowry being great should not be transported out of the land; in which marriage (more politic than Scripturelike) he was dispensed by Pope Julius at the request of Ferdinandus. The reign of this king continued with great fame the space of thirty-eight years; during whose time was great alteration of things, as well to the civil state of the realm as especially to the state ecclesiastical. For by him was abolished out of the realm the usurped power of the Bishop of Rome, idolatry and superstition somewhat repressed, images and pilgrimages defaced, monasteries pulled down, sects rooted out, Scriptures reduced to the vulgar tongue, and the state of the Church redressed.

The history of divers good men and women persecuted for religion

Besides the faithful martyrs of Christ that gave their lives for the testimony of his truth I find recorded in the register of London, between 1509 and 1527, the names of divers men and women who were persecuted and imprisoned for the same.

The chiefest objection against Joan Baker was that she would not only herself not reverence the crucifix, but had also persuaded a friend of hers lying at the point of death not to put any trust in the crucifix but in God who is in heaven, who only worketh all the miracles that be done, and not the dead images which be but stocks and stones; and therefore she was sorry that she had gone so often on pilgrimage to St Saviour and other idols; also that she did hold opinion that the Pope had no power to give pardons, and that Lady Young, who was not long before that time burned, died a true martyr; and therefore she wished that she herself might do no worse than Lady Young had done.

Great displeasure was conceived against Richard Wolman, for that he termed the Church of Paul's a house of thieves, affirming that the priests there were not liberal givers unto the poor but rather takers-away from them of what they could get.

It was alleged against William Couper and Alice his wife that they had spoken against pilgrimages and worshipping of images; but chiefly the woman, who having her child hurt by falling into a ditch, and being earnestly persuaded by her ignorant neighbours to go to St Laurence for help, said that neither Laurence nor any other saint could help her child, and therefore none ought to go to any image made with man's hands, but only to Almighty God; for pilgrimages were nothing worth, saving to make priests rich.

Unto John Household, Robert Rascall, and Elizabeth Stamford, as well the article against the sacrament of the altar was objected as also that they had spoken against praying to saints, and had despised the authority of the Bishop of Rome and others of his clergy. But especially Household was charged to have called them Antichrists and whoremongers, and the Pope himself a strumpet and a common bawd unto the world, who with his pardons had drowned in blindness all Christian realms, and that for money.

About the same time there were certain articles objected against John Hig, amongst which were these: that he had affirmed that it was as lawful for a temporal man to have two wives at once as for a priest to have two benefices; that he had in his custody a book of the four evangelists in English and did often read therein; that he favoured the opinions of Martin Luther, openly pronouncing that Luther had more learning in his little finger than all the doctors in England in their whole bodies; and that all the priests were blind and led the people the wrong way. Likewise it was alleged that he had denied purgatory, and had said that while he was alive he would do as much for himself as he could, for after his death he thought that prayers and alms-deeds could little help him.

These and suchlike matters were they wherewith these simple men and women were chiefly charged, and as heinous heretics excommunicated, imprisoned, and compelled to recant. Some of them, besides the ordinary bearing of faggots, were enjoined to appear once every year before their ordinary, as also to wear the sign of a faggot painted upon their sleeves all their lives, or as long as it pleased their ordinary to appoint. By which rigorous and open punishing they meant to terrify and keep back all others from the true knowledge of Jesus Christ. But the Lord be praised, what effect their wicked purposes have taken these our lightsome days of God's glorious gospel do joyfully declare.

Thus have I summarily collected the principal articles objected against these weak and earthy vessels, not minding to excuse or condemn them in their falls and defections, but leaving them unto the rich mercies of the Lord. Now, leaving to say any further herein, I will go forthward with other somewhat serious matters.

The martyrdom of William Sweeting, John Brewster, and John Browne

In searching the register for the collection of the names before recited, I find that within the compass of the same years there were some others who, after they had once showed themselves as frail as the rest, became again as earnest professors of Christ as ever they were before, and were the second time apprehended, examined, condemned, and most cruelly burned. Of which number were William Sweeting and John Brewster, who were burned together in Smithfield, the 18th of October 1511. Let us here adjoin the story of John Browne, burnt at Ashford about this fourth year of King Henry VIII.

The occasion of the first trouble of John Browne was by a priest sitting in Gravesend barge. Browne, being at the same time in the barge, came and sat by him; thereupon the priest asked him, 'Dost thou know who I am? Thou sittest too near me, thou sittest on my clothes.'

'No, sir; I know not what you are.'

'I tell thee I am a priest.'

'What, sir! Are you a parson, or vicar, or a lady's chaplain?'

'No. I am a soul-priest. I sing for a soul.'

'Do you so, sir? That is well done; I pray you, sir, where find you the soul when you go to mass?'

'I cannot tell thee.'

'I pray you, where do you leave it, sir, when the mass is done?'

'I cannot tell thee.'

'How can you then have the soul?'

'Go thy ways, thou art an heretic and I will be even with thee.'

So at the landing the priest rode straightways to Archbishop Warham. Hereupon Browne three days after, his wife being churched the same day, he bringing in a mess of potage to his guests was sent for, and his feet bound under his own horse, and so brought to Canturbury, neither his wife nor he nor any of his knowing whither he went; and there continuing from Low Sunday till the Friday before Whitsunday, his wife not knowing all this while where he was, he was set in the stocks overnight, and on the morrow went to death at Ashford, *an* 1517. As he was in the stocks his wife, then hearing of him, came and sat by him all the night before he should be burned; to whom he declaring the whole story how he was handled, showed that he could not set his feet to the ground; and told her how by the two bishops, Warham and Fisher, his feet were heated upon the hot coals and burnt to the bones 'to make me,' said he, 'deny my Lord, which I will never do; for if I should deny my Lord in this world, he would hereafter deny me. I pray thee therefore, good Elizabeth, continue as thou hast begun, and bring up thy children virtuously and in the fear of God.'

The next day, on Whitsunday Even, this godly martyr was burned. Standing at the stake this prayer he made, holding up his hands:

'O Lord, I yield me to thy grace,
Grant me mercy for my trespass;
Let never the fiend my soul chase.
Lord, I will bow and thou shalt beat;
Let never my soul come in hell heat.

'Into thy hands I commend my spirit; thou hast redeemed me, O Lord of truth.' And so he ended. *Ex testimonio Aliciae Browne eius filiae*. At the fire one Chilton, the bailey arrant, bade cast in his children also, for they would spring, said he, of the ashes.

William Sweeting first dwelt with Lady Percy at Dalington in the county of Northampton and from thence went to Boxted in Essex, where he was the holy water clerk seven years: after that he was bailiff and farmer to Mrs Margery Wood the term of thirteen years. From Boxted he came to St Osithe, where he served the prior sixteen years or more; where he so turned the prior by his persuasions that the said prior was afterwards compelled to abjure. Sweeting, coming up to London with the prior, for suspicion of heresy was committed to the Lollards' Tower, and being abjured in the Church of St Paul was constrained to bear a faggot at Paul's Cross and at Colchester, and afterwards to wear a faggot upon his coat all his life; which he did two years together till the parson of Colchester required him to help him in the service of the church, and so plucked the badge from his sleeve; and there he remained two years, being the holy water clerk. From thence departed, and travelling abroad came to Rederith in the diocese of Winchester, where he was holy water clerk the space of a year. Then went to Chelsea, where he was their neatherd and kept the town beasts; in which town, as he went forth with his beasts to the field, the good man was apprehended and brought before the bishop, and his chamber searched for books. This was *an.* 1511.

The crimes whereupon he was examined be these:

First, for having much conference with one William Man in a book called Mathew.

Item, that he frequented the company of James Brewster, who had been abjured.

Item, that when his wife should go on pilgrimage he asked her what good she would receive, adding that it were better for her to keep at home and attend to her business.

Item, that he had received of William Man that the sacrament of the altar was not the very body, but bread in substance, received in memorial of Christ.

Item, because he had reprehended his wife for worshipping images and setting up candles before them.

Thus have you the crimes laid against William Sweeting wherefore he was condemned; who being asked what cause he had why he should not be judged for relapse, said he had nothing else but that he committed himself to the mercy of God.

With William Sweeting the same time was examined and condemned James Brewster of the parish of St Nicholas in Colchester. Brewster was a carpenter, who being unlettered could neither read nor write, and was apprehended in one Walker's house in St Clement's parish. Six years before, *an.* 1505, he had been abjured by William

Warham, Archbishop of Canturbury, the See of London being then vacant; and after other penance done at Colchester was enjoined to wear a faggot upon his upper garment during his life; which badge he did bear upon his left shoulder near the space of two years, till the controller of the Earl of Oxford plucked it away, because he was labouring in the works of the earl.

The crimes which he confessed were these:

First, that he had been with William Sweeting in the fields hearing him read many good things out of a book.

Item, for having a little book of Scripture in English.

Item, that he had conference with Henry Hert against images, and that it was better bestowed money which was given to the poor than that which was offered in pilgrimage.

Item, that when William Sweeting and he were talking of the sacrament of the Lord's body Brewster should say, 'Now the Son of the living God help us,' unto whom Sweeting should answer, 'Now Almighty God do so.'

Then being asked, as the Romish manner is, whether he had any cause why he should not be judged for relapse, he said that he submitted him to the mercy of God and to the favourable goodness of his judge. Likewise did William Sweeting submit himself; trusting belike that they should find some favour in this humble subjecting themselves unto their goodness. But note the unmerciful and unchristian dealing of these catholic fathers, who upon their submission were contented to give out a solemn commission, the tenor whereof was to release them from the sentence of excommunication whereinto they had incurred; but immediately after the bishop notwithstanding pronounced the sentence of death and condemnation; whereupon they were delivered to the secular power, and together burnt in Smithfield at one fire, the 18th of October 1511.

John Stilman, martyr

It would be tedious to recite the great multitude of good men and women which recanted and abjured about the beginning of King Henry's reign; among whom some there were whom the Lord reduced again, and made strong in the profession of his truth and constant unto death: one was John Stilman, who about the 24th of September 1518 was brought before Richard Fitzjames, then Bishop of London, at his manor of Fulham, and by him was there examined and charged, that notwithstanding his abjuration made about eleven years then past before Edmund Bishop of Salisbury, as well for speaking against the worshipping, praying, and offering unto images, as also for denying the carnal and corporal presence in the sacrament of Christ's memorial, yet since that time he had fallen into the same opinions again; and further he had praised John Wickliffe, affirming that he was a saint in heaven, and that his book *The Wicket* was good and holy. Soon after his examination he was sent unto the Lollards' Tower in London, and the 22nd of October was brought into the consistory at Paul's, and then judicially examined by Thomas Hed, the bishop's vicar-general. His constant persevering in the truth perceived, Dr Hed, the 25th of October, by his sentence definitive did condemn him for a relapsed heretic, and delivered him the same day unto the Sheriffs of London, to be burned in Smithfield.

Among persons which submitted themselves and were put to penance certain there which in 1521, because they had been abjured before, were now condemned for relapse and were committed to the secular arm to be burned, whose names here follow: Thomas Bernard, James Morden, Robert Rave, John Scrivener. Touching the burning of John Scrivener, here is to be noted that his children were compelled to set fire unto their father, in like manner as Joan Clerke, daughter of William Tilsworth, was constrained to give fire to the burning of her own natural father, as is above specified; the example of which cruelty, as it is contrary both to God and nature, so it has not been seen or heard of in the memory of the heathen.

CHAPTER 3

LUTHER, TINDALL, AND THEIR DISCIPLES

The reformation of the Church

Although it cannot be sufficiently expressed into what desolation the Church was brought in those latter days, yet by the reading of these stories aforepast some intelligence may be given in what darkness the world was drowned during these 400 years. The religion of Christ, which consisteth in spirit and verity, was turned into outward observation, ceremonies, and idolatry. So many saints we had, so many gods; so many monasteries, so many pilgrimages; so many relics, forged and feigned; so many lying miracles. Instead of the living Lord we worshipped stocks and stones. How the people were led, so the priests were fed, no care was taken. Instead of God's word, man's word was set up; instead of Christ's testament, the canon law. The law of God was little read, the end thereof less known; the difference between gospel and law was not understood, the benefit of Christ not considered, the effect of faith not expended.

The foundation of all our Christianity is this—the promise of God in the blood of Christ His Son, giving life to all that believe in him by grace, not by works. Upon this foundation of God's free promise and grace first builded the patriarchs, kings, and prophets; upon the same foundation Christ builded His church; upon which foundation the apostles likewise builded the church apostolical or catholical. This foundation so long as the Church did retain, it continued sound. But in process of years, through wealth and negligence, came in new builders, who would build upon a new foundation a new church more glorious, the Church of Rome; who laid the groundwork upon the strength of Law and works. A new church with a new foundation hath been erected, not upon God's promise and His free grace in Christ Jesus, nor upon free justification by faith, but upon merit of men's working. Hereof have they planted all their new devices; as masses, trecenaries, *diriges*, obsequies, vigils, midnight rising, barefoot-going, fish-tasting, stations, jubilees, advocation of saints, praying to images, pilgrimage-walking, works of supererogation, pardons, relations, indulgences, satisfactions, auricular confession.

Moreover, as this new-found church was deformed in doctrine, so was it corrupted in order of life and deep hypocrisy. Under the pretence of Peter's chair they exercised a majesty above emperors and kings. Under the visor of their vowed chastity reigned adultery; under the cloak of professed poverty they possessed the goods of the temporalty; under the title of being dead to the world they reigned in the world; under colour of the keys of heaven they brought all the states of the world under their girdle. Yet neither did their pride cease to ascend nor could their avarice be satisfied. If the example of Wolsey and other cardinals and popes cannot satisfy thee, turn over the Ploughman's Tale in Chaucer, where thou shalt understand much more of their demeanour than I have here described.

In these miserable days of darkness and ignorance thou seest, good reader, how necessary it was that reformation of the Church should come, which now most happily began to work through the merciful providence of Almighty God; who although he suffered his Church to wander through the seduction of pride and prosperity a long time, yet at length it pleased his goodness to respect his people and to reduce his Church into the pristine frame again, from whence it was piteously decayed. Whereof I have now to entreat, intending by the grace of Christ to declare how this reformation first began and how it proceeded by little and little unto this perfection which now we see, and more I trust shall see.

Herein we have first to behold the admirable work of God's wisdom. For as the first decay of the Church began of rude ignorance, and lack of knowledge in teachers, so to restore the Church by doctrine and learning it pleased God to open to man the art of printing, the time whereof was shortly after the burning of Hus. Printing being opened incontinent ministered unto the Church the tools of learning and knowledge; which were good books, which before lay hid and unknown. The science of printing being found, immediately followed the grace of God, which stirred up good wits aptly to conceive the light of knowledge; by which light darkness began to be espied and ignorance detected; truth from error, religion from superstition, to be discerned.

After these wits stirred up of God followed other more, increasing daily in science, in tongues, and perfection of knowledge; who now were able not only to discern in matters of judgment, but also were so furnished with the help of good letters that they did encounter with the adversary, sustaining the cause of learning against barbarity, of verity against error, of religion against superstition. In number of whom were Picus and Franciscus Mirandula, Laurentius Valla, Franciscus Petrarcha, Dr Wesalianus, Revelinus, Grocinus, Dr Coletus, Rhenanus, Erasmus etc. Here began the first push to be given against the ignorant faction of the Pope's pretensed church; who after that by their learned writings and laborious travail they had opened a window of light unto the world and had made a way more ready for other to come after, immediately followed Martin Luther, with other after him; by whose ministry it pleased the Lord to work a more full reformation of his Church. Luther diligently reduced the minds of men to the Son of God: as John Baptist demonstrated the Lamb of God that took away the sins of the world, so Luther, shining in the Church as the bright daylight after a long and dark night, expressly showed that sins are freely remitted for the love of the Son of God, and that we ought faithfully to embrace this bountiful gift.

Martyrs of Coventry

Mrs Smith, widow; Robert Hatchets, shoemaker; Archer, shoemaker; Hawkins, shoemaker; Thomas Bond, shoemaker; Wrigsham, glover; Landsdale, hosier; martyred at Coventry *an.* 1519. Their persecutors: Simon Mourton, the bishop's sumner; also the Bishop of Coventry, and Friar Stafford, warden of the Grey Friars.

The principal cause of the apprehension of these persons was teaching their children the Lord's Prayer and Ten Commandments in English, for which they were upon Ash Wednesday put in prison till Friday. Then they were sent to Mackstock Abbey six miles from Coventry; during which time their children were sent for before Friar Stafford; who examining them of their belief charged them, upon pain of suffering such death as their fathers should, in no wise to meddle any more with the Lord's Prayer, the Creed, and Commandments, in English. Which done, upon Palm Sunday the fathers of these children were brought back to Coventry, and there condemned to be burned.

Only Mrs Smith was dismissed for the present. Because it was somewhat dark as she should go home, Simon Mourton offered to go home with her. As he was leading her by the arm and heard the rattling of a scroll within her sleeve, 'Yea,' saith he, 'what have ye here?' And so took it from her and espied that it was the Lord's Prayer &c in English. Which when the wretched sumner understood, 'Ah sirrah!'

said he, 'come: as good now as another time'; and so brought her back to the bishop, where she was immediately condemned, and burned with the six men the 4th of April 1519.

In the number of these Coventry men was also Robert Silkeb, who at the apprehension of these fled away and escaped. But two years after he was taken again and brought to Coventry, where he was burned the morrow after he came thither, about the 13th of January 1521.

When these were dispatched, immediately the sheriffs went to their houses and took all their goods and cattle to their own use, not leaving their wives and children any parcel thereof. And as the people began to grudge somewhat at the cruelty showed and at the unjust death of these martyrs, the bishop caused it to be noised abroad that they were not burned for having the Lord's Prayer and the Commandments in English, but because they did eat flesh on Fridays; which could not be proved, nor was any such matter objected to them in their examinations. The witnesses of this history be yet alive, of whom one is Mother Hall, dwelling now in Bagington two miles from Coventry.

Thomas Bilney and Thomas Arthur, which abjured at Norwich

Thomas Bilney was brought up in the University of Cambridge even from a child, profiting in all kind of liberal science unto the profession of both laws. But having gotten a better schoolmaster, the Holy Spirit of Christ, he came at last unto this point, that forsaking the knowledge of man's laws he converted his study to those things which tended more unto godliness than gainfulness. As he himself was inflamed with the love of true religion, so again was in his heart an incredible desire to allure many unto the same, desiring nothing more than that he might stir up any to the love of Christ. Neither was his labours vain; for he converted many of his fellows unto the knowledge of the gospel, amongst which number were Thomas Arthur and Mr Hugh Latimer; which Latimer at that time was cross-keeper at Cambridge, bringing it forth upon procession days.

Bilney forsaking the university went into many places teaching and preaching, being associate with Arthur, which accompanied him from the university. The authority of Thomas Wolsey, Cardinal of York, at that time was great in England, but his pomp and pride much greater; which did evidently declare to all wise men the vanity of all the bishops and clergy; whereupon Bilney with other good men, marvelling at the incredible insolency of the clergy which they could no longer abide, began to reprove this excessive pomp, and also to pluck at the authority of the Bishop of Rome. It was time for the cardinal to awake and look about his business; neither lacked he any craft or subtlety of a serpent, for he understood well enough upon how slender a foundation their ambitious dignity was grounded, neither was he ignorant that their Luciferous and proud kingdom could not long continue against the manifest word of God; especially if the light of the gospel should once open the eyes of men. He did not greatly fear the displeasure of princes: only this he feared, the voice of Christ in his gospel, lest it should disclose their hypocrisy and deceits. Wherefore he thought good speedily to withstand these beginnings; whereupon he caused Bilney and Arthur to be cast into prison.

The 27th of November 1527 the cardinal, accompanied with a great number of bishops with many divines and lawyers, came into the chapterhouse of Westminster, where Bilney and Arthur were brought before them; and the cardinal there inquired of Bilney whether he had taught the people the opinions of Luther or any other condemned by the Church; whereunto Bilney answered that wittingly he had not taught any of Luther's opinions, or any other, contrary to the Catholic Church. Then the cardinal asked him whether he had once made an oath that he should not preach or defend any of Luther's opinions, but should impugn the same everywhere. He answered that he had made such an oath, but not lawfully. These answers made, the cardinal caused him to swear to answer plainly to the articles set forth by him in the diocese of London, the diocese of Norwich, and other places, without any craft or leaving out any part of the truth.

After he was thus sworn and examined, the cardinal proceeded to the examination of Thomas Arthur, causing him to take the like oath. This done, he asked him whether he had not once told Sir Thomas More that in the sacrament of the altar there was not the very body of Christ. This he denied. Then the cardinal gave him time to deliberate till noon, and to bring his answer in writing. After noon, what time the examination of Arthur was ended, the cardinal and bishops did call in for witness before Bilney John Huggen, chief provincial of the friars-preachers, Geffrey Julles, and Richard Jugworth, Professors of Divinity, which were sworn that they should speak their minds upon the articles laid against him. And because he was occupied about the affairs of the realm, he committed the hearing of the matter to the

Bishop of London and other bishops there present, to proceed against all men, as also against writings set forth by Martin Luther, and root out their errors and opinions; and all such as were found culpable, to compel them to abjuration, or if the matter so required, to deliver them unto the secular power.

On the 28th of November the Bishop of London with the Bishops of Ely and Rochester came unto the Bishop of Norwich's house, where likewise they did swear certain witnesses, and so proceeded to the examination of Mr Arthur; which being ended, the Bishop of London warned him that he should not reveal his examinations, nor his answers nor any part thereof.

On the 2nd of December the bishops assembled again in the same place and swore more witnesses against Mr Bilney: that done, they called for Arthur. The said Arthur did revoke and condemn the articles against him ministered, and submitted himself to the judgment of the Church.

On the 4th of December the bishops assembled in the chapterhouse of Westminster, whither Mr Bilney was brought and exhorted to recant; who answered that he would stand to his conscience. On the 5th the bishops assembled there again, before whom Bilney was brought; whom the Bishop of London asked whether he would return to the Church and acknowledge his heresies. Bilney answered that he trusted he was not separate from the Church, and required time and place to bring in witnesses; which was refused. Then the bishop again required of him whether he would return to the Catholic Church: he answered that if they could prove that he was convict he would submit himself; and other answer he would give none.

On the 7th of December the bishops being assembled Bilney appeared; whom the Bishop of London asked whether he would now return to the unity of the Church and revoke the heresies whereof he stood convicted. He answered that now he was persuaded by Mr Dancaster and other friends, he would submit himself, trusting they would deal gently with him. Then he desired that he might read his abjuration; which the bishop granted. When he had read the same secretly by himself, being demanded what he would do he answered that he would abjure; and there openly read his abjuration, and subscribed, and delivered it to the bishop, which then did absolve him, and for his penance enjoined him that he should abide in a prison appointed by the cardinal, till he were by him released; and moreover the next day he should go before the procession in the Cathedral Church of St Paul bareheaded with a faggot on his shoulder, and should stand before the preacher at Paul's Cross all the sermon time. *Ex Regist. Lond.*

After which abjuration made, about 1529 Bilney took such repentance and sorrow that he was near the point of utter despair, as by Mr Latimer is testified; whose words I thought here to annex, written in his seventh sermon preached before King Edward: 'I knew a man myself, Bilney, little Bilney, that blessed martyr of God who, what time he had borne his faggot and was come again to Cambridge, had such conflicts within himself that his friends were afraid to let him be alone. They were fain to be with him day and night and comfort him as they could; but no comforts would serve. As for the comfortable places of Scripture, to bring them unto him was as though a man would run him through the heart with a sword. Yet for all this he was revived and took his death patiently, and did well against the tyrannical See of Rome.' Again Mr Latimer in another of his sermons hath these words: 'Mr Bilney, which was burnt here in England for God's sake, was induced by his friends to bear a faggot at the time when the cardinal was aloft and bare the swinge. When Bilney came to Cambridge again a whole year after, he was in such anguish that nothing did him good, neither eating nor drinking, nor even any communication of God's word; for he thought that all the Scriptures were against him and sounded to his condemnation; so that I many a time communed with him, for I was familiarly acquainted with him; but all things whatsoever any man could allege to his comfort seemed to him to make against him. Yet for all that afterwards he came again. God endued him with such strength that he not only confessed his faith in the gospel of our Saviour, but also suffered his body to be burned for that same gospel's sake.'

By this it appeareth how vehemently this good man was pierced with sorrow and remorse for his abjuration the space almost of two years, from 1529 to 1531. Then he by God's grace came at length to some quiet of conscience, being resolved to give his life for the confession of that truth which before he had renounced. Thus being determined and setting his time, he took his leave in Trinity Hall at ten o'clock at night of certain of his friends and said that he would go to Jerusalem, alluding to the example of Christ in the gospel, what time he was appointed to suffer his passion. So Bilney departed to Norfolk, and there preached first privately in households to confirm the brethren and sisters, and the anchoress whom he had converted to Christ. Then preached he openly in the fields, confessing his fact and preaching publicly that doctrine which he before had abjured, and willed all men to beware by him, and never to trust their fleshly friends in causes of religion. And so, setting forward on his journey toward the celestial Jerusalem, he departed from thence to the anchoress in Norwich, and gave her a New Testament of Tindall's translation and *The Obedience of a Christian Man*; whereupon he was apprehended and carried to prison, there to remain till the blind bishop Nixe sent up for a writ to burn him.

In the mean season the friars, with doctors, civil and canon, resorted to him, labouring to persuade him not to die in those opinions, saying he should be damned body and soul if he so continued; among whom were sent to him of the bishop, Dr Call, provincial of the Grey Friars, and Dr Stokes, an Augustine Friar, who lay with him in prison in disputation till the writ came. Dr Call, through Bilney's doctrine and good life, whereof he had experience, was somewhat reclaimed to the gospel's side. Dr Stokes remained obdurate, and doth to this day. Another great doer against him was one Friar Bird, with one eye, provincial of the White Friars. This Bird was a suffragan in Coventry and afterwards Bishop of Chester, and was he that brought apples to Boner, mentioned in the story of Haukes. Another was a Black Friar called Hodgkins who married, and in Queen Mary's time put away his wife. These four orders of friars were sent to bait Bilney, who notwithstanding, as he had planted himself upon the firm rock of God's word, was at a point; and so continued unto the end.

Now for testimony of this matter, forsomuch as Mr More allegeth none to prove that Bilney at his death did recant, I have searched out and procured the true certificate of Bilney's burning, with all the circumstances thereto belonging, testified not by some-says and hear-says, as More useth, but truly witnessed and faithfully recorded by one (Dr Parker, Archbishop of Canturbury) who, as in place and degree he surmounteth the estate of More, so being also both a spiritual person and there present the same time, coming for the purpose the day before to see his burning, was a present beholder of his martyrdom. The order of which martyrdom was as followeth.

Bilney, after examination and condemnation before Dr Pelles, chancellor, first was degraded by Suffragan Underwood according to their Popish manner. This done, he was committed to the lay power and to the two sheriffs of the city, of whom Thomas Necton was one. This Necton was Bilney's special friend, and sorry to accept him to such execution as followed; but such was the dread of the chancellor and friars that he could no otherwise do, but he must receive him; who notwithstanding, as he could not bear to be present at his death, so for the time that he was in his custody, he caused him to be more friendly looked unto, and more wholesomely kept concerning his diet, than he was before.

The Friday following at night, which was before the day of his execution, Bilney had divers of his friends resorting unto him in the Guild Hall, where he was kept. One of the said friends, finding him eating an ale-brew with such a cheerful heart as he did, said that he was glad to see him so shortly before his painful departure so heartily refresh himself. 'Oh,' said he, 'I follow the example of the husbandmen of the country, who having a ruinous house to dwell in yet bestow cost as long as they may to hold it up. And so do I now with this ruinous house of my body, and with God's creatures in thanks to him refresh the same as you see.' Then sitting with his friends in godly talk to their edification, some put him in mind that though the fire which he should suffer the next day should be of great heat unto his body, yet the comfort of God's Spirit should cool it to his everlasting refreshing. At this word Thomas, putting his hand towards the flame of the candle burning before them and feeling the heat thereof, 'Oh,' said he, 'I feel by experience, and have known it long by philosophy, that fire by God's ordinance is naturally hot; yet I am persuaded by God's holy word, and by the experience of some spoken of in the same, that in the flame they felt no heat and no consumption; and I constantly believe that however the stubble of this my body shall be wasted by it, my soul shall be purged thereby: a pain for the time, whereon followeth joy unspeakable.' And here he much treated of this place of Scripture, 'Fear not, for I redeemed thee, and called thee by thy name; thou art mine own. When thou goest through the water I will be with thee, and the strong floods shall not overflow thee. When thou walkest in the fire, it shall not burn thee, and the flame shall not kindle upon thee; for I am the Lord thy God, the Holy One of Israel.'[1] Which he did most comfortably entreat of, as well in respect of himself as applying it to the particular use of his friends there present; of whom some took such sweet

[1] Is. xliii. 1-2, specially marked in Bilney's own Bible, now in Corpus Christi College Library, Cambridge.—Ed.

fruit therein that they caused the whole sentence to be fair written in tables, and some in their books; the comfort whereof, in divers of them, was never taken from them to their dying day.

The Saturday following, when the officers with their glaives and halberds were ready to receive him and to lead him to the place of execution without the city gate called Bishop's Gate, in a low valley called the Lollards' Pit under St Leonard's Hill, environed about with great hills (which place was chosen for the people's quiet sitting to see the execution), at the coming forth of Bilney out of the prison door one of his friends came to him and prayed him in God's behalf to be constant, and to take his death as patiently as he could. Whereunto Bilney answered with a mild countenance, 'When the mariner is entered his ship to sail on the troublous sea, he for a while is tossed in the billows; yet in hope that he shall once come to the quiet haven he beareth in better comfort the perils which he feeleth: so am I now toward this sailing; and whatsoever storms I shall feel, yet shortly after shall my ship be in the haven, as I doubt not thereof, desiring you to help me with your prayers.'

So he, going forth in the street, giving much alms by the way by the hands of one of his friends, and accompanied by Dr Warner, parson of Winterton, whom he did choose as his old acquaintance to be with him for his ghostly comfort, came at last to the place of execution and descended from the hill to the same, apparelled in a layman's gown with his sleeves hanging down and his arms out, his hair being piteously mangled at his degradation, and drew near to the stake prepared; and somewhat tarrying the preparation of the fire, he desired that he might speak some words to the people, and there standing thus he said: 'Good people, I am come hither to die, and born I was to live under that condition, naturally to die again; and that you may testify that I depart out of this present life a true Christian man, in a right belief towards God, I will rehearse unto you the articles of my creed;' then began to rehearse them as they be in the common creed; and at the article of Christ's incarnation and coming to the word 'crucified' he humbly bowed himself; then coming to 'I believe the Catholic Church' he paused and spake these words, 'Good people, I must here confess to have offended the Church, in preaching once against the prohibition of the same at a poor cure belonging to Trinity Hall in Cambridge, where I was Fellow, entreated thereunto by the curate and other good people of the parish, showing that they had no sermon there of long time before; so in my conscience moved I did make a poor collation unto them. Howbeit I trust at the general day charity, that moved me to this act, shall bear me out at the judgment seat of God.' And so he proceeded, without any recantation.

This done, he put off his gown and went to the stake, and kneeling upon a little ledge coming out of the stake, whereon he should afterwards stand to be better seen, he made his private prayer in so good and quiet behaviour that he seemed not much to consider the terror of his death, and ended his prayers with the psalm beginning 'Hear my prayer, O Lord, consider my desire.' The next verse he repeated in deep meditation thrice, 'And enter not into judgment with thy servant, for in thy sight shall no man living be justified.' And so finishing that psalm he ended his private prayers.

After that he turned himself to the officers asking if they were ready, and they answered 'Yea'. Whereupon he put off his jacket and doublet and stood in his hose and shirt, and went unto the stake, standing upon that ledge, and the chain was cast about him; and standing thereon Dr Warner came to bid him farewell, who spake but few words for weeping: upon whom Bilney did most gently smile, and inclined his body to speak a few words of thanks; and the last were these, 'O Master Doctor! *Pasce gregem tuum, pasce gregem tuum; ut cum venerit Dominus, inveniat te sic facientem*;' that is 'Feed your flock, feed your flock; that when the Lord cometh he may find you so doing'; and 'Farewell, good Master Doctor, and pray for me.' And so he departed sobbing and weeping. While Bilney thus stood upon the ledge, certain friars and priors came to him and said, 'O Master Bilney, the people be persuaded that we be the causers of your death, and therefore it is likely that they will withdraw their alms from us, except you discharge us of the matter'; whereupon Bilney spake with a loud voice to the people and said, 'I pray you, good people, be never the worse to these men for my sake, as the authors of my death: it was not they.'

Then the officers put reeds and faggots about his body and set fire to the reeds, which made a great flame that sparkled and deformed the visor of his face; which flame was blown away from him by the violence of the wind which was that day notable great; in which it was said that the fields were marvellously plagued by the loss of corn; and so for a little pause he stood without flame, the flame departing and recoursing thrice ere the wood took strength to consume him; and then he gave up the ghost, and his body, being withered, bowed downward upon the chain. Then one of the officers with his halberd smote out the staple in the stake behind him, and suffered his body to fall into the bottom of the fire, laying wood upon it; and so he was consumed.

Thus have ye, good readers, the true history of this good man; that is, of blessed Saint Bilney, as Mr Latimer doth call him, without any recantation, testified by the authority above said; by which authority being there present and yet alive it is furthermore affirmed that Bilney not only did never recant, but also that he never had any such bill, script, or scroll in his hand to read either softly or apertly, as Mr More *per licentiam poeticam* would bear us down. Wherefore even as ye see More deal in this, so ye may trust him in his other tales, if ye will.

The story of Mr Simon Fish

Before the time of Mr Bilney I should have placed the story of Simon Fish, with the book called *The Supplication of Beggars*; declaring by what means it came to the king's hand, and what effect followed in the reformation of many things, especially the clergy. But the missing of a few years breaketh no great square in our story, though it be now entered here which should have come in six years before.

After the light of the gospel, working mightily in Germany, began to spread his beams here in England, great stir followed in the hearts of many; so that coloured hypocrisy, false doctrine, and painted holiness, began to be espied more and more by the reading of God's word. The authority of the Bishop of Rome and the glory of his cardinals were not so high, but such as had fresh wits, sparkled with God's grace, began to espy Christ from Antichrist; in the number of whom was Simon Fish, a gentleman of Gray's Inn. It happened about 1525 that there was a play by one Mr Roo of the same Inn, in which partly was matter against Cardinal Wolsey; and where none durst play that part which touched the cardinal, Mr Fish took upon him to do it. Whereupon great displeasure ensued against him, insomuch as he, being pursued by the cardinal the night that this tragedy was played, was compelled to void his own house, and so fled over the sea to Tindall. The year following this book was made; and in the year, as I suppose, 1528 was sent over to Lady Anne Bullen, who then lay at a place not far from the Court. Which book her brother seeing in her hand, took and read it and gave it to her again, willing her earnestly to give it to the king, which she did. The king demanded of her who made it: whereunto she answered and said one Fish, who was fled out of the realm for fear of the cardinal.

After the king had kept the book in his bosom three or four days, such knowledge was given by the king's servants to the wife of Simon Fish, that she might send for her husband without all danger: whereupon she came first and made suit to the king for the safe return of her husband; who showed a marvellous gentle countenance towards her, asking where her husband was. She answered, 'If it like your Grace, not far off.' 'Then,' said he, 'fetch him, and he shall come and go without peril, and no man shall do him harm;' saying moreover that he had much wrong that he was from her so long; who had been absent now two years and a half. In the meantime the cardinal was deposed and Mr More sat in his place of the Chancellorship.

Thus Fish's wife, emboldened by the king's words, went immediately to her husband, being lately come over and lying privily within a mile of the Court, and brought him to the king, which appeareth to be about *an.* 1530. When the king saw him and understood he was the author of the book, he came and embraced him with loving countenance. After long talk for three or four hours, as they were riding together on hunting, the king at length dimitted him and bade him take home his wife, for she had taken great pains for him; who answered the king and said he durst not do so for fear of Sir Thomas More, then Chancellor, and Stokesley, Bishop of London. The king, taking his signet off his finger, willed him to have him recommended to the Lord Chancellor, charging him not to be so hardy to work him any harm. Fish, receiving the signet, went and declared his message to the Lord Chancellor, who took it as sufficient for his own discharge but asked if he had anything for the discharge of his wife. For she had displeased the friars by not suffering them to say their gospels in her house unless they would say it in English. Whereupon the Lord Chancellor, leaving not his grudge towards the wife, sent his man for her to appear before him; who had it not been for her young daughter, who lay sick of the plague, had been like to come to much trouble. Of which plague her husband deceasing within half a year, she afterwards married Mr James Bainham, Sir Alexander's son, a worshipful knight of Gloucestershire: which James not long after was burned, as in process of this story shall appear.

Thus much concerning Simon Fish, author of *The Book of Beggars*, who also translated a book called *The Sum of the Scripture* out of Dutch. Against *The Book of the Beggars* another contrary book was written shortly by one Sir Thomas More under the title of *The Poor Silly Souls*

Puling out of Purgatory. After the writer had first divided the world into four parts, heaven, hell, earth, and purgatory, he maketh dead men's souls by a rhetorical *prosopopoeia* speak out of purgatory pinfold, scoffing at the author of the *Beggars' Book*, calling him fool, an ass, a goose, a mad dog, an heretic, and all that naught is. Yet these purgatory souls must take heed how they call a man fool so often; for if the gospel doth pronounce them guilty of hell fire which say 'Fool', it may be doubted lest those silly souls, calling this man fool so oft, do bring themselves thereby out of purgatory to the fire of hell. But as I do not think that there is any such place of purgatory as Mr More's poetical vein doth imagine, I cease to burden the souls departed and lay all the wit in Mr More, for not keeping *decorum personae* as a poet should have done. Some will think Mr More to have missed some part of his *decorum* in making the devil to be messenger between earth and purgatory, bringing tidings to the prisoned souls of the book and of the name of the maker. As touching the manner how this devil came into purgatory, it makes me laugh to see the merry antics of Mr More. Belike this was some merry devil, or else had eaten some *nasturtium* before; which coming into purgatory to show the name of this man could not tell his tale without laughing. 'But this was,' saith he, 'an enmious and an envious laughing, joined with grinning and gnashing of teeth.' Belike this was in Utopia, where Mr More's purgatory is founded; but because Mr More is hence departed, I leave him with his merry antics. As touching his book of purgatory, because John Frith hath effectuously overthrown the same, I will refer the reader to him while I repair again to the history.

After the clergy, and especially the cardinal, understood these books of *The Beggars' Supplication* to be strawed abroad in the streets of London, the cardinal caused not only his servants to gather them up, but also, when he understood that the king had received one of them, he came unto the King's Majesty saying, 'If it please your Grace, here are divers seditious persons who have scattered abroad books containing errors and heresies'; desiring his Grace to beware of them. Whereupon the king putting his hand in his bosom took out one of the books and delivered it unto the cardinal. Then the cardinal with his bishops consulted how they might provide a remedy for this mischief, and determined to give out a commission to forbid the reading of all English books, and namely this *Book of Beggars* and the New Testament of Tindall's translation, which was done out of hand by Cutbert Tonstall,

Bishop of London, who sent out his prohibition unto his archdeacons with all speed.

The New Testament began first to be translated by Tindall and came forth in print about *an.* 1529, wherewith Cutbert Tonstall with Sir Thomas More being sore aggrieved, devised how to destroy that false, erroneous translation, as he called it. It happened that one Augustine Packington, a mercer, was then at Antwerp where the bishop was. This man favoured Tindall but showed the contrary unto the bishop. The bishop, desirous to bring his purpose to pass, communed how he would gladly buy the New Testaments. Packington hearing him say so said, 'My Lord, I can do more in this matter than most merchants that be here, if it be your pleasure; for I know the Dutchmen and strangers that have bought them of Tindall and have them here to sell; so that if it be your Lordship's pleasure I must disburse money to pay for them or else I cannot have them; and I will assure you to have every book of them that is printed and unsold.' The bishop thinking he had God by the toe said, 'Do your diligence, gentle Mr Packington. Get them for me and I will pay whatsoever they cost; for I intend to burn them all at Paul's Cross.' Packington went unto Tindall and declared the whole matter; and so the bishop had the books, Packington had the thanks, and Tindall had the money. Tindall corrected the New Testaments again and caused them to be newly imprinted, so that they came thick and threefold into England. When the bishop perceived that, he sent for Packington and said to him, 'How cometh this, that there are so many New Testaments abroad? you promised me that you would buy them all.' Then answered Packington, 'Surely, I bought all that were to be had; but I perceive they have printed more since. It will never be better so long as they have letters and stamps; wherefore you were best to buy the stamps too, and so you shall be sure.' At which the bishop smiled, and so the matter ended.

Richard Bayfield, martyr

Following the order of years and times, next after the consummation of Bilney we have to treat of the martyrdom of Richard Bayfield, who in the same year 1531 was burned in Smithfield. Bayfield, a monk of Bury, was converted by Dr Barnes and two London brickmakers, Mr Maxwell and Mr Stacy, who through their godly conversation converted many men and women, and once a year of their own cost went about to visit the brethren and sistern scattered abroad. Dr Barnes much resorted to the Abbey of Bury where Bayfield was, to one Dr Ruffam; who had been at Lovaine together students. At that time it happened that Bayfield was chamberlain of the house, to provide lodging for the strangers and to see them well entertained; who delighted much in Dr Barnes' talk. At last Dr Barnes gave him a New Testament in Latin, and the other two gave him Tindall's Testament in English, with a book called *The Wicked Mammon*, and *The Obedience of a Christian Man*; wherein he prospered so mightily in two years' space that he was cast into the prison of his house, there sore whipped with a gag in his mouth, and then stocked; and continued in the same torment three quarters of a year before Dr Barnes could get him out, which he brought about by means of Dr Ruffam; and so he was committed to Dr Barnes to go to Cambridge with him. By that time he had been there a good while, he tasted so well of good letters that he never returned to his abbey but went to London, to Maxwell and Stacy, and they kept him secretly a while and so conveyed him beyond the sea; Dr Barnes being then in the Fleet for God's word. Bayfield was beneficial to Tindall and Frith; for he brought substance with him, and was their own hand, and sold all their works both in France and in England. At last, coming to London to Mr Smith's house in Buckler's Bury, there was he bewrayed, and dogged from that house to his bookbinder's in Mark Lane, and there taken and carried to Lollards' Tower and from thence to the coalhouse; by reason that one Parson Patmore of Much Haddam in Essex, then lying in Lollards' Tower, was in the doctrine of Christ there confirmed by him. Patmore after long trouble was abjured and condemned by the bishop to perpetual prison. He was taken because he married his priest. He had always corn in plenty, and when the markets were very dear he would send his corn thither to pluck down the prices thereof.

Bayfield, being in the coalhouse, was worser handled than he was before in the Lollards' Tower; for he was tied by the neck, middle, and legs, standing upright by the walls, divers times manacled, to accuse other that had bought his books. But he accused none, but stood to his religion and confession of his faith unto the very end, and was in the consistory of Paul's thrice put to his trial, whether he would abjure or no. He said he would dispute for his faith, and so did to their great shame, Stokesley being his judge, with Winchester and other bishops.

On the 20th of November 1531, in the choir of the Cathedral Church of St Paul, before John Bishop of London judicially sitting, assisted with

John Abbot of Westminster, Robert Abbot of Waltham, and Nicholas Prior of Christ's Church in London, Richard Bayfield was brought forth by Thomas Turnor his keeper. Then the bishop, after long deliberation, read the sentence against him; by which he condemned him as an heretic, and declared that he should be degraded. The sentence being read, he proceeded immediately to the actual degrading and there solemnly degraded him before the people; which being done, he dismissed him from the ecclesiastical court; whereupon the secular power received him unto their jurisdiction without any writ in that behalf obtained, but only by virtue of the bishop's letters, by the statute of King Henry IV directed unto them under the bishop's seal.

And so he was delivered to the sheriffs to carry to Newgate, being commanded to bring him upon Monday following into Paul's upper choir, there to give attendance upon the bishop with the residue till they had done with him; by and by the sheriffs were commanded to have him into the vestry, then to bring him forth in Antichrist's apparel to be degraded before them. When the bishop had degraded him, kneeling upon the highest step of the altar, he took his crosier staff and smote him on the breast, that he threw him down backwards and brake his head, that he swooned: when he came to himself he thanked God that he was delivered from the malignant church of Antichrist, and was come into the true Church, militant here in earth. So was he led forth through the choir to Newgate, and there rested about an hour in prayer, and so went to the fire in his apparel, manfully and joyfully, and there for lack of a speedy fire was three quarters of an hour alive. When the left arm was on fire, he rubbed it with his right hand and it fell from his body, and he continued in prayer to the end without moving.

Sir Thomas More, after he had brought this good man to his end, ceased not to rave in his ashes, to spy out what sparks he could find of reproach and contumely, whereby to rase out all good memory of his name. He found two things to lay against him; the one, that Bayfield went about to assure himself of two wives at once; the second, that all the while that he was not in utter despair of pardon, he was content to forswear his doctrine and letted not to disclose his brethren. For answer whereof, although there were no more to be said, yet this were enough to say, that Mr More thus saith of him; a man so blinded in the zeal of Popery, so deadly set against the one side and so partially affectionate unto the other, that in them whom he favoureth he can see nothing but fair roses and sweet virtue; in the other which he hateth there is never a thing can please his fantasy, but all is black as pitch, vice, abomination, heresy, and folly. But as touching the defence of Bayfield, as of other moe, I will defer the defence of them to a several apology by itself.

The story of the apprehension of Edward Freese, a painter

Edward Freese was born in York and was prentice to a painter in the same city; and by reason of working for his master in Bearsy Abbey was known unto the abbot; for he was a boy of a pregnant wit, and the abbot favoured him so much that he bought his years of his master and would have made him a monk. The lad not liking that kind of living, and not knowing how to get out because he was a novice, ran away and came to Colchester, and remaining there according to his former vocation was married and lived there like an honest man. After he had been there a good time, he was hired to paint certain cloths for the New Inn, which is in the middle of the market place; and in the upper border of the cloths he wrote certain sentences of the Scripture: by that he was known to be one of them which they call heretics.

On a time, he being at work in the same inn, they of the town when they had seen his work went about to take him: he, having some inkling thereof, thought to shift for himself, but was taken forcibly in the yard of the inn. After this he was brought to London and so to Fulham to the bishop's house, where he was cruelly imprisoned, with one Johnson and his wife, Wylie and his wife and son, and Father Bate of Rowshedge. They were fed with fine manchet made of sawdust, or at least a great part thereof; and were so straitly kept that their wives and friends could not come at them. After the painter had been there a long space, he was removed to Lollards' Tower. His wife whiles he was yet at Fulham being desirous to see her husband, being then big with child, the porter lift up his foot and struck her on the belly, that at length she died of the same; but the child was destroyed immediately. After that they were all stocked for a long time; then they were let loose in their prisons again. Some had horselocks on their legs, some other irons. This painter would ever be writing on the walls with chalk or a coal, and in one place he wrote, 'Dr Dodipoll would make me believe the moon were made of green cheese.' Because he would be writing, he was manacled by the wrists so long that the flesh of his arms was grown higher than his irons. He could not kemb his head, and he remained so long manacled that his hair was folded together.

After the death of his wife, his brother sued to the king for him, and after a long suit he was brought out in the consistory at Paul's and kept three days without meat before he came to his answer. What by the long imprisonment and evil handling, and for lack of sustenance, the man was in that case that he could say nothing, but gaze upon the people like a wild man; and if they asked him a question he could say nothing but 'My Lord is a good man.' Thus when they had spilt his body and destroyed his wits, they sent him back to Bearsy Abbey; but he would not tarry amongst them; albeit he never came to his perfect mind to his dying day.

His brother Valentine and his wife gave their lives at one stake in York for the testimony of Jesus Christ.

The wife of Father Bate, while he was at Fulham, made many supplications to the king without redress, and at last she delivered one to his own hands and he read it himself, whereupon she was appointed to go into Chancery Lane to one Mr Selyard; and at last she got a letter of Selyard to the bishop, and thought her suit well bestowed, hoping that some good should come to her husband thereby. And because the officers in those days were very crafty and desirous of blood, as others had proved, her friends would needs see the contents of her letter and not suffer her to deliver it to the bishop: as they thought so they found indeed; for it was after this manner: 'Look what you can gather against Father Bate; send me word by Sir William Saxy, that I may certify the king's Majesty etc.' Thus the poor woman, when she thought her suit had been done, was in less hope of her husband's life than before. But within short space it pleased God to deliver him; for he gat out in a dark night and was caught no more, but died a short time after.

In the beginning of this year, through the complaint of the clergy to the king, the translation of the New Testament with a great number of other books were forbidden. For the bishops coming into the Star Chamber the 25th of May, and communing with the king's Council, alleged that the translations of Tindall and Joy were not truly translated, and that in them were prefaces that smelled of heresy and railed against the bishops: wherefore all such books were prohibited, and commandment given by the king to the bishops that they, calling to them the best learned men of the universities, should cause a new translation to be made, so that the people might not be ignorant of the law of God. Notwithstanding the bishops did nothing at all to the setting forth of any new translation, which caused the people much to study Tindall's translation, by reason whereof many things came to light.

This year also in May the Bishop of London caused all the New Testaments of Tindall's translation, and many other books which he had bought, to be brought into Paul's churchyard and there burned.

James Bainham, lawyer and martyr

James Bainham, gentleman, son to a knight of Gloucestershire, being brought up by his parents in the studies of good letters had knowledge both of Latin and Greek. After that he gave himself to the study of the law, being a man of virtuous disposition and godly conversation, mightily addicted to prayer, an earnest reader of Scriptures, a visitor of prisoners, liberal to scholars, merciful to his clients, diligent in giving counsel to the needy, widows, fatherless, and afflicted, without reward; briefly a singular example to all lawyers. This Bainham, as above noted, married the wife of Simon Fish, for which he was suspected, and at last accused to Sir Thomas More, and arrested with a sergeant at arms, and carried out of the Middle Temple to the Chancellor's house at Chelsea, where he continued in free prison till Sir Thomas More saw he could not prevail in perverting him to his sect. Then he cast him in prison in his own house, whipped him at the tree in his garden called the tree of troth, and sent him to the Tower to be racked, Sir Thomas being present himself, till he had lamed him, because he would not accuse the gentlemen of the Temple of his acquaintance, nor show where his books lay; and because his wife denied them to be at his house she was sent to the Fleet and their goods confiscate.

After they had thus practised against him what they could by tortures then was he brought before John Stokesley, Bishop of London, the 15th of December 1531, in the town of Chelsea, and there examined. The next day Bainham appeared again before the bishop; where his former articles with his answers were repeated and his hand brought forth. Which done, they asked whether he would persist in that which he had said or would return to the Catholic Church; adding many fair and alluring words, that he should reconcile himself, saying the time was yet that he might be received; the bosom of his Mother was open for him: otherwise there was no remedy. Now was the time either to save or else utterly to cast himself away. Which of these ways he would take, the case required a present answer, for the sentence definitive was ready to be read. To conclude long matter in few words, Bainham, wavering in perplexity between life and death, at length giving over to the adversaries gave answer that he was contented to submit himself in those things wherein he had offended, excusing that he was deceived by ignorance.

So Bainham was returned to his prison; who the fifth day after appeared as before in the consistory; whom the Chancellor asked if he would abjure and submit himself; who answered that he would submit himself, and as a Christian man should, and being commanded to lay his hand upon the book he read his abjuration openly. After the reading whereof he protested that by his oath he intended not to go from such defence which he might have had before his oath. The Chancellor, taking the definitive sentence in his hand, said, 'Take your oath and kiss the book; or else I will do mine office against you.' And so he took the book and kissed it and subscribed the same. Which done, the Chancellor put him to his fine, to pay twenty pound to the king. After that he enjoined him penance, to go before the cross in procession at Paul's and to stand before the preacher during the sermon with a faggot upon his shoulder; and to return with the sumner to prison, there to abide the bishop's determination. So the 17th of February he was dismissed home; where he had scarce a month continued but he bewailed his abjuration, and was never quiet in conscience until he had uttered his fall to all his acquaintance and asked God and all the world forgiveness before the congregation in a warehouse in Bow Lane. The next Sunday after he came to St Austen's with the New Testament in his hand in English and *The Obedience of a Christian Man* in his bosom, and stood up in his pew, declaring openly with tears that he had denied God; and prayed the people to beware of his weakness, and not to do as he did: 'For,' said he, 'if I should not return unto the truth'—having the New Testament in his hand—'this word of God would damn me body and soul at the day of judgment.' He prayed everybody rather to die by and by than to do as he did; for he would not feel such an hell again as he did feel, for all the world's goods. Besides this he wrote letters to the bishop and others, so that shortly after he was apprehended and committed to the Tower of London.

The 20th of April Bainham was brought before the vicar-general in the Church of All Saints of Barking. The sentence of condemnation was given against him, the which here to repeat word for word is not necessary, forsomuch as the tenor thereof is all one with that which passed before in the story of Bayfield. After this sentence given, Bainham was delivered into the hands of Sir Richard Gresham, sheriff, who caused him to be carried unto Newgate; and the said James Bainham was burned in Smithfield the last day of April at three o'clock at afternoon.

Bainham during his imprisonment was very cruelly handled: for almost a fortnight he lay in the bishop's coalhouse in the stocks with irons upon his legs. Then he was carried to the Lord Chancellor's and there chained to a post two nights; then to Fulham, where he was cruelly handled the space of a sennight; then to the Tower, where he lay a fortnight, scourged with whips to make him revoke his opinions. Thence he was carried to Barking, then to Chelsea, and there condemned; and so to Newgate to be burned. At his burning, as he was at the stake in the midst of the fire, which had half consumed his arms and legs, he spake these words: 'O ye papists, behold, ye look for miracles and here now you may see a miracle; for in this fire I feel no more pain than if I were in a bed of down: it is to me as sweet as a bed of roses.'

The death and martyrdom of John Frith

Amongst all other chances there hath been none a long time more grievous than the lamentable death and cruel handling of John Frith, a young man who had so profited in all learning and knowledge that scarcely there was his equal amongst all his companions; and withal had such godliness of life joined with his doctrine that it was hard to judge in which of them he was more commendable. Of the godliness this may serve for experiment sufficient, that notwithstanding his manifold and singular ornaments of the mind, wherewithal he might have opened an easy way unto honour and dignity, he rather chose wholly to consecrate himself unto the Church of Christ, showing forth and practising the precept so highly commended of the philosophers touching the life of man: life, they say, is given unto man in such sort that how much the better a man is, so much the less he should live unto himself, but unto others, serving for the common utility; and that we should think a great part of our birth to be due unto our parents, a greater part unto our country, and the greatest part of all to be bestowed upon the Church. He began his study at Cambridge; in whom nature had planted, being but a child, marvellous instinctions and love unto learning. He had also promptness of wit and a ready capacity to receive and understand anything; neither was there any diligence wanting in him; whereby it came to pass that he was not only a lover of learning but became an exquisite learned man; in which exercise when he had laboured certain years, he fell into acquaintance with William Tindall, through whose instructions he first received into his heart the seed of the gospel.

At that time Thomas Wolsey, Cardinal of York, prepared to build a college in Oxford, marvellously sumptuous, which had the name of Frideswide but now named Christ's Church, not so much, it is thought, for the zeal that he bare unto learning as for an ambitious desire of glory and renown. But that building—he being cut off by the stroke of death; for he was sent for unto the king, accused of certain crimes, and in the way by immoderate purgations killed himself—left partly begun, partly imperfect, and nothing save the kitchen was finished. Whereupon Rodulphus Gualterus, being then in Oxford and beholding the college, said, '*Egregium opus, cardinalis iste instituit collegium et absolvit popinam.*' How large and ample those buildings should have been may easily be perceived by that which is already builded, the kitchen, the hall, and certain chambers, where there is such curious graving and workmanship of stonecutters that all things did glister for the excellency of the workmanship, for the fineness of the matter, with the gilt antics and embossings: if all had been furnished as it was begun, it might well have excelled not only all colleges of students but also palaces of princes. This ambitious cardinal gathered together into that college whatsoever excellent thing there was in the whole realm, vestments, vessels, ornaments, all kind of precious things. Besides that he appointed unto that company all such men as were found to excel in any kind of learning.

Chief of them which were called from Cambridge were Mr Clarke, Mr Sumner, Mr Bettes, John Frith, Bayly, Goodman; also Taverner of Boston, the good musician; picked young men of grave judgment and sharp wits; who conferring together upon the abuses of religion were accused of heresy unto the cardinal, and cast into prison within a deep cave under the ground of the college, where their salt fish was laid; so that through the filthy stench they were all infected, and certain of them upon being taken out of prison into their chambers there deceased. Clarke, Sumner, and Bayly, eating nothing but salt fish from February to August, died all three within one week: Goodman, being sick in the prison with the others, was had out and died in the town. Bettes, having no books found in his chamber, through entreaty and surety got out of prison and at last slipped away to Cambridge, and afterwards was chaplain to Queen Anne. Taverner, although he was suspected for hiding Clarke's books under the boards in his school, yet the cardinal excused him, saying he was but a musician.

John Frith with other by the cardinal's letter, which sent word that he would not have them so straitly handled, were dismissed out of prison upon condition not to pass above ten miles out of Oxford. Frith went over the sea, and after two years came over for exhibition of the Prior of Reading, and had the prior over with him. At Reading he was taken for a vagabond and brought to examination; where the simple man, which could not craftily enough cover himself, was set in the stocks. After he had sitten there a long time and was almost pined with hunger, and would not for all that declare what he was, at last he desired that the schoolmaster of the town might be brought to him, which was one Leonard Cox, a man very well learned. As soon as he came Frith began in Latin to bewail his captivity. The schoolmaster, overcome with his eloquence, did not only take pity upon him but began to love such an excellent wit, unlooked for in such a state and misery. Afterwards conferring together as touching universities, schools and tongues, they fell from Latin into Greek, wherein Frith did so inflame the love of that schoolmaster towards him that he brought him into a marvellous admiration, especially when the schoolmaster heard him so promptly by heart rehearse Homer's verses out of the Iliad: whereupon the schoolmaster went with all speed unto the magistrates, complaining of the injury which they did show unto so excellent a young man.

Thus Frith through the help of the schoolmaster was dimitted out of the stocks and set at liberty. Albeit his safety continued not long, through the great hatred and deadly pursuit of Sir Thomas More, who persecuted him by land and sea, besetting all the ways and havens and promising great rewards if any man could bring tidings of him. Thus Frith not knowing which way to turn seeketh some place to hide in. Thus fleeting from one place to another and often changing his garments, yet could he be in safety in no place; so at last, being traitorously taken, he was sent unto the Tower of London, where he had many conflicts with the bishops, but especially in writing with Sir Thomas More. The first occasion of his writing was this: he had communication with a certain old familiar friend of his touching the sacrament of the body and blood of Christ; and as the treatise of this disputation seemed somewhat long, his friend desired him that such things as he had reasoned upon he would briefly commit unto writing, and give unto him for the help of his memory. Frith, albeit unwilling and not ignorant how dangerous it was to enter into such a contentious matter, at last being overcome by the entreaty of his friend rather followed his will than looked to his own safeguard.

There was at that time in London a tailor named William Holt, who feigning great friendship toward the party instantly required of him to give him licence to read over that writing of Frith's; which when he inadvisedly did, the other by and by carried it unto More: which thing afterwards was occasion of great trouble and also of death unto Frith; for when More had gotten a copy of this treatise he sharpened his pen all that he might to answer this young man—for so he calleth him throughout his book; but when the book was set forth and showed unto the world, he endeavoured to keep it from printing, lest any copy should come into Frith's hands. Notwithstanding when at last Frith had gotten a copy by means of his friends, he answered him out of the prison, omitting nothing that any man could desire to the perfect handling of the matter. I think it not necessary to repeat all his arguments or the testimonies which he had gathered out of the doctors; specially as Cranmer in his *Apology* against the Bishop of Winchester collected them abundantly; and I doubt whether the archbishop gave more credit unto any author of that doctrine than unto Frith.

What dexterity of wit was in him and excellency of doctrine may appear not only by his books which he wrote of the sacrament, but also in those entitled *Of Purgatory*. In which quarrel he withstood the violence of three most obstinate enemies, Rochester, More, and Rastall, whereof the one by the help of the doctors, the other by wresting the Scriptures, the third by the help of natural philosophy, had conspired against him. But he as a Hercules fighting not against two only but with all three at once, did so confound them that he converted Rastall to his part. Besides these commendations there was in him friendly and prudent moderation in uttering the truth, joined with learned godliness; which virtue hath always so prevailed in the Church of Christ that without it all other gifts of knowledge, be they never so great, cannot greatly profit, but oftentimes do much hurt. Would God that all things in all places were so free from all dissension that there were no mention made amongst Christians of Zuinglians and Lutherans, when neither Zuinglius neither Luther died for us; but that we might be all one in Christ. Neither do I think that anything more grievous could happen unto those worthy men than their names to be abused to sects and factions, who so greatly strove against all factions. Neither do I here discourse which part came nearest unto the truth, nor so rashly intermeddle in this matter that I will detract anything from either part, but rather wish of God I might join either part unto the other. But now forsomuch as we entreat of John Frith, I must needs embrace the moderation which was in that man, who maintaining this quarrel of the sacrament of the Lord's Supper no less godly than learnedly did it so moderately, without contention, that he would never seem to strive against the Papists except he had been driven to it.

Frith, after he had sufficiently contended in his writings with More, Rochester, and Rastall, More's son-in-law, was carried to Lambeth before the Bishop of Canturbury, and afterwards unto Croydon before the Bishop of Winchester, to plead his cause. Last of all he was called before the bishops in a common assembly at London, where he constantly defended himself, if he might have been heard. The order of his judgment, with the manner of his examination and the articles objected against him, are set forth by himself in a letter written and sent unto his friends whilst he was prisoner in the Tower.

When no reason would prevail against the cruelty of these furious foes, on the 20th of June 1533 he was brought before the Bishops of London, Winchester, and Lincoln; who sitting in St Paul's ministered certain interrogatories upon the sacrament and purgatory unto Frith; to which when he had answered and showed his mind, he subscribed to his answers in these words: 'I Frith thus do think; and as I think so have I said, written, and affirmed, and in my books have published.' When by no means he could be persuaded to recant these articles, but said, '*Fiat judicium & justitia*,' he was condemned by the Bishop of London to be burned, and sentence given against him. This sentence read, the bishop directed his letter to Sir Steven Pecocke, Mayor of London, and the sheriffs, for receiving John Frith into their charge; who, being delivered unto them, the 4th of July was carried into Smithfield to be burned.

When he was tied unto the stake, it sufficiently appeared with what constancy and courage he suffered death; for when the faggots and fire were put unto him he willingly embraced the same, thereby declaring with what uprightness of mind he suffered death for Christ's sake. The wind made his death somewhat longer, which bare away the flame from him unto his fellow that was tied to his back; but he had established his mind with such patience, God giving him strength, that as though he had felt no pain in that long torment he seemed rather to rejoice for his fellow than to be careful for himself. This truly is the power and strength of Christ, striving and vanquishing in his saints; who sanctify us together with them to the glory of his holy name. Amen.

Andrew Hewet burned with Mr Frith

Andrew Hewet, born in Feversham in the county of Kent, a man of four and twenty years, was apprentice with a tailor in Watling Street. As he went upon a holy day into Fleet Street toward St Dunstan's, he met one William Holt, which was foreman with the king's tailor; and being suspected by Holt, who was a dissembling wretch, to be one that favoured the gospel, after a little talk he went into an honest house about Fleet Bridge, which was a bookseller's. Then Holt sent for officers and searched the house, and finding Andrew apprehended him and carried him to the Bishop's House, where he was cast into irons; and being there a good space he had a file conveyed unto him wherewith he filed off his irons, and when he spied his time got out of the gate. But being unskilful to hide himself for lack of good acquaintance, he went into Smithfield and there met one Wythers, a hypocrite as Holt was. Wythers, understanding how he had escaped and pretending a fair countenance unto him, willed him to go with him, promising that he should be provided for; and so kept him in the country where he had to do, from Low Sunday till Whitsuntide, and then brought him to London to the house of John Chapman in Hosier Lane, and there left him for two days.

Then he came to Chapman's house again and brought Holt with him. And when they met with Andrew they seemed as though they meant to do him very much good; and Holt said that if he should bring any man in trouble it were pity but that the earth should open and swallow him up; insomuch that they would needs sup there that night, and prepared meat of their own charges. At night they came and brought guests with them, because they would have the matter seem as though it had come out by others. When they had supped they went their way, and Holt took out of his purse two groats and gave them to Andrew, and embraced him in his arms. As they were gone out there came in one John Tibauld, which was banished from his own house by an injunction, for he had been four times in prison for Christ's cause. Within an hour after Holt and Wythers were gone, the bishop's chancellor and one Sergeant Wever came and brought with them the watch and searched the house, where they found John Chapman, Andrew, and John Tibauld, whom they bound with ropes and carried to the Bishop's House; but Andrew they sent unto the Lollards' Tower, and kept Chapman and Tibauld asunder, watched with two priests' servants. The next day Bishop Stokesley came from Fulham, and after they were examined with threatening words Chapman was committed to the stocks with this threat, that he should tell another tale or else sit there till his heels did drop off. Tibauld was shut by in a close chamber; but by God's provision he was delivered out of prison; albeit he could not enjoy his house and land because of the bishop's injunction, but was fain to sell all that he had in Essex; for his injunction was that he should not come within seven miles of his own house. Chapman, after five weeks' imprisonment (whereof three weeks he sat in the stocks) by much suit made unto the Lord Chancellor, Lord Audley, was delivered; but Hewet, after long and cruel imprisonment, was condemned to death and burned with Frith.

When they were at the stake one Dr Cooke, a parson in London, openly admonished the people that they should in no wise pray for them, no more than they would do for a dog; at which words Frith, smiling, desired the Lord to forgive him. These words did not a little move the people unto anger, and not without good cause. Thus these two blessed martyrs committed their souls into the hands of God.

The persecution and death of Thomas Benet, testified by John Vowel

Thomas Benet was born in Cambridge and there made Master of Art, and as some think was a priest, a man very well learned and of a godly disposition, being of the familiarity of Thomas Bilney, the glorious martyr of Christ. This man, the more he did grow in the knowledge of God and his holy word, the more he did abhor the corrupt state of religion; and thinking his own country no safe place for him to remain in, and being desirous to live in more freedom of conscience, he did forsake the university and went into Devonshire in 1524, and first dwelled in a market town named Torrinton; where for the maintenance of himself and his wife he kept a school. But that town not serving his expectation, after one year he came to Exeter, and hiring a house in Bocher Row did exercise the teaching of children. He was of quiet behaviour and of a very courteous nature, offensive to nobody. The time which he had to spare from teaching he gave to private study in the Scriptures, having no dealings with anybody saving with such as he could learn to be favourers of the gospel and zealous of true religion: of such he would be inquisitive, and desirous to join himself unto them. Therefore understanding that William Strowde of Newnham was committed to the bishop's prison in Exeter upon suspicion of heresy, although he was never before acquainted with him yet did he send letters of consolation unto him; wherein, to avoid all suspicion which might be conceived of him, he did disclose himself and utter what he was, and the causes of his being in the country, writing among other things these words: 'Because I would not be a whoremonger I married a wife, with whom I have hidden myself in Devonshire these six years.'

But as every tree hath his due time to bring forth his fruit, so did this man. For he, daily seeing the glory of God blasphemed, idolatrous religion maintained, and that usurped power of the Bishop of Rome extolled, was so troubled in spirit that he could not be quiet till he did utter his mind therein. Wherefore, dealing privately with certain friends, he did disclose how God was dishonoured, his word contemned, and his people carried headlong to damnation: therefore he must needs utter their abominations, and for the testimony of his conscience and the defence of true religion would yield himself patiently, as God would give him grace, to die therein: his death should be more profitable to the Church of God than his life. His friends promised to pray for him, that he might continue a faithful soldier to the end; which done, he gave order for the bestowing of such books as he had, and shortly after, in October, he wrote his mind in certain scrolls which he set upon the doors of the Cathedral Church; in which was written, 'The Pope is Antichrist, and we ought to worship God only and no saints.'

These bills being found, there was no small ado, and no little search made for the heretic that set up these bills; and the bishop and his doctors were as hot as coals and enkindled as though stung with wasps. To keep the people in their blindness order was taken that the doctors should up to the pulpit every holy day and confute this heresy. Nevertheless Benet, keeping his doings secret, went the Sunday following to the Cathedral Church and sat down by two men who were the busiest in all the city in searching for this heretic. They said one to the other, 'Surely this fellow is the heretic that set up the bills, and it were good to examine him.' Nevertheless, when they saw the sober behaviour of the man, his attentiveness to the preacher, his godliness in the church, being occupied in his book, a Testament in Latin, they were astonied, and had no power to speak unto him, but left him reading his book. To be short, the brains of canons and priests, officers and commons, were earnestly busied how such an enormous heretic might be espied and known; but it was long first.

At last the priest found out a toy to curse him, whatsoever he were, with book, bell, and candle; which curse at that day seemed most fearful and terrible. One of the priests, apparelled all in white, ascended into the pulpit. The other rabblement, with certain friars and monks standing round and the cross being holden up with holy candles fixed to the same, he began his sermon with this theme of Joshua, 'There is blasphemy in the army,' and made a long protestation, tedious and superstitious; and concluded that that foul and abominable heretic who put up such blasphemous bills was damnably accursed; and besought God, our Lady, St Peter, with all the holy company of martyrs, confessors, and virgins, that it might be known what heretic had put up such blasphemous bills, that God's people might avoid the vengeance.

This fantasy and mocking being done, Benet could no longer forbear, but fell to great laughter within himself and could not cease; by which the poor man was espied. Those that were next to him, wondering at that great curse and believing that it could not but light on one or other, asked Benet for what cause he should laugh. 'My friends,' said he, 'who can forbear, seeing such merry conceits played by the priests?' Straightway a noise was made, 'Here is the heretic, hold him fast!' With that there was confusion of voices and clapping of hands, and yet they were uncertain whether he were the heretic or no. His enemies, being uncertain, departed, and he went home to his house; where he renewed the bills and caused his boy, early in the morning following, to set the bills upon the gates of the churchyard. As the boy was setting one upon a gate called the Little Style, one W.S., going to the church to hear a mass which was daily said about five o'clock in the morning, found the boy at the gate, and asking him whose boy he was did charge him to be the heretic; wherefore pulling down the bill he brought the same with the boy before the mayor; thereupon Benet, being known and taken, was violently committed to ward.

On the morrow began the canons and heads of the city to fall to examination; with whom for that day he had not much communication but confessed to them, 'It was I that put up those bills, and I would do it again; for in them I have written nothing but truth.' The next day he was sent unto the bishop, who committed him to the prison called the Bishop's Prison, where he was kept in irons with as much favour as a dog should find. Then the bishop, with his chancellor and other of his clergy and friars, began to examine him, and burdened him that contrary to the Catholic Faith he denied praying to saints, and the supremacy of the Pope. Whereunto he answered in such sober manner and so learnedly defended his assertions, that he did not only silence his adversaries but also brought them in great admiration of him, the most part having compassion on him. The friars took great pains to persuade him to recant and acknowledge his fault touching the bills; but they but dig after day; for God had appointed him to be a witness of his holy name, and to be at defiance with all their persuasions.

To declare with what cruelty the officers searched his house for books, how shamefully they handled his wife, it were too long to write. She like a good woman took all things patiently that they did to her; like as in other things she was contented to bear the cross with him, as to fare hardly with him at home and to live with coarse meat and drink, that they might be the more able to help the poor, as they did to the uttermost of their power.

Amongst all other priests and friars Gregory Basset was most busy with him. This Gregory was fervent with the poor man to please the canons, and tormented his brains how to turn him from his opinion: he would not depart the prison but lay there night and day, who notwithstanding lost his labour; for Benet was at a point not to deny Christ before men. So Gregory lost his spurs, insomuch that he said in open audience that there was never so obstinate an heretic. A whole week night and day was Benet applied of these hypocrites. It were an infinite matter to declare all things done and said to him in his imprisonment; and the hate of the people by means of ignorance was hot against him; notwithstanding they could never move his patience: he answered every matter soberly, and that more by the aid of God's Spirit than by any worldly study. He was at least fifty years old. Being in prison, his wife provided sustenance for him; and when she lamented he comforted her, and prayed her to move him nothing to apply unto his adversaries.

When these canons and priests with the monks and friars had done what they could, and perceived that he would by no means relent, then they proceeding unto judgment drew out their bloody sentence against him, condemning him to be burned. The writ which they had procured *de comburendo* being brought from London, they delivered him on the 15th of January 1531 unto Sir Thomas Denis, Sheriff of Devonshire. The mild martyr, rejoicing his end to approach so near, yielded himself with all humbleness to suffer the cross of persecution; and being brought to his execution in a place called Livery Dole without Exeter, he made his humble confession and prayers unto God, and requested the people to do the like for him; whom he exhorted with such a pithy oration to seek the true honouring of God, and to leave the devices and imaginations of man's inventions, that all the hearers were in great admiration; insomuch that most of the people, as also the scribe who wrote the sentence of condemnation, did confess that he was God's servant and a good man.

Nevertheless two esquires, Thomas Carew and John Barnehouse, standing at the stake by him, first with fair promises but at length through rough threatenings, willed him to revoke his errors and to call to our Lady and the saints. To whom he answered, 'No, it is God only on whose name we must call; and we have no other advocate unto him but Jesus Christ: by him must we offer our prayers to God if we will have them heard.' With this answer Barnehouse was so enkindled that he took a furze-bush upon a pike and having set it on fire thrust it unto his face, saying, 'Whoreson heretic, pray to our Lady, or by God's wounds I will make thee do it.' Benet patiently answered, 'Alas, sir, trouble me not'; and holding up his hands said, '*Pater, ignosce illis.*' Whereupon the gentleman caused the wood to be set afire, and therewith this godly man lift up his eyes, saying, '*Domine, recipe spiritum meum.*' And he did never stir nor strive, but patiently abode the cruelty of the fire until his life was ended. For which the Lord God be praised and send us his grace that at the latter day we may with him enjoy the bliss prepared for the elect children of God.

Thus we have as in a gross sum compiled together the names and causes, though not of all, yet of a great and too great number of good men and women which in these sorrowful days from 1527 to 1533, that is till the coming of Queen Anne, were vexed and prosecuted under the tyranny of the Bishop of Rome. During the time of Queen Anne we read of no great persecution nor any abjuration in the Church of England, save that the registers make mention of certain Dutchmen, counted for Anabaptists, of whom ten were put to death *an.* 1535. Where note that two, albeit the definitive sentence was read, notwithstanding were pardoned by the king; which was contrary to the Pope's law.

After the bishops and heads of the clergy had a long time taken their pleasure, exercising their cruel authority against the poor wasted flock of the Lord, and began to molest also greater persons of the temporalty, in 1534 a parliament was called by the king about the 15th of January; in which parliament the Commons complained of the cruelty of the prelates and ordinaries, for calling men before them *ex officio*. For such was then the usage of the ordinaries and their officials that they would send for men and lay accusations to them of heresy, only declaring to them that they were accused, and would minister articles to them; but no accuser should be brought forth: whereby the commons were grievously oppressed; for the party ascited must either abjure or do worse: purgation he might none make.

As these matters were long debating in the Common House, it was agreed that the temporal men should put their griefs in writing and deliver them to the king. The 18th of March the Common Speaker, accompanied with certain knights and burgesses, came to the king's presence and declared how the temporal men of his realm were sore aggrieved with the cruel demeanour of the prelates and ordinaries, which touched their bodies and goods so near that they were enforced to make their humble suit by their Speaker unto his Grace, to take such order and redress as to his high wisdom might seem convenient. Unto this request of the Commons although the king gave no present grant, but suspended them with a delay, yet this sufficiently declared the grudging minds of the temporal men against the spiritualty, lacking nothing but God's helping hand to work in the king's heart. Neither did divine Providence fail, but eftsoons ministered a ready remedy. He saw the pride and cruelty of the clergy grown to such an height as was intolerable. He saw the bitter afflictions of his oppressed flock, his truth decayed, his religion profaned, his Church lamentably wasted. It was time for his high Majesty to look upon the matter; as he did indeed by a strange means, which was the king's divorcement from Lady Katherine and marrying with Lady Anne Bullen; which was the beginning of all this reformation which hath followed since in the Church of England.

CHAPTER 4

THE BREAK WITH ROME

The marriage between King Henry and Anne Bullen

Ye heard before how after the death of Prince Arthur Lady Katherine, Princess Dowager and wife to Prince Arthur, to the end her dowry might remain within the realm, was espoused after the decease of her husband to his brother Henry. This marriage seemed very strange and hard; but what can be so hard wherewith the Pope, the omnipotent vicar of Christ, cannot dispense if it please him? The Pope which then ruled at Rome was Julius II, by whose dispensation this marriage, which neither nature would admit nor God's law would bear, was approved and ratified; and continued as lawful without doubt or scruple near twenty years, till a doubt began to be moved by the Spaniards themselves *an.* 1523; at what time Charles the Emperor promised to marry Lady Mary, daughter to the king; with which promise the Spaniards were not well contented, objecting that Lady Mary was begotten of the king by his brother's wife. Whereupon the Emperor, forsaking that marriage, did couple himself with Lady Isabel of Portugal *an.* 1526. The year following King Henry, disappointed of the Emperor, entered talk for Lady Mary to be married to the French king's son, Duke of Orleance. After long debating at length the matter was put off by a doubt of the President of Paris, casting the like objection as the Spaniards had done before, whether the marriage between the king and the mother of Lady Mary were good or no. So the marriage, twice attempted, brake off again in 1527.

The king, perplexed in his conscience and careful for the commonwealth, could not rest, but inquired further what the word of God, and learning, would say unto it. Neither was the case so hard, after it began to come in public question, but that by the word of God, the judgments of learned clerks, and the censure of the chief universities of all Christendom, it was soon discussed to be unlawful. All these censures and writings, albeit they might suffice to have resolved the king's conscience, yet would he not straightway use that advantage unless he had the assent of the Pope, as also the Emperor; wherein he perceived no little difficulty. For the Pope, seeing the marriage was authorised by his predecessor, would hardly turn his keys about to undo that which the Pope before him had locked: again the Emperor, he thought, would be no less hard for his part, forsomuch as the Lady Katherine was the Emperor's near aunt. His purpose was to feel what they both would say, and therefore he sent Stephen Gardiner to weigh with Pope Clement: to the Emperor was sent Sir Nicholas Harvey, ambassador in the Court of Gaunt. Pope Clement, not waying the sequel of the matter, sent Cardinal Campeius into England, joined with the Cardinal of York.

The king, opening unto them the grief of his conscience, seemed with great persuasions to have drawn those two legates to his side; who of their own accord pretended no less but to show a willing inclination to further the king's cause. But the mouths of the common people, in especial of women and such other as favoured the queen, were not stopped. To satisfy the blind surmises of these also which cast out such lewd words, that the king would for his own pleasure have another wife, with like unseeming talk, he, willing that all should know the truth, caused his nobility, judges, and Councillors, to resort to his palace of Bridewell the 8th of November 1529, where he, openly speaking in his great chamber, stirred the hearts of a number.

The next year, 1530, at the Black Friars of London was prepared a solemn place for the two legates, who coming with their crosses, pillars, axes, and other Romish ceremonies, were set in two chairs covered with cloth of gold. The king and queen were ascited before the legates the 28th of May; where the king was called by name, who appeared by two proctors. Then the queen was called, who with four bishops and a great company of ladies came personally before the legates; who after her obeisance, with sad gravity of countenance appealed from the legates, as judges not competent, to the Court of Rome, and so departed. Notwithstanding the cardinals sat weekly, and every day arguments on both sides were brought, but nothing was determined. Cardinal Campeius conveyed himself home to Rome again. The king, seeing himself thus defeated and deluded by the cardinals, took it to no little grief: whereupon the fall of the Cardinal of York followed not long after. This was *an.* 1530. It happened the same year that the king was advertised that the Emperor and the Pope were together at Bononie. Wherefore he directed Sir Thomas Bullen, late created Earl of Wiltshire, Dr Stokesley, afterward Bishop of London, and Dr Lee, afterward Bishop of York, with his message to the Pope's court. Clement, understanding the king's request, and fearing what might follow if learning and Scripture should take place against the authority of their dispensation, and moreover doubting the Emperor's displeasure bare himself strange off from the matter, answering the ambassadors with this delay, that he would hear the full matter disputed when he came to Rome.

Although the king ought no such service to the Pope, to stand to his arbitrament in this case or any other, having the Scripture to lead him and his law in his own hands to warrant him, yet for that he would not rashly break order he bare so long as conveniently he might. At length when he saw no hope of redress, he began to look about him, what was best both for his own conscience and the stablishment of his realm to do.

When the king could get no favourable grant from the Pope touching his cause, he was forced to take the redress of his right into his own hands; and seeing this Gordian knot would not be loosed at Rome, he was driven against his will to play the noble Alexander himself, and with the sword of his princely authority knapped the knot at one stroke clean asunder, loosing as it were with one solution infinite question. For where the doctors had long disputed, and yet could never thoroughly discuss the largeness of the Pope's two swords, temporal and spiritual, the king with one sword did cut off both clean out of England, as we shall see anon. But first the king began with the cardinal, casting him by the law of *praemunire* out of his possessions; and so at length, by poisoning himself, he procured his own death *an.* 1530.

In the year of our Lord 1532 divers preachings were in the realm, one contrary to another, concerning the king's marriage; in especial Thomas Abel the queen's chaplain, to please her withal both preached and wrote a book in defence of the marriage, whereby divers simple men were persuaded. Whereupon the king caused to be reduced into a book the determination of the universities with the judgments of great clerks; which book being set abroad did satisfy all reasonable persons which were not too much wedded to their wills.

About the same time died William Warham, Archbishop of Canturbury; in whose room succeeded Thomas Cranmer, the king's chaplain and a great disputer against the unlawful marriage of Lady Katherine.

An. 1533 by authority of parliament it was consulted and considered concerning the legality of the lawful succession unto the crown, in ratifying and enabling the heirs of the king's body and Queen Anne.

Moreover the degrees of marriage plainly and clearly were explained and set forth, such as be expressly prohibited by God's laws. Also being in the same parliament concluded that no man of what estate, degree, or condition soever hath any power to dispense with God's laws, it was therefore assented that the marriage aforetime solemnised between the king and Lady Katherine, being before wife to Arthur the king's brother, and carnally known by him, should be deemed and adjudged unlawful and against the law of God, and also reputed and taken to be of no value nor effect; and that the separation thereof by Thomas Cranmer Archbishop of Canturbury should stand good and effectual to all intents; and also that the lawful matrimony between the king and Lady Anne his wife should be established, approved, and ratified for good and consonant to the laws of Almighty God. And further also, for the establishing of this king's lawful succession, it was by the said parliament adjudged that the inheritance of the crown should remain to the heirs of their two bodies, that is of the king and Queen Anne his wife.

These things being done in parliament, the king proceeded to the marriage of Lady Anne Bullen, mother to our most noble queen now, who was a comforter and aider of all the professors of Christ's gospel, as well the learned as the unlearned; her life being also directed according to the same, as her weekly alms did manifestly declare; who besides the ordinary of a hundred crowns and apparel that she gave weekly to both men and women, gave wonderful much privy alms to widows and poor householders continually till she was apprehended; and she ever gave three or four pound at a time to poor people to buy them kine withal, and sent her subamner to the towns about where she lay, that the parishioners should make a bill of all poor householders in their parish: some towns received seven, eight, or ten pound to buy kine withal. She also maintained many learned men in Cambridge. Likewise did the Earl of Wiltshire her father and Lord Rochford her brother, and by them these men were brought in favour with the king; of whom some are yet alive and can testify the same; which would to God they were now as great professors of the gospel of Christ as then they appeared to be; which were Dr Heath and Dr Thurlby; with whom was joined Lord Paget, who at that present was an earnest Protestant and gave unto one Raynold West Luther's books and Franciscus Lambertus *De Sectis*, and read Melancthon's *Rhetoric* openly in Trinity Hall in Cambridge, and was with his master Gardiner a maintainer of Dr Barnes and all the protestants then in Cambridge, and holp many religious persons out of their cowls.

It hath been reported unto us by divers persons who were about this queen and daily acquainted with her doings how her Grace carried ever about her a little purse, out of which she was wont daily to scatter abroad some alms to the needy, thinking no day well spent wherein some man had not fared the better by some benefit at her hands. This I write by the relation of certain noble personages who were the chief of her waiting maids, especially the Duchess of Richmond.

Thus the king being divorced from his brother's wife married this gracious lady, making a happy change for us, being divorced from the princess and also from the Pope, both at one time. Notwithstanding, as good purposes are never without some trouble following, so it happened that the princess, procuring from Rome the Pope's curse, caused both the king and the realm to be interdicted.

Queen Anne, shortly after her marriage being great with child, the next year, 1533, was crowned at Westminster; and not long after her coronation, the 7th of September she was delivered of a fair lady; for whose good deliverance *Te Deum* was sung in all places, and great preparation made for the christening. The mayor and his brethren with forty of the chief citizens were commanded to be present with all the nobles and gentlemen. The king's palace and all the walls between that and the Friars was hanged with arras, and the Friars' Church. The font was of silver and stood in the midst of the church covered with a fine cloth, and gentlemen with aprons and towels about their necks gave attendance about it. Over the font hung a fair canopy of crimson satin fringed with gold. Between the choir and the body of the church was a close place with a pan of fire to make the child ready in. The old Duchess of Norfolk bare the child in a mantle of purple velvet with a long train furred with ermine. The Duke of Norfolk with his marshal rod went on the right hand of the duchess, the Duke of Suffolk on the left. The Countess of Kent bare the long train of the child's mantle. Over the child was borne a canopy by Lord Rochford, Lord Hussey, Lord William Haward, and Lord Thomas Haward. In this order they came unto the church door, where the Bishop of London met it with divers abbots and bishops, and began the observances of the sacrament. The Archbishop of Canturbury was godfather, the Duchess of Norfolk and the Marchioness of Dorset godmothers, and the child was named Elizabeth. After all things were done at the church door, the child was brought to the font and christened. This done, Garter King of Arms cried aloud, 'God of his infinite goodness send prosperous life and long to the high and mighty Princess of England, Elizabeth.' Then the trumpets blew, and the child was brought up to the altar and immediately confirmed by the archbishop. After a solemn banquet ended with hypocras, wafers, and suchlike in plenty, they returned unto the Court with the princess.

The abolishing of the Pope out of England

Next followeth the year 1534, in which was assembled the high court of parliament again, upon the 3rd of February; wherein was made an Act of Succession, to which every person of lawful age should be sworn. During this parliament time every Sunday preached at Paul's Cross a bishop, which declared the Pope not to be head of the Church. Commissioners were sent over all England to take the oath of all men and women to the Act of Succession; at which few repined, except John Fisher Bishop of Rochester, Sir Thomas More late Lord Chancellor, and Dr Nicholas Wilson parson of St Thomas Apostle's in London. These three, after long exhortation to them made by the Bishop of Canturbury at Lambeth refusing to be sworn, were sent to the Tower. But the bishop and Sir Thomas More excused them by their writings, in which they said that they had written before Lady Katherine to be queen, and could not well go from that which they had written. Likewise the doctor excused that he in preaching had called her queen, and could not withsay it again. Howbeit at length he was contented to dissemble the matter and so escaped; but the other two stood against all the realm in their opinion.

From March this parliament was prorogued to the 3rd of November; at what time it was enacted that the Pope and all his cardinals, with his pardons and indulgences which so long had clogged this realm of England to the slaughter of so many good men, was now eradicate and exploded out of this land, and sent home to their own country of Rome. God be praised.

An act concerning the King's Highness to be supreme head of the Church of England

'Albeit the King's Majesty justly and rightly is and ought to be the supreme head of the Church of England, and so is recognised by the clergy of this realm in their convocations; nevertheless for corroboration and confirmation thereof, and for increase of virtue in Christ's religion within this realm of England, and to repress and extirp all errors, heresies, and other enormities and abuses heretofore used in the same: be it enacted by authority of this present parliament that the King our sovereign Lord, his heirs and successors, shall be taken, accepted, and reputed the only supreme head in earth of the Church of England, called *Anglicana Ecclesia*: and that our sovereign Lord, his heirs and successors, shall have power and authority to visit, repress, redress, reform, order, correct, restrain, and amend, all errors, abuses, offences, contempts, and enormities, whatsoever they be.'

That no man shall surmise this ruin of the Pope to have come rashly upon the king's own partial affection or by temerity of a few, and not by the grave and advised judgment and consent, as well of the Nobles and Commons temporal as also upon substantial ground, by the discussion and consultation of the spiritual and most learned persons of this realm, it shall be requisite to adjoin the testimony of the bishops' own oaths made to the king, rendering unto him only the style of supreme head, next under Christ, of the Church of England, as by their own words and handwriting may appear.

The oath of Stephen Gardiner to the king

'I Stephen Bishop of Winchester do purely, of mine own voluntary accord, and absolutely, on the word of a bishop, profess and promise to your princely Majesty, my singular and chief Lord and Patron, Henry VIII, by the grace of God King of England and France, Defender of the Faith, Lord of Ireland, and in earth of the Church of England Supreme Head immediately under Christ, that from this day forward I shall swear, promise, give, or cause to be given to no foreign potentate, emperor, king, prince, or prelate, nor yet to the Bishop of Rome whom they call Pope, any oath or fealty, directly or indirectly, either by word or writing. I profess the Papacy of Rome not to be ordained of God by Holy Scripture, but declare it to be set up only by man. Neither shall I consent that the Bishop of Rome shall have or exercise here any authority or jurisdiction. Furthermore, that the Bishop of Rome is not to be called Pope, nor Supreme Bishop, or Universal Bishop, but only Bishop of Rome and fellow-brother, this I shall to my power openly maintain and defend.

'For the confirmation hereof I give my faith and truth by firm promise and in the faith of a bishop, that against this my profession and promise made I shall defend myself by no dispensation, exception, nor any remedy by cautel of law or example, during my natural life. Whereunto I have subscribed the name both of myself and of my bishopric with my proper hand; and thereto have put my seal, in perpetual and undoubted testimony.

'Given the 10th day of February 1534–5.

Stephen Winton.'

So likewise all the other bishops, after the same order and form of oath, were bound to the king as supreme head of the Church of England under Christ, renouncing utterly the Pope's usurped jurisdiction in this realm, testifying the same with their own hand and with their seal.

Moreover Gardiner, in the book *De Vera Obedientia*, what constancy he pretendeth, what arguments he inferreth, how earnestly he disputeth on the king's side against the Bishop of Rome's authority, by the words of his book it may appear. To this book we will adjoin for good fellowship the Preface of Edmund Boner, Archdeacon then of Leicester. What man, reading this book with Boner's preface before the same, would ever have thought any alteration could so work in man's heart to make these men turn the cat, as they say, in the pan, and start so suddenly from the truth so manifestly known, so pithily proved, so vehemently defended, and—as it seemed—so faithfully subscribed? If they dissembled all this that they wrote and sware unto, what perjury most execrable was it before God and man? If they meant good faith and spake then as they thought, what pestilent blindness is this so suddenly fallen upon them, to make that false now which was true before, or that to be now true which before was false? Thus to say and unsay and then to say again, to do and undo, and to play fast or loose with truth, truly is not the doing to a man to be trusted. But here a man may see what man is of himself, when God's good Spirit lacketh to be his guide.

When all other the king's subjects and the learned of the realm had taken the oath of the king's supremacy, only Fisher Bishop of Rochester and Sir Thomas More refused to be sworn; who falling into the danger of the law were committed into the Tower and executed for the same *an.* 1535. Fisher had been a great persecutor of John Frith, whom he and Sir Thomas caused to be burned a year and a half before. For his learning and other virtues this bishop was well reputed by many. But pity it was that he, endued with that knowledge, should be so far drowned in superstition; more pity that he was so obstinate in his ignorance; but most pity of all that he so abused the learning he had, to such cruelty as he did. But this commonly we see come to pass, that 'whoso striketh with the sword shall perish with the sword', and they that stain their hands with blood seldom bring their bodies dry to the grave; as commonly appeareth by the end of bloody tyrants, especially such as be persecutors of Christ's poor members; in the number of whom was this bishop and Sir Thomas More, by whom Frith, Teukesbury, Hytten, Bayfield, with divers other saints of God, were brought to their death. The Pope, to recompense Fisher for his faithful service, had elected him cardinal and sent him a cardinal's hat as far as Calice, but the head that it should stand upon was as high as London Bridge ere the hat could come to him. Thus Fisher and More, which had put Frith to death for heresy against the Pope, were beheaded for treason against the king.

More was also recounted a man both witty and learned; but whatsoever he was besides, a bitter persecutor he was of good men, and a wretched enemy against the truth of the gospel, as by his books may appear; wherein most slanderously he writeth against Luther, Zuinglius, Tindall, Frith, Barnes, Bayfield, Bainham, Teukesbury, falsely belying their doctrine, as I have sufficient matter to prove against him. As he was a sore persecutor of them that stood in defence of the gospel, so on the other side such a blind devotion he bare to the Pope-holy see of Rome, and so wilfully stood in the Pope's quarrel against his own prince, that he would not give over till he had brought the scaffold of Tower Hill, axe and all, upon his own neck.

Edward Hall in his Chronicle, writing of the death and manners of Sir Thomas More, seems to stand in doubt whether to call him a foolish wise man or a wise foolish man; for as by nature he was endued with a great wit, so the same was so mingled, saith he, with taunting and mocking that it seemed to them that best knew him that he thought nothing to be well spoken except he had ministered some mock in the communication; insomuch that at his coming to the Tower, one of the officers demanding his upper garment for his fee, meaning his gown, he answered that he should have it and took him his cap, saying that it was the uppermost garment that he had. Even going to his death, a poor woman called unto him and besought him to declare that he had certain evidences of hers in the time that he was in office, and that he would entreat that she might have them again, or else she was undone. He answered, 'Good woman, have patience awhile, for the king is good unto me, that within this half hour he will discharge me of all businesses and help thee himself.' When he went up the stair on the scaffold he desired one of the sheriff's officers to help him up, and said, 'When I come down again, let me shift for myself so well as I can.' The hangman kneeled down to him, asking forgiveness of his death, as the manner is; to whom he said, 'I forgive thee, but I promise that thou shalt never have honesty of the striking off my head, my neck is so short.' Even when he should lay down his neck on the block, he, having a great grey beard, striked out his beard and said to the hangman, 'I pray you, let me lay my beard over the block, lest you should cut it.' Thus with a mock he ended his life.

There is no doubt but that the Pope's Holiness hath hallowed these two persons long since for catholic martyrs; neither is it to be doubted but after a hundred years they shall be also shrined and portused, dying as they did in taking the Bishop of Rome's part against their own ordinary and natural prince.

Shortly after the overthrow of the Pope began by little and little the ruin of religious houses in England. For neither could the fall of monasteries have followed after unless that suppression of the Pope had gone before; neither could any reformation of the Church have been attempted unless the subversion of those superstitious houses had been joined withal. In the year 1536, in the month of October, the king, having then Thomas Cromwell of his Council, sent Dr Lee to visit the abbeys, priories, and nunneries in all England, and to set at liberty all such religious persons as desired to be free, and all others under the age of twenty-four years; providing withal that such as were dismissed should have given them by the abbot or prior, instead of their habit, a secular priest's gown and forty shillings, likewise the nuns to have such apparel as secular women did commonly use, and to go where they would; at which time also from the abbeys and monasteries were taken their chief jewels and relics.

To go forward in our story, as the order and computation of years do give, we have now to enter into the story of the martyr William Tindall, this present year betrayed and put to death; which Tindall as he was a special organ of the Lord appointed, and as God's mattock to shake the inward roots of the Pope's proud prelacy, so the prince of darkness with his impious imps, having special malice against him, left no way unsought how to trap him and spill his life, as by the process of his story here following may appear.

The life and story of the true servant and martyr of God, William Tindall

William Tindall was born about the borders of Wales, and brought up from a child in the University of Oxford, where he by long continuance increased as well in the knowledge of tongues and other liberal arts as specially in the knowledge of the Scriptures, whereunto his mind was singularly addicted; insomuch that he, lying then in Magdalen Hall, read privily to certain students and fellows of Magdalen College some parcel of divinity, instructing them in the truth of the Scriptures. Whose manners and conversation, being correspondent to the same, were such that all they which knew him esteemed him to be a man of most virtuous disposition, and of life unspotted. He removed from thence to the University of Cambridge, where being further ripened in the knowledge of God's word, leaving that university also he resorted to one Mr Welch, a knight of Gloucestershire, and was there schoolmaster to his children and in good favour with his master. This gentleman, as he kept a good ordinary commonly at his table, there resorted unto him abbots, deans, archdeacons, with other doctors and great beneficed men; who there, together with Tindall sitting at the same table, did use to talk of learned men, as of Luther and Erasmus; also of controversies and questions upon the Scriptures. Tindall spared not to show them plainly his judgment in matters; and when they at any time did vary from Tindall in opinions, he would lay before them the manifest places of the Scriptures to confirm his sayings. Thus continued they for a season, contending together sundry times, till they waxed weary and bare a secret grudge against him.

Not long after this certain of these great doctors invited Mr Welch and his wife to a banquet, where they had talk at pleasure, uttering their ignorance without any gainsaying. Then Mr Welch and his wife, coming home and calling for Tindall, began to reason with him about those matters whereof the priests had talked at their banquet. Tindall answering by the Scriptures reproved their false opinions. Then said Lady Welch, a stout and wise woman, 'Well, there was such a doctor which may dispend one hundred pounds, and another two hundred pounds, and another three hundred pounds: were it reason, think you, that we should believe you before them?' Tindall gave her no answer, nor after that, because he saw it would not avail, he talked but little in those matters. At that time he was about the translation of a book of Erasmus, called *Enchiridion Militis Christiani*, which, being translated, he delivered to his master and lady; who after they had perused the same, the prelates were no more so often called to the house, neither had they the cheer and countenance when they came as before they had; which thing they well perceiving, and supposing it came by means of Mr Tindall, refrained themselves and at last utterly withdrew.

As this grew on, the priests of the country clustering together began to storm against Tindall in alehouses and other places; of whom Tindall himself testifieth, and reporteth that he suffered much in that country by a sort of unlearned priests, full rude and ignorant, 'who have seen no more Latin than that which they read in their portues and missals (which many of them can scarcely read) except it be Albertus, *De Secretis Mulierum*, in which they pore day and night, and make notes therein, and all to teach the midwives, as they say; and another called Lyndwood, a book of constitutions to gather tithes, mortuaries, offerings, customs, and other pillage, which they call not theirs but God's part, the duty of Holy Church, to discharge their consciences withal. For they are bound that they shall increase all things unto the uttermost of their powers, which pertain to Holy Church.' Thus these blind priests, flocking to the alehouse (for that was their preaching place) raged against him, affirming that his sayings were heresy; adding unto his sayings, of their own heads, more than ever he spake; and so accused him secretly to the chancellor and other of the bishop's officers.

Not long after this there was a sitting of the chancellor appointed, and warning was given to the priests to appear, amongst whom Tindall was also warned to be there. Whether he had any misdoubt by their threatenings, or knowledge given him that they would lay things to his charge, it is uncertain; but certain this is, that he doubted their privy accusations; so that he in going thitherwards cried in his mind to God, to give him strength fast to stand in the truth of his word. When the time came for his appearance, the chancellor threatened him grievously, rating him as though he had been a dog, and laid to his charge many things whereof no accuser could be brought forth, notwithstanding the priests of the country were present. Thus Tindall escaping out of their hands returned to his master.

There dwelt not far off a doctor that had been chancellor to a bishop, who had been of old familiar acquaintance with Tindall and favoured him well; unto whom Tindall opened his mind upon divers questions of the Scripture; for to him he durst disclose his heart. The doctor said, 'Do you not know that the Pope is very Antichrist, whom the Scripture speaketh of? But beware what you say; for if you be perceived to be of that opinion, it will cost you your life;' and said moreover, 'I have been an officer of his; but I have given it up, and defy him and all his works.'

Not long after, Tindall happened to be in the company of a certain divine, recounted for a learned man, and in disputing with him drave him to that issue that the great doctor burst out into these blasphemous words: 'We were better to be without God's laws than the Pope's.' Tindall replied, 'I defy the Pope and all his laws,' and added that if God spared him life, ere many years he would cause a boy that driveth the plough to know more of the Scripture than he did. After this the grudge of the priests increasing more and more, they never ceased barking at him and laid many things to his charge, saying that he was an heretic in sophistry, in logic, in divinity; and that he bare himself bold of the gentlemen in that country, but shortly he should be otherwise talked withal. To whom Tindall answering said that he was contented they should bring him into any country in all England, giving him £10 a year to live with, and binding him to no more but to teach children and preach.

To be short, Tindall being so molested by the priests was constrained to leave that country and seek another place; and so coming to Mr Welch he desired that he might depart from him, saying in this wise, 'Sir, I perceive that I shall not be suffered to tarry long in this country, neither shall you be able to keep me out of the hands of the spiritualty; and what displeasure might grow thereby to you God knoweth; for the which I should be right sorry.' In fine Mr Tindall with the good will of his master departed and came up to London, and there preached awhile as he had done in the country before, especially about the town of Bristow, and in the common place called St Austin's Green. At length he bethinking himself of Cutbert Tonstall, Bishop of London, especially for the commendation of Erasmus, who in his annotations so extolleth him for his learning, thus cast with himself, that if he might attain unto his service he were a happy man. So coming to Sir Henry Gilford, the king's Controller, and bringing with him an oration of Isocrates which he had translated into English, he desired him to speak to the bishop for him; which he did, and willed him to write to the bishop and to go himself with him. Which he did likewise, and delivered his epistle to a servant of his named Hebilthwaite. But God saw that was not the best for Tindall's purpose nor for the profit of his Church, and therefore gave him to find little favour in the bishop's sight; the answer of whom was this: his house was full; he had moe than he could well find; and advised him to seek in London abroad. So remained he in London almost a year, marking the course of the world and especially the demeanour of the preachers, how they boasted themselves and set up their kingdom; beholding also the pomp of the prelates, with other things which greatly misliked him; insomuch that he understood not only there to be no room in the bishop's house for him to translate the New Testament, but that there was no place in all England.

Therefore having by God's providence some aid and provision ministered unto him by Humfrey Mummoth and other good men, he departed into Germany where the good man, inflamed with a tender care of his country, refused no travail nor diligence how by all means possible to reduce his brethren of England to the same understanding of God's holy word and verity which the Lord had endued him withal. Whereupon he, considering in his mind, and conferring also with Frith, thought no way more to conduce thereunto than if the Scripture were turned into the vulgar speech, that poor people might also read the plain word of God. For he perceived that it was not possible to stablish the lay people in any truth, except the Scripture were so plainly laid before their eyes in their mother tongue that they might see the meaning of the text; else, whatsoever truth should be taught them, these enemies of the truth would quench it again, either with reasons of sophistry and traditions of their own making, founded without ground of Scripture, either juggling with the text, expounding it in such a sense as it were impossible to gather if the right meaning thereof were seen. He considered this chiefly to be the cause of all mischief in the Church, that the Scriptures of God were hidden from the people's eyes; for the idolatries maintained by the clergy would not be espied; and therefore all their labour was to keep it down, that either it should not be read at all, or if it were, they would darken the sense with the mist of their sophistry, and entangle those who despised their abominations with worldly similitude and apparent reason of natural wisdom; and wresting the Scripture unto their own purpose would so delude them in descanting upon it with allegories, and amaze the unlearned lay people, that though thou felt in thy heart and wert sure that all were false that they said, yet couldst thou not solve their subtle riddles.

For such considerations this good man was moved to translate the Scripture into his mother tongue, for the utility and profit of the simple people of his country, first setting in hand the New Testament, which he first translated about 1527. After that he took in hand to translate the Old Testament, finishing the five books of Moises, with learned and godly prologue prefixed before every one, worthy to be read and read again by all good Christians, as the like also he did upon the New Testament. He wrote divers other works, amongst which is that most worthy monument entitled *The Obedience of a Christian Man*, wherein with singular dexterity he instructeth all men in the duty of Christian obedience, with other treatises, as *The Wicked Mammon*, *The Practice of Prelates*, with expositions upon parts of the Scripture, and books answering Sir Thomas More and other adversaries of the truth, no less delectable than fruitful to be read: which partly being unknown unto many, partly worn out by time, the printer hereof, good reader, for conserving such singular treasures hath collected and set forth in one general volume, as also the works of Frith, Barnes, and other, most profitable for thy reading.

These books of Tindall's compiled, published, and sent over into England, it cannot be spoken what a door of light they opened to the eyes of the whole nation, which before were many years shut up in darkness.

At his first departing out of the realm he took his journey into the farther parts of Germany, as into Saxony, where he had conference with Luther and other learned men. After a season he came down from thence into the Neatherlands, and had his most abiding in Antwerp until his apprehension, whereof more shall be said hereafter.

Amongst his other books one work he made for the declaration of the sacrament of the altar, which he kept by him, considering how the people were not yet fully persuaded in other matters tending to superstitious ceremonies. He thought time was not come to put forward that work, but rather that it should hinder the people from other instructions, supposing that it would seem to them odious to hear any such thing at that time, sounding against their mass, had everywhere in great estimation as was the goddess Diana among the Ephesians, whom they thought to come from heaven. Wherefore Tindall, being prudent in his doings and no less zealous in the setting forth of God's truth after such sort as it might take most effect with the people, did forbear the putting forth of that work, not doubting but by God's grace a time should come to have that abomination openly declared, as it is at this present day, the Lord be praised.

These books of Tindall, especially the New Testament of his translation, after they began to come into men's hands and to spread abroad, as they wrought great profit to the godly, so the ungodly, fearing lest their works of darkness should be discerned, began to stir with no small ado; like as at the birth of Christ, Herod and all Jerusalem was troubled with him. But especially Satan, maligning the success of the gospel, set to his might also, how to hinder the blessed travails of that man. For at what time Tindall had translated *Deuteronomium*, minding to print the same at Hamborough he sailed thereward; where upon the coast of Holland he suffered shipwreck, by which he lost all his books and copies, and so was compelled to begin all anew, doubling his labours. Having lost both money, his copies, and his time, he came in another ship to Hamborough, where Mr Coverdale tarried for him, and helped him in translating the five books of Moises, from Easter till December, in the house of a worshipful widow, Mrs Margaret Van Emmerson, *an.* 1529; a great sweating sickness being at the same time in the town. Having dispatched his business at Hamborough he returned to Antwerp.

When God's will was that the New Testament in the common tongue should come abroad, Tindall the translator thereof added to the end an epistle wherein he desired them that were learned to amend, if aught were found amiss. Wherefore if any such default had been, it had been the part of courtesy for men of knowledge to have showed their learning and redressed that was to be amended. But the spiritual fathers, not willing to have that book to prosper, cried upon it that there were a thousand heresies in it, and that it was not to be corrected but utterly to be suppressed. Some said it was not possible to translate the Scripture into English; some that it was not lawful for lay people to have it in their mother tongue; some that it would make them all heretics. To reduce the temporal rulers unto their purpose they said it would make the people rise against the king. All this Tindall himself declareth, and addeth further, showing what pains was taken in examining that translation and comparing it with their own imaginations, that with less labour they might have translated themselves a great part of the Bible; showing moreover that they scanned every tittle and point in the translations so narrowly that there was not one 'i' therein, but if it lacked a prick over his head they numbered it unto the ignorant people for an heresy. So great were the devices of the clergy to drive the people from the knowledge of the Scripture, which neither would they translate themselves nor yet abide it to be translated of others.

The prelates of the realm, thus incensed against the Old and New Testament translated by Tindall, and conspiring together how to repeal the same, never rested before they had brought the king to their consent; by reason whereof a proclamation was set forth under public authority, but no just reason showed, that Tindall's translation with other works both of his and other writers were inhibited; which was about 1527. Not contented herewith they proceeded further how to entangle him in their nets and bereave him of life.

Tindall, being in Antwerp, had been lodged about one year in the house of Thomas Pointz, an Englishman, who kept an house of English merchants; about which time came one out of England whose name was Henry Philips, a comely fellow like as he had been a gentleman, having a servant with him; but for what purpose he was sent thither no man could tell. Tindall divers times was desired forth to dinner and supper among merchants; by means whereof Philips became acquainted with him, so that within short space Tindall had great confidence in him and brought him to his lodging, and had him once or twice to dinner and supper, and further entered such friendship with him that through his procurement he lay in the same house; to whom he showed his books and other secrets of his study, so little did Tindall mistrust this traitor.

But Pointz, having no great confidence in the fellow, asked Tindall how he came acquainted with this Philips. Tindall answered that he was an honest man, handsomely learned and very comformable. Pointz said no more, thinking that he was brought acquainted with him by some friend of his. Philips, being in the town three or four days, desired Pointz to walk with him forth of the town to show him the commodities thereof, and in walking together without the town had communication of divers things, and some of the king's affairs. Pointz as yet suspected nothing, but by the sequel of the matter he perceived more what he intended. Meantime this he well perceived, that he bare no great favour either to the setting forth of any good thing either to the proceedings of the king. But when the time was past, Pointz perceived this to be his mind, to feel if he could perceive whether he might break with him, for lucre of money, to help him to his purpose; for he perceived before that he was monied and would that Pointz should think no less; but by whom, it was unknown. For he had desired Pointz before to help him to divers things; and such things as he named he required might be of the best, 'for,' said he, 'I have money enough;' but of this talk came nothing but that men should think he had some things to do; for nothing else followed of his talk. So it was to be suspected that Philips was in doubt to move this matter to any of the officers of Antwerp, for doubt it should come to the knowledge of some Englishmen, and Tindall should have had warning.

So Philips went from Antwerp to the Court of Bruxels, which is from thence twenty-four miles, the king having there no ambassador; for the king and the Emperor were at a controversy for the question betwixt the king and Lady Katherine, who was aunt to the Emperor; and the discord grew so much that it was doubted lest there should have been war; so that Philips, a traitor both against God and the king, was thus the better retained, as other traitors besides him; who after he had betrayed Tindall into their hands showed himself likewise against the king's own person. To make short, Philips did so much there that he procured to bring from there with him to Antwerp that procuror-general which is the Emperor's attorney, with other officers; which was not done with small expenses, from whomsoever it came.

Within a while after, Pointz sitting at his door, Philips' man came unto him and asked whether Mr Tindall were there, and said his master would come to him, and so departed; but whether Philips were in the town or not was not known: at that time Pointz heard no more neither of the master nor of the man. Within three or four days Pointz went to Barrow, eighteen miles from Antwerp, where he had business to do for a month or six weeks; in his absence Philips came again to Antwerp, to the house of Pointz, and coming in spake with his wife, asking for Mr Tindall, and whether he would dine there with him, saying, 'What good meat shall we have?' She answered, 'Such as the market will give.' Then went he forth again to provide, and set the officers whom he brought with him from Bruxels about the door. Then about noon he came again, and went to Tindall and desired him to lend him forty shillings; 'for,' said he, 'I lost my purse this morning, coming over at the passage, between this and Machelin.' So Tindall took him forty shillings, which was easy to be had of him if he had it; for in the subtleties of this world he was unexpert.

Then said Philips, 'Mr Tindall, you shall be my guest here this day.' 'No,' said Tindall, 'I go forth this day to dinner and you shall go with me and be my guest where you shall be welcome.' So when it was dinner-time Tindall went forth with Philips, and at the going forth of Pointz's house was a long narrow entry, so that two could not go in a front. Tindall would have put Philips before him, but Philips would in no wise, but put Tindall before, for he pretended to show great humanity. So Tindall, a man of no great stature, went before, and Philips, a tall person, followed behind him; who had set officers on either side of the door upon two seats, which might see who came in the entry; and coming through the same entry Philips pointed with his finger over Tindall's head down to him, that the officers might see that it was he whom they should take, as the officers afterwards told Pointz, and said, when they had laid him in prison, that they pitied his simplicity when they took him. Then they took him and brought him to the Emperor's procuror-general, where he dined. Then came the procuror-general to the house of Pointz, and sent away all that was there of Tindall's, as well his books as other things; and from there Tindall was had to the castle of Filford, eighteen miles from Antwerp, and there remained till he was put to death.

Then incontinent, by the help of English merchants, were letters sent in favour of Tindall to the Court of Bruxels. Also not long after letters were directed out of England to the Council at Bruxels, and sent to the merchant-adventurers to Antwerp, commanding them to see that with speed they should be delivered. Then such of the chief of the merchants as were there at that time required Pointz to take in hand the delivery of those letters, with letters also from them in favour of Tindall, to the Lord of Barrow and others; which lord, as it was told Pointz by the way, was departed from Bruxels, as chief conductor of the eldest daughter of the King of Denmark, to be married to the palsgrave, whose mother was sister to the Emperor. Pointz, after he heard of his departure, did ride after the next way and overtook him at Akon, where he delivered to him his letters; which when he had read he made no direct answer, but somewhat objecting said there were of their countrymen that were burned in England not long before, as indeed there were Anabaptists burned in Smithfield; so Pointz said, 'Whatsoever the crime was, if his Lordship or any other nobleman had written requiring to have had them, he thought they should not have been denied.' 'Well,' said he, 'I have no leisure to write, for the princess is ready to ride' Then said Pointz, 'If it please your Lordship, I will attend you unto the next baiting-place,' which was at Mastright. 'If you do so,' said the lord, 'I will advise myself by the way what to write.' So Pointz followed him from Akon to Mastright, fifteen miles; and there he received letters of him, one to the Council there, another to the merchant-adventurers, and another to Lord Cromwell in England.

Pointz rode from thence to Bruxels, and then and there delivered to the Council the letters out of England with the Lord of Barrow's letters, and received eftsoons answer into England of the same by letters which he brought to Antwerp to the English merchants, who required him to go with them into England. He, very desirous to have Tindall out of prison, let not to take pains, with loss of time in his own business, but diligently followed with the letters, which he there delivered to the Council, and was commanded by them to tarry until he had other letters, of which he was not dispatched thence in a month after. At length the letters being delivered him, he returned and delivered them to the Emperor's Council at Bruxels, and there tarried for answer. When Pointz had tarried three or four days, it was told him by one that belonged to the Chancery that Tindall should have been delivered to him according to the tenor of the letters; but Philips, hearing he should be delivered to Pointz and doubting lest he should be put from his purpose, knew no other remedy but to accuse Pointz, saying that he had been a succourer of Tindall and was of the same opinion; and that this was only his own suit, to have Tindall at liberty, and no man's else.

Upon his accusation Pointz was attached and delivered to the keeping of two sergeants of arms; and the same evening was sent to him one of the Chancery, with the procuror-general, who ministered unto him an oath that he should truly make answer to all such things as should be inquired of him. The next day they came again and had him in examination, and so five or six days, upon not so few as an hundred articles, as well of the king's affairs as of the message concerning Tindall, of his aiders, and of his religion; out of which examination the procuror-general drew twenty-four articles and declared the same against Pointz, the copy whereof he delivered to him to make answer thereunto, and permitted him to have an advocate and proctor; and order was taken that eight days after he should deliver unto them his answer, and from eight days to eight days to proceed till the process were ended. Also that he should send no messenger to Antwerp where his

Lord open the King of Englãds eies.

‘The Martyrdome and burning of maister William Tindall, in Flaunders, by Filford Castle.’

house was, nor to any other place, but by the post of Bruxels; nor to send any letters, nor any to be delivered to him, but written in Dutch; and the procuror-general, who was party against him, to examine them thoroughly, contrary to all right and equity, before they were sent or delivered; neither might any be suffered to speak with Pointz in any other tongue except only Dutch, so that his keepers, who were Dutchmen, might understand what the contents of the letters or talk should be; saving that at one time the provincial of the White Friars came to dinner where Pointz was prisoner, and brought with him a young novice, an Englishman, whom the provincial of his own accord did bid to talk with Pointz; so with him he was licensed to talk. The policy therein was easy to be perceived. Between Pointz and the novice was much pretty talk, as of Sir Thomas More and the Bishop of Rochester and their putting to death; whose death he seemed greatly to lament, especially dying in such a quarrel, worthy he said to be accounted martyrs; with other noble doctrine and deep learning, meet to feed swine withal; such blindness in those days reigned amongst them. After this Pointz delivered up his answer to the procuror-general, and then at the days appointed went forth with replication duplic, with other answers each to other in writing what they could.

As the commissioners came to Pointz, Philips the traitor accompanied them to the door in following the process against him, as he also did against Tindall; for so they that had Pointz in keeping showed him. Thus Pointz for Tindall was sore troubled and long kept in prison; at length, when he saw no other remedy, by night he made his escape and avoided their hands. But Tindall could not escape their hands, but remained in prison still; who being brought unto his answer was offered an advocate and a proctor; for in any criminal cause there it shall be permitted to have counsel, to make answer in the law. But he refused to have any such, saying that he would answer for himself; and so he did.

At last after much reasoning, when no reason would serve, although he deserved no death, he was condemned by virtue of the Emperor's decree made in the Assembly at Ausbrough, and upon the same brought to the place of execution was tied to the stake, and then strangled first by the hangman and afterwards with fire consumed, in the morning, at the town of Filford, *an.* 1536, crying at the stake with fervent zeal and a loud voice, 'Lord, open the king of England's eyes.'

Such was the power of his doctrine and sincerity of his life that during his imprisonment, which endured a year and a half, it is said that he converted his keeper, his daughter, and other of his household. The rest that were with him in the castle reported of him that if he were not a good Christian man, they could not tell whom to trust. The procuror-general left this testimony of him, that he was *homo doctus, pius, & bonus*, a learned, good, and godly man.

The death of Lady Katherine, and of Queen Anne

The same year in which Tindall was burned, 1536, died Lady Katherine in January. In May followeth the death of Queen Anne, who had now been married to the king three years. The king, being in his jousts at Greenwich, suddenly departed to Westminster, and the next day Queen Anne was had to the Tower with Lord Rochford her brother and certain other, and the 19th day after was beheaded. The words of this Christian lady at her death were these:

'Good Christian people, I am come hither to die, for by the law I am judged to death; and therefore I will speak nothing against it. I am come hither to accuse no man, nor to speak anything of that whereof I am accused; but I pray God save the king and send him long to reign over you, for a gentler, more merciful prince was there never: to me he was ever a good, gentle, and sovereign lord. If any person will meddle of my cause, I require them to judge the best. And thus I take my leave of the world and of you all, and I heartily desire you all to pray for me. Lord, have mercy on me.' And so she kneeled down, saying, 'To Christ I commend my soul; Jesu receive my soul,' repeating the same divers times till at length the stroke was given and her head strucken off.

This was the end of that godly lady. Godly I call her for sundry respects, whatsoever the cause was or quarrel objected against her. First, her last words declared no less her faith in Christ than did her modesty utter forth the goodness of the cause, whatsoever it was. Besides that, this also may seem to give a great clearing unto her, that the king the third day after was married in his whites unto another. Certain this was, that for the singular gifts of her mind, so well instructed and given toward God, joined with like gentleness and pity toward all men, there hath not been many such queens before her borne the crown of England. Principally, this commendation she left behind her, that during her life the religion of Christ had a right prosperous course. What a zealous defender she was of Christ's gospel her acts declare; amongst which acts this is one, that she placed Hugh Latimer in the bishopric of Worcester.

This I cannot but marvel, why the parliament holden this year, which parliament three years before had confirmed this marriage as most lawful, should now so suddenly and contrary to their own doings repeal and disable the marriage as unlawful. But more I marvel why parliament, after the illegitimation of the marriage enacted, not contented with that should further proceed, and charge her with such carnal desires as to misuse herself with her own natural brother Lord Rochford and others, being so contrary to all nature that no natural man will believe it.

Incontinent after the suffering of Queen Anne the king within three days married Lady Jane Semer, of whom came King Edward; shortly after whose birth his mother died in childbed, and left the king a widower, who so continued two years together.

The history of the worthy martyr of God, John Lambert

Immediately upon the destruction of the monasteries, the same year in November followed the condemnation of John Lambert, the servant of Jesus Christ and martyr of blessed memory. Lambert, born and brought up in Norfolk, was converted by Bilney and studied in the University of Cambridge; where after he had sufficiently profited in Latin and Greek and had translated out of both tongues sundry things into English, being forced at last by violence he departed to parts beyond the seas to Tindall and Frith, and there remained a year and more, being preacher and chaplain to the English house at Antwerp till he was disturbed by Sir Thomas More, and by the accusation of one Barlow was carried to London. He was brought to examination first at Lambeth, then at the bishop's house at Otford, before Warham, Archbishop of Canturbury; having forty-five articles ministered against him, whereunto he rendered answer by writing. These answers were delivered to Dr Warham about 1532, at which time Lambert was in custody in the archbishop's house at Otford, destitute of all furniture of books, as by his own words is to be gathered. But within short space, August 23rd, the archbishop died; whereby it seemeth that Lambert for that time was delivered. Meanwhile Cranmer was sent over in embassage with the Earl of Wiltshire, Stokesley, Kerne, Benet, and other learned men, to the Bishop of Rome lying then at Bononie, to dispute the matter of the king's marriage, first in the Court of Rome, then in the Court of the Emperor; where after sundry appointments made, when the time came, no man there appeared to dispute with them. But of this more copiously we will entreat in the sequel of the story.

After the death of Warham succeeded Dr Cranmer. Lambert in the mean season being delivered, partly by the death of this archbishop, partly by the coming in of Queen Anne, returned unto London and there exercised himself about the Stocks, teaching children Greek and Latin. And forsomuch as priests in those days could not be permitted to have wives, he left his priesthood and applied himself to teaching, intending shortly after to be free of the Grocers and to be married. But God did both intercept his marriage and also his freedom, and married him to his Son Christ Jesus.

After Lambert now had continued in this vocation of teaching with great commendation and no less commodity to the youth, it happened this year 1538 he was present at a sermon in St Peter's Church. He that preached was Dr Tailor, which afterwards in the time of King Edward was made Bishop of Lincoln, and in the time of Queen Mary was deprived from the same, and ended his life among the confessors of Jesu Christ. When the sermon was done Lambert went gently unto the preacher to talk with him, and uttered divers arguments wherein he desired to be satisfied. The whole matter was concerning the sacrament of the body and blood of Christ. Tailor, excusing himself at that present for other business, willed him to write his mind and to come again at more leisure. Lambert was contented and so departed; who when he had written his mind came again unto him. Tailor desiring to satisfy Lambert conferred with Dr Barnes. Barnes persuaded Tailor to put the matter to Cranmer. Lambert was sent for by the archbishop, brought into open court, and forced to defend his cause. For the archbishop had not yet favoured the doctrine of the sacrament whereof afterwards he was an earnest professor. It is said that Lambert did appeal from the bishop to the King's Majesty. But however the matter was, the rumour of that disputation spread throughout the Court.

At that time Stephen Gardiner, Bishop of Winchester, was in authority amongst the king's Councillors, who, as he was of cruel nature, so was he of a crafty wit, ever gaping for some occasion how to hinder the gospel; albeit a long time he was not so greatly esteemed with the king that he could achieve his purpose. But at length, upon this matter advising himself, he thought he had apt occasion to accomplish his desire: he went straight unto the king, with flattering words giving him most pernicious counsel, declaring how great hatred was raised upon him in all places; first, for abolishing the Bishop of Rome's authority; then for subversion of the monasteries; and also for that the divorcement of Queen Katherine was fresh in men's minds; now the time served, if he would take it, to remedy all these matters and pacify the minds of them that were offended with him, if only in this matter of John Lambert he would manifest unto the people how stoutly he would resist heretics.

The king, giving ear more willingly than prudently to this siren, sent out a general commission, commanding all the nobles and bishops of this realm to come with all speed to London to assist the king against heretics, which the king himself would sit in judgment upon. A day was set for Lambert, where a great assembly of the nobles was gathered from all parts of the realm, not without much wonder in this so strange a case. All the seats were full of men round about the scaffold. Lambert was brought from the prison with a guard of armed men, as a lamb to fight with many lions, and placed over against where the king's seat was, so that now they tarried but for the king's coming.

At last the king himself did come as judge of that great controversy, with a great guard, clothed all in white, as covering by that dissimuling all bloody judgment. On his right hand sat the bishops and behind them the lawyers, clothed all in purple according to the manner. On the left hand sat the peers of the realm, justices, and other nobles in their order; behind whom sat the gentlemen of the king's privy chamber. When the king was set in his throne, he beheld Lambert with a stern countenance; and then he called forth Dr Day, Bishop of Chichester, commanding him to declare the causes of this assembly. When he had made an end of his oration, the king, standing up upon his feet, leaning upon a cushion of white cloth of tissue, turning towards Lambert with brows bent, as it were threatening some grievous thing, said, 'Ho, good fellow, what is thy name?' Then the man of Christ, humbly kneeling, said, 'My name is John Nicolson, although of many I be called Lambert.'

'What? have you two names? I would not trust you, having two names, although you were my brother.'

'Most noble prince, your bishops forced me to change my name.'

After much talk in this manner the king commanded him to declare his opinion, what he thought touching the sacrament of the altar. Then Lambert gave God thanks which had so inclined the heart of the king that he would not disdain to hear the controversies of religion; for it happeneth oftentimes, through the cruelty of bishops, that innocent men in many places are put to death without the king's knowledge. But now, forsomuch as that eternal King of kings in whose hands are the hearts of all princes hath inspired the king's mind that he himself will be present to understand the causes of his subjects, specially whom God hath endued with so great gifts of judgment and knowledge, he doth not mistrust but that God will bring some great thing to pass through him, to the glory of his name.

Then the king, with an angry voice interrupting his oration, 'I came not hither,' said he, 'to hear mine own praises thus painted; briefly go to the matter, without any more circumstance.' Thus he spoke in Latin. But Lambert, abashed at the king's angry words contrary to all expectation, stayed awhile, considering whither he might turn in these extremities. The king with anger and vehemency said, 'Why standest thou still? Answer touching the sacrament of the altar, whether dost thou say that it is the body of Christ or wilt deny it.' With that word the king lifted up his cap.

'I answer with St Augustine that it is the body of Christ after a certain manner.'

'Answer me neither out of St Augustine neither by the authority of any other: tell me plainly whether thou sayest it is the body of Christ or no.' These words the king spake again in Latin.

'Then I deny it to be the body of Christ.'

'Mark well; for now thou shalt be condemned by Christ's own words, *Hoc est corpus meum*.'

Then he commanded Cranmer to refute his assertion; who began his disputation very modestly, saying, 'Brother Lambert, let this matter be handled between us indifferently, that if I do convince your argument to be wrong by the Scriptures, you will willingly refuse the same; but if you shall prove it true by manifest testimonies of the Scripture, I promise I will willingly embrace the same.'

When they had contended, Lambert so answering that the king seemed greatly to be moved therewith and the bishop himself that disputed to be entangled and all the audience amazed, the Bishop of Winchester, which was appointed the sixth place of the disputation, fearing lest the argument should be taken out of his mouth, before the archbishop had made an end unshamefacedly alleged a place out of the twelfth chapter to the Corinthians: 'Have I not seen Jesus?' After the

Bishop of Winchester had done, Tonstall Bishop of Durham took his course and after a long preface spake much of God's omnipotency. Next stepped forth Stokesley Bishop of London, who afterward at the point of death rejoiced, boasting that in his lifetime he had burned fifty heretics. After this the other bishops as they were appointed supplied their places of disputation.

Lambert meantime, compassed with perplexities, vexed with taunts and threats, wearied with long standing, which continued five hours, and seeing no hope in speaking, was at this point that he chose rather to hold his peace. Hereby it came to pass that those bishops who last of all disputed spoke without interruption, save that now and then Lambert would allege somewhat out of St Augustine. But for the most part he held his peace, defending himself rather with silence than with arguments, which he saw would nothing prevail.

At last, when torches began to be lighted, the king said unto Lambert, 'What sayest thou now after all the instructions of these learned men? art thou not yet satisfied? wilt thou live or die? thou hast yet free choice.'

'I submit myself wholly unto the will of your Majesty.'

'Commit thyself unto the hands of God, not unto mine.'

'I commend my soul unto the hands of God, but my body I submit unto your clemency.'

'If you do commit yourself unto my judgment, you must die; for I will not be a patron unto heretics. Cromwell, read the sentence of condemnation against him.'

Here it is much to be marvelled at that through the pestiferous counsel of this one Bishop of Winchester Satan did here perform the condemnation of Lambert by no other ministers than gospellers themselves, Tailor, Barnes, Cranmer, and Cromwell; who afterwards in a manner all suffered the like for the gospel's sake; of whom we will speak more hereafter.

Thus was John Lambert by the king judged and condemned to death; whose judgment now remaineth with the Lord against that day when before that great Judge both princes and subjects shall stand, not to judge but to be judged, according as they have deserved. *Ex testimonio cujusdam αὐτόπτου.* A.G.

Upon the day that was appointed for this holy martyr to suffer, he was brought out of prison at eight o'clock in the morning unto the house of Lord Cromwell and carried into his inner chamber, where it is reported of many that Cromwell desired of him forgiveness for that he had done. At last Lambert being admonished that the hour of his death was at hand, he was greatly cheered; and being brought out into the hall he saluted the gentlemen and sat down to breakfast with them, showing no sadness or fear. When breakfast was ended, he was carried straightway to the place of execution where he should offer himself unto the Lord, a sacrifice of sweet savour. Touching the terrible fashion of the burning of this blessed martyr, here is to be noted that of all which have been burned at Smithfield there was none so cruelly handled as he. For after his legs were consumed up to the stumps, and the wretched tormentors had withdrawn the fire from him so that but a small fire and coals were left under him, two that stood on each side of him with their halberds pitched him upon their pikes as far as the chain would reach. Then he lifting up such hands as he had, and his fingers flaming with fire, cried unto the people, 'None but Christ, none but Christ'; and so, being let down from their halberds, fell into the fire and there gave up his life.

The martyrdom of Lancelot, John, and Giles Germaine, and one Stile

About the year 1539 one John, a painter, and Giles Germaine were accused of heresy; and while they were in examination at London before the bishop and other judges, by chance there came in one of the king's servants named Lancelot, a very tall man, and of no less godly disposition than strong and tall of body. This man standing by seemed by his countenance and gesture to favour both the cause and the poor men; whereupon he being apprehended was examined and condemned with them, and the next day at five o'clock in the morning was carried with them into St Giles in the Field and there burned, being but a small concourse of people at their death.

In the fellowship of these blessed martyrs of Christ, who suffered for the testimony of God's word, another good man cometh to mind who was with like cruelty oppressed, and burned in Smithfield about the latter end of Cutbert Tonstall's time Bishop of London; whose name was Stile, as is credibly reported by a worthy and ancient knight named Robert Outred, who was present at his burning. With him there was burned also a book of the Apocalypse which he was wont to read upon. This book when he saw fastened unto the stake to be burned with him, lifting up his voice, 'O blessed Apocalypse,' said he, 'how happy am I that shall be burned with thee!' And so this good man and the blessed Apocalypse were together in the fire consumed.

The Act of the Six Articles

Wily Winchester, with his crafty fetches by pestilent persuasion creeping into the king's ears, ceased not to seek all means to overthrow religion, first bringing him in hatred with the German princes, then putting him in fear of the Emperor, of the French king, of the Pope, of the King of Scots; but especially of commotions within this realm, which of all things he most dreaded, by reason of innovation of religion and dissolving of abbeys. Which being so, he exhorted the king for his own safeguard and public quiet to see betimes by what policy these mischiefs might be prevented. Against which no shift could be better devised than if he would show himself severe against these new sectaries, Anabaptists and Sacramentaries as they called them, and would set forth such articles confirming the ancient faith as whereby he might recover his credence with Christian princes, and all the world might judge him to be a right Catholic. By such suggestions the king being seduced began to withdraw his defence from true religion; and although he had rejected the Pope out of this realm, first he stretched out his hand to the burning of Lambert, and in the year following, 1540, he summoned a solemn parliament to be holden the 28th of April; also a convocation of all the bishops and learned clergy. In which parliament or convocation articles were decreed by certain prelates commonly called the Six Articles (or the Whip with Six Strings) in pretence of unity. What unity followed, the groaning hearts of a great number and the cruel death of divers, both in the days of King Henry and Queen Mary, can so well declare as I pray God never the like be felt hereafter.

The doctrine of these wicked articles although it deserveth to be buried in perpetual oblivion, yet for that the office of history compelleth us, for the more light of posterity, faithfully to comprise things done in the Church as well one as another, this shall be briefly to recapitulate the sum and effect of the Six Articles as they were given out.

First—In the sacrament of the altar by the efficacy of Christ's word, being spoken by the priest, is present really under the form of bread and wine the natural body and blood of Jesus Christ, conceived of the Virgin Mary; and after the consecration there remaineth no substance of bread or wine, or any other substance but the substance of Christ, God and man.

Second—Communion in both kinds is not necessary by the law of

God to all persons: in the flesh under form of bread is the very blood, and with the blood under form of wine is the very flesh, as well apart as they were both together.

Third—Priests may not marry by the law of God.

Fourth—Vows of chastity made to God advisedly ought to be observed by the law of God; and it exempteth them from other liberties of Christian people, which without that they might enjoy.

Fifth—It is necessary that private masses be continued, whereby Christian people receive consolations and benefits: it is agreeable also to God's law.

Sixth—Auricular confession is necessary to be retained and frequented.

After these articles were consented upon, the prelates perceiving that such a violent Act could not prevail until bloody penalties were set upon them, they caused to be enacted by the King, Lords, and Commons as followeth:

If any person within the king's dominions by word, writing, imprinting, ciphering, or otherwise, should publish, preach, teach, say, affirm, declare, dispute, argue, or hold any opinion that in the sacrament of the altar, under form of bread and wine after consecration, there is not present really the natural body and blood of Jesus Christ conceived of the Virgin Mary, or that there remaineth any substance of bread and wine, or any other substance but the substance of Christ, God and man, or that in the flesh under the form of bread is not the very blood of Christ, or that with the blood of Christ under the form of wine is not the very flesh of Christ, as well apart as though they were both together; every person so offending, their aiders, consenters, and abettors, should be adjudged heretics; and should suffer death by burning without abjuration, benefit of the clergy, or sanctuary; and also should forfeit to the King's Highness all his honours, manors, castles, lands, tenements, rents, reversions, services, possessions and all other hereditaments, goods, and chattels, farms, and freeholds.[1]

Touching the other five articles, the penalties were these: every person or persons which do maintain or defend anything contrary to the same, or being in orders did marry, should be adjudged as felons and lose both life and forfeit goods: if any within order of priesthood before the time of the parliament had contracted matrimony, the said matrimony should be dissolved.

[1] This sentence in its original form runs to 371 words.—Ed.

These six articles although they contained manifest errors and absurdities, such was the power of darkness that the cause of truth was left desolate. For every man seeing the king's mind so addict, upon politic respects, to have these articles pass forward, few in all that parliament durst defend that they understood to be true save only Cranmer, who then being married (as is supposed) took upon him the earnest defence of the truth, three days together disputing against those wicked articles. Wherefore the king, well liking his zealous defence, only willed him to depart out of the parliament-house (for safeguard of his conscience) till the act should pass; which he with humble protestations refused to do. Which articles after they were passed by parliament, the king, for the favour which he ever bare to Cranmer and reverence to his learning, being desirous to know what he had objected in parliament against these articles, required a note of the archbishop. This word was sent to him by Cromwell and other lords, whom the king then sent to dine with him at Lambeth, to comfort his troubled spirit. Dinner finished, the next day the archbishop, collecting his arguments, authorities of Scriptures, and doctors together, caused his secretary Rafe Morice to write a fair book thereof, which was delivered to the King's Majesty by Lord Cromwell.

The year following, 1541, in April was holden a parliament which after divers prorogations continued till July, in which month Cromwell, being in the Council-chamber, was suddenly apprehended and committed to the Tower; whereat as many good men, who knew nothing but truth by him, did lament, so more there were that rejoiced, especially of the religious sort, such as had been in some dignity before in the Church and now by his means were put from it. For such was his nature that he could not abide any kind of popery, or of false religion creeping under hypocrisy; and less could he abide the ambitious pride of popish prelacy, which professing all humility was so elated in pride that kings could not rule their own realms for them. These snuffing prelates hated him, which was the cause to bring him to his end, so that on the 19th day of the month aforesaid he was attainted by parliament. In which attainder, sundry crimes, surmises, objections, and accusations were brought against him: above all he was accused of heresy, for that he was a supporter of them whom they accounted for heretics, as Barnes, Clarke, and many other, whom by his authority and letters to sheriffs and justices in divers shires he had rescued out of prison.

Howsoever the cause of Cromwell standeth true or false, this is certain, that Stephen Gardiner lacked not privy assisters, which cunningly could fetch this matter about and watch their time when the king, being disposed to marry another wife, Katherine Haward, immediately after the beheading of Cromwell did repudiate Lady Anne of Cleve, which during the life of Cromwell could not so well be brought to pass.

But these things being done and past, let us return to Cromwell now committed to the Tower; who, so long as he went with full sail of fortune, how temperately he did ever bear himself in his estate before hath been declared. So now Cromwell, by the wind of adversity being overblown, received the same with no less patience of a Christian heart. Amongst the commissioners who came unto him one there was whom Cromwell desired to carry a letter to the king; which, when he refused, saying that he would carry no letter from a traitor, Cromwell desired him at least to do a message to the king. To that the other was contented, and granted, so it were not against his allegiance. Then Cromwell, taking witness of the other lords what he had promised, 'You shall commend me,' said he, 'to the king, and tell him by that he hath tried and proved you as I have done, he shall find you as false a man as ever came about him.' Besides this he wrote a letter to the king, whereof when none durst take the carriage upon him, Sir Rafe Sadler went unto the king to understand whether he would permit him to bring the letter or not; which when the king had granted, Sadler presented the letter unto the king, which he commanded thrice to be read unto him, insomuch as the king seemed to be moved therewith.

Notwithstanding, the worthy and noble Lord Cromwell, oppressed by his enemies and condemned in the Tower, on the 28th of July 1541 was brought to the scaffold on Tower Hill. His prayer made, after he had lovingly exhorted them that were about him on the scaffold, he quietly committed his soul into the hands of God; and so patiently suffered the stroke of the axe, by a ragged and butcherly miser, which very ungoodly performed the office.

Of the Bible in English, and of Edmund Boner

When Edmund Boner, Bishop of Herford and ambassador resident in France, began to be nominate by Lord Cromwell to the bishopric of London *an.* 1540, Cromwell procured of the king of England letters to the French king to license a subject of his to imprint the Bible in

English within the University of Paris; because paper was there more apt to be had, and also there were more store of good workmen. At the same time the king wrote to Boner that he should aid the doers thereof; which bishop outwardly showed great friendship to the imprinters, and did command the said persons to be daily at his table both dinner and supper; and so much rejoiced in the workmanship of the said Bible that he would visit the house where the Bibles were printed. Further he caused the Englishmen to put in print a New Testament in English and Latin, and took a great many of them and paid for them and gave them to his friends.

While the Bible was in printing Henry VIII preferred Boner to be Bishop of London; at which time Boner took his oath to the king acknowledging his supremacy, and called one of the Englishmen that printed the Bible, Richard Grafton; to whom Boner said, 'Mr Grafton, before God the greatest fault I ever found in Stokesley was vexing poor men for having the Scripture in English; and, God willing, he did not so much hinder it but I will as much further it: I will have of your Bibles set up in the Church of Paul's at least six; and I will pay you for them and give you hearty thanks.'

After the letters were delivered, the French king was well content to permit the doing thereof; and so the printer printed the book to the last part: then was the quarrel picked and he was sent for to the inquisitors and charged with heresy. Then were sent for the Englishmen that were at the cost and charge thereof; but having some warning what would follow, the said Englishmen posted away as fast as they could, leaving behind all their Bibles to the number of 2500, and never recovered any, saving that the lieutenant-criminal, having them delivered unto him to burn in a place of Paris like Smithfield, called Maulbert Place, was moved with covetousness and sold four great dry-fats of them to a haberdasher to lap caps in, and those were bought again; but the rest were burned, to the great loss of those that bare the charge of them. Notwithstanding, after they had recovered some part of the books and were encouraged by Cromwell, the Englishmen went again to Paris and got the presses, letters, and servants of the printer, and brought them to London; there they became printers themselves and printed the Bible in London, not without great trouble for the hatred of Stephen Gardiner and his fellows.

In those days there were two bibles in English, printed in divers places. The first was called Mathew's Bible, printed at Hamborough about 1532. In the translation of this bible the greatest doer was William Tindall, who with the help of Miles Coverdale had translated all the books except the Apocrypha. But because Tindall was apprehended before this bible was perfected, it was thought good to change the name of Tindall and to father it by a strange name Thomas Mathew, John Rogers being corrector to the print, who had translated the Apocrypha. Which Bible after it was presented to Cromwell and Cranmer, who liked very well of it, Cromwell presented it to the king, and obtained that the same might freely be read of his subjects; so that there was printed upon the book one line in red letters: 'Set forth with the king's most gracious licence.'

This book did not a little offend the bishops, both for the prologues and chiefly about the marriage of priests and the mass, which there was said not to be found in Scripture. After the restraint of this Bible another began to be printed at Paris *an.* 1540, called the Bible of the Large Volume. A great helper thereto was Cromwell. The chiefest overseer was Coverdale, who taking the translation of Tindall conferred the same with the Hebrew and amended many things.

After this the bishops brought Cromwell out of favour and shortly to his death; and not long after complaint was made to the king of the translation of the Bible, and of the preface; then was the sale of the Bible stayed, the bishops promising to amend it but never performing the same. Then Grafton was called, charged with the printing of Mathew's Bible, then examined of the Great Bible. He was sent to the Fleet, and before he came out was bound in £300 that he should neither sell nor imprint any more bibles until the king and clergy should agree upon a translation. Thus was the Bible stayed during the reign of King Henry VIII.

After the imprinters had lost their bibles they continued suitors to Boner, and Boner fed them with fair words but did nothing for them, till at last Boner was discharged of his ambassade and returned home, where he was welcomed by Cromwell who loved him dearly. So long as Cromwell remained in authority, so long was Boner at his beck, friend to his friends and enemy to his enemies; as at that time to Gardiner, Bishop of Winchester, who never favoured Cromwell, and therefore Boner and Winchester were the greatest enemies that might be. But so soon as Cromwell fell, Boner and Winchester pretended to be the greatest men that lived; and no good word could Boner speak of Cromwell, but the vilest and bitterest that he could speak. Such as

Boner knew to be in favour with Cromwell, he could never abide their sight; insomuch as the day after Cromwell was apprehended Grafton met Boner and said that he was sorry to hear the news. 'Are ye sorry for that?' said he; 'It had been good that he had been dispatched long ago.' Afterward Grafton, being charged for the imprinting of a ballet in favour of Cromwell, was called before the Council, where Boner charged him with the words that he spake to him of Cromwell. But Audley who was Lord Chancellor discreetly cut off the matter.

The history of Robert Barnes, Thomas Garret, and William Hierome

Like as in battles the chief point of victory consisteth in the safety of the general, so when the standard-bearer of the Church of England, Thomas Cromwell, was made away, pity it is to behold what slaughter of good men and women ensued. For Winchester, having now free swing to exercise his cruelty, wonder it was to see what troubles he raised in the Lord's vineyard. He made his first assaults upon Robert Barnes, Thomas Garret, and William Hierome, whom two days after Cromwell's death he caused to be put to execution.

Barnes, after he came from the University of Lovaine, came to Cambridge, where he was made prior of the house of the Augustines. At that time the knowledge of good letters was scarcely entered into the university, all things being full of rudeness and barbarity: whereupon Barnes began in his house to read Terence, Plautus, and Cicero, so that he caused the house to flourish with good letters. After these foundations laid, then did he read openly Paul's epistles and put by Duns and Dorbell, and turned their fruitless disputations to better matter of the Holy Scriptures, and thereby made divers good divines. The order of disputation which he kept in his house he observed likewise in the university, when he should dispute with any man in the schools. Thus Barnes became mighty in the Scriptures, preaching ever against bishops and hypocrites; and yet did not see his idolatry, which he taught and maintained till Mr Bilney converted him wholly unto Christ.

The first sermon that he preached of this truth was the Sunday before Christmas Day at Edward's Church by the Peas Market, whose theme was the epistle of the day *Gaudete in Domino &c.*; and so postilled the whole epistle, following Luther's postil: for that sermon he was accused of heresy by two Fellows of King's Hall. Then the learned in Christ flocked together in open sight in the schools, at St Mary's, and at the Austins', and conferred continually together. The house that they resorted most commonly unto was the White Horse, which to bring God's word into contempt was called Germany. Much trouble began to ensue. The adversaries of Barnes accused him in the Regent House before the vice-chancellor, where his articles were presented, he promising to make answer at the next convocation; and so it was done. Dr Nottoris moved Dr Barnes to recant; but he refused.

This tragedy continued in Cambridge, one preaching against another, until within six days of Shrovetide. Then was sent down to Cambridge a sergeant at arms who arrested Barnes openly to make others afraid; and they had determined to search for Luther's books. But Dr Farman of the Queens' College sent word to those who were suspected, in number thirty persons. But, God be praised, they were conveyed by that time that the sergeant at arms, the vice-chancellor, and the proctors were at every man's chamber; and that night they gave him his answer, which he carried to London the next morning, and lay at Mr Parnell's house by the Stocks. In the morning he was carried to Cardinal Wolsey, to Westminster. Then by reason of Dr Gardiner, secretary to the cardinal, he spake the same night with the cardinal in his chamber of estate. 'What, Mr Doctor,' said the cardinal; 'had you not sufficient scope in the Scriptures to teach the people, but that my golden shoes, pole-axes, pillars, golden cushions, crosses did so sore offend you that you must make us *ridiculum caput* amongst the people? we were jollily that day laughed to scorn.' Barnes answered, 'I spake nothing but the truth.' The cardinal answered, 'Do you think it more necessary that I should have all this royalty, because I represent the king's person to the keeping down of rebellions, treasons, all the wicked members of this commonwealth, or to sell all these things and give it to the poor, which will piss it against the wall?' He answered, 'I think it necessary to be sold and given to the poor. For the King's Majesty is not maintained by your pomp and pole-axes, but by God who saith, "*Per me reges regnant.*" '

Then answered he, 'Lo, Mr Doctors, here is the wise man that you told me of,' Then they kneeled down and said, 'We desire your Grace to be good unto him, for he will be reformable.' Then said he, 'Stand you up; for your sakes we will be good unto him. How say you, Mr Doctor? do you not know that I am *legatus de latere*, able to dispense in all matters concerning religion in this realm as much as the Pope may?'

'I know it to be so.'

'Will you then be ruled by us, and we will do all things for your honesty?'

'I thank your Grace: I will stick to God's book according to the simple talent God hath lent me.'

'Well, thou shalt have thy learning tried to the uttermost, and thou shalt have the law.'

So he came home to Parnell's house again and in the morning to York Place, and was committed to the sergeant of arms, to bring him into the chapterhouse at Westminster before the bishops. The same time when Dr Barnes should appear before the cardinal there were five Stillyard men to be examined for Luther's books; but after they spied Barnes they set the others aside, and the sergeant at arms presented his articles and his accusers. Then they sware him and laid his articles to him. He offered the book of his probations unto them, who took it and said they should have no leisure to dispute with him at that present, and committed him to the Fleet with the other. On Saturday he came again before them and there remained till five o'clock at night, and after long disputations they called him to know whether he would abjure or burn. He was in great agony and thought rather to burn than to abjure. But then was he sent to have the counsel of Gardiner and Foxe, and they persuaded him to abjure, because, they said, he should do more in time to come; and with other reasons mighty in the sight of foolish flesh. Upon that he consented to abjure, and subscribed with his own hand.

Then they commanded the Warden of the Fleet to carry him to the place whence he came, to be kept in close prison, and in the morning to provide five faggots for Barnes and the four Stillyard men. The fifth Stillyard man was commanded to have a taper of five pound weight to be provided for him, to offer to the rood of Northern in Paul's. By eight o'clock in the morning they were all ready in Paul's Church, the church being so full that no man could get in. The cardinal had a scaffold made on the top of the stairs for himself, with thirty-six abbots, mitred priors, and bishops, and he in his pomp, mitred, sat enthronized, his chaplains in damask and satin and himself in purple like a bloody Antichrist. There was a new pulpit erected on the top of the stairs for the Bishop of Rochester to preach against Luther and Dr Barnes; and great baskets full of books, which were commanded, after the fire was made before the rood of Northern, there to be burned; and these heretics after the sermon to go thrice about the fire and cast in their faggots. Barnes was commanded at the end of the sermon to declare that he was more charitably handled than he deserved; his heresies were so horrible. And so the cardinal departed under a canopy with his mitred men with him, till he came to the second gate of Paul's, and there he took his mule. Then these poor men being commanded to come down from the stage, the bishops sat down again and commanded the Knight-Marshal to carry them about the fire. And so they were brought to the bishops, and Rochester declared unto the people how many days of pardon they had, for being at that sermon; and there did assoil Barnes with the others, and showed the people that they were received into the Church again. This done, the Warden of the Fleet and the Knight-Marshal were commanded to have them to the Fleet again, there to remain till the cardinal's pleasure were known.

After Barnes there had continued half a year, he was committed to be a free prisoner at the Austen Friars. When those caterpillars had undermined him, they complained to their Lord Cardinal; whereupon he was removed to Northampton, there to be burned. He himself, understanding nothing thereof, one Mr Horne, his special friend, having intelligence of the writ which should shortly be sent down to burn him, gave him counsel to feign himself to be desperate, and that he should write a letter to the cardinal and leave it on his table where he lay, to declare whither he was gone to drown himself, and to leave his clothes in the same place; and there another letter to be left to the mayor, to search for him in the water, because he had a letter written in parchment about his neck, closed in wax, which should teach all men to beware by him. Upon this they were seven days in searching for him, but he was conveyed to London in a poor man's apparel, and took shipping, and went to Antwerp and so to Luther; and there fell to study, till he had made answer to the bishops entitled *Acta Romanorum Pontificum*, and another book with a supplication to King Henry. It was told the cardinal that he was drowned, and he said, '*Perit memoria ejus cum sonitu*'; but this did light upon himself shortly after, which wretchedly died at Leicester.

In the mean season Barnes got favour with the learned in Christ and with foreign princes, and was great with Luther, Melancthon, the Duke of Saxon, and the King of Denmark; which king, in the time of More and Stokesley, sent him with the Lubecks as an ambassador to King Henry VIII. He lay with the Lubecks' chancellor at the Stillyard. More, then Chancellor, would feign have entrapped him, but the king would not let him, for Cromwell was his great friend. The Lubecks and he disputed with the bishops in defence of the truth; and so he departed without restraint. After going again to Wittemberg he remained there to set forward his works in print; he returned again in the beginning of the reign of Queen Anne and continued a faithful preacher in this city, being all her time well entertained and promoted. After that, he was sent ambassador by King Henry to the Duke of Cleve, for the marriage of the Lady Anne of Cleve, and well accepted in the ambassade, and in all his doings, until Gardiner came out of France. After he came, neither religion prospered, nor the Queen, nor Cromwell, nor the preachers; who after the marriage of Lady Anne of Cleve never ceased until he had grafted the marriage in another stock, by occasion whereof he began his bloody broil. For not long after Dr Barnes with his brethren were apprehended and carried before the King to Hampton Court, where the king, seeking the means of his safety, at Winchester's request granted him leave to go home with the bishop to confer with him. But they not agreeing Gardiner and his co-partners sought how to entangle them in further danger, which not long after was brought to pass; for they were enjoined to preach three sermons the Easter following at the Spittall, at which sermons Gardiner was present, to hear record of their recantation or trip them in their talk if they had spoken anything awry.

Now let us likewise consider the story of Thomas Garret, recorded by Anthony Dalaber, who was there present. About the year 1526, in February, Mr Garret, curate of Honey Lane in London, came unto Oxford and brought with him books in Latin treating of the Scripture, and Tindall's first New Testament, which books he sold to divers scholars, whose names he wrote in a small book of accounts. After a while news came that he was searched for through all London to be taken as an heretic and imprisoned for selling those heretical books, as they termed them. For it was known to Cardinal Wolsey and the Bishop of London that Garret had a great number of those books and that he was gone to Oxford to make sale of them there. Wherefore they determined to search all Oxford, to imprison him if they might and to burn all his books, and him too if they could; so burning hot was the charity of those holy fathers. But at that time one of the proctors, Cole of Magdalen, was well acquainted with Garret, and gave secret warning unto a friend or two of Garret's, and willed that he should forthwith secretly depart out of Oxford; for if he were taken he should be sent up unto the cardinal and committed unto the Tower. So in the morning Garret departed out of Oxford toward Dorsetshire. How far he went, and by what occasion so soon he returned, I know not. But in the night he came again where he lay before, and so in the search which was made for him he was taken in his bed by the two proctors and delivered unto Dr Cotisford, commissary of the university, who kept him prisoner in his own chamber.

Thus far Dalaber hath prosecuted this story, who before finishing departed, the year 1562; the residue, as we could gather it of ancient and credible persons, so have we added here.

Garret was convented before the commissary, Dr London, and Dr Higdon, into St Mary's Church, where they convicted him as an heretic and compelled him to carry a faggot in open procession to Frideswide's, and Dalaber with him, Garret having his red hood on his shoulders like a Master of Art. After that they were sent to Osney, to be kept in prison till further order was taken.

The third who suffered with Barnes and Garret was William Hierome, Vicar of Stepney. Hierome for the comfort of the people had preached sermons, wherein to plant in the consciences of men the truth of Christian religion he laboured to weed out the roots of men's traditions, doctrines, dreams, and fantasies. In so doing it could not otherwise be but he must needs provoke much hatred against him among the adversaries of Christ's gospel. It happened that Hierome, preaching at Paul's, mentioned Agar and Sara, declaring what these two signified; he showed further how Sara and Isaac and all they that were Isaac's and born of the free woman Sara were freely justified: contrary, they that were born of Agar the bondwoman were bound and under the law. What was here spoken but that St Paul himself expoundeth in his Epistle to the Galatians? What could here be gathered of any reasonable hearer but consonant to sound doctrine? Now see what malice armed with sophistry can do. The sermon finished, it was not long but he was convented before the king at Westminster, and there accused for erroneous doctrine. Who doubteth here but if Saint Paul himself had been at Paul's Cross and had preached the same words which he wrote, he had been apprehended for an heretic?

Thus much concerning the several stories of these three men. Now let us see the order of their martyrdom, joining them all together.

Ye heard before how Barnes, Hierome, and Garret were caused to preach at Easter at the Spittall; the occasion whereof, as I find it reported by Gardiner, writing against George Joye, I thought good here to discourse more at large. Gardiner, hearing that Barnes, Hierome, and Garret should preach the Lent following, *an.* 1541, at Paul's Cross, to stop the course of their doctrine sent his chaplain to the Bishop of London to have a place for him to preach at St Paul's, which was granted, and time appointed that he should preach the Sunday following; which Sunday was appointed before for Barnes to occupy that room. Gardiner therefore, determining to declare the Gospel of that Sunday containing the devil's three temptations, began to note the abuse of Scripture amongst some, as the devil abused it to Christ. This sermon finished, Dr Barnes had his day apppointed to make his sermon; who taking the same text was on the contrary side no less vehement in setting forward the true doctrine than Winchester had been in plucking men backward from truth to lies, from religion to superstition. In which sermon he, calling out Gardiner by name to answer him, alluded in a pleasant allegory to a cockfight, terming Gardiner a fighting cock and himself another; but the Garden Cock, he said, lacketh good spurs.

With this sermon Gardiner was so tickled in the spleen that he went to the king to complain, showing how he, a prelate of the realm, was reviled at Paul's Cross. The king, giving too much ear to Gardiner's grief, was incensed against Barnes, and with many high words rebuked his doings in his privy closet. Unto whom when Barnes had submitted himself, 'Nay,' said the king, 'yield thee not to me: I am a mortal man'; and therewith rising up, turning to the sacrament, and putting off his bonnet, said, 'Yonder is the Master of us all, author of truth: yield in truth to him, and that truth will I defend; and otherwise yield thee not unto me.' Much ado there was, and great matter laid against Barnes. In conclusion this order was taken, that Barnes should go apart with Winchester to confer together of their doctrine, witnesses being appointed to be indifferent hearers, of whom one was Dr Cockes, the other Dr Robinson, with two other which should be reporters to the king of the disputation.

The question between them propounded, Gardiner came forth with his arguments which, saith Gardiner, Barnes could not answer, but desired to be spared that night, and the next morning he would answer. In the morning Barnes went about to assoil his arguments. Gardiner replied, and thus continued they in this altercation two hours. In the end of this cock-fight Winchester croweth up the triumph, declaring how Barnes besought him to forgive him and to take him to be his scholar; whom Winchester receiving not as scholar but as companion, offered him a portion of his living, £40 a year. The king was content that Barnes should repair to the bishop's house at London the Monday following. Upon the Monday the bishop, studying to instruct Barnes, uttered to him certain articles to the number of ten. Forsomuch as they be sufficiently answered by George Joye in his Joinder and Rejoinder against Winchester, I shall not need to cumber this work with any new ado.

Barnes, hearing the talk of the people and having conference with certain learned men, two days after his coming to the bishop's house waxed weary thereof, and signified unto him that if he would take him as one that came to confer he would come still, but else he would come no more. This being known unto the king, Barnes again was sent for and convented before the king, who incensed against him enjoined him, Hierome, and Garret, at the Easter sermons at St Mary Spittall to revoke the doctrine they had taught; at which sermons Gardiner was present to hear their recantation. First Barnes solemnly began to make his recantation; which done, he with much circumstance and obtestation called upon the bishop, and asking forgiveness required him in token of a grant to hold up his hand. Which when the bishop at first refused to do, Barnes again called for it, desiring him to show his charity; which when he had done with much ado, wagging his finger a little, Barnes entering to his sermon beginneth the process of the matter, preaching contrary to that which before he had recanted; insomuch that the mayor, when the sermon was finished, sitting with the bishop, asked him whether he should from the pulpit send him to ward for that his bold preaching. The like also did Hierome and Garret after him.

The king had appointed certain to report the sermons. Besides them there was one who writing to a friend in the Court declared how gaily they had all handled the matter, to satisfy the recantations and in the same sermons to utter the truth. Wherefore Barnes with his fellows were apprehended and committed to the Tower. Gardiner in his book against Joye would needs clear himself that he was in no cause of their casting into the Tower, for that he had no access to the king's secret counsel; notwithstanding Gardiner cannot persuade us but that his privy complaining to the king and other workings by his fautors about the king was a great sparkle to set their faggots afire. Thus Barnes, Hierome, and Garret being committed to the Tower after Easter there remained till the 30th of July, two days after the death of Cromwell. Then ensued process against them by the king's Council, to which process Gardiner confesseth that he was privy. Whereupon all three were brought from the Tower to Smithfield, where they had there at the stake sundry exhortations. Barnes desired all men to forgive him if he had said any evil at any time whereby he had offended any man, and to bear witness that he abhorred all doctrines against the word of God, and that he died in the faith of Jesu Christ. He desired them all to pray for him, and then turned about and put off his clothes, making him ready to the fire, patiently to take his death. The like confession made Hierome and Garret, reciting all the articles of the Christian Faith, declaring their minds upon every article as time would suffer; whereby the people might understand that there was no error in their faith wherefore they ought to be condemned; protesting moreover that they denied nothing in the Old or New Testament set forth by their sovereign lord the king, whom they prayed the Lord long to continue amongst them, with his son Prince Edward.

And so, their prayers made, wherein they desired the Lord Jesus to establish them with faith, constancy, and patience, they, taking themselves by the hand and kissing one another, quietly and humbly offered themselves to the hands of the tormentors and took their death both Christianly and constantly.

Wherein is to be noted how mightily the Lord worketh in the hearts of his servants, especially in such which suffer with a guiltless conscience; example whereof we have not only in these three but also in Lord Cromwell who suffered two days before. What a guiltless conscience he bare to his death his Christian patience declared; who first calling for his breakfast and cheerfully eating the same, and after that passing out of his prison down the hill within the Tower, and meeting Lord Hungerford going to his execution, and perceiving him all doleful, with cheerful countenance asking why he was so heavy willed him to pluck up his heart; 'For,' said he, 'there is no cause for fear: if you be heartily sorry for that you have done, there is mercy enough with the Lord, who for Christ's sake will forgive you.' So went they together to the place of execution and took their death patiently.

The same time and place where and when these three did suffer, three other were executed, though not for the same cause, but rather the contrary—for denying the king's supremacy—whose names were Powell, Fetherstone, and Abel; which spectacle brought the people into doubt which part to take, as might well happen amongst simple people, seeing two contrary parts suffer, the one for popery, the other against popery, both at one time. A stranger there present, seeing three on one side and three on the other, said, '*Deus bone, quomodo hic vivunt gentes? hic suspenduntur Papistae, illic comburuntur Antipapistae!*' But to remove all doubt from posterity how this happened, the cause did rise by reasons of discord among the King's Council, who were so divided that one half seemed to hold with one religion, the other with the contrary. This division of the Council caused both parts above mentioned to suffer together. For as one part of the Council called for the execution of Barnes, Garret, and Hierome, so the other part called for execution of the law upon Powell, Fetherstone, and Abel; which six, condemned and drawn to the place of execution two upon an hurdle, one a Papist the other a Protestant, thus after a strange manner were brought into Smithfield, where all six together for contrary doctrine suffered death, three by fire for the gospel, three by hanging, drawing, and quartering for popery.

The story of John Porter, cruelly martyred for reading the Bible in Paul's

In the same year 1541 John Porter for reading the Bible in Paul's Church was cruelly handled, and that unto death. It was declared above how Edmund Boner, Bishop of London, in the days of Cromwell being ambassador at Paris, was a great doer in setting forward the printing of the Bible in the Great Volume, promising that he would have six Bibles in the Church of St Paul; which at his coming home he performed according to the king's proclamation. The Bibles thus standing in Paul's, many people used to resort to the hearing thereof, especially when they could get any that had an audible voice to read unto them, misdoubting no danger; and no more there was, so long as the days of Cromwell lasted. After he was gone, it happened amongst divers persons who frequented there the reading of the Bible that Porter used sometimes to be occupied in that godly exercise to the edifying as well of himself as of others. Porter was a fresh young man of big stature, who by diligent reading of the Scripture became very expert. The Bible being set up by Boner upon divers pillars in Paul's Church, fixed with chains for all to read that would, great multitudes would resort thither to hear Porter, because he could read well and had an audible voice.

Boner grieved withal sent for Porter and rebuked him very sharply for his reading. Porter answered that he trusted he had done nothing contrary to the law, neither contrary to his advertisements which he had fixed over every Bible. Boner then laid unto his charge that he had made expositions upon the text, and gathered great multitudes about him to make tumults. He answered he trusted that should not be proved by him. But Boner sent him to Newgate, where he was miserably fettered in irons, both legs and arms, with a collar of iron about his neck fastened to the wall in the dungeon, being so cruelly handled that he was compelled to send for a kinsman whose name is also Porter, and yet alive and can testify that is true, and dwelleth yet without Newgate. Who seeing his kinsman in this miserable case entreated Jewet, then keeper of Newgate, that he might be released out of those cruel irons; and so, through friendship and money, had him up among other prisoners, which lay there for felony and murder. Porter, hearing and seeing their wickedness and blasphemy, exhorted them to amendment of life, and gave them such instructions as he had learned of the Scriptures: for so doing he was complained on, and so carried down and laid in the lower dungeon of all, oppressed with bolts and irons, where six or eight days after he was found dead.

A note of one Thomas Sommers, imprisoned for the gospel

Amongst Londoners troubled by the clergy we will add, though a little out of place, a note of Thomas Sommers, who died in the Tower of London for confessing the gospel. Thomas, a very honest merchant and wealthy, was sent for by the cardinal and committed to the Tower for that he had Luther's books. The cardinal's judgment was that he should ride from the Tower into Cheapside, carrying a book in his hand and heaped with books hanging about him, with three or four other merchants after the same order. When Sommers should be sent on a collier's nag as his fellow-prisoners were, a friend brought him a very good gelding fair dressed with bridle and saddle; and when the bishop's officer came to dress him with books as they had trimmed the other, and would have made holes in his garment to have thrust the strings of the books therein, 'Nay,' said Sommers, 'I have always loved to go handsomely in my apparel;' and taking the books he bound them together and cast them about his neck (the leaves being all open) like a collar; and rode foremost through the streets till they came about the Standard in Cheapside, where a great fire was made to burn their books in, and a pillory set up for four persons in token that they deserved it.

In the meantime, by the way as they should come, it was appointed that one should go before them with a basin; at the noise whereof Mr Sommers' horse, being a lofty gelding and fierce, was in such a rage that he which rung the basin was fain to go alone a great space before any horseman followed. At length, when they came to the fire, every one of them having a book in his hand, they were commanded to cast their books into the fire. But when Sommers saw that his New Testament should be burned, he threw it over the fire; which was seen by some of God's enemies and brought to him again, commanding him to cast it into the fire; which he would not do, but cast it through the fire; which thing was done three times; but at last a stander-by took it up and saved it from burning. But not long after Sommers was cast again into the Tower by the cardinal through the cruelty of the bishops; who soon after died in the prison for the testimony of his faith.

The fourth and fifth marriage of King Henry VIII

In the month next following the apprehension of Cromwell, which was *an.* 1541, the king immediately was divorced from Lady Anne of Cleve. The separation being wholly committed to the clergy of the convocation, it was by them concluded that the king, being freed from that pretensed matrimony as they called it, might marry where he would, and so might she likewise; whom also consenting to the divorcement herself was after that taken no more for queen, but only called Lady Anne of Cleve. The king the same month was married to his fifth wife, Lady Katherine Haward, niece to the Duke of Norfolk. This marriage likewise continued not long; for in the year next following Lady Katherine was accused to the king of incontinent living, not only (before her marriage) with Francis Direham, but also of spouse-breach sith her marriage, with Thomas Culpeper. For the which both men were by act of parliament attainted and executed for high treason; and Lady Katherine, with Jane Rochford, late wife to George Bullen Lord Rochford, brother to Anne Bullen, were beheaded within the Tower. *Ex Hallo & aliis.*

After the punishment of this lady, his fifth wife, the king, calling to remembrance the words of Cromwell and missing more and more his old counsellor, and partly also smelling somewhat the ways of Winchester, began a little to set his foot again in the cause of religion. And although he ever bare a special favour to Thomas Cranmer, as you shall hear hereafter, yet now the more he missed Cromwell, the more he inclined to the archbishop. Therefore in October next after the execution of the queen the king, understanding some abuses yet to remain unreformed, namely pilgrimages and idolatry, directed letters unto the archbishop for the speedy reformation of the same. Furthermore the next year, 1543, in February, followed another proclamation by the king's authority, wherein the Pope's law forbidding white meats to be eaten in Lent was repealed for the behoof of the king's subjects.

The persecution of Testwood, Filmer, Person, and Marbecke

When the time came nigh that the king (newly married to that virtuous lady, Katherine Parre) should make his progress abroad, Stephen Gardiner had so compassed his matters that no man bare so great a swinge about the king as he did; wherewith the gospellers were so quailed that the best of them looked every hour to be clapped in the neck; for the saying went abroad that the bishop had bent his bow to shoot at some of the head deer. In the meantime three of four of the poor rascals were caught, Anthony Person, Henry Filmer, and John Marbecke, and sent to Windsor by the sheriff's men, and laid fast in the town gaol; and Robert Testwood, who had kept his bed, was brought out of his house upon crutches and laid with them. As for Bennet who should have been the fifth man, his chance was to be sick of the pestilence, and having a great sore upon him he was left behind in the Bishop of London's gaol, whereby he escaped the fire. These men being brought to Windsor, there was a sessions specially procured to be holden, against which were all the farmers belonging to the College of Windsor warned to appear, because they could not pick out Papists enough in the town to go upon the jury. The judges were Dr Capon Bishop of Salisbury, Sir William Essex, Sir Thomas Bridges, Sir Humfrey Foster, Mr Franklin, Dean of Windsor, and Fachel of Reading.

When these had taken their places and the prisoners brought before them, the Clerk of the Peace called Anthony Person and read his indictment. To this Anthony answered, 'I will be tried by God and by the true Church of Christ, whether this be heresy whereof ye have indicted me. So long as I preached the Bishop of Rome and his filthy traditions I was never troubled; but since I have taken upon me to preach Christ and his gospel ye have always sought my life. But it maketh no matter; for when you have taken your pleasure of my body I trust it shall not lie in your powers to hurt my soul.' 'Thou callest us thieves,' quoth the bishop. 'I say,' quoth Anthony, 'ye are not only thieves but murderers, except ye preach the word of God sincerely to the people; which ye do not nor never did; but have allured them to idolatry, superstition, and hypocrisy, for your own lucre and glory's sake, through which ye are become rather bite-sheeps than bishops, devouring the poor sheep of Christ like ravening wolves, never satisfied with blood; which God will require of your hands one day, doubt it not.' Then spake Symons his accuser, 'It is a pity this fellow had not been burned long ago as he deserved.' 'In faith,' quoth Anthony, 'if you had as you deserved, you were more worthy to stand in this place than I. When we shall both appear before the tribunal seat of Christ, it will be known which of us two hath best deserved this place.'

Then was Testwood called and his indictment read, which was that he should say in the time that the priest was lifting up the sacrament, 'Take heed; let him not fall.' Testwood answered it was a thing maliciously forged of his enemies to bring him to his death. 'Yes,' quoth the bishop, 'thou hast been seen that when the priest should lift up the sacrament over his head, then wouldst thou look down upon thy book, because thou wouldst not abide to look upon the blessed sacrament.' 'My Lord,' quoth Testwood, 'whereon did *he* look that marked me so well?' 'Marry,' quoth the king's attorney, 'he could not be better occupied than to mark such heretics.'

Then was Filmer called and his indictment read; that he should say, 'If God be in the sacrament of the altar, I have eaten twenty gods in my days.' These words were gathered of certain communications which should be between Filmer and his brother, a very poor labouring man. This tale was no sooner brought to Dr London but he sent for the poor man home to his house, where he cherished him with meat and money, telling him that he should never lack so long as he lived. When Dr London had thus won the poor man, he retained him as one of his household until the court day was come, and then sent him up to witness this tale against his brother. Which tale Filmer denied utterly, saying that Dr London had set him on and made him say what his pleasure was: 'My Lord, there is no man in all this town that will testify with him that ever he heard any such talk: if he can bring any that will witness the same with him, I refuse not to die.' But say what he could, it would not prevail.

Then was Marbecke called and his indictment read, which was that he should say that the mass is robbery of the glory of God, and that Christ is made in the mass man's laughing-stock. He answered that the words were not his but the words of John Calvin, which he had but written out, and that long before the Six Articles came forth; so that he was discharged of that offence by the king's general pardon.

Then was the jury called, which were all farmers whereof none had ever seen those men before upon whose life and death they went. Wherefore the prisoners desired to have such as did know them and had seen their daily conversations, in place of the farmers or joined with them; but the matter was otherwise determined. When the jury had taken their oath, the king's attorney began to speak, making every man's cause as heinous as he could devise. When he had done, Sir Humfrey Foster spake in favour of Marbecke. 'Masters,' quoth he, 'ye see there is no man here that layeth anything to the charge of this poor man Marbecke, saving that he hath written other men's sayings, whereof he is discharged by the king's pardon.' Then started up Fachel and said, 'What can we tell whether they were written before the pardon or after?' These words were the cause of Marbecke's casting that day.

Then went the jury up to the chamber over the place where the judges sat, and in the meantime went all the knights and gentlemen abroad saving the bishop, Essex, and Fachel. When the jury had been in the chamber about a quarter of an hour, up goeth Symons unto them and tarried there a pretty while. After that came one of the jury down to the bishop and talked with him and the other twain a good while, whereby many conjectured that the jury could not agree of Marbecke. Not long after his going up again they came down to give their verdict, and one Hyde, dwelling in a lordship belonging to the College of Windsor, speaking in the mouth of the rest, said they were all guilty. Then the judges made courtesy who should give judgment. Fachel requiring the bishop to do it, he said he mought not. The other also said they would not. Then said Fachel, 'One must do it; and if no man will, then will I.' So Fachel, being lowest of the bunch, gave judgment.

The prisoners, condemned and had away, prepared themselves to die on the morrow, comforting one another in the death and passion of their Master Christ, trusting that the same Lord which had made them worthy to suffer so far for his sake would give them power to overcome those fiery torments, and of his mercy and goodness receive their souls. Such heavenly talk was amongst them that night that the hearers watching the prison without, whereof the sheriff himself was one, were constrained to shed plenty of tears, as they themselves confessed. On the morrow word was brought that they should not suffer that day. The Bishop of Sarum had sent a letter to the Bishop of Winchester in favour of Marbecke; at the sight of which the bishop straightway went to the king and obtained his pardon; which being granted he caused a warrant to be made for the sheriff's discharge delivering the same to the messenger, who with speed returned, bringing good news to the town of Marbecke's pardon: whereat many rejoiced.

The morning that the prisoners should go to execution, taking leave of Marbecke they praised God for his deliverance, and besought him to help them with prayer unto God to make them strong in their afflictions; and kissing him one after another they departed, and came to the place of execution, where Person embraced the post in his arms and kissing it said, 'Welcome mine own sweet wife; this day shall thou and I be married together in the love and peace of God.' And being all three bound to the post, a young man of Filmer's acquaintance brought him a pot of drink. 'I thank you,' quoth Filmer, 'and now, my brother, I desire you in the name of the Lord to stand fast in the truth of the gospel.' And so, taking the pot at his hand, he asked his brother Anthony if he would drink. 'Yea, brother Filmer,' quoth he, 'I pledge you in the Lord.' When he had drunk, he gave the cup to Anthony, and Anthony likewise to Testwood. When Anthony and Testwood had both drunken, Filmer rejoicing in the Lord said, 'Be merry, my brethren, and lift up your hearts unto God, for after this sharp breakfast I trust we shall have a good dinner in the Kingdom of Christ our Redeemer.' At which words Testwood, lifting up hands and eyes to heaven, desired the Lord to receive his spirit; and Person, pulling the straw unto him, laid a good deal upon the top of his head, saying, 'This is God's hat; now am I dressed like a soldier of Christ, by whose merits only I trust this day to enter into his joy.' So yielded they up their souls to the Father of heaven in the faith of his dear Son, with such steadfastness that many who saw their patient suffering confessed that they could have found in their heart to have died with them.

Kerby and Roger Clarke of Suffolk, martyrs

Coming now to the year 1546, first passing over the priest Saxye, hanged in the porter's lodge of Stephen Gardiner; to pass over also one Henry with his servant burned at Colchester; I will proceed to the story of Kerby and Roger Clarke of Mendlesham, who were apprehended at Ipswich the Saturday before Gang Monday and brought before Lord Wentworth, with other commissioners appointed to sit upon their causes. Kerby and Roger being in the gaoler's house, came in Mr Robert Wingfield with Mr Bruesse of Wennenham; who then having conference with Kerby, Wingfield said, 'Remember the fire is hot: take no more upon thee than thou shalt be able to perform. The pain will be extreme, and life is sweet. Better to stick to mercy while there is hope of life than rashly to begin and then to shrink.' He answered, 'Be at my burning, and you shall say, "There standeth a Christian soldier in the fire." I know that God will suffer no more to be laid upon us than he will give us strength to bear.' 'Ah, Kerby,' said Wingfield, 'If thou be at that point I will bid thee farewell; for I am not so strong that I am able to burn.' And so both gentlemen, saying they would pray for them, shook hands and so departed.

When they came to the judgment-seat, Wentworth with the rest of the justices there ready, Kerby and Roger lifted up eyes and hands to heaven, making their prayers to God. That done, their articles were declared unto them; then it was demanded whether they believed that after the words spoken by a priest there were not the very body and blood of Christ, flesh, blood, and bone, as he was born of the Virgin Mary, and no bread. They answered No; but they did believe the sacrament which Christ Jesus did institute was only to put all men in remembrance of his precious death and blood-shedding for the remission of sins; and that there was neither flesh nor blood to be eaten with the teeth, but bread and wine; yet more than bread and wine, for it was consecrated to an holy use. Then with much persuasions and threats were these poor men hardly laid to at the hands of Foster, an inferior justice; but these two continued faithful unto the end. Then sentence was given upon them both, Kerby to be burned in the said town on the next Saturday and Roger at Bury the Gang Monday after. Kerby, when his judgment was given by Lord Wentworth, bowing himself devoutly said, 'Praised be Almighty God,' without any more words. Then did Wentworth talk secretly, putting his head behind another justice that sat between them. Roger perceiving that said with a loud voice, 'Speak out, my Lord: if you have done anything contrary to your conscience, ask God mercy: we for our parts forgive you: speak not in secret, for ye shall come before a Judge and then make answer openly.' Then was Kerby and Roger sent forth, Kerby to prison there and Roger to St Edmund's Bury.

The next day about 10 o'clock Kerby was brought to the market-place, where a stake was ready, wood, broom, and straw, and did off his clothes unto his shirt, having a nightcap upon his head, and so was fastened to the stake with irons, there being in the gallery Lord Wentworth with most of the justices of those quarters, where they might see his execution and hear what Kerby did say; and a great number of people, about two thousand by estimation. Then said the under-sheriff to Kerby, 'Hast thou anything to say?' 'Yea, sir,' said he, 'if you will give me leave.' 'Say on,' said the sheriff. Then Kerby taking his nightcap from his head was putting it under his arm, as though it should have done him service again; but remembering himself he cast it from him, and lifting up his hands he said the *Te Deum* and the Belief with other prayers, in English. Lord Wentworth, whilst Kerby was thus doing, did shroud himself behind one of the posts of the gallery and wept, and so did many other. Then said Kerby, 'I have done: execute your office, good Mr Sheriff.' Then fire was set to the wood, and with a loud voice he called unto God, knocking on his breast, and holding up his hands, as long as remembrance would serve, and so ended his life; the people giving shouts and praising God, with great admiration of his constancy, being so simple and unlettered.

On Gang Monday Roger Clarke was brought out of prison and went on foot to the gate called Southgate in Bury, and by the way the procession met them; but he went on and would not bow cap nor knee, but wite vehement words rebuked that idolatry and superstition, the officers being much offended. And without the gate, where was the place of execution, the stake being ready and the wood lying by, he kneeled down and said *Magnificat* in English, making a paraphrase wherein he declared that the blessed Virgin, who might well rejoice in pureness, yet humbled herself to her Saviour. 'And what sayest thou, John Baptist,' said he, 'the greatest of all men's children? "Behold, the Lamb of God, which taketh away the sins of the world."' Thus with a loud voice he cried unto the people while he was in fastening to the stake, and then the fire was set to him, where he suffered unmercifully;

for the wood was green and would not burn, so that he was choked with smoke. Moreover, being set in a pitch barrel with some pitch sticking still by the side, he was therewith sore pained till he had got his feet out of the barrel. At length one standing by took a faggot-stick, and striking at the ring of iron about his neck so pashed him that he shrank down on one side into the fire, and so was dissolved.

The story of Queen Katherine Parre

After these stormy stories, the course as well of the time as the matter of the story doth require now to entreat touching the troubles of the excellent lady Katherine Parre, the last wife to King Henry.

The year after the king returned from Bullein he was informed that Katherine was much given to the study of the Scriptures, and had retained divers learned persons to instruct her in the same; with whom as at all times convenient she used to have private conference touching spiritual matters, so especially in Lent every afternoon for an hour one of her chaplains made some collation to her and to her gentlewomen or others that were disposed to hear; in which sermons they of times touched such abuses as in the Church were rife. Which things as they were not secretly done, so neither were their preachings unknown unto the king, whereof for a great time he seemed very well to like. Which made her the more bold to debate with the king touching religion and to discover herself, oftentimes exhorting the king that as he had to his eternal fame begun a good work in banishing that monstrous idol of Rome, so he would finish the same, purging his Church of England clean from the dregs thereof, wherein remained great superstition. And albeit the king grew, towards his latter end, very stern and opinionate, so that of few he could be content to be contended withal by argument, notwithstanding towards her he refrained his accustomed manner as appeared by great respects, either for the reverence of the cause, whereunto he seemed well inclined, or else to the singular affection which until a very small time before his death he always bare her. For never handmaid sought with more diligence to please her mistress than she did apply herself in all things to please his humour.

Besides the virtues of the mind, she was endued with rare gifts of nature, as singular beauty and comely personage, things wherein the king greatly delighted; and so enjoyed she the king's favour, to the great likelihood of the setting at large of the gospel within this realm, had not the malicious practice of enemies professed against the truth prevented the same, to the alienating of the king's mind from religion and almost to the ruin of the queen. The conspirers of her death were Gardiner Bishop of Winchester, Wrisley Lord Chancellor, and others. These, seeking to kindle pernicious humours in their sovereign lord, to the intent to deprive her of this favour which then she stood in with the king, and thereby to stop the passage of the gospel and invade the small remainder of that poor flock, made their entry into this mischievous enterprise after this manner.

The king, as you have heard, misliked to be contended withal in any kind of argument. This humour of his the queen would not stick, entering with him into discourse, with sound reasons of Scripture now and then to contrary; the which the king took in good part, or at least did never show countenance of offence thereat; which did not a little appal her adversaries. Perceiving her so grounded in the king's favour they durst not for their lives once open their lips unto the king either in her presence or behind her back. So long she continued this her accustomed usage without all peril, until at last by reason of his sore leg he waxed sickly, froward, and difficult to be pleased. In the time of his sickness he left his accustomed manner of visiting the queen; therefore she, according as she understood him to be disposed to have her company, would visit him after dinner or after supper, as was most fit for her purpose; at which times she would not fail to use all occasions to move him to proceed in the reformation of the Church. The sharpness of the disease had sharpened the king's patience, so that he began to show some tokens of misliking; and contrary unto his manner, upon a day, breaking off that matter, he took occasion to enter into other talk, which somewhat amazed the queen; notwithstanding in her presence he knit up all arguments with gentle words and loving countenance; and after other pleasant talk she took her leave of his Majesty; who after his manner bidding her 'Farewell, sweetheart,' licensed her to depart.

At this visitation chanced the Bishop of Winchester to be present, and thought that if the iron were beaten whilst it was hot, such misliking might follow towards the queen as might overthrow her and all her endeavours. His expectation did nothing fail him; for the king showed himself no less ready to receive information than the bishop was maliciously bent to stir up the king's indignation against her. The king, immediately upon her departure, used these or like words: 'A good hearing it is when women become clerks; and a thing much to my comfort, to come in mine old days to be taught by my wife.' The bishop hearing this seemed to mislike that the queen should take upon her to stand in argument with his Majesty, whom he extolled for his rare virtues, and especially his judgment in matters of religion; it was unseemly for any of his Majesty's subjects to argue with him so malapertly and grievous to his Majesty's Councillors to hear the same: inferring moreover how perilous it is for a prince to suffer such insolent words at his subjects' hands; who, as they take boldness to contrary their sovereign in words, so want no will but only power to overthwart them in deeds. Besides this, the religion by the queen maintained did not only dissolve the politic government of princes, but also taught the people that all things ought to be in common; their opinions were so odious, and for the prince's estate so perilous, that the greatest subject in this land, defending those arguments that she did defend, had by law deserved death. For his part he would not speak his knowledge in the queen's case—the uttering thereof might through her and her faction be the destruction of him and of such as did chiefly tender the prince's safety—without his Majesty would be their protector; which if he would do, he with other faithful Councillors could disclose such treasons cloaked with this heresy that his Majesty should easily perceive how perilous it is to cherish a serpent within his own bosom. Therewithal with heavy countenance and whispering together with them of that sect there present, he held his peace.

Thus Winchester with flattering words so far crept into the king, and with doubtful fears he with his fellows so filled the king's mistrustful mind, that before they departed the king had given commandment to consult together about the drawing of articles against the queen, wherein her life might be touched, which the king pretended to be fully resolved not to spare. During the time of deliberation they failed not to use all kind of mischievous practices, as well to suborn accusers as to understand what books by law forbidden she had in her closet. They thought it best to begin with some of those ladies whom they knew to be great with her, the chiefest whereof and privy to all her doings were Lady Harbert, sister to the queen and chief of her privy chamber; Lady Lane, of her privy chamber and also her cousin germane; Lady Tyrwit, of her privy chamber and in great favour with her. It was devised that these three should first have been brought to answer unto the Six Articles, and upon their apprehension their closets and coffers should have been searched, that somewhat might have been found whereby the queen might be charged, and carried by barge by night unto the Tower. The king was made privy to the device by Winchester and Wrisley, and his consent demanded; who like a politic prince was contented dissemblingly to give his consent; knowing notwithstanding in the end what he would do. Thus the time and place of these apprehensions was appointed.

The king lay at White Hall and used very seldom, being not well at ease, to stir out of his chamber; and few of his Council but by especial commandment resorted unto him; these only except who by reason of this practice used oftener than of ordinary to repair unto him. This purpose so finely was handled that within few days of the time appointed for execution of the matter the poor queen knew not nor suspected anything at all, and therefore used when she came to visit the king to deal with him touching religion as before. The king gave her leave to utter her mind without contradiction, not to have her speedy dispatch but to try out the uttermost of Winchester's fetches. Thus it chanced that the king, upon a night of her being with him and her leave taken of him, in misliking her religion brake the whole practice unto one of his physicians, Dr Wendy as is supposed, pretending he intended not any longer to be troubled with such a doctress as she was, and declaring what trouble was in working against her by certain enemies, yet charging him upon peril of his life not to utter it to any creature living; and thereupon declared unto him the parties above named, with all circumstances.

The queen all this while perceived nothing of all this, nor what was working against her and what traps were laid for her. But see what the Lord God did for his poor handmaiden, in rescuing her from the pit of ruin whereinto she was ready to fall unawares. For it came to pass that the bill of articles drawn against the queen and subscribed with the king's own hand, although dissemblingly, falling from the bosom of one of the aforesaid Councillors was found and brought to the queen; who reading the articles and perceiving the king's hand unto the same fell incontinent into a great agony, taking on in such sort as was lamentable to see, as certain of her ladies yet alive can testify.

The king hearing what perplexity she was in, almost to the peril of her life, sent his physicians unto her, who did what they could for her recovery. Then Wendy, who knew the case better than the other, for the comforting of her heavy mind began to break with her in secret manner touching the articles devised against her, which he knew to be true; although he stood in danger of his life if ever he were known to utter the same to any living creature. Nevertheless he could not but give her warning of that mischief that hanged over her head, beseeching her to use all secrecy in that behalf; and exhorted her somewhat to conform herself unto the king's mind; if she would do so she should find him favourable unto her. Not long after this the king, hearing of the dangerous state wherein she still remained, came unto her himself; unto whom after she had uttered her grief, fearing lest his Majesty had taken displeasure with her and utterly forsaken her, he, like a loving husband, with comfortable words so refreshed her careful mind that she began somewhat to recover; and the king, after he had tarried there about an hour, departed.

After this the queen, remembering the words that Wendy had said, devised how she might repair to the king's presence. So first commanding her ladies to convey away their books which were against the law, the next night after supper she, waited upon only by Lady Harbert her sister, and Lady Lane, who carried the candle before her, went unto the king's bed-chamber, whom she found talking with certain gentlemen of his chamber; whom when the king did behold, very courteously he welcomed her, and breaking off the talk with the gentlemen began of himself, contrary to his manner before accustomed, to enter into talk of religion, seeming desirous to be resolved by the queen of certain doubts which he propounded. The queen, perceiving to what purpose this talk did tend, with such answers resolved his questions as the time did require, answering again after this manner:

'Where I have with your Majesty's leave been bold to hold talk with your Majesty, I have not done it so much to maintain opinion as to minister talk, not only to the end your Majesty might with less grief pass over this painful time of your infirmity, but also that I, hearing your Majesty's learned discourse, might receive some profit thereof, always referring myself unto your Majesty, as by ordinance of nature it is convenient for me to do.'

'And is it even so, sweetheart?' quoth the king, 'and tended your arguments to no worse end? Then perfect friends we are now again, as ever at any time heretofore.' And as he sat in his chair embracing her in his arms and kissing her, he added this, that it did him more good to hear those words of her own mouth than if he had heard news of an hundred thousand pounds fallen unto him. And with great tokens of joy and liking, with promises never again to mistake her, entering into other very pleasant discourse with the queen and the lords, in the end, being far on the night, he gave her leave to depart; whom, in her absence, to the standers-by he gave as affectuous commendation as beforetime to the bishop and the Chancellor he seemed to mislike of her. Now the king's mind was clean altered, and he detested, as afterwards he plainly showed, this tragical practice of those cruel Cayphases; who, nothing understanding of the king's good disposition towards the queen, were busily occupied about providing for their next day's labour, which was the day determined to have carried the queen to the Tower.

The day and almost the hour being come, the king being disposed in the afternoon to take the air went into the garden, whither the queen also came, being sent for by the king, the three ladies above named waiting upon her; with whom the king disposed himself to be as pleasant as ever he was in all his life; when suddenly in the midst of their mirth in cometh the Lord Chancellor with forty of the king's guards at his heels, with purpose to have taken the queen, together with the three ladies, whom they had before purposed to apprehend alone even then unto the Tower. Whom the king sternly beholding, breaking off his mirth with the queen, stepping a little aside called the Chancellor unto him; who upon his knees spake certain words unto the king. What they were is not well known, but it is most certain that the king's replying unto him was, 'Knave! arrant knave! beast! fool!' With that the king commanded him to avaunt out of his presence. These words were so vehemently whispered out that the queen did easily with her ladies overhear them. Thus departed the Lord Chancellor as he came, with all his train, the whole mode of his device utterly broken.

The king immediately returned to the queen; whom she perceiving to be very much chafed—albeit he enforced himself to put on a merry countenance—with as sweet words as she could utter endeavoured to qualify the king's displeasure, with request unto his Majesty in behalf of the Lord Chancellor. 'Ah, poor soul,' quoth he, 'thou little knowest how evil he deserveth this grace at thy hands. Of my word, sweetheart, he has been towards thee an arrant knave, and so let him go.' To this the queen in charitable manner replying in few words, ended that talk; having for that time and ever escaped the dangerous snares of her cruel enemies for the gospel's sake.

The death of King Henry the Eighth

Thus through the gracious supportation of Christ our Lord we have run over these thirty-seven laborious years of King Henry's reign; under whose governance such acts and records, troubles, persecutions, recantations, practices, alterations, and reformations as then happened in the Church we have here discoursed, with such statutes, injunctions, and proclamations as by him were set forth; not comprehending all things as fully as might be, yet pretermitting so few things as we could of such matters as came to our hands.

I will now proceed to the reign of King Edward his son, after that first I shall intermit a few words touching the death of his father; who after long languishing, infirmity growing more and more upon him, lay from St Steven's Day to the end of January. His physicians at length perceiving that he would away, and yet not daring to discourage him for fear of the act passed in parliament that none should speak of the king's death, moved them that were about the king to put him in remembrance of his mortal state and fatal infirmity; which when the rest were in dread to do Denie, who was specially attendant upon him, boldly coming to the king told him what case he was in, to man's judgment not like to live; and exhorted him to prepare himself to death, calling to remembrance his former life, and to call upon God betime for grace and mercy, as becometh every Christian man to do.

Although the king was loth to hear any mention of death, yet perceiving the same to rise upon the judgment of his physicians and feeling his own weakness, he disposed himself to hearken to his exhortation and to consider his life past; which although he much accused, 'Yet,' said he, 'is the mercy of Christ able to pardon all my sins, though they were greater than they be.' Denie, glad to hear him thus speak, required to know whether he would have any learned men sent for to open his mind unto. The king answered that if he had any he would have Dr Cranmer, then lying at Croydon. Denie asking the king whether he would have him sent for, 'I will first,' said the king, 'take a little sleep; and then as I feel myself I will advise upon the matter.' After an hour or two the king awaking, and feeling feebleness to increase upon him, commanded Cranmer to be sent for; but before he could come the king was speechless and almost senseless. Notwithstanding, perceiving Cranmer to be come, he reaching his hand to Cranmer did hold him fast, but could utter no word and scarce was able to make any sign. The archbishop, exhorting him to put his trust in Christ and call upon his mercy, desired him, though he could not speak, to give some token with his eyes or with his hand that he trusted in the Lord. Then the king did wring his hand in his as hard as he could, and shortly after departed, after he had reigned thirty-seven years and nine months, leaving behind him three children, Edward, Mary, and Elizabeth.

CHAPTER 5

THE BRIEF ASCENDANCY OF CRANMER

KING EDWARD VI

After the death of King Henry succeeded Edward his son, being of the age of nine years. He began his reign the 28th of January 1547; and reigned six years, five months, and nine days; and deceased *an.* 1553, the 6th of July. Of whose excellent virtues and singular graces although nothing can be said enough to his commendation, yet because the fame of such a worthy prince shall not pass our story without some grateful remembrance, I thought in few words to touch some little portion of his praise, taken out of great heaps of matter which might be inferred. For to stand upon all that might be said of him would be too long; and yet to say nothing were too unkind. If princes which have wisely and virtuously governed have found in all ages writers to celebrate their acts and memory, such as never knew them nor were subject unto them, how much are we Englishmen bound not to forget our duty to King Edward; a prince tender in years, yet for his sage and mature ripeness in wit and all princely ornaments, as I see but few to whom he may not be equal, so I see not many to whom he may not justly be preferred.

After the godly disposition of this king briefly declared, we will intermeddle something to describe the order which he followed in his government of both the states, as well politic as especially ecclesiastic; who after the decease of his father coming unto the crown, because he was of tender age he was committed to sixteen governors. Amongst them especially Lord Edward Semer Duke of Somerset, his uncle, was assigned to him as protector of him and of the commonwealth; a man not so highly advanced for his consanguinity as for his noble virtues, and especially for his favour to God's word worthy of his vocation. Through the industry of this man that monstrous hydra with six heads (the Six Articles) which devoured so many men before, was abolished; by reason whereof the counsels of Winchester began to decay; who storming at the matter wrote to the Lord Protector in the cause thereof, as by his letters is to be seen.

The Holy Scriptures he restored to the mother tongue; masses he extinguished. Furthermore after softer beginnings by little and little greater things followed in the reformation of the churches. Such as were in banishment for the danger of the truth were again received to their country. To be short, a new face of things began now to appear, as it were in a stage, new players coming in, the old being thrust out; for the most part the bishops were changed; such as had been dumb prelates before were compelled to give place to others that would preach and take pains. Besides others out of foreign countries men of notable knowledge were sent for, among whom was Peter Martyr, Martin Bucer, and Paulus Phagius; of whom the first taught at Oxford, the other two professed at Cambridge, and that with no small commendation of the whole university. Of the old bishops some were committed to one ward, some to another. Boner, Bishop of London, was committed to the Marshalsea, and eftsoons for contempt and misdemeanour deposed from his bishopric, as in further process followeth to be seen. Gardiner, Bishop of Winchester, with Tonstall Bishop of Duresme, was cast into the Tower for his disobedience, where he kept Christmas three years together; more worthy of some other place without the Tower, if it had pleased God not to have meant a further plague to this realm by that man.

But those gentle times of King Edward, under the government of this noble Protector, have this one commendation proper unto them, that amongst the whole number of this popish sort, of whom some privily did steal out of the realm, many were crafty dissemblers, some were open adversaries, not one man lost his life. In sum, during the whole time of this king much tranquillity and as it were a breathing time was granted to the whole Church of England; so that the rage of persecution ceasing and the sword taken out of the adversary's hand, there was now no danger to the godly, unless it were by wealth and prosperity, which many times bringeth more damage in corrupting men's minds than any time of persecution or affliction. Briefly, during all this time, neither in Smithfield nor any other quarter of this realm any was heard to suffer for religion, either Papist or Protestant, except only two, one an English woman called Joan of Kent, and the other a Dutchman named George, who died for articles not much necessary here to be rehearsed.

Matter concerning Edmund Boner Bishop of London

Now, forsomuch as we have to enter into the story of Boner, for the better understanding of the whole order thereof it shall be requisite to rip up the matter from the beginning of King Edward's time. King Edward in the first year of his reign, 1547, the 1st of September for the order of his visitation directed out commissioners, who sitting in Paul's Church, there being present Edmund Bishop of London, Polydore Virgil, and others of the Cathedral Church, after the sermon made and the commission read ministered an oath unto the bishop to renounce the Bishop of Rome with his usurped authority and to swear obedience unto the king, according to the statute made in the 31st year of King Henry VIII; also that he should redress all such things as were needful within the said church to be reformed. The bishop desired that he might see their commission, only, as he said, that he might the better put in execution the things wherein he was charged by them. The commissioners said they would deliberate more upon the matter; and so they called the other ministers of the church before them and ministered the like oath unto them. Which done, the commissioners delivered unto the bishop injunctions and homilies set forth by the king, which the bishop received under this protestation, 'I will observe them if they be not repugnant to God's law and the statutes and ordinance of the Church'; and added with an oath that he never read the homilies and injunctions.

Which protestation made, Boner required Peter Lilly the register to register and enact the same. So the commissioners, delivering the injunctions and the homilies to Mr Bellassere, Archdeacon of Colchester, and Gilbert Bourne, Archdeacon of London, Essex, and Middlesex, and enjoining them under pains therein contained to put the same in speedy execution, did continue the visitation till three o'clock. At which hour the commissioners being set, and the canons and priests of the said church appearing before them and being examined upon oath for their doctrine and conversation; first John Painter, one of the canons, openly confessed that he viciously and carnally had often the company of a certain man's wife; in which crime divers other canons and priests confessed in like manner, and could not deny themselves to be culpable. After the commissioners had delivered to Mr Royston, prebendary, and to the proctor of the Dean and Chapter, the king's injunctions and homilies, they prorogued their visitation until seven.

By this visitation it appeareth, gentle reader, how Boner made his protestation and how he required the same to be put in public record. Furthermore thou hast to note the unchaste conversation of these popish votaries. What followed their protestation remaineth to be declared; wherein first thou shalt understand that the bishop shortly after his protestation went unto the king, where he submitted himself, and recanting his protestation craved pardon for his inordinate demeanour towards his Grace's commissioners; which pardon, notwithstanding it was granted unto him for the acknowledging of his fault, yet for the evil example of the fact it was thought good that he should be committed to the Fleet; where he did not long continue, but was restored to house and living in the first year of the king. In a second and a great part of the third he demeaned himself—although not forward in advancing the king's proceedings, yet in such sort as no great advantage by any law could be taken against him—both in swearing obedience to the king and in receiving his injunctions; also in professing his assent touching the state of religion then, and in directing letters according to the archbishop's precepts to his sumner, to the Bishop of Westminster and other bishops, for abolishing images, for abrogation of the mass, for bibles to be set up, and for ministering in both kinds; till he, hearing of the death of the Lord Admiral, the Lord Protector's brother, and of the rising of the king's subjects in sundry tumults, began as he durst to slack his pastoral diligence, so that in many places of his diocese the people not only were negligent in resorting to divine service but also did frequent foreign rites of masses and other orders than in this realm appointed; and he himself, contrary to his wonted manner, upon principal feasts refused in his own person to execute.

This disobedient dealing, as it greatly offended most of the king's loving subjects, so did it much mislike the minds, as well of that faithful preacher John Hooper, afterwards Bishop of Worcester and Gloucester, as of William Latimer, Bachelor of Divinity: they did thereupon exhibit unto the king a bill of denunciation against the bishop. The king, having thus intelligence of the contemptuous negligence of this bishop, thought it necessary to look severely unto the punishment of such dangerous obstinacy, and by the advice of the Lord Protector and the rest of his Council directed his commission under his broad seal unto the Archbishop of Canturbury, the Bishop of Rochester, and other Councillors, authorizing them to call before them the Bishop of London as also the aforesaid denouncers, and upon due examination to proceed against him summarily according to law either to suspension, excommunication, prison, or deprivation; or to use any censure ecclesiastical which might to their wisdoms seem more pertinent.

Upon Wednesday the 10th of September 1549, in the third year of King Edward VI, Thomas Cranmer Archbishop of Canturbury, with Nicholas Ridley Bishop of Rochester, Sir William Peter (one of the king's principal secretaries), and William May, Doctor of Civil Law and Dean of Paul's, sat judicially upon Edmund Boner Bishop of London, within the archbishop's Chamber of Presence at his house in Lambeth. The commissioners, showing their commission, requested Sir William that he would openly read the same. Which done, the archbishop in the name of the rest declared unto the bishop that complaint had been made against him in writing unto the King's Majesty and his honourable Council, and that his Highness had committed the examination thereof unto him and his colleagues there present, as also unto Sir Thomas Smith, the other of his Majesty's principal secretaries, though then absent; and therewithal showed a bill of complaint exhibited unto the king by William Latimer and John Hooper, ministers, which they likewise requested Sir William to read. These things ended, the bishop pulled out of his bosom a protestation ready written, which he exhibited unto the commissioners, requesting that the same might be openly read. This protestation read, he requested the commissioners that he might have the bill of complaint delivered him; which when he had perused, he said that the same was so general that he could not directly answer thereunto. The archbishop answered that the special complaint against him was that he had transgressed the king's commandment in that he in his sermon at Paul's Cross did not set forth unto the people the king's royal power in his minority, according to the article delivered unto him for that purpose; and for proof thereof called Latimer and Hooper. The bishop said, 'As for this merchant Latimer, I know him very well and have borne with him and winked at his evil doings a great while. As touching this other merchant Hooper, I have not seen him before; howbeit I have heard much of his naughty preaching.' Then turning to the archbishop he required to have a copy of the commission and the denunciation, with time to answer thereunto; which the commissioners granted, assigning him to appear again before them upon Friday next, to answer the denunciation.

Upon Friday the 13th September four commissioners, with Sir Thomas Smith, the other of the king's principal secretaries, sat judicially in the archbishop's chapel; before whom appeared the Bishop of London. The archbishop first said, 'My Lord of London, the last time you were before us we laid certain articles to your charge touching your disobedience to the King's Majesty, and you have this day to make your answer thereunto; wherefore now show us what you have to say for your defence.' The bishop made answer, 'My Lord, the last day that I appeared before you there sat in the king's commission your Grace, my Lord of Rochester, Mr Secretary Peter, and Mr Dean of Paul's; now, I perceive, there sitteth also Mr Secretary Smith, who because he sat not at the beginning ought not so to do; for by the law they which begin must continue the commission.' The archbishop answered that he was no lawyer; 'But,' said he, 'if the law be so indeed I take it to be unreasonable.' 'Well,' said the bishop, 'there be here that knoweth the law; and yet I say not this to the intent to stick much in this point, but to tell it you by the way; for I have here mine answer ready.'

Then said Peter, 'My Lord, in good sooth although I have professed the law, yet by disuse thereof, and having been occupied a long time in other matters, I have perhaps forgotten what the law will do precisely in this point. But admit the law were so as you say, yet yourself knoweth that this is our certain rule in law, *quod consuetudo est juris interpres optimus*; and I am sure you will not deny that the custom is commonly in this realm in all judgments and commissions used to the contrary; and in very deed we all together at the Court, having the commission presented unto us, take it upon us; and therefore for you to stick in such trifling matters you shall rather in my judgment hurt yourself than otherwise.' 'Truly, Mr Secretary,' said the bishop, 'I have also of long while been disused in the study of law, but having occasion to turn my books I find the law to be as I say; yet, as I said, I tell you hereof but by the way.'

At which words Smith said, 'Well, my Lord, as cunning as you make yourself in the law, there be here that knoweth the law as well as you; for my part I have studied the law too and I promise you these be but quiddities and quirks invented to delay matters; but our commission is to proceed summarily and *de plano*, and to cut off such frivolous allegations.' 'Well,' said the bishop, 'look well on your commission and you shall find these words, "To proceed according to law and justice," and I ask both law and justice at your hands.'

Then Mr Secretary Peter willed him to stand no more thereupon but to proceed unto his answer; whereupon he took forth a writing wherein was contained his answer to the denunciation exhibited by Latimer and Hooper, and delivering it unto the archbishop said that it was of his own handwriting, and for lack of sufficient time written so hastily that it could scarcely be read of any other, and therefore he desired to read it himself; and so taking it again read it openly. Wherein he alleged that his denouncers were vile, infamed, and notorious criminous persons, and also open and manifest heretics; and were for the same excommunicated and accursed, and were so taken of all the Catholics of this realm, and especially Hooper, who besides other his poisoned doctrines among the people had also, before the denunciation, made divers heretical books against the true presence of Christ's body in the sacrament of the altar; which books and doctrine William Latimer had and then likewise did allow, believe, and teach, to the loss of both their own souls and their believers'; and therefore were not now nor ought at any time to be admitted either in this their denunciation against him or in any other judicial act.

Monday the 16th the archbishop, with the Bishop of Rochester, Secretary Smith, and Dr May, sat judicially within his chapel at Lambeth; before whom appeared the Bishop of London. He exhibited in writing his answers unto the last former articles. But before the same were read the archbishop said that his late answers unto the denunciation were very obscure, and contained much slander against Latimer and Hooper, and much untruth. With this the bishop, in a raging heat, turned himself about unto the people, saying, 'Now hear what the Bishop of London saith for his part.' But the commissioners, seeing his inordinate contumacy, denied him to speak any more. And so, he still protesting of the invalidity of their proceedings, they did for that present depart. It was assigned that upon Monday following, being the 23rd of the month, the bishop should again appear before the commissioners, to show final cause why he should not be declared *pro confesso* upon the articles whereunto he had not fully answered.

The 23rd of September the bishop was brought before them by the undermarshal, to whom for his disobedient behaviour he was before committed, and there did first declare that his appearance was not voluntary but coacted; and therewith did again intimate a general recusation of all the commissioners, alleging that the archbishop with his colleagues had neither observed the order of their commission nor yet proceeded against him after any laudable fashion, but contrariwise had attempted many things unlawfully against his person, dignity, and estate, especially in committing him to strait prison and yet commanding him to make answer. Therefore he intended to submit himself under the protection of the King's Majesty. Notwithstanding the archbishop with the rest told him plain that they would be still his judges and proceed against him according to the king's commission until they did receive a *supersedeas*, which if he did obtain they would gladly obey. The bishop said that he would stand unto his recusations and appellations before made, and would not make other answer. Whereupon the archbishop pronounced him *contumax*, and in pain thereof declared him *pro confesso*.

Upon the first of October the bishop appearing before them, the commissioners determined that the archbishop should at that present read and publish their sentence definitive against him; which he did, pronouncing him to be deprived from the bishopric of London; which ended, the bishop did therefrom appeal by word of mouth, alleging that the sentence was *lex nulla*; the tenor of whose words I thought here to express, as they were by him uttered:

'I Edmund Bishop of London do, under my former protestation heretofore made, and to the intent it may also appear that I have not consented or agreed to anything done against me and in my prejudice, allege and say that this sentence given here against me is *lex nulla*; and so far forth as it shall appear to be *aliqua*, I do say it is *iniqua* and *injusta*, and that therefore I do from it, as *iniqua* and *injusta*, appeal to the most excellent and noble King Edward VI, by the grace of God King of England, France, and Ireland, Defender of the Faith and of the Church of England (next under God here on earth) supreme Head.'

Thereupon they committed him again to his keeper in prison, where he remained till the death of King Edward VI; after which he wrought most horrible mischief and cruelties against the saints of God, as appeareth hereafter, throughout the whole reign of Queen Mary. This done, and the supplication perused, the king eftsoons giveth commandment to certain men of honour and worship, and persons skilful in the law, that they, perusing all such acts and muniments of Boner by him exhibited and alleged, with all his protestations, recusations, and appellations, should upon mature consideration thereof give their direct answer whether the appellation of Boner were to be deferred unto, and whether the sentence defined against him stood by the law sufficient and effectual, or not: who after diligent discussion and considerate advisement of all the premises gave their resolute answer, that the appellation of Edmund Boner was naught and unreasonable, and that the sentence by the commissioners was rightly and justly pronounced.

Thus then leaving Boner in the Marshalsea with his keeper, we will proceed further in the course of our story, as the order of time requireth, and although the trouble of the Lord Protector falleth here jointly with the deprivation of Dr Boner, yet because he was shortly delivered out of the same, I will delay the tractation thereof till the time of his second trouble, which was two years after; and so in the meantime returning into our discourse, intend by the Lord's leave to continue the matters begun touching the king's proceedings for reformation of religion in the foresaid year, 1549.

It followeth then in story that certain of the vulgar multitude, hearing of the apprehension of the Lord Protector, and supposing the alteration of public service into English, and administration of the sacrament and other rites lately appointed in the Church, had been the act only of the Lord Protector, began to noise abroad that they should now have their old Latin service, with holy bread and holy water, and other superstitious ceremonies; whereupon the king directed strait commandment to the bishops to warn prebendaries, vicars, and curates, with the churchwardens of every parish, to bring in all antiphoners, missals, grails, manuals, legends, pixes, portuasses, journals, and ordinals. In the year following other letters were sent out, for the taking down of altars in churches and setting up the table instead, unto Nicholas Ridley, who being Bishop of Rochester before was then made Bishop of London in Boner's place.

The story of Stephen Gardiner

Although the first imprisonment of Stephen Gardiner, Bishop of Winchester, was before the deprivation of Bishop Boner, yet forsomuch as he was not deposed from his bishopric till the second year after, which was 1551, I have driven off the history of the Bishop of Winchester to this present place, intending not to extend the explication of the matter so amply as I might, partly for that being done in my first volume of Acts and Monuments may here suffice the reader, being disposed there to search and further to read, partly considering how this present volume is grown already very large, I thought not to pester the same with any more superfluity than needs must. Therefore I mind here to excerp only the principal effects. Briefly therefore we will set before the reader the evidence against the bishop, wherein in brief sum is described the whole manner of his misordered demeanour, copied out of public records.

'Whereas the King's Majesty did about ten months past address forth commissions, and appointed injunctions to be generally observed; which being such as touched the reformation of many abuses and concerned the quiet of the realm, were of all men obediently received and reverently observed and executed, saving only of the Bishop of Winchester, who showed such wilful disobedience as might have bred much unquietness: he being sent for and his lewd proceedings laid to his charge in the presence of the whole Council so used himself as he was thought worthy most sharp punishment; yet he was only sequestered to the Fleet, where after he had remained a certain time as much at his ease as if he had been at his own house, upon his promise of conformity he was set at liberty and licensed to remain in his diocese. Where forgetting his promise he began forthwith to set forth such matters as bred more strife and contention in that one small shire than was almost in the whole realm. Wherefore being admonished by his Grace and their Lordships he did not only promise to conform in all things like a good subject, but offered to declare to the world his conformity, and promised in an open sermon so to open his mind in sundry articles agreed upon that such as had been offended should be well satisfied. Notwithstanding at the day appointed he did not only most arrogantly, and that in the presence of his Majesty, speak contrary to an express commandment given to him on his Majesty's behalf, but also used such a manner of utterance as was like to have stirred a great tumult, and showed himself very seditious. Forsomuch as these proceedings might breed innumerable inconveniences, it was determined by their Grace and Lordships that he should be committed to the Tower.'

Certain of the Council by the king's appointment had access to him in the Tower to persuade with him; which were these—the Duke of Somerset, the Lord Treasurer, the Lord Privy Seal, the Lord Great Chamberlain, and Mr Secretary Peter. These articles also were delivered to the bishop:

'Whereas I Stephen Bishop of Winchester, having certain things appointed for me to do and preach, have not done that as I ought to do, although I promised to do the same; I am right sorry therefore, and do most heartily thank his Majesty that of his great clemency it hath pleased his Highness to deal with me not according to rigour but mercy. And I affirm of mine own will, without any compulsion, as ensueth:

1. The king and his successors are the supreme heads of the Churches of England and Ireland.
2. The appointing of holy days and fasting days or to dispense therewith is in the king's authority.
3. The king hath most Christianly set forth with the consent of the whole parliament a devout book of service, which is to be accepted of all bishops and ministers and observed of all the king's subjects.
4. I acknowledge the king to be my sovereign Lord, and in this his tender age to be my entire king. I and all other subjects are bound to obey all his laws and commandments, as though his Highness were thirty or forty years old.
5. I acknowledge that the Statute of the Six Articles for just causes is by authority of parliament repealed.
6. His Majesty and his successors have authority to alter all abuses and all ceremonies as shall seem most convenient for the edification of the people; so that the alteration be not contrary to the law of God.'

To these articles although Winchester with his own hand did subscribe, yet because he stuck in the first point touching his submission, it was thought good to the king that the Master of the Horse and Mr Secretary Peter should repair unto him again with the same request of submission; and in case the words seemed too sore, to refer it unto himself with what words he should devise to submit him, that upon the acknowledgment of his fault the king might extend his mercy towards him. When the Master of the Horse and Secretary Peter had been with him in the Tower according to their commission, returning from him again they declared unto the king and his Council how precisely the bishop stood in justification of himself, that he had never offended the King's Majesty; wherefore he utterly refused to make any submission at all. Whereupon it was agreed that he should be sent for and examined once again, whether he would stand at this point or no. Which if he did, then to denounce unto him the sequestration of his benefice and consequently the intimation, in case he were not reformed within three months; as in the day of his appearance shall appear. After this sequestration the bishop was convented unto Lambeth before the Archbishop of Canturbury and other the king's commissioners, by them to be examined; by whom were objected against him nineteen special articles.

After these articles were exhibited unto him, and he having leave to say for himself, wherein he used all the cautels, shifts, and remedies of the law to his most advantage, by protesting, recusing, and excepting against the commission, and requiring the copies, as well of the articles as of his protestation, of the actuaries, W. Say and Thomas Argall, time was assigned unto him to answer the articles in writing. But he so cavilled and dallied from day to day to answer directly, although he was sufficiently laboured and persuaded to the same by sundry callings and acts, and abundantly convicted by depositions and witnesses, especially by matter induced by Lord Paget, Andrew Beynton, and Mr Chalenor (all which I refer to in my first book) that at last he appealed from them—reputing them not to be competent and indifferent judges to determine his cause—unto the king's royal person, always reserving to himself the benefit of his appellation. So proceeded he to the answering of the foresaid articles, but in such crafty and obstinate manner as before he had been accustomed. Briefly to conclude, such exceptions he used against the witnesses produced against him, and he himself produced such a number of witnesses in his defence, and used so many delays and cavillations, that in the end the commissioners, seeing his stubbornness, proceeded to the sentence definitive against him, as followeth:

'We Thomas Archbishop of Canturbury, Primate of all England and Metropolitan, with the Right Reverend Fathers in God Nicholas Bishop of London, Thomas Bishop of Ely, and Henry Bishop of Lincoln, William Peter, knight, James Hales, knight, Griffith Leison and John Oliver, Doctors of Civil Law, Richard Goodrick and John Gosnold, esquires, judges appointed and lawfully proceeding in the presence of you, Stephen Bishop of Winchester, do proceed to our final judgment in the manner following.

'Forasmuch as we find that you have of long time notwithstanding many admonitions remained a person much grudging, speaking against the godly reformations of abuses set forth by the king's authority, and forasmuch as you contemptuously refuse to recognise your notorious misbehaviours and disobediences, remaining incorrigible and without hope of amendment, contrary both to your oath and also your bounden duty of allegiance; we judge and determine you to be removed from the bishopric of Winchester, and from all rights, emoluments, and other appurtenances to the said bishopric belonging; and declare the said bishopric void.'

This sentence definitive being given, the bishop dissented from the same as unjust of no efficacy or effect in law; and in that the same containeth excessive punishment, and for other causes expressed in his appellation, he did then and there by word of mouth appeal to the King's Majesty, first, secondly, and thirdly, instantly, more instantly, most instantly; and asked apostles or letters dimissorials to be given unto him, and also a copy of the sentence; the judges declaring that they would first know the king's pleasure.

And thus an end of Winchester for a while, till we come to talk of his death hereafter; whom as we number among good lawyers, so is he to be reckoned amongst ignorant divines, proud prelates, and bloody persecutors, as both by his cruel life and pharisaical doctrine may appear, especially in the article of the sacrament, and of our justification, and images, and also in crying out of the Paraphrase, not considering in whose person the things be spoken; but what the paraphrast uttereth in the person of Christ or of the evangelist, and not in his own, that he wresteth unto the author and maketh thereof heresy and abomination.

The tragical history of the Lord Protector

After so many troublous matters in this history aforepassed, coming now to the lamentable narration of Lord Edward Duke of Somerset, the king's uncle and protector of his person and his realm, I could not well enter into the story without some premonition first to all noble personages within this realm, briefly to admonish them, no man to plant any trust upon the brickle pillars of worldly prosperity, how high soever it seemeth, considering that there is no state so high but it hath his ruin; no wisdom so circumspect but it may be circumvented; no virtue so perfect but it may be envied; neither any man's trade so simple but it may be beguiled. Therefore seeing that no man can always stand in this so ruinous a world, the surest way is for every man to choose his standing so, that his fall may be the easier. But because my purpose is to abridge and make short, I will here stay; and falling into the story of the Lord Protector will declare the occasion of his trouble from the beginning.

King Edward had three uncles by his mother's side, Edward, Thomas, and Henry Semer: of the two first, one was made Protector, the other High Admiral. These two, so long as they were knit together in amity, preserved themselves, their nephew, and the commonwealth from all danger. But the subtle old serpent sought to sow matter first of discord between them, then of suspicion, last of all extreme hatred; insomuch that the Protector suffered his brother being accused to be condemned and to lose his head. Whereby it came to pass that not long after he was overthrown of his enemies and cast into the Tower, and at last lost his head also, to the lamentation of many good men, as in the sequel of this history followeth to be declared. To begin with Sir Thomas, here is to be understood that he had married Queen Katherine, late wife to King Henry VIII. Now it happened that there fell a displeasure betwixt the Queen and the Duchess of Somerset, and thereupon in behalf of their wives grudge began between the brethren, to the trouble of the realm and the confusion of them both. First to the Lord Admiral's charge it was laid that he purposed to destroy the young king and translate the crown unto himself; and for the same being attainted and condemned, did suffer at Tower Hill the 20th of March 1549. Many reported that the duchess had wrought his death: many moe affirmed that the fall of the one brother would be the ruin of the other; the experiment whereof eftsoons ensued.

After the beheading of the Lord Admiral insurrections began to kindle the same year in divers quarters of the realm; by occasion whereof Lord Russell was sent to the west parts and Lord Dudley Earl of Warwick was sent with an army into Norfolk, where he and a great number of gentlemen meeting the rebels were in great danger. In the end the overthrow was given to the rebels about the beginning of September 1549. In October how the matter fell out between the Lord Protector and certain other lords I know not, but at the return of the Earl of Warwick great consultation there was among the lords against the Lord Protector. When the king with his Council at Hampton Court heard thereof, Secretary Peter with the king's message was sent unto them; whom the lords detained, making no answer to the message. The reasonable condition of the Lord Protector not much regarded of the lords, they persisting in their purpose took this advice, to keep themselves in the City of London, as strong as they might; and calling upon the mayor and aldermen, they willed them to provide a substantial watch by night and a good ward by day for the safeguard of their city; which was consented unto, and the companies of London in their turns warned to watch and ward.

Then the lords demanded 500 men to aid them to fetch the Lord

Protector out of Windsor; but the mayor answered that he could grant none aid without the assent of the common council of the city; whereupon the next day a common council was warned. Meanwhile the Lords of the Council assembled themselves at the Lord Mayor's house, and there did agree and publish a proclamation forthwith, the effect of which was that the Lord Protector was a great traitor. The lords came the next day to the Guild Hall and communed a long while with the mayor. At last the mayor came forth to the common council, where was read the king's letter to the mayor and citizens, commanding them to aid him with a thousand well appointed men out of their city, and to send the same with all speed to his castle at Windsor. This letter was not so secretly devised but the Lords had knowledge immediately thereof; who forthwith addressed their letters in semblable wise to the Lord Mayor and aldermen in the king's name, not only for a supportation of armed men to serve their purposes, but that they should not obey any injunctions from the duke. After receiving these two letters, one from the king, the other from the lords, which came both at one instant with contrary commandment to the Lord Mayor and citizens, the case seemed hard to them what way to take. On one side the authority of the king was much; on the other the power and garrisons of the lords lying then in London was not little.

The case thus standing perplexedly, by the mouth of the Recorder it was requested that the citizens would grant their aid unto the lords, for that the Protector had abused the King's Majesty and the whole realm; and that without he were taken from the king and made to understand his folly this realm was in great hazard; and therefore required that the citizens would aid the lords with 500 men. Hereunto of a great part in the common council was no other answer made but silence; but the Recorder still cried upon them for answer. At last stepped up a wise and good citizen named George Stadlowe and said, 'In the time of King Henry the Third the barons, as our lords do now, demanded aid of the City of London, and that in a rightful cause. The city did aid them, and it came to an open battle, and the lords took the king and his son prisoners. Upon certain conditions the lords restored the king and his son to their liberties, and among all conditions this was one, that the king should pardon the citizens of London; the which was granted. But what followed? The liberties of the city were taken away and the citizens miserably afflicted. Such a thing is it to enter into the wrath of a prince. Wherefore forasmuch as this aid is required of the king, whose voice we ought to hearken unto rather than unto the lords—and yet I would not wish the lords to be clearly shaken off—my counsel is that they and we join in suit and make our humble petition to the king, that it may please his Highness to hear such complaint against the government of the Lord Protector as may be justly alleged and proved; and I doubt not but this matter will be so pacified that neither shall the king nor the lords have cause to seek for further aid, neither we to offend any of them both.'

After this tale the commons stayed, and the Lord Mayor and his brethren brake up till they had further communed with the lords. The conclusion was that the Lords sat next day in the Star Chamber and from thence sent Sir Philip Hobby with their letter of credence to the king, requesting his Majesty to give credit to that which Sir Philip should declare in their name. The king gave him liberty to speak and most gently heard all that he had to say; who so handled the matter that in the end the Lord Protector was commanded from the king's presence and shortly was committed to ward in a tower within the Castle of Windsor called Bewchamp Tower; and soon after were stayed many gentlemen that attended upon the Lord Protector. The same day the Lords of the Council resorted to the king: the next day they brought from thence the Lord Protector and the other that were there stayed, and conveyed them through the City of London unto the Tower, and there charged the Lord Protector with sundry articles. Yet the Lord above so ordered the matter by means of the king labouring for his uncle that in short while he was let out of the Tower and the proclamation which had made him a traitor within three days was called in again. So the Duke of Somerset was restored, though not to the former office, yet unto liberty, wherein he continued two years and two days. After which time the Duke was apprehended and committed again to the Tower. At length the time being come of his arraignment the good Duke, being brought from the Tower, was conveyed through London with the axe before him, and with great preparance of bills, halberds, pikes, and polaxes in most forcible wise; a watch also set before every man's door through the high street of London. So was he brought into Westminster Hall, where the Lords of the Council, sitting as his judges upon a new scaffold, he was before them arraigned and charged both with treason and felony.

I pass over the vile taunts, without modesty or honesty, used by certain of the sergeants and justices, and other sitting there. All which he patiently did suffer, neither storming inwardly nor reviling them with words, but contented to take all things at their hands, and with no less patience bare now their cruel railings than he did before their glavering words and flattering in time of his prosperity. And as the patience of this good duke was marvellous in forbearing his enemies, so was his temperance no less seen in answering the articles to him objected; whereunto he wisely and substantially replied, putting himself in the end to be tried by his peers; who after consultation did frame their verdict thus: of treason they discharged him, but they accounted him guilty of felony. When the people, which were present to a great number, heard the lords say 'Not guilty' (meaning by the case of treason), supposing that he had been clearly acquitted and seeing the axe carried away, for joy they made an outcry, declaring their affection and favour unto the duke, whose life they greatly desired. But this opinion of the people was deceived, and the innocent duke condemned to die for felony; which Act of Felony had been made a little before against rebels and unlawful assemblies, such as should seek the death of any Councillor. By virtue of which act the duke being accused to purpose the death of the Duke of Northumberland, was condemned of felony, and so was returned towards the Tower; at whose passage through the city great outcries were made again of the people. Thus the good duke, landing at the Crane of the Vinetrie, was conveyed to the Tower where he endured till the 22nd of January; upon which day, at the coming down of the letter of execution from the King and the Council, the duke was delivered unto the sheriffs and brought to the place of execution.

Touching which execution a few words here would be bestowed in describing the wonderful manner thereof, as it hath faithfully been suggested to us upon the credit of a certain noble personage, who not only was present at the deed doing but next unto him upon the scaffold, beholding all things with his eyes, and with his pen reporting the same as here followeth.

'In the year of our Lord 1552, the 22nd of January, in the sixth year of the reign of King Edward VI, the noble Duke of Somerset was brought out of the Tower of London and delivered to the sheriffs of the city, and compassed about with a great number of armed men was brought unto the scaffold on Tower Hill, where he, nothing changing neither voice nor countenance, kneeling down and lifting up his hands commended himself unto God. Standing up again and turning himself towards the east side of the scaffold, nothing abashed with the sight of the axe, but with the like cheerfulness as beforetimes he was accustomed to hear the causes of other, he uttered these words to the people: "Dearly beloved friends, I am brought hither to suffer death, albeit that I never offended against the king neither by word nor deed. But I willingly offer myself, with hearty thanks unto God that hath given me this time of repentance, who might through sudden death have taken away my life, that neither I should have acknowledged him nor myself. Moreover there is somewhat that I must put you in mind of touching Christian religion, which I always furthered to my power. Neither I repent me of my doings but rejoice therein, sith now the state of religion cometh most near unto the order of the primitive Church. Which thing I esteem as a great benefit given of God, exhorting you all that this which is most purely set forth unto you you will with thankfulness embrace, and set out the same in your living. Which if you do not, without doubt calamity will follow."

'When he had spoken, suddenly there was a terrible noise heard, as it had been the noise of some tempest, which unto some seemed to be heard from above; as if a great deal of gunpowder, enclosed in an armoury and having caught fire, had violently broken out. Unto some again it seemed as though it had been a great multitude of horsemen coming upon them, albeit they saw nothing. Thereby it happened that they ran away, some into the ditches and puddles, some into the houses thereabouts; other some fell grovelling unto the ground with their polaxes and halberds; and most of them cried out, "Jesus save us." Those which tarried in their places know not where they were, and I myself, being also afraid in this hurly-burly, stood still altogether amazed, looking when any man would knock me on the head. It happened here as the evangelists write it did unto Christ, when the officers of the high priests and pharisees, coming with weapons to take him, being astonied ran backward and fell to the ground.

'Meantime the people spied Sir Anthony Browne riding unto the scaffold; which was the occasion of a new noise. For when they saw him coming they conjectured that which was not true but which they all wished for, that the king by that messenger had sent his uncle pardon; and casting up their caps they cried, "Pardon, pardon is come; God save the king!" Thus this good duke, although destitute of all man's help, saw before his departure in how great love and favour he was with all men. And truly I do not think that in so great slaughter of dukes as hath been in England within these few years there was so many weeping eyes at one time, and not without cause. For all men did see in the decay of this duke the ruin of all England, except such as indeed did perceive nothing.

'The duke meantime standing still in the same place made a sign to the people that they would keep themselves quiet. Silence obtained, he spake unto them in this manner, "Friends, there is no such matter here as you vainly hope. Wherefore I pray you to be contented with my death, which I am most willing to suffer. Let us join in prayer for the preservation of the King's Majesty, unto whom I have showed myself a faithful subject. I have always been diligent in his affairs at home and abroad, and no less diligent in seeking the common commodity of the whole realm." At which words all the people cried out it was most true.

'Then the duke proceeding said, "If there be any that hath been offended by me, I humbly ask him forgiveness, but especially Almighty God, whom all my life I have most grievously offended; and all that have offended me I do with my whole heart forgive. Now I once again require you that you will keep yourselves quiet and still, lest through your tumult you might trouble me. For albeit the spirit be willing and ready, the flesh is frail and wavering, and through your quietness I shall be much quieter. Moreover I desire you all to bear me witness that I die in the faith of Jesus Christ, desiring you to help me with your prayers, that I may persever constant in the same unto my life's end."

'After this he kneeled down. Then Dr Cox, which was there to counsel him, delivered a scroll into his hand, wherein was contained a brief confession unto God. Which being read, he stood up again, and first bade the sheriffs farewell, then the Lieutenant of the Tower, and other, taking them all by the hand which were upon the scaffold with him. Then he gave the hangman money. Which done, he put off his gown and kneeling down again in the straw untied his shirt-strings. After that the hangman turned down his collar about his neck, and all other things which did hinder him. Then covering his face with his own handkercher he laid himself down along, showing no token of fear, neither did his countenance change, but that before his eyes were covered there began to appear a red colour in the midst of his cheeks. Because his doublet covered his neck, he was commanded to rise and put it off; then laying himself down again upon the block and calling thrice, "Lord Jesu save me," as he was the third time repeating the same, even as the name of Jesu was in uttering, in a moment he was bereft both of head and life, and slept in the Lord Jesus.'

Thus, gentle reader, thou hast here the true history of this worthy and noble duke, and if any man report it otherwise, let it be counted as a lie.

Touching the life and conversation of the duke what shall we need to speak, when he cannot be sufficiently commended according to the dignity of his virtues? There was in him great humanity, and such meekness as is rare in so high estate. He was ready to give ear to the complaints of the poor, and no less attentive unto the affairs of the commonwealth. Which if he had lived together with King Edward, was like to do much good in reforming many misorders within this realm. He was ignorant of all craft and deceit, and as far void of pride and ambition as he was from doing of injury. He was of a gentle disposition, not coveting to be revenged; more apt to be deceived than to deceive. His ancient love of the gospel and of religion he brought with him to the state of this his dignity. The proof whereof was seen in his constant standing to God's truth and zealous defence thereof against the Bishops of Chichester, Norwich, Lincoln, London, and others moe. As he was a courteous duke at home, so was he no less fortunate a captain in warfare abroad; under whose guiding not only divers rebellious commotions were happily suppressed here at home, but in Scotland such a victory was given him of God that with the loss scarce of six hundred of his own men there were of the enemies little less than ten thousand slain and put to flight, the very same day in which all the idolatrous images were here burnt at London. Yet he was a man of nature singularly given to peace, as may be seen by the sweet and peaceable exhortation by him set forth and sent to the realm of Scotland.

But as there is nothing in this world so perfect which is not blotted with some spot of vice, so amongst the manifold commendations of this duke one thing there was which both distained his honour and impaired his safety; which was that he in condescending to the death of his brother followed too rashly the persuasion of some more craftily than godly disposed persons. Credible it is that the duke, in suffering or procuring the death of his brother, not only endamaged himself and weakened his own power, but provoked the chastisement of God's scourge which did so light upon him.

The decease of King Edward VI

Thus having discoursed things done under the reign of King Edward, such as seemed not unfruitful to be known, we will now draw to the end and death of this blessed king, our young Josias; who about a year and a half after the death of the Duke of Somerset his uncle, in 1553 entering into the seventeenth year of his age and the 7th of his reign, in the month of June[1] was taken from us, for our sins no doubt; whom if it had so pleased the Lord to have spared with longer life, not unlike it was but proceeding as he began he would have reformed such a commonwealth here in the realm of England as by good cause it might have been said of him that was said of the noble Emperor Augustus, in reforming the empire of Rome, 'which empire he received, he said, of brick, but he left it of fine marble.' But the condition of this realm and the customable behaviour of English people, whose property is commonly to abuse the light of the gospel when it is offered, deserved no such benefit of so blessed a reformation, but rather a plague of deformation, such as happened after his reign in the next queen's days that followed.

Thus then this godly and virtuous imp was cut from us, whose worthy life and virtues have been partly afore declared. Nevertheless, to have some monument of him remaining to testify of the good nature and gentle disposition of that prince, we will add here for a remembrance the report of the prince's schoolmaster to the archbishop.

'Right honourable and my singular good Lord, after my most hearty commendations, the opportunity of this messenger forceth me to write at this time, having little matter but only to signify unto your Grace that my Lord's Grace your godson is merry and in health, and of such towardness in learning, godliness, gentleness, and all honest qualities, that both you and I and all this realm ought to take him for a singular gift sent of God, an imp worthy of such a father; for whom we are bound *sine intermissione* to render to God most hearty thanks; with most humble request of his long and prosperous continuance. He hath learned almost four books of Cato to construe, to parse, and to say without book. And of his own courage now in the latter book he will needs have at one time fourteen verses, which he conneth pleasantly and perfectly, besides things of the Bible, *Satellitium Vivis*, Aesop's

[1] A printer's error: Foxe twice gave the date as 6th July.—Ed.

Fables, and Latin making, whereof he hath sent your Grace a little taste. *Dominus Jesus te diutissime servet.*'

Now to return from whence we have digressed, which is to signify some part of the manner of his godly departing. As the time approached when it pleased Almighty God to call this young king from us, which was the 6th of July the year abovesaid, about three hours before his death this godly child, his eyes being closed, speaking to himself and thinking none to have heard him, made this prayer which followeth.

'Lord God, deliver me out of this miserable and wretched life, and take me among thy chosen: howbeit not my will but thy will be done. Lord, I commit my spirit to thee. O Lord, thou knowest how happy it were for me to be with thee; yet for thy chosen sake send me life and health that I may truly serve thee. O my Lord God, bless thy people and save thine inheritance. O Lord God, save thy chosen people of England. O my Lord God, defend this realm from papistry, and maintain thy true religion, that I and my people may praise thy holy name, for thy Son Jesus Christ's sake.'

Then turned he his face, and seeing who were by him said unto them, 'Are ye so nigh? I thought ye had been further off.' Then Dr Owen said, 'We heard you speak to yourself, but what you said we know not.' He then, after his fashion smilingly, said, 'I was praying to God.' The last words of his pangs were these: 'I am faint; Lord, have mercy upon me and take my spirit.' And thus he yielded up the ghost, leaving a woeful kingdom behind unto his sister. Albeit he in his will had excluded his sister Mary from the succession of the crown because of her corrupt religion, yet the plague which God had destinate unto this sinful realm could not so be voided but that she, being the elder daughter to King Henry, succeeded in possession of the crown; of whose dreadful and bloody regiment it remaineth now to discourse.

CHAPTER 6

THE REVERSION TO ROME

The first entering of Queen Mary to the crown

QUEEN MARY

What time King Edward by long sickness began to appear more feeble, meanwhile a marriage was solemnized in May between Lord Gilford, son to the Duke of Northumberland, and Jane, the Duke of Suffolk's daughter, whose mother was daughter to Mary, King Henry's second sister; who first was married to the French king and afterwards to Charles Duke of Suffolk. The king waxing every day more sick, whereas indeed there seemed in him no hope of recovery, it was brought to pass, by consent not only of the nobility but also of the chief lawyers of the realm, that the king by his testament did appoint Lady Jane to be inheritrix unto the crown of England, passing over his sisters Mary and Elizabeth. To this order subscribed all the king's Council, the chief of the nobility, the Mayor and City of London, and almost all the judges and chief lawyers, saving only Justice Hales of Kent, a man favouring true religion and an upright judge as any in this realm. Of this man you shall hear more in the sequel. The causes laid against Mary were for that it was feared she would marry a stranger and thereby entangle the crown; also that she would clean alter religion and bring in the Pope, the destruction of the realm, which indeed came to pass. Much probable matter they had thus to conjecture of her, by reason of her stubbornness showed in her brother's days.

The matter thus concluded, King Edward not long after departed by the vehemency of his sickness, when he was sixteen years of age; with whom also decayed in a manner the whole flourishing estate of the English nation. When Edward was dead, Jane was established in the kingdom by the nobles' consent, and was forthwith published queen by proclamation at London, and in other cities where there was any great resort. Between this damsel and Edward there was little difference in age, though in learning and knowledge of the tongues she was not only equal but superior unto him. If her fortune had been as good as her bringing up, joined with fineness of wit, she might have seemed comparable not only to your Aspasias and Sempronias, yea to any other women that deserved high praise for their singular learning, but also to the university men, which have taken many degrees of the schools.

In the meantime while these things were a working at London, Mary, who had knowledge of her brother's death, speedeth herself secretly away far from the city, hoping chiefly upon the good will of the commons, yet perchance not destitute of the secret advertisements of some of the nobles. When the Council heard of her departure, they gathered a power of men together and assigned that the Duke of Suffolk should have the leading of the band. Afterwards altering their minds, they thought it best to send the Duke of Northumberland, and that the Duke of Suffolk should keep the Tower, where Lord Gilford and Lady Jane the same time were lodged. In which expedition the guard also, albeit unwilling at the first, were induced to assist the duke and set forward with him.

Mary meanwhile withdrew herself into Norfolk and Suffolk, where she understood the duke's name to be had in much hatred for the service done there of late in subduing the rebels; and gathering to her such aid of the commons as she might, kept herself close within Fremingham Castle. To whom first of all resorted the Suffolk men; who, being always forward in promoting the proceedings of the gospels, promised her their help so that she would not attempt the alteration of the religion which her brother had established by laws publicly enacted and received by consent of the whole realm. Unto this condition she agreed, with such promise made unto them—that no innovation should be made of religion—that no man could have misdoubted her. Which promise if she had as constantly kept as they did willingly preserve her with their bodies and weapons, she had done a deed worthy of her blood. Thus Mary, guarded with the power of the gospellers, did vanquish the duke and all that came against her. In consideration whereof, it was methinks an heavy word that she answered to the Suffolk men afterwards, which did make supplication of her Grace to perform her promise: 'Forsomuch as you, being but members, desire to rule your head, you shall one day well perceive that members must obey their head.' To cause the more terror unto other, a gentleman named Dobbe, dwelling about Wyndam, for advertising her of her promise was three times set on the pillory to be a gazingstock unto all men. Others delivered her supplications made out of the Scripture, to exhort her to continue in the true doctrine, and were sent to prison. But such is the condition of men's nature that we are more ready to seek friendship when we stand in need of help than to requite a benefit once received.

On the contrary side the Duke of Northumberland was now forward in his way. What ado there was, what stirring on every side, what riding and posting, what messages and instructions went to and fro, what talking among the soldiers, what heartburning among the people, what speeding of ordnance hourly out of the Tower, what rumours and coming of soldiers from all quarters there was; a world it was to see, enough to make a whole Ilias.

The greatest help that made for Lady Mary was the short journeys of the duke, which by commission were assigned to him. For the longer the duke lingered in his voyage, Lady Mary the more increased in puissance, the hearts of the people being mightily bent unto her; which after the Council at London perceived, and understood how the multitude did withdraw their hearts to stand with her, and that certain noblemen began to go the other way, they turned their song and proclaimed for Queen Lady Mary, eldest daughter to King Henry VIII and appointed by parliament to succeed King Edward, dying without issue. And so the duke was left destitute, and forsaken alone at Cambridge with some of his sons and a few other; who there were arrested and brought to the Tower as traitors to the Crown.

Thus have you Mary now made a queen, and the sword of authority put into her hand, which how she afterwards did use we may see in the sequel of this book. When she saw all quiet, sending the duke to the Tower the 25th of July she followed not long after, being brought the 3rd of August to London, with the great rejoicing of many but a greater fear of moe. Her first lodging she took at the Tower, where Jane with her husband a little before her coming were imprisoned; they remained waiting her pleasure almost five months. But the duke within a month after his coming was brought forth to the scaffold and beheaded; albeit he, being put in hope of pardon if he would recant and hear mass, consented thereto and denied in words that true religion which, as well in King Henry VIII's days as in King Edward's, he had oft declared himself to favour; whose recantation the Papists did forthwith publish, rejoicing at his conversion, or rather subversion. Thus the duke, with Sir John Gates and Sir Thomas Palmer (which

Palmer on the other side confessed his faith as he had learned in the gospel) being put to death, Mary entering thus her reign with the blood of these men, besides hearing mass in the Tower gave signification hereby, but especially by the sudden delivering of Gardiner out of the Tower, that she was not minded to stand to that which she so deeply had promised to the Suffolk men. Other things followed which more and more discomforted the people; not only the releasing of Gardiner, being then made Lord Chancellor of England and Bishop of Winchester, Dr Poynet being put out, but also that Boner was restored to his bishopric and Dr Ridley displaced. Item, Day to Chichester, Scory being put out. Item, Tonstall to Duresme. Item, Heath to Worcester and Hooper committed to the Fleet. Item, Vesie to Exeter and Coverdale put out. Ridley in time of Queen Jane had made a sermon at Paul's Cross, so commanded by the Council, declaring his mind touching Lady Mary, alleging the inconveniences which might rise by receiving her to be queen. Shortly after this sermon Queen Mary was proclaimed; whereupon despoiled of all his dignities he was sent upon a lame horse to the Tower.

The 13th of September Hugh Latimer appeared before the Council, and was committed to the Tower close prisoner. The same day the Archbishop of Canturbury appearing before the Council was commanded to appear the next day before them in the Star Chamber, where they charging him with treason, committed him to the Tower, there to remain till further justice at the queen's pleasure.

The 1st of October Mary was crowned at Westminster and the 10th day begun parliament with a solemn mass of the Holy Ghost after the popish manner, celebrated with great pomp in the Palace of Westminster. Mass being done, the queen was brought into Parliament House to begin the consultation; at which were repealed all statutes made in the time of King Henry VIII for *praemunire*, and in King Edward's time for common prayer and sacrament in English.

In November Archbishop Cranmer, notwithstanding he had refused to subscribe to the king's will disinheriting his sister, alleging many grave and pithy reasons for her legitimation, was in Guild Hall arraigned and attainted of treason, with Lady Jane and three of the Duke of Northumberland's sons, which were had again to the Tower and there kept for a time. Notwithstanding Cranmer, pardoned of treason, stood only in the action of doctrine which they called heresy. The people, especially the churchmen, perceiving the queen so set upon her old religion, to show themselves no less forward to serve the queen's appetite, began in their choirs to set up the pageant of St Katharine, and of St Nicholas, and of their procession in Latin, after all their old solemnity, with gay gardeviance and grey amices.

When December was come, parliament brake up; in which parliament communication was moved of the queen's marriage with Philip, the Emperor's son. Meanwhile Cardinal Poole, being sent for by Queen Mary, was by the Emperor requested to stay with him, that his presence in England should not be a let to the marriage; for the making whereof he sent a most ample ambassade, which took such success that after they had communed of the matters a few days they knit up the knot. This mention of marriage was very evil taken of the people and many of the nobility, who for this and for religion conspiring among themselves, made a rebellion, whereof Sir Thomas Wyat was one of the chief beginners; who being in Kent said that the queen would by foreign marriage bring upon this realm most miserable servitude and establish popish religion. About the 25th of January news came to London of this stir in Kent, and shortly after the Duke of Suffolk, who was fled into Warwickshire and Leicestershire, there to gather a power. The queen caused them both to be proclaimed traitors, and sent against Wyat Thomas Duke of Norfolk, who being about Rochester Bridge forsaken of them that went with him returned to London without bloodshed on either party. To apprehend the Duke of Suffolk was sent the Earl of Huntington in post, who entering Coventry before the Duke, disappointed him of his purpose. The duke in great distress committed himself to the keeping of a servant of his named Underwood, in Astley Park, who like a false traitor betrayed him. And so was brought to the Tower. The other were taken; and Wyat came towards London in the beginning of February. The queen, hearing of Wyat's coming, came into the city to the Guild Hall where she made a vehement oration against Wyat. Here is to be noted that at the coming of Mary to the Guild Hall, it being bruited before that she was coming with harnessed men, a number of Londoners, fearing lest they should be there entrapped and put to death, made out of the gate before her entering. Furthermore note that when she had ended her oration (which she seemed to have perfectly conned without book), Winchester standing by her cried to the people, 'Oh how happy are we, to whom God hath given such a wise and learned prince!'

Two days after, which was the 3rd of February, Lord Cobham was committed to the Tower, and Wyat entered Southwark; who forsomuch as he could not enter that way into London, returning another way to Kingston with his army came through the streets into Ludgate, and returning thence was resisted at Temple Bar, and there yielded himself to Sir Clement Parson, and was brought by him to the Court, and with him the residue of his army (for before almost half his men ran away at Kingston Bridge) were also taken and about an hundred killed. They that were taken were had to prison and a great many were hanged, and he himself executed at Tower Hill and then quartered; whose head being set upon Hay Hill was stolen away and great search made for the same (of which story ye shall hear more hereafter).

The 12th of February was beheaded Lady Jane, to whom was sent Mr Fecknam, alias Howman, from the queen two days before her death, to commune with her and reduce her from the doctrine of Christ to Queen Mary's religion; but it would not be. Fecknam took his leave, saying that he was sorry for her: 'For I am sure,' quoth he, 'that we two shall never meet.' 'True it is,' said she, 'that we shall never meet, except God turn your heart, for you are in an evil case. And I pray God to send you his Holy Spirit; for he hath given you his great gift of utterance, if it pleased him also to open the eyes of your heart.'

It remaineth now to infer the manner of her execution. These are the words that Lady Jane spake upon the scaffold at the hour of her death. When she mounted the scaffold she said to the people standing thereabout, 'Good people, I pray you all to bear me witness that I die a true Christian woman, and that I look to be saved by no other mean but the mercy of God in the blood of his only Son Jesus Christ. I confess that when I did know the word of God I neglected the same, loved myself and the world; and therefore this punishment is worthily happened unto me for my sins: yet I thank God that of his goodness he hath given me respite to repent. And now, good people, while I am alive, I pray you assist me with your prayers.' Then kneeling down she turned to Fecknam saying, 'Shall I say this psalm?' He answered 'Yea.' Then said she the *Miserere mei Deus* in English in most devout manner to the end; then she stood up and gave her maiden, Mistress Ellen, her gloves and handkercher, and her book to Mr Bruges. Then she untied her gown and the hangman pressed upon her to help her off with it; but she desiring him to let her alone turned towards her two gentlewomen, who helped her off therewith and also with her frowes, paste, and neckerchief, giving her a fair handkerchief to knit about her eyes.

Then the hangman kneeled down and asked her forgiveness, whom she forgave most willingly. Then he willed her to stand upon the straw; which doing she saw the block. Then she said, 'I pray you dispatch me quickly.' Then she kneeled down saying, 'Will you take it off before I lay me down?' The hangman said, 'No, madam.' Then tied she the handkerchief about her eyes, and feeling for the block she said, 'Where is it? where is it?' One of the standers-by guiding her thereunto, she laid her head upon the block and stretched forth her body and said, 'Lord, into thy hands I commend my spirit'; and so finished her life, in the year of Our Lord 1554, the 12th day of February.

Thus was beheaded Lady Jane, and with her also Lord Gilford her husband; too innocents in comparison of them that sat upon them. For they did but ignorantly accept that which others had willingly devised, and by open proclamation consented to take from others and give to them. Touching the condemnation of Lady Jane, here is to be noted that Judge Morgan, who gave sentence against her, shortly after fell mad, and in his raving cried out continually to have Lady Jane taken away from him; and so ended his life. And not long after the death of Lady Jane, upon the 21st of the same month was Henry Duke of Suffolk her father also beheaded at Tower Hill, the fourth day after his condemnation; about which time also were condemned for this conspiracy many gentlemen and yeomen, whereof some were executed at London, some in the country; in the number of whom was Lord Thomas Gray, brother to the duke, being apprehended in North Wales and executed for the same.

The 24th of the same month Boner Bishop of London sent a commission to all curates and pastors of his diocese, for taking the names of such as would not come the Lent following to auricular confession, and to the receiving at Easter. The next month there was a letter sent from the queen to Boner with articles annexed to be put in speedy executing, containing as here followeth:

That no bishop in any ecclesiastical writings do put in this clause, *Regia authoritate fulcitus.*

That no bishop do hereafter exact any oath touching the primacy or succession.

That every bishop do travail for the repressing of heresies, duly punishing the same.

That every bishop shall deprive all such persons from their benefices who have married wives; that all such persons be also divorced every one from his woman, and due punishment otherwise taken for the offence.

That all manner of processions be used after the old order of the Church in Latin.

That the bishop of the diocese do compel the parishioners to hear divine service.

About the same time there came from the queen a proclamation against foreigners within this realm, the purpose of which proclamation chiefly concerned religion. Upon the proclamation not only the strangers in King Edward's time received into the kingdom for religion, among whom was Peter Martyr, but many Englishmen fled, some to Frieseland, some to Cleveland, some to High Germany, where they scattered into companies and congregations at Wesel, Frankford, Emden, Strausborough, Basil, Zurich, Geneva, and other places, near to the number of 800 persons.

How Cranmer, Ridley, and Latimer were sent down to Oxford to dispute

About the 10th of March Cranmer, Ridley, and Latimer were conveyed as prisoners from the Tower to Windsor and from thence to Oxford, there to dispute with the learned men of both universities about the presence, substance, and sacrifice of the sacrament. Appointed to dispute against them were these: of Oxford, Weston, Tresham, Cole, Oglethorpe, Pie, Harpsfield, Fecknam; of Cambridge, Young, Glyn, Seaton, Watson, Sedgewick, Atkinson, etc. The questions whereupon they should dispute were these:

Whether the natural body of Christ be really in the sacrament;

Whether after the consecration any other substance do remain;

Whether in the mass be a sacrifice propitiatory for the quick and the dead.

On Saturday the 14th of April the commissioners, doctors, and many other dined with the mayor. After dinner they went to St Mary's Church, and sat on seats before the altar to the number of thirty-three persons; and first they sent to the mayor that he should bring in Dr Cranmer. The archbishop, brought before the commissioners, reverenced them with much humility, and having a stool offered him refused to sit. Then the prolocutor began with a short preface in praise of unity in the Church; declaring withal his bringing up and taking degrees in Cambridge, and how he was promoted by King Henry and had been his counsellor and a catholic man, one of the same unity, but of late years did separate himself from it by teaching erroneous doctrine: therefore it pleased the queen to send them to bring him to this unity again. Then showed he him how they had agreed on certain articles whereunto they willed him to subscribe. The archbishop answered the preface very modestly and learnedly, showing that he was very glad to come to a unity, so that it were in Christ and agreeable to his holy word.

When he had thus spoken his mind, the prolocutor caused the articles to be read unto him. The bishop read them over three or four times, and touching the first article asked what they meant by *verum & naturale*, true and natural. 'Do you not mean,' saith he, '*corpus organicum*, a sensible body?' Some answered, '*idem quod natum est ex Virgine*, the same that was born of the Virgin.' The bishop denied it utterly; and when he had looked upon the other two he said they were all false, and therefore would not agree in that unity with them. Which done, the prolocutor, first willing him to write his mind of them that night, said moreover that he should dispute in them, and caused a copy to be delivered him, assigning him to answer thereunto on Monday next; and so charged the mayor with him again to be had to Bocardo.[1] The archbishop was greatly commended of everybody for his modesty; insomuch that some Masters of Art were seen to weep for him, who in judgment were contrary to him.

Then was Dr Ridley brought in, who hearing the articles read answered without any delay, they were all false and sprang out of a sour root. Then did they lay to his charge a sermon made when he was Bishop of Rochester, wherein, they said, he spake with transubstantiation. He denied it, and asked whether they could bring any that heard him. They could bring no proof at all. After that he was asked whether he desired not my Lord Chancellor that now is to stick to the mass. He said that my Lord would say no such things of him. Then he was asked whether he would dispute or no. He answered that as long as God gave him life he should not only have his heart but also his mouth and pen to defend his truth. They said he should dispute on Thursday, and gave him the articles and bade him write his mind of them that night; and so did command the mayor to have him from whence he came.

Last of all came in Latimer, with a kerchief and two or three caps on

[1] A prison in Oxford.—Ed.

his head, his spectacles hanging by a string at his breast, and a staff in his hand, and was set in a chair. After his denial of the articles, when he had Wednesday appointed for disputation, he alleged age, sickness, and lack of books, saying that he was almost as meet to dispute as to be captain of Calice; but he would declare his mind either by writing or word, and would stand to all they could lay upon his back; complaining moreover that he was permitted to have neither pen nor ink, nor any book but the New Testament there in his hand, which he had read over seven times deliberately, yet could not find the mass in it, neither the marrow bones nor sinews of the same. At which words the commissioners were not a little offended; so they put him to silence. There was a very great press of people, and one of the beadles swooned by reason thereof and was carried into the vestry. After this the Cambridge men went to the Cross Inn to supper. On Sunday Mr Harpsfield preached at St Mary's, the University Church, at nine o'clock. After the sermon they went all to Magdalen College and there had a great dinner. They supped at Lincoln College with the prolocutor, whither Cranmer sent answer upon the articles in writing.

On Monday, the 16th Mr Say and Mr White, notaries, went about in the morning to the colleges to get subscriptions to the articles. About eight o'clock the prolocutor, with the doctors and vice-chancellor, met at Exeter College; and so they went into the schools, and when the vice-chancellor, the prolocutor, and doctors were placed, and four appointed to be *exceptores argumentorum* set at a table in the midst, and four notaries sitting with them, Cranmer came to the answerer's place, the mayor and aldermen sitting by him; and so the disputation began, with a short *praeludium*. Chedsey began to argue first; and as he left, the prolocutor, Tresham, Oglethorpe, Marshall, Pie, Cole, and Harpsfield did interrupt and press him with their arguments, so that every man said somewhat, disorderly, sometime in Latin, sometime in English, so that three hours of the time was spent ere the Vice-chancellor of Cambridge began; who was interrupted as before. He began with three or four questions subtly. Here the beadles had provided drink and offered the answerer, but he refused with thanks. The prolocutor offered him, if he would make water or otherwise ease himself he should. Thus the disputation continued until almost two o'clock. Then were all the arguments, written by the four appointed, delivered into the hands of Mr Say, register; the prisoner was had away by the mayor; and the doctors dined at University College.

The next day, the 17th, was brought forward Dr Ridley to dispute; against whom was set Dr Smith to be principal opponent. Smith could get nothing at his hand; insomuch that other did take his arguments and prosecuted them. He showed himself learned and a great clerk; they could bring nothing but he knew it as well as they. After this Dr Glyn began to reason, who (notwithstanding Ridley had always taken him for his friend) made a very contumelious preface against him. This Ridley did the more take to heart, because it proceeded from him. Howbeit he thought that Glyn's mind was to serve the turn; for afterwards he came to the house where Ridley was kept, and desired him to pardon his words; which Ridley did from the very heart, and wished earnestly that God would give not only unto him but unto all other the knowledge of God's evangelical sincerity, that they being fully reconciled might meet in the house of the heavenly Father.

Then Tresham began to speak, moved with great zeal, and desired that he might be in the stead of John Baptist, in converting the hearts of the fathers and reducing Bishop Ridley again to Mother Church. At first, not knowing the person, he thought he had been some good old man which had the zeal of God although not according to knowledge, and began to answer him with mansuetude and reverence; but afterwards he smelled a fox under a sheep's clothing. Then came in another, whom Ridley knew not, and said, 'The universal Church both of the East and the West agreed in the Council of Florence that in the sacrament of the altar there is the real body.' Here cried out Dr Cole and said they agreed concerning transubstantiation of bread into the body of Christ. Ridley said that could not be. Here start up another unknown to Ridley, who affirmed with him that indeed there was nothing decreed concerning transubstantiation, but the Council left that, as a matter not worthy to disturb the concord of the Church; to whom Ridley answered that he said the truth.

After these disputations of Bishop Ridley, next was brought out Mr Latimer, upon Wednesday the 18th; which disputation began at eight o'clock in such form as before; but it was most in English. For Latimer alleged that he was out of use with Latin and unfit for that place. There replied unto him Mr Smith of Oriall College; Cartwright, Harpsfield, and divers other had snatches at him and gave him bitter taunts. He escaped not hissings and scornful laughings, no more than they that went before him. He was very faint and desired that he might not long tarry.

He durst not drink for fear of vomiting. The disputation ended before eleven o'clock. Latimer was not suffered to read that he had painfully written; but it was exhibited and the prolocutor read part thereof, and proceeded unto the disputation.

After the disputation of Mr Latimer, the Friday following, which was the 20th, the commissioners sat in St Mary's Church, and Dr Weston used particularly dissuasions with every of them, and would not suffer them to answer, but directly to say whether they would subscribe or no. First to the Bishop of Canturbury he said he was overcome in disputations. The bishop answered that whereas Dr Weston said he had answered and opposed, and could neither maintain his own errors nor impugn the verity, all that he said was false. For he was not suffered to oppose as he would, nor could answer as he was required unless he would have brawled with them; so thick their reasons came one after another. Ever four or five did interrupt him, that he could not speak. Ridley and Latimer were asked what they would do; they said they would stand to that they had said. Then were they all called together and sentence read over them; that they were no members of the Church, and therefore they, their fautors and patrons, were condemned as heretics. In reading of it they were asked whether they would turn or no: they bade them read on, for they were not minded to turn. So they were condemned all three. After the sentence they were separated: the archbishop was returned to Bocardo, Ridley was carried to the sheriff's house, Latimer to the bailiff's.

The Saturday following they had a mass with a general procession and great solemnity. Cranmer was caused to behold the procession out of Bocardo, Ridley out of the sheriff's house. Latimer, brought to see it from the bailiff's house, thought that he should have gone to burning, and spake to Augustine Cooper, a catchpole, to make a quick fire; but when he came to Karfor and saw the matter, he ran as fast as his old bones would carry him to one Spenser's shop, and would not look towards it. Last of all Dr Weston carried the sacrament, and four doctors carried the canopy over him.

These disputations being thus discoursed and ended, which were at Oxford in the month of April, now let us return to the prosecuting of our story touching other things that happened in other parts of the realm in this tumultuous time. Because things that happened were so many that it is hard to keep a perfect order in reciting them, we have thought here a little to interrupt the order of time, returning to July

1553. In which month I showed before how the Duke of Northumberland was apprehended by the guard, and brought to London on the 25th of July and so to the Tower. These be the names of them that were committed to the Tower with the duke—the Earl of Warwick, the Earl of Huntington, Lord Ambrose Dudley and Lord Henry Dudley, Sir John Gates, Sir Henry Gates, Sir Andrew Dudley, Sir Thomas Palmer, and Dr Sands, Chancellor of Cambridge.

The 26th of July the Marques of Northampton, the Bishop of London, Lord Robert Dudley, and Sir Richard Corbet; the 27th the Lord Chief Justice of England and the Chief Justice of the Common Pleas; on the 28th the Duke of Suffolk and Sir John Cheeke, were committed to the Tower. The 30th Lord Russell was committed to the Sheriff of London's custody; the 31st the Earl of Rutland was committed to the Fleet. On the 3rd of August the queen entered London at Aldgate, and so to the Tower, where she remained seven days, and then removed to Richmond. On the 5th Lord Ferres was committed to the Tower, Boner was delivered out of the Marshalsea, Dr Cockes was committed to the Marshalsea, and Edward Underhill to Newgate; Tonstall and Gardiner were delivered out of the Tower, and Gardiner received into the Privy Council and made Lord Chancellor. On the 7th Henry Dudley, captain of the guard at Guises, was taken and brought to the Tower. On the 8th the king's body was brought to Westminster and there buried. The same day a mass of requiem was sung within the Tower by the Bishop of Winchester, who had on his mitre and did all things as in time past was done; at which mass the queen was present. On the 18th the Duke of Northumberland, the Marques of Northampton, and the Earl of Warwick were arraigned at Westminster and the same day condemned, the Duke of Norfolk being the judge. On the 19th Andrew Dudley, John Gates, Henry Gates, and Thomas Palmer were arraigned, and condemned the same day, the Marques of Winchester being judge. On the 21st Northumberland, Northampton, Dudley, John Gates, and Palmer heard mass within the Tower and received the sacrament in one kind only. On which day also Queen Mary set forth a proclamation signifying that she could not any longer hide the religion which she from her infancy had professed, inhibiting in the proclamation printing and preaching. On the 22nd Northumberland, John Gates, and Palmer were beheaded on Tower Hill. The 13th of September Hugh Latimer, the 14th the Bishop of Canturbury, was committed to the Tower.

Sunday the 1st of October the queen went from White Hall to Westminster Abbey, accompanied with most of the nobility, the ambassadors of divers countries, and the Mayor of London with the Aldermen. Out of the abbey to receive her came three silver crosses and fourscore singing men, all in gorgeous copes. Amongst whom were the Dean and divers of her chaplains, and after them followed ten bishops, mitred all. In this order they returned from Westminster Hall to the abbey, where she was crowned by Gardiner Bishop of Winchester.

The 26th of October the Vice-chancellor of Cambridge went to Clare Hall and displaced Dr Madew and placed Mr Swynborne in the mastership, for that he was *uxoratus*, married. The 28th the papists in King's College had their whole service in Latin, contrary to the law then in force. The 3rd of November the Vice-chancellor sent for the curate of the Round Parish, saying he would have one uniform order of service throughout the town, and that in Latin. The 15th of December there were two proclamations at London, one repealing certain acts made by King Edward and setting up the mass, the other that no man should interrupt any of those who would say mass. About this time a priest at Canturbury said mass one day, and the next came into the pulpit and desired the people to forgive him; he said he had betrayed Christ as Peter did; and made a long sermon against the mass.

Passing to February, here is to be noted that upon the 15th there was seen within the City of London, about nine in the forenoon, strange sights. There was seen two suns both shining at once, the one a good way distant from the other. At the same time was seen a rainbow turned contrary, and a great deal higher than hath been accustomed. The common standing of the rainbow is thus ∩, but this stood thus ∪, with head downward and feet upward. Both these sights were seen as well at Westminster, in Cheapside, on the south side of Paul's as in many other places, and that by a great number of honest men. Certain aldermen went out of the Guild Hall to behold the sight.

On the 23rd of February 1554 Lord Henry Gray Duke of Suffolk was brought forth of the Tower unto the scaffold on Tower Hill. There accompanied him Dr Weston as his ghostly father, against the will of the duke. For when the duke went up to the scaffold, Weston pressed to go up with him. The duke with his hand put him down again off the stairs, and Weston taking hold of the duke forced him down likewise. As they ascended the second time, the duke again put him down. Then Weston said that it was the queen's pleasure he should do so. Wherewith the duke casting his hands abroad ascended the scaffold. Then he desired all men to forgive him, saying that the queen had forgiven him. Weston declared with a loud voice that the queen *had* forgiven him. With that divers of the standersby said with audible voice, 'Such forgiveness God send *thee*!' Then the duke kneeled down and said the psalm *Miserere mei Deus* unto the end, looking up to heaven. When he had ended the psalm he said, '*In manus tuas, Domine, commendo spiritum meum.*' Then he stood up and delivered his cap and scarf unto the executioner. The executioner kneeled down and asked the duke forgiveness. The duke said, 'God forgive thee, and I do; when thou dost thine office, I pray thee do it well and bring me out of this world quickly.' Then stood there a man and said, 'My Lord, how shall I do for the money that you owe me?' The duke said, 'Alas, good fellow; I pray thee trouble me not now, but go to my officers.' Then he knit a kercher about his face, and kneeled down and said, 'Our Father' unto the end. Then he said, 'Christ have mercy upon me,' and laid his head on the block. The executioner took the axe, and at the first chop stroke off his head and held it up to the people.

In this week all such priests within the diocese of London as were married were divorced from their livings, and commanded to bring their wives within a fortnight that they might be likewise divorced from them. This the bishop did of his own power.

On the 18th of March Lady Elizabeth the queen's sister was brought to the Tower.

The 8th of April there was a cat hanged upon a gallows at the cross in Cheap apparelled like a priest ready to say mass, with a shaven crown. Whereon arose great evil will against the city; for the queen and the bishops were very angry. The same afternoon there was a proclamation that whosoever could bring forth the party that did hang up the cat should have twenty nobles, which reward was afterwards increased to twenty marks; but none could or would earn it.

The 11th of April was Sir Thomas Wyat beheaded and quartered at Tower Hill, where he uttered these words: 'Concerning what I said of other in my examination, to charge any as partakers of my doings, I accuse neither my Lady Elizabeth nor my Lord of Devonshire. I cannot accuse them, neither am I able to say that they knew anything of my rising.' When Dr Weston told him that his confession was otherwise before the Council, he answered, 'That which I said then, I said; but that which I say now is true.' Upon the 17th Sir James Croft and Mr Winter were brought to the Guild Hall, with whom also was brought Sir Nicholas Throgmorton, and arraigned of treason for that he was suspected of conspiring with the Duke of Suffolk and the rest; where he so learnedly behaved himself in clearing his own case that the quest which was charged with this matter could not but find him not guilty; for the which the persons of the quest, being substantial men of the city, were bound in the sum of 500 pounds apiece to appear before the queen's Council at a day appointed, there to answer for his acquitting; which quest appeared accordingly before the Council in the Star Chamber, whence they were committed to prison.

Concerning the condemnation of Thomas Archbishop of Canturbury, Dr Ridley, and Mr Latimer, which was the 20th of this month, because we have said enough before, it shall not need now to bestow any further rehearsal thereof. The Friday following the condemnation of them, the 27th of April Lord Thomas Gray, the late Duke of Suffolk's brother, was beheaded at Tower Hill. On the 28th Sir James Croft was arraigned and condemned. On the 17th of May William Thomas was arraigned at the Guild Hall and condemned. Who the day after was hanged, drawn, and quartered. His accusation was for conspiring the queen's death; how true it was I have not to say. This is certain, that he made a right godly end, and wrote many fruitful exhortations, letters, and sonnets in the prison before his death. The 19th day of the month Lady Elizabeth was brought out of the Tower and committed to the custody of Sir John Williams, of whom her Highness was courteously entreated; who afterwards was had to Woodstock, and there committed to the keeping of Sir Henry Benifield, of Oxborough in Norfolk; who forgetting her estate and his own duty (as it is reported) showed himself more hard unto her than either cause was given of her part or reason of his own part would have led him, if wisdom in him might have seen before what danger might have ensued thereof. Whereof we have to entreat more at large hereafter.

Upon the 20th of July the Prince of Spain landed at Southampton; who as he set foot upon the land drew his sword, and carried it naked in his hand a good way. Then met him the mayor, who delivered the keys of the town unto the prince, who removed his sword into his left hand and received the keys without any word or countenance of thankfulness, and after a while delivered the keys to the mayor again. At the town gate met him the Earl of Arundel and Lord Williams, and so he was brought to his lodging. Upon the 25th Philip Prince of Spain and Mary Queen of England were married in the Cathedral Church at Winchester by the Bishop of Winchester, in the presence of a great number of noblemen of both realms. The first day of August following there was a proclamation that from that time forth the style of all writings should be altered and this following should be used:

'Philip and Mary, by the grace of God King and Queen of England, France, Naples, Jerusalem, and Ireland; Defenders of the Faith; Princes of Spain and Cicill; Archdukes of Austrich; Dukes of Millaine, Burgundy, and Brabant; Counties of Haspurge, Flanders, and Tyroll.'

Of this marriage as the papists chiefly seemed to be very glad, so divers of them to show forth their inward affections, some made interludes and pageants, some drew forth genealogies deriving his pedigree from Edward III and John of Gaunt, some made verses. Amongst all other Mr White, then Bishop of Lincoln (his poetical vein being drunken with the joy of the marriage), spued out certain verses, the copy whereof we have here inserted.

Philippi & Mariae Genealogia

Ille parens regum Gandava ex urbe Johannes
Somersetensem comitem profert Johannem:
Somersetensis venit hoc patre dux Johannes,
Qui Margaretā Richemundi habuit Comitissam.
Haec dedit Henricum, qui regni septimus hujus
Henrico octavo solium regale reliquit.
Hoc patre propitio & fausto quasi sidere nata
Iure tenes sacram, teneasque Maria coronam.

After the consummation of which marriage they removed from Winchester to sundry other places, and by easy journeys came to Windsor Castle, where he was stalled in the Order of the Garter. At which time an herald took down the arms of England at Windsor and in place of them would have set up the arms of Spain, but he was commanded to set them up again by certain lords. From thence they removed to Richmond, and from thence by water came to London and landed at the Bishop of Winchester's house, through which they passed into Southwark Park and so to Southwark House, where they lay that night. The next day, being the 19th of August, the king and queen rode through the City of London to White Hall; and at London

Bridge was a vain spectacle set up, two images representing two giants, Corineus and Gogmagog, holding between them certain Latin verses which for the vain ostentation of flattery I overpass. As they passed over the bridge, there was a number of ordnance shot at the Tower, such as by old men's report the like hath not been heard or seen these hundred years.

The 17th of September was a proclamation in London that all vagabonds and masterless men, as well strangers as Englishmen, should depart the city within five days; and straitly charging all innholders, victuallers, taverners, and alehouse-keepers that they, after the said five days, should not sell any meat, drink, or any kind of victual to any servingman whatsoever, unless he brought a testimonial from his master to declare whose servant he was, and were in continual household with his said master; upon pain to run in danger of the law if they offended herein.

On the 7th of November Lord Paget and Sir Edward Hastings were sent as ambassadors to Cardinal Poole at Bruxels: it was thought they were sent to conduct him to England, where at that time he was appointed Bishop of Canturbury. Cardinal Poole landed at Dover upon the 21st, on which day one act passed in parliament for his restoration in blood, repealing that act made against him in King Henry VIII's time, and on the next day the king and queen came both to Parliament House to give their royal assent. Upon the 24th the cardinal came by water to London and so to Lambeth House.

Upon the 28th there was general procession in Paul's for joy that the queen was conceived and quick with child, as declared in a letter sent from the Council to the Bishop of London. At this procession were ten bishops with all the prebendaries of Paul's, also the Lord Mayor with the aldermen, and a great number of commons in their best array. Of this child a great talk began to rise in every man's mouth, with busy preparation and much ado, especially amongst such as seemed to carry Spanish hearts in English bodies. In number of whom is not to be forgotten one Sir Richard Southwell, who being in the Parliament House when the Lords were occupied in other matters of importance, suddenly starting up, for fulness of joy brast out in these words: 'Tush, my masters; what talk ye of these matters? I would have you take some order for our young master that is now coming into the world apace, lest he find us unprovided.' By which words it may appear what an assured opinion was then conceived in men's heads of Queen Mary to be conceived and quick with child; insomuch that in the same parliament there was eftsoons a bill exhibited and an act made upon the same. Thus we see how man doth purpose but God disposeth as pleaseth him. For all this labour, provision, and order taken in parliament for their young master long looked for, coming so surely into the world, in the end appeared neither young master nor young mistress that any man to this day can hear of. Furthermore, as the labour of the lay sort was herein deluded, so no less ridiculous it was to behold what little effect the prayers of the Pope's churchmen had with Almighty God, who travailed no less with their processions, masses, and collects, for the happy deliverance of this young master.

Upon the 26th of January parliament was dissolved. In this parliament the Bishop of Rome was established, and all such laws as were made against him since the 20th year of King Henry VIII were repealed, and Cardinal Poole and other were restored to their blood. Also there was an act made that whosoever should speak anything against the king or queen, or might move any sedition or rebellion, at the first time to have one of his ears cut off or forfeit 100 marks, and at the second time to have both his ears cut off or forfeit 100 pound; and whosoever should write or print any of the premises to have their right hand cut off.

CHAPTER 7

THE BEGINNING OF THE TERROR

The story of Mr John Rogers

The 4th of February suffered the constant martyr of God, John Rogers. Rogers, brought up in the University of Cambridge, was chosen by the merchant adventurers to be their chaplain in Brabant at Antwerp, where he served to their contentation many years. It chanced him there to fall in company with Tindall and Coverdale, which both for the hatred they bare to popish superstition and love to true religion had forsaken their native country. In conferring with them he came to great knowledge in the gospel of God, insomuch that he cast off the yoke of popery and joined himself with them in that painful and most profitable labour of translating the Bible into English, which is entitled *The Translation of Thomas Mathew*. He, knowing by the Scriptures that unlawful vows may lawfully be broken and that matrimony is honourable among all men, joined himself in lawful matrimony and so went to Wittenberg in Saxony, where he did not only greatly increase in all good learning, but so much profited in the knowledge of Dutch that a congregation was committed to his cure. In which ministry he served many years until it pleased God, by the travail of his chosen servant Edward, to banish all popery forth of England and to receive in true religion. He then, having a ready will to help forward the work of the Lord in his native country, left such honest and certain conditions as he had in Saxony, and came into England to preach the gospel without certainty of any condition. In which office after he had faithfully travailed, Ridley, then Bishop of London, gave him a prebend in the Cathedral Church, and the Dean and Chapter chose him to be the reader of the divinity lesson there; therein he diligently travailed until Queen Mary banished the gospel and true religion and brought in the Antichrist of Rome.

After the queen was come to the Tower, he, being called thereunto, made a vehement sermon at Paul's Cross, confirming such true doctrine as he and other had there taught in King Edward's days, exhorting the people to beware of popery and superstition. The Council called him to account; to whom he made a stout answer, yet in such sort handled himself that at that time he was dismissed. But after proclamation was set forth by the queen to prohibit true preaching he was called again before the Council; for the bishops thirsted after his blood. The Council quarrelled with him concerning his doctrine, and in conclusion commanded him as prisoner to keep his own house; and so he did, although by flying he might easily have escaped their cruel hands, and many things might have moved him thereunto. He did see the recovery of religion in England for the present desperate; he knew he could not want a living in Germany; and he could not forget his wife and ten children. But after he was called to answer in Christ's cause he would not depart, but for the trial of that truth was content to hazard his life. Thus he remained in his own house as prisoner a long time, till at length through the procurement of Boner, who could not abide honest neighbours to dwell by him, he was removed to Newgate, where he was lodged among thieves and murderers for a great space, during which what business he had with the adversaries of Christ is not known, further than he himself did leave in writing.

After Rogers had been long imprisoned, often examined, and at length most cruelly by wicked Winchester condemned the 4th of February 1555, he was warned suddenly by the keeper's wife of Newgate to prepare himself for the fire; who being asleep scarce with much slogging could be awaked. At length being raised and waked, and bid to make haste, 'Then,' said he, 'I need not tie my points;' and so was had down first to Boner to be degraded. That done, he craved but one petition. Boner asking what that should be. 'Nothing,' said he, but that he might talk a few words with his wife before his burning. But that could not be obtained of him. So he was brought into Smithfield, where he showed most constant patience, not using many words but exhorting the people to remain in that faith which he had taught, for confirmation whereof he was not only content to bear all such cruelty as had been shown him, but gladly to give his flesh to the fire for the testimony of the same.

Briefly to comprehend the whole order of his martyrdom: first Rogers was committed to prison as is above said, and there continued a year and a half. In prison he was merry. He wrote much; his examinations he penned with his own hand, which else had never come to light; wherein is to be noted the memorable working of God's providence. For notwithstanding that during his imprisonment strait search there was to take away his writings; yet after his death his wife and one of her sons coming into the place where he lay, it chanced her son to spy a black thing (for it had a black cover) lying in a blind corner under a pair of stairs; who, willing his mother to see what it was, found it to be the book written with his own hand, containing his examinations and answers.

To proceed further in describing the doings of this man while he remained prisoner in Newgate, he was to the prisoners liberal; for whom he devised that he with his fellows should have but one meal a day, they paying notwithstanding for the whole: the other meal should be given to them that lacked on the other side of the prison. The Sunday before he suffered he drank to Mr Hooper, being then underneath him, and bade them commend him unto him and tell him there was never little fellow better would stick to a man than he would stick to him, presupposing they should both be burned together, although it happened otherwise; for Rogers was burned alone.

Now when the time came that he should be brought to Smithfield, first came to him Mr Woodrofe, one of the sheriffs, and asked him if he would revoke his abominable doctrine. Rogers answered, 'That which I have preached I will seal with my blood.' 'Then,' quoth Woodrofe, 'thou art an heretic.' 'That shall be known,' quoth Rogers, 'at the day of judgment.' 'Well,' quoth Woodrofe, 'I will never pray for thee.' 'But I will pray for you,' quoth Rogers; and so was brought by the sheriffs towards Smithfield, saying the *Miserere* by the way, all the people rejoicing at his constancy, with great praises to God for the same. And there in the presence of Mr Rochester, Controller of the Queen's Household, Sir Richard Southwell, both the sheriffs, and a wonderful number of people, he was burned into ashes, washing his hands in the flame as he was burning. A little before his burning at the stake, his pardon was brought if he would have recanted, but he utterly refused it. He was the *protomartyr* of all the blessed company that suffered in Queen Mary's time. His wife and children, eleven in number, ten able to go and one sucking at her breast, met him as he went towards Smithfield. This sorrowful sight of his own flesh and blood could nothing move him, but that he cheerfully took his death in defence of Christ's gospel.

The history of Laurence Sanders

After Queen Mary in the first year of her reign had inhibited the preaching of God's word, divers ministers of the word did notwithstanding according to their bounden duty feed their flock, not as teachers authorised by public authority, as in the happy days of blessed King Edward, but as private pastors of particular flocks; among whom Laurence Sanders was one, a man of worshipful parentage. His bringing up was in learning from his youth, in places meet for that purpose, as namely in the school of Eaton; from whence, according to the manner there used, he was chosen to go to the King's College in Cambridge, where he continued scholar three whole years and profited in learning very much. Shortly after that he did forsake the university and went to his parents, upon whose advice he minded to become a merchant, for that his mother, having a good portion for him among his brethren, thought to set him up wealthily. So he, coming up to London, was bound prentice with a merchant named Sir William Chester, who afterwards chanced to be Sheriff of London the year that Sanders was burned at Coventry. Thus by the mind of his friends Laurence should have been a merchant; but God saw better for his servant, as it fell out in the end. For the Lord so wrought in his heart that he could find no liking in that vocation; so that when his fellows were occupied about that kind of trade, he would withdraw himself into some privy corner and there fall into lamentations, as one not liking that kind of life.

His master, hearing his prentice thus in secret prayers to mourn by himself, called him unto him to know the cause; who then perceiving his mind nothing to fantasy that kind of life, and his whole purpose to be bent to the study of his book and spiritual contemplation, directed letters unto his friends, and giving him his indenture set him free. Thus Laurence, ravished with the love of learning and especially with the reading of God's word, returned to Cambridge, where he began to couple to the knowledge of Latin the study of Greek. Therewith also he joined the study of Hebrew. Then gave he himself wholly to the study of Holy Scripture, to furnish himself to the office of a preacher. As his exercises were special teachings, so in the end they proved singular consolations; so that he was able to comfort other who were in any affliction. Thus continued he in the university till he proceeded Master of Art, and a long space after.

In the beginning of King Edward's reign, after licence obtained he began to preach, and was so well liked of them which then had authority that they appointed him to read a divinity lecture in the college at Fothringa. He married about that time and in the married state led a life unblamable. The college being dissolved, he was placed to be Reader in the minster at Lichfield. After a certain space he departed to a benefice in Leicestershire called Church Langton, whereupon he, keeping residence, taught diligently. Thence he was called to take a benefice in London named All Hallows in Bread Street. Then minded he to give over his cure in the country, and after he had taken possession of his benefice in London he departed into the country to discharge himself thereof. At that time began the broil about the claim that Queen Mary made to the crown, by reason whereof he could not accomplish his purpose.

In this trouble he preached at Northampton, nothing meddling with the state, but boldly uttered his conscience against popish doctrine. The queen's men which were there and heard him were highly displeased with his sermon, and for it kept him among them as prisoner; but because there was no law broken by his preaching they dismissed him. He, seeing the dreadful days at hand, inflamed with godly zeal, preached at both benefices as time could serve him, seeing he could resign neither of them now but into the hands of a Papist. Thus passed he to and fro preaching until that proclamation was put forth of which mention is made at the beginning. At which time he was at his benefice in the country where he, notwithstanding the proclamation, taught diligently God's truth until he was not only commanded to cease but also with force resisted. Some of his friends counselled him to fly out of the realm, which he refused to do. But seeing he was with violence kept from doing good in that place, he returned towards London to visit the flock of which he had there the charge.

On the 14th of October as he was coming nigh to the city Sir John Mordant, a Councillor to Queen Mary, did overtake him and asked him whither he went. 'I have,' said Sanders, 'a cure in London; and I go to instruct my people according to my duty.' 'I would counsel you,' quoth the other, 'not to preach.' 'If you forbid me by lawful authority, then must I obey,' said Sanders. 'Nay,' quoth he, 'I will not forbid you; but I give you counsel.' Thus entered they both the city and departed each from other. Mordant went to give warning to Boner that Sanders would preach in his cure the next day. Sanders resorted to his lodging, with a mind bent to do his duty; where, because he seemed to be somewhat troubled, one which was there asked him how he did. 'In very deed,' saith he, 'I am prison till I be in prison,' meaning that his mind was unquiet until he had preached, and that then he should have quietness of mind though he were put in prison.

The next day in the forenoon he made a sermon in his parish. In the afternoon he was ready in his church to have given another exhortation to his people. But the bishop interrupted him by sending an officer for him. This officer charged him upon pain of contumacy forthwith to come to his master. Thus, as the apostles were brought out of the temple where they were teaching unto the rulers of the priests, so was Sanders brought before this bishop in his palace, who had in his company Mordant and some of his chaplains. The bishop laid no more to Sanders' charge but treason for breaking the queen's proclamation, heresy and sedition for his sermon!

After much talk had, the bishop willed him to write what he believed of transubstantiation. Sanders did so, saying, 'My Lord, ye do seek my blood, and ye shall have it. I pray God that ye may be so baptized in it that ye may thereafter loathe blood-sucking and become a better man.' This writing the bishop kept for his purpose—even to cut the writer's throat, as shall appear hereafter. The bishop, when he had his will, sent Sanders to the Lord Chancellor, as Annas sent Christ to Cayphas. But the Chancellor being not at home, Sanders was constrained to tarry for him four hours in the utter chamber, where he found a chaplain of the bishop's very merrily disposed, with certain gentlemen playing at the tables, with divers other occupied in the same exercise. All this time Sanders stood modestly at the cupboard bare-headed, Mordant walking up and down near him. At last the bishop returned from the Court, Sanders, brought to the place of examination, meekly kneeled down and made courtesy; unto whom the bishop spake on this wise: 'How happeneth it that notwithstanding the queen's proclamation you have enterprised to preach?' Sanders denied not that he did preach, saying that forasmuch as he saw the perilous time now at hand he did but (as he was warned by Ezekiel) exhort his flock to persever in the doctrine which they had learned, saying also that he was pricked forward thereunto by the place of the apostle wherein he was commanded rather to obey God than man; moreover nothing more moved him thereunto than his own conscience.

'A goodly conscience surely,' said the bishop. 'Your conscience could make our queen a bastard or misbegotten, would it not?' Then said Sanders, 'We do not say that the queen is misbegotten. For that, let them care whose writings are yet in the hands of men witnessing the same, not without the great shame of the author'; taunting the bishop himself, who had before to get the favour of King Henry VIII written a book *Of True Obedience*, wherein he had declared Mary to be a bastard. 'We do only teach the sincerity of the word; which albeit it is now forbidden us to preach with our mouths, yet I do not doubt but our blood shall manifest the same.' The bishop prettily nipped and touched said, 'Carry this frenzy fool to prison.' Sanders answered that he did give God thanks, which had given him at last a place of rest and quietness, where he might pray for the bishop's conversion.

Sanders continued in prison a year and three months. Strait charge was given to the keeper that no man should speak with him. His wife yet came to the prison gate with her young child in her arms to visit her husband. The keeper, though he durst not suffer her to come into the prison, yet did take the babe out of her arms and brought him unto his father. Sanders seeing him rejoiced greatly, saying that he rejoiced more to have such a boy than he should if two thousand pound were given him. Unto the standers-by, which praised the goodliness of the child, he said, 'What man would not lose his life rather than by prolonging it adjudge this boy to be a bastard, his wife a whore, and himself a whoremonger? If there were no other cause for which a man of my estate should lose his life, who would not give it to avouch this child to be legitimate, and his marriage lawful and holy?'

And now to come to the examination of this good man: after the bishop had kept him one whole year and a quarter in prison, at length they called him to be examined. This examination being ended, the officers led him out of the place, and so stayed until his fellows were likewise handled, that they might have them altogether to prison. Sanders, standing among the officers, seeing a multitude of people opened his mouth and spake freely, warning them of that which by their falling from Christ to Antichrist they did deserve, and exhorting them by repentance to rise again, and to embrace Christ with stronger faith, to confess him to the end in defiance of death and the devil. Copies of his examination and excommunication came to the hands of such as do keep them still in secret. After he was delivered to the secular power, he was brought by the Sheriff of London to the prison called the Counter in his own parish in Bread Street, whereat he rejoiced because out of prison as before out of a pulpit he might preach to his parishioners.

The 4th of February the Bishop of London did come to the prison to disgrade him; which when he had done, Sanders said, 'I thank God I am none of your church.' The day following the sheriff delivered him to certain of the queen's guard which were appointed to carry him to Coventry, there to be burned. The first night they came to St Albon's, where Mr Grimoald, a man who had more store of good gifts than of great constancy, did speak with him. Sanders took a cup in his hand, and asked him if he would pledge him of that cup of which he would begin to him. Grimoald shrugging and shrinking said, 'Of that cup which is in your hand I will pledge you; but of that other which you mean I will not promise you.' 'Well,' said Sanders, 'my dear Lord Jesus hath begun to me of a more bitter cup than mine shall be; and shall I not pledge my most sweet Saviour?'

After they were come to Coventry, a poor shoemaker came to him and said, 'O my good master, God strengthen and comfort you!' 'Gramercies, good shoemaker,' quoth Sanders, 'I pray thee pray for me; for I am the unmeetest man for this high office that ever was appointed to it; but my gracious God and most dear Father is able to make me strong enough.' That same night he was put into the common gaol among other prisoners, where he slept little but spent the night in prayer. The next day, the 8th of February, he was led to the place of execution in the park without the city, going in an old gown and a shirt, bare-footed. When he was come nigh to the place, the officer appointed to see the execution done said to Sanders that he was one of them which marred the queen's realm with false doctrine and heresy, 'Wherefore thou hast deserved death; yet if thou wilt revoke thine heresies the queen hath pardoned thee; if not, yonder fire is prepared for thee.' Sanders answered, 'It is not I nor my fellow-preachers of God's truth that have hurt the queen's realm, but yourself and such as you are, which have always resisted God's holy word. I hold no heresies; but the blessed gospel of Christ, that hold I; that have I taught; and that will I never revoke.' With that this tormentor cried, 'Away with him!' And away went Sanders with a merry courage towards the fire. He fell to the ground and prayed; he rose up again and took the stake in his arms and kissed it saying, 'Welcome the cross of Christ. Welcome everlasting life'; and being fastened to the stake and fire put to him, full sweetly he slept in the Lord.

The life and martyrdom of John Hooper

John Hooper, graduate in the University of Oxford, after the study of other sciences, wherein he had abundantly profited, was stirred with fervent desire to the love and knowledge of the Scriptures; in searching whereof there lacked in him no diligence, neither wanted unto him the grace of the Holy Ghost to open unto him the light. Thus Hooper, growing more and more in spiritual understanding and showing some sparkles of his fervent spirit in the time of King Henry VIII, fell into hatred of certain rabbins in Oxford, who began to stir coals against him; whereby he was compelled to void the university, and removing from thence was retained in the house of Sir Thomas Arundell, and was his steward till Arundell, having intelligence of his opinions, which he in no case did favour, yet favouring the person of the man, found means to send him in a message to the Bishop of Winchester, by conference of learning to do some good upon him; but in any case to send home his servant to him again. Winchester, after long conference with Hooper four or five days together, when he perceived that neither he could do good to him, nor that he would take any good at his hand, according to Arundell's request he sent home his servant again, commending his learning and wit but bearing in his breast a grudging spirit against Hooper still.

Not long after this intelligence was given to Hooper to provide for himself, for danger that was working against him. Whereupon Hooper, leaving Arundell's house and borrowing an horse from a friend, took his journey to the seaside to go to France, sending back the horse by one which indeed did not deliver him to the owner. Hooper being at Paris tarried there not long, but in short time returned into England, and was retained of Mr Sentlow till he was again laid for; whereby he was compelled, under pretence of being captain of a ship going to Ireland, to take the seas. And so escaped he through France to the higher parts of Germany, where he was lovingly entertained at Zurick of Mr Bullinger his singular friend. There also he married his wife, a Burgonian, and applied very studiously the Hebrew tongue.

At length, when God saw it good to stay the bloody time of the Six Articles and to give us King Edward to reign over this realm, amongst many other exiles which then repaired homeward Hooper thought not to absent himself, but offered to help forward the Lord's work to the uttermost of his ability. So coming to Bullinger and other of his acquaintance in Zurick to give them thanks for their singular kindness and humanity toward him, with like humanity purposed to take his leave of them, and so did. 'You shall be sure,' said he, 'from time to time to hear from me, and I will write unto you as it goeth with me. But the last news of all I shall not be able to write; for there,' said he, taking Bullinger by the hand, 'where I shall take most pains, there shall you hear of me to be burned to ashes.'

When Hooper had taken farewell of his friends in Zurick, he made his repair again into England, where he coming to London used continually to preach, most times twice every day, and never failed. The people in great flocks daily came to hear his voice, insomuch that oftentimes when he was preaching the church would be so full that none could enter further than the doors. In doctrine he was earnest, in tongue eloquent, in the Scriptures perfect, in pains indefatigable. Moreover as he began, so he continued unto his life's end. For neither could labour and pains-taking break him, neither promotion change him, neither dainty fare corrupt him. His life was so pure and good that no kind of slander could fasten any fault upon him. He was of body strong, his health sound, his wit pregnant, his invincible patience able to sustain whatsoever sinister fortune and adversity could do. He was constant of judgment, a good justicer, spare of diet, sparer of words, and sparest of time; in housekeeping very liberal, and sometime more free than his living would extend unto. Briefly, of all those virtues and qualities required of St Paul in a good bishop in his epistle to Timothy, I know not one in this good bishop lacking. He bare in countenance and talk always a certain grave grace, which might peradventure be wished sometimes to have been a little more popular and vulgar-like; but he knew what he had to do best himself.

After he had thus practised this common kind of preaching, at length he was called to preach before the King's Majesty, and soon after made Bishop of Gloucester by the king's commandment. In that office he continued two years, and behaved himself so well that his very enemies —except for his sharp correcting of sin—could find no fault with him; after that he was made Bishop of Worcester. As for the revenues of both his bishoprics, although they did not greatly exceed, yet if anything surmounted thereof he pursed nothing but bestowed it in hospitality. Twice I was in his house in Worcester, where in his common hall I saw a table spread with good store of meat, and beset full of beggars and poor folk of the city, who were served by four at a mess with hot and wholesome meats; and when they were served (being afore examined of the Lord's Prayer, the articles of their faith, and Ten Commandments) then he himself sat down to dinner and not before. After this manner Hooper executed the office of a most vigilant pastor so long as the state of religion did safely flourish: would God that all other bishops would use the like diligence in their function!

King Edward being dead and Mary crowned queen, religion being changed, this good bishop was one of the first sent for to London, first to answer to Dr Heath, then appointed bishop of that diocese, secondarily to render account to Dr Boner, Bishop of London, for that he in King Edward's time was one of his accusers, in that he showed himself not conformable to ordinances prescribed by the king and his Council. And although Hooper was not ignorant of the evils that should happen towards him, he tarried still saying, 'Once I did flee; but now, because I am called to this vocation, I am thoroughly persuaded to tarry, and to live and die with my sheep.' When at the day of his appearance, the 1st of September, he was come to London, before he could come to Drs. Heath and Boner he was intercepted to appear before the queen and her Council, to answer to certain obligations wherein they said he was bound unto her; and when he came before them, Winchester received him very opprobriously, and railing and rating of him accused him of religion. He, again, boldly told his tale and purged himself. But it came to this conclusion, that by then he was commanded to ward, it being declared unto him that his imprisonment was only for certain sums of money for which he was indebted to the queen, and not for religion. This how false and untrue it was, shall in his place appear.

The next year, 1554, the 19th of March, he was called again to appear before Winchester and other the queen's commissioners, where when he could not be permitted to plead his cause, he was deprived of his bishoprics. The 22nd of January 1555 Babington, the Warden of the Fleet, was commanded to bring Hooper before the Bishop of Winchester. The bishop moved Hooper to forsake the corrupt doctrine preached in the days of King Edward and acknowledge the Pope to be head of the Church. Hooper answered that he would in no wise condescend to any such usurped jurisdiction, neither esteemed he the church whereof they call him head to be the Catholic Church of Christ. Whereupon Babington was commanded to bring him to the Fleet again; who shifted him from his former chamber into another, and his former chamber was searched for writings which Hooper was thought to have made, but none were found.

The 28th of January the commissioners sat in judgment at St Mary Overy's, where Hooper appeared before them, and after much disputation was commanded aside till Rogers (which was then come) had been examined. Examinations ended, the two sheriffs were commanded to carry them to the Counter in Southwark, to see whether they would relent and come home to their catholic church. Hooper went before with one of the sheriffs, Rogers came after with the other, and being out of the church door Hooper looked back and stayed till Rogers drew near, unto whom he said, 'Come, brother Rogers; must we two take this matter first in hand and begin to fry these faggots?' 'Yea, sir,' said Rogers, 'by God's grace.' 'Doubt not,' said Hooper, 'but God will give strength.' So going forwards, there was such a press of people in the streets who rejoiced at their constancy that they had much ado to pass. By the way the sheriff said to Hooper, 'I wonder that ye were so hasty with my Lord Chancellor and did use no more patience.' He answered, 'Mr Sheriff, I was nothing at all impatient, although I was earnest in my Master's cause, and it standeth to me so in hand, for it goeth upon life and death; not the life and death of this world only, but of the world to come.' Then were they committed to the keeper of the Counter and appointed to several chambers, with commandment that they should not be suffered to speak one with another, neither any other permitted to come at them that night.

The next day they were brought again before the commissioners. After long and earnest talk, when they saw that Hooper would by no means condescend unto them, they condemned him to be degraded and read his condemnation. That done, Rogers was brought before them and in like manner entreated, and so they delivered both of them to the two sheriffs, who were willed to carry them to the Clink, a prison not far from Winchester's house, there to remain till night. When it was dark, Hooper was led with many bills and weapons through Winchester's house, and over London Bridge through the city to Newgate. Some of the sergeants were willed to go before and put out the costermongers' candles, who used to sit with lights in the streets; fearing that the people would have made attempt to have taken him away from them by force. But notwithstanding this device, the people having foreknowledge of his coming, many came forth of their doors with lights and saluted him, praising God for his constancy in the true doctrine, and desiring God to strengthen him to the end. Hooper required the people to make their earnest prayers for him, and so went through Cheapside to the place appointed and was delivered as close prisoner to the keeper of Newgate, where he remained six days, nobody being permitted to come to him or talk to him.

The 4th of February, in the chapel in Newgate, the Bishop of London there sitting with his notary and other witnesses, came Alexander Andrew the gaoler, bringing Hooper and Rogers; where the bishop at the request of Winchester proceeded to the degradation of Hooper and Rogers. First he put upon them all the vestures and ornaments belonging to a priest, as though they should solemnly execute in their office. Thus they being invested, the bishop beginneth to pluck off first the uppermost vesture; and so by degrees coming down to the lowest vesture; and so being stript he deprived them of all benefits belonging to the clergy, and pronounced the parties so degraded to be given to the secular power, the sheriffs; who receiving first Mr Rogers had him away, bringing him to the place of execution where he suffered. The same night his keeper gave him[1] an inkling that he should be sent to Gloucester to suffer death, whereat he rejoiced very much, praising God that he saw it good to send him amongst the people over whom he was pastor, there to confirm with his death the truth which he had taught them. And immediately he sent for his boots, spurs, and cloak, that he might be in readiness to ride when he should be called.

Next day about four o'clock in the morning the keeper came and searched him and the bed wherein he lay, to see if he had written anything; then he was led by the sheriffs and their officers to a place not far from St Dunstan's Church in Fleet Street, where six of the queen's guards were appointed to receive him and carry him to Gloucester, there to be delivered unto the sheriff who with Lord Shandoys and other commissioners were appointed to see execution done. Which guard brought him to the Angel, where he brake his fast with them, eating more liberally than he had used to do. About break of day he leaped cheerfully on horseback without help, having a hood under his hat that he should not be known. And so he took his journey joyfully towards Gloucester, and always by the way the guard learned of him where he was accustomed to lodge, and ever carried him to another inn.

[1] Hooper.—Ed.

On the Thursday following he came to a town in his diocese called Ciceter about eleven o'clock, and there dined at a woman's house which had always hated the truth and spoken all evil she could of Hooper. This woman, perceiving the cause of his coming, showed him all the friendship she could and lamented his case with tears, confessing that she had often reported that if he were put to the trial he would not stand to his doctrine. After dinner he rode forwards and came to Gloucester about 5 o'clock. A mile without the town was much people assembled, which lamented his estate, insomuch that one of the guard rode post into the town to require aid of the mayor and sheriffs, fearing lest he should have been taken from them. The officers and their retinue repaired to the gates with weapons and commanded the people to keep their houses; but no man once gave any signification of rescue or violence. So was he lodged at one Ingram's house in Gloucester; and that night, as he had done all the way, he did eat his meat quietly, and slept his first sleep soundly. After his first sleep he continued all night in prayer until the morning, and then desired that he might go into the next chamber (for the guards were in the chamber where he lay) that there being solitary he might talk with God; so that all that day, saving a little at meat and when he talked with such as the guard licensed to speak with him, he bestowed in prayer.

The sheriffs were determined to have lodged him in the common gaol called Northgate, if the guard had not made intercession for him, who declared at large how quietly and patiently he had behaved himself in the way; adding that any child might keep him, and that they would rather take pains to watch with him than that he should be sent to the common prison. So it was determined that he should remain in Robert Ingram's house, and the sheriffs, sergeants, and other officers did appoint to watch with him themselves. His desire was that he might go to bed that night betimes, saying that he had many things to remember; and so he did at five o'clock, and slept one sleep soundly, and bestowed the rest of the night in prayer. In the morning he desired that no man should be suffered to come into the chamber, that he might be solitary till the hour of execution.

About eight o'clock came Lord Shandoys with a great band of men, Sir Anthony Kingston, and other commissioners appointed to see execution done. At nine Hooper was willed to prepare himself, for the time was at hand. Immediately he was brought down from his chamber by the sheriffs, accompanied with bills, glaives, and weapons.

When he saw the multitude of weapons, he spake on this wise: 'Mr Sheriffs, I am no traitor, neither needed you to have made such a business to bring me where I must suffer, if ye had willed me, I would have gone alone to the stake and have troubled none of you.' Afterwards, looking upon the people assembled, being by estimation 7000 (for it was market-day, and many also came to see his behaviour towards death) he spake unto those that were about him, saying, 'Why be these people assembled? Peradventure they think to hear something of me now as in times past; but alas, speech is prohibited me. Notwithstanding, the cause of my death is well known unto them. When I was appointed to be their pastor, I preached unto them true doctrine out of the word of God; because I will not now account the same to be untrue, this kind of death is prepared for me.'

So he went forward between the sheriffs in a gown of his host's, his hat upon his head and a staff in his hand to stay himself withal; for the *sciatica* which he had in prison caused him somewhat to halt. All the way, being straitly charged not to speak, he could not be perceived once to open his mouth, but beholding the people, which mourned bitterly for him, he would sometimes lift up his eyes and look very cheerfully upon such as he knew; he was never known, during the time of his being amongst them, to look with so cheerful and ruddish a countenance as he did at that present. When he came to the place where he should die, smilingly he beheld the stake and preparation made for him, near the great elm tree over against the College of Priests, where he was wont to preach. The place round about the houses and the boughs of the trees were replenished with people; and in the chamber over the college gate stood the priests of the college. Then kneeled he down to prayer, and beckoned unto him whom he knew well to hear the prayer, to make report thereof in time to come; who, pouring tears upon his shoulder, gave attentive ears unto the same; which prayer he made upon the whole creed, wherein he continued half an hour. After he was somewhat entered into his prayer, a box was brought and laid before him upon a stool, with his pardon from the queen if he would turn. At the sight whereof he cried, 'If you love my soul away with it, away with it!' The box being taken away Lord Shandoys said, 'Seeing there is no remedy, dispatch quickly.' Hooper said, 'Good my Lord, I trust your Lordship will give me leave to make an end of my prayers.' Then said my Lord Shandoys to Sir Edmund Bridges his son, which gave ear before to Hooper's prayer at his request, 'Edmund, take heed that he do nothing else but pray: if he do, tell me and I shall quickly dispatch him.'

Prayer being done, he prepared himself to the stake, put off his host's gown and delivered it to the sheriffs, requiring them to see it restored to the owner, and put off the rest of his gear unto his doublet and hose, wherein he would have burned. But the sheriffs would not permit that, such was their greediness; unto whose pleasures he obediently submitted himself, and his doublet, hose, and petticoat were taken off. Then being in his shirt he took a point from his hose himself and trussed his shirt between his legs, where he had a pound of gunpowder in a bladder, and under each arm the like quantity, delivered him by the guard. So desiring the people to say the Lord's Prayer with him and to pray for him—who performed it with tears during the time of his pains—he went up to the stake. Three irons made to bind him to the stake were brought; one for his neck, another for his middle, and the third for his legs. But he refusing them said, 'Ye have no need thus to trouble yourselves: I doubt not but God will give strength sufficient to abide the fire without bands; notwithstanding, suspecting the frailty of the flesh but having assured confidence in God's strength, I am content ye do as ye think good.' So the hoop prepared for his middle was brought, which being somewhat too short (for his belly was swollen by imprisonment) he shrank and put in his belly with his hand until it was fastened; when they offered to have bound his neck and legs with the other two hoops he utterly refused them, saying, 'I am well assured I shall not trouble you.'

Thus being ready, he looked upon the people, of whom he might be well seen (for he was tall and stood on an high stool) and beheld round about him: in every corner there was nothing to be seen but weeping people. Then he prayed to himself. By and by he that was appointed to make the fire came to him and did ask forgiveness. Of whom he asked why he should forgive him, saying that he knew never any offence he had committed against him. 'Oh, sir,' said the man, 'I am appointed to make the fire.' 'Therein,' said Hooper, 'thou dost nothing offend me; do thine office, I pray thee.' Then the reeds were cast up, and he received two bundles in his own hands, kissed them, and put under either arm one of them, and showed with his hands how the rest should be bestowed, and pointed to the place where any did lack.

Anon commandment was given that fire should be set to, and so it was. But because there were put to no fewer green faggots than two horses could carry, it kindled not by and by, and was a pretty while also before it took the reeds upon the faggots. At length it burned about him, but the wind having full strength—it was a lowering and cold morning—it blew the flame from him, so that he was no more but touched by the fire. A few dry faggots were brought, and a new fire kindled with faggots; for there were no more reeds. That burned at the nether parts but had small power above because of the wind, saving that it did burn his hair and scorch his skin a little. In the time of which fire he prayed, saying mildly, as one without pains, 'Lord Jesus, have mercy upon me and receive my soul.' After the second was spent, he did wipe his eyes with his hands and said with an indifferent loud voice, 'For God's love, good people, let me have more fire.' All this while his nether parts did burn: the faggots were so few that the flame did not burn strongly at his upper parts. The third fire was kindled within a while, more extreme than the other two; then the bladders of gunpowder brake, which did him small good, the wind had such power. In which fire he prayed with somewhat a loud voice, 'Lord Jesus, receive my spirit.' These were the last words he was heard to utter. But when he was black in the mouth, and his tongue swoln that he could not speak, his lips went till they were shrunk to the gums; and he knocked his breast with his hands until one of his arms fell off, and then knocked still with the other, what time the fat, water, and blood dropped out at his fingers' ends, until his strength was gone and his hand did cleave fast to the iron upon his breast. So bowing forwards he yielded up his spirit.

Thus was he three-quarters of an hour or more in the fire. Even as a lamb patiently he abode the extremity thereof, neither moving forwards, backwards, nor to any side; but having his nether parts burned and his bowels fallen out he died as quietly as a child in his bed. He now reigneth, I doubt not, as a blessed martyr in the joys of heaven prepared for the faithful in Christ before the foundations of the world.

When I see the patience of these martyrs in our days, so constantly abiding the torments ministered unto them for God's cause, methinks I may worthily compare them unto the martyrs of the primitive Church; in the number of whom, if comparison be to be made between saint and saint, martyr and martyr, with whom might I better match John Hooper than with Polycarpus the ancient Bishop of Smyrna, of whom Eusebius maketh mention in *The Ecclesiastical Story*? For as both agreed in one kind of punishment, being both put to the fire, so which of them showed more patience in the time of suffering, it is hard to be said. And though Polycarpus being set in the flame was kept by miracle from the torment of the fire till he was stricken down with weapon and dispatched; Hooper, by no less miracle armed with fervent spirit of God's comfort, despised the violence thereof, as though he had felt little more than did Polycarpus the fire flaming round about him. Moreover as is written of Polycarpus, when he should have been tied to the stake he required to stand untied saying, 'Let me alone, I pray you; for he that gave me strength to come to this fire will give me patience to abide in the same without your tying;' so likewise Hooper, when he should have been tied with three chains to the stake, requiring them to have no such mistrust of him was tied with but one; who, if he had not been tied at all, no doubt would have no less answered to that great patience of Polycarpus.

The history of Dr Rowland Taylor

The town of Hadley was one of the first that received the word of God in all England, at the preaching of Thomas Bilney; by whose industry the gospel of Christ had such gracious success and took such root there that a great number of that parish became exceeding well learned in the Holy Scriptures, as well women as men, so that a man might have found among them many that had often read the whole Bible through, and could have said a great part of St Paul's epistles by heart, and readily given a learned sentence in any matter of controversy. Their children and servants were also trained so diligently in the knowledge of God's word that the whole town seemed rather an university of the learned than a town of clothes-making or labouring people; and that most is to be commended, they were for the more part faithful followers of God's word in their living.

In this town was Rowland Taylor, Doctor in both Civil and Canon Laws and a right perfect divine; who at his entering into his benefice did not, as the common sort do, let out his benefice to a farmer that should gather in the profits and set in an ignorant priest to serve the cure, and, so they have the fleece, little or nothing care for feeding the flock; contrarily he forsook Archbishop Cranmer, with whom he was in household, and made his personal abode in Hadley among the people committed to his charge; where he gave himself wholly to the study of Holy Scriptures, faithfully endeavouring to fulfil that charge which the Lord gave unto Peter: 'Feed my lambs, feed my sheep.' This love of Christ so wrought in him that no Sunday nor holy day passed, nor other time when he might get the people together, but he preached to them the doctrine of salvation.

Not only was his word a preaching unto them, but all his life was an example of unfeigned holiness. He was void of pride, meek as any child, so that none were so poor but they might boldly resort unto him; neither was his lowliness fearful, but as occasion required he would be stout in rebuking evildoers. None was so rich but he would tell him his fault, with such earnest rebukes as became a good pastor. He was ready to do good to all men, readily forgiving his enemies, and never sought to do evil to any. To the poor that were blind, lame, sick, or that had many children he was a very father and diligent provider; insomuch that he caused the parishioners to make general provision for them, and he himself, beside the relief that they always found at his house, gave an honest portion to the common alms-box. His wife also was a discreet and sober matron, and his children brought up in the fear of God and good learning.

Thus continued this good shepherd among his flock, leading them through the wilderness of this wicked world, all the days of King Edward VI. But after it pleased God to take Edward from this vale of misery unto his blessed rest, a petty gentleman, a lawyer called Foster, being a steward and keeper of courts, a man of no great skill but a bitter persecutor, with one John Clerke of Hadley, conspired to bring in the Pope and his maumetry again into Hadley church. For as yet Dr Taylor had retained in his church the service and reformation made by King Edward, and earnestly preached against popish corruptions. Foster and Clerke hired John Averth, parson of Aldam, a very money mammonist and an open advouterer and whoremonger, to come to Hadley and there begin again the popish mass. To this purpose they builded up with all haste possible the altar, intending to bring in their mass again about Palm Monday. But in the night the altar was beaten down; therefore they built it up the second time, and laid watch, lest any should again break it down. The day following came Foster and Clerke, bringing with them their popish sacrificer, who brought all his implements and garments to play his popish pageant, whom they and their men guarded with swords and bucklers, lest any man should disturb him in his missal-sacrifice.

When Dr Taylor, who sat studying the word of God, heard the bells ringing, he arose and went into the church, supposing something had been there to be done, and found the doors fast barred, saving the chancel door, which was only latched. He, entering in and coming into the chancel, saw a popish sacrificer in his robes, with a broad new-shaven crown, beset round about with drawn swords and bucklers. Then said Taylor, 'Thou devil! Who made thee so bold to enter into this church of Christ to profane it with this abominable idolatry?' With that start up Foster, and with a furious countenance said to Taylor, 'Thou traitor! What doest thou here to perturb the queen's proceedings?' Taylor answered, 'I am no traitor, I am the shepherd that Christ hath appointed to feed this his flock: I have authority to be here; and I command thee, thou popish wolf, to avoid hence.' Then said Foster, 'Wilt thou, traitorly heretic, make a commotion and resist the queen's proceedings?' Taylor answered, 'I make no commotion; I resist only your idolatries which are against God's word, the queen's honour, and tend to the subversion of this realm. And further, thou dost against the canon law, which commandeth that no mass be said but at a consecrate altar.'

When the parson of Aldam heard that, he began to shrink back and would have left his saying of mass; then start up Clerke and said, 'Mr Averth, be not afraid, you have a *superaltare*;[1] go forth with your business, man.' Then Foster with his armed men took Dr Taylor and led him with strong hand out of the church; and the popish prelate proceeded in his idolatry. Taylor's wife, who followed her husband into the church, when she saw her husband thus violently thrust out of his church, kneeled down and held up her hands and with loud voice said, 'I beseech God to avenge this injury that this idolater doth to the blood of Christ.' Then they thrust her out of the church also and shut the doors; for they feared that the people would have rent their sacrificer in pieces. Notwithstanding one or two threw in great stones at the windows and missed very little the popish masser.

A day or two after, Foster and Clerke made a complaint of Dr Taylor, by a letter written to Stephen Gardiner. When the bishop heard this, he sent a letter to Taylor commanding him to appear before him to answer complaints made against him. When Taylor's friends heard this they were exceeding sorry, foreseeing to what end the matter would come, and earnestly counselled him to fly, declaring that he

[1] A stone consecrated by the bishops, which the Papists carry instead of an altar when they mass for money in gentlemen's houses.

could neither be indifferently heard to speak his mind, nor look for justice at the Chancellor's hands, who was most fierce and cruel; but must needs, if he went up to him, wait for imprisonment and death at his hands. Then said Taylor, 'Dear friends, I heartily thank you for that ye have so tender a care over me. And although there is neither justice nor truth to be looked for at my adversaries' hands, but imprisonment and cruel death, yet know I my cause to be so good, and truth so strong upon my side, that I will go and appear before them and to their beards resist their false doings.' Then said his friends, 'Mr Doctor, we think it not best so to do. You have sufficiently done your duty in resisting the parson of Aldam. And forasmuch as our Saviour biddeth us that when they persecute us in one city we should fly into another, we think in flying ye should do best, keeping yourself against another time, when the Church shall have great need of such teachers and pastors.' 'Oh,' quoth Taylor, 'what will ye have me to do? I have already lived too long, to see these terrible and wicked days. Fly you and do as your conscience leadeth you; I am determined to go to the bishop. God shall hereafter raise up teachers of his people, which shall with much more diligence and fruit teach them than I have done. God will not forsake his Church. As for me, I shall never be able to do God so good service as I may do now; nor shall I ever have so glorious a calling as I now have, nor so great mercy proffered me as is now at this present.'

When his friends saw him determined to go, they with weeping eyes commended him unto God. He within a day or two prepared himself to his journey, leaving his cure with an old priest, Sir Richard Yeoman, who afterwards for God's truth was burnt at Norwich. There was also in Hadley one Alcocke, who after Yeoman was driven away used daily to read a chapter and say the English litany in Hadley church. But him they fet up to London and cast in prison in Newgate, where after a year he died.

Taylor, accompanied with a servant named John Hull, took his journey towards London. By the way Hull laboured to persuade him to fly, and proffered himself to go with him, to serve him and in all perils to venture his life for him. But in no wise would Taylor agree thereunto, but said, 'Oh, John, shall I give place to thy worldly persuasion and leave my flock in this danger? Remember the good Shepherd Christ which died for his flock. Him must I follow. Therefore, good John, pray for me, and if thou seest me weak at any time, comfort me.'

Thus they came to London, and Taylor presented himself to Gardiner, Lord Chancellor of England. For this hath been one great abuse these many years, that offices of most importance have commonly been committed to bishops, whereby three mischiefs have happened, to the dishonour of God and neglecting of the flock of Christ. First, they have had small leisure to attend to their pastoral cures; secondly, it hath puffed up many bishops into such pride that they have thought no nobleman in the realm worthy to be their fellow; thirdly, where they by this means knew the secrets of princes they have caused the same to be known in Rome afore the kings could accomplish their intents in England. By this means hath the Papacy been so maintained, and things ordered after their pleasure, that much mischief hath happened in this realm and others.

Now when Gardiner saw Taylor, he reviled him, calling him knave, traitor, heretic, with many other villainous reproaches; which all Taylor heard patiently, and at last said, 'My Lord, I am neither traitor nor heretic, but a true subject and a Christian man; and am come according to your commandment to know the cause that your Lordship hath sent for me.'

'Art thou come, villain? How darest thou look me in the face? Knowest thou not who I am?'

'Yes; ye are Dr Stephen Gardiner, Bishop of Winchester and Lord Chancellor; and yet but a mortal man, I trow. But if I should be afraid of your lordly looks, why fear you not God, the Lord of us all? How dare ye look *any* Christian man in the face, seeing ye have denied our Saviour Christ and his word and done contrary to your own oath and writing? With what countenance will ye appear before the judgment seat of Christ, and answer to your oath made first unto Henry VIII of famous memory and afterward unto Edward his son?'

'Tush! That was Herod's oath; unlawful and worthy to be broken. I have done well in breaking it, and I thank God I am come home to our Mother the Catholic Church of Rome; and so I would thou shouldst do.'

'Should I forsake the Church of Christ, founded upon the apostles and prophets, to approve those lies, errors, superstitions, and idolatries that the Popes and their company so blasphemously approve? God forbid. Let the Pope and his return to Christ and his word; then will Christian men turn unto him. You wrote truly against him and were sworn against him.'

'I tell thee it was Herod's oath; and our Holy Father hath discharged me of it.'

'But you shall not be so discharged before Christ, who will require it at your hands as a lawful oath made to our sovereign Lord the king, from whose obedience no man can assoil you.'

'Thou art an arrogant lunatic and very fool.'

'My Lord, leave your railing, which is not seemly for one in authority. I am a Christian man, and he that saith to his brother, "Thou fool," is in danger of hell fire.'

'Thou art married?'

'I thank God I am, and have had nine children, all in lawful matrimony. Blessed be God that ordained matrimony and commanded that every man that hath not the gift of continency should marry a wife and not live in adultery or whoredom.'

Then called the bishop his men and said, 'Have this fellow hence! Carry him to the King's Bench and charge the keeper he be straitly kept.' Then kneeled Taylor down and said, 'Lord, I thank thee. From the tyranny of the Bishop of Rome and his detestable errors and abominations good Lord deliver us, and God be praised for good King Edward.' So they carried him to the King's Bench, where he lay prisoner almost two years. He found therein the vigilant preacher of God's word Mr Bradford. After a while he was cited to appear in the Arches at Bow Church, when he stoutly defended his marriage, affirming by the Scriptures of God, by the doctors of the primitive Church, by laws civil and canon, that it is lawful for a priest to marry. This did he so plainly prove that the judge could give no sentence of divorce against him; but gave sentence he should be deprived of his benefice because he was married. Hadley benefice was given or sold to one Newall, whose virtues were altogether unlike Taylor, as the poor parishioners full well have proved.

After a year and three quarters, in which the Papists got certain old laws put down by King Henry VIII and King Edward revived by parliament, so that they might *ex officio* cite whom they would and charge him with what articles they lusted, they sent for Dr Taylor with certain other prisoners, which were convented before the Chancellor and other commissioners about the 22nd of January. After Taylor with great spirit had answered for himself and rebuked his adversaries for breaking their oath, they committed him to prison again, where he endured till the last of January.

On the day aforesaid Taylor, Bradford, and Sanders were called to appear before the Bishop of Winchester, the Bishops of Norwich, London, Salisbury, and Duresme, and were charged with heresy and schism. A determinate answer was required, whether they would submit themselves to the Roman bishop; or else they would proceed to their condemnation. When Taylor and his fellows heard this, they answered boldly that they would not depart from the truth which they had preached in King Edward's days, neither submit themselves to the Romish Antichrist: they thanked God for so great mercy, that he would call them to be worthy to suffer for his word and truth. When the bishops saw them so unmovably fixed in the truth, they read the sentence of death upon them; which when they heard, they said, 'We doubt not, but God will require our blood at your hands.'

So was Taylor bestowed in the Clink till it was toward night, and then removed to the Counter by the Poultry. When he had lien in the Counter a sevennight or thereabouts, the 4th of February 1555 Boner Bishop of London with others came to disgrade him, bringing such ornaments as appertain to their mummery. He called for Taylor to be brought unto him; so Taylor was brought down from the chamber above. At his coming the bishop said, 'Mr Doctor, I would you would remember yourself and turn to your Mother, Holy Church; so I will sue for your pardon.' Taylor answered, 'I would you and your fellows would turn to Christ.' 'Well,' quoth the bishop, 'I am come to disgrade you: put on these vestures.' 'No,' quoth Taylor, 'I will not.' 'Wilt thou not?' said the bishop; 'I shall make thee ere I go.' Then he charged him upon his obedience to do it, but he would not; so he willed another to put them on his back. When he was furnished therewith, he set his hands by his side, walking up and down, and said, 'How say you, my Lord? am not I a goodly fool? If I were in Cheap, should I not have boys enough to laugh at these apish toys?' So the bishop scraped his fingers, thumbs, and the crown of his head, and did the rest of such-like devilish observances. When he should have given Taylor a stroke on the breast with his crozier staff, the bishop's chaplain said, 'My Lord, strike him not, for he will sure strike again,' 'Yea, by St Peter will I,' quoth Taylor; 'I were no Christian if I would not fight in my Master's quarrel.' So the bishop laid his curse upon him but stroke him not. Then Taylor said, 'You curse me, yet God doth bless me. You have done me wrong and violence; yet I pray God forgive you. But from the tyranny of the Bishop of Rome and his detestable enormities good Lord deliver us.' Going up to his chamber he told Bradford that he had made the bishop afraid; 'for,' saith he laughingly, 'his chaplain gave him counsel not to strike me, for that I would strike again; and by my troth I made him believe I would do so indeed.'

The night after he was disgraded, his wife and his son Thomas resorted unto him, and were by the gentleness of the keepers permitted to sup with him. For this difference was ever found between the keepers of the bishops' prisons and the keepers of the king's prisons: the bishops' keepers were ever cruel like their masters; but the keepers of the king's prisons showed for the most part as much favour as they possibly might. So came Taylor's wife, his son, and John Hull his servant to sup with him; and afore supper they kneeled down and prayed, saying the litany.

After supper he gave God thanks that had so called him and given him strength to abide by his holy word; and turning to Thomas he said, 'My dear son, God bless thee and give thee his Holy Spirit, to be a true servant of Christ, to learn his word, and to stand by his truth all thy life long. See that thou fear God always. Flee from sin and wicked living: serve God with daily prayer and apply thy book. Be obedient to thy mother, love her and serve her: be ruled by her now in thy youth and follow her counsel in all things. Beware of lewd company, of young men that fear not God but follow their lusts and vain appetites. Fly from whoredom and hate all filthy living, remembering that I thy father die in defence of holy marriage. Another day, when God shall bless thee, love and cherish the poor, and count thy chief riches to be rich in alms. When thy mother is old, forsake her not, but provide for her to thy power and see that she lack nothing; for so will God bless thee.'

Then turning to his wife: 'My dear wife,' quoth he, 'continue steadfast in the fear and love of God. I have been unto you a faithful yokefellow, and so have you been unto me; for which I pray God to reward you. Now the time is come that I shall be taken from you, and you discharged of the wedlock-bond towards me: therefore I will give you my counsel. You are yet a child-bearing woman, and therefore it will be most convenient for you to marry. For doubtless you shall never be at a convenient stay for yourself and our poor children, nor out of trouble, till you be married. Therefore, as soon as God will provide it, marry some faithful man that feareth God. Doubt not, God will provide an honest husband for you, and will be a merciful Father to you and to my children; whom I pray you bring up in the fear of God and in learning, to the uttermost of your power.'

When he had thus said, they prayed together and kissed one the other; and he gave his wife a book of the church service set out by King Edward, and his son a Latin book containing the notable sayings of the old martyrs, gathered out of *Ecclesiastica Historia*.

On the morrow after Taylor had supped with his wife, which was the 5th of February, the sheriff with his officers came to the Counter by two in the morning, brought forth Dr Taylor, and without any light led him to the Woolsack, an inn without Aldgate, Taylor's wife, suspecting that her husband should that night be carried away, watching all night in St Butolph's church porch, having with her two children, Elizabeth, 14 years of age (whom being left without father or mother Taylor had brought up of alms from three years old), the other Mary, Taylor's own daughter. When the sheriff and his company came against St Butolph's, Elizabeth cried, 'Oh my dear father! Mother, mother, here is my father led away.' Then cried his wife, 'Rowland, Rowland, where art thou?' For it was a very dark morning. Taylor answered, 'Dear wife, I am here,' and stayed. The sheriff's men would have led him forth; but the sheriff said, 'Stay a little, masters, and let him speak with his wife'; and so they stayed. Then came she to him, and he took Mary in his arms; and he, his wife, and Elizabeth kneeled down and said the Lord's Prayer. The sheriff wept apace, and so did others of the company. After they had prayed, he rose and kissed his wife and shook her by the hand, and said, 'Farewell my dear wife; be of good comfort, for I am quiet in my conscience. God shall stir up a father to my children.' Then he kissed Mary and said, 'God bless thee and make thee his servant'; and kissing Elizabeth he said, 'God bless thee. I pray you all stand strong and steadfast unto Christ and his word, and keep you from idolatry.' Then said his wife, 'God be with thee, dear Rowland; I will with God's grace meet thee at Hadley.'

So was he led to the Woolsack, and his wife followed him. He was put into a chamber with four yeomen of the guard and the sheriff's men. Taylor, as soon as he was come into the chamber, fell on his knees and gave himself to prayer. The sheriff, seeing Taylor's wife there, would in no case grant her to speak any more with her husband, but gently desired her to go to his house and take it as her own, and promised her she should lack nothing, and sent two officers to conduct her thither. Notwithstanding she desired to go to her mother's, whither the officers led her, and charged her mother to keep her there till they came again. Thus remained Dr Taylor in the Woolsack till eleven o'clock, at which time the sheriff was ready to receive him; so they set him on horseback within the inn, the gates being shut. At the coming out of the gates John Hull stood at the rails with Thomas. When Taylor saw them he called them, and Hull lifted the child and set him on the horse before his father; and Taylor put off his hat and said to the people that stood there, 'Good people, this is mine own son, begotten in lawful matrimony; God be blessed for lawful matrimony.' Then lifted he up his eyes and prayed for his son, laid his hat upon the child's head and blessed him, and delivered the child to Hull, whom he took by the hand and said, 'Farewell John Hull, the faithfulest servant that ever man had.' And so they rode forth, the Sheriff of Essex with four yeomen of the guard and the sheriff's men leading him.

When they were come almost at Burntwood, Arthur Faysie, who before had been Dr Taylor's servant, met them, and supposing him to have been at liberty said, 'Mr Doctor, I am glad to see you again at liberty,' and took him by the hand. 'Soft, sir,' quoth the sheriff, 'he is a prisoner.' 'I cry you mercy,' said Arthur, 'I knew not so much and thought it no offence to talk to a true man.' The sheriff was very angry with this, and threatened to carry Arthur to prison; notwithstanding he bade him get quickly away. And so they rode to Burntwood, where they caused to be made for Taylor a close hood, with holes for his eyes and a slit for his mouth, that no man should know him. All the way Taylor was merry, as one going to a banquet or bridal. He spake many notable things to the sheriff and yeomen, and often moved them to weep through his calling upon them to amend their wicked living. Oftentimes also he caused them to wonder and rejoice, to see him so void of fear, joyful in heart, and glad to die. Of these yeomen three used Taylor friendly, but the fourth, whose name was Homes, used him very churlishly.

At Chelmsford met them the Sheriff of Suffolk, there to receive him. At supper the Sheriff of Essex earnestly laboured him to return to the popish religion and said, 'Good Mr Doctor, we are right sorry for you, considering what loss is of such one as ye might be if ye would. God hath given you great learning and wisdom; wherefore ye have been in great favour in times past with the highest of this realm. Besides, ye are a man of goodly personage and by nature like to live many years; and ye should in time to come be in as good reputation as ever ye were, or better. For ye are beloved of all men, and it were great pity ye should cast away yourself willingly, and come to such a painful and shameful death. Ye should do much better to revoke your opinions and return to the Catholic Church of Rome, acknowledge the Pope's Holiness to be supreme head of the Universal Church, and reconcile yourself to him. Doubt not but ye shall find favour at the queen's hands. I and all these your friends will be suitors for your pardon, which no doubt ye shall obtain. This counsel I give you of good will toward you; and therefore I drink to you.' In like manner said all the yeomen of the guard.

When they had all dronk to him and the cup was come to him, he stayed a little as one studying what answer he might give. At last he said, 'My masters all, I heartily thank you of your good will; I have hearkened to your words and marked well your counsels. To be plain with you, I perceive that I have been deceived myself, and am like to deceive a great many of Hadley of their expectation.' 'Good Mr Doctor,' quoth the sheriff, 'God's blessing on your heart! Hold you there still. It is the comfortablest word that we heard you speak yet. What? should ye cast away yourself in vain? Play a wise man's part, and I warrant ye shall find favour.' Thus they rejoiced at the word and were very merry. At last 'Mr Doctor,' quoth the sheriff, 'what meant ye by this, that ye say ye think ye have been deceived yourself, and shall deceive many one in Hadley?' Then said Taylor, 'I will tell you. I am as you see, a man that hath a very great carcase, which I thought should have been buried in Hadley churchyard, if I had died in my bed as I hoped. But herein I was deceived; and there are a great number of worms in Hadley churchyard which should have had jolly feeding upon this carrion, which they have looked for many a day. But now I know we be deceived, both I and they; for this carcase must be burnt to ashes, and so shall they lose their bait and feeding that they looked to have had of it.' When the company heard him say so, they were amazed and looked one on another, marvelling at the man's constant mind that without all fear made a jest at the cruel torment now prepared for him. Thus was their expectation clean disappointed.

When they were come to Lanham, the sheriff stayed there two days; and thither came a great number of gentlemen and justices appointed to aid the sheriff. These laboured Taylor very sore to reduce him to the Romish religion, promising him his pardon. They promised him promotions—yea, a bishopric if he would take it; but their words were in vain. For he had not built his house upon the sand, but on the sure and immovable rock. After two days the sheriff led Taylor towards Hadley; and coming within a mile of Hadley he desired to light off his horse to make water: which done, he leaped and fet a frisk or twain as men do in dancing. 'Why, Mr Doctor,' quoth the sheriff, 'how do you now?' He answered, 'Well, Mr Sheriff—never better; for now I know I am almost at home. I lack not past two stiles to go over, and I am at my Father's house. But Mr Sheriff, shall not we go through Hadley?' 'Yes,' said the sheriff, 'you shall go through Hadley.' Then said he, 'Good Lord, I thank thee I shall once ere I die see my flock, whom I have most heartily loved and truly taught. Good Lord, bless them and keep them steadfast in thy truth.'

When they were come to Hadley and came riding over the bridge, at the bridge foot waited a poor man with five small children. When he saw Taylor, he and his children fell upon their knees and held up their hands, and cried, 'Dear father and good shepherd Dr Taylor, God succour thee as thou hast many a time succoured me and my poor children.' Such witness had the servant of God of his charitable alms given in his lifetime. The sheriff and others that led him to death were astonied at this, and the sheriff sore rebuked the poor man. The streets of Hadley were beset on both sides with men and women of the town and country who waited to see him; whom when they beheld so led to death, with weeping eyes and lamentable voices they cried, 'Ah good Lord, there goeth our good shepherd from us, that so faithfully hath taught us, so fatherly hath cared for us, and so godly hath governed us. Merciful God, what shall we poor scattered lambs do? Good Lord, strengthen him and comfort him.' Wherefore the people were rebuked by the sheriff and catchpoles. Dr Taylor said to the people, 'I have preached to you God's word and truth, and am come this day to seal it with my blood.' Coming against the almshouses he cast to the poor people money which remained of that good people had given him in time of his imprisonment. As for his living, they took it from him at his first going to prison, so that he was sustained all the time of his imprisonment by the alms of people that visited him. The money that now remained he put in a glove and gave to the almsmen standing at their doors to see him. Coming to the last of the almshouses, and not seeing the poor that there dwelt ready in their doors as the other were, he asked, 'Is the blind man and blind woman that dwelt here alive?' It was answered, 'Yea, they are within.' Then threw he glove and all in at the window, and so rode forth.

At last coming to Aldam Common, where he should suffer, and seeing a multitude of people, he asked, 'What place is this, and what meaneth it that so much people are gathered hither?' It was answered, 'It is Aldam Common, the place where you must suffer; and the people are come to look upon you.' Then said he, 'Thanked be God I am at home'; and so light from his horse and with both hands rent the hood from his head. Now was his head notted evil favouredly and clipped like a fool's head, which cost good Bishop Boner had bestowed upon him when he disgraded him. But when the people saw his reverend and ancient face, with a long white beard, they burst out with tears and cried, 'God save thee, good Dr Taylor! Christ strengthen and help thee; the Holy Ghost comfort thee'; with other godly wishes. Then would he have spoken to the people, but the yeomen of the guard were so busy about him that as soon as he opened his mouth one or other thrust a tipstaff into his mouth, and would in no wise permit him to speak. Then desired he licence of the sheriff to speak; but the sheriff bade him remember his promise to the Council. 'Well,' quoth Taylor, 'promise must be kept.' What this promise was is unknown; but the common saying was that after he and others were condemned the Council sent for them and threatened they would cut their tongues out of their heads, except they would promise that at their deaths they would not speak to the people.

Taylor, perceiving that he could not be suffered to speak, sat down, and seeing one named Soyce, called him and said, 'Come and pull off my boots, and take them for thy labour. Thou hast long looked for them, now take them.' Then rose he up, put off his clothes unto his shirt, and gave them away; which done, he said with a loud voice, 'Good people, I have taught you nothing but God's holy word, and those lessons that I have taken out of God's holy book: I am come hither to seal it with my blood.' With that word Homes, who had used Taylor cruelly all the way, gave him a great stroke upon the head with a waster, and said, 'Is that the keeping of thy promise, thou heretic?' Then he kneeled down and prayed, and a poor woman among the people stepped in and prayed with him; but her they thrust away, and threatened to tread her down with horses; notwithstanding she would not remove, but abode and prayed with him. When he had prayed, he went to the stake and kissed it, and set himself into a pitch-barrel which they had set for him to stand in, and stood with his back upright against the stake, his hands folded together and his eyes toward heaven, and continually prayed.

Then they bound him with chains, and the sheriff called one Doningham, a butcher, and commanded him to set up faggots; but he refused to do it and said, 'I am lame, sir, and not able to lift a faggot.' The sheriff threatened to send him to prison; notwithstanding he would not do it. Then appointed he Mulleine of Carsey, a man for his virtues fit to be a hangman; Soyce, a drunkard; and Warwick, who in King Edward's days lost one of his ears for seditious talk; also one Robert King, a deviser of interludes, who had doings with the gunpowder. These four were appointed to set up the faggots and make the fire, which they most diligently did; and Warwick cruelly cast a faggot at him, which brake his face, that the blood ran down his visage. Then said Taylor, 'Oh friend, I have harm enough; what needed that?' Furthermore Sir John Shelton standing by as Taylor was saying the psalm *Miserere* in English, struck him on the lips. 'Ye knave,' said he, 'speak Latin: I will make thee.' At last they set to fire; and Taylor, holding up both hands, said, 'Merciful Father of heaven, for Jesus Christ my Saviour's sake receive my soul into thy hands.' So stood he still without crying or moving, his hands folded, till Soyce with an halberd struck him on the head that the brains fell out, and the dead corpse fell into the fire.

Thus rendered the man of God his blessed soul into the hands of his merciful Father, and to his most dear and certain Saviour, whom he entirely loved, faithfully and earnestly preached, obediently followed in living, and constantly glorified in death.

The history of Thomas Tomkins, William Hunter, with others

After that Gardiner had got the laws and the secular arm on his side with full power to rule as he listed, and had brought these bishops and preachers under foot, namely the Archbishop of Canturbury, Ridley, Latimer, Hooper, Rogers, Sanders, Taylor, and Bradford, he supposed all had been cocksure and Christ conquered for ever, so that the people, terrified with the example of these great men condemned, never would once rout against their violent religion. But eight or nine days after Gardiner had given sentence against Hooper, Rogers, Sanders, Taylor, and Bradford, being the 8th of February, six other men were brought before the bishop to be examined, whose names were W. Pigot, butcher; Stephen Knight, barber; Th. Tomkins, weaver; Th. Haukes, gentleman; John Laurence, priest; William Hunter, apprentice. Gardiner, seeing thus his device disappointed, gave over the matter utterly discouraged, and from that day meddled no more in such kind of condemnations, but referred the whole doing thereof to Boner; who supplied that part right doughtily, as in the process of this history may appear. Boner taking the matter in hand called before him in his consistory at Paul's the persons aforenamed, and the next day, the 9th of February, read the sentence of condemnation, as appeareth in Boner's own registers; such speed these men could make in dispatching their business.

Now remaineth severally to entreat of the martyrdom of these six persons, of which the first was Tomkins, burned in Smithfield the 16th of March 1555. Tomkins, a weaver by occupation, dwelling in Shorditch, was of disposition so godly that if any woman had come to him with her web, or if any other had come to talk of any matter, he would begin with prayer. If any had sought unto him to borrow money, he would show him such money as he had in his purse and bid him take it. When they came to repay it, so far off was he from strait exaction of his due that he would bid them keep it while they were better able. These were the conditions of Tomkins, testified to this day by most of his neighbours; of whom moe than half a dozen came to me reporting the same; recording moreover that Boner kept Tomkins in prison half a year, during which he beat him about the face whereby his face was swelled. Whereupon the bishop caused his beard to be shaven, and gave the barber twelve pence. Touching which shaving this is to be added: Boner, having Tomkins with him at Fulham in July, set him to make hay; and seeing him labour so well the bishop, sitting him down, said, 'I like thee well, for thou labourest well: I trust thou wilt be a good Catholic.' 'My Lord,' said he, 'St Paul saith "He that doth not labour is not worthy to eat."' Boner said, 'Ah! St Paul is a great man with thee.' After other talk the bishop wished his beard off, saying he would look like a Catholic. 'My Lord,' said Tomkins, 'before my beard grew I was, I trust, a good Christian, and so I trust to be, my beard being on.' But Boner sent for the barber and caused his beard to be shaven off. The very cause was that Boner had plucked off a piece of his beard before.

The rage of this bishop was not so great against him but the constancy of the party was much greater with patience to bear it; who, although he had not learning, was so endued with God's Spirit that by no means he could be removed from the confession of truth. Boner, when he saw that by no persuasions could he prevail against him, devised another practice to try his constancy, to the intent that he might overthrow him by some forefeeling of death. So with Harpsfield and other standing by he called for Tomkins, who coming before the bishop and standing in defence of his faith, the bishop fell from beating to burning. Who having a wax candle of three or four wicks standing upon the table took Tomkins by the fingers and held his hand over the flame, supposing that by the pain of the fire being terrified he would leave off the defence of his doctrine. Tomkins, thinking there presently to die, began to commend himself unto the Lord. In the time that his hand was burning he afterwards reported to one James Hinse that his spirit was so rapt that he felt no pain. In which burning he never shrunk till the veins shrunk, the sinews burst, and the water did spurt in Harpsfield's face, insomuch that Harpsfield desired the bishop to stay, saying he had tried him enough. This burning was in the hall at Fulham, and Boner, not contented with burning his hand, rested not until he had consumed his whole body into ashes.

Tomkins, after half a year in prison, the 8th of February was brought with certain other before Boner, sitting in his consistory, to be examined. When the bishop saw that he could not convince him, he brought forth articles and interrogatories, whereunto he should the next day answer. The next day he was brought before the Bishops of London, Bath, and St David's; where he was earnestly exhorted by the Bishop of Bath to revoke his opinions. He answered, 'My Lord, I was born and brought up in ignorance until now of late years; now I know the truth, wherein I will continue unto the death.' Then Boner caused his articles and confession to be read, and persuaded with him to recant. To whom he said, 'My Lord, I cannot see but that you would have me forsake the truth and fall into heresy.' The bishop seeing he would not recant gave sentence of condemnation upon him. Then he delivered him to the Sheriff of London, who carried him unto Newgate, where he remained until the 16th of March; on which day he was conveyed into Smithfield and there sealed his faith in the flaming fire, to the glory of God's holy name, and confirmation of the weak.

The 26th of March followed the martyrdom of William Hunter, a young man of nineteen years, born of godly parents by whom he was not only instructed in true religion but confirmed unto death. Wherein may appear a singular spectacle, not only of marvellous fortitude in the party so young, but also in his parents, to behold nature in them striving with religion and overcome of the same; example whereof in the sequel of this story we have here before our eyes. Which history faithfully drawn out by Robert his brother, who being present with William till his death sent the true report unto us, we have here with like faithfulness recorded.

'William, a prentice in London in the first year of Queen Mary, was commanded at the Easter following to receive communion at a mass by the priest of the parish where he dwelt; which because he refused to do, he was threatened that he should be brought before the Bishop of London. Wherefore William's master, Thomas Taylor, a silk weaver, required William to depart from him lest he should come in danger because of him. William took leave of his master and came to Burntwood where his father dwelt, with whom he remained about half a quarter of a year. It happened within five or six weeks that William, going into the chapel of Burntwood and finding a Bible on a desk, read therein. There came in one Father Atwell, a sumner, which hearing William read in the Bible said, "What meddlest thou with the Bible? Canst thou expound the Scriptures?"

' "Father Atwell, I take not upon me to expound the Scriptures; but I, finding the Bible here when I came, read in it to my comfort."

' "It was never merry world since the Bible came abroad in English. I perceive your mind well enough: you are one of them that misliketh the queen's laws. You must turn another leaf, or else you and a great sort more heretics will broil for this gear, I warrant you."

' "God give me grace that I may believe his word and confess his name, whatsoever come thereof."

' "Confess his name? ye will go to the devil and confess *his* name!"

' "You say not well, Father Atwell."

'Atwell went out of the chapel in a fury saying, "I am not able to reason with thee, but I will fetch one straightway which shall talk with thee, thou heretic." And he, leaving William reading in the Bible, straightway brought Thomas Wood, Vicar of Southwell, which was at an alehouse over against the chapel; who hearing old Atwell say that William was reading the Bible came by and by, and finding him reading took the matter very heinously, saying, "Sirrah, who gave thee leave to read the Bible and expound it?"

' "I expound not the Scriptures, sir, but read them for my comfort."

' "What meddlest thou with them at all?"

' "I will read the Scriptures while I live: you ought, Mr Vicar, not to discourage any man for that matter, but rather exhort men diligently to read the Scriptures."

'Immediately after, this Vicar told Justice Browne of the communication which William and he had together. Browne immediately sent for William's father and the constable. For after William and the vicar had reasoned together he took leave of his father and fled. When the constable and William's father were come, Browne asked where William was. His father answered, "If it please you, sir, I know not where he is."

' "No? I will make thee tell where he is, and fetch him also, ere I have done with thee. Why didst thou not bring him when thou hadst him? If thou wilt not fetch him, I will send thee to prison till I get him. See thou promise to fetch him; else it is not best to look me in the face any more nor to rest in Burntwood."

' "Sir, would you have me seek out my son to be burned?"

' "If thou bring him to me thou shalt not need to care for the matter. Fetch him, and see what I will do for him."

'After Father Hunter had ridden a two or three days' journey to satisfy Browne's expectation, it happened that William met his father in the highway, and told him that he thought he sought him. His father confessing it wept sore and said that Browne charged him to bring him to him. "Howbeit," said he, "I will return home and say I cannot find you." But William said, "I will go home with you and save you harmless, whatsoever cometh of it." Thus they came home together; but William, as soon as he was come, was taken by the constable and laid in the stocks till the day, when Browne sent for him, and when William was come commanded the Bible to be brought and began to reason with William on this manner. "I hear you are a Scripture man and can reason of the 6th of St John. How say you to another place?"—turning to the 22nd of St Luke—"Look here; for Christ saith that the bread is his body." William answered, "Though Christ call the bread his body, as he doth also say that he is a vine, a door, etc., yet is not his body turned into bread, no more than he is turned into a door or vine. Christ called the bread his body by a figure." At that Browne said, "Thou art a villain indeed. Wilt thou make Christ a liar?" and was in such a fury that William could not speak a word. William, seeing him in such a fury, desired that he would either hear him quietly or send him away. Browne answered, "Indeed I will send thee tomorrow to my Lord of London, and he shall have thee under examination"; and thus left off the talk, made a letter, and sent William with the constable to Boner.

'After he had read the letter, the bishop began, "I understand by Mr Browne's letter that you have had communication with the Vicar of the Wield about the blessed sacrament of the altar; whereupon Mr Browne sent for thee, to bring thee to the Catholic Faith from which he saith thou art gone." William answered, "I am not fallen from the Catholic Faith of Christ, but confess it with all my heart."

' "Why, wilt thou not recant thy saying that Christ's body is not in the sacrament, the same that was born of the Virgin Mary?"

' "My Lord, Mr Browne hath certified you of the talk which he and I had together, and ye know what I said to him; the which I will not recant."

' "I think thou art ashamed to bear a faggot and recant openly, but if thou wilt recant thy sayings thou shalt not be put to open shame: speak the word here between me and thee, and I promise thee it shall go no further, and thou shalt go home without any hurt."

' "If you will leave me to my conscience, I will go to my father and dwell with him, or else with my master again."

' "I am content, so thou wilt go to church and receive and be shriven."

' "No, I will not do so."

' "Then I will make you sure enough, I warrant you."

'Then the bishop commanded his men to put William in the stocks in his gatehouse, where he sat two days and nights with a crust of bread and a cup of water. At the two days' end the bishop came to him, and finding the water and the bread still by him said to his men, "Take him out of the stocks and let him break his fast with you." Then they let him forth of the stocks, but would not suffer him to eat with them. And he said he was as loth to be in their company as they were to be in his. After breakfast the bishop sent for William and demanded whether he would recant or no. William made him answer that he would never recant that which he had confessed concerning his faith in Christ. The bishop said he was no Christian, but denied the faith in which he was baptized. William answered, "I was baptized in the faith of the Holy Trinity, the which I will not go from." Then the bishop sent him to the convict prison, and commanded the keeper to lay irons on him, as many as he could bear; and moreover asked him how old he was. William said he was nineteen. "Well," said the bishop, "you will be burned ere you be twenty." Then he parted, the bishop allowing him a halfpenny a day to live on in bread or drink.

'Thus he continued in prison three-quarters of a year; in which time he had been before the bishop five times, besides the time when he was condemned in the consistory in Paul's, the 9th of February: at which time I his brother Robert was present, when I heard the bishop condemn him and five other. The bishop calling William asked if he would recant, then pronounced sentence upon him; how that he should go to Newgate for a time and from thence to Burntwood, "where," said he, "thou shalt be burned." Then the bishop called for another, and when he had condemned them all he called for William and persuaded with him saying, "If thou wilt recant I will make thee a freeman in the City, and give thee forty pound in good money to set up thine occupation withal; or I will make thee steward of my house and set thee in office; for thou hast wit enough." But William answered, "I thank you for your offers; notwithstanding I cannot find in my heart to turn from God for love of the world: I count all things worldly but loss and dung in respect of the love of Christ." Then said the bishop, "If thou diest in this mind thou art condemned for ever." William answered, "God justifieth them whom man condemneth unjustly." Thus departed William and the rest to Newgate, where they remained about a month; which afterward were sent, William to Burntwood, the others into divers places.

'When William was come to Burntwood, the Saturday before the Annunciation that followed on the Monday after, William remained till Tuesday, because they would not put him to death then for the holiness of the day. Meanwhile William's father and mother came to him, and desired of God that he might continue to the end in that good way which he had begun; and his mother said to him that she was glad that ever she was so happy to bear such a child, which could find in his heart to lose his life for Christ's name's sake. Then William said, "For my little pain which I shall suffer, which is but a short braid, Christ hath promised me a crown of joy: may you not be glad of that, mother?" With that his mother kneeled down saying, "God strengthen thee, my son, to the end. Yea, I think thee as well bestowed as any child that ever I bare."

'Thus they continued in their inn, the Swan in Burntwood; and many of William's acquaintance came to him and reasoned with him and he with them, exhorting them to come away from Popish superstition and idolatry. Thus passing away Saturday, Sunday, and Monday, at night William dreamed that he met his father as he went to the stake, and that there was a priest at the stake who went about to have him recant. To whom he cried, "Away, false prophet!" and exhorted the people to beware of him and such as he was.

'Now when it was day, the sheriff, Mr Brocket, called on to set forward to the burning of William Hunter. Then came the sheriff's son to William and embraced him saying, "William, be not afraid of these men with bows, bills, and weapons, ready to bring you to the place where you shall be burned." William answered, "I am not afraid: I have cast my count what it will cost me." Then the sheriff's son could speak no more for weeping. Then William plucked up his gown, stepped over the parlour groundsel, and went forward cheerfully, the sheriff's servant taking him by one arm and I by another. Thus going he met his father, according to his dream; and he spake to his son, weeping and saying, "God be with thee, son William." And William said, "God be with you, good father, and be of good comfort; for we shall meet again, when we shall be merry." Then William kneeled down and said the 51st psalm.

'Then said the sheriff, "Here is a letter from the queen. If thou wilt recant, thou shalt live." "No," quoth William, "I will not recant." Then William rose and went to the stake and stood upright to it. Then came a bailiff and made fast the chain about William. Then said Browne, "Here is not wood enough to burn a leg of him." Then said William, "Pray for me while ye see me alive, good people, and I will pray for you." "Now," quoth Browne, "pray for thee? I will pray no more for thee than for a dog." William answered, "Mr Browne, now you have that which you sought for, and I pray God it be not laid to your charge in the last day." Then said William, "Son of God, shine upon me"; and immediately the sun in the element shone out of a dark cloud so full in his face that he was constrained to look another way; whereat the people mused, because it was so dark a little time before. Then William took up a faggot of broom and embraced it in his arms. Then the priest which William dreamed of came to his brother Robert with a popish book to carry to William that he might recant. Which book his brother would not meddle withal. William seeing the priest said, "Away, thou false prophet! Beware of them, good people, and come away from their abominations." "Then," quoth the priest, "how thou burnest here, so shalt thou burn in hell." William answered, "Thou liest! away, thou false prophet, away!"

'Immediately fire was made. Then William cast his psalter into his brother's hand, who said, "William, think on the passion of Christ and be not afraid." William answered, "I am not afraid." Then he lift up his hands and said, "Lord, Lord, Lord, receive my spirit"; and casting down his head again into the smothering smoke, he yielded up his life for the truth.'

William Pigot, Stephen Knight, and John Laurence

In the story of Tomkins and his fellows, mention was made of six, condemned together by Boner the 9th of February. Of the six two, Tomkins and Hunter, were executed, one the 16th of February,[1] the other upon the 26th of March. Other three, to wit William Pigot and Stephen Knight, suffered upon the 28th, and John Laurence the 29th.

The 9th of February they were all three, with Tomkins and Hunter, brought into the consistory, and had the same articles propounded unto them which were propounded unto Tomkins, and thereto also subscribed these words, 'I do so believe'. They were exhorted to recant and revoke their doctrine and receive the Faith. They answered they would not, but would stick to that Faith that they had subscribed unto; for they believed that the contrary thereof was heresy. When the bishop saw that neither fair flattering nor cruel threatenings would prevail, he gave them severally their judgments. Because Laurence had been one of their anointed priests he was solemnly degraded. Their condemnation and this degradation ended, they were committed into the custody of the sheriffs, who sent them unto Newgate, where they remained with joy together until they were carried into Essex, and there Pigot was burned at Braintree, Knight at Maldon.

The next day, the 29th, Laurence was brought to Colchester and there, being not able to go (for his legs were worn with heavy irons, his body weakened with evil keeping) was borne to the fire in a chair, and so sitting was in his constant faith consumed with fire. At the burning of this Laurence young children came about the fire and cried, as well as young children could speak, 'Lord, strengthen thy servant and keep thy promise'; which thing as it is rare, so it is no small manifestation of the glory of God, who wrought this in the hearts of these little ones; nor

[1] The date was previously given as 16th March.—Ed.

yet a little commendation to their parents, which from their youth brought them up in the knowledge of God.

The history of Dr Robert Farrar

The day after Laurence's death followed the martyrdom of the Bishop of St David's in Wales, Robert Farrar, the next bishop that suffered after Hooper. Farrar by favour of the Lord Protector was first promoted to that dignity. This man I may well call twice a martyr, not only for the cruel death of the fire which he suffered in the days of Queen Mary, but for divers injuries and molestations in King Edward's time which he sustained at the hands of his enemies after the fall of the Duke of Somerset.

Through the procurement of his adversaries Hugh Rawlins, priest, and Thomas Lee did exhibit to the King's Council certain articles and informations to blemish the bishop's credit and pull him from his bishopric. After these wrangling articles were given up, then was the bishop called for to answer, the hearing whereof was committed unto Dr Wootton and Sir John Mason, who likewise received the bishop's answers to the articles. Then came in for witness upon the articles George Constantine and the chanter of St David's; against whom the bishop laid first exceptions, then exhibited matter justificatory. Then he was appointed by the commissioners, before his departure from London to pay two hundred pound (arrearages) into the Court of First-fruits and Tenths at Bartlemew Day next following; which payment he made accordingly, notwithstanding that his adversaries sought means to have made him break his day. 'One Edward Harbert, who hath a parsonage of his to farm, kept back his rent to the very last day, because that money should not help to serve his turn; and so by crafty cavillation detaineth it still in his hand with a year's rent and an half more; for Harbert is an adherent of the bishop's adversaries.'

Thus ye have heard the first trouble of this martyr in King Edward's days. Briefly to conclude this process, Farrar, partly upon the importunate suit of his adversaries, partly upon the infortunate fall of the good Duke of Somerset, was detained in prison till the death of King Edward and the coming in of Queen Mary, whereby a new trouble rose upon him, being now accused and examined for his doctrine. He was called before the Bishop of Winchester with Hooper, Rogers, Bradford, Sanders, and other, the 4th of February. On which day he should with them have been condemned; but because leisure or list did not then serve the bishop, his condemnation was deferred and he sent to prison again, where he continued till the 14th of February, and then was sent into Wales, there to receive sentence of condemnation. Who then upon the 26th in the church of Carmarthen was presented before Henry Bishop of St David's and Constantine the notary. Henry received him into his own custody, committing him to the keeping of Owen Jones; and thereupon declared unto Farrar the great mercy and clemency that the King and Queen's Highness' pleasure was to be offered unto him; that is to say, that if he would submit himself to the laws of this realm and conform himself to the unity of the Catholic Church, he should be pardoned. After that seeing Farrar give no answer to the promises the bishop committed him to the keeper, to be kept in prison till a new monition, and meantime to deliberate with himself for his further answer to the premises.

The last of February Morgan, the pretensed Bishop of St David's, sitting as judge ministered unto Bishop Farrar certain articles and interrogatories in writing, which Farrar refused to answer till he might see his commission and authority. Whereupon the pretensed bishop did pronounce him *contumax*, to be counted *pro confesso;* which done, he committed the bishop to the custody of Owen Jones. Upon Monday the 11th of March he, appearing again before the bishop and the notary Constantine, exhibited in a written paper his answer to the articles, to which he did so subscribe, adding these words, *tenens se de aequitate & justitia esse Episcopum Menevensem*, that the bishop assigned the next Wednesday to hear his definitive sentence. Which day Farrar was demanded of the pretensed bishop whether he would recant his heresies, schisms, and errors, and subscribe to the Catholic articles. After this Farrar did exhibit a schedule written in English, appealing withal by word of mouth from the bishop to Cardinal Poole. All which notwithstanding, the bishop proceeding in his rage pronounced the definitive sentence against him contained in writing; by which sentence he pronounced him an heretic excommunicate, to be given up forthwith to the secular power.

Thus this godly bishop, condemned and degraded, not long after was brought to the place of execution in Carmarthen, where he in the market-place in the south side of the market cross, the 30th of March, most constantly sustained the torments of the fire.

The history of Rawlins White, reported by John Dane

Forsomuch as we have here passed the history of Mr Farrar, I have thought to adjoin the history of Rawlins White, a fisherman, which in the like cause and in the same country of Wales, and about the same month, gave his life like a valiant soldier of Jesus Christ, and was burned at Cardiff; the process of whose story here followeth:

'After God of his mercy had raised up the light of his gospel through the blessed government of King Edward VI, Rawlins began to mislike that which before he had embraced, and to have some good opinion of that which before had been concealed from him; and he began to be a diligent hearer and searcher-out of the truth. But because the good man was unlearned, he knew no ready way how he might satisfy his great desire. At length it came in his mind to take a special remedy to supply his necessity, which was this. He had a little son, which he sent to school to learn to read. After the little boy could read indifferently well, his father every night after supper would have the boy read a piece of Holy Scripture, and now and then of some other good book; in which exercise the old man had such delight that he rather practised himself in the study of Scripture than in the trade which beforetime he had used; so that Rawlins in few years went forward in such sort that he was able to instruct other, and when occasion served would go from one place to another, visiting such as he had best hope in. He became an open and notable professor of the truth, not without the company of his little boy, whom he used as an assistance to his good purpose. To this great industry God did add a singular gift of memory, so that he could do that in rehearsing the text which men of riper knowledge, by notes and other helps, could very hardly accomplish; insomuch that he upon the alleging of Scripture would often cite the book, the leaf, and the very sentence; such was the working of God in this unlearned father.

'When he had thus continued five years, King Edward died. Mary succeeded, and with her papistry crept in. Howbeit Rawlins continued in his purpose till he was taken by the officers of the town as a man suspected of heresy. He was convented before the bishop of Llandaff, by whom after divers combats this good father was committed to prison in Chepstowe. At last he was removed to the castle of Cardiff, where he continued one whole year. Whereupon the bishop caused him to be brought to his own house beside Chepstowe, and assayed many ways to reduce him to conformity. But when all means were to no purpose, the bishop willed him to advise with himself, either to recant his opinions or to bide the rigour of the law, and gave him a day of determination; which day being come, the bishop with his chaplains went into the chapel. When the bishop with his retinue were placed in order, poor Rawlins was brought before them. The bishop used a long kind of talk to him, declaring that he was known to hold heretical opinions, and that through his instruction many were led into error. He exhorted him to consider his own estate wherein he stood; "For," said the bishop, "ye seem altogether obstinate and wilful. Now we thought good to send for you, to see if there were any conformity in you; if you will show yourself repentant for that which you have done against God and the prince's law, we are ready to use favour towards you; but if by no means we can persuade you, we are minded to minister the law unto you."

'"Proceed in your law a God's name," said Rawlins; "but for an heretic you shall never condemn me while the world standeth." The bishop with hot words reproved him, and forthwith was ready to read the sentence. Howbeit upon advice given by his chaplains he thought best first to have a mass, thinking that by so doing some wonderful work should be wrought in Rawlins: thereupon a priest began mass. Meantime poor Rawlins betook himself to prayer in a secret place thereby. Mass ended, Rawlins was called for again. The bishop used many persuasions, but to no purpose; whereupon he caused the definitive sentence to be read. Which being ended, Rawlins was dismissed; and from thence he was carried again to Cardiff to be put into the prison called Cockmarell, a dark, loathsome, and most vile prison.

'Now when he perceived his time was near, he sent to his wife and willed her that she should send him his wedding-garment, meaning a shirt, which afterward he was burned in; which request his wife with great sorrow did perform, and early in the morning did send it to him, which he received most joyfully. When the hour of his execution was come, Rawlins was brought out of prison having on his body the long shirt which he called his wedding-garment, and an old russet coat. He had upon his legs an old pair of leather buskins. He was guarded with a great company of bills and glaives; which when he beheld, "Alas," quoth he, "what meaneth all this? I will not start away: I give unto God most hearty thanks that he hath made me worthy to abide all this for his name's sake." So he came to a place where his wife and children stood weeping, the sudden sight of whom so pierced his heart that tears trickled down his face. But he soon began to be angry with himself, insomuch that striking his breast with his hand he used these words, "Ah flesh, wouldst thou fain prevail? Do what thou canst, thou shalt not have the victory." By this time this poor innocent came to the very altar of his sacrifice, and there found a stake ready, with wood toward the making of the fire; which when he beheld, he set forward very boldly, but fell down and kissed the ground. In rising again the earth a little sticking on his nose, he said, "Earth unto earth, and dust unto dust: thou art my mother and unto thee I shall return." Then went he cheerfully and set his back close unto the stake; when he had stood there awhile he cast his eye upon this reporter and said, "I feel a great fighting between the flesh and the spirit, and the flesh would fain have his swinge: I pray you, when you see me tempted hold your finger up to me, and I shall remember myself."

'As he was standing with his back close unto the stake, a smith came with a great chain of iron; whom when he saw, he cast up his hand and gave God thanks. Then the smith cast the chain about him; and as he was making it fast Rawlins said, "I pray you, friend, knock in the chain fast; for it may be that the flesh would strive mightily; but God give me strength to abide the extremity." When the smith had made him sure, the officers began to lay on more wood with a little straw and reed; wherein the good old man was no less occupied than the best: as far as he could reach he would pluck the straw and reed, and lay it about him in places most convenient for his speedy dispatch, with such a cheerful countenance that all present were astonished. Then some that stood by cried out, "Set to fire"; which being set to, the straw and reed cast up a great and sudden flame; in which this blessed man bathed his hands until the sinews shronk and the fat dropped away; saving that once he did as it were wipe his face with one of them. All this while, which was somewhat long, he cried with a loud voice, "O Lord, receive my soul," until he could not open his mouth. At last the fire was so vehement against his legs that they were consumed almost before the rest of his body was burned, which made the whole body fall over the chain into the fire sooner than it would have done. Thus died this godly old man for the testimony of God's truth, being now rewarded no doubt with the crown of everlasting life.'

It is recorded furthermore of Father Rawlins by this reporter that as he was going to his death he seemed to be altered in nature. For as before he was wont to go stooping through the infirmity of age, having a sad countenance and a very feeble complexion, and withal very soft in speech and gesture, now he went not only bolt upright but also bore a most pleasant and comfortable countenance, not without great courage and audacity both in speech and behaviour. The hairs of his head and his beard were more white than grey, which gave such a show to his whole person that he seemed altogether angelical. He was of the age of threscore years or thereabouts.

John Cardmaker, John Warne, John Ardeley, and John Simson

Upon the 30th of May suffered together in Smithfield John Cardmaker, otherwise called Taylor, prebendary of Wells, and John Warne, upholsterer, of the parish of St John in Walbrook. Cardmaker first was an Observant Friar before the dissolution of the monasteries; then a married minister; and in King Edward's time appointed Reader in Paul's, where the Papists were so much aggrieved with his doctrine that in his reading they mangled his gown with their knives. Cardmaker, apprehended in the beginning of Queen Mary's reign, with Barlow, Bishop of Bath, was brought to London and laid in the Fleet, King Edward's laws yet being in force. After the Pope was again admitted as supreme head of the Church, and the bishops had gotten authority *ex officio* to exercise their tyranny, these two were brought before Winchester and others appointed by commission to examine the faith of prisoners, and the Chancellor offered the queen's mercy if they would be conformable.

To this they made such answer as the Chancellor with his fellow-commissioners allowed them for Catholics. Whether they of weakness answered, or he of subtlety would so understand their answer that he might have some forged example of a shrinking brother to lay in the dish of the rest which were to be examined, it may easily be perceived by this, that to all which followed they objected the example of Barlow and Cardmaker, commending their discretion and learning. But whatsoever their answer was, Barlow was led again to the Fleet, from whence he afterward being delivered did by exile bear witness to Christ's gospel. Cardmaker was conveyed to the Counter, the Bishop of London procuring it to be published that he should be delivered after he had subscribed to transubstantiation and other articles. To the same prison Laurence Sanders was brought after condemnation; when these two had such Christian conference that, whatsoever the bishops blustered and the tickle ears of the people too lightly believed, they both showed themselves worthy martyrs of Christ, as of Sanders is already written. After whose departure Cardmaker remained prisoner to be baited of the Papists, which would seem to have certain hope that Cardmaker was theirs. Continued conference divers of them had with him, to none effect. To the end their doings might appear, he required them to put their reasons in writing, and promised to answer them.

Next I thought best to infer the articles and answers of John Warne, his fellow-martyr. Warne, examined upon the articles the 23rd of May, did answer to the same, confessing the contents to be true in every part, subscribing the same. The bishop, exhorting him to leave his heresies and return to the bosom of Mother Church, commanded him to appear again next day; at what time he was earnestly exhorted to recant his opinions. He answered that he would not depart from his profession unless he were persuaded by the Holy Scriptures. The next day the bishop examined him again upon his former articles, to which he most constantly did stick. 'I am persuaded,' quoth he, 'to be in the right opinion and see no cause to repent; for all filthiness and idolatry is in the Church of Rome.' The bishop, seeing he could not prevail, finished this examination with the definitive sentence against Warne, and charged the sheriffs with him, under whose custody he remained in the prison of Newgate until the 30th. Upon which day John Cardmaker with John Warne were brought to the place where they should suffer.

The sheriffs called Cardmaker aside and talked with him so long that in the meantime Warne had made his prayers, was chained to the stake, and had wood and reed set about him, so that nothing wanted but the firing. The people, which before had heard that Cardmaker would recant, were in a marvellous dump and sadness, thinking indeed that Cardmaker should now recant at the burning of Warne. At length Cardmaker departed from the sheriffs, came towards the stake, kneeled down, and made a long prayer in silence; yet the people confirmed themselves in their fantasy of his recanting, seeing him in his garments, praying secretly, and no semblance of any burning. His prayers ended, he rose, put off his clothes unto his shirt, went with courage to the stake, and kissed it sweetly: he took Warne by the hand and comforted him heartily; and gave himself to be bound to the stake most gladly. The people seeing this so suddenly done, contrary to their fearful expectation, cried out for joy, saying, 'God be praised! The Lord strengthen thee, Cardmaker.' This continued while the executioner put fire to them, and they both passed through the fire to blessed rest among God's holy martyrs, to enjoy the crown of victory prepared for the elect soldiers of Christ Jesus in his kingdom. To whom be glory for ever. Amen.

With Cardmaker and Warne was also condemned John Ardeley and John Simson. Before we come to the story of them, first is to be noted the king and queen's letter sent by a post to the bishop. This letter made him the more hasty to the condemnation, as well of others as of these men of whom we have presently to entreat; which being both of one town and of one trade, being husbandmen in Wigborow in Essex, and almost of one age, were brought together by the undersheriff of Essex to Boner upon the accusation of heresy. Touching the manner of their examinations: as the articles were much like, so their answers were not much discrepant. These articles being to them objected and their answers made, the bishop beginning with Ardeley did urge to recant. To whom Ardeley gave answer, 'My Lord, neither you nor any other of your religion is of the Catholic Church: you be of a false faith.' The bishop demanding whether he would relinquish his erroneous opinions and be reduced to the unity of the Church, he answered, 'God foreshield that I should do so, for then I should lose my soul.' After this the bishop read the condemnation, as he also did against Simson. And so they were both committed to the sheriffs to be executed. But before I come to their execution, here is a thing not unworthy the looking upon, which happened in the examination of these two martyrs.

At the examination there was assembled such a multitude that because the consistory was not able to hold them they were fain to stand in the church, waiting to see the prisoners when they should depart. Meantime the bishop, in a heat with the bold answers of the two prisoners, especially Simson, burst out in his loud and angry voice, 'Have him away, have him away!' The people, thinking that the prisoners had their judgment, desirous to see the prisoners had to Newgate, severed themselves, one running one way, another another way, which caused such a noise in the church that they in the consistory marvelled what it should mean; the bishop also, afraid of this sudden stir, asked what was to do. The standers-by said there was like to be some tumult, for they were together by the ears. When the bishop heard this his heart was in his heels, and he with the rest of the court betook them to their legs, hastening with all speed possible to recover the door that went into the bishop's house; but the rest, being lighter of foot than my Lord, did sooner recover the door, and thronging hastily to get in kept the bishop out, and cried, 'Save my Lord!' meaning first to save themselves; whereby they gave the standers-by good matter to laugh at. But of this enough.

Simson and Ardeley were shortly after sent to Essex, where both in one day (about the 10th of June) were put to death, albeit in several places; Simson suffered at Rochford; Ardeley was had to Railey, where he finished his martyrdom.

The ridiculous handling of John Tooly

About the same time fell out a solemn process about the Pope's spiritualty against John Tooly. The story is this. About the time that the Spaniards began to keep a stir in England, Tooly, a poulter in London, conspired with certain other to rob a Spaniard at St James's; and although the deed were heinous of itself, yet was it made greater, being committed against such a person and such a country, which the queen and her Court did highly favour. Tooly was found guilty and judged to be hanged, notwithstanding in this realm there are many more thefts committed than thieves executed. Tooly being led to the gallows fast by Charing Cross, standing upon the cart read a prayer in a printed book and two other prayers in two several papers; then, having the halter about his neck, desired the people to pray for him and to bear witness that he died a Christian man, and trusted to be saved only by the merits of Christ's passion—not by masses or trentals, images or saints: as Tooly did steal for covetousness, so the Bishop of Rome did sell masses and trentals for covetousness. 'From the tyranny of the Bishop of Rome and his detestable enormities; from false doctrine and heresy, and from contempt of thy word and commandment, good Lord deliver us!' adding further, 'All you that be Christian men, say Amen.' Immediately 300 persons and more said 'Amen' three times at least.

As soon as the bruit of this fact came into the ears of the priests, they were not a little mad that so great a reproach should be done against the Holy Father. Calling therefore a council together, Tooly's talk at his death was debated among themselves. At last, after much *pro* and *contra* they all consented to those men's judgments who thought that the violating of the Pope's Holiness should be revenged with fire and faggots. I believe that Cardinal Poole was no small doer in this sentence;

for as Winchester and Boner did always thirst after the blood of the living, so Poole's lightning was for the most part kindled against the dead. Peradventure being loth to be so cruel as the other he thought by this means to discharge his duty to the Pope. By the Cardinal's fiery fist the bones of Martin Bucer and Paulus Phagius, which had lien almost two years in their graves, were taken up and burned at Cambridge as Tooly's carcase was here at London. Besides this, because he would show some token of his diligence in both universities, he caused Peter Martyr's wife to be digged out of the churchyard and buried on the dunghill. Of these prodigious acts ye shall hear more hereafter. But now to Tooly, who was hanged and put into his grave, out of which he was digged again by commandment of the bishops; and because he was bold to derogate the authority of the Bishop of Rome at the time of his death, it pleased them to condemn him as an heretic.

Anon a citation was set upon Paul's church door under the bishop's great seal, the tenor whereof here ensueth.

'Edmund Bishop of London to all parsons, vicars, curates, clerks, and learned men within our diocese of London; salutation and benediction. Forsomuch as it is come to our hearing that one John Tooly, the son of perdition and iniquity, coming to the profundity of malice, in the self same time in the which he should go to hanging for the great theft by him committed, did utter divers and sundry damnable, blasphemous, and heretical opinions and errors repugnant to the verity of the Catholic Faith, and did exhort the people to hold the same errors and opinions; we do command that ye will cite the wife of Tooly that is dead, his kindred, friends, and familiars, and all other and every of them, that they appear before us to defend the good name of him that is dead, and to allege and propose in due form of law a cause reasonable, if they have or can tell of any, why the said Tooly that is dead ought not to be determined and declared an heretic and excommunicate person, and his remembrance condemned, in the detesting and condemning of so heinous a deed and crime, and his body or carcase to lack church burial as a rotten member cut off from the Church, and the same to be committed to the arm and power secular, and they compelled hereafter for ever to hold their peace.'

When the time of this citation was expired, and Tooly being cited did not appear, next in order of law came the suspension (whereas one suspension had been enough for him!) and after that the excommunication, that is, that no man should eat and drink with him; if any met him by the way he should not bid him good morrow; and he should be excluded from the communion of the Church. Then he was for an heretic condemned and committed to the sheriffs of London, which with like diligence went about to execute their charge. Receiving the man (suspended, excommunicated, condemned as an heretic, and besides that dead) they laid him on the fire to be burned *ad perpetuam rei memoriam*. This was done the 4th of June.

The martyrdom of Thomas Haukes

Immediately after the story of Dr Taylor mention was made of six men brought before Boner upon the 8th of February. In which number was Thomas Haukes, condemned with them the 9th of the month. But because his execution did not follow with theirs but was prolonged to this month of June, it followeth now to enter tractation thereof.

He was of the country of Essex, born of honest stock, in profession a courtier, brought up daintily from childhood. Besides that he was of such comeliness and stature, so well endued with excellent qualities, that he might seem a man made for the purpose. But his gentle behaviour towards other, and especially his fervent study and singular love unto true religion and goodness, did surmount all the rest. First Haukes, following the guise of the Court, entered service with the Lord of Oxford, where he remained a good space, being esteemed and loved of all the household so long as Edward VI lived. But he dying, all things began to go backwards, religion to decay, godliness to be in danger everywhere, and chiefly in the houses of great men. Haukes, misliking the state of things, rather than change the profession of true godliness which he had tasted, thought to change the place; and forsaking the nobleman's house departed to his own home, where he might use his own conscience.

But what place in this world shall a man find so secret whither that old wicked serpent cannot creep? Haukes, keeping his house at home, had born unto him a son, whose baptism was deferred to the third week, for that he would not suffer him to be baptized after the papistical manner; which thing the adversaries not able to suffer, laying hands upon him did bring him to the Earl of Oxford, to be reasoned with as not sound in religion, in that he seemed to contemn the sacraments of the Church. The earl, either intending not to trouble himself in such matters or else seeing himself not able to weigh with him in cases of religion, sent him to London with letters, and put him in the hands of Boner.

After private conferences and long debatings in the bishop's house, the bishop, seeing no hope to win him, was fully set to proceed openly against him. Haukes was cited with his fellows to appear in the bishop's consistory the 8th of February. Upon which appearance was laid against him the bill of his confession written with Boner's hand. He standing to the said confession, the bishop assigned him with the other five the day following to appear before him again to give a resolute answer what they would stick unto. Which day being come and these six prisoners severally called before the bishop, at the coming of Haukes the bishop willed him to remember what was said to him yesterday, and to advise with himself what he would answer, for he stood upon life and death. 'Well,' quoth Haukes, 'I will willingly receive whatsoever shall be put upon me.' Being exhorted with many fair words to return to the bosom of Mother Church: 'No, my Lord,' said he, 'that will I not; for if I had an hundred bodies I would suffer them all to be torn in pieces rather than recant.' Continuing in the same song, notwithstanding that the doctors were ever calling him to come again to the unity of the Church, he ever kept them off with this answer, that he would never go from the belief he was in so long as he lived. Whereupon Boner read the sentence of death upon him; so was he condemned the same day with his fellows, the 9th of February. Nevertheless his execution was prolonged and he remained in prison till the 10th of June. Then was he committed to the hands of Lord Rich, who being assisted with power sufficient of the worshipful of the shire had Haukes into Essex with six other whose stories hereafter follow, there to suffer martyrdom, Haukes at Coxehall, the other in other places.

A little before his death certain of his friends seemed not a little concerned by the example of his constancy; yet being feared with the sharpness of the punishment which he was going to, privily desired that in the midst of the flames he would show them some token, whereby they might be the more certain whether the pain were so great that a man might not therein keep his mind quiet and patient. Which thing he promised to do, and it was agreed that if the pain were tolerable he should lift up his hand above his head before he gave up the ghost. When the hour was come Haukes was led to the place appointed by Lord Rich and his assistance; who being come unto the stake addressed himself to the fire, having a strait chain cast about his middle, with people on every side compassing him about; unto whom after he had spoken many things, especially unto Lord Rich, reasoning with him of the innocent blood of the saints, at length after his fervent prayers poured out unto God the fire was set unto him. In which he continued long, and when his speech was taken away by violence of the flame, his skin also drawn together and his fingers consumed, so that now all men thought he had been gone, suddenly the blessed servant of God, mindful of his promise, reached up his hands burning on a light fire over his head, and with great rejoicing as it seemed clapped them three times together. At the sight whereof there followed such applause and outcry of the people, especially of them which understood the matter, that the like hath not commonly been heard. And so the blessed martyr, straightway sinking down into the fire, gave up his spirit, a faithful witness of Christ's holy gospel.

Thomas Osmund, William Bamford, and Thomas Osborne, martyrs

Mention was made in the story of Thomas Haukes of six prisoners sent with him to Essex; of which six three were sent to be burned, three to recant and do penance. The names were these: Thomas Osmund, fuller; William Bamford, weaver; Thomas Osborne, fuller; Nicholas Chamberlaine, weaver; Thomas Brodehill, weaver; Richard Web, weaver; all of the town of Coxehall. Which six men were sent to Boner to be examined, by the Earl of Oxford and Sir Philip Paris. The prisoners, being sent up the 1st of May, were brought before the bishop the 17th, to be examined upon sundry articles, whereunto they were compelled to answer and put their hand. These articles propounded and answered, they were until the afternoon dismissed; at what time they did again appear, and were travailed with by flattering speeches to revoke their opinions; who notwithstanding remained constant and firm, and therefore were sent away until the next day. Then the bishop condemned them as heretics and delivered them to the sheriffs, in whose custody they remained until they were delivered to the sheriff of Essex, and by him were executed, Chamberlaine at Colchester the 14th of June, Osmund at Manningtree the 15th, and Bamford at Harwich the same day.

CHAPTER 8

FURTHER VICTIMS OF GARDINER AND BONER

The history of Mr John Bradford

John Bradford was born at Manchester. His parents did bring him up in learning from infancy, until he attained such knowledge in Latin and skill in writing that he was able to gain his own living in some honest condition. He became servant to Sir John Harrington, who in the great affairs of King Henry and King Edward, which he had in hand when he was treasurer of the king's camp in Bullonois, had such experience of Bradford's activity in writing, of expertness in the art of auditors, as also of his trustiness, that not only in those affairs, but in his private business, above all other he used his faithful service.

Thus continued Bradford certain years in an honest and good trade. But the Lord, which had elected him unto a better function and preordained him to preach the gospel, called his chosen child to the understanding and partaking of the same gospel. Bradford did forsake his worldly affairs, and after account given to his master of all his doings departed from him, and gave himself wholly to the study of the Scriptures. Which purpose to accomplish the better he departed from the Temple at London, where the temporal law is studied, and went to Cambridge, to learn by God's law how to further the building of the Lord's temple. In Cambridge his diligence so pleased all men that within one year the university did give him the degree of Master of Art. Immediately after, the master and fellows of Pembroke Hall did give him a fellowship in their college: Martin Bucer so liked him that he had him not only most dear unto him, but oftentimes exhorted him to bestow his talent in preaching. Bradford answered that he was unable to serve in that office through want of learning. Bucer was wont to reply, 'If thou have not fine manchet bread, give the people barley bread, or whatsoever the Lord hath committed unto thee.' Whiles Bradford was thus persuaded to enter the ministry, Dr Ridley called him to take the degree of deacon. This done, he obtained for him a licence to preach, and did give him a prebend in St Paul's.

In this office by the space of three years how diligently he laboured many parts of England can testify. Sharply he reproved sin, sweetly he preached Christ crucified, pithily he impugned errors, earnestly he persuaded to godly life. When Queen Mary had gotten the crown, still continued Bradford diligent in preaching until he was deprived both of office and liberty. They took occasion to do this injury for such an act as among Turks and infidels would have been with thankfulness rewarded. The fact was this. The 13th of August in the first year of Queen Mary, Bourne, then Bishop of Bath, made a seditious sermon at Paul's Cross to set popery abroad, in such sort that it moved the people to no small indignation, being almost ready to pull him out of the pulpit. Neither could the reverence of the place, nor the presence of Boner who was then his master, nor the commandment of the mayor, stay their rage: the more they spake, the more the people were incensed. Bourne seeing himself in peril, whereof he was sufficiently warned by the hurling of a dagger at him, desired Bradford, who stood in the pulpit behind him, to stand in his place and speak to the people. Bradford was content, and spake to the people of godly obedience. So glad were they to hear him that they cried with a great shout, 'Bradford, Bradford; God save thy life, Bradford!' well declaring not only what affection they bare unto him, but what regard they gave unto his words. For after he had entered a little to exhort them to quiet, all raging ceased, and they in the end quietly departed, each man to his house. Yet Boner thought himself not sure of his life till he were safely housed, notwithstanding that the mayor and sheriffs were there to help. Wherefore he desired Bradford not to depart till he were in safety; which Bradford according to his promise performed. For while the mayor and sheriffs did lead Bourne to the schoolmaster's house, which is next to the pulpit, Bradford went at his back, shadowing him from the people with his gown.

Let the reader consider the peril of Bourne, the charity of Bradford, the headiness of the multitude, and also the grudging minds of certain which remained behind, grieved not a little to see that so good a man should save the life of such a popish priest, so impudently railing at King Edward; among whom one gentleman said, 'Ah Bradford, Bradford, thou savest him that will help to burn thee. If it were not for thee I would run him through with my sword.' Thus Bourne through Bradford's means escaped death.

The same Sunday in the afternoon Bradford preached at Bow Church in Cheapside, and reproved the people sharply for their misdemeanour. After this he did abide still in London with an innocent conscience. Within three days he was sent for to the Tower, where the queen was, to appear before the Council. There was he charged with saving Bourne, which act they called seditious, and also objected against him for preaching; and so he was committed first to the Tower, then unto other prisons, out of which neither his innocency nor charitable dealing could purchase liberty of body, till by death he obtained the heavenly liberty of which neither Pope nor Papist shall ever deprive him.

From the Tower—where he remained from August 1553 to the 22nd of January 1555, upon which day he was called out to examination before Winchester and other commissioners—he came to the King's Bench in Southwark; and after his condemnation he was sent to the Counter in the Poultry in London; in which two places he did preach twice a day unless sickness hindered him; where also the sacrament was often ministered, and such resort of good folks was daily to his lecture and to the sacrament that commonly his chamber was wellnigh filled. Preaching, reading, and praying was his whole life. He did not eat above one meal a day: in the midst of dinner he often used to muse with himself, having his hat over his eyes, whence came tears dropping on his trencher. Very gentle he was to man and child, and in so good credit with his keeper in Southwark that he had licence, upon his promise to return that night, to go into London without any keeper to visit one that was sick, lying by the Stillyard. Neither did he fail his promise, but returned to prison rather preventing his hour than breaking his fidelity. He counted that hour not well spent wherein he did not some good. He was no niggard of his purse, but would liberally participate that he had to his fellow-prisoners. Once a week he visited the thieves, pick-purses, and such others that were with him in prison, unto whom he would give godly exhortation, to learn amendment of their lives by their troubles, and that done distribute among them some portion of money to their comfort.

The night before he was had to Newgate he was troubled by dreams, how the chain for his burning was brought to the Counter gate, and how the next day, Sunday, he should be had to Newgate and on the Monday burned in Smithfield, as indeed it came to pass. Vexed oftentimes with these dreams, about three in the morning he waked him that lay with him and told him what he was troubled withal. Then after a little talk Bradford rose out of bed and gave himself to his old exercise of reading and prayer. At dinner he did eat his meat and was very merry, nobody being with him from morning to night but he that lay with him, with whom he had many times that day communication of death, of the kingdom of heaven, and of the ripeness of sin in that time. In the afternoon the keeper's wife came up, and much troubled, being almost windless, said, 'Oh Mr Bradford, I bring you heavy news.' 'What is that?' said he. 'Marry,' quoth she, 'tomorrow you must be burned: your chain is now a-buying, and soon you must go to Newgate.' Bradford put off his cap, and lifting his eyes to heaven said, 'I thank God for it; I have looked for the same a long time, and therefore it cometh not suddenly; the Lord make me worthy thereof': and so, thanking her for her gentleness, departed into his chamber and called his friend with him, who when he came thither, he went himself alone a long time and prayed. Which done, he came again to him that was in his chamber and took him divers writings, and showed him what he would have done, and after they had spent the afternoon in such things, at last came to him half a dozen of his friends, with whom all the evening he spent the time in prayer and other good exercise.

A little before he went out of the Counter he made a notable prayer of his farewell that ravished the mind of the hearers. Also when he shifted himself with a clean shirt made for his burning by one Walter Marlar's wife, who was a good nurse unto him, he made such a prayer of the wedding-garment that their eyes were as thoroughly occupied in looking on him as their ears gave place to hear his prayer. At his departing out of the chamber he gave money to every servant and officer of the house, with exhortation to them to fear and serve God. That done, he turned him to the wall and prayed vehemently that his words might not be spoken in vain. Then being beneath in the court, all the prisoners cried out to him and bid him farewell, as the rest of the house had done before with tears. The time they carried him to Newgate was about eleven or twelve in the night, when it was thought none would be stirring abroad; yet contrary to expectation was there in Cheapside and other places between the Counter and Newgate a multitude of people that came to see him, which gently bade him farewell, praying for him with pitiful tears; he as gently bade them farewell, praying heartily for them and their welfare.

It was nine o'clock of the day before Bradford was brought into Smithfield; which in Newgate spied a friend of his, unto whom he reached his hand over the people and plucked him to him, and delivered to him from his head his velvet nightcap with other things besides. And after a little secret talk with him immediately came to him a brother-in-law of his, Roger Beswick, which as soon as he had taken Bradford by the hand, one of the sheriffs, called Woodrofe, came with his staff and break Roger's head that the blood ran about his shoulders; which sight Bradford beholding with grief bade his brother farewell, willing him to commend him to his mother and the rest of his friends, and to get him to some surgeon betimes. Then was he led to Smithfield with a great company of weaponed men, as the like was not seen at any man's burning; for in every corner of Smithfield there were some besides those which stood about the stake. Bradford, being come to the stake, fell flat to the ground, secretly making his prayers to Almighty God. Then rising and putting off his clothes to his shirt he went to the stake, and there suffered joyfully and constantly.

With whom also was burnt one John Leafe, apprentice to Humfrey Gawdie, tallow-chandler in London, of the age of nineteen years, born at Kirkeby Moreside in the county of York; who upon the Friday before Palm Sunday was committed to the Counter in Bread Street by an alderman who had charge of that ward where Leafe did dwell. He coming to examination before Boner gave firm and Christian testimony of his doctrine, answering to such articles as were objected to him by the bishop. As touching his belief in the sacrament of the altar, he answered that after the words of consecration spoken by the priest there was not the natural body and blood of Christ in substance, but bread and wine as before; the communicants received the same in remembrance of Christ's death and passion, and spiritually, in faith, they received Christ's body and blood. Also he believed auricular confession not to be necessary to be made unto a priest, neither that the priest hath any authority given him by Scripture to remit sin. Upon these answers he at that time being dismissed was bid the Monday next, the 10th of June, to appear again to hear sentence; at what time the bishop, essaying all ways to revoke him to his own trade, found him the same man still, so planted upon the rock of truth that no words or deeds of men could remove him. Whereupon the bishop proceeded to read the sentence of condemnation; whereby this young man, committed to the secular power, was then adjudged, and not long after suffered with Bradford, confirming with his death that which he had professed in his life.

It is reported by one that was in the Counter the same time and saw the thing, that after his examination, when two bills were sent unto him, one containing a recantation, the other his confessions, to know to which of them he would put his hand, first hearing the bill of recantation read to him (because he could not read nor write himself) that he refused. But when the other was read unto him, which he well liked, instead of a pen he took a pin, and pricking his hand sprinkled the blood upon the bill, willing the reader to show the bishop that he had sealed the bill with his blood already.

When they came to the stake in Smithfield, Bradford on one side of the stake, Leafe on the other side, they lay flat on their faces praying the space of a minute off an hour. Then one of the sheriffs said, 'Arise and make an end; for the press of the people is great.' At that they both stood up, and Bradford took a faggot in his hand and kissed it, likewise the stake. When he had so done, he desired of the sheriffs that his servant might have his raiment; 'For,' said he, 'I have nothing else to give him, and he is a poor man.' The sheriff said he should have it. Forthwith Bradford put off his raiment and went to the stake; and holding up his hands said, 'O England, England, repent thee of thy sins. Beware of false Antichrists; take heed they do not deceive you.' The sheriff bade tie his hands if he would not be quiet. 'O Mr Sheriff,' said Bradford, 'I am quiet: God forgive you this.' One of the officers which made the fire said, 'You are a fool and were best hold your peace.' Bradford gave no answer, but prayed the people to pray for him; and turned his head unto the young man that suffered with him and said, 'Be of good comfort, brother: we shall have a merry supper with the Lord this night'; and embracing the reeds said thus, 'Strait is the way and narrow is the gate that leadeth to eternal salvation, and few there be that find it.'

Thus they both ended their mortal lives, without any alteration of their countenance, being void of all fear, hoping to obtain the prize of the game that they had long run at, to the which I beseech Almighty God to conduct us through the merits of Jesus Christ our Saviour.

James Trevisam buried in the fields

On the third of July 1555 died James Trevisam in the parish of St Margaret in Lothbery, who being impotent kept his bed. Trevisam had a servant, John Small, which read on the Bible; and as he was reading Berd the promoter came to the house and would needs go up the stairs, where he found four persons besides him and his wife; to wit, the young man that read and two men and a woman; all which folks Berd apprehended and carried to the Counter, where they remained about a fortnight. Moreover Berd would have had James himself to Newgate in a cart but for neighbours. Nevertheless the poor man was fain to put in two sureties for his forthcoming; for he could not go out of his bed, being not only impotent but also very sick. So within a few days, James lying in extremities, the parson of the church, Mr Farthing, came to him, had communication with him, agreed well, and departed. After the priest was come down into the street there met him one Toller, a founder. 'Yea,' saith he, 'be ye agreed? I will accuse you, for he denieth the sacrament of the altar.' Upon that the parson went to him again, and then the priest and he could not agree. So the parson went to the bishop and told him. The bishop answered that he should be burnt; and if he were dead he should be buried in a ditch. So when he died the parson was against his wife as much as he could, neither would let her have the coffin to put him in nor anything else, but was fain to bear him upon a table to Morefield, and there was he buried. The same night the body was cast up above the ground, his sheet taken from him, and he left naked. The owner of the field seeing him buried him again; a fortnight after, the sumner came to his grave and summoned him to appear at Paul's before his ordinary, to answer to such things as should be laid against him. But what more befell him I have not certainly to say.

The history of John Bland, preacher

The 12th of July J. Bland, J. Frankesh, Nicholas Sheterden, and Humfrey Middleton were burnt at Canturbury together. Frankesh and Bland were ministers and preachers, the one being parson of Adesham, the other vicar of Rolvindon. Bland was a man so little born for his own commodity that no part of his life was separated from the common utility of all men; for his first doings were employed to the bringing up of children in learning and virtue; under whom were trained divers towardly young men which even at this present do handsomely flourish, in the number of whom is Dr Sands, now Archbishop of York. After this he coming to the ministry in the Church was inflamed with incredible desire to profit the congregation; which may appear by this, that whereas he was cast into Canturbury prison for preaching the gospel and delivered once or twice at the suit of his friends, yet would he needs preach again as soon as he was delivered.

Whereupon being the third time apprehended, when his friends yet again would have found means to have him delivered if he would have promised to abstain from preaching, he would accept no such condition.

Bland, tossed to and fro from prison to prison, from session to session, at last was brought before the Bishop of Dover, the commissary, and the archdeacon at Canturbury, the 13th of June. The bishop was Richard Thornton, the commissary Robert Collins, the archdeacon Nicholas Harpsfield. Under these a great sort of innocent lambs of Christ were slain at Canturbury. Bland was one of the first, who being brought before the bishop was examined of articles. To whom it was objected by the commissary whether he believed that Christ is really in the sacrament. He answered that he believed that Christ is in the sacrament as he is in all other good bodies; so that he judged not Christ to be really in the sacrament. Whereupon he was deferred to the 20th, then to hear what should be done in case he would not relent. Which day he appearing as before was required to say his mind plainly to the articles, being again repeated to him. This done and his answers taken, respite was given him yet a few days to deliberate with himself. The 25th of June he making his appearance again openly and boldly withstood the authority of the Pope; whereupon his sentence was read and he committed to the secular power.

Having now passed over the examinations of Bland let us proceed to the rest of his concaptives, Frankesh, Sheterden, Middleton, and Thacker, of whom Thacker only gave back. The rest were condemned by the suffragan of Canturbury, touching whose examinations I shall not need long to stand, forsomuch as the articles ministered against them were all one, so in their answers they little or nothing disagreed, as hereafter you shall hear. To seven articles propounded to the five persons above named first answered Frankesh somewhat doubtfully, desiring further respite of fourteen days to deliberate with himself; which was granted. Bland answered flatly and roundly, as before ye heard. Sheterden and Middleton answered to the first and second articles affirmatively. The third after a sort they granted. To the fourth, fifth, and sixth, touching the real presence and the sacrament to be ministered in Latin and in one kind, they refused to answer. Sheterden said he would not answer before the case were determined why he was imprisoned before the laws of parliament received. Thacker only relented and was contented to take penance. Thus the four upon these answers were condemned by the Bishop of Dover the 25th of June 1555.

So being given to the secular power they were burned at Canturbury the 12th of July, at two stakes but all in one fire, where they, in the sight of God and his angels and before men, like true soldiers of Christ gave a constant testimony to the truth of his holy gospel.

Nicholas Hall and Christopher Waide, martyrs

Next after the suffering of the Kentish men above named followed the martyrdom of Nicholas Hall, bricklayer, and Christopher Waide of Dartford, which were condemned by Maurice Bishop of Rochester about the last day of June. Hall was burned at Rochester about the 19th of July. With Hall and Waide three other were condemned, Joane Beach, widow, John Harpolle of Rochester, and Margery Polley; of which Margery here followeth in story.

Margery Polley, widow of Richard Polley of Pepingbery, was brought before the bishop about the beginning of June; which bishop, according to the pontifical solemnity of that church, rising up out of the chair of his majesty, in high swelling style to dash the poor woman beginneth: 'We Maurice Bishop of Rochester, proceeding of our mere office against thee, Margery Polley, of the parish of Pepingbery, of our diocese and jurisdiction of Rochester, do lay and object against thee all and singular these articles ensuing. To the which, and to every parcel of them, we require of thee a true, full, and plain answer, by virtue of thine oath thereupon to be given etc.' The oath being ministered and the articles commenced against her, she so framed her answers that she neither allowed the deity of their sacrament nor the absurdity of their mass. For the which sentence was read against her and she condemned. But because her death followed not upon the same, we will defer tractation thereof to the due time, first setting down in order of history the execution of Christopher Waide.

Christopher Waide, linen-weaver, was condemned by Maurice Bishop of Rochester and appointed to be burned at Dartford. At the day appointed, which was in July, there was betimes in the morning carried out of the town in a cart a stake and many bundles of reeds, to a place a quarter of a mile out of the town called the Brimth, into a gravel pit, the common place of the execution of felons. Thither also was brought a load of broom-faggots and tall wood; unto which place resorted the people of the country in great number and there tarried his coming, insomuch that thither came divers fruiterers with horseloads of cherries and sold them. About ten o'clock cometh riding the sheriff with a great many other gentlemen and their retinue, and with them Waide, riding pinioned, and by him Margery Polley, both singing a psalm. Margery, as soon as she espied afar off the multitude gathered about the place where he should suffer, said unto him very loudly and cheerfully, 'You may rejoice, Waide, to see such a company gathered to celebrate your marriage this day.' And so passing by the place, which joined hard to the highway, they were carried straight down to the town, where she was kept until the sheriff returned from Waide's execution. Waide, made ready and stripped out of his clothes in an inn, had brought unto him a fair long white shirt from his wife, which being put on and he pinioned, was led up on foot again to the foresaid place. Coming straight to the stake took it in his arms and kissed it, setting his back unto it, and standing in a pitch barrel taken from the beacon hard by. Then a smith brought a hoop of iron and with two staples made him fast to the stake under his arms.

As soon as he was thus settled, he spake with a cheerful and loud voice the last verse of the 86th psalm, 'Show some good token upon me, O Lord, that they which hate me may see it and be ashamed, because thou, Lord, hast helped me and comforted me.' Near the stake was a little hill, upon the top whereof were pitched four staves quadrangle-wise, with a covering round about like a pulpit; into which place as Waide was praying at the stake entered a friar with a book in his hand; whom when Waide espied, he cried earnestly unto the people to take heed of the doctrine of the whore of Babylon, exhorting them to embrace the doctrine of the gospel; whom the sheriff interrupted saying, 'Be quiet, Waide, and die patiently.' 'I am,' said he, 'I thank God, quiet, Mr Sheriff; and so trust to die.' All this while the friar stood still, looking over the coverlet as though he would have uttered somewhat; but Waide mightily admonished the people to beware of that doctrine; which when the friar perceived, he withdrew himself immediately without speaking any word, and went away. Then the reeds being set about him he pulled them and embraced them in his arms, with his hands making a hole against his face that his voice might be heard, which they perceiving that were his tormentors cast faggots at the hole, which notwithstanding he still as he could put off, his face being hurt with the end of a faggot cast thereat. Then fire being put unto him he cried, 'Lord Jesus, receive my soul,' without any sign of impatiency in the fire, till at length he was heard by no man to speak, still holding his hands up over his head even when dead and altogether roasted, as though they had been stayed up with a prop.

This sign did God show unto him, whereby his very enemies might perceive that God had according to his prayer showed such a token upon him. This was the order of this martyr's execution, this was his end; whereby God seemed to confound and strike with the spirit of dumbness the friar, that locust which was risen up to have spoken against him; and no less wonderfully sustained those hands which he lifted up to him for comfort in his torment.

Spectatores praesentes Richardus Fletcher pater, nunce minister Ecclesiae Crambroke; Richardus Fletcher filius, minister Ecclesiae Riensis.

The burning of Dirick Carver and John Launder

The 22nd of July was burned at Lewes in the county of Sussex Dirick Carver, of the parish of Brighthamstead. The next day was burned at Stening John Launder, of Godstone in Surrey. Which two men were about the end of October 1554 apprehended by Edward Gage as they were at prayer within the dwelling house of Dirick, and by him sent up unto the queen's Council, who after examination sent them to Newgate, there to attend the leisure of Bishop Boner; whence they were brought the 8th of June into the bishop's chamber. There they made their several confessions, signing them with their own hands. Which being read, the bishop objected unto them certain other articles, which they confessed to be true. This done, after long persuasions they were demanded whether they would stand to their answers. Launder said, 'I will never go from these answers so long as I live.' The other confirmed the same, and they were commanded to appear again before the bishop in the consistory at Paul's.

Upon the tenth of June these two persons were brought unto the consistory, where the bishop beginning with Carver caused his confession and answers to be read unto him, asking him whether he would stand to the same. Dirick answered that he would; 'for your doctrine is poison and sorcery. If Christ were here you would put him to a worse death than he was put to before. You say you can make a god: ye can make a pudding as well'; with divers other such words. The bishop seeing this constancy pronounced his usual blessing towards this Dirick as also upon John Launder, who after like process remained in the same constancy; and therefore were both delivered unto the sheriffs there present; but afterwards were conveyed to the places above named, and there joyfully gave their bodies to be burned in the fire, and their souls into the hands of God.

Dirick was a man whom the Lord had blessed as well with temporal riches as with spiritual treasures; which riches were no clog unto his professing of Christ; of which there was such havoc made by the greedy raveners of that time that his wife and children had little or none thereof. During his imprisonment, although he was well stricken in years and, as it were, past the time of learning, he so spent his time that being at his apprehension ignorant of any letter of the book he could before his death read perfectly any printed English; whose diligence is worthy no small commendation.

At his coming into Lewes to be burned, the people called upon him, beseeching God to strengthen him in the faith of Jesus Christ. He thanked them, and prayed God that he would strengthen them in the like faith. When he came to the sign of the Star, the sheriff said that he had found him a faithful man in all his answers. As he came to the stake he kneeled down and made his prayers, and the sheriff made haste. Then his book was thrown into the barrel, and when he had stripped himself, as a joyful member of God he went into the barrel himself. As soon as ever he came in he took up the book and threw it among the people. Then the sheriff commanded on pain of death to throw in the book again. Immediately that faithful member spake with a joyful voice saying, 'Dear brethren and sistern, witness to you all that I am come to seal with my blood Christ's gospel, because I know that it is true. As many of you as believe upon the Father, the Son, and the Holy Ghost, unto everlasting life, see you do the works appertaining to the same. As many of you as believe upon the Pope of Rome, you believe to your utter condemnation.' Immediately the sheriff said, 'If thou dost not believe on the Pope, thou art damned body and soul. Speak to thy God that he may deliver thee now; or else to strike me down, to the example of this people.' But this faithful member said, 'The Lord forgive you your sayings.'

Then spake he again to all the people present saying, 'All you whom I have offended in words or in deed, I ask you for the Lord's sake to forgive me; and I heartily forgive all which offended me in thought, word, or deed.' He said further in his prayer as followeth: 'O Lord my God, thou hast written, "He that will not forsake, wife, children, house, and all that he hath, and take up thy cross and follow thee, is not worthy of thee." But thou, Lord, knowest that I have forsaken all to come unto thee: Lord, have mercy upon me, for unto thee I commend my spirit; and my soul doth rejoice in thee.'

These were the last words of that faithful member of Christ before the fire was put to him. After that the fire came to him he cried, 'O Lord, have mercy upon me,' and sprong up in the fire, calling upon the name of Jesus, and so ended.

James Abbes, a martyr of blessed memory

Among many that travailed in these troublesome days to keep a good conscience was James Abbes, a young man who through compulsion of the tyranny then used was enforced to have his part with his brethren in going from place to place in peril of apprehending. But when the Lord had another work for him to do, he was brought before the Bishop of Norwich, Dr Hopton, who examining him of his religion and charging him very sore both with threats and fair speech, at last poor James did yield to their naughty persuasions, although his conscience consented not thereto. When he was dismissed, the bishop calling him again gave him a piece of money, 60d or 20d, whether I know not; which when James had received and was gone from the bishop, his conscience began to throb and to accuse his fact, how he had displeased the Lord by consenting unto their beastly illusions; in which combat with himself being piteously vexed he went immediately to the bishop again and threw him his money, and said it repented him that ever he gave consent to their wicked persuasions, and that he gave his consent in taking his money. The bishop with his chaplains did labour afresh to win him, but in vain: James would not yield for none of them all, although he had played Peter before through infirmity; but stood manfully in his Master's quarrel to the end, and abode the force of the fire to the consuming of his body into ashes, which was done in Bury the 2nd of August 1555.

John Denley, John Newman, and Patrick Pachingham

In the midst of this tempestuous rage of malignant adversaries, persecuting and destroying the flock of Christ, many there were who though not spiritual men yet thought to help forward for their parts, and as one would say to heap up moe coals to this furious flame of persecution, whether of blind zeal or parasitical flattery I know not. One was Edmund Tyrrell, a justice of peace within the county of Essex, an assister to cruel murderers of God's saints, who as he came from the burning of certain martyrs met John Denley, gentleman, and John Newman (both of Maidstone) travelling upon the way and going to visit friends in Essex; and upon the sight of them, as he yet braggeth, upon suspicion apprehended and searched them, and finding confessions of their faith in writing about them sent them unto the queen's commissioners. They receiving these prisoners, after they saw they could little prevail with their own persuasions, sent them unto Boner to be handled after his fatherly and charitable discretion: how favourable it was the sequel doth manifestly declare. The 28th of June he caused Denley and Newman with one Patrick Pachingham to be brought into his chamber, there examining them upon their confessions, objecting also articles of his own. They all answered in effect one thing, although Denley answered more largely than the others. This done, the bishop used his customary persuasions, to which Denley said, 'God save me from your counsel and keep me in the mind that I am in, for that you count heresy I take to be the truth.' Thereupon they were commanded to appear in the bishop's consistory the 5th of July.

The first of July he proceeded against them with his usual form of law, reading first their confessions, articles, and answers, then tempting them, sometimes with promises, otherwhiles with threatenings, always his chiefest argument. In the end, seeing their unmovable constancy, upon the 5th of July he condemned them as heretics and gave them unto the sheriffs as to his common executioners, who kept them until they were commanded by writ to send them to their several places of suffering; which was for Denley Uxbridge, where the 8th of August he was burned. Being set in the fire with the burning flame about him, he sung a psalm. Then cruel Dr Story commanded one of the tormentors to hurl a faggot at him, whereupon, being hurt therewith upon the face that he bled again, he left his singing and clapped both his hands on his face. 'Truly,' quoth Story to him that hurled the faggot, 'thou hast marred a good old song.' Denley, still in the flame of the fire, put his hands abroad and sung again, yielding at last his spirit into the hands of God.

After the martyrdom of Denley at Uxbridge, suffered also Pachingham at the same town, about the 28th of the month. Pachingham was charged of Boner for his behaviour in the bishop's chapel, who at mass time there standing would not put off his cap, which was taken for an heinous offence. Pachingham also, being much laboured by Boner to recant, protested that the church which he believed was no Catholic church but the church of Satan.

The other, John Newman, pewterer, dwelling at Maidstone, was burned the last of August at Saffron Walden in Essex.

W. Coker, W. Hopper, H. Laurence, R. Colliar, R. Wright, and W. Stere

Mention was made in the story of Bland and Sheterden of certain other Kentish men with them, examined by Thornton Bishop of Dover. The condemnation and execution of them was deferred till the end of August. Coming therefore now to the time of their suffering, we will briefly touch some part of their examination and answers as we find them in the registers. The names of these were William Coker, William Hopper, Henry Laurence, Richard Colliar, Richard Wright, and William Stere.

First Coker said he would answer no otherwise than he had already answered: being offered respite of six days he refused it; and so sentence of condemnation was read against him the 11th of July. Hopper first seemed to grant the determination of the Catholic Church. After calling himself better to mind, constantly sticking to the truth he was condemned the 16th of July. Laurence, examined the 16th, answered to the articles objected against him, denying auricular confession and that he would receive the sacrament, 'because the order of the Holy Scriptures is changed in the sacrament.' Sentence was given against him the 2nd of August. Colliar, examined of the sacrament of the popish altar, said he did not believe that after the consecration there is the real and substantial body of Christ, but only bread and wine, and that it is most wicked to believe otherwise. Upon this sentence was read against him and he condemned the 16th of August. After his condemnation he sung a psalm, wherefore the priests and their officers railed at him, saying he was out of his wits. Wright, the same day appearing, and required of the judge what he believed of the real presence, answered that as touching the mass he was ashamed to speak of it as it was used in the Church. Against whom sentence was also read the day aforesaid. Stere likewise was brought to appear the 16th of August, where he, being required to make answer to the judge, made answer that he should command his dogs and not him; and declared that Dick of Dover had no authority to sit against him in judgment, and asked where his authority was. Who then showed him certain writings from Rome. Stere denying that to be of sufficient force, the said Dick said he had authority from the queen. Then the martyr alleging that the Archbishop of Canturbury, then in prison, was his diocesan, urged him to show his authority from the archbishop, or else he denied his authority to be sufficient. Thus sentence was pronounced against him.

Thus these six witness-bearers to the truth, condemned by the bloody suffragan, the archdeacon of Canturbury, Mr Collins and Mr Faucet, were burned altogether in Canturbury at three stakes and one fire, about the end of August.

The persecution of ten martyrs together

After the burning of these six followeth the persecution of ten other saints of the Lord; not such saints as the Pope maketh but such as are spoken of in the Apocalypse: 'These be they that follow the Lamb whithersoever he goeth, and which have washed their stoles in the blood of the Lamb.' The names of these ten were Elizabeth Warne, George Tankerfield, Robert Smith, Steven Harwood, Thomas Fust, William Hale, Thomas Leyes, George King, John Wade, Joan Layshford. The prisons of London being now to be replenished with God's saints, and moe and moe coming in, the Council caused these ten to be sent to Boner, by him to be examined and rid out of the way.

Now severally to prosecute the stories of these ten, we will begin with Elizabeth Warne, who in this month of August was burnt at Stratford Bowe nigh unto London, widow of John Warne, upholsterer, who also was burned in May last past, as before is recorded. Elizabeth had been apprehended the first of January in a house in Bowe churchyard in London, as they were gathered in prayer, and was carried to the Counter, where she lay as prisoner until the 11th of June; at which time she was brought unto Newgate, and remained there unto the second of July. Then she was sent by the commissioners to Boner, who the 6th of the month caused her with divers others to be brought before him and examined upon sundry articles. In the end, when she had divers times been brought before him and exhorted to recant, she said, 'Do what ye will; for if Christ was in error, then am I in error.' Upon which answer she was the 12th of July condemned as an heretic and delivered to the secular power to be put to death, which thing was accomplished in her the same month.

George Tankerfield of London, cook, born in York, about the age of twenty-seven, was a very Papist till Queen Mary came in; then perceiving the cruelty used of the Pope's side was brought into misdoubt of their doings and began to abhor them. And so he was moved to read the Testament, whereby the Lord lightened his mind with the knowledge of the truth, working lively faith in him to believe the same and to detest all Papistry; and so he came no more to their doings. Not only that, but this lively faith kindled such a flame in him as would not be kept in, but utter itself by confession thereof, reproving his former doings to his friends, exhorting them likewise to turn to the truth; thus he began to be smelled out till at last he was sent for as followeth.

It pleased God to strike him with sickness, whereby he lay long sick; and on a certain day, to take the air, he rose and walked into the Temple Fields to see the shooters. In the mean season came Beard to his house and enquired for him, pretending to his wife that he came only to have him come and dress a banquet at Lord Paget's. The wife, because his apparel was very brave, took him to be some honest gentleman and with all speed prepared to fetch her husband, having good hope he should now earn some money; and lest this gentleman should be noyed with tarrying she fet him a cushion to set him soft, laid a fair napkin before him, set bread thereon, and came to her husband, who when he heard it said, 'A banquet, woman! It is such a banquet as will not be very pleasant to the flesh; but God's will be done.' When he came home, he saw who it was and called him by his name; which when his wife perceived and wherefore he came, like a tall woman would play Peter's part, and instead of a sword took a spit, and had run him through, had not the constable, which Beard had sent for by his man, come in withal, who rescued him; yet she sent a brick-bat after him and hit him on the back. And so Tankerfield was delivered to the constable, and brought to Newgate about the last day of February 1555, by Beard, yeoman of the guard, and Simon Ponder, constable, sent in by Roger Cholmley, knight, and Dr Martin.

Tankerfield, thus brought to prison by his adversaries, at length was brought before Boner, who ordered his articles and positions unto him. To these he answered, declaring his mind touching auricular confession and the mass; and to these assertions he said he would stand; whereupon the bishop reading the sentence of his Popish condemnation gave him to the secular power. And so this blessed servant of God was had to St Albon's, and there with patience and constancy ended his life, the 26th of August, for the defence of the truth.

Robert Smith was brought unto Newgate the 5th of November by John Matthew, yeoman of the guard, by commandment of the Council. This Smith first gave himself unto service in the house of Sir Thomas Smith, Provost of Eaton: from thence he was preferred to Windsor, having there in the college a clerkship of ten pound a year. He was tall and slender, active about many things but chiefly delighting in the art of painting, which rather for his mind's sake than for lucre he did practise. In religion he was fervent after he had once tasted the truth; wherein he was confirmed by the preachings and readings of one Mr Turner and other. Whereupon at the coming of Queen Mary he was deprived of his clerkship by her visitors, and not long after was apprehended and brought before Boner, as here followeth written and testified by his own hand.

'The 12th of July I was with my brethren brought into the consistory, and mine articles read before my Lord Mayor and the Sheriffs with all the assistances; to which I answered. . . . Then began the sentence *In Dei nomine*. To which I answered that he began in a wrong name, requiring of him where he learned in Scriptures to give sentence of death against any man for his conscience' sake. To which he made no answer, but went forward to the end, and immediately cried away with me. . . . Then was I with the rest of my brethren carried away to Newgate.

'Thus, gentle reader, as near as I can I have set out the truth of my examination and the verity of mine unjust condemnation for the truth, requiring God that it may not be laid to the charge of thee, O England; requiring your hearty prayers unto God for his grace and spirit of boldness; with hope even shortly to set my seal at Uxbridge, the 8th of August, by God's grace. Pray that it may be to his honour, my salvation, and your consolation, I pray you. *Da gloriam Deo*.'

About this time died also Steven Harwood at Stratford and Thomas Fust at Ware, which two, as they were about one time burned with Smith and Tankerfield although in sundry places, so were they also examined and condemned with them. Their process, because it was joined with the process of Smith and others above mentioned, I thought it superfluous to repeat. To be short, after their answers made, both were condemned by the bishop as heretics to be burned, and so finished they their martyrdom, the one at Stratford, the other at Ware.

In the same company was also William Hale of Thorpe in Essex, who being examined with the rest the 12th of July received with them the

'The picture describing the strait handling of the close prisoners in Lollards Tower.'

sentence of condemnation, giving this exhortation withal to the lookers-on: 'Ah good people, beware of the idolater and this Antichrist,' pointing unto the bishop. So was he delivered unto the sheriffs as an heretic to be burned; who sent him to Barnet, where about the end of August he sealed his faith with the consuming of his body by cruel fire, yielding his soul unto his sure Redeemer.

Other three, to wit King, Leyes, and Wade, sickening in Lollards' Tower, were so weak that they were removed into sundry houses within the City of London and there departed, and were cast out into the fields and there buried by night of faithful brethren, when none in the day durst do it *propter metum Judaeorum*. The last that remained was Joan Laysh or Layshford, daughter-in-law to John and Elizabeth Warne; but because she was reprieved to a longer day, her story we will defer till January the next year.

The like Catholic charity was showed upon William Andrew of Horsley in Essex, carpenter, who was brought to Newgate the 1st of April 1555. Through strait handling in the prison, there he lost his life. And so after the popish manner he was cast out into the fields and by night was privily buried by the hands of faithful brethren.

The martyrdom of Robert Samuel, preacher

Master Foster, justice, dwelling at Cobdock in Suffolk, did not only not cease to study how to bring those in thrall that were godly inclined to religion, but also whatever they were that once came in his claws, they escaped not without clog of conscience or else loss of life, so greedy was he of blood. Among many whom he troubled was one Samuel, in King Edward's days a faithful preacher of God's word, who seemeth worthy of high admiration. He was minister at Barfolde, where he taught fruitfully so long as the time would suffer him to do his duty. Being removed from the ministry and put from his benefice, yet would he not give over his care that he had for his flock, but would teach them privily when he could not openly be suffered so to do; at what time order was taken by the queen that all priests which had married in King Edward's days, putting their wives from them, should be compelled to return to single life. This would not Samuel stand unto, for that he knew it to be wicked and abominable; but determining that God's laws were not to be broken for man's tradition he kept his wife still at Ipswich. Foster having intelligence hereof foreslacked no diligence, but eftsoons sendeth out his espials, laying wait for Samuel, that if he came home to his wife at any time they might apprehend him.

When such as should betray him espied him at home with his wife, they came immediately flocking about his house and beset it with a great company, and took him in the night because they durst not do it in the daytime for fear of tumult, although Samuel did nothing withstand them but meekly yielded himself into their clutches. They put him into Ipswich gaol, where he passed his time meekly among his godly brethren, so long as he was permitted to continue there. Howbeit not long after being taken from thence, he was carried to Norwich, where Dr Hopton (or Dr Dunning, his chancellor) exercised great cruelty against him, as indeed they had not their matches for cruel tormenting the bodies of the saints. For although the other were sharp enough in their generation, yet could they be satisfied with imprisonment and death and would go no further. Neither did I ever hear of any besides these, which so far exceeded all bounds of compassion in tormenting their poor brethren as this bishop did, in such sort that many of them he perverted and brought quite from the truth, and some from their wits also. The bishop therefore, thinking he might as easily prevail with Samuel as with other, kept him in a very strait prison, where he was chained bolt upright to a great post, in such sort that standing only on tiptoe he was fain to stay up the whole weight of his body thereby. They added far more grievous torments, keeping him without meat and drink, whereby he was unmercifully vexed through hunger and thirst; saving that he had every day two or three mouthfuls of bread and three spoonfuls of water, to the end rather that he might be reserved to farther torments than that they would preserve his life.

At last when he was brought forth to be burned, which was but a trifle in comparison of those pains that he had passed, certain heard him declare what strange things had happened unto him during his imprisonment. After he had been famished two or three days together he fell into a sleep, as it were one half in a slumber: one clad all in white seemed to stand before him which ministered comfort unto him in these words: 'Samuel, take a good heart unto thee; for after this day shalt thou never be hungry or thirsty.' Which thing came to pass; for from that time till he should suffer he felt neither hunger nor thirst. And this declared he, to the end that all men might behold the wonderful works of God.

As this godly martyr was going to the fire, there came a certain maid to him which took him about the neck and kissed him; who, being marked by them that were present, was sought for the next day to be had to prison and burned, as the party herself informed me; however she escaped their fiery hands, keeping herself secret in the town a good while after. But as this maid, Rose Nattingham, was preserved by the providence of God, so there were two other honest women did fall into the fury of that time. One was a brewer's wife, the other a shoemaker's wife, but both now espoused to a new husband, Christ. With these two was this maid very familiar, who giving counsel to one of them that she should convey herself away while she had time, had this answer at her hands: 'I know well that it is lawful to fly; which remedy you may use if you list. But my care standeth otherwise. I am tied to a husband and have a sort of young children at home; and I know not how my husband, being a carnal man, will take my departure from him; therefore I am minded to stand to the extremity of the matter.'

So the day after Samuel suffered, these two wives, one called Anne Potten, the other Joan Trunchfield, were apprehended and had into prison together; which as they were by sex and nature somewhat tender, so they were at first less able to endure the straitness of the prison; and especially the brewer's wife was cast into great agony of mind thereby. But Christ, beholding the infirmity of his servant, did not fail to help her in this necessity; so at length they both suffered, *an.* 1556, February 19. Samuel suffered the 31st of August 1555.

Thomas Hayward and John Goreway; Robert and John Glover

Although this terrible persecution in Queen Mary's days did chiefly light in London, Essex, Norfolk, Suffolk, and Kent, we find few parts of this realm free from this fatal storm, but some good martyrs there shed their blood. To begin with the diocese of Lichfield and Coventry, there we find two condemned and burned about the midst of September at Lichfield, Thomas Hayward and John Goreway. Unto this month pertaineth also the memorable martyrdom of Robert Glover, gentleman; of whose troubles I cannot well entreat but must intermix some mention of his brother John, forsomuch as this privy commission was chiefly sent for John and not for Robert, albeit John escaped and Robert in his stead was apprehended. I thought therefore in one story to comprehend them both. To begin with John, the eldest, who being a gentleman born and heir to his father, dwelling in Manceter, was endued with fair possessions of worldly goods, but much more plentifully enriched with God's heavenly grace and inward virtues; which grace so working in him, he with his two brethren, Robert and William, not only embraced the happy light of Christ's holy gospel, but most zealously professed and no less diligently in their living followed the same.

Touching John Glover, so it pleased God to lay his heavy hand of inward affliction upon this man, that though he suffered not the pains of outward fire as his brother did, yet if we consider what in spirit and mind this man suffered, he may well be counted with his brother for a martyr, being no less desirous of the same martyrdom; yea, and in comparison may seem to be chronicled for a double martyr. For as Robert was speedily dispatched with the torments of the fire in a short time, so this saint of God, how much more grievous pangs, what boiling heats of the fire of hell inwardly he felt, no speech is able to express. I remember I was once or twice with him, who I perceived to be so worn and consumed that neither any pleasure of life and almost no kind of senses was left in him. Yet the occasion thereof was not of great moment. But this we see common among holy and blessed men: the more devout and godly they are, the more mistrust they have of themselves; often they are terrified and perplexed with small matters as though they were huge mountains; whereas others there be whom heinous crimes do nothing touch or stir at all. The occasion was that he being called by the Holy Spirit to the knowledge of the gospel, and having received a wondrous sweet feeling of Christ's heavenly kingdom, his mind falling a little to cogitation of his former affairs belonging to his vocation, began to misdoubt himself. He persuaded himself that he had sinned against the Holy Ghost, so that he despaired of salvation. This good servant of God albeit he suffered many years so sharp buffetings of Satan, yet the Lord at last did rid him of all discomfort, in such sort as he like one placed in heaven already and dead in this world led a life altogether celestial.

In the days of Queen Mary, as soon as the Bishop of Coventry heard the fame of this John, being so ardent in the gospel of Christ, he wrote to the mayor to apprehend him. But God, who seeing his trusty servant with so many torments broken and dried up would in no wise heap too many sorrows upon one poor wretch, neither would commit him to the fire who had been already scorched with the fires of inward affliction so many years, did graciously provide that his brother, being both stronger of body and better furnished with learning to answer the adversaries, should sustain that conflict; and so it came to pass. For as soon as the mayor received the bishop's letters, he sent forthwith a privy watchword to John to convey away himself; who with his brother William was not so soon departed out of his house but the searchers rushed in to take him. But when John could in no place be found, one of the officers going into an upper chamber found Robert lying on his bed, sick of a long disease, who was incontinent brought before the sheriff; which favouring Robert and his cause would fain have dismissed him and wrought what means he could, saying he was not the man for whom they were sent; nevertheless being feared with the stout words of the officer he was constrained to carry him away against his will, and so laid him fast while the bishop came.

Thus much concerning John Glover. Now to consider the story of Robert; forsomuch as the whole narrative of the same by his own testimony in writing was sent unto his wife, it shall seem best to exhibit his own words. Much did this worthy martyr leave behind him in writing concerning his entreating in prison and his conflicts with the bishop and his chancellor. Moe examinations he had no doubt when he was brought forth to be condemned, which he would have left unto us if length of life had permitted him to finish that he intended. Only this, which I could learn by relation of Austen Bernher, a familiar friend of his, concerning the going to his death, I can report; that Robert Glover, after he was condemned by the bishop and was at a point to be delivered out of this world, it so happened that two or three days before, his heart being lumpish and desolate of all spiritual consolation, felt in himself no aptness nor willingness but rather a heaviness and dullness of spirit, full of much discomfort to bear the bitter cross of martyrdom ready to be laid upon him. Whereupon fearing lest the Lord had utterly withdrawn his favour from him he made his moan to Austen, signifying unto him how earnestly he had prayed, yet could receive no sense of any comfort. Austen desired him patiently to wait the Lord's pleasure, and exhorted him to play the man, nothing misdoubting but the Lord in his good time would visit him; and therefore desired him, whensoever any feeling of God's mercies should begin to touch his heart, that he should show some signification thereof, whereby he might witness with him the same.

The next day, when the time came of his martyrdom, as he was going to the place and was now come to the sight of the stake, although all the night before praying for courage he could feel none, suddenly he was so mightily replenished with God's holy comfort and heavenly joys that he cried out, clapping his hands to Austen and saying, 'Austen, he is come, he is come!' and that with such joy and alacrity as one seeming rather to be risen from some deadly danger to life than as one passing out of the world by any pains of death. Such was the marvellous working of the Lord's hand upon that good man.

In the same fire was burned also Cornelius Bongey, a capper of Coventry, about the 20th of September.

After the martyrdom of Robert Glover, although John seeing his brother apprehended for him would gladly have put himself in his brother's stead, if friends had not otherwise persuaded him, showing that in so doing he might entangle himself but should do his brother no good; he thus in great vexation endured, rubbing out as well as he could, till about the latter end of Queen Mary the sheriffs with their officers, being sent to seek him, came into his house where he and his wife were. As he was in his chamber by himself, the officers, bursting into the house and searching other rooms, came to the chamber door where John was, who holding the latch softly with his hand perceived the officers buckling about the door, amongst whom one having the string in his hand was ready to pluck at the same. Meantime another coming by bade them come away, saying they had been there before. Whereupon they went to search other corners of the house, where they found Agnes his wife; who being had to Lichfield and examined before the bishop, after much ado was constrained to give place to their tyranny. John meantime, partly for care of his wife, partly through cold taken in the woods where he did lie, took an ague, whereupon not long after he left this life, which the Papists so long had sought for.

What befell after his death both to him and William is not unworthy to be remembered; who after he was dead and buried in the churchyard without priest or clerk, Dr Draicot, then chancellor, six weeks after sent for the parson of the town and demanded how it chanced that he was there buried. The parson answered that he was then sick and knew not of it. The chancellor commanded the parson to go home, and cause the body of John Glover to be taken up and cast over the wall into the highway. The parson answered that he had been six weeks in the earth and so smelled that none was able to abide the savour of him. 'Well,' quoth Draicot, 'then take this bill and pronounce him in the pulpit a damned soul, and a twelve-month after take up his bones and cast them over the wall, that carts and horses may tread upon them: then will I come and hallow again that place in the churchyard where he was buried.'

Recorded by the parson, who told the same to Hugh Burrowes, dwelling at Fynden in Darbyshire, by whose information we received the same.

Not much unlike usage was practised by these Catholic children of Mother Church upon William. The good people of Weme in Shropshire, where he died, brought the body unto the parish church intending there to have it buried. But Bernard, curate of the church, to stop the burial rode to the bishop, Rafe Bane, to certify him of the matter and to have his advice. Meantime the body lying there a whole day, in the night Richard Morice, a tailor, would have interred him, but then came John Thorlyne with other moe, and would not suffer the body to be buried; so that after he had lain there two days cometh Bernard with the bishop's letter, the contents of which here followeth:

'Understanding that one Glover, an heretic, is dead in the parish of Weme, I thought it good not only to command the curate that he should not be buried in Christian burial, but also command all the parish that no man procure, help, nor speak to have him buried in holy ground. I charge the churchwardens in special, and all the parish, that they assist the curate in procuring that he be not buried neither in the church nor within the wainables of the churchyard; and I charge those that brought the body to carry it away again, and that at their charge, as they will answer at their peril.'

By virtue of this letter they which brought the corpse were fain to carry it back again. But forsomuch as the body was corrupted and smelt so strongly that unneth any man might come near it, they were forced to draw it with horses unto a broom-field, and there was he buried.

The martyrdom of William Wolsey and Robert Pigot

After the suffering of Robert Glover and Cornelius Bongey at Coventry, followeth next the condemnation of other two, condemned at Ely by John Fuller, the bishop's chancellor, Dr Shaxton his suffragan, Robert Steward Dean of Ely, John Christopherson Dean of Norwich, 1555, October 9, the names of which martyrs were William Wolsey and Robert Pigot, dwelling both in Wisbich. Wolsey, a constable dwelling in Wells, was there brought to death by procurement of Richard Everard, a justice, who extremely handled Wolsey and bound him to the good bearing, causing him to put in sureties upon his good behaviour until the next sessions holden within the Isle of Ely. So Wolsey, dispatched of his office, removed his house, coming to dwell in Wisbich. Then being called again at the next sessions he was constrained to put in new sureties, which he refused to do, and so was commanded to gaol at the syze holden at Ely in Lent.

In Easter Week there repaired to confer with him Dr Fuller with Christopherson and one Dr Young, who laid to his charge that he was out of the Catholic Faith, willing him to meddle no further with the Scriptures than did become a layman. Wolsey, suffering them to say their pleasures, at last answered, 'Good Mr Doctor, what did our Saviour mean when he spake these words: "Woe unto you, scribes and pharisees, hypocrites, for ye shut up the kingdom of heaven before men; ye yourselves go not in, neither suffer ye them that come to enter in." ' 'Yea,' saith Fuller, 'you must understand that Christ spake to the scribes and pharisees.' 'Nay, Mr Doctor,' saith Wolsey, 'Christ spake even to you and to all other like you.'

The syze holden at Wisbich drawing nigh, Fuller cometh again to Wolsey, and speaketh on this manner: 'Thou dost much trouble my conscience; I pray thee depart and rule thy tongue, so that I hear no more complaint of thee: come to church when thou wilt, and if thou be complained upon, so far as I may I will not hear of it.' 'Mr Doctor,' quoth Wolsey, 'I was brought hither by a law, and by a law I will be delivered.' Then being brought to the sessions, Wolsey was laid in the castle at Wisbich, thinking to him and all his friends that he should have suffered there at that present time; but it proved nothing so.

Then Pigot the painter, being at liberty, was there presented by some evil-disposed person for not coming to church. Pigot, being called in the sessions, would not absent himself but did appear before Sir Clement Higham, who said unto him, 'Ah! are you the holy father the painter? how chance ye came not to church?' 'Sir,' quoth the painter, 'he that is in the true Faith of Jesus Christ is never absent, but present in the Church of God.' 'Sirrah,' said the judge, 'you are too learned for me to talk withal; I will send you to them that be better learned than I'; straightways commanding him to the gaol where Wolsey lay. So, the sessions being ended, Wolsey and Pigot were carried again to Ely into prison, where they both did remain till the day of their death. Meantime certain of their neighbours at Wisbich being at Ely came to see how they did. There came also a chaplain of Bishop Goodrick's, a Frenchman born, Peter Valentius, who said to Wolsey and Pigot, 'My brethren, according to my office I am come to talk with you, for I have been amner here these twenty years and before. Wherefore I must desire you to take it in good part that I am come to talk with you, I promise you, not to pull you from your faith; but I both require and desire in the name of Jesus Christ that you stand to the truth of the gospel; and I beseech Almighty God to preserve both you and me in the same unto the end. For I know not myself, my brethren, how soon I shall be at the same point that you are now.'

Pigot and Wolsey were called to judgment about the 9th of October before Fuller, Shaxton, Christopherson, and others, who laid earnestly to their charge for their belief in divers articles, but especially of the sacrament of the altar. Then Christopherson called for pen and ink and wrote these words: 'I Robert Pigot do believe that after the words of consecration spoken by the priest there remaineth no more bread and wine, but the very body and blood of Christ really and substantially, the selfsame that was born of the Virgin Mary'; and reading it to the painter he said thus: 'Dost thou believe all this according as it is written?' 'No, sir,' said the painter, 'that is your faith not mine.' So immediately judgment was given upon them to die; which done, they were sent again to the prison, where they did lie till the day of their death. At which day one Peacocke, being appointed to preach, took his text out of the First Epistle to the Corinthians, chapter five, of one that had lived unordinately by abusing his father's wife, likening Pigot and Wolsey to the same man, oftentimes saying that such members must be cut off from the congregation.

His sermon ended, Pigot and Wolsey being brought to the place of execution and bound to the stake with a chain, cometh one to the fire with a great sheet knit full of books to burn, like as they had been New Testaments. 'Oh,' said Wolsey, 'give me one of them,' and Pigot desired another; both of them clapping them close to their breasts, saying the 106th Psalm, desiring all the people to say Amen; and so received the fire most thankfully.

Dr Nicholas Ridley and Mr Hugh Latimer

The same year, month, and day which Wolsey and Pigot suffered at Ely, 1555, October 16th, followed at Oxford the slaughter of two singular captains and principal pillars of Christ's Church, Ridley Bishop of London and Latimer Bishop sometime of Worcester, of whose memorable learning and incomparable gifts of grace, joined with sincerity of life, all the realm can witness; so it needeth not that we should stand exactly in setting forth a full description of the same, but only to comprehend in a few words, touching the order of their lives, so much as necessarily serveth to the instruction of the reader and maketh to the use of this present history, in declaring first their beginnings and bringing up; then their studies and acts in the university; their preferments to higher dignity; at last their travail in setting forth religion and in maintaining the same to the shedding of their blood. And to begin with the life of Mr Ridley.

Among many other worthy histories of such as have been murdered for the gospel of Christ in Queen Mary's reign, the tragical story of Dr Ridley I thought good to chronicle and leave to perpetual memory; beseeching thee, gentle reader, with care to peruse, diligently to consider, and deeply to print the same in thy breast, seeing him to be a man beautified with such excellent qualities, ghostly inspired and now written doubtless in the Book of Life with the blessed saints, crowned and throned amongst the glorious company of martyrs. Descending of a stock right worshipful, he was born in Northumberlandshire, who being a child learned his grammar with great dexterity in Newcastle, and was removed from thence to Cambridge, where he in short time became so famous that for his singular aptness he was called to higher offices of the university, and was called to be head of Pembroke Hall, and made Doctor of Divinity. Departing thence he travelled to Paris; who at his return was made chaplain to King Henry VIII, and promoted afterwards by him to the Bishopric of Rochester; and from thence translated to the Bishopric of London in King Edward's days.

In which offices he so occupied himself by preaching the wholesome doctrine of Christ that never child was more loved of his parents than he of his diocese. Every holy day and Sunday he preached in one place or other, except he were letted by weighty business; to whose sermons the people resorted, swarming about him like bees, and coveting the sweet flowers and wholesome juice of the fruitful doctrine, which he did not only preach but showed by his life, as a glittering lantern to the eyes of the blind, in such chastity of life (declining from all evil concupiscences) that even his enemies could not reprove him in one jot thereof. Besides this he was passing learned, his memory was great, and he of such reading that he deserved to be comparable to the best of our age, as can testify his notable works, pithy sermons, and sundry disputations; his very adversaries will say no less.

He, using all ways to mortify himself, was given to much prayer and contemplation; every morning, as soon as his apparel was done upon him, he went forthwith to his bedchamber, and prayed the space of half an hour; which being done, immediately he went to his study, if there came no other business to interrupt him, where he continued till ten o'clock, and then came to the common prayer daily used in his house. Prayers being done, he went to dinner, where he used little talk, except occasion by some had been ministered; then was it discreet and wise, sometimes merry, as cause required. Dinner done, he used to sit an hour or thereabouts, talking or playing chess. That done, he returned to his study and there would continue, except suitors or business abroad were occasion of the contrary, until five at night, and then would come to common prayer as in the forenoon; which being finished, he went to supper, behaving himself there as at his dinner before. After supper recreating himself in playing chess the space of an hour, he would return to his study, continuing there till eleven, which was his common hour to go to bed, then saying his prayers upon his knees, as in the morning when he rose.

Now remaineth a word or two to be declared of his gentle nature and kindly pity in the usage of an old woman called Mrs Boner, mother to Dr Boner, which I thought good to touch, as well for the rare clemency of Dr Ridley as the unworthy immanity and ingrateful disposition of Boner. Ridley, at his manor at Fulham, always sent for Mrs Boner, dwelling in an house adjoining his house, to dinner and supper, with Mrs Mungey, Boner's sister, saying, 'Go for my mother Boner;' who coming was ever placed in the chair at the table's end, being so gently welcomed as though he had been born of her own body, being never displaced of her seat although the king's Council had been present; saying, when any of them were there, 'By your Lordship's favour this place of right and custom is for my mother Boner'. How well he was recompensed for this singular gentleness at the hands of Boner, the least child that goeth by the ground can declare. For who afterwards was more enemy to Ridley than Boner? who more went about to seek his destruction? recompensing his gentleness with extreme cruelty; as well appeared by the strait handling of Ridley's sister and George Shipside her husband: Boner, restored again, would not suffer the brother and natural sister of Ridley to enjoy that which they had by their brother, but currishly without all order of law or honesty, by extort power wrested from them all the livings they had.

Now concerning God's vocation, how Ridley was first called to the savouring of Christ and his gospel, it may appear that the occasion of his conversion was by reading Bertram's *Book of the Sacrament;* whom also conference with Cranmer and Peter Martyr did confirm in that behalf; who being thoroughly won to the new way, as he was before blind and zealous in his ignorance, so was he constant and faithful in the knowledge which the Lord had opened unto him, and did much good while authority of extern power might defend the peace of the Church and proceedings of the gospel. But after it pleased God to call from us King Edward, as the Church of England was left open to the enemy's hand, so Ridley eftsoon and with the first was laid hands upon and committed to prison, as before hath been expressed; first in the Tower, then translated with the Archbishop of Canturbury and Latimer to Oxford, was with them enclosed in the common prison of Bocardo, while at length dissevered from them he was committed to custody in the house of one Irish, where he remained till his martyrdom, which was from 1554 till 1555 and 16th of October,

Now after the life of Bishop Ridley followeth likewise the life and doings of the worthy champion and soldier of Christ, Hugh Latimer. He was the son of Hugh Latimer of Thirkesson in the county of Leicester, a husbandman of right good estimation, with whom he was brought up until he was of the age of four years; at which time his parents (having him left for their only son, with six daughters) seeing his ready wit, purposed to train him up in the knowledge of good literature; wherein he so profited at the common schools of his own country that at fourteen years he was sent to the University of Cambridge; where after some continuance of exercises in other things he gave himself to the study of School divinity. Zealous he was in the popish religion, and so scrupulous that being a priest he was so servile an observer of the Romish decrees that he thought he had never sufficiently mingled his massing wine with water; and moreover that he should never be damned if he were once a professed friar. In this blind zeal he was a very enemy to the professors of Christ's gospel, as his oration, made when he proceeded Bachelor of Divinity, against Philip Melancthon did plainly declare. Especially his popish zeal could in no case abide Mr Stafford, Reader of the Divinity Lectures, spitefully railing against him and willing the youth of Cambridge in no wise to believe him.

Notwithstanding such was the merciful purpose of God, that when he thought to have utterly defaced the professors of the gospel he was himself by a member of the same prettily caught in the net of God's word. For Thomas Bilney, being at that time a trier out of Satan's subtleties, seeing Latimer to have a zeal in his ways was stricken with brotherly pity towards him, and bethought by what means he might best win this zealous ignorant brother to the knowledge of Christ. Wherefore he came to Latimer's study and desired him to hear him make his confession. Which thing he willingly granted, by hearing whereof he was so touched that he forsook the School doctors and other such fopperies and became an earnest student of true divinity, as he himself in his first sermon upon the *Paternoster* doth confess. So that whereas before he was an enemy of Christ, he was now a zealous seeker after him, changing his old manner of cavilling and railing into diligent conferring with Bilney and others, and came also to Stafford before he died, and desired him to forgive him.

After his winning to Christ he was not satisfied with his own conversion only, but became both a public preacher and a private instructor to the rest of his brethren within the university by the space of three years, spending his time partly in the Latin tongue among the learned, partly among the simple people in his natural language. Howbeit as Satan never sleepeth when he seeth his kingdom begin to decay, so now, seeing that this member of Christ would be a shrewd shaker thereof, he raised up his impious imps to molest him. Amongst these was an Augustine friar, who took occasion upon certain sermons that Latimer made about Christenmass 1529, as well in the church of St Edward as in St Augustine's, to inveigh against him for that Latimer, alluding to the common usage of the season, gave the people cards out of the 5th, 6th, 7th chapters of St Mathew, whereupon they might occupy their time. For the chief triumph in the cards he limited the heart as the principal thing they should serve God withal, whereby he overthrew all external ceremonies not tending to the necessary furtherance of God's word and sacraments. For the better attaining hereof he wished the Scriptures to be in English, whereby the people might the better learn their duties, as well to God as their neighbours. The handling of this matter was so apt for the time that not only it declared a singular towardness of wit in the preacher, but also wrought in the hearers much fruit, to the overthrow of superstition and setting up of religion.

It would ask a long discourse to declare what a stir there was in

Cambridge upon this preaching of Latimer. First came out the Prior of the Black Friars, who thinking to make a great hand against Latimer, about the time when Latimer brought forth his cards brought out his Christenmas dice, casting to his audience *cinq* and *quatre*, meaning by *cinq* five places in the New Testament and the four Doctors by the *quatre;* by which *cinq, quatre* he would prove it not expedient the Scripture to be in English, lest the vulgar sort might be brought in danger to leave their vocation; for example the ploughman when he heareth this: 'No man that layeth his hand on the plough and looketh back is meet for the kingdom of God', might hearing this cease from his plough. Likewise the baker, when he hears that a little leaven corrupteth a whole lump of dough, may leave our bread unleavened, and so our bodies shall be unseasoned. Also the simple man, when he heareth in the gospel 'If thine eye offend thee, pluck it out and cast it from thee', may make himself blind and so fill the world full of beggars. These with other moe this clerkly friar brought out, to the number of five, to prove his purpose.

Latimer hearing this sermon of Dr Buckneham cometh shortly after to the church to answer the friar, where resorted unto him a great multitude as well of the university as of the town, with great expectation to hear what he could say; among whom, directly in face of Latimer underneath the pulpit, sat Buckneham with his friar's cowl about his shoulders. Then Latimer, first repeating the reasons of Dr Buckneham whereby he would prove it dangerous for the vulgar people to have the Scripture in the vulgar tongue, so refuted the friar, so answered his objections, so dallied with his bald reasons of the ploughman looking back and the baker leaving his bread unleavened, that the vanity of the friar might to all men appear, proving to the people how there was no such danger for the Scriptures to be in English. Proceeding in his sermon, he began to discourse of the figurative phrases common in Scripture, and in Hebrew most commonly used; 'and not only in Hebrew: every speech hath his metaphors and figurative significations, so common to all men that the painters paint them on walls and in houses; for example,' saith he looking towards the friar, 'when they paint a fox preaching out of a friar's cowl, none is so mad to take this to be a fox that preacheth, but know well enough the meaning of the matter, which is to paint out unto us what hypocrisy, craft, and subtle dissimulation lieth hid many times in these friars' cowls.' In fine Friar Buckneham with this sermon was so dashed that never after he durst peep out of the pulpit against Latimer.

Then came at last Dr West Bishop of Ely, who preaching against Latimer at Barwell Abbey forbade him within the churches of that university to preach any more. Notwithstanding Dr Barnes, Prior of the Augustine Friars, did license Latimer to preach in his church of the Augustines, and he himself preached at the church by called St Edward's, which was the first sermon of the gospel which Barnes preached. Whereupon certain articles were gathered out of his sermon and commenced against him by Mr Tyrell, fellow of King's Hall, and by the vice-chancellor presented to the cardinal.

Latimer, baited by the friars, doctors, and masters of that university, notwithstanding the malice of these malignant adversaries continued yet in Cambridge, preaching three years together with such favour of the godly, also with such admiration of his enemies that heard him, that the bishop himself, coming and hearing his gift, wished himself to have the like and was compelled to commend him upon the same. So Latimer, with Bilney, continued yet in Cambridge a space, where he with Bilney used much to confer together, insomuch that the place where they most used to walk in the fields was called long after The Heretics' Hill.

After Latimer had thus travailed in Cambridge about three years, he was called up to the cardinal for heresy, where he was content to grant such articles as then they propounded unto him. He returned to the university, where by means of Dr Buts, the king's physician, he laboured in the cause of the king's supremacy. Then went he to the Court, where he remained a certain time, preaching in London very often. At last being weary of the Court, having a benefice offered by the king at the suit of Cromwell and Buts, contrary to the mind of Buts he would needs depart and be resident of the same. This benefice was in Wilshire, the name of which town was West Kington, where this good preacher did exercise himself to instruct his flock, and his diligence extended to all the country about. His teaching was so zealous that he could not escape without enemies. It chanced that whereas he, preaching upon the blessed Virgin, had declared his mind, referring all honour to Christ our only Saviour, certain popish priests therewith offended wrought much trouble against him, drawing out articles which they falsely imputed unto him. The chief molesters of him, besides these country priests, were Dr Powell of Salisbury, Dr Wilson, Mr Hubberdin, and Dr Sherwood; of whom some preached against him, some also did write against him; insomuch that he was cited to appear before William Warham Archbishop of Canturbury, and John Stokesley Bixhop of London, *an.* 1531, January 29.

Against this citation Latimer did appeal to his own ordinary; notwithstanding he was had up to London before Warham and the Bishop of London, where he was detained a long space from his cure. There he, called thrice every week before the bishops to answer for his preaching, had articles laid to him whereunto they required him to subscribe. At length he writeth to the archbishop, partly excusing his infirmity, whereby he could not appear at their commandment, partly expostulating with them for detaining him from his duty, for no cause but preaching the truth against vain abuses crept into religion.

In these dangerous straits and snares, hard it had been for him to have escaped so long, had not the hand of the Highest preserved him through the favour of his prince, who with his mere power rescued him out of the crooked claws of his enemies. At length also he advanced him to the dignity of a bishop, making him Bishop of Worcester, who so continued a few years, instructing his diocese with wholesome doctrine and example of perfect conversation agreeing to the same. But as before both in the university and at his benefice he was tossed and turmoiled by evil-disposed persons, so in his bishopric he was not clear of some that sought his trouble. One especially, and that no small person, accused him to the prince for his sermons. It were a long process to story out all the doings and travails of this Christian bishop, but this I thought sufficient for this present.

He continued in this laborious function of a bishop till the coming in of the Six Articles. Then he did of his own free accord resign his pastorship. Shaxton Bishop of Salisbury resigned likewise his bishopric. These two remained a great space unbishoped, keeping silence till the time of King Edward. At what time he first put off his rochet in his chamber among his friends, suddenly he gave a skip on the floor for joy, being discharged of such a heavy burden. But troubles followed him wheresoever he went. A little after he renounced his bishopric he was almost slain, but sore bruised, and with the fall of a tree. Coming up to London for remedy he was molested of the bishops, whereby he was again in no little danger: and at length was cast into the Tower, where he remained prisoner till Edward entered his crown, by means whereof the golden mouth of this preacher was opened again. So he, beginning afresh to set forth his plough, continued all the time of the said king, labouring in the Lord's harvest most fruitfully, discharging his talent in divers places of the realm, as also at London in the convocation house, and before the king at the Court. In the inward garden before applied to lascivious and courtly pastimes he dispensed the glorious gospel of Jesus Christ, preaching before the king and his whole Court.

In this painful travail he occupied himself all King Edward's days, preaching for the most part every Sunday twice, to no small shame of loitering and unpreaching prelates which occupy great rooms and do little good; and that so much more to their shame because he, being a sore bruised man and above sixty-seven years of age, took so little care of sparing himself, to do the people good. Now to speak of his indefatigable diligence in his private studies, who every morning, winter and summer, about two in the morning was at his book. How careful his heart was of the preservation of the Church and the success of the gospel his letters testify, wherewith he continually admonished such as were then in authority of their duty, and assisted them with his counsel.

Among other doings in him to be noted this is not to be overpassed, that God not only gave him his Spirit plenteously to preach his word, but by the same Spirit he did so evidently foreshow all those plagues which ensued, that if ever England had a prophet he might seem to be one. Touching himself he ever affirmed that preaching the gospel would cost him his life, to which he no less cheerfully prepared himself than was persuaded that Winchester was kept in the Tower for the same purpose, as the event did too truly prove. For not long after Queen Mary was proclaimed, a pursuivant was sent (by means no doubt of Winchester) into the country to call him up; of whose coming although Latimer lacked no forewarning, being premonished about six hours before by John Careless, whose story followeth, so far off was it that he thought to escape that he prepared himself towards his journey before the pursuivant came to his house.

Latimer, coming up to London through Smithfield, where merrily he said that Smithfield had long groaned for him, was brought before the Council, where he, patiently bearing all the taunts given him by the scornful Papists, was cast again into the Tower, where he sustained imprisonment a long time, notwithstanding the unmerciful handling of the lordly Papists, which thought then their kingdom would never fall; yet he showed himself not only patient but also cheerful in and above all that they could work against him. Such a valiant spirit the Lord gave him that he was able not only to despise prison and torments, but to deride the doings of his enemies. When the Lieutenant's man came to him, the aged father, kept without fire in the frosty winter and wellnigh starved with cold, merrily bade the man tell his master that if he did not look the better to him perchance he would deceive him. The Lieutenant, hearing this and fearing lest he thought to make some escape, began to look more straitly to his prisoner, and coming to him beginneth to charge him with his words. 'Yea, Mr Lieutenant, so I said,' quoth he, 'for you look, I think, that I should burn; but except you let me have some fire, I am like to deceive your expectation, for I am like here to starve for cold.'

Latimer, passing a long time in the Tower, was transported to Oxford with Cranmer and Ridley, there to dispute upon articles sent down from Gardiner Bishop of Winchester, as is before touched. Latimer with his fellow-prisoners were condemned and committed again to prison, and there they continued from April to October; where they were occupied with conference, prayer, or writing. Latimer by reason of his age wrote least of them in this latter time of his imprisonment; yet in prayer he was fervently occupied, wherein oftentimes so long he continued kneeling that he was not able to rise without help. These were three principal matters he prayed for: first, that God would give him grace to stand for his doctrine until death, that he might give his heart blood for the same; secondly, that God would restore his gospel to England once again. The third matter was to pray for the preservation of the queen that now is, whom he with tears desired God to make a comfort to his comfortless realm of England. These were the matters he prayed for. Neither were these things desired of him in vain, for the Lord most graciously did grant all his requests.

Touching the memorable acts of this worthy man this is not to be neglected, what a bold enterprise he attempted in sending to King Henry a present, the manner whereof is this. There was then, and remaineth still, a custom received from the old Romans that upon New Year's Day, the 1st of January, every bishop with some handsome gift should gratify the king; and so they did, some with gold, some with silver, some with a purseful of money, some one thing, some another. But Latimer presented a New Testament for his New Year's gift, with a napkin having this posy about it, *Fornicatores & adulteros judicabit Dominus*.

Thus hast thou, gentle reader, the whole life both of Ridley and Latimer since their first springing years to this present time and month, October 1555; in which month they were brought forth together to their final examination and execution. As we have heretofore declared their lives distinctly one from the other, so now jointly to couple them together, as they were together joined in one cause and martyrdom, we will prosecute the rest that remaineth concerning their later examination, degrading, and suffering.

After the appearing of Cranmer before the Pope's delegate and the queen's commissioners about the 12th of September, whereof more shall be said when we come to the death of the archbishop, upon the 28th was sent to Oxford another commission from Cardinal Poole, legate *a latere*, to John White Bishop of Lincoln, Dr Brookes Bishop of Gloucester, and Dr Holyman Bishop of Bristow, the contents of which commission was that they or two of them should have full authority to ascite, examine, and judge Hugh Latimer and Dr Ridley, pretensed Bishops of Worcester and London, for sundry erroneous opinions which Latimer and Ridley did maintain in disputations had in Oxford in May, June, and July 1554. Which opinions if the named persons would now recant, yielding themselves to the determination of the Catholic Church planted by Peter in the blessed See of Rome, the judges should have power to receive the said penitent persons and minister unto them the reconciliation of the Holy Father. But if Latimer and Ridley would stubbornly maintain these opinions, the said lords should proceed in form of judgment according to the law of heretics, that is, degrading them from their dignity of bishop, priest, and all other orders should pronounce them heretics, cut them off from the Church, and yield them to receive punishment due to all such heresy and schism.

The last day of September Ridley and Latimer were ascited to appear before the said lords in the Divinity School at Oxford at eight o'clock. Thither repaired the lords, placing themselves in the high seat made for public lectures, being then fair set, and trimmed with cloth of tissue and cushions of velvet. After the lords were set, Latimer and Ridley were sent for. But because it seemed good severally to examine them, Latimer was kept back until Ridley was thoroughly examined. Soon after the coming of Ridley the commission was read. But Ridley standing bare-headed, humbly expecting the cause of his appearance, eftsoons as he heard the cardinal named and the Pope's Holiness, put on his cap. Then the Bishop of Lincoln after the third admonition commanded one of the beadles to pluck his cap from his head. Ridley, bowing his head to the officer, gently permitted him to take off his cap. After this the bishop in a long oration exhorted Ridley to recant and 'to acknowledge the supremacy of our Most Reverend Father in God the Pope's Holiness, which lineally taketh his descent from Peter, upon whom Christ promised to build his Church.'

Ridley desired his patience to suffer him to speak somewhat of the premises, lest the multitude of things might confound his memory, and said, 'As touching the saying of Christ whence your Lordship gathereth the foundation of the Church upon Peter, the place is not to be understood as you take it. For after Christ had asked his disciples whom men judged him to be, and they answered that some said he was a prophet, some Helias, some one thing, some another, he said, "Whom say ye that I am?" Then Peter, "Thou art Christ, the Son of God." Christ answered, "Thou art Peter, and upon this stone I will build my church"; that is to say, upon this stone—not meaning Peter himself, as though he would have constitute a mortal man, so frail and brickle a foundation of his stable and unfallible church; but upon this rock-stone—that is, this confession of thine that I am the Son of God—I will build my church. For this is the foundation and beginning of all Christianity, with word, heart, and mind to confess that Christ is the Son of God.'

With that the bishop interrupting him said, 'Well, Mr Ridley, you wrest places to your own pleasure. I am sure you know that there are two powers, the one declared by the sword, the other by the keys. The sword is given to kings and rulers of countries; the keys were delivered by Christ to Peter, and of him left to all the successors. As touching our goods and lives, we with you acknowledge us subjects to the king and queen, who hath the temporal sword; but as concerning matters of religion, we acknowledge another head; and as the king and queen do in all worldly affairs justly challenge the primacy, so in spiritual matters they acknowledge themselves not to be heads and rulers, but members of Christ's body. But we came not in this sort to reason the matter with you, but have certain instructions according to which we must proceed, proposing certain articles unto which we require your answer directly either denying them either granting them without farther reasoning; which articles you shall hear now, and tomorrow at eight o'clock in St Mary's Church we will take your answers. If you require a copy of them you shall have it, pen, ink, and paper; also such books as you shall demand, if they be to be gotten in the university.'

So he charging the mayor with him dismissed Ridley and sent for Latimer, who being brought to the Divinity School there tarried till they called for him; who eftsoons as he was placed said, 'My Lords, if I appear again I pray you not to send for me till you be ready, for I am an old man, and it is great hurt to mine old age to tarry so long gazing upon the cold walls.' Then the Bishop of Lincoln said, 'I was sorry you were brought so soon: it is the bailiff's fault, not mine; but it shall be amended.' Then Latimer bowed his knee down to the ground, holding his hat in his hand, having a kerchief on his head and upon it a nightcap or two, and a great cap with two broad flaps to button under the chin, wearing a threadbare Bristow frieze gown girded with a penny leather girdle, at which hanged by a long string of leather his Testament, and his spectacles without case depending about his neck upon his breast.

The bishop began, 'Mr Latimer, you shall understand that I and my Lords here have a commission from my Lord Cardinal Poole to examine you upon certain assertions of yours. Consider, Mr Latimer, that without the unity of the Church is no salvation, and in the Church can be no errors. What should stay you to confess that which all the realm confesseth, to forsake that which the king and queen have renounced and all the realm recanted? It shall be no more shame to you than it was to us all. The See of Rome is no usurped power, but founded upon Peter by Christ, as by the express word of God may be proved.' With that Latimer began to remove his cap from his ears. The bishop proceeded, 'Christ spake expressly to Peter saying *Rege oves meas*, the which word doth not only declare a certain ruling of Christ's flock, but includeth also a certain pre-eminence and government; so that in saying *Rege* Christ declared a power which he gave to Peter, which power Peter delivered to Clement, and so in all ages hath it remained in the See of Rome. If you shall acknowledge your errors, then shall we receive you, acknowledge you one of the Church, and minister unto you upon due repentance the benefit of absolution. But if you persever in your blindness, then must we separate you from us, and as a rotten member cut you off from the Church, and commit you to the temporal judges. Therefore consider your estate: you are an old man; spare your body, accelerate not your death, remember your soul's health, consider that if you die in this state you shall be a stinking sacrifice to God; for it is the cause that maketh the martyr and not the death; consider that if you die in this state you die without grace, for without the Church can be no salvation.'

Latimer lift up his head, for before he leaned on his elbow, and asked whether his Lordship had said. The bishop answered 'Yea.'

Latimer: 'Your Lordship exhorted me to come to the unity of the Church. I confess, my Lord, a Catholic Church spread throughout all the world without which unity of the Church no man can be saved; but I know by God's word that this church is in all the world and hath not his foundation in Rome only, as you say. Methought your Lordship brought a place out of the Scriptures to confirm the same, that there was jurisdiction given to Peter, in that Christ bade him *regere*, govern his people. Indeed, my Lord, St Peter did well and truly his office in that he was bid *regere*; but the Bishops of Rome have taken a new kind of *regere*. Indeed they ought to *regere*, but how? not as they will themselves; but this *regere* must be hedged and digged in. They must *regere*, but *secundum verbum Dei*; they must rule, but according to the word of God. Thus the Bishops of Rome have turned *regere secundum verbum Dei* into *regere secundum voluntatem suam*; they have turned rule according to the word of God into rule according to their own pleasures.'

The bishop, not attending to this saying of Latimer, proceeded in rehearsing the articles before proposed to Ridley, and required Latimer's answer to the first. Latimer, making his protestation that notwithstanding these his answers it should not be taken that he would acknowledge any authority of the Bishop of Rome, saying that he was their Majesties' subject and not the Pope's, neither could serve two masters at one time, required the notaries so to take his protestation that, whatever he should say, he should not be taken as though he did agree to any authority that came from the Bishop of Rome. The bishop said that his protestation should be so taken, but required him to answer affirmatively or negatively to each article and recited the same again. The notaries took his answers to be affirmatively. Forthwith the bishop charged the mayor with Latimer and brake up their session for that day.

The next day the lords repaired to St Mary's Church, and after they were set in a high throne trimmed with cloth of tissue and silk, then appeared Mr Ridley, who was set at a framed table a good space from the bishops' seat, which table had a silk cloth cast over it, the which place was compassed about with framed seats in quadrate form, partly for gentlemen which repaired thither (for this was the session day also of gaol-delivery) and heads of the university to sit, and partly to keep off the press of the audience; for the whole body, as well of the university as of the town, came to see the end of these two persons. After Ridley's appearance and the silence of the audience the bishop recited the first article and required Ridley's answer. Ridley said that his answer was there in writing and desired that it might be published, but the bishop would not read the whole, but here and there a piece of it. So the notaries took his answer, that he referred him to his answer in writing exhibited now, and before at the disputation. Likewise the bishop recited the second article and required an answer; Ridley referred him to his answer in writing, and like answers were taken to the residue of the articles.

These answers in this manner rehearsed, and penned of the notaries, the Bishop of Gloucester endeavoured in many words, amplifying and enlarging the matter eloquently with sundry points of rhetoric to move affections, to persuade Ridley to recant and forsake his religion. Likewise the Bishop of Lincoln, holding his cap in his hand, desired him to turn. But Ridley made an absolute answer that he was fully persuaded the religion which he defended to be grounded upon God's word: therefore without great offence towards God, great peril and damage of his soul, he could not forsake his Master, but desired the bishop to perform his grant, in that his Lordship said the day before that he should have licence to show why he could not with a safe conscience admit the authority of the Pope. But the bishop said that whereas then he had demanded licence to speak three words, he was contented that he should speak forty, and that grant he would perform.

Then stepped forth Dr Weston which sat by, and said, 'Why, he hath spoken four hundred already!' Ridley confessed he had, but they were not of that matter. The Bishop of Lincoln bade him take his licence; but he should speak but forty, and he would tell them upon his fingers. Ridley began to speak, but before he had ended half a sentence, the doctors cried that his number was out, and he was put to silence. The bishop forthwith read the sentence of condemnation, written in a long process, which because it is sufficiently expressed before we thought meet to omit. Howbeit the effect was that they did condemn Ridley as an heretic, and adjudged him to be degraduated from all ecclesiastical order, and committed him to the secular powers to receive due punishment.

Ridley was committed as a prisoner to the mayor, and Latimer was sent for; but in the mean season the cloth which lay upon the table whereat Ridley stood was removed, because Latimer had never the degree of Doctor, as Ridley had. Eftsoons as Latimer appeared, perceiving no cloth upon the table he laid his hat, an old felt, under his elbows and immediately spake to the commissioners saying, 'I beseech your Lordships to set a better order at your entrance; I am an old man and have a very evil back, so that the press doth me much harm.' Lincoln: 'I am sorry, Mr Latimer, for your hurt. At your departure we will see to better order.'

Latimer thanked his Lordship, making a very low courtesy. After this the bishop began: 'Mr Latimer, although yesterday, after we had taken your answers to those articles which we proposed, might have justly proceeded to judgment against you, yet we, desiring not your destruction, but rather that you would revoke your errors and turn to the Catholic Church, deferred farther process till this day; and now we have called you here before us to hear whether you are content to revoke your heretical assertions and submit yourself to the determination of the Church—and I for my part most earnestly do exhort you—or to know whether you persever still the man that you were, for which we would be sorry. Therefore we will propose unto you the same articles, and require of you a determinate answer without farther reasoning'; and eftsoons recited the first article. The notaries took his answer to be affirmatively. In like manner did he answer to the other articles, not varying from his answers made the day before.

After the bishop had exhorted him to recant and Latimer had answered that he ne could ne would deny his Master Christ, the bishop read his condemnation, after the publication of which the three bishops brake up their sessions and dismissed the audience. But Latimer required the bishop to perform his promise that he should have licence briefly to declare why he refused the Pope's authority. But the bishop said that now he could not hear him. Then Latimer asked him whether it was not lawful for him to appeal from this judgment. The bishop asked him to whom he would appeal. 'To the next General Council,' quoth Latimer, 'which shall be truly called in God's name.' With that appellation the bishop was content; but he said it would be a long season before such a convocation would be called. Then the bishop committed Latimer to the mayor. Because the press was not yet diminished, the bishop commanded avoidance and willed Latimer to tarry lest he should take hurt at his egression as he did at his entrance. So continued Ridley and Latimer in durance till the 16th of October.

Upon the 15th the Bishop of Gloucester, Dr Brookes, and the Vice-chancellor of Oxford, with many others moe, came unto Mr Irish's house, then Mayor of Oxford, where Ridley was close prisoner. When the bishop came into the chamber where Ridley did lie, he told him that yet once again the queen's Majesty did offer him her gracious mercy if he would receive the same and come home to the Faith which he was baptized in, and revoke his erroneous doctrine that he had taught: if he would not recant, they must needs proceed according to the law. 'My Lord,' quoth Ridley, 'you know my mind. As for the doctrine which I have taught, my conscience assureth me that it was sound and according to God's word; which doctrine, the Lord being my helper, I will maintain so long as my tongue shall wag and breath is within my body, and in confirmation thereof seal the same with my blood.' And here Ridley would have reasoned with Brookes of the Bishop of Rome's authority, but could not be suffered; yet he spake so earnestly against the Pope that the bishop told him if he would not hold his peace he should be compelled. 'And seeing that you will not receive the queen's mercy but stubbornly refuse the same, we must against our wills proceed according to our commission to disgrading, taking from you the dignity of priesthood. For we take you for no bishop and therefore will the sooner have done with you. So, committing you to the secular power, you know what doth follow.'

In saying these words they put upon Ridley the surplice with all the trinkets appertaining to the mass. As they were putting on the same, Ridley did vehemently inveigh against the Romish bishop and all that foolish apparel, calling him Antichrist and the apparel foolish and abominable—yea, too fond for Vice in a play; insomuch that Brookes was exceeding angry with him and said, 'You were best to hold your peace lest your mouth be stopped.' At which words one Edridge said to Brookes, 'Sir, the law is he should be gagged.' Ridley looking earnestly upon him wagged his head at him and with a sigh said, 'Oh well, well, well!' So they proceeded in their doings; nevertheless Ridley was ever talking things not pleasant to their ears.

When they came to that place where Ridley should hold the chalice and the wafer-cake called the singing-bread, they bade him hold the same in his hand. Ridley said, 'They shall not come in my hands: if they do, they shall fall to the ground.' Then was one appointed to hold them in his hand while Brookes read a certain thing in Latin touching the degradation of spiritual persons. Afterward they put a book in his hand, and read a certain thing in Latin; the effect thereof was, 'We do take from you the office of preaching the gospel.' Ridley gave a great sigh, looking up towards heaven, saying, 'O Lord, forgive them this their wickedness.' As they put upon him the mass gear, so they began with the uppermost garment in taking it away again, reading a thing in Latin according to the order contained in the book of the Pope's law. When all was taken from him saving the surplice on his back, as they were reading and taking it away, Ridley said, 'What power be you of, that you can take from a man that which he never had? I was never singer in all my life; yet you will take from me that which I never had!'

This degradation finished, Brookes called the bailiffs, delivering to them Mr Ridley with this charge, to keep him from any man speaking with him, and that he should be brought to the place of execution when they were commanded. Then Ridley brast out with these words, 'God, I thank thee, and to thy praise be it spoken, there is none of you all able to lay to my charge any notorious crime; for if you could, it should surely be laid in my lap!' Brookes said he played the part of a proud pharisee, praising himself; but Ridley said, 'No, no, no! To God's glory be it spoken. I confess myself to be a miserable sinner and have great need of God's mercy, and do daily cry for the same; therefore, I pray you, have no such opinion in me.' Then they departed, and in going away a warden of a college, of whose name I am not sure, bade Ridley repent and forsake that erroneous opinion. Whereunto Ridley said, 'Sir, repent you; for you are out of the truth. I pray God grant you understanding of his word.' Then the warden in a chafe thereat said, 'I trust I shall never be of your devilish opinion, neither be in that place whither you shall go. He is,' said he, 'the obstinatest man that ever I heard talk since I was born.'

The night before he suffered his beard was washed and his legs; and as he sat at supper at Mr Irish's he bade his hostess and the rest at the board to his marriage; 'For,' saith he, 'tomorrow I must be married'; and so showed himself as merry as ever he was before. And wishing his sister at his marriage he asked his brother whether she could find in her heart to be there. He answered, 'Yea, I dare say, with all her heart.' At this talk Mrs Irish wept; but Ridley comforted her and said, 'Oh Mrs Irish, you love me not now, I see well enough; for in that you weep it doth appear you will not be at my marriage, neither are content therewith. Indeed you be not so much my friend as I thought you had been. But quiet yourself: though my breakfast shall be somewhat sharp and painful, I am sure my supper shall be more pleasant and sweet.' When they arose from the table, his brother offered to watch all night with him. But he said, 'That you shall not. I mind to go to bed and to sleep as quietly tonight as ever I did in my life.'

Upon the north side of the town, in the ditch[1] over against Balliol College, the place of execution was appointed, and for fear of any tumult that might arise to let the burning, Lord Williams was commanded by the queen's letters, and the householders of the city, to be there assistant sufficiently appointed. When everything was in readiness, the prisoners were brought forth by the mayor and the bailiffs.

Ridley had a fair black gown, furred and faced with foins, such as he was wont to wear being bishop, and a tippet of velvet furred likewise about his neck, a velvet nightcap upon his head and a corner cap upon the same, going in a pair of slippers to the stake. After him came Latimer in a poor Bristow frieze frock all worn, with his buttoned cap and a kerchief on his head, all ready to the fire, a new long shroud hanging over his hose down to the feet; which at first sight stirred men's hearts to rue upon them, beholding on one side the honour they sometime had, on the other the calamity whereunto they were fallen.

Dr Ridley, as he passed towards Bocardo, looked upon where Cranmer did lie, hoping to have seen him at the glass window and to have spoken unto him. But Cranmer was busy with Friar Soto and his fellows, disputing together, so that he could not see him. Then Ridley looking back espied Latimer coming after, unto whom he said, 'Oh, be ye there?' 'Yea,' said Latimer, 'have after as fast as I can follow.' So he following a pretty way off, at length they came to the stake one after the other, where first Ridley entering the place, holding up both hands looked towards heaven. Then espying Latimer, with a wondrous cheerful look ran to him, embraced and kissed him; and as they that stood near reported, comforted him, saying, 'Be of good heart, brother, for God will either assuage the fury of the flame or strengthen us to abide it.' With that went he to the stake, kneeled down by it,

[1] In 1837 a quantity of ashes and burnt sticks was found three feet below the surface of Broad Street, opposite the door of the Master's Lodgings.—Ed.

kissed it, and most effectuously prayed; behind him Latimer kneeled, as earnestly calling upon God as he. After they arose, the one talked with the other a little while, till they which were appointed to see the execution removed themselves out of the sun. What they said I can learn of no man.

Then Dr Smith, of whose recantation in King Edward's time ye heard before, began his sermon to them upon this text, 'If I yield my body to the fire to be burnt, and have not charity, I shall gain nothing thereby.' He alleged that the goodness of the cause, not the order of death, maketh the holiness of the person; which he confirmed by the example of Judas, and of a woman in Oxford that of late hanged herself, for that they might then be adjudged righteous which desperately sundered their lives from their bodies, as he feared that those men that stood before him would do. He cried to the people to beware of them, for they were heretics and died out of the Church. He ended with a short exhortation to them to recant and save their lives and souls, which else were condemned. His sermon was scant; in all, a quarter of an hour.

Ridley said to Latimer, 'Will you begin to answer the sermon or shall I?' Latimer said, 'Begin you first, I pray you.' Ridley and Latimer kneeled down towards Lord Williams, the vice-chancellor, and other commissioners, who sat upon a form thereby; unto whom Ridley said, 'I beseech you, my Lord, for Christ's sake, that I may speak but two or three words.' Whilst my Lord bent his head to the mayor and vice-chancellor, to know whether he might give him leave to speak, the bailiffs and Dr Marshall, vice-chancellor, ran hastily up to him and with their hands stopped his mouth, and said, 'Mr Ridley, if you will recant, you shall not only have liberty so to do, but also have your life.' 'Not otherwise?' said Ridley. 'No,' quoth Marshall, 'if you will not so do you must suffer for your deserts.' 'Well,' quoth Ridley, 'so long as the breath is in my body I will never deny my Lord Christ and his known truth: God's will be done in me.' With that he rose up and said with a loud voice, 'I commit our cause to Almighty God, which shall indifferently judge all.' To whose saying Latimer added his old posy, 'There is nothing hid but it shall be opened'; and he said he could answer Smith well enough if he might be suffered.

Incontinently they were commanded to make them ready, which they with all meekness obeyed. Ridley took his gown and his tippet and gave it to his brother-in-law in Shepside, who all his time of imprisonment, although he might not be suffered to come to him, lay there at his own charges to provide him necessaries, which from time to time he sent him by the sergeant that kept him. Some other of his apparel that was little worth he gave away; other the bailiffs took. He gave away besides divers small things to gentlemen standing by, divers of them pitifully weeping. To Sir Henry Lea he gave a new groat, and to Lord Williams' gentlemen napkins, nutmegs, and races of ginger, his dial, and such other things as he had about him. Some plucked the points off his hose; happy was he that might get any rag of him. Latimer gave nothing, but very quietly suffered his keeper to pull off his hose and other array, which was very simple; and being stripped into his shroud he seemed as comely a person to them that were present as one should lightly see; and whereas in his clothes he appeared a withered and crooked, silly old man, he now stood bolt upright, as comely a father as one might behold. Then Ridley, standing as yet in his truss, said to his brother, 'It were best for me to go in my truss still.' 'No,' quoth his brother, 'it will put you to more pain, and the truss will do a poor man good.' Whereunto Ridley said, 'Be it, in the name of God,' and unlaced himself. Then, being in his shirt, he stood upon the stone, held up his hands, and said, 'O Heavenly Father, I give thee most hearty thanks, for that thou hast called me to be a professor of thee, even unto death. I beseech thee, take mercy upon this realm of England, and deliver the same from all her enemies.'

Then the smith took a chain of iron and brought the same about both Ridley's and Latimer's middles. As he was knocking in a staple, Ridley took the chain in his hands and shaked the same, for it did gird in his belly, and looking aside to the smith said, 'Good fellow, knock it in hard, for the flesh will have his course.' Then his brother did bring him gunpowder in a bag, and would have tied the same about his neck. Ridley asked what it was. His brother said, 'Gunpowder.' Then said he, 'I take it to be sent of God; I will receive it as sent of him. And have you any for my brother?' meaning Latimer. 'Yea, sir, that I have,' quoth his brother. 'Then give it unto him,' said he, 'betime, lest ye come too late.' So his brother went, and carried of the same gunpowder unto Latimer. Meantime Ridley spake unto Lord Williams: 'My Lord, I must be a suitor unto your Lordship in behalf of divers poor men, and especially in the cause of my poor sister; I have made a supplication to the queen's Majesty in their behalfs. I beseech your Lordship for Christ's sake to be a mean to her Grace for them. My brother here hath the supplication and will resort to your Lordship to certify you hereof. There is nothing in all the world that troubleth my conscience, I praise God, this only excepted. Whiles I was in the See of London, divers poor men took leases of me and agreed with me for the same. Now I hear say the bishop that now occupieth the same room will not allow my grants unto them made, but contrary to all law and conscience hath taken from them their livings, and will not suffer them to enjoy the same. I beseech you, my Lord, be a mean for them, and God will reward you.'

Then they brought a faggot kindled with fire and laid the same down at Ridley's feet. To whom Latimer spake in his manner: 'Be of good comfort, Mr Ridley, and play the man. We shall this day light such a candle by God's grace in England, as I trust shall never be put out.' When Ridley saw the fire flaming up towards him he cried with a wonderful loud voice, '*In manus tuas, Domine, commendo spiritum meum; Domine, recipe spiritum meum*'; and repeated this latter part often in English, 'Lord, receive my spirit'; Latimer crying as vehemently on the other side, 'O Father of heaven, receive my soul.' Who received the flame as it were embracing of it. After he had stroked his face with his hands, and as it were bathed them in the fire, he soon died (as it appeared), with very little pain or none. And thus much concerning the end of this old and blessed servant of God, Mr Latimer, for whose laborious travails, fruitful life, and constant death, the whole realm hath cause to give great thanks to Almighty God.

But Ridley, by reason of the evil making of the fire unto him, because the wooden faggots were laid about the gorse, and over-high built, the fire burned first beneath, being kept down by the wood; which when he felt, he desired them for Christ's sake to let the fire come unto him. Which when his brother-in-law heard but not well understood, intending to rid him out of his pain, as one in such sorrow not well advised what he did, heaped faggots upon him so that he clean covered him, which made the fire more vehement beneath, that it burned clean all his nether parts before it touched the upper: that made him leap up and down under the faggots, and often desire them to let the fire come unto him, saying 'I cannot burn.' Which indeed appeared well; for after his legs were consumed by reason of his struggling through the pain (whereof he had no release, but only his contentation in God) he showed that side toward us clean, shirt and all untouched with flame. Yet in all this torment he forgat not to call unto God, 'Lord, have mercy upon me,' intermeddling his cries, 'Let the fire come unto me, I cannot burn.' In which pangs he laboured till one of the standers-by with his bill pulled off the faggots above, and where he saw the fire flame up, he wrested himself unto that side. When the flame touched the gunpowder he was seen stir no more, but burned on the other side, falling down at Latimer's feet.

The end of Stephen Gardiner

The next month after the burning of Ridley and Latimer, which was November, Stephen Gardiner, bishop and chancellor, a man hated of God and all good men, ended his wretched life; concerning the qualities and disposition of which man forsomuch as somewhat hath been declared in the story of King Edward's reign, I shall need the less now to stand upon the same. First, this viper's bird crept out of Bury in Suffolk, brought up most of his youth in Cambridge; his wit, capacity, memory, and other enduements of nature not to be complained of if he had rightly applied the same. Through this promptness and towardness of his he profited not a little in such studies as he gave his head unto, as first in civil law, then in languages and such other like, especially those arts and faculties which had any prospect to dignity and preferment. Besides other ornaments of nature, memory chiefly seemed in him beneficial, rather than diligence of study.

To these gifts and qualities were joined his great or greater vices, which not so much followed him as overtook him, not so much burdened him as made him burdenous to the whole realm. He was of a proud stomach and high-minded, in his own opinion flattering himself too much; in wit crafty and subtle; toward his superior flattering and fair-spoken; to his inferiors fierce; against his equal stout and envious if in judgment he anything withstood him, as appeared between good Lord Cromwell and him in the reign of King Henry, being of like haughtiness of stomach as the poets write of Pelides, *cedere nescius;* who although would give no place to men, yet I wish he would have given place to truth, according as he seemed not altogether ignorant of that truth. What his knowledge was therein is evident as well by his book *De Vera Obedientia* as by his sermon before King Edward; also by his answers to the Council the same time; and moreover by his own words may be gathered in sundry places, as more plainly may appear by that which hereafter followeth.

As touching divinity he was so variable, wavering with time, that no constant censure may be given what to make of him. If his doings and writings were according to his conscience, no man can say whether he was Protestant or Papist. If he wrote otherwise than he thought, for fear or to bear with time, then was he a double deep dissembler before God and men, to say and unsay, to write and unwrite, to swear and unswear, so as he did. For first, in the beginning of Queen Anne's time, who was so forward or so busy in the matter of the king's divorce as was Gardiner, who was first sent to Rome and then to the Emperor as chief agent in behalf of Lady Anne? by whom also he was preferred to the Bishopric of Winchester (and Boner to the Bishopric of London). Again, at the abolishing of the Pope, who so ready to swear or so vehement to write against the Pope as he, as not only by his sermons but also by his book *De Obedientia* may appear? in which book lest any should think him drawn thereunto otherwise than by own consent, he plainly declareth how, not rashly nor upon a sudden, but upon long deliberation about the matter, he at length uttered his judgment. Moreover so he uttered his judgment in writing against the usurped supremacy of the Pope, that coming to Lovaine afterward he was there accounted for a person excommunicate and a schismatic, insomuch that he was not permitted in their church to say mass, and in their public sermons they cried out against him.

Thus long continued he firm and forward, so that who but Winchester during all the time of Queen Anne? After her decease time by little and little carried him away, till at length emulation of Cromwell's estate, and especially (as it seemeth) for his so much favouring of Boner, whom Winchester at that time in no case could abide, made him an utter enemy both against him and also his religion; till again in King Edward's days he began a little to rebate from certain points of popery and somewhat to smell of the gospel, and no doubt he would have further turned had not the unlucky decay of the Duke of Somerset clean turned him away from true divinity to plain popery; wherein he continued a cruel persecutor to his dying day.

But whatsoever he was, seeing he is gone I refer him to his judge, to whom he shall stand or fall. Concerning his death and manner thereof, I would they which were present would testify to us what they saw. This we have all to think, that his death happened so opportunely that England hath a mighty cause to give thanks to the Lord therefore; not so much for the great hurt he had done in times past in perverting his princes, in bringing in the Six Articles, in murdering God's saints, in defacing Christ's religion, as especially for that he had thought to have brought to pass in murdering also our noble queen that now is. For whatsoever danger it was of death that she was in, it did no doubt proceed from that bloody bishop.

Of things uncertain I must speak uncertainly for lack of fuller information, or else peradventure they be in the realm that can say more than here I have expressed. For as Boner, Story, Thornton, Harpsfield, Dunning, with other, were occupied in putting the poor branches of Christ's saints to death, so this bishop bent all his devices and spent all his powder in assailing the root, and in casting such a platform (as he himself at his death is said to confess) to build his popery upon, as he thought should have stood for ever and a day. But, as I said, of uncertain things I can speak but uncertainly. Wherefore as touching the manner of his death, how rich he died, what words he spake, what little repentance he showed; whether he died with his tongue swoln and out of his mouth as did Thomas Arundell, or whether he stonk before he died as Wolsey did, or whether he died in despair as Latomus and others did; all this I refer either to their reports of whom I heard it, or leave it to the knowledge of them which know it better.

Notwithstanding I thought not to overpass a certain hearsay, which not long since came to me by information of a worthy gentlewoman and a gentleman of the same name and kindred, which Mrs Munday, wife of Mr Munday, secretary sometime to old Lord Thomas Duke of Norfolk, a present witness of this that is testified, thus openly reported in the house of a worshipful citizen bearing yet office in the city, in words as followeth.

The same day when Bishop Ridley and Mr Latimer suffered at Oxford, about the 19th of October there came into the house of Stephen Gardiner the old Duke of Norfolk[1] with Master Munday, reporter thereof. The aged duke there waiting for his dinner, the bishop, being not yet disposed to dine, deferred the time to three or four at afternoon. At length about 4 o'clock cometh his servant posting in all possible speed from Oxford, bringing intelligence to the bishop what he had heard and seen; of whom the bishop diligently inquiring the truth of the matter, and hearing by his man that fire most certainly was set unto them, cometh out rejoicing to the duke. 'Now,' saith he, 'let us go to dinner.' Whereupon they being set down, meat immediately was brought and the bishop began merrily to eat. But what followed?

[1] ob. 1554.—Ed.

The bloody tyrant had not eaten a few bits, but the sudden stroke of God's terrible hand fell upon him, in such sort as immediately he was taken from the table and brought to his bed; where he continued 15 days in such intolerable anguish and torments that all those 15 days he could not avoid, by urine or otherwise, anything that he received; whereby his body being miserably inflamed within (who had inflamed so many martyrs) was brought to a wretched end. And thereof, most like it is, came the thrusting out of his tongue from his mouth so swoln and black with the inflammation of his body. A spectacle worthy to be noted of all such bloody burning persecutors.

The burning of John Web, George Roper, and Gregory Parke

Next after the martyrdom of the two most worthy standardbearers of Christ's army, Nicholas Ridley and Hugh Latimer, followed three other stout soldiers, John Web, gentleman, George Roper, and Gregory Parke. Web was brought before the Bishop of Dover and Nicholas Harpsfield the 16th of September, and had propounded unto him such articles as were commonly ministered by Boner to those of his jurisdiction. Being invited to deliberate upon the matter, he made answer that he would no otherwise say than he had already said, which was this: 'As touching the sacrament of Christ's body I believe to be left unto his Church in commemoration of his death and passion until his coming again. It is left in remembrance of his body, not by the words of consecration to be made his body really, substantially, and the same that was born of Mary—I utterly deny that.' The 3rd of October Web, Roper, and Parke were brought all three together before the said judge; who there and then agreeing and steadfastly allowing the answer made before by Web, were adjudged heretics, and in the latter end of November they were brought out of prison to the place of martyrdom. Roper was a younger man of fresh colour and complexion, the other two somewhat more elderly. Roper, at his coming to the stake, putting off his gown fet a great leap. So soon as the flame was about him he put out both his arms like a rood and stood steadfast in that manner, not plucking his arms in till the fire burnt them off. Thus these martyrs, brought to the stake and compassed about with a chain, were consumed all three together in one fire at Canturbury, counting themselves happy that they were made worthy to suffer for Christ's gospel's sake.

William Wiseman

The 13th of December in Lollards' Tower died William Wiseman, a clothworker of London, where he was in bonds for the word of God. How he deceased is not fully certain. Some thought that either through famine or ill handling he was made away; by reason whereof the crowner, John Gibbes, with an inquest of twelve men, were fain to sit upon him; who although to the outward appearance were said to find nothing in him but God's visitation, yet what privy causes there might be of his death the Lord knoweth. After William was departed in the Tower, the Holy Catholic Church men cast him out into the fields, commanding that no man should bury him; according as their devout manner is to do with all such as die in like sort, whom they count as profane and worthy of no burial, but to cast to dogs and birds, *ἑλώρια κύνεσσι*, as the poet saith, Yet their merciless commandment notwithstanding, some good Tobies there were which buried him in the evening, as commonly they did all the rest thrown out in like sort, whom they were wont privily by night to cover; and many times the archers in the fields standing by and singing together psalms at their burial.

The history of Mr John Philpot

Next followeth the martyrdom of Mr John Philpot. He was a knight's son, born in Hampshire, brought up in the New College in Oxford, where he studied civil law six or seven years, besides other liberal arts, especially the tongues, wherein very forwardly he profited. In wit he was pregnant and happy, of singular courage, in spirit fervent, in religion zealous, of nature and condition plain and apert, far from all flattery, farther from all hypocrisy and dissimulation. What his learning was his own examinations penned with his own hand can declare.

From Oxford, desirous to see other countries as occasion served, he went into Italy, where he coming from Venice to Padua was in danger through a Franciscan friar accompanying him, who coming to Padua sought to accuse him of heresy. At length returning into England as the time ministered more boldness to him in the days of King Edward, he had divers conflicts with Gardiner in Winchester. After that, having an advowson by the said bishop he was made Archdeacon of Winchester under Dr Poynet, who succeeded Gardiner in that bishopric. Thus during the time of King Edward he continued to no small profit of those parties thereabout. When that blessed king was taken away and Mary his sister came in place, whose study was wholly bent to alter the state of religion in the woeful realm of England, she caused a convocation of prelates and learned men to be congregate to the accomplishment of her desire. In which convocation Philpot with a few others sustained the cause of the gospel manfully against the adversary part; for which cause, notwithstanding the liberty promised before, he was called to account before Gardiner the Chancellor, then being his ordinary, by whom he was first examined. From thence he was removed to Boner and other commissioners, with whom he had divers conflicts. Many of Philpot's examinations and privy conferences are come to light, faithfully written with his own hand. He was divers other times after this examined, both openly in the consistory at Paul's and secretly in the bishop's house; yet what was there said is not sufficiently known, either because Philpot was not suffered to write, or for that his writings are by some kept close and not brought forth.

The bishop, having sufficiently taken his pleasure with Philpot in private talks and seeing his immutable constancy, thought it high time to rid his hands of him, and on the 13th and 14th of December, sitting judicially in the consistory he caused him to be brought before him and others, more for order's sake than for any affection to right judgment. The bishop recited unto him an exhortation in English; and after this they had great conference together, as well out of the Scriptures as also out of the Doctors. But when Boner saw that by learning they were not able to convince Mr Philpot, he thought by defamations to bring him out of credit; and turning to the Lord Mayor brought forth a knife and a bladder full of powder and said, 'My Lord, this man had a roasted pig brought unto him, and this knife was put secretly between the skin and the flesh thereof, and so was it sent unto him in prison. Also this powder was sent unto him, under pretence that it was good and comfortable to eat or drink; which powder was only to make ink to write withal. When his keeper did perceive it he brought it unto me. Which when I did see, I thought it had been gunpowder and put fire to it, but it would not burn. Then I took it for poison and gave it to a dog, but it was not so. Then I took a little water, and it made as fair ink as ever I did write withal. Therefore, my Lord, you may understand what a naughty fellow this is.'

Philpot: 'Ah, my Lord, have you nothing else to charge me withal but these trifles, seeing I stand upon life and death? Doth the knife in the pig prove the Church of Rome to be a Catholic church, etc.?'

Then the bishop brought forth an instrument containing articles and questions agreed upon in Oxford and Cambridge. Also he did exhibit two books in print: one was the catechism made in King Edward's days, 1552, the other concerning the disputation in the Convocation House. Moreover he did bring forth and laid to Philpot's charge two letters, one touching Bartlet Greene, the other containing exhortations and comforts, both written unto him by friends. These books, letters, and other matters being read, the bishop demanded if the book entitled *The True Report of the Disputation*, etc., were of his penning. Philpot answered that it was a good and true book of his own penning and setting forth.

The bishop waxing weary, and being not able by any ground either of God's word or of the Catholic Fathers to overcome him, fell by flattering speech to persuade with him; promising that if he would revoke his opinions and come home to their church he should not only be pardoned that which was past, but they would with all favour receive him again as a true member thereof. Which words when Boner saw would take no place, he demanded of Philpot whether he had any just cause to allege why he should not condemn him as an heretic. 'Well,' quoth Philpot, 'your idolatrous sacrament which you have found out ye would fain defend; but ye cannot nor never shall.' In the end the bishop seeing his unmovable steadfastness did pronounce the sentence of condemnation against him. Philpot said, 'God give you grace to repent your wicked doings; and let all men beware of your bloody church.' Moreover whiles Boner was about the midst of the sentence the Bishop of Bath pulled him by the sleeve and said, 'My Lord, my Lord, know of him first whether he will recant or no.' Boner said, 'Oh, let me alone'; and read forth the sentence.

When he had done he delivered him to the sheriffs; and two officers brought him into Paternoster Row, and there his servant met him, and when he saw him he said, 'Ah, dear master.' Philpot said, 'I shall do well enough; thou shalt see me again.' The officers thrust him away and had his master to Newgate: as he went he said to the people, 'Good people, blessed be God for this day.' So the officers delivered him to the keeper. His man thrust to go in after his master, and one of the officers said unto him, 'Hence, fellow! what wouldst thou have?' He said, 'I would speak with my master.' Then Philpot turned him about and said, 'Tomorrow you shall speak with me.' Then the underkeeper said to Philpot, 'Is this your man?' He said, 'Yea.' So he did license his man to go in with him; and Philpot and his man were turned into a little chamber and there remained until Alexander the chief keeper did come unto him; who greeted him with these words: 'Ah! hast thou not done well to bring thyself hither?'

'Well, I must be content, for it is God's appointment. I shall desire you to let me have your gentle favour; for you and I have been of old acquaintance.'

'Well, I will show thee gentleness and favour, so thou wilt be ruled by me.'

'I pray you show me what you would have me do.'

'If you would recant I will show you any pleasure I can.'

'Nay, I will never recant that which I have spoken, for it is most certain truth, and I will seal it with my blood.'

'This is the saying of the whole pack of you heretics.'

Whereupon he commanded him to be set upon the block, and as many irons upon his legs as he might bear, for that he would not follow his wicked mind. Then the clerk told Alexander in his ear that Philpot had given his man money. Alexander said to his man, 'What money hath thy master given thee?'

'My master hath given me none.'

'No! Hath he given thee none? That I will know, for I will search thee.'

'Do with me what you list, and search me all that you can. He hath given me a token or two to send to his friends, as to his brother and sister.'

'Ah!' said Alexander unto Philpot, 'thou art a maintainer of heretics; thy man should have gone to some of thine affinity; but he shall be known well enough.'

'Nay, I do send it to my friends; there he is, let him make answer to it. But, good Mr Alexander, be so much my friend that these irons may be taken off.'

'Well, give me my fees, and I will take them off: if not, thou shalt wear them still.'

'Sir, what is your fee?'

'Four pound.'

'I have not so much: I am but a poor man, and I have been long in prison.'

'What wilt thou give me then?'

'I will give you twenty shillings, and that I will send my man for; or else I will lay my gown to gage. For the time is not long that I shall be with you: the bishop said I should be soon dispatched.'

Then said Alexander, 'What is that to me?' and departed from him, and commanded him to be had into Limbo. So his commandment was fulfilled; but before he could be taken from the block, the clerk would have a groat. Then one Wittrence, steward of the house, took him on his back and carried him down, his man knew not whither. Wherefore Philpot said to his man, 'Go to Mr Sheriff, and show him how I am used.' So his servant went straightway, and took an honest man with him. When they came to Mr Sheriff, which was Mr Macham, and showed him how Philpot was handled in Newgate, the sheriff took his ring from his finger and delivered it unto that honest man which came with Philpot's man, and bade him go unto Alexander and command him to take off his irons and handle him more gentle, and to give his man that which he had taken from him. When they came to Alexander and told their message from the sheriff, Alexander took the ring and said, 'Ah, I perceive that Mr Sheriff is a bearer with him and all such heretics as he is; therefore tomorrow I will show it to his betters.' Yet he went in to Mr Philpot where he lay and took off his irons, and gave him such things as he had taken before from his servant.

At supper, the 17th of December, there came a messenger from the sheriffs and bade Philpot make him ready, for the next day he should be burned at a stake. Philpot answered, 'I am ready; God grant me strength and a joyful resurrection.' So he went into his chamber and poured out his spirit unto God, giving him hearty thanks that he had made him worthy to suffer for his truth. In the morning the sheriffs came and calleth for him, and he most joyfully came down unto them. There his man did meet him and said, 'Ah, dear master! Farewell.' His master said unto him, 'Serve God, and he will help thee.' So he went to the place of execution; and when he was entering into Smithfield the way was foul, and two officers took him up to bear him to the stake. Then he said merrily, 'What! will you make me a Pope? I am content to go to my journey's end on foot.' But first, coming into Smithfield, he kneeled down saying these words, 'I will pay my vows in thee, O Smithfield.' When he was come to the place of suffering, he kissed the stake and said, 'Shall I disdain to suffer at this stake, seeing my Redeemer did not refuse to suffer a vile death upon the cross for me?' Then he said the 106th, 107th, and 108th Psalms. When he had made an end he said to the officers, 'What have you done for me?' Everyone of them declared what they had done, and he gave to every of them money. Then they bound him unto the stake and set fire unto that constant martyr, who in the midst of the flames yielded his soul into the hands of God.

CHAPTER 9

IMPRISONMENTS, TORMENTS, AND DEATH

The story of seven martyrs

The Catholic prelates of the Pope's band, not satisfied with their one year's bloody murdering of the reverend, learned, and principal members of Christ's Church (whereof there were now very few which were not consumed by fire or compelled to fly their natural country) continued this next year also, 1556, in no less cruelty towards the more simple and inferior sort of people (I mean in degree, though God be praised, not in steadfastness), having yet sometimes amongst them such as were both learned and of good estimation. As the firstfruits thereof, about the 27th of January were burned in Smithfield these seven persons: Thomas Whittle, priest; Bartlet Greene, gentleman; John Tudson, artificer; John Went, artificer; Thomas Browne; Isabel Foster, wife; Joan Warne, alias Lashford, maid. All which seven, as they were burned in one fire, so were they all upon one form of articles condemned in one day. Howbeit forasmuch as the gifts of God in them were diverse, their dealings were also diverse, as shall be more plainly perceived in their several processes hereafter following.

Whittle, a married priest, after he had been expulsed from the place in Essex where he served, went abroad where he might, here and there as occasion was ministered, preaching the gospel of Christ. At length being apprehended by one Edmund Alabaster in hope of reward which he miserably gaped after, he was brought before the Bishop of Winchester, who was fallen lately sick of his disease, whereof not long after he died most strangely. But the apprehender for his proffered service was rated of the bishop, asking if there were no man unto whom he might bring such rascals but to him. 'Out of my sight, thou varlet! What dost thou trouble me with such matters?' The greedy cormorant being thus defeated of his prey, yet thinking to hunt further, carried his prisoner to the Bishop of London, with whom what an evil mess of handling Whittle had, and how he was by the bishop all to beaten and buffeted about the face, by his own narration in a letter sent unto his friend manifestly may appear.

'Upon Thursday the tenth of January the Bishop of London sent for me out of the porter's lodge, where I had been all night, lying upon the earth, upon a pallet, where I had as painful a night of sickness as ever I had, God be thanked. When I came before him, he talked with me many things of the sacrament so grossly as is not worthy to be rehearsed and amongst other things he asked me if I would have come to mass that morning if he had sent for me. I answered that I would have come to him at his commandment, "but to your mass," said I, "I have small affection." At which answer he was displeased sore, and said I should be fed with bread and water. And as I followed him through the great hall, he turned back and beat me with his fist, first on one cheek, then on the other, as the sign of my beating did many days appear. Then he led me into a little salthouse, where I had no straw nor bed, but lay two nights on a table and slept soundly, I thank God.'

At his last examination before the bishop, upon the 14th of January, Boner with his fellow-bonerlings, sitting in his consistory, called forth Whittle, with whom he began as followeth: 'Because ye be a priest, as I and other bishops here be, and did receive the order of priesthood after the rite and form of the Catholic Church, ye shall not think but I will minister justice as well unto you as unto others.' Then Boner did charge him that when in times past he had said mass according to the order then used, Whittle of late had railed against the same, saying that it was idolatry and abomination. Whereunto Whittle said that at such time as he so said mass he was ignorant, adding that the elevation of the sacrament giveth occasion of idolatry to them that be unlearned. Then the servant of our Saviour was again admonished, and with persuasions entreated by the bishop; who because he would not agree unto the same, the bishop proceeded first to his degradation, that is, to unpriest him of all his priestly trinkets and clerkly habit. After this, according to his accustomed proceedings, the bishop assayed him yet again, with words rather than substantial arguments, to conform him to his religion, who denying so to do said, 'As for your religion, I cannot be persuaded that it is according to God's word.' The bishop then asked what fault he found in the administration of the sacrament. Whittle answered, 'It is not used according to Christ's institution, in that it is privately and not openly done; and also for that it is ministered but in one kind to the lay people, against Christ's ordinance. Further, Christ commanded it not to be elevated nor adored; for the adoration and elevation cannot be approved by Scripture.'

'Well,' quoth Boner, 'my Lords here have shown great learning for thy conversion, wherefore if thou wilt yet return to the faith of the Catholic Church I will receive thee thereunto and not commit thee to the secular power.' To make short, Whittle strengthened with the grace of the Lord stood unmovable in that he had affirmed. Wherefore the sentence being read, the next day he was committed to the secular power, and in few days after brought to the fire with the other six, sealing up the testimony of his doctrine with his blood.

After the martyrdom of Whittle next followeth to speak of Bartlet Greene, who the next day after Whittle was likewise condemned. Greene was of a good house and having such parents as both favoured learning and were willing to bring up their child in the same; who after some entrance in inferior schools was sent unto the University of Oxford, where within short time he attained as well to the knowledge of sundry profane sciences, as also in his last years unto the understanding of Divinity; whereunto he was at first an utter enemy, until God of his mercy opened his eyes by his repairing unto the lectures of Peter Martyr, Reader of the Divinity Lecture in the University, so that thereby he saw the true light of Christ's gospel. Whereof when he had once tasted, it became unto him as the fountain of lively water that our Saviour spake of to the woman of Samaria, so as he never thirsted any more, but had a well springing unto everlasting life; insomuch as when he was called by his friends from the university, and placed in the Temple at London to attain to the knowledge of the common laws of the realm, he continued in his former study of the gospel. Howbeit through the fellowship of such worldly young gentlemen as are commonly in that and the like houses, he became by little and little a compartner of their follies and youthful vanities, as well in his apparel as also in banquetings and other excesses; which he afterwards did sore lament, as appeareth by his own testimony, left in a book of a friend of his, a little before his death, written with his own hand.

For the better maintenance of himself in his studies and other affairs he had a large exhibition of his grandfather Dr Bartlet, who during the time of Greene's imprisonment made unto him large offers of great livings if he would recant and come home to the Church of Rome. But those persuasions took small effect in his faithful heart, as the sequel did declare. He was beloved of all men, for he was of a meek, discreet, and gentle behaviour to all. Injurious he was to none, beneficial to many; as appeareth amongst other by his friendly dealing with Christopher

Goodman, at that present a poor exile beyond the seas; with whom Greene had often society in Oxford in the days of King Edward; which now notwithstanding his friend's banishment he did not lightly forget. That turned as it chanced to the great grief of both, the one of heart for the loss of his friend, the other of body in suffering the murdering rage of Papists. The cause was a letter which Greene did write unto Goodman, containing as well the report of certain questions cast abroad in London as also an answer to a question made by Goodman in a letter, in which he required to have the certainty of the report spread amongst them on the other side of the seas that the queen was dead. Whereunto Greene answered simply that she was not dead.

These letters, with many other written to exiles by their friends in England, came by the apprehension of the bearer unto the hands of the king and queen's Council, who perused the whole number and amongst them espied this letter of Green's, in the contents whereof they found these words: 'The queen is not yet dead.' Which words were only written as an answer to Goodman; howbeit to some of the Council they seemed very heinous; yea, treason they would have made them if the law would have suffered. Which when they could not do, they examined him upon his faith. His answers little pleased them; and after they had long detained him in prison they sent him unto Boner to be ordered according to his ecclesiastical law. Many conferences and public examinations they brought him unto. But in the end, seeing his steadfastness to be such against which neither threatenings nor promises could prevail, the 15th of January the bishop caused him with the rest above named to be brought into the consistory in Paul's; where being set in his judgment seat accompanied with Fecknam, then Dean of the same church, and other his chaplains, after he had condemned the other six he then calling for Greene read the articles generally objected to all seven prisoners. But when Greene would have answered them particularly he was put to silence, with promise that he should have time to answer; and the bishop proceeding asked Greene if he would recant and return to their Romish mother; which when he denied, the bishop pronounced the sentence definitive against him and committed him to the sheriffs, who caused him to be carried to Newgate. As he was going thither there met him two gentlemen, his special friends, minding to comfort their persecuted brother; but at their meeting their loving hearts were manifested by the abundance of their tears. When Greene saw them he said, 'My friends, is this your comfort you are come to give me in my heaviness? Must I, who needed to have comfort ministered to me, become now a comforter of you?' Thus declaring his most quiet mind, he cheerfully spake to them and others until he came to the prison door, into which he joyfully entered, and there remained always either in prayer or in other godly exercises unto the 27th of January, when he with his brethren went most cheerfully unto the place of their torments, often repeating as well by the way as at the stake these verses:

Christe Deus, sine te spes est mihi nulla salutis:
Te duce vera sequor, te duce falsa nego.

Thomas Browne, born in the parish of Histon within the diocese of Ely, came to London, where he dwelled in the parish of St Bride's in Fleet Street, a married man of the age of thirty-seven; who because he came not to his parish church was presented by the constable of the parish to Boner. Browne being had to Fulham, with the other there to be examined, was required upon the 26th of September to come into the chapel to hear mass, which he refusing to do went into the warren and kneeled among the trees. For this he was greatly charged of the bishop as for an heinous matter done in contempt of their mass. At length being producted to his last examination the 15th of February to hear sentence definitive against him, he was required with many fair words and glozing promises to revoke his doctrine. The bishop said, 'Browne, ye have been before me many times and oft, and I have travailed with thee to win thee from thine errors; yet thou and suchlike report that I go about to seek thy blood.' 'Yea, my Lord,' saith he, 'indeed ye be a bloodsucker, and I would I had as much blood as is water in the sea for you to suck.'

Boner then proceeding to the articles, when he had read them unto him again, asked him whether he was content to relinquish his heresies and return to the unity of the Catholic Faith. He made answer again, saying if they were heresies he would forsake them. 'They be heresies,' quoth the bishop. 'How will ye prove it?' said Browne; 'for I will not go from mine answer except you can prove them to be heresies, which ye shall never do; for that which you call heresy is no heresy.' Boner, not able or else not disposed to supply the part of a sufficient teacher in proving that which the other had denied by good authority of the Scripture, read the sentence definitive against him. This done, he was committed to the sheriffs, and burned the 27th of January, constantly abiding with the other the Pope's torments for the true confession of his Christian faith.

The same day and time when Brown was condemned was also producted John Tudson unto like condemnation. Tudson was born in Ipswich, after that apprentice in London, dwelling with George Goodyear of the parish of St Mary Botolph; who being complained of to Sir Richard Cholmley and Dr Story, was by them sent unto Boner and was divers times before him in examination. After this he was brought unto the open consistory; where the said true servant of the Lord was moved with sundry persuasions to go from his opinion and to persist in the unity of the church which they were of. But he persisting in that which he had received in King Edward's time refused so to do, saying there was no heresy in his answers. The bishop still used his accustomed persuasions, promising him all his offences and errors to be forgiven him if he would return. Then said Tudson, 'Tell me wherein I have offended, and I will return.' Then said the bishop, 'In your answers.' 'No,' said Tudson, 'I have not therein offended; and ye, my Lord, pretend charity, but nothing thereof appeareth in your works.' Thus after a few words the bishop did likewise promulgate against him sentence of condemnation; which being read, the martyr was committed to the secular power, and so with much patience finished his life with the other, the 27th of January.

John Went, born in Langham in Essex, of the age of twenty-seven, and a shearman by occupation, first was examined by Dr Story upon the sacrament of the Popish altar; and because the poor man did not accord with him thoroughly in the real presence of the body and blood of Christ, Story did send him up to Boner; who after divers examinations in the consistory attempted the like persuasions with him as he did to the other, to recant and return. To whom in few words Went answered he would not: by the leave of God he would stand firm in that he had said. When the bishop notwithstanding did still urge him with words and fair glozes to give over himself to their opinion, he could have no answer of him but this: 'I say as I have said.' Whereupon being condemned by the bishop's sentence he was committed unto the sheriffs (whom that shameless shaveling abused for his servile butchers) and so brought to his martyrdom, which he with no less constancy suffered to the end with the rest of that blessed society of martyrs.

With these five persons above recited were also two women

condemned the same time and burned for the same cause; the one a wife, Isabel Foster, the other a maid, Joan Warne, otherwise Lashford. Isabel was born in Grafestocke in the diocese of Carlile and married to John Foster, cutler, of the parish of St Bride's in Fleet Street, being of the age of fifty-five. She likewise, for not coming to the church being sent to Boner and imprisoned, was sundry times examined by the bishop, but never overcome nor removed from the confession of Christ's gospel. At length coming unto her final examination in the consistory the 15th of January, she was moved again whether she would go from her former answers. Whereunto she gave a resolute answer in few words: 'I will not go from them, by God's grace'; and thereunto did adhere, neither being cast down by the menacing threats of the bishop, nor yielding through his alluring enticements, promising both life and liberty if she would associate herself in the unity of the Catholic Church. Whereunto she said that she trusted she was never out of the Catholic Church; and so she continued constant till the sentence definitive was pronounced; then she was committed to the secular power, and brought a few days after to the stake, the seven and twentieth day of the month; where she, like a faithful witness of the Lord's truth, with the other five aforesaid ended her troubles here, to find rest in the kingdom of Christ.

In a certain place of these *Acts and Monuments* mention was made of Elizabeth Warne, who with her husband John in the beginning of Queen Mary's reign was apprehended in Bow Churchyard for being there at a communion. Both suffered for the same, the man in May, the wife in July. Now the daughter in January followed her parents in the same martyrdom. This Joan Lashford was the daughter of Robert Lashford, cutler, and the foresaid Elizabeth, who afterward was married to John Warne, upholsterer. Joan, about the age of twenty years, ministering to her father and mother in prison, inspected and known to be of the same doctrine and religion, was sent to Boner by Dr Story, and so committed to the Counter in the Poultry, where she remained five weeks, and from thence had to Newgate, where she continued certain months. After that, remaining prisoner in the custody of Boner, her confession was, being examined, that the whole twelvemonth before she came to no popish mass service in the church neither would do, either to receive the sacrament or to be confessed, because her conscience would not suffer her so to do. This godly damosel, feeble and tender of age yet strong by grace, in this confession stood so firm that neither flattering promises nor violent threats could turn her; but being exhorted by the bishop to return to the Catholic unity of the Church saith boldly to him again, 'If ye will leave off your abomination I will return: otherwise I will not.' Thus she constantly persevering in the Lord's holy truth was by the sentence definitive condemned, and committed unto the sheriffs, by whom the foresaid seven and twentieth day of January she with the rest, being brought unto the stake, there washed her clothes in the blood of the Lamb, to whom most lovingly she espoused herself.

Five martyrs in Canturbury

After these seven martyred together in Smithfield, shortly after in the same month, the 31st of January, followed another like fellowship of martyrs at Canturbury, four women and one man, whose names be these: John Lomas, a young man; Anne Albright, Joan Catmer, Agnes Snoth, widow; Joan Sole, wife. These five persons were burnt at two stakes and one fire together; who when the fire was flaming about their ears did sing psalms. Whereat the good knight Sir John Norton being there present wept bitterly at the sight thereof.

The story of Thomas Cranmer

Concerning the life and estate of that Most Reverend Father in God and Prelate Thomas Cranmer, late Archbishop of Canturbury, and of the occasion of his preferment unto his archiepiscopal dignity, who of many hath been thought to have procured the same by friendship only, and of some other esteemed unworthy so high a vocation: it is first to be noted that Cranmer, coming of an ancient parentage, from the Conquest to be deducted, and continuing sithence in the name and family of a gentleman, was born in a village called Arselacton in Nottinghamshire. Who being from infancy kept at school and brought up not without much good civility, came in process of time unto the University of Cambridge, and there prospering in good knowledge amongst the better sort of students was chosen fellow of Jesus College. And so being Master of Art it chanced him to marry a gentleman's daughter; by means whereof he lost his fellowship, and became the Reader in Buckingham College;[1] and for that he would with more diligence apply that his office of reading, he placed his wife in an inn called the Dolphin, the wife of the house being of affinity unto her. For

[1] Now called Magdelene.—Ed.

his often resort unto his wife in that inn he was marked of some popish merchants; whereupon rose the slanderous report against him after he was preferred to the Archbishopric of Canturbury, raised up by the malicious disdain of certain malignant adversaries to Christ and his truth, bruiting abroad everywhere that he was but an hostler and without all good learning.

Whilst Cranmer continued as a Reader in Buckingham College his wife died in childbed. After whose death the masters and fellows of Jesus College, desirous again of their old companion for his towardliness in learning, chose him again fellow of the same college; where he remaining at his study became in few years after the Reader of Divinity Lecture in the same college, and in such special estimation with the whole university that being Doctor of Divinity he was commonly appointed one of the heads (two or three of the chiefest learned men) to examine such as yearly profess in Commencement, either Bachelors or Doctors of Divinity, by whose approbation the whole university licenseth them to proceed unto their degree; again by whose disallowance the university also rejecteth them for a time to proceed, until they be furnished with more knowledge. Now Dr Cranmer, ever much favouring the knowledge of the Scripture, would never admit any to proceed in Divinity unless they were substantially seen in the story of the Bible; by means whereof certain friars and other religious persons, principally brought up in the study of School authors without regard to the authority of Scriptures, were commonly rejected by him, so that he was of the religious sort much hated; yet in the end divers of them being thus compelled to study the Scriptures became very well learned and well affected; insomuch that when they proceeded Doctors of Divinity could not overmuch extol Dr Cranmer's goodness towards them, who had for a time put them back to aspire unto better knowledge and perfection.

Like as he was neither in fame unknown nor in knowledge obscure, so was he greatly solicited by Dr Capon to have been one of the fellows in the foundation of Cardinal Wolsey's College in Oxford, which he utterly refused, not without danger of indignation. Notwithstanding, foreseeing that which after chanced to the utter confusion of many learned men there, because man's glory was there more sought for than God's, he stood to the danger of the said indignation, which chanced more prosperously unto him within few years after than he looked for. For whiles he continued in Cambridge the great and weighty cause of King Henry VIII, his divorce with Lady Katherine Dowager of Spain, came into question; which being many ways by the space of two or three years amongst the canonists, civilians, and other learned men diversely debated, it came to pass that Cranmer by reason that the plague was in Cambridge resorted to Waltham Abbey, to one Mr Cressey's house, whose wife was of kin to Cranmer. And for that he had two sons of Cressey at Cambridge as his pupils, he rested at Waltham Cross at the house of Mr Cressey with the said two children during that summer whiles the plague reigned.

Cardinal Campeius and Cardinal Wolsey, being in commission from the Pope to determine that great cause in controversy between the king and the queen, dallied and delayed all the summer in hearing the cause debated. When August was come, the cardinals, little minding to proceed to sentence-giving, took occasion to finish their commission and not further to determine therein, pretending not to be permitted by the laws to keep courts of ecclesiastical matters in harvest time; which sudden giving over of the commission by both the cardinals being unknown to the king, it so much moved him that he commanded the Dukes of Norfolk and Suffolk to dispatch forthwith Campeius home again to Rome; and so in haste removed himself from London to Waltham for a night or twain, whiles his household removed to Greenwich; by means whereof it chanced that the harbingers lodged Dr Stephens, secretary, and Dr Foxe, almoner (the chief furtherers on the king's behalf of the said cause), in the house of Mr Cressey, where Cranmer was resident. When supper time came all three doctors met together, Stephens and Foxe much marvelling at Cranmer's being there. As they were of old acquaintance the secretary and the almoner well entertained Dr Cranmer, minding to understand his opinion touching their great business they had in hand. So whiles they were at supper they conferred with Cranmer concerning the king's cause, requesting him of his opinion.

Cranmer answered that he could say little to the matter, for that he had not studied it. Notwithstanding in his opinion they made more ado in prosecuting the law ecclesiastical than needed. 'It were better that the question whether a man may marry his brother's wife were decided by the divines and by the authority of the word of God, whereby the conscience of the prince might be better satisfied, than thus from year to year by frustrating delays to prolong the time, leaving the truth of the matter unbolted out by the word of God. There is but one truth in it, which the Scriptures will soon declare, being by learned men well handled, and that may be as well done in the universities here as at Rome: you might this way have made an end of this matter long since.' When Cranmer had thus ended his tale, the other two well liked of his devices and wished that they had so proceeded aforetime; and thereupon conceived some matter of that device to instruct the king withal, who was then minded to send to Rome for a new commission. The next day, when the king removed to Greenwich, like as he took himself not well handled by the cardinals, so desirous of an end of his tedious suit he called unto him Stephens and Foxe, saying unto them, 'What now, my masters, shall we do in this infinite cause of mine? I see there must be a new commission procured from Rome, and when we shall have an end God knoweth.'

When the king had said his mind, the almoner said unto the king again, 'We trust that there shall be better ways devised for your Majesty than to travel to Rome any more in your Highness's cause. At Waltham this other night we met an old acquaintance of ours, Dr Cranmer, with whom having conference concerning your Highness's cause, he thought that the next way were to instruct your Majesty's conscience by trying your Highness's question by the authority of the word of God, and thereupon to proceed to a final sentence.' 'Marry,' said the king, 'I will surely speak with him: let him be sent for out of hand. I perceive that that man hath the sow by the right ear. If I had known this device two years ago it had been in my way a great piece of money, and had rid me out of much disquietness.'

Whereupon Cranmer was sent for, and being removed to Cambridge and so towards his friends in Nottinghamshire, a post went for him. But when he came to London he began to quarrel with these two his acquaintances, that he by their means was thus troubled and brought thither to be cumbered in a matter wherein he had nothing travailed in study; and therefore entreated them that they would make his excuse in such sort that he might be dispatched away from coming in the king's presence. They promised so to do if by any means they might compass it. But all was in vain; for the more they began to excuse Cranmer's absence the more the king chid with them, for that they brought him not out of hand to his presence, so that no excuse serving he was fain undelayedly to come to the Court; whom the gentle prince benignly accepting demanded his name, and said, 'Were you not at Waltham such a time in the company of my secretary and my almoner? Cranmer affirming the same, the king said again, 'Had you not conference with them concerning our matter of divorce now in question?'

'True, if it please your Highness.'

'I perceive that you have the right scope of the matter. You must understand that I have been long troubled in conscience, and now I perceive that by this means I might have been long ago relieved one way or other, if we had this way proceeded. Therefore, Mr Doctor, I pray you, and because you are a subject I charge and command you, all other business set aside to take pains to see my cause furthered according to your device, as much as it may lie in you. For I protest before God and the world that I seek not to be divorced from the queen, if by any means I might justly be persuaded that our matrimony were inviolable and not against the laws of God; for otherwise there was never cause to move me to seek any such extremity. Neither was there ever prince had a gentler, more obedient and loving companion and wife than the queen is, nor I never fancied woman in all respects better, if this doubt had not risen; assuring you that for the singular virtues wherewith she is endued, besides the consideration of her noble stock, I could be right well contented still to remain with her, if so it would stand with the will of Almighty God. I therefore pray you, with an indifferent eye and with as much dexterity as lieth in you that you for your part do handle the matter, for the discharging of both our consciences.'

Cranmer, much disabling himself to meddle in so weighty a matter, besought the king to commit the examining of this matter by the word of God unto the best learned men of both his universities, Cambridge and Oxford. 'You say well,' said the king, 'and I am content therewith. Nevertheless I will have you specially to write your mind therein.' So calling the Earl of Wiltshire to him, said, 'Let Dr Cranmer have entertainment in your house at Durham Place for a time, to the intent he may be there quiet to accomplish my request; and let him lack neither books nor anything requisite for his study.' After the king's departure Cranmer went with my Lord of Wiltshire unto his house, wherein he incontinent wrote his mind concerning the king's question; adding besides the authorities of the Scriptures, of general councils, and of ancient writers, also his opinion, which was this; that the Bishop of Rome had no authority whereby he might dispense with the word of God. When Cranmer had made this book and committed it to the king, the king said to him, 'Will you abide by this that you have here written before the Bishop of Rome?' 'That will I do,' quoth Cranmer, 'if your Majesty do send me thither.' 'Marry,' quoth the king, 'I will send you to him in a sure ambassage.'

Thus by means of Cranmer's handling of this matter not only certain learned men were sent abroad to most of the universities in Christendom to dispute the question, but also the same being disputed by the divines in Cambridge and Oxford, it was there concluded that no such matrimony was by the word of God lawful. A solemn ambassage was then prepared and sent to the Bishop of Rome, then at Bononie, wherein went the Earl of Wiltshire, Cranmer, Stokesley, Carne, Bennet, and other learned men and gentlemen. When the time came that they should come before the Bishop of Rome to declare the cause of their ambassage, the Bishop sitting on high in his cloth of estate and in his rich apparel, with his sandals on his feet, offering as it were his foot to be kissed of the ambassadors, the earl disdaining thereat stood still and made no countenance thereunto, so that all the rest kept themselves from that idolatry.

Howbeit one thing is not here to be omitted, as a prognosticate of our separation from the See of Rome, which then chanced by a spaniel of the earl. For he having there a great spaniel which came out of England with him, stood directly between the earl and the Bishop of Rome. When the Bishop had advanced his foot to be kissed, whether the spaniel perceived the Bishop's foot of another nature than it ought to be, so taking it to be some kind of repast, or whether it was the will of God to show some token by the dog unto the Bishop of his inordinate pride, that his feet were more meet to be bitten of dogs than kissed of Christian men; the spaniel, I say, when the Bishop extended his foot to be kissed, went directly to the Pope's feet, and not only kissed the same unmannerly but as some plainly affirm took fast with his mouth the great toe of the Pope, so that in haste he pulled in his glorious feet. Whereat our men smiling in their sleeves, what they thought God knoweth. But in fine, the pontifical Bishop after that sought no more at that present for kissing his feet, but without further ceremony gave ear to the ambassadors; who offered on the king's behalf to be defended that no man *jure divino* could marry his brother's wife, and that the Bishop of Rome by no means ought to dispense to the contrary. Divers promises were made, and sundry days appointed wherein the question should have been disputed; and when our part was ready to answer no man appeared to dispute in that behalf. So in the end, the Bishop making to our ambassadors good countenance and gratifying Cranmer with the office of the Penitentiaryship, dismissed them undisputed withal. Whereupon the earl and the other commissioners saving Cranmer returned home into England.

Cranmer went to the Emperor, being in his journey towards Vienna in expedition against the Turk, there to answer such learned men of the Emperor's council as could say anything to the contrary part. Amongst the rest was Cornelius Agrippa, an high officer in the Emperor's Court, who having private conference with Cranmer in the question was so fully satisfied in the matter that afterwards there was never disputation openly offered to Cranmer in that behalf. The matter thus prospering, as well touching the king's question as concerning the invalidity of the Bishop of Rome's authority, Bishop Warham Archbishop of Canturbury departed this life, whereby that dignity then being in the king's gift was immediately given to Dr Cranmer.

Thus much touching the preferment of Cranmer unto his dignity, and by what means he achieved unto the same; not by flattery, nor by bribes, nor by other unlawful means; which thing I have more at large discoursed to stop the railing mouths of such who, being themselves obscure and unlearned, shame not to detract so learned a man most ignominiously with the surname of an hostler, whom for his zeal unto sincere religion they ought with much humility to have had in regard and reputation.

Now concerning his behaviour and trade of life towards God and the world, being now entered into his said dignity, and forsomuch as the Apostle St Paul writing to two bishops, Timothy and Titus, setteth out unto us a perfect description of a true bishop, unto which exemplar it shall be hard in these strange days to find the image of any bishop correspondent; yet for example sake let us take this Archbishop of Canturbury and try him by the rule thereof, to see how near he cometh to the description of St Paul, or else how far off he swerveth from the common course of other in his time, of his calling. The rule of St Paul is to be found 1 Tim. 3, also in Titus 1, in these words: 'A bishop must be faultless, as becometh the minister of God. Not stubborn, nor angry, no drunkard, no fighter, nor given to filthy lucre; but harborous, one that loveth goodness, sober-minded, righteous, holy, temperate, and such as cleaveth unto the true word and doctrine.'

Unto this rule and touchstone to lay now the life and conversation of this archbishop, we will begin with 'A bishop must be faultless, as becometh the minister of God.' Like as no man is without sin and every man carrieth with him his especial vice and fault; so nevertheless the Apostle meaneth that the bishop must be faultless in comparison of the common conversation of men of the world, which seem more licentiously to live at their own liberties and pleasures than the bishop ought to do, having small regard unto good example giving, which a bishop most carefully ought to consider, lest by his dissolute life the word of God be evil spoken of. Which thing to avoid, and the better to accomplish this precept of the Apostle, this worthy man gave himself to continual study, not breaking that order that he in the university commonly-used, that is, by five o'clock in the morning at his book, and so consuming the time in study and prayer until nine. No hour of the day was spent in vain, but the same was so bestowed as tended to the glory of God, the service of the prince, or the commodity of the Church. Which by well bestowing of his time procured to him most happily a good report of all men, to be in respect of other men's conversation faultless, as became the minister of God.

Secondly, 'A bishop ought not to be stubborn.' With which vice this archbishop in no wise ought to be charged; whose nature was such as none more gentle, or sooner won to an honest suit, specially in such things wherein by word, writing, counsel, or deed he might gratify any gentle or noble man, or do good to any mean person, or relieve the needy and poor.

Then followeth 'Not angry.' Surely if overmuch patience may be a vice, this man may seem to offend rather on this part than on the contrary. Albeit for all his doings I cannot say: for the most part, such was his mortification that way that few we shall find in whom the saying of our Saviour Christ so much prevailed as with him; who would not only have a man to forgive his enemies but also to pray for them: that lesson never went out of his memory. For he had many cruel enemies, not for his own deserts but only for his religion's sake; yet whatsoever he was that sought his hindrance, either in goods, estimation, or life, and upon conference would seem never so slenderly to relent or excuse himself, he would both forget the offence committed and evermore friendly entertain him, and show such pleasure to him as by any means possible he might perform or declare: insomuch that it came into a common proverb, 'Do unto my Lord of Canturbury displeasure or a shrewd turn; then you may be sure to have him your friend whiles he liveth.'

'Not given to filthy lucre, but harborous.' The contrary whereof was so odious unto St Paul that he esteemed the same no less than idolatry, in that it maketh men forget their duty to God, and instead of him to worship their treasure. How little this prelate we speak of was infected with this vice, and how he was no niggard, all kind of people that knew him, as well learned beyond the seas and on this side, to whom yearly he gave in exhibition no small sums of money, as other, both gentlemen, mean men, and poor men, who had in their necessity that which he could spare, lend, or make, can testify. And albeit such was his liberality towards all sorts of men that no man did lack whom he could do for, either in giving or lending; yet such was again his circumspection that when he was apprehended and committed by Queen Mary to the Tower, he ought no man living a penny that could or would demand any duty of him, but satisfied every man to the utmost; where else no small sums of money were owing him of divers persons, which by breaking their bills he freely forgave before his attainder.

'Harborous.' As touching this word, whereby is meant the maintenance of hospitality, so little was this property lacking in him that some men misliking the same thought it rather a house of overmuch lavishing and unprofitable expense. But as nothing can be so well done which by some or other shall not be maligned and detracted, so neither did this man lack his cavillers, some finding fault with his prodigality, some on the contrary part complaining of his spare house and strait order, much under the state of his revenues and calling.

Now followeth together these virtues, 'One that loveth goodness, sober-minded, righteous, holy, and temperate.' Concerning these qualities, the trade of his life, joined with his benign and gentle disposition, testify that he could not be void of these virtues reigning in him, which was so abundantly adorned with the other which above we have declared.

Then concludeth St Paul with the most excellent virtue to be wished in a prelate of the Church. For if this constancy be not in him to this end, that is, 'to cleave fast unto the true word of doctrine that he may be able to exhort with wholesome learning, and to reprove them that say against it'; if he be void, I say, of these gifts and graces, he is worthy of no commendation but shall seem an idol and deceiver of the world.

Neither shall he deserve the name of bishop if either for dread or meed, affection or favour, he do at any time or in any point swerve from the truth. In this behalf the constancy of this archbishop never, for the most part, shronk for any manner of storm, but was so many ways tried that neither favour of his prince nor fear of the indignation of the same, nor any other worldly respect could change his purpose, grounded upon that infallible doctrine of the gospel. Notwithstanding, his constant defence of God's truth was ever joined with such meekness towards the king that he never took offence against him.

At the time of setting forth the Six Articles, mention was made before in the story of King Henry VIII how adventurously Cranmer did oppose himself, standing as it were post alone against the whole parliament, disputing three days together against the articles; insomuch that the king, when neither he could mislike his reasons and yet would needs have these articles to pass, required him to absent himself out of the Chamber while the act should pass, and so he did; and how the king afterward sent all the Lords of the parliament unto the archbishop to Lambeth to cheer his mind again. This was done during the time of Cromwell's authority. After the apprehension of Cromwell certain of the Council, by the enticement of his ancient enemy the Bishop of Winchester and other of the same sect, attempted the king against him, declaring that the realm was so infected with heresies that it was dangerous for his Highness farther to permit it, lest such contention should arise among his subjects that thereby might spring horrible commotions, as in Germany not long ago. The enormity whereof they could not impute to any so much as to the archbishop, who by his preaching had filled the realm full of pernicious heresies. The king would needs know his accusers. They answered that as he was a Councillor no man durst accuse him; but if it would please his Highness to commit him to the Tower for a time, there would be accusations and proofs enough against him: otherwise testimony against him would not appear. 'Therefore your Highness must give us leave to commit him to durance.'

The king, perceiving their importunate suit against the archbishop but not meaning to have him wronged, granted that they should the next day commit him to the Tower for his trial. When night came, the king sent Sir Anthony Denie about midnight to the archbishop, willing him forthwith to resort unto him. The archbishop speedily addressed himself to the Court, and coming into the Gallery where the king tarried for him, his Highness said, 'Ah, my Lord of Canturbury, I can tell you news. It is determined by me and the Council that you tomorrow at nine o'clock shall be committed to the Tower, for that you have preached and sown within the realm such a number of execrable heresies that it is feared, the whole realm being infected with them, no small contention will rise thereby amongst my subjects, as of late in divers parts of Germany; and therefore the Council have requested me, for the trial of the matter, to suffer them to commit you to the Tower, or else no man dare come forth as witness, you being a Councillor.'

The archbishop kneeled down and said, 'I am content, if it please your Grace, to go thither at your Highness' commandment, and I humbly thank your Majesty that I may come to my trial; for there be that have many ways slandered me, and now this way I hope to try myself not worthy of such report.'

The king, perceiving the man's uprightness joined with such simplicity, said, 'O Lord, what manner a man be you? what simplicity is in you? I had thought that rather you would have sued to us to have taken the pains to have heard you and your accusers together for your trial, without any such indurance. Do you not know what state you be in with the whole world, and how many great enemies you have? Do you not consider what an easy thing it is to procure three or four false knaves to witness against you? Think you to have better luck that way than your Master Christ had? I see you would run headlong to your undoing if I would suffer you. Your enemies shall not so prevail against you; for I have otherwise devised with myself to keep you out of their hands. Notwithstanding tomorrow when the Council shall sit and send for you, resort unto them, and if in charging you with this matter they commit you to the Tower, require of them, because you are one of them, that you may have your accusers brought before them without any further indurance, and use for yourself as good persuasions as you may devise; and if no entreaty will serve, then deliver unto them this my ring and say, "If there be no remedy, my Lords, but I must needs go to the Tower, then I revoke my cause from you and appeal to the king's own person by this his token"; for so soon as they shall see my ring, they shall understand that I have resumed the whole cause into mine own hands.'

The archbishop perceiving the king's benignity to himwards had much ado to forbear tears, and humbling himself with thanks took his leave. On the morrow about nine o'clock the Council sent a gentleman usher for the archbishop, who when he came to the Council Chamber door could not be let in, but was compelled to wait among the pages, lackeys, and serving-men. Dr Buts the king's physician, resorting that way and espying how my Lord of Canturbury was handled, went to the king and said, 'My Lord of Canturbury, if it please your Grace, is well promoted: he is become a lackey or a serving-man, for he standeth this half hour at the Council Chamber door amongst them.' 'It is not so,' quoth the king, 'I trow; the Council hath not so little discretion as to use the Metropolitan of the realm in that sort, specially being one of their own number. But let them alone and we shall hear more soon.'

Anon the Archbishop was called into the Chamber, to whom was alleged as before is rehearsed. The archbishop answered as the king had advised him: when he perceived that no persuasion or entreaty could serve, he delivered them the king's ring, revoking his cause into the king's hands. The whole Council being thereat amazed, the Earl of Bedford with a loud voice, confirming his words with a solemn oath, said, 'When you first began the matter, my Lords, I told you what would come of it. Do you think that the king will suffer this man's finger to ache? Much more, I warrant you, will he defend his life against brabling varlets. You do but cumber yourselves to hear tales and fables against him.' And so incontinently they all rose and carried to the king his ring, surrendering the matter, as the use was, into his hands.

When they were come to the king's presence his Highness with a severe countenance said unto them, 'Ah, my Lords, I thought I had wiser men of my Council than now I find you. What discretion was this in you, to make the Primate of the realm, and one of you in office, wait at the Chamber door amongst serving-men? You had no commission of me so to handle him. I was content that you should try him as a Councillor and not as a mean subject. But now I well perceive that things be done against him maliciously; and if some of you might have had your mind you would have tried him to the uttermost. But I do you all to wit that if a prince may be beholding unto his subject, by the faith I owe to God I take this man here, my Lord of Canturbury, to be of all other a most faithful subject unto us, and one to whom we are all much beholding.' With that one or two of the chiefest of the Council, making their excuse, declared that in requesting his indurance it was rather meant for his trial, and his purgation against the common fame and slander of the world, than for any malice conceived against him.

'Well, well,' quoth the king, 'take him and well use him, as he is worthy to be, and make no more ado.' With that every man caught him by the hand and made fair weather of altogethers, which might easily be done with that man.

Although he was compassed about with mighty enemies and by many crafty trains impugned, yet through God's mighty providence working in the king's heart to favour him, he rubbed out all King Henry's time without blemish or soil, by means of the king's supportation; who not only defended the archbishop against all his conspired adversaries, but extended such special favour unto him that he, being not ignorant of his wife whom he had married before at Noremberge, keeping her also all the Six Articles time contrary to the law, both permitted the same and kept his counsel. Then after the death of Henry immediately succeeded his son Edward, under whose government the state of this archbishop, his godfather, was nothing impaired but rather advanced.

Until the entering of King Edward Cranmer was scarcely yet thoroughly persuaded in the right knowledge of the sacrament, or at least was not yet fully ripened in the same; wherein shortly after he being more groundedly confirmed by conference with Ridley, in process of time did so profit in more riper knowledge that at last he took upon him the defence of the whole doctrine, that is, to refute first the corporal presence; secondly, transubstantiation; thirdly, idolatrous adoration; fourthly, the false error that men do eat the natural body of Christ; and lastly, the blasphemous sacrifice of the mass. Whereupon he wrote five books for the public instruction of the Church of England, which instruction to this day standeth and is received in this Church of England. Against these five books of the archbishop Stephen Gardiner, the arch-enemy of Christ and his gospel, being then in the Tower, slubbereth up an answer, such as it was, which he in open court exhibited at Lambeth, being there examined by the archbishop and other the king's commissioners in King Edward's days, which book was entitled *An Explication and Assertion of the Catholic Faith*. Against this explication, or rather cavilling sophistication, the archbishop learnedly and copiously replying again maketh answer, which also he published to the eyes and judgments of all men in print. The unquiet spirit of Gardiner being not yet contented thrusteth out another book in Latin of the like Popish argument but after another title, named *Marcus Antonius Constantinus*. Whereunto the archbishop again intending a full confutation had already absolved three parts of his answer in prison: two perished in Oxford; the other remaineth in my hands ready to be set forth, as the Lord shall see good.

Thus much concerning the doings and travails of this archbishop during the lives of King Henry and King Edward. Which two kings so long as they continued, this archbishop lacked no stay of maintenance against his maligners. Afterward Edward falling sick, when he perceived that his death was at hand, knowing that his sister Mary was wholly wedded to Popish religion, bequeathed the succession to Lady Jane (a lady of great birth but greater learning, niece to Henry by his sister) by consent of the Council and lawyers of this realm. To this testament of the king's when all the nobles, states, and judges had subscribed, they sent for the archbishop and required that he also would subscribe. But he excusing himself said that it was otherwise in the testament of King Henry, and that he had sworn to the succession of Mary, by which oath he was so bound that without manifest perjury he could not go from it. The Council answered that they were not ignorant of that, and that they had a conscience as well as he, and moreover that they were sworn to that testament, and therefore he should not think there was any danger therein, or that he should be in more peril of perjury than the rest. The archbishop answered that he was judge of no man's conscience but his own; and concerning subscription, before he had spoken with the king himself he utterly refused to do it. The king therefore, being demanded of the archbishop, said that the nobles and lawyers counselled him unto it, and persuaded him that the bond of the first testament could nothing let but that Jane might succeed him and the people acknowledge her as queen. Who then demanding leave of the king that he might first talk with certain lawyers, when they all agreed that by law it might be so, returning to the king, with much ado he subscribed.

Not long after this King Edward died, being almost sixteen years old, to the great sorrow but greater calamity of the whole realm. Immediately it was demanded that Lady Jane, which was unwilling thereunto, should be proclaimed queen; which much misliked the common people, not that they did so much favour Mary as for the hatred conceived against some whom they could not favour. Besides this, other causes there happened also of discord between nobles and commons; for what injuries of commons and enclosures wrongfully holden, with other inordinate pollings and uncharitable dealing between landlords and tenants, I cannot tell. But in fine Mary, hearing of the death of her brother and shifting for herself, was so assisted by the commons that eftsoons she prevailed; who being established in possession of the realm came to London; and after she had caused the two fathers, Northumberland and Suffolk, to be executed, she caused Jane, being both in age tender and innocent from this crime, after she could by no means be turned from her faith, together with her husband to be beheaded. The rest of the nobles, paying fines, were forgiven, the archbishop only excepted; who, though he desired pardon by means of friends, could obtain none; the queen would not once vouchsafe to see him; for the old grudges against the archbishop for the divorcement of her mother lay hid in the bottom of her heart. Besides this, she remembered the state of religion changed, which was imputed to the archbishop.

While these things were in doing, a rumour was in all men's mouths that the archbishop, to curry favour with the queen, had promised to say a *dirige* mass in the funeral of her brother. This rumour Cranmer thinking speedily to stay, gave forth a writing in his purgation, the tenor whereof I need not here recite. This bill being written and lying openly in a window in his chamber, cometh in by chance Mr Scory, Bishop of Chichester, who after he had perused the same required of the archbishop a copy. The archbishop when he had granted the same, Scory lending it to some friend of his, there were divers copies taken and the thing published abroad; insomuch that every scrivener's shop was occupied in writing out the same; and some copies coming to the bishops' hands and brought to the Council, and they sending it to the commissioners, the matter was known and he commanded to appear. Cranmer at his day prefixed appeared before the commissioners, bringing a true inventory, as he was commanded, of all his goods. A bishop of the Privy Council, being one of the commissioners, 'My Lord,' said he, 'there is a bill put forth in your name wherein you seem to be aggrieved with setting up the mass again: we doubt not that you are sorry that it is gone abroad.' The archbishop answered, 'As I do not deny myself to be the author of that bill, so I confess that I am sorry that the bill went from me in such sort as it did; for I had intended to have made it in a more ample manner and to have set it on the doors of all the churches in London with mine own seal joined thereto.' At which words, when they saw the constantness of the man, they dismissed him, affirming that shortly he should hear further.

Not long after this he was sent to the Tower, and soon after condemned of treason. The queen, when she could not honestly deny him pardon, seeing all the rest were discharged, and specially seeing he last of all others subscribed to King Edward's request, and that against his will, released to him his action of treason and accused him only of heresy; which liked the archbishop right well, because the cause was not now his own but Christ's; not the queen's but the Church's. At length it was determined by the queen and the Council that he should be removed to Oxford, there to dispute with the doctors and divines. And privily word was sent before to them of Oxford to make them ready to dispute. And although the queen and the bishops had concluded before what should become of him, it pleased them that the matter should be debated, that under some honest show of disputation the murder of the man might be covered. Neither could their revengement abide any long delay, and therefore in all haste he was carried to Oxford. What this disputation was and how it was handled, and also touching his condemnation, because sufficiently it hath been declared, we mind now to proceed to his final condemnation the 12th of September 1555, seven days before the condemnation of Ridley and Latimer. The story whereof followeth, faithfully corrected by the report of one who being both present thereat and a devout favourer of Rome can lack no credit.

After the disputations done in Oxford between the doctors of both universities and the three bishops, Cranmer, Ridley, and Latimer, sentence was ministered against them by Dr Weston and other of the university, whereby they were judged to be heretics and committed to the mayor and sheriffs. But forasmuch as the sentence was void in law—for the authority of the Pope was not yet received into the land—therefore was a new commission sent from Rome and a new process framed for the conviction of these men. In which commission was Dr James Brookes Bishop of Gloucester, the Pope's subdelegate, with Dr Martin and Dr Story, commissioners in the king and queen's behalf. Touching Dr Martin, although he was used as an instrument of the Pope's side, yet neither was he so bitter an enemy in this persecution as other commissioners were; and also in the time of Queen Elizabeth, where divers other Doctors of the Arches refused to be sworn against the Pope, he denied not the oath.

Upon Thursday the 12th of September 1555 in the Church of St Mary and at the high altar was erected a solemn scaffold for Bishop Brookes, ten foot high. The seat was made that he might sit under the sacrament of the altar. On the right hand of the Pope's delegate beneath him sat Dr Martin, on the left hand Dr Story, and underneath them other doctors, scribes, and pharisees also, with the Pope's collector and a rabblement of suchlike. These bishops being placed in their pontificalibus, the Bishop of Canturbury was sent for. He having intelligence of them that were there thus ordered himself. He came forth of the prison to the church, set forth with bills and glaives for fear he should start away, clothed in a fair black gown with his hood on both shoulders, such as Doctors of Divinity use to wear. After he was come into the church, he did not put off his cap to any of them but stood still till he was called. Anon one of the proctors to the Pope called, 'Thomas Archbishop of Canturbury, make answer to that shall be laid to thy charge, that is to say, blasphemy, incontinency, and heresy; and make answer to the Bishop of Gloucester, representing the Pope's person.'

Upon this he being brought more near unto the scaffold where the foresaid bishops sat, he first well viewed the place of judgment, and spying where the king and queen's proctors were, putting off his cap he, first humbly bowing his knee to the ground, made reverence to the one, and after to the other. That done, beholding the bishop in the face he put on his bonnet again, making no token of obedience to him at all. Whereat the bishop being offended said that it might beseem him right well, weighing the authority he did represent, to do his duty unto him. Cranmer answered that he had taken a solemn oath never to consent to the admitting of the Bishop of Rome's authority into this realm of England again; and that he meant by God's grace to keep it; and therefore would commit nothing either by sign or token which might argue his consent to the receiving of the same. So he desired the bishop to judge of him: he did it not for any contempt of his person, which he would have honoured as well as any of the other if his commission had come from as good an authority as theirs.

When after many means used they perceived that the archbishop would not move his bonnet, the bishop proceeded, and finishing his oration sat down. After whom Dr Martin taking the matter in hand, when he had ended his oration, the archbishop kneeling down towards the west said the Lord's Prayer. Then rising up he reciteth the Creed. Which done, he entereth with his protestation. When the standers-by began to murmur against him, the judges willed him to answer directly to the interrogatories articulated against him in form of law. After he had answered and the public notary had entered the same, the judges and commissioners were about to rise and depart. But the Bishop of Gloucester, thinking it not the best so to dismiss the people somewhat stirred with the words of the archbishop, began in the hearing of the people to declame. After whom Dr Story taketh the matter, and seeking to make an end of that session he eftsoons called for witnesses to be produced, who should be sworn upon the book to declare next day whatsoever they knew or could remember against Dr Cranmer's heresy.

The depositions of which witnesses being taken, Dr Story admonished the archbishop, permitting him to make his exceptions if he thought any of the witnesses were to be refused. Who would admit none of them all, being perjured. 'For if to swear against the Pope were unlawful, they should rather have given their lives than their oath. But if it were lawful, then they are perjured to defend him whom they forsware before.' Nevertheless this answer being lightly regarded as little to the purpose, he was commanded again to the place from whence he came. Who at his departing out like as at his coming in showed low obedience to Dr Martin and Dr Story, the queen's commissioners. Then Dr Story pointing to the Bishop of Gloucester said that he ought rather to give reverence to him. The archbishop departing without any obeisance to the bishop, all rose up and departed everyone to his own. Thus brake up the session for that day about two o'clock.

After they had received his answers to all their objections, they cited him to appear at Rome within fourscore days to make there his personal answers; which he said, if the king and queen would send him, he would be content to do, and so was carried to prison again, where he continually remained. Wherein all men that have eyes to see may easily perceive the crafty practice of these prelates and the vizored face of their justice, as though the Court of Rome would condemn no man before he answered for himself, as all law and equity required. But the very same time that unholy father, contrary to all justice, sent his letter executory unto the king and queen to deprive him of his dignity; which thing he did not only before the eighty days were ended but before there were twenty days spent. Furthermore whereas the archbishop was first detained in strait prison so that he could not appear, and therefore had a most just excuse of his absence by all laws, popish and other; yet in the end of the fourscore days was that worthy martyr decreed *contumax*, that is, sturdily, frowardly, and wilfully absent, and in pain of the same absence condemned and put to death.

This letter or sentence definitive of the Pope was dated about the first of January and delivered here in England about the midst of February; upon the receipt of which another session was appointed for the archbishop to appear the 14th of February before commissioners sent down by the queen, the chief whereof was the Bishop of Ely, Dr Thurlby. Albeit he was not the archbishop's household chaplain, yet he was so familiarly acquainted with him, so dearly beloved, like a natural brother, that there was never anything in the archbishop's house so dear, were it plate, jewel, horse, maps, or anything else, but if Thurlby did never so little commend it—a subtle kind of begging—the archbishop either gave it to him or sent it to his house. So greatly was the archbishop enamoured with him that whosoever would obtain anything of him most commonly would make their way before by Thurlby. Which bye-matter I thought here to recite; not so much to upbraid the man with the vice of unthankfulness as to admonish him of benefits received, whereby he may the better remember his old benefactor.

With Thurlby was also assigned in the commission Dr Boner Bishop of London; which two coming to Oxford upon St Valentine's Day as the Pope's delegates with a new commission from Rome, by virtue thereof commanded the archbishop to come before them in the choir of Christ's Church before the high altar, where they sitting in their pontificalibus first began to read their commission; wherein was contained how that in the Court of Rome all things being indifferently examined, both the articles laid to his charge with the answers made unto them, witnesses examined on both parts, and counsel had as well on the king and queen's behalf as on behalf of Cranmer, so that he wanted nothing pertaining to his defence, etc. 'O Lord,' said the archbishop, 'what lies be these, that I, being in prison and never suffered to have advocate at home, should produce witness and appoint my counsel at Rome? God must needs punish this shameless lying.' They read on the commission, which came from the Pope *plenitudine potestatis*, giving them full authority to proceed to deprivation of him, and upon excommunication to deliver him to the secular power *omni appellatione remota*.

They proceeding thereupon to his degradation first disguised him, putting on him a surplice and then an alb; after that the vestment of a subdeacon and every other furniture, as a priest ready to mass. 'What,' said he, 'I think I shall say mass.' 'Yea,' said Cosins, one of Boner's chaplains, 'I trust to see you say mass for all this.' 'Do you so?' quoth he; 'That shall you never see.' Then they invested him in all manner of robes of a bishop and archbishop as he is at his installing, saving that as everything then is most rich and costly, so everything in this was of canvas and old clouts, with a mitre and pall of the same suit done upon him in mockery; then the crozier was put in his hand. This done, Boner, who by the space of many years had borne no great good will towards him, and now rejoiced to see this day wherein he might triumph over him and take his pleasure at full, began to stretch out his eloquence, making his oration to the assembly after this sort.

'This is the man that hath ever despised the Pope's Holiness, and now is to be judged by him; this is the man that hath pulled down so many churches, and now is come to be judged in a church; this is the man that contemned the blessed sacrament of the altar, and now is come to be condemned before that blessed sacrament hanging over the altar; this is the man that like Lucifer sat in the place of Christ upon an altar to judge other, and now is come before an altar to be judged himself.' Boner went on in his rhetorical repetition, lying and railing against the archbishop, beginning every sentence with 'This is the man,' till at length there was never a man but was weary of his unmannerly usage of him; insomuch that the Bishop of Ely divers times pulled him by the sleeve to make an end, and said to him afterwards when they went to dinner that he had broken promise with him; for he had entreated him earnestly to use him with reverence.

After all this done, they began to bustle towards his degrading, and first to take from him his crozier, which he held fast and refused to deliver, and imitating the example of Martin Luther pulled an appeal out of his left sleeve, which he there and then delivered unto them saying, 'I appeal to the next General Council; and herein I have comprehended my cause, which I desire may be admitted,' and prayed divers of the standers-by to be witnesses. This appeal being put up to the Bishop of Ely, he said, 'My Lord, our commission is to proceed against you *omni appellatione remota*, and therefore we cannot admit it.' 'Why,' quoth he, 'then you do me the more wrong, for the matter is between the Pope and me *immediate*, and no man ought to be judge in his own cause.' 'Well,' quoth Ely, 'if it may be admitted it shall,' and so received it of him. Then began he to persuade earnestly with the archbishop to consider his state while there was time to do him good, promising to become a suitor to the king and queen for him; and so protested his love and friendship that had been between them, heartily weeping, so that for a time he could not go on with his tale. After going forward, he earnestly affirmed that if it had not been the king and queen's commandment no worldly commodity should have made him to have done it. The archbishop, gently seeming to comfort him, said he was well content withal. So proceeded they to his degradation.

When they came to take off his pall, then said he, 'Which of you hath a pall, to take off my pall?' which imported as much as they being his inferiors could not degrade him. Whereunto one of them said, in that they were but bishops they were his inferiors, but being the Pope's delegates they might take his pall. And so they did, and proceeding took everything in order from him as it was put on. Then a barber clipped his hair round about, and the bishop scraped the tops of his fingers where he had been anointed, wherein Boner behaved himself as roughly as the other bishop was gentle. 'All this,' quoth the archbishop, 'needed not; I had myself done with this gear long ago.' Last of all they stripped him of his gown and put upon him a poor yeoman-beadle's gown, bare and nearly worn and evil favouredly made, and a townsman's cap on his head; and so delivered him to the secular power. Then spake Boner: 'Now are you no lord any more.' And whensoever he spake to the people of him (as he was continually barking against him) ever he used this term, 'This gentleman here.'

While the archbishop was thus remaining in durance, whom they had kept now in prison almost three years, the doctors and divines of Oxford busied themselves all that ever they could about Cranmer to have him recant, assaying by all crafty allurements they might devise to bring their purpose to pass. And to the intent they might win him easily they had him to the Dean's house of Christ's Church, where he lacked no delicate fare, played at the bowls, had his pleasure for walking, and all other things that might bring him from Christ. Over and besides all this, secretly and sleightly they suborned certain men, which when they could not expugn him by arguments and disputation should by entreaty and fair promises or any other means allure him to recantation; perceiving what a great wound they should receive if the archbishop stood steadfast; and again how great profit they should get if he the principal standard-bearer should be overthrown. By reason whereof the wily Papists flocked about him with threatening, flattering, entreating, promising, and all other means; specially Henry Sydall and Friar John de Villa Carcina.[1]

First they set forth how acceptable it would be to the king and queen and how gainful to him. They added moreover how the Council and noblemen bare him good will. They put him in hope that he should not only have his life but also be restored to his ancient dignity, saying it was but a small matter that they required him to do, only that he would subscribe to a few words with his own hand; which if he did, there should be nothing in the realm that the queen would not easily grant him, whether he would have riches or dignity, or else he had rather live a private life in quiet rest in whatsoever place he listed, only that he would set his name in two words to a little leaf of paper. But if he refused there was no hope of pardon; for the queen would have Cranmer a Catholic or else no Cranmer at all. Therefore he should choose whether he thought it better to end his life in the flames now ready to be kindled than with much honour to prolong his life until the course of nature did call him: there was no middle way. Moreover they exhorted him that he would look to his wealth, his estimation and quietness, saying that he was not so old but that many years yet remained in his lusty age; and if he would not do it in respect of the queen, yet he should do it in respect of his life, and not suffer that other men should be more careful for his health than he was himself. This was agreeable to his notable learning and virtues, which being adjoined with his life would be profitable to many, but being extinct by death should be fruitful to no man. Therefore they would him to lay hold upon the occasion of his health while it was offered, lest he might hereafter seek it when he could not have it. Finally, if the desire of life did nothing move him, he should remember that to die is grievous in all ages, and in his years and flower of dignity it were more grievous; but to die in the fire is most grievous of all.

With these and like provocations these flatterers ceased not to solicit and urge him, using all means they could to draw him to their side; whose force his manly constancy did a great while resist. But at last when they made no end of calling upon him, the archbishop being overcome, whether through their importunity or by his own imbecility, at length gave his hand. It might be supposed that it was done for the hope of life, and better days to come. But as we may perceive by a letter of his sent to a lawyer, the most cause why he desired

[1] A Dominican theologian with exceptional powers of persuasion.—Ed.

his time to be delayed was that he would make an end of *Marcus Antonius*, which he had already begun. But howsoever it was, plain it was to be against his conscience.

This recantation was not so soon conceived, but the doctors and prelates without delay caused the same to be imprinted and set abroad in all men's hands. Whereunto for better credit first was added the name of Thomas Cranmer; then followed the witnesses, Sydall and Friar John. The queen, having now gotten a time to revenge her old grief, received his recantation very gladly; but of her purpose to put him to death she would nothing relent.

Now was Cranmer's cause in a miserable taking, who neither inwardly had any quietness in his own conscience nor outwardly any help in his adversaries. Besides this, on the one side was praise, on the other side scorn, on both sides danger, so that neither could he die honestly nor yet unhonestly live. And whereas he sought profit he fell into double disprofit, that neither with good men he could avoid secret shame nor yet with evil men the note of dissimulation.

The queen, taking secret counsel how to dispatch Cranmer out of the way, appointed Dr Cole and secretly gave him commandment that against the 21st of March he should prepare a funeral sermon for Cranmer's burning. Cole returned to Oxford, ready to play his part; who as the day of execution drew near came into the prison to Cranmer, to try whether he abode in the Catholic Faith wherein he had left him. When Cranmer had answered that by God's grace he would daily be more confirmed in the Catholic Faith, Cole departing for that time the next day repaired to the archbishop again, giving no signification yet of his death that was prepared: in the morning, the day appointed for Cranmer's execution, Cole coming to him asked if he had any money. When he answered that he had none, he delivered him fifteen crowns to give the poor, to whom he would; and exhorting him so much as he could to constancy in faith departed thence about his business, as to his sermon appertained.

By this and other arguments the archbishop began to surmise what they went about. Then because the day was not far past, and the lords and knights that were looked for were not yet come, there came to him the Spanish friar, witness of his recantation, bringing a paper with articles which Cranmer should openly profess in his recantation before the people; desiring him that he would write the instrument with the articles with his own hand and sign it with his name; which when he had done, the friar desired that he would write another copy thereof which should remain with him, and that he did also. But the archbishop being not ignorant whereunto their secret devices tended, and thinking that the time was in hand in which he could no longer dissemble the profession of his faith with Christ's people, he put secretly in his bosom his prayer with his exhortation written in another paper, which he minded to recite to the people before he should make the last profession of his faith, fearing lest if they had heard the profession of his faith first they would not afterward have suffered him to exhort the people.

Soon after nine o'clock Lord Williams, Sir Tho. Bridges, Sir John Browne, and the other justices with certain noblemen of the queen's Council, came to Oxford with a great train of waiting men. Also of the other multitude, as is wont in such a matter, was made a great concourse and greater expectation. For first of all, they that were of the Pope's side were in great hope to hear something of Cranmer that should stablish the vanity of their opinion; the other part could not yet doubt that he which for so many years had set forth the doctrine of the gospel either would or could now in the last act of his life forsake his part. Briefly, as every man's will inclined either to this or that, so every man wished and hoped for, their minds hanging between hope and doubt; so that the greater the expectation was in so doubtful a matter, the more was the multitude gathered thither to hear and behold.

In this great frequency and expectation Cranmer at length cometh from the prison Bocardo unto St Mary's Church, because it was a foul and rainy day, in this order. The mayor went before, next the aldermen in their place and degree; after them was Cranmer brought between two friars, which mumbling to and fro certain psalms in the streets answered one another until they came to the church door, and there they began the *Nunc dimittis*, and entering into the church brought him to his standing and there left him. There was a stage set up over against the pulpit, of a mean height from the ground, where Cranmer had his standing, waiting until Cole made him ready to his sermon. The lamentable case of that man gave a sorrowful spectacle to all Christian eyes that beheld him. He that late was Archbishop, Metropolitan, and Primate of England, and the king's Privy Councillor, being now in a bare and ragged gown with an old square cap, exposed to the contempt of all men, did admonish men not only of his own calamity but also of their state and fortune. For who would not pity his case and fear his own chance, to see such a prelate, so grave a Councillor, after so many dignities, in his old years, deprived of his estate, adjudged to die and in so painful a death to end his life?

When he had stood a good space upon the stage, turning to a pillar adjoining thereunto he lifted up his hands unto heaven and prayed unto God, till at length Dr Cole coming into the pulpit and beginning his sermon entered first into mention of Tobias and Zachery. Whom after he had praised for their perseverance in the true worshipping of God, he divided his sermon into three parts according to the custom of the Schools, intending to speak first of the mercy of God; secondly of his justice; and last of all how the prince's secrets are not to be opened. Proceeding a little from the beginning he took occasion to turn his tale to Cranmer, and with many hot words reproved him that he being endued with wholesome and Catholic doctrine fell into pernicious error; which he not only defended by writings but also allured other men to do the like, with great liberality of gifts, as it were, appointing rewards for error; and after he had allured them, by all means did cherish them.

Cranmer meantime, with what grief of mind he stood hearing this sermon his countenance did better express than any man can declare. Twenty several times the tears gushed out abundantly, dropping down marvellously from his fatherly face. Commiseration and pity moved all men's hearts, that beheld so heavy a countenance and such abundance of tears in an old man of so reverend dignity.

Cole after he had ended his sermon called back the people that were ready to depart. 'Brethren,' said he, 'lest any man should doubt of this man's conversion and repentance, you shall hear him speak before you. I pray you, Mr Cranmer, that you will now perform that you promised not long ago; namely that you would openly express the true and undoubted profession of your faith, that you may take away all suspicion from men, and that all may understand that you are a Catholic indeed.' 'I will do it,' said the archbishop, 'and that with a good will'; who rising and putting off his cap began to speak thus unto the people: 'I desire you, beloved brethren in the Lord, that you will pray to God for me to forgive me my sins, which above all men both in number and greatness I have committed. But among all the rest there is one offence which most of all at this time doth vex and trouble me, whereof in process of my talk you shall hear more in his proper place.' Then putting his hand into his bosom he drew forth his prayer, which he recited to the people. Then he said:

'Every man, good people, desireth at the time of their death to give some good exhortation, that other may remember the same and be the better thereby; so I beseech God grant me grace that I may speak something at this my departing whereby God may be glorifed and you edified. First, it is a heavy case to see that so many folk be so much doted upon the love of this false world, and so careful for it, that of the love of God or of the world to come they seem to care little or nothing. Therefore this shall be my first exhortation—that you set not your minds overmuch upon this glozing world, but upon God and upon the world to come. The second exhortation is that next under God you obey your king and queen willingly and gladly, without murmuring or grudging; not for fear of them only, but much more for the fear of God, knowing that they be God's ministers, appointed by God to rule and govern you; and therefore whosoever resisteth them resisteth the ordinance of God. The third exhortation is that you love altogether like brethren and sisters. For alas, pity it is to see what contention and hatred one Christian man beareth to another, not taking each other as brother and sister but rather as strangers and mortal enemies. But I pray you learn and bear well this one lesson, to do good unto all men as much as in you lieth, and to hurt no man, no more than you would hurt your own natural brother or sister.

'The fourth exhortation shall be to them that have great substance and riches of this world, that they will well consider and weigh three sayings of the Scripture. One is of our Saviour Christ himself, who saith, "It is hard for a rich man to enter into the kingdom of heaven." A sore saying, yet spoken of him that knoweth the truth. The second is of St John, whose saying is this: "He that hath the substance of this world, and seeth his brother in necessity, and shutteth up his mercy from him, how can he say that he loveth God?" The third is of St James, who speaketh to the covetous rich man after this manner: "Weep you and howl for the misery that shall come upon you: your riches do rot, you clothes be moth-eaten, your gold and silver doth canker and rust; and their rust shall bear witness against you and consume you like fire. You gather a hoard or treasure of God's indignation against the last day." Let them that be rich ponder well these three sentences; for if they ever had occasion to show their charity, they have it now at this present, the poor people being so many and victuals so dears.

'And now forasmuch as I am come to the last end of my life, whereupon hangeth all my life past and all my life to come, either to live with my Master Christ for ever in joy, or else to be in pain for ever with wicked devils in hell, and I see before mine eyes presently either heaven ready to receive me or else hell ready to swallow me up; I shall therefore declare unto you my very faith how I believe, without any colour or dissimulation; for now is no time to dissemble, whatsoever I have said or written in time past.

'First, I believe in God the Father Almighty, maker of heaven and earth, etc. And I believe every article of the Catholic Faith, every word and sentence taught by our Saviour Jesus Christ, his apostles and prophets, in the New and Old Testament.

'And now I come to the great thing that so troubleth my conscience, more than anything that ever I did or said in my whole life, and that is the setting abroad of a writing contrary to the truth, which now here I renounce and refuse, as things written with my hand contrary to the truth which I thought in my heart, and written for fear of death, and to save my life if it might be; and that is, all such bills and papers which I have written or signed with my hand since my degradation; wherein I have written many things untrue. And forasmuch as my hand offended, writing contrary to my heart, my hand shall first be punished therefore; for may I come to the fire, it shall be first burned. As for the Pope, I refuse him as Christ's enemy and Antichrist, with all his false doctrine. And as for the sacrament, I believe as I have taught in my book against the Bishop of Winchester, the which my book teacheth so true a doctrine of the sacrament that it shall stand at the last day before the judgment of God, where the Papistical doctrine contrary thereto shall be ashamed to show her face.'

Here the standers-by were all astonied, marvelled, were amazed, did look one upon another, whose expectation he had so notably deceived. Some began to admonish him of his recantation and to accuse him of falsehood. Briefly, it was a world to see the doctors beguiled of so great an hope. I think there was never cruelty more notably deluded; for they looked for a glorious victory by this man's retractation; who as soon as they heard these things began to let down their ears, to rage, fret, and fume; and so much the more because they could not revenge their grief; for they could now no longer threaten or hurt him. For the most miserable man in the world can die but once, and he must needs die that day. So, when they could do nothing else unto him, yet, lest they should say nothing, they ceased not to object unto him his falsehood and dissimulation. Unto which accusation he answered, 'Ah, my masters, do not take it so. Always I have been a hater of falsehood and a lover of simplicity, and never before this time have I dissembled.' In saying this all the tears that remained in his body appeared in his eyes. And when he began to speak more of the sacrament and of the Papacy, some of them began to yelp, and bawl, and Cole cried, 'Stop the heretic's mouth and take him away.'

Then Cranmer being pulled down from the stage was led to the fire, accompanied with those friars, vexing and threatening him most cruelly. 'What madness,' say they, 'hath brought thee again into this error, by which thou wilt draw innumerable souls with thee into hell?' To whom he answered nothing, but directed all his talk to the people, saving that to one troubling him in the way he spake, and exhorted him to get him home to his study and apply his book diligently, saying if he did diligently call upon God, by reading more he should get knowledge. But the other Spanish barker, raging and foaming, was almost out of his wits, always having this in his mouth, '*Non fecisti*? Didst thou it not?'

But when he came to the place where the holy bishops and martyrs, Latimer and Ridley, were burnt before him for the confession of the truth, kneeling down he prayed to God; and not long tarrying in his prayers, putting off his garments to his shirt he prepared himself to death. His shirt was made long, down to his feet. His feet were bare; likewise his head, when both his caps were off, was so bare that one hair could not be seen upon it. His beard was long and thick, covering his face with marvellous gravity. Such a countenance moved the hearts both of his friends and of his enemies.

Then the Spanish friars, John and Richard, began to exhort him and play their parts with him afresh, but with lost labour. Cranmer, with steadfast purpose abiding in the profession of his doctrine, gave his hand to certain old men and others that stood by, bidding them farewell. And when he had thought to have done so likewise to Ely, Ely drew back his hand and refused, saying it was not lawful to salute heretics, specially such a one as returned unto the opinions that he had forsworn. And if he had known before that he would have done so, he would never have used his company so familiarly; and chid those sergeants and citizens which had not refused to give him their hands. This Ely was a priest lately made, being then one of the fellows of Brasennose.

Then was an iron chain tied about Cranmer, whom when they perceived to be more steadfast than that he could be moved from his sentence, they commanded the fire to be set unto him. When the wood was kindled and the fire began to burn near him, stretching out his arm he put his right hand into the flame, which he held so immovable (saving that once with the same hand he wiped his face) that all men might see his hand burned before his body was touched. His body did so abide the burning of the flame with such constancy that, standing always in one place without moving his body, he seemed to move no more than the stake to which he was bound. His eyes were lifted up into heaven, and oftentimes he repeated his 'unworthy right hand' so long as his voice would suffer him; and using often the words of Steven, 'Lord Jesus, receive my spirit,' in the greatness of the flame he gave up the ghost.

Thus have you the full story concerning the life and death of this archbishop and martyr, Thomas Cranmer, and also of divers other the learned sort of Christ's martyrs burned in Queen Mary's time, of whom this archbishop was the last, being burnt about the middle time of the reign of that queen, and almost the middle man of all the martyrs burnt in all her reign.

Persecution in Suffolk

In the story of Robert Samuel mention was made of two women of the same town of Ipswich, which shortly after him suffered likewise, the names of whom was Agnes, wife of Robert Potten, and Joan, wife of Michael Trunchfield, shoemaker; who about the same time that the archbishop was burned at Oxford suffered likewise in Ipswich. Their persuasion was this, that in the sacrament was the memorial only of Christ's death and passion; 'for,' said they, 'Christ is ascended into heaven and is on the right hand of God the Father, and not in the sacrament as he was born of the Virgin Mary.' For this they were burned; who being simple women manfully stood to the confession and testimony of God's word; insomuch that when they had prepared and undressed themselves ready to the fire, with comfortable words of the Scripture they earnestly required the people to lay hold on the word of God, and not upon man's invention, despising the ordinances of the Romish Antichrist, with all his superstitions and rotten religion; and so continuing in the torments of fire they held up their hands and called unto God so long as life did endure.

Potten's wife a little before her death, being asleep in her bed, saw a bright burning fire, right up as a pole, and on the side of the fire she thought there stood a number of Queen Mary's friends looking on. Then she seemed to muse with herself whether her fire should burn so bright or no; and indeed her suffering was not far unlike to her dream. This also I thought further to note, how these two being always together in prison, Michael's wife seemed to be nothing so ardent as Potten's, although (God be thanked) they did stoutly stand to the confession of the truth both; but when Michael's wife came to the stake and saw nothing but present death before her, she much exceeded the other in joy and comfort; albeit both of them did joyfully suffer, as it was marvelled at of those that knew them and did behold their end. Thus these two martyrs ended their lives with great triumph: the Lord grant we may do the like. Amen.

Persecution in the diocese of Salisbury

After these two women of Ipswich succeeded three men, which were burnt the same month at one fire in Salisbury, whom in the like quarrel with the others spared not their bodies, to bring their souls to the celestial felicity, whereof they were thoroughly assured in Christ Jesus. Their names were John Spicer, freemason; William Coberley, tailor; John Maundrell, husbandman.

Maundrell, the son of Robert Maundrell of Rowde in Wiltshire, was from his childhood brought up in husbandry; and after he came to man's estate did abide in a village called Buchamton, where he had wife and children. Maundrell, after that the Scripture was translated into English by Tindall, became a diligent hearer, so that he delighted in nothing so much as to hear and speak of God's word, never being without the New Testament about him, although he could not read. When he came into any company that could read, his book was always ready, having a very good memory, so that he could recite by heart most places of the New Testament; his conversation being honest and charitable, as his neighbours are able to testify. So it was that in the days of King Henry, at what time Dr Trigonion and Dr Lee did visit abbeys, Maundrell was brought before Trigonion at an abbey called Edyngton, where he was accused that he had spoken against the holy water and holy bread and suchlike ceremonies, and for the same did wear a white sheet, bearing a candle in his hand about the market, in Devises. Nevertheless his fervency did not abate; for in the days of

Queen Mary, when popery was restored, Maundrell left his house and departed into the county of Gloucester and the north part of Wiltshire, wandering from one to another to such men as he knew feared God, with whom as a servant to keep their cattle he did remain; but after a time he returned to his country, and coming to the Vyes, to a friend name Anthony Clee, had talk with him of returning to his house. When the other exhorted him by the words of Scripture to fly from one city to another, he replying by the words of the Apocalypse about them that be fearful, etc., said that he must go home, and so did; where he with Spicer and Coberley used at times to confer together.

The Sunday following they agreed to go to the parish church called Kevell, where Maundrell and the other two, seeing the parishioners in the procession follow and worship the idol there carried, advertised them to leave the same, and return to the living God, namely speaking to Robert Barksdale, headman of the parish; but he took no regard to these words. After this the vicar came into the pulpit, who being about to read his bead-roll and pray for the souls in purgatory, Maundrell said that that was the Pope's pinfold, the other two affirming the same. After which by commandment of the priest they were had to the stocks, where they remained till their service was done, and they were brought before a Justice of Peace, and the next day carried to Salisbury and presented before Bishop Capon and W. Geffrey, chancellor of the diocese; by whom they were imprisoned and oftentimes examined of their faith, but seldom openly.

At the last examination the chancellor, accompanied with the sheriff of the shire and other priests, in the parish church of Fisherton Anger demanding how they did believe, they answered, 'As Christian men ought to believe: they believed in God the Father, and in the Son, and in the Holy Ghost, the twelve articles of the Creed, the Holy Scriptures from Genesis to the Apocalypse.' But that faith the chancellor would not allow. He opposed them in particular articles: first, whether they did not believe that after the words of consecration spoken by the priest at mass there remained no substance of bread and wine, but Christ's flesh and blood as he was born of the Virgin Mary. They answered negatively, saying that the popish mass was abominable idolatry, but confessing that in a faithful congregation, receiving the sacrament of Christ's body and blood duly ministered according to Christ's institution, Christ's body and blood is spiritually received of the faithful believer. Asked whether the Pope was supreme head of the

Church and Christ's vicar on earth, they answered that the Bishop of Rome doth usurp over emperors and kings, being Antichrist and God's enemy. The chancellor said, 'Will you have the Church without head?' They answered Christ was head of his Church, and under Christ the queen's Majesty. 'What,' said the chancellor; 'a woman head of the Church?' 'Yea,' said they, 'within her Grace's dominions.' Also, that souls in purgatory were delivered by the Pope's pardon and the suffrages of the Church. They said they believed that the blood of Christ had purged their sins, so that they feared nothing the Pope's purgatory or esteemed his pardons.

The articles thus answered, the chancellor read their condemnation and delivered them to the sheriff. Then spake John Spicer saying, 'Oh Master Sheriff, now must you be their butcher, that you may be guilty also with them of innocent blood.' This was the 23rd of March 1556, and the 24th they were carried out of the common gaol to a place betwixt Salisbury and Wilton, where were two posts set for them to be burnt at. Which men coming to the place kneeled down and made their prayers secretly together, and then being disclothed to their shirts, Maundrell spake with a loud voice, 'Not for all Salisbury'; which word men judged to be an answer to the sheriff, which offered him the queen's pardon if he would recant. In like manner spake John Spicer saying, 'This is the joyfullest day that I ever saw.' Thus were they three burnt at two stakes, where most constantly they gave their bodies to the fire, and their souls to the Lord for testimony of his truth. As touching Coberley, who being somewhat learned, and being at the stake was somewhat long a burning as the wind stood: after his body was scorched with the fire and his left arm taken from him by the violence of the fire, the flesh being burnt to the white bone, at length he stooped over the chain and with the right hand, being somewhat starkened, knocked upon his breast softly, blood and matter issuing out his mouth. Afterward, when they all thought he had been dead, suddenly he rose right up with his body again. Thus much concerning these three Salisbury martyrs.

Six martyrs at London

About the 24th of April were burned in Smithfield at one fire Robert Drakes, minister; William Tyms, curate; Richard Spurge, shearman; Thomas Spurge, fuller; John Cavell, weaver; George Ambrose, fuller. They were all of Essex and so of the diocese of London, and were sent up by Lord Rich and others unto Stephen Gardiner, Chancellor of England, about the 22nd of March 1555. Who upon small examination sent them, some unto the King's Bench, others unto the Marshalsea, where they remained almost the whole year unto the death of the bishop, and had during that time nothing said unto them. After Dr Heath, Archbishop of York, was chosen for the Lord Chancellorship, four of these persecuted brethren, weary of their long imprisonment, made their supplication unto Dr Heath, requiring his aid for their deliverance. This supplication was subscribed with the names of these four—Richard Spurge, Thomas Spurge, George Ambrose, John Cavell.

Upon the receipt hereof Sir Richard Reade, one of the officers of the Court of the Chancery, the 16th of January was sent unto the Marshalsea to examine the four prisoners; and beginning with Richard Spurge received his answers, the effect whereof was that he with others were complained upon by the parson of Bocking unto Lord Rich for that they came not unto their parish church, and thereupon was by Lord Rich sent unto the late Lord Chancellor. He said that he came not to the Church sithence the alteration of the English service into Latin, because he misliked both the same and the mass also, as not consonant with God's holy word. Thomas being next examined made the same answer in effect: he absented himself from the church because the word of God was not there truly taught, nor the sacraments of Christ duly administered in such sort as was prescribed by the same word. The like answer made George Ambrose, adding moreover that after he had read the late Bishop of Winchester's book *De Vera Obedientia*, with Boner's preface, inveighing both against the authority of the Bishop of Rome, he did much less set by their doings than before. John Cavell, agreeing in other matters with them, answered that the cause why he did forbear coming to the church was that the parson had preached two contrary doctrines. In a sermon made at the queen's first entry to the crown he did exhort the people to believe the gospel; for it was the truth, and if they did not believe it they should be damned. But in a second sermon he preached that the Testament was false in forty places.

About the 4th of March Robert Drakes also was examined, who was parson of Thundersley in Essex and had there remained three years. He was presented unto the benefice of Thundersley by Lord Rich, and now notwithstanding was sent up by the said Lord Rich with the others and at his coming to the bishop of Winchester was by him demanded whether he would conform himself to the laws of the realm then in force. He said he would abide all laws that stood with the laws of God; and thereupon was committed to prison.

Now remaineth likewise to declare the examination of William Tyms, deacon and curate of Hockley in Essex. Tyms was apprehended of Mr Tyrrell the Justice, and sent to the ordinary of the diocese, Bishop Boner; who after certain talk he had with him directed him to the Bishop of Winchester, and was commanded by him to the King's Bench. Tyms, as he was but a deacon, was simply, not priestly, apparelled, forasmuch as he went not in a gown, but in a coat; and his hosen were of two colours, the upper part white and the nether stocks of sheep's russet. The proud prelate, seeing his simple attire, began to mock him:

'Ah, sirrah! are you a deacon?'

'Yes, my Lord, that I am.'

'So methinketh you are decked like a deacon.'

'My Lord, my vesture doth not so much vary from a deacon, but methinketh your apparel doth as much vary from an apostle.'

Then spake one of the bishop's gentlemen: 'My Lord,' said he in mockage, 'give him a chair, a toast, and drink, and he will be lusty.' But the bishop bade have him away, and commanded him to come before him the next day. But Winchester, for lack of leisure, or because of sickness growing upon him, or for what cause I know not, either would not or could not attend unto him but returned him to his ordinary, Bishop Boner. So William was placed with the other five, and with them brought to public examination the 21st of March in the Bishop's Palace of London, where the bishop enquired of them their faith upon the sacrament of the altar. They answered that the body of Christ was not in the sacrament really and corporally after the words of consecration spoken by the priest.

After this the bishop falling to entreating and persuasions exhorted Tyms to revoke his heresies, as he termed them, and reform himself unto the Church of Rome, and not to stick so much to the literal sense of the Scriptures but to use the interpretation of the old Fathers. He answered, 'I will not reform myself thereunto. The See of Rome is the See of Antichrist, and to that church I will not conform myself nor once consent unto it.' Then the bishop seeing his boldness to be unmovable pronounced the sentence definitive upon him, and gave him over to the secular power.

After, calling for Robert Drakes he used the like manner of exhortation that he did before. Drakes said, 'As for your Church of Rome, I utterly defy and deny it with all the works thereof, even as I deny the devil and all his works.' The bishop then using the accustomed order of law gave him the like blessing that Tyms had, and so charged the sheriff with him. In fine, calling the rest in their courses and upon the like demands receiving the like answers, the bishop gave unto each of them their several judgments, and so ridding his bloody hands committed them unto the sheriffs, who sent them unto Newgate, whither they went all most joyfully, abiding there the Lord's good time wherein they should seal their faith with their blood; which they most stoutly performed the 24th of April.

The story of John Harpole and Joan Beach

Touching the examination of Joan Beach, widow, and John Harpole within the diocese of Rochester by Maurice, Bishop of the diocese, remembrance was made before in the story of Nicholas Hall, wherein was declared the four articles consistorial of the bishop, objected and laid, as unto Hall and his company, so also to Joan Beach. The same four articles were also the same time and place ministered to John Harpole by Bishop Maurice; who after the like answers received of him as of the other condemned them both to death by one form of sentence. Thus these two Christian martyrs coupled in one confession suffered together at one fire in the town of Rochester, about the 1st of April.

John Hullier, minister and martyr

Next ensueth the martyrdom of John Hullier, minister, who being brought up in the school of Eaton was afterward scholar and then conduct in the King's College at Cambridge, and suffered under Dr Thurlby Bishop of Ely and his chancellor, for the sincere setting out of the light of God's gracious gospel revealed in these our days. In whose behalf this is to be lamented, that among so many fresh wits and stirring pens in that university so little matter is left unto us touching the process of his judgment and order of his suffering, which so innocently gave his life among them. By certain letters which he himself left behind it appeareth that he was zealous and earnest in that doctrine of truth which every true Christian man ought to embrace. His martyrdom was about the 2nd of April.

The death of six constant professors of Christ

Not long after the death of Drakes, Tyms, and the other Essex martyrs executed in Smithfield, followed in the same order of martyrdom at one like fire in Colchester, where most of them did inhabit, six other blessed martyrs, whose names be these—Christopher Lyster of Dagneham, husbandman; John Mace of Colchester, apothecary; John Spenser of Colchester, weaver; Symon Joyne, sawyer; Richard Nichols of Colchester, weaver; John Hamond of Colchester, tanner. Of these the bishop, because he, as it seemed by the process recorded by his register, waxed weary, made a very quick dispatch. For soon after that they were delivered unto John Kingstone, Bachelor of Civil Law and commissary to the bishop, by the Earl of Oxford and other commissioners, as appeareth by a bill dated 28th of March 1556, and by him sent unto his master, the bishop caused them to be brought unto his house at Fulham; where in the open church were ministered unto them the same articles that were propounded unto Bartlet Greene and others; to which they made their several answers agreeing in one truth. These answers made, the bishop did dismiss them until the afternoon. At which time having first their articles and answers read unto them again, and they standing most firmly unto their profession, they were by divers means assayed if they would revoke their faith and return to the unity of Antichrist's Church. When they refused, the bishop pronounced the sentence of condemnation, committing them unto the temporal power; who upon receipt of the king and queen's writ sent them unto Colchester, where the 28th of April most cheerfully they ended their lives, to the glory of God's holy name and the encouragement of other.

Hugh Laverock, John Apprice, burned at Stratford the Bowe

In the discourse of this part of history I know not whether more to marvel at the unsearchable mercies of God (with whom there is no respect of persons, but he chooseth as well the poor, lame, and blind, as the rich, mighty, and healthful, to set forth his glory), or else to note the unnatural doings of these unmerciful Catholics (I mean Boner and his complices), in whom was so little mercy that they spared neither impotent age, neither lame nor blind, as may well appear by these two poor creatures whose stories hereunder follow—Hugh Laverock of the parish of Barking, painter, a cripple; John Apprice, a blind man. These accused by some promoting neighbour unto the bishop and other commissioners, were sent for by their officer, and being delivered into the hands of the bishop were the 1st of May examined in his palace at London; where he first objected against them those nine articles whereof mention is made before. They answered in effect as Lyster, Mace, and others had done. Whereupon they were again sent to prison, and the 9th of the month in the consistory of Paul's were again openly producted, and there travailed withal to recant their opinions against the sacrament of the altar. Whereunto Laverock said, 'I will stand to mine answers; and I cannot find in the Scriptures that the priests should lift up over their head a cake of bread.'

The bishop then turned him unto John Apprice and asked what he would say. He answered, 'Your doctrine is so agreeable with the world that it cannot be agreeable with the Scripture of God. And ye are not of the Catholic Church; for ye make laws to kill men and make the queen your hangman.' The bishop somewhat tickled and therefore loth to delay their condemnation any longer—such was his burning charity—commanded that they should be brought after him unto Fulham, whither he before dinner did go. There in the afternoon, after his solemn manner he pronounced the definitive sentence against them; and delivering them into the hands of the temporal officer thought to dispatch his hands of them, but could not so dispatch his conscience before the judgment of God from the guiltiness of innocent blood.

The poor men, now in the temporal officer's hands, might not there be suffered long to remain; the 15th of May, very early in the morning, they were carried from Newgate in a cart to Stratford the Bowe, and most quietly in the fire, praising God, yielded up their souls into his hands. At their death Laverock after he was chained cast away his crutch; and comforting his fellow-martyr said, 'Be of good comfort, my brother; for my Lord of London is our good physician. He will heal us both shortly; thee of thy blindness and me of my lameness.' And so patiently these two saints of God together suffered.

Three women burned in Smithfield

The next day after the martyrdom of this lame and blind man, were brought to the fire three women, with whom was adjoined another, who being in the same constancy with them was partaker of the said condemnation. These were Katherine Hut of Bocking, widow; Joan Hornes of Billerica, maid; Elizabeth Thackvel of Great Bursted, maid;

Margaret Ellis of Billerica, maid. These with divers more were persecuted and sent up, especially by Sir John Mordant and Edmund Tyrrell Esquire, Justices of Peace. Boner, entering into examination of these four women, objected the like articles to them as are before expressed; thereunto the woman accorded in their answers, agreeing unto the other before them.

They were produced again about the 13th of April to further examination, and so to final judgment; where Katherine Hut, standing before the bishop, boldly stood to that which she had said before, neither yielding to his fair promises nor overthrown with his terror; who, being required of the sacrament to say her mind, openly protested, 'I deny it to be God; because it is a dumb god and made with men's hands.' Wherein the faithful martyr firmly persisting received her sentence, being condemned of Boner to the fire; which she with great constancy sustained by the grace and strength of the Lord and for the love of Christ.

Joan Hornes, producted likewise to her judgment and condemnation, with like fortitude declared herself a follower of Christ's Testament, giving no place to the adversary. Being charged that she did not believe the sacrament of Christ's body and blood to be Christ himself, she said, 'If you can make your god shed blood or show any condition of a true lively body, then will I believe you; but it is but bread, as touching the substance thereof'; and concerning the Romish see she said, 'I forsake all his abominations: from them, Good Lord, deliver us.' From this stable and constant assertion when the bishop was too weak to remove her, and too ignorant to convince her, he knocked her down with the butcherly axe of his sentence. And so the virgin and martyr, committed to the shambles of the secular sword, was offered up with her fellows a burnt sacrifice to the Lord 'in the savour of a sweet smell'.

Margaret Ellis, likewise persevering in her confession, and resisting the errors and heresies of the Papists, was by Boner adjudged and condemned; but before the time of her burning came, prevented by death in Newgate prison, departed and slept in the Lord. No less strength appeared in the other maid, Elizabeth Thackvel, whose mind the Lord had so confirmed in his truth, so armed with patience, that as her adversaries could with no sufficient knowledge of Scripture convince her affirmation, so by no forcible attempts they could remove her confession.

These three innocent women, thus wrongfully by men condemned for the just cause of God's gospel, were had to Smithfield, and there, cruelly bound to the stake, gave their bodies to the tormentors: their spirits they commended to God, for whose glory they were willing to suffer whatsoever the cruel hands of their enemies should work against them, dying more joyfully in the fire than some that burned them did peradventure in their beds.

Thomas Drowry and Thomas Croker, martyrs

Ye heard a little before of two men, one blind the other lame, which suffered about the 15th of May. Here is not to be forgotten another as godly a couple, which suffered the like martyrdom at Gloucester: one was a blind boy named Thomas Drowry. How long he was in pain I am not certain. Of this, credible intelligence I have received by the testimony of the Register of Gloucester, John Taylor, that the boy at his last examination and condemnation was brought before Dr Williams, Chancellor of Gloucester, sitting judicially with the register in the consistory. The chancellor ministered unto the boy such articles as are accustomed in such cases; amongst which he chiefly urged the article of transubstantiation, as followeth:

'Dost thou not believe that after the words of consecration there remaineth the real body of Christ in the sacrament?'

'No, that I do not.'

'Then thou art an heretic and shalt be burned. But who hath taught thee this heresy?'

'You, Mr Chancellor.'

'Where, I pray thee?'

'In yonder place,' pointing towards the pulpit.

'When did I teach thee so?'

'When you preached a sermon upon the sacrament. You said the sacrament was to be received spiritually by faith, and not carnally and really, as the Papists have taught.'

'Then do as I have done, and thou shalt live as I do.'

'Though you can so easily dispense with yourself and mock with God, the world, and your conscience, yet will I not do so.'

'Then God have mercy upon thee; for I will read the sentence against thee.'

'God's will be fulfilled.'

The register being somewhat moved stood up and said to the chancellor, 'Fie for shame, man! Will you read the sentence against him and condemn yourself? Away, away, and substitute some other to give judgment.'

'No, register, I will obey the law and give sentence myself according to mine office.'

And so he read the sentence against the boy, with an unhappy tongue and a more unhappy conscience, delivering him unto the secular power. Who the sixth day of May brought the blind boy to the place of execution at Gloucester, together with Tho. Croker, a bricklayer, condemned for the like testimony of the truth. Both together in one fire most joyfully yielded their souls into the hands of the Lord Jesus. *Ex testimonio Jo. Loud.*

Three burnt at Beckles

After the death of these were three men burnt at Beckles in Suffolk in one fire, about the 21st of May 1556—Thomas Spicer, John Deny, Edmund Poole. Spicer was a single man of nineteen years, by vocation a labourer, dwelling in Winston in Suffolk, and there taken in his master's house in summer, being in his bed, by James Ling and John Keretch of the same town and William Davies of Debnam. The occasion of his taking was that he would not go to hear mass and receive their idol at the commandment of Sir John Tyrrell, of Gipping Hall, and certain other justices, who sent both him and them to Eye dungeon, till at length they were all brought before Dunning, then Chancellor of Norwich, and Mings the register, sitting at Beckles. The chancellor persuading what he could to turn them from the truth could by no means prevail. Wherefore minding in the end to give sentence he burst out in tears, entreating them to turn again to the Holy Mother Church, and not wilfully cast away themselves. As he was thus labouring them and seemed very loth to read the sentence, the register, being weary of tarrying or else perceiving the martyrs to be at a point, called upon the chancellor to rid them out of the way and make an end. At which words the chancellor read the condemnation over them with tears, and delivered them to the secular power. The next day they were all burnt together in Beckles. Whereupon it is to be thought that the writ *De comburendo* was not yet come down nor could not be, the Lord Chancellor being at London; which if it be true, it is plain that both they went beyond their commission that were the executioners, and also the clergy which were the instigators thereof cannot make good that they now pretend, saying they did nothing but by law.

While these good men were at the stake and had prayed, they said their belief; and when they came to 'Catholic Church' Sir John Silliard spake to them. 'That is well said, sirs,' quoth he: 'I am glad to hear you say you believe the Catholic Church. That is the best word I have heard of you yet.' To which Poole answered that though they believe the Catholic Church they do not believe in their popish church, which is no part of Christ's Catholic Church. When they rose from prayer they all went joyfully to the stake; and being bound thereto and the fire burning about them, they praised God in such an audible voice that it was wonderful to all those which heard them. Then one Robert Bacon, an enemy of God's truth and a persecutor of his people, willed the tormentors to throw on faggots to stop the knaves' breaths, as he termed them; so hot was his burning charity. But these good men not regarding their malice confessed the truth, and yielded their lives to the death for the testimony of the same, gloriously and joyfully. Which constancy in the like cause the Lord grant we may imitate and follow to the end, whether it be death or life, to glorify the name of Christ. Amen.

Thirteen martyrs burned at Stratford the Bowe

Not long after there followed in this blessed order of martyrs eleven men and two women, whose dwellings were in sundry places in Essex and whose names followeth—Henry Adlington, Laurence Parnam, Henry Wye, William Hallywel, Thomas Bowyer, George Searles, Edmund Hurst, Lyon Cawch, Rafe Jackson, John Derifal, John Routh, Elizabeth Pepper, Agnes George. Unto whom the 6th of June 1556 Dr Darbyshire, Boner's chancellor, ministered the same articles mentioned before; to which they made their several answers in simplicity and in a good conscience. When these thirteen were condemned and the day appointed they should suffer, which was the 27th day of June, they were carried from Newgate to Stratford the Bowe and there divided into two parts, in two several chambers. The sheriff came to the one part and told them that the other had recanted and their lives therefore should be saved, willing them to do the like and not to cast away themselves. They answered that their faith was not builded on man but on Christ crucified. The sheriff perceiving no good to be done with them went to the other part, and said like a liar the like to them. They answered as their brethren had done before. When he saw that it booted not to persuade, for they were grounded on the Rock, he led them to the place where they should suffer; and being all there together they prayed unto God, and joyfully went to the stake and embraced it heartily. The eleven men were tied to three stakes, the two women loose in the midst without any stake; and so they were all burnt in one fire, with such love to each other and constancy in our Saviour Christ that it made all the lookers-on marvel.

The death of John Careless

The 1st of July amongst other prisoners who died the same year in the King's Bench was one John Careless of Coventry, a weaver; who though he were by the secret judgment of Almighty God prevented by death, so that he came not to the full martyrdom of his body, is no less worthy to be counted in honour and place of Christ's martyrs than other that suffered cruel torments, as well for that he was a long time imprisoned as for his willing mind and zealous affection thereunto if the Lord had so determined it, as well may appear by his examination before Dr Martin. He endured prisoner two whole years, having wife and children. In his captivity first being in Coventry gaol, he was in such credit with his keeper that upon his word he was let out to play in the pageant about the city with his companions. That done, keeping touch with his keeper, he turned again into prison at his hour appointed. After that being brought to London, he was endued with such patience and fortitude that he longed for nothing more earnestly than to come to the promotion to die in the fire for the profession of his faith; yet it pleased the Lord to prevent him with death that he came not to it but died in prison—and after was buried in the fields in a dunghill.

The martyrdom of Julins Palmer, John Gwin, and Thomas Askine

About the 16th of the same month suffered these three martyrs at Newbery, in which number was Julins Palmer, sometime student and fellow of Magdalen College in Oxford, and afterwards schoolmaster in Reading. As God's works be wonderful, which chooseth some of all sorts to confess his gospel, so there is no example in the whole fellowship of martyrs more to be wondered at than this: that one which all King Edward's days was a Papist within the university, and so obstinate that he did utterly abhor all godly prayer and sincere preaching, did after in Queen Mary's time suffer most cruel death at the Papists' hands at Newbury in Barkshire for the zealous profession of the blessed truth.

His name was Julins Palmer, born in Coventry, where his father had sometime been mayor and was an upholsterer by his mystery. How he was brought up in his tender years we know not, but he was sometime scholar to Mr Harley, which taught the free school of Magdalen College; by whose diligence and his own capacity he became a toward young scholar in prose and verse; for he had a very prompt and ready memory, a wit sharp and pregnant. He spake Latin with great facility and wanted not competent knowledge in Greek; insomuch that divers times he supplied the room of the Greek Reader in his house. He was a subtle disputer both in the public Schools and also at home. He used to say that he was never so pleasantly occupied as when he came to the hard debating of profound questions in philosophy; so that he oftentimes spent the whole night in discussing deep and diffuse questions, as *de principiis, de infinito, de vacuo, de tempore, de casu et fortuna*, etc. And although he applied divinity very lately he recompensed the small time of his study with the greatness of his diligence, and his late coming to the truth with his zealous proceeding therein. For by the inspiration of God's Holy Spirit he gave an apparent signification in his young years that, if God had spared his life to age, he would have grown to such maturity and ripeness of judgment whereby he should have been an ornament to Christ's Church and an honour to his country.

In private study he was so indefatigable that he arose every morning at four o'clock and went not lightly to bed before ten at night. As he grew in years and understanding he came to be a Bachelor of Arts, and at length to a fellowship in Magdalen College, where also he was admitted to the office of Reader in Logic *anno* 1550. Now if he had at the first favoured sincere religion, then had we had less matter to note in him. But he was so addicted to the Romish faith that his company and conversation were altogether with such as were utter enemies to the gospel of Christ. Sermons would he hear none himself, nor suffer his scholars to resort unto them. The preachers themselves he did both disdain and despise, and all such as were setters-forth of sound doctrine; for which contumacy he was so oft called before the officers of the college and punished, sometime by the purse, sometime by the lack of his commons, and otherwhile by tasks and exercises of learning, that divers supposed him to have endeavoured of set purpose to be counted a sufferer for that fantasied religion of the Romish Church.

Not long before the death of King Edward certain slanderous libels and railing verses were privily fixed to the walls and doors of the college, against the President, Dr Haddon, whereby was ministered further matter of trouble to Palmer. Inquisition was made to search out the author of so despiteful a deed, but nothing could be found and proved against Palmer or any of his companions. Now Palmer being hereupon examined by the officers did not only deny the fact to have been his, but also spake many reproachful words touching the said officers and sent the same to them in writing, whereby he was by them adjudged to be an unworthy member of that society. And so for this and other Popish pranks he was expelled the house. After he was thus dispatched, he was fain for his own maintenance to apply himself to be a teacher of children in the house of Sir Francis Knolles, in which trade he continued until the coming-in of Queen Mary. When her visitors were sent to Magdalen College under a title of reformation to displace divers of the fellows that were learned and to put right Catholics, as they called them, in their rooms, then came Palmer, waiting to be restored to his living again, thinking by good right to be restored of them whose religion, as he said, he did to the uttermost of his power defend and maintain. At length he obtained the same. Then after he was restored again to his house in Queen Mary's reign, God dealt so mercifully with him that in the end he became of an obstinate Papist an earnest gospeller.

When he was restored to his college he became very inquisitive and careful to hear and understand how the martyrs were apprehended, what articles they died for, how they were used, and after what sort they took their death. He spared not at his own charges to send one of his scholars to Gloucester, to understand the whole order of Bishop Hooper's death and bring him true report thereof; which some think he did because he was wont in King Edward's time to say that none of them would stand to death for their religion. Thus he learned with what horrible cruelty the martyrs of God were tried, and how valiantly they overcame all kind of torments; whereof he himself did see more experience afterward at the death of those holy confessors which were burned at Oxford before his eyes; insomuch that the first hope which the godly conceived of him was at his return from the burning of Ridley and Latimer, at what time in the hearing of his friends he brast out, 'Oh tyranny tragical and more than barbarous!'

From that day forward he studiously sought to understand the truth, and within short space he had yielded up his fellowship in Oxford. He was placed schoolmaster by patent in the grammar school of Reading, where he was well accepted as well for his good learning and knowledge as for his earnest zeal and profession of the truth. But Satan envying his good proceeding and prosperous success would not suffer him long to be quiet. He stirred up against him certain double-faced hypocrites, which by crafty insinuation had crept in to understand his secrets, under pretence of zeal to the gospel; which men he suspecting no deceit joyfully embraced, making them privy of all his doings. For as he himself was then inflamed with the love of heavenly doctrine, so had he an incredible desire by all means possible to encourage others to a profession of the same. These trusty brethren, so soon as they had found opportunity, spared not in his absence to rifle his study of certain books and writings; among which was his replication to Morwin's verses touching Winchester's epitaph, and other arguments both in Latin and English written by him against Popish proceedings, and specially against their brutish tyranny towards the martyrs. When they had thus done, they were not ashamed to threaten him that they would exhibit the same to the Council, unless he would without delay depart out of their coasts and give over the school to a friend of theirs.

Thus then was this silly young man for the safeguard of his life forced to depart upon the sudden from Reading, leaving behind in the hands of his enemies his stuff and one quarter's stipend. So he took his journey toward Ensham where his mother dwelt, hoping to obtain at her hands certain legacies due to him by his father's will, which he should have received years before; and taking his journey by Oxford he requested certain friends to accompany him thither. His mother understanding his errand by his brother whom he had sent before to entreat for him, as soon as she beheld him on his knees asking her blessing as he had been accustomed to do: 'Thou shalt,' said she, 'have Christ's curse and mine wheresoever thou go.' He amazed at so heavy a greeting at length said, 'Oh mother, your own curse you may give me, which God knoweth I never deserved; but God's curse you cannot give me, for he hath already blessed me.' 'Nay,' saith she, 'thou wentest from God's blessing into the warm sun, when thou wast banished for an heretic out of that worshipful house in Oxford; and now for the like knavery art driven out of Reading too. As for money and goods, I have none of thine: thy father bequeathed nought for heretics. Faggots I have to burn thee: more thou gettest not at my hands.'

Thus poor Palmer, destitute of worldly friendship and cruelly repelled of her whom he took to have been his surest friend, wist not which way to turn his face. As he went alone, musing and pondering, it came in his head to leave his appointed journey and return closely to Reading, trusting there by the help of friends to receive his quarter's stipend and convey his stuff to the custody of some trusty body. To Reading he cometh, and taketh up his lodging at the Cardinal's Hat, desiring his hostess to assign him a close chamber where he might be alone. He came not so closely but that this viperous generation had knowledge thereof: without delay they laid their heads together and consulted what way they might most safely proceed against him to bring their cankered malice to pass. Soon it was concluded that one Hampton should resort to him under pretence of friendship to fish out the cause of his repair to Reading. Palmer, as he was a man simple and without all wrinkles of cloaked collusion, opened to him his whole intent. Hampton earnestly persuaded him to the contrary, declaring what danger might ensue if this were attempted. Palmer replied, and as they waxed hot in talk Hampton flang away in a fury and said, as he had fished so should he fowl for him. Palmer called for his supper and went to bed; but within short space after the officers and their retinue came rushing in with lanterns and bills, requiring him in the king and queen's name to make ready himself and depart with them. So this silly young man perceiving that he was Judasly betrayed was led away and committed to ward; whom the keeper brought down into a vile, stinking, and blind dungeon prepared for thieves and murderers. There he left him hanging by the hands and feet in a pair of stocks, so high that well near no part of his body touched the ground. In this dungeon he remained about ten days.

After this he was brought before the mayor, and by the procurement of certain false brethren who had been conversant with Palmer and robbed his study grievous crimes were laid to his charge, as treason, sedition, murder, and adultery. Palmer answered that if such heinous crimes might be proved against him, he would patiently submit himself to all kind of torments that could be devised. 'But, O ye cruel bloodsuckers,' said he, 'ye follow the practices of your progenitors, the viperous and wolfish generation of pharisees and Papists; but be well assured, God already seeth your cruel devices and crafty packing, and will not suffer the outrageous fury of your venomous tongues and fiery hearts to escape unpunished.' All this while no mention was made of heresy or heretical writings. When the evidence was given the mayor dismissed them and went to dinner, commanding Palmer to the cage, to make him an open spectacle of ignominy to the eyes of the world.

In the afternoon Palmer came to his answer, and did so mightily and clearly deface their evidence and defend his own innocency that the mayor was much ashamed that he had given such credit unto them, so that he sought means how they might convey him out of the country privily. When they saw the matter frame so ill-favouredly, fearing that if he should escape secretly their doings would tend no less to their shame and danger than to the mayor's dishonesty, they devised a new policy to bring to pass their festered malice against him, which was their extreme refuge. For whereas before they were partly ashamed to accuse him of heresy, seeing they had been accounted earnest brethren themselves, and partly afraid because they had broken up his study and committed theft, yet now lest their iniquity should have been revealed to the world they put both fear and shame aside, and began to refricate and rip up the old sore, the scar whereof had been but superficially cured, as you have heard; and so to colour their former practices with the pretence of his reformation in religion, they charged him with the writings that they had stolen out of his study.

Thus Palmer was once again called out of the prison to appear before the mayor, and Bird the official, and two other justices, to render an account of his faith before them, to answer to such informations as were laid against him. When they had gathered of his mouth sufficient matter to entrap him, they devised a bill of instructions against him, to be directed to Dr Jeffrey, who had determined to hold his visitation the next Tuesday at Newbery, the 16th of July. Thus were the false witnesses and bloody accusers winked at and the innocent delivered to the lion to be devoured. It was therefore concluded that Palmer should be sent to Newbery, Thomas Askine, *alias* Roberts, being fellow-prisoner with him in Christ's cause. To Newbery they came on Monday night, and were committed to the comfortable hostry of the blind house, where they found John Gwin, their faithful brother in the Lord.

In the year 1556, the 15th of July, four or five seats were prepared in the choir of the parish church of Newbery for the visitors, Dr Jeffrey for the Bishop of Sarum, Sir Richard Abridges, high sheriff of the shire, Sir William Rainsford, John Winchcombe, Esquire, and the parson of Inglefield. The prisoners were presented, the commission read, and other things done in order. We are credibly informed that Sir Richard, the same day after dinner, sent for Palmer to his lodging, and there, in the presence of divers persons yet alive, friendly exhorted him to revoke his opinions, to spare his young years, wit, and learning. 'If thou wilt show thyself corrigible and repentant, I promise thee before this company I will give thee meat and drink and books, and ten pound yearly, so long as thou wilt dwell with me. And if thou wilt set thy mind to marriage, I will procure thee a wife and a farm and help to stuff and frit thy farm for thee. How sayest thou?' Palmer thanked him very courteously and made him further answer concerning his religion, somewhat at large but very modestly, concluding that as he had already in two places renounced his living for Christ's sake, so he would with God's grace be ready to yield up his life for the same when God should send time. Then was Palmer commanded again to the blind house; but the other two were led again the same afternoon to the consistory, and there were condemned and delivered to the sheriff, Sir Richard.

The next morning, the 16th of July, Palmer was required to subscribe to certain articles which they had drawn out, touching the cause of his condemnation; in the front whereof were heaped together many heinous terms, as horrible, heretical, damnable, devilish, and execrable doctrine. He subscribed; whereupon Dr Jeffrey read the sentence of condemnation, and so was he delivered to the secular power, and was burned the same afternoon about five o'clock. One hour before they went to the place of execution Palmer did not only comfort his brethren that were with him appointed as sheep to be slain, but wrested plentiful tears from the eyes of many that heard him. And as they were singing a psalm, came the sheriff and the bailiffs of the town with a great company of harnessed and weaponed men, to conduct them to the fire. When they were come to the place where they should suffer they fell all three to the ground, and Palmer with an audible voice pronounced the 31st psalm: the other two made their prayers secretly to God. As Palmer began to arise, there came behind him two popish priests, exhorting him to recant and save his soul. Palmer answered, 'Away, away! Tempt me no longer. Away from me, all ye that work iniquity; for the Lord hath heard the voice of my tears.' And so forthwith they put off their raiment, and went to the stake and kissed it. When they were bound to the post, Palmer said, 'Good people, pray for us, that we may persever to the end. And beware of Popish teachers, for they deceive you.'

As he spake this, a servant of one of the bailiffs threw a faggot at his face, that the blood gushed out in divers places; for which fact the sheriff reviled him, calling him cruel tormentor, and with his staff brake his head, that the blood likewise ran about his ears. When the fire was kindled and began to take hold upon their bodies, they lifted up their hands towards heaven, and cheerily, as if they felt no smart, they cried, 'Lord Jesu, strengthen us; Lord Jesu, receive our souls.' And so they continued without any struggling, holding up their hands and knocking their hearts, and calling upon Jesu until they had ended their mortal lives. This is also to be noted, that after their three heads by force of the raging fire were fallen together in a cluster, and they all were judged to have given up the ghost, suddenly Palmer, as a man wakes out of sleep, moved his tongue and jaws and was heard to pronounce this word, 'Jesu'. So being resolved into ashes he yielded to God as joyful a soul as anyone that ever was called to suffer for his blessed name. God grant us all to be moved with the like spirit. *Justus ut Palma florebit.*

A tragical, lamentable, and most pitiful history, full of most cruel and tyrannical murder

Amongst all and singular histories touched in this book before, as there be many pitiful, divers lamentable, some horrible and tragical, so there is none either in cruelty to be compared, or so far off from all compassion and humanity, as this merciless fact of the Papists done in the Isle of Garnsey upon three women and an infant, whose names be these—Katherine Cawches, the mother; Guillemine Gilbert, the daughter; Perrotine Massey, the other daughter; an infant, son of Perrotine. Before I come to the purpose of this story it shall be necessary to begin with the circumstances, whereupon the first original and occasion did rise of this tragical cruelty.

The 27th of May 1556 in the Isle of Garnsey, which is a member of England, in St Peter's Port, was a naughty woman named Vincent Gosset, who being evil disposed went to the house of Nicholas le Conronney about ten o'clock at night, and taking the key of the house (lying under the door) entered into a chamber toward the street, where she espying a cup of silver within a cupboard took it away, and conveyed herself out of the house again; who immediately after brought the cup to Perrotine Massey, an honest woman dwelling in the town, desiring her to lend her sixpence upon the same. Perrotine seeing the cup and suspecting the same to be stolen answered that she would not take it, yet having knowledge of the owner thereof took it to restore it to whom it did appertain, and to the end she should not carry it to another gave her sixpence. It is to be noted that Thomas Effart testifieth that knowledge was given by Perrotine to Conronney touching the stealing of this piece, who eftsoons attached Vincent Gosset of the trespass; who being apprehended and examined immediately confessed the fact, desiring to have one sent with her (Collas de Loutre) with 6d to fetch the goblet, and so did.

The next day the king's officers being informed of the premises by Nicholas Cary, constable, assembled the justices to enquire further, as well upon that fact of Vincent Gosset as upon other things there amiss. After declaration made by officers and constable before the justices, for that the constable did report to have found certain vessel of pewter in the house of Perrotine Massey (who dwelt with her mother Katherine Cawches and her sister Guillemine Gilbert), which vessel did bear no mark, and especially for that there was a pewter dish whereof the name was scraped out, their bodies were attached and put in prison, and their movable goods taken by inventory. A few days after, these three silly women, abiding thus in durance in the castle, made supplication unto the justices to have justice ministered unto them; *viz.* if they had offended the law, to let them have the law; if not, to grant them the benefit of subjects. Thereupon they were appointed to come to their answer the 5th of June; upon which day, after strait examining of the matter and the honest answering of the cause by the women, at last they submitted themselves to the report of their neighbours, that they were no thieves nor evil disposed persons, but lived honestly as became Christian women, the false report of their accusers notwithstanding. The cause being thus debated, they were found by the neighbours not guilty, but had lived always as honest women among them; saving only that to the commandments of Holy Church they had not been obedient. Upon this verdict it was in fine adjudged that Vincent Gosset, being attainted of felony and condemned for the same, should be whipped, and after, her ear being nailed to the pillory, should be banished out of the isle without further punishment. As touching the other three woman, the mother with her two daughters, for their not coming to the church they were returned prisoners again into the castle the 1st of July.

Thus far concerning the true discourse of this matter in every point as the case stood, according to the faithful testimony of the Garnsey men written with their own hands both in French and English; wherein you see what false, surmised matter was pretended against these women, and nothing proved; and how by the attestation of their neighbours they were fully cleared of the fact, and should by the temporal court have been dismissed had not the spiritual clergymen, picking matter of religion against them, exercised such extremity in persecuting these miserable prisoners that in no case should they escape their bloody hands till they had brought them to their end. For after they were purged of all other things, being known of their not coming to the church, the bailiff, the lieutenant, and the jurats, thinking the matter not to pertain to them but to the clergy, forthwith wrote their mandate to the dean, Jaques Amy, and the curates of the isle. The women were convented before the justice aforesaid with his assistants. Being examined concerning the ordinances of the Romish Church they made answer that they would keep the ordinances of the king and queen and the commandments of the Church, notwithstanding that they had done the contrary in the time of King Edward, in showing obedience to his ordinances and commandments. After which answer they were returned to prison until the others had an answer of their letter from the dean and his complices. During which time the dean and curates gave their information touching the women to the bailiff and jurats, condemning them for heretics, the women neither hearing of any information neither yet being examined of their faith. When the bailiffs and jurats understood that the dean and curates had not examined the women, they would not sit in judgment that day, but ordained the women first to be examined of their faith. So the officers did fetch and present them before the dean and curates. Which being done, they were examined severally; after which they were returned into prison.

The 14th of July after the examination before Elyer Gosselin, bailiff, Sir Jaques Amy, dean, and the curates did deliver before the justice under the seal of the dean a certain sentence, the sum whereof was that Katherine Cawches and her daughters were found heretics, and they have delivered them to justice to do execution according to the sentence. This done, commandment was given to the king's officers to fetch the women to hear the sentence in the presence aforesaid. They appearing before them said in the ears of all the auditory that they would see their accusers and know them that have deposed against them, because they might make answers and have their libel accordingly; for they knew not that they had offended the king and queen, nor the Church, but entirely would obey the king and queen and the Church, as all true subjects are bound to do. For any breach of the laws that they had done they required justice. All which notwithstanding, the poor women were condemned, and adjudged to be burnt to ashes, according to a sentence given by Gosselin. After which the women did appeal to the king and queen and their Council, saying that against reason and right they were condemned. Notwithstanding they could not be heard, but were delivered by the bailiff to the officers, to see execution done on them.

The time being come when the innocent mother with her two daughters should suffer, in the place where they should consummate their martyrdom were three stakes set up. At the middle post was the mother, the eldest daughter on the right hand, the youngest on the other. They were first strangled, but the rope broke before they were dead, and the poor women fell in the fire. Perrotine, who was great with child, did fall on her side, where happened a rueful sight, not only to the eyes of all that there stood, but also to the ears of all true-hearted Christians that shall read this history. For as the belly of the woman brast asunder by the vehemency of the flame, the infant, a fair man child, fell into the fire, and being taken out of the fire by one W. House was laid upon the grass. Then was the child had to the provost, and from him to the bailiff, who gave censure that it should be carried back again and cast into the fire. And so the infant baptized in his own blood, to fill up the number of God's innocent saints was both born and died a martyr, leaving behind to the world, which it never saw, a spectacle wherein the whole world may see the Herodian cruelty of this graceless generation of Catholic tormentors, *ad perpetuam rei infamiam.*

Forsomuch as this story percase, for the horrible strangeness of the fact, will be hardly believed of some, but thought to be forged, or else more amplified of me than truth will bear me out, therefore to discharge my credit herein I have not only told thee before how I received this story by the faithful relation, both in French and English, of them which were present witnesses and lookers-upon, but also have hereto annexed the true supplication of the inhabitants of Garnsey and of the brother to the mother of the two sisters, complaining to the queen and her commissioners concerning the horribleness of the act. This supplication being presented to the commissioners in 1562, such order was taken that the matter being returned to the said country farther to be examined, the dean thereupon was committed to prison and dispossessed of all his livings. In conclusion both he and all other partakers of that bloody murder, whether of conscience or for fear of

'A lamentable spectacle of three women, with a sillie infant brasting out of the mothers wombe, being first taken out of the fire, and cast in againe, and so all burned togither in the Isle of Garnsey. 1556. July 18.'

the law, were driven to acknowledge their trespass and submit themselves to the queen's pardon.

Joan Waste

The 1st of August suffered at Darby a poor honest woman, blind from birth and unmarried, about the age of twenty-two, named Joan Waste, of the parish of All Hallows. Of them that sat upon this innocent woman's blood the chiefest was Rafe Bane bishop of the diocese, and Dr Draicot his chancellor. After the bishop had caused Joan to be apprehended in Darby, suspecting her to be guilty of certain heresies, she was divers times privily examined by Finch the official; after that brought to public examination before the bishop; at last burnt in Darby.

Joan was the daughter of William Waste, a barber, who sometime also used to make ropes. His wife had Joan and one other at one birth, and she was born blind. When she was about twelve or fourteen years old she learnt to knit hosen and sleeves and other things, which in time she could do very well. Furthermore she would help her father to turn ropes, and do such other things as she was able, and in no case would be idle. Thus continued she with her father and mother during their lives. After whose departure then kept she with Roger her brother; who in the time of King Edward of blessed memory gave herself daily to go to the church to hear divine service in the vulgar tongue. Thus by hearing homilies and sermons she became marvellously well affected to the religion then taught. At length, having by her labour gotten and saved so much money as would buy her a New Testament, she caused one to be provided for her. And though she was unlearned and by reason of her blindness unable to read, yet for the great desire she had to have printed in her memory the sayings of Holy Scriptures contained in the New Testament she acquainted herself with one John Hurt, then prisoner in the common hall of Darby for debts.

John, being a grave man of threescore and ten years, being prisoner and many times without company, did daily read unto her one chapter of the New Testament. If at any time he was otherwise occupied or letted through sickness, she would repair unto John Pemerton, clerk of the parish church, or some other person which could read, and sometimes she would give a penny or two to such persons as would not freely read unto her, appointing unto them aforehand how many chapters they should read, or how often they should repeat one chapter, upon a price. Moreover this was notorious, that she being utterly blind could without a guide go to any church within the town, or to any other place or person with whom she had any such exercise. By which exercise she so profited that she was able not only to recite many chapters without book but also could aptly impugn by divers places of Scriptures as well sin as such abuses in religion as then were too much in use.

As this godly woman thus daily increased in the knowledge of God's holy word and in her life expressed the fruits of the same, not long after through the fatal death of King Edward followed the woeful ruin of religion in the reign of his sister. In which alteration, notwithstanding the general backsliding of the greatest part of the whole realm into the old Papism, yet this poor blind woman proceeded still in her former exercise, both being zealous in that she had learned and also refusing to communicate in religion with those which taught contrary doctrine to that she had learned. For which she was convented before the bishop and Dr Draicot, with divers other called to bear witness. Pressed by the bishop with many arguments of Christ's omnipotency, as why was not Christ able as well to make the bread his body as to turn water into wine, raise Lazarus from the dead, and suchlike arguments; and many times threatened with imprisonment, torment, and death; the poor woman, half astonied through their terror and threats and desirous, as it seemed, to prolong her life, offered unto the bishop that if he would before that company take it upon his conscience that the doctrine which he would have her believe was true, and that he could at the dreadful day of judgment answer for her therein, she would then further answer them. The bishop answered he would; but his chancellor said, 'My Lord, you know not what you do: you may in no case answer for an heretic'; unto whose sayings the bishop reformed himself. The poor woman answered that if they refused to take of their conscience that it was true they would have her believe, she would answer no further but desired them to do their pleasure. So they pronounced sentence and delivered her unto the bailiffs of Darby; who after they had kept her about five weeks, at length there came a writ *De Haeretico comburendo*, by virtue whereof they were appointed by the bishop to bring her to the parish church of All Saints at a day appointed, where Draicot should make a sermon.

When the day and time were come, first cometh to the church Dr Draicot accompanied with divers gentlemen. All things now in readiness, at last the poor blind creature was brought and set before the pulpit, where the doctor, being entered into his sermon and inveighing against divers matters which he called heresies, said that she was not only blind of her bodily eyes but also blind in the eyes of her soul. And as her body should be presently consumed with material fire, so her soul should be burned in hell with everlasting fire world without end: it was not lawful for the people to pray for her. The sermon ended, the blessed servant of God was carried away from the church to the Windmill Pit near the town; and holding Roger her brother by the hand she prepared herself, and desired the people to pray with her, and said such prayers as she before had learned, and cried upon Christ to have mercy upon her, as long as life served. In this mean season Draicot went to his inn for sorrow of her death, and there laid him down and slept during all the time of her execution.

William Dangerfield and Joan his wife

When I had finished the story of the Garnsey women, with the infant with them burned, and also had passed the burning of poor Joan Waste, I hoped I should have found no more such stories of unmerciful cruelty showed upon silly women and infants; but now, coming to the persecution of Gloucestershire, I find another story of such unmercifulness showed against a woman in childbed, as far from all humanity as any story hitherto rehearsed.

In Wotton Underhedge not far from Bristow was dwelling one William Dangerfield, a right honest poor man, who by Joan his wife had nine children, and she now lying in childbed of the tenth. William, after he had been abroad from his house a certain space for fear of persecution, hearing that his wife was brought to bed repaired home as natural duty required, she being delivered four days before. The return of this man was not so soon known to some of his uncharitable neighbours, but they incensed with the spirit of Papistry beset the house, took William, and carried him to prison. So at length he was brought to the bishop Dr Brookes; in whose cruel handling he remained till his legs almost were fretted off with irons. The wife likewise was taken with her child, being but fourteen days old, and carried into the common gaol and placed amongst thieves and murderers, where both she and her poor innocent found so small charity among the Catholic men that she never could come to any fire, but was driven to warm the clothes that she should put about the child in her bosom.

While they remained thus enclosed in several prisons, the husband and wife, the bishop beginneth to practise not with the woman first, as the serpent did with Eve, but with the man, deceiving his simplicity with fair, glozing words, falsely persuading him that his wife had recanted, and asking him wherefore he should more stand in his own conceit than she, being as well learned as he; and so subtly drew out a form of recantation wherewith he deceived the simple soul; whereunto after he had once granted that he would consent, although he had not yet recanted they suffered him to go to his wife, where she lay in the common gaol. Then they opening their minds one to another, when he saw his wife not released, perceiving that he had not done well he declared unto her how he was circumvented by the subtle flatterings of the bishop, bearing him in hand that she had recanted; 'and thus deceiving me,' said he, 'brought this unto me'; and plucked out of his bosom the copy of the recantation whereunto he had granted his promise. At the sight whereof the wife hearing what her husband had done, her heart clave asunder saying, 'Alack! thus long have we continued one; and has Satan so prevailed to cause you to break your first vow made to Christ in baptism?' And so departed William and Joan, with what hearts the Lord knoweth. Then began he to bewail his promise made to the bishop, and to make his prayer to God, desiring him that he might not live so long as to call evil good and good evil; and so he departed towards his house, where by the way homeward he took his death, and shortly after departed, according to his prayer, after he had endured in prison twelve weeks.

His wife continued still in prison with her tender infant, till at last she was brought before the bishop to be examined: what her answers were it is not certainly known. Whatsoever they were, they pleased not the bishop, as appeared by his ire increased against the poor woman and her continuance in the prison, together with her babe, which remained with her in the gaol, partaker of her martyrdom, so long as her milk would serve to give it suck, till at length the child, starved for cold and famine, was sent away when it was past all remedy, and shortly after died; and not long after the mother followed, besides the mother of the husband, of the age of eighty years and upward; who, being left in the house after their apprehension, for lack of comfort perished also.

Thus have ye in one story the death of four together; first of the old woman, then of the husband, after that of the innocent child, lastly of the mother. What became of the other nine children I am not sure. This story is testified as well by others as by Mrs Bridges, dwelling in the same town and partaker of like afflictions, and hardly escaped with her life.

Five famished in Canturbury Castle

As among all the bishops Boner of London principally excelled in persecuting the saints of Christ, so of all archdeacons Nicholas Harpsfield of Canturbury was the sorest and of least compassion, only Dunning of Norwich excepted; by whose unmerciful nature very many were put to death in that diocese, not only in the bloody time of that queen but also in the blessed beginning of our most renowned queen that now is. In the beginning of November were together in the castle of Canturbury fifteen innocent martyrs, of which none escaped with their lives, but they were either burned or else famished in prison: of the two sorts which is the easier death God knoweth. Of these fifteen ten suffered in the fire, of whom more shall follow hereafter. The other five were pined most unmercifully in the strait prison, of whom we have here presently to entreat; whose names were these: John Clerke, Dunston Chittenden (which two were yet uncondemned), William Foster of Stone, Alice Potkins, wife, of Staplehurst, John Archer of Crambroke, weaver. The first two were uncondemned; the other three were condemned and should have been burned, but suffered no less torments, being macerate and pined to death by famine. What their articles and answers were I need not here recite, seeing all they in that time of Queen Mary commonly suffered for one sort of cause, that is, for holding against the seven sacraments, against the reality of Christ's being in his supper, against the Church of Rome, against images worshipped in church; for not coming to church, etc.

First William said that he believed all articles of the Creed; but to believe that there be more sacraments than two, and to pray to saints either to profit us or to pray for souls in purgatory to profit them that faith and works do justify, or to allow popish ceremonies in church, that he denied. This William was a labouring man of forty years. He was apprehended and imprisoned by Sir Thomas Moyle. Alice for the like confession was condemned to be burnt, for that she was not neither would be confessed to the priest; for that she received not the sacrament of the altar; because she would not pray to the saints nor creep to the cross. Being demanded of her age, she said that she was forty-nine years old according to her old age, and according to her young age since she learned Christ she was of one year's age; and was committed by Mr Roberts to prison. The answer of John Archer was in like sort. Concerning the not praying to saints and for the dead in purgatory, for faith only to justify, and suchlike, he granted as the other had done. This Archer, of the age of fifty years, was attached and imprisoned by Sir John Gilford.

Thus have ye the cause and imprisonment of these five. Touching the cruelty of their death, that ye shall not surmise the relation thereof to proceed from myself, you shall hear their own testimony and certification by their own letter thrown out of the prison. The copy of their letter is this:

'We, the poor prisoners of the Castle of Canturbury for God's truth, lie in cold irons, and our keeper will not suffer any meat to be brought to us to comfort us. If any man do bring us bread, butter, cheese, or any other food, the keeper will charge them that bring us anything except money or raiment to carry it with them again; if he do receive any food for us he doth keep it for himself, and he and his servants spend it so that we have nothing thereof. Thus the keeper keepeth away our victuals from us; insomuch that there are four of us prisoners there famished already, and thus it is his mind to famish us all. We think he is appointed of the bishops and priests, and also of the justices, so to famish us; and not only us, but all other prisoners in other prisons for the like cause. Notwithstanding we write not these letters to that intent we might not afford to be famished for the Lord Jesus' sake, but that the murderers' hearts should be known to all the world, and all men may know of what church they are and who is their father.'

Thus have ye the whole persecution of this year declared, the year of our Lord 1556 and the fourth of Queen Mary's reign, with the names and causes of all them which suffered martyrdom within the compass of the said year. The number slain and martered in divers places of England at sundry times this year came to above eighty-four persons, whereof many were women—wives, widows and maidens; besides them which otherwise by secret practice were made away, or driven out of goods and houses or out of the realm, or else within the realm were put to penance and coacted by violence to recant.

CHAPTER 10

THE CRUELTY OF BONER AND HIS COMPLICES

Ten martyrs within the diocese of Canturbury

Mention was made a little before of the persecution in Kent. We declared that fifteen were in the Castle of Canturbury imprisoned for God's word; of which fifteen we showed five to be famished unto death within the castle and buried by the highway, about the beginning of November. The other ten in the first month of the next year, 1557, were committed unto the fire and consumed to ashes by Thornton, Bishop suffragan of Dover, otherwise called Dick of Dover, and by Nicholas Harpsfield, Archdeacon of the province. The names of these martyrs be these—John Philpot of Tenterden, William Waterer of Bedingden, Stephen Kempe of Norgate, William Haye of Hithe, Thomas Hudsonne of Salenge, Matthew Bradbridge of Tenterden, Thomas Stephens of Bedingden, Nicholas Final of Tenterden, William Lowick of Crambroke, William Prowting of Thornham. Of these ten, six were burned at Canturbury about the 15th of January, that is, Kempe, Waterer, Prowting, Lowick, Hudson, and Haye; other two, Stephens and Philpot, at Wye, about the same month; other two, Final and Bradbridge, at Ashford, the 16th of the same.

Five martyrs burned in Smithfield

Next in order follow five other burned at London, in Smithfield, April 12th, whose names were these—Thomas Loseby, Henry Ramsey, Thomas Thirtel, Margaret Hyde, and Agnes Stanley. Who being, some by Lord Rich, some by other justices of peace, and constables (their own neighbours) accused and apprehended for not coming to their parish churches, were sent unto Boner, and by his commandment the 27th of January examined before Dr Darbyshire, chancellor to the bishop, upon the former general articles. Whose answers were that as they confessed there was one true and Catholic Church whereof they steadfastly believed, and thought the Church of Rome to be no part; so in the same church they believed there were but two sacraments, Baptism and the Supper of the Lord. These answers taken by the chancellor, they were for that time dismissed; but the bishop, taking the matter into his own hands, the 6th of March propounded unto them certain other articles.

The first of April they were again convented before the bishop in his palace, where little appeareth to be done except to know whether they would stand by their answers and whether they would recant or no. When they refused to recant and deny the truth, the bishop caused them to be brought into the open consistory the third of the month. The bishop first called for Loseby, and after his accustomed manner willed his articles and answers to be read. In reading thereof when mention was made of the sacrament of the altar, the bishop with his colleagues put off their caps. Whereat Loseby said, 'My Lord, seeing you put off your cap I will put on my cap,' and therewithal put on his cap. After, the bishop continuing in his customary persuasions, Loseby said, 'My Lord, I trust I have the spirit of truth, which you abhor; for the wisdom of God is foolishness unto you.' Whereupon the bishop pronounced sentence of condemnation against him, and delivering him unto the sheriff called for Margaret Hyde, with whom he used the like exhortations. Notwithstanding she said, 'I will not depart from my sayings till I be burned; and, my Lord, I would see you instruct me with some part of God's word, and not give me instructions of holy bread and holy water, for it is no part of the Scripture.' But he, being neither himself nor any of his able to accomplish her request, used his final reason of convincement, the sentence of condemnation, and leaving her off called for Agnes Stanley, who upon the bishop's like persuasions made this answer: 'My Lord, where you say I am an heretic, I am none; neither will I believe you, nor any man that is wise will believe as you do. As for these that ye say be burnt for heresy, I believe they are true martyrs before God; therefore I will not go from my faith as long as I live.' Her talk thus ended, she received the like reward.

The bishop then turning his tale unto Thomas Thirtel received of him this answer: 'My Lord, I will not hold with your idolatrous ways; for I say the mass is idolatry, and will stick to my belief so long as the breath is in my body.' Upon which words he was also condemned as an heretic. Last of all was Henry Ramsey demanded if he would stand unto his answers, or recanting the same come home again and be a member of their church. He answered, 'I will not go from my religion as long as I live. And, my Lord, your doctrine is naught; for it is not agreeable to God's word.' The bishop, to conclude, pronouncing sentence against him and the rest, charged the sheriff with them; who the 12th day of the same month brought them into Smithfield, where all together in one fire most joyfully and constantly they ended their temporal lives, receiving therefore the life eternal.

Five women and two men burned at Maidstone

Now to return to the diocese of Canturbury. June the 18th were seven martyrs burned at Maidstone—Joan Bradbridge of Staplehérst; Walter Appleby of Maidstone; Petronill his wife; Edmund Allen of Fritenden; Katherine his wife; Joan Manning, wife, of Maidstone; Elizabeth, a blind maiden. Touching their accusers and manner of apprehension, and their private conflicts with the adversaries, I find no great matter coming to my hands, save only of Allen some intimation is given me, how his troubles came and what was his cause and answer before the justices.

Allen was a milner, and in a dear year when many poor people were like to starve he fed them, and sold his corn better cheap by half than others did; and also fed them with the food of life, reading to them the Scriptures and interpreting them. This being known to the popish priests thereabout dwelling, by the procurement of them, namely John Tailor, parson of Fritenden, and Thomas Henden, parson of Stapleherst, he was eftsoons complain of to the justices and brought before Sir John Baker; who sending for them committed both him and his wife to ward. Not long after they were let out, I know not how, and went over unto Calice. After a certain space he began to be troubled in conscience; and meeting with one John Web of the same parish, who was likewise fled from the tyranny of Baker and Tailor, said unto him that he could not be in quiet there; for God, said he, had something for him to do in England. Thus shortly he returned home to Fritenden.

Parson Tailor, informed by his brother Sextan that Edmund Allen the milner and his wife were returned and were not at mass-time in the church; as he was the same time in the midst of his mass, a little before the elevation, he turned him to the people in a great rage, and commanded them with all speed to go unto their house and apprehend them, and he would come to them with as much haste as might be possible. Which promise he well performed; for he had not so soon made an end of *Ite, missa est,* and the vestments off his back, but he was at the house; and laying hand of Allen caused him again to be brought to Sir John, with a grievous complaint of his reading the Scriptures to the people. So were he and his wife sent to Maidstone prison. Witnessed by Richard Fletcher, vicar of Crambroke, and John Web of Fritenden.

They were not so soon in prison but Mr Baker sent unto their house certain of his men with Tailor and Henden to take an inventory of all the goods that were in the house, where they found in the bedstraw a casket locked with a padlock; and cutting the wisp thereof opened it and found a sackcloth bag of money, thirteen or fourteen pound in gold and silver; which money after they had told and put in the bag again, they carried away. Also they found psalters, Bibles, and other writings; all which with the money were delivered to Henden, and after, in the reign of this queen, were by law recovered from him. Thus Allen and his wife, maliciously accused, wrongfully imprisoned, and cruelly spoiled of their goods, were brought before Sir John to be examined; who taunting and reviling him without all mercy asked if those were the fruits of his gospel, to have conventicles to gather people together, to make conspiracies, to sow sedition and rebellion.

Thus was he carried to prison and afterward burned. And thus much touching the particular story of Edmund Allen and his wife; who with the five other above named were altogether burned at Maidstone the year and month aforementioned and the 18th day of the month.

John Hullier, burned at Cambridge

Concerning the story of John Hullier, martyr, partly mentioned before, for the more full declaration of the death and martyrdom of that good man I thought thereunto to add that which since hath come to my hand.

Hullier was brought up at Eaton College; and after, according to the foundation of that house, he was elected scholar in the King's College, where not tarrying full three years of probation before he was fellow of the college, he after a little season was one of the ten conducts in the college, *anno* 1539. In process of time he came to be curate of Babram three miles from Cambridge, and went afterward to Linne; where he having divers conflicts with the Papists was carried to Ely, to Dr Thurlby, then bishop; who after divers examinations sent him to Cambridge Castle, where he remained but a while. Thence he was conveyed to the town prison called the Tolboth, lying there almost a quarter of a year. At length he was cited to appear at Great St Mary's on Palm Sunday Even before divers doctors, amongst whom was chiefest Dr Shaxton; where after examination he was condemned. Then he was degraded after their Popish manner with scraping crown and hands. When they had degraded him he said cheerfully, 'This is the joyfullest day that ever I saw: I thank you all that you have lightened me of all this paltry.' Meantime, whilst it was doing, one standing by asked Hullier what book he had in his hand; who answered, 'A Testament;' whereat this man in a rage took it and threw it violently from him. Then was he given to the secular powers, who carrying him to prison again took from him all his books and papers.

On Maundy Thursday coming to the stake, he exhorted the people to pray for him. Then going to a stool prepared for him to sit on to have his hosen plucked off he desired the people to pray for him again, and also to bear witness that he died in the right faith and would seal it with his blood; certifying them that he died in a just cause and for the testimony of the truth, and that there was no other rock but Jesus Christ to build upon, under whose banner he fought and whose soldier he was. Which done, he went meekly himself to the stake, and with chains being bound was beset with reed and wood, standing in a pitch-barrel; and the fire being set to, not marking the wind, it blew the flame to his back. He feeling it began earnestly to call upon God. Nevertheless his friends, perceiving the fire to be ill kindled, caused the sergeants to turn it, and fire it in that place where the wind might blow it to his face. That done, there was a company of books cast into the fire; and by chance a communion-book fell between his hands, who receiving it joyfully opened it, and read so long as the force of the flame and smoke caused him that he could see no more. Then he fell again to prayer, holding his hands up to heaven and the book between his arms next his heart, thanking God for sending him it. At that time, the day being fair and hot, yet the wind was somewhat up, and it caused the fire to be the fiercer; and when all the people thought he had been dead, he suddenly uttered these words: 'Lord Jesus, receive my spirit.'

The place where he was burned was called Jesus Green, not far from Jesus College. Seagar gave him gunpowder, but he was dead before it took fire. All the people prayed for him, and many a tear was shed; which the Papists seeing cried he was not to be prayed for; and being damned it could profit him nothing. Nevertheless they continued praying; whereat the Papists fell into such a rage that they menaced them with terrible threatenings. His flesh being consumed, his bones stood upright as if they had been alive. Of the people, some took as they could get of him, as pieces of bone. One had his heart, which was distributed as far as it could go; one took the scalp and looked for the tongue, but it was consumed except the very root.

Simon Miller and Elizabeth Cooper, burnt at Norwich

In July ensued the martyrdom of Simon Miller and Elizabeth Cooper. Simon, dwelling in Linne, a zealous man in the knowledge of the Lord and of his truth, detesting the enforced religion then set forth, came to Norwich, where he standing in the press and hearing of the people coming out from their Popish service, began to ask them where he might go to have the communion. Divers much marvelling to see his boldness, an evil disposed Papist said that if he would needs go to a communion he would bring him where he should be sped of his purpose. Whereupon he was brought to the Chancellor of Norwich, Dunning, who after a few words passed with the examinate committed him to ward. Meanwhile as he was in examination he had in his shoe his confession written in a paper, whereof a piece appearing above his shoe was spied and taken out. The chancellor asking if he would stand to the confession of the faith therein contained, he affirmed the same; whereupon he was committed. At length he, constantly abiding in his professed purpose and defence of God's truth, was by the bishop and his chancellor condemned, and committed to the fire about the 13th of July.

With Miller also was burnt Elizabeth Cooper, a pewterer's wife dwelling in St Andrew's parish, where she had before recanted. Being unquiet for the same and greatly troubled inwardly, at last she came into St Andrew's Church, the people being at their popish service: there standing she revoked her recantation before made in that place, willing the people not to be deceived, neither to take her doings before for an example. Then cried one Bacon, laying his arms abroad, 'Mr Sheriff, will you suffer this?' and urged him to go from the church to her house, at whose knocking she came down, and was taken and sent to prison. The sheriff, named Thomas Sutterton, and she had been servants together in one house, and for the friendship he bare unto her, and the more for the gospel's sake, he was very loth to do it, but was enforced by other persons much against his own conscience, which he now earnestly repenteth.

The good woman being condemned, and at the stake with Simon, when the fire came unto her she a little shrank thereat, crying one

'Ah!' When Simon heard the same, he put his hand behind him toward her and willed her to be strong and of good cheer; whereat she stood as still and quiet as one most glad to finish that good work which most happily she had begun. So, in fine, she ended her life with her companion joyfully, committing her soul into the hands of Almighty God.

Five men and five women burnt at Colchester

As it is no new thing in those whom we call prelates and priests of the Church to be raisers-up of persecution against Christ and his poor flock, so is it much to be marvelled that men of honour and worship would be made ministers to serve the affections of these tyrants as well in all the sorrowful days of the late queen as namely in this present story is to be marked.

Twenty-two were sent up prisoners together from Colchester to London by the Earl of Oxford, Lord Darcy, Mr Tyrrell of St Osithe's, and other commissioners and justices, etc. The which twenty-two through a gentle submission put unto them were afterward released. In the number of these was one Will. Mount of Muchbentley in Essex, husbandman, with Alice his wife and Rose Allin, maid, the daughter of Alice Mount; which coming home again to their house refrained themselves from the unsavoury service of the popish church, and frequented the company of men and women which gave themselves diligently to reading and calling upon God through Christ; whereby they so fretted the priest of that town, Sir Thomas Tye, and other like unto him, that casting their heads together they made a pestilent supplication to Lord Darcy in the name of the whole parish.

When this wicked priest had thus wrought his malice against the people of God, the storms began to arise against William Mount and his company, whereby they were forced to hide themselves from the heat thereof. At last, the 7th day of March 1557, the first Sunday in Lent, by two o'clock in the morning Edmund Tyrrell (who came of the house of those Tyrrells which murdered King Edward the Fifth and his brother) took with him the bailiff of the hundred and the two constables of Muchbentley with divers other a great number; and besetting the house of William Mount called to them to open the door. Which done, Tyrrell went into the chamber where Mount and his wife lay, willing them to rise; 'For,' said he, 'ye must go with us to Colchester Castle.' Mother Mount being very sick desired that her daughter

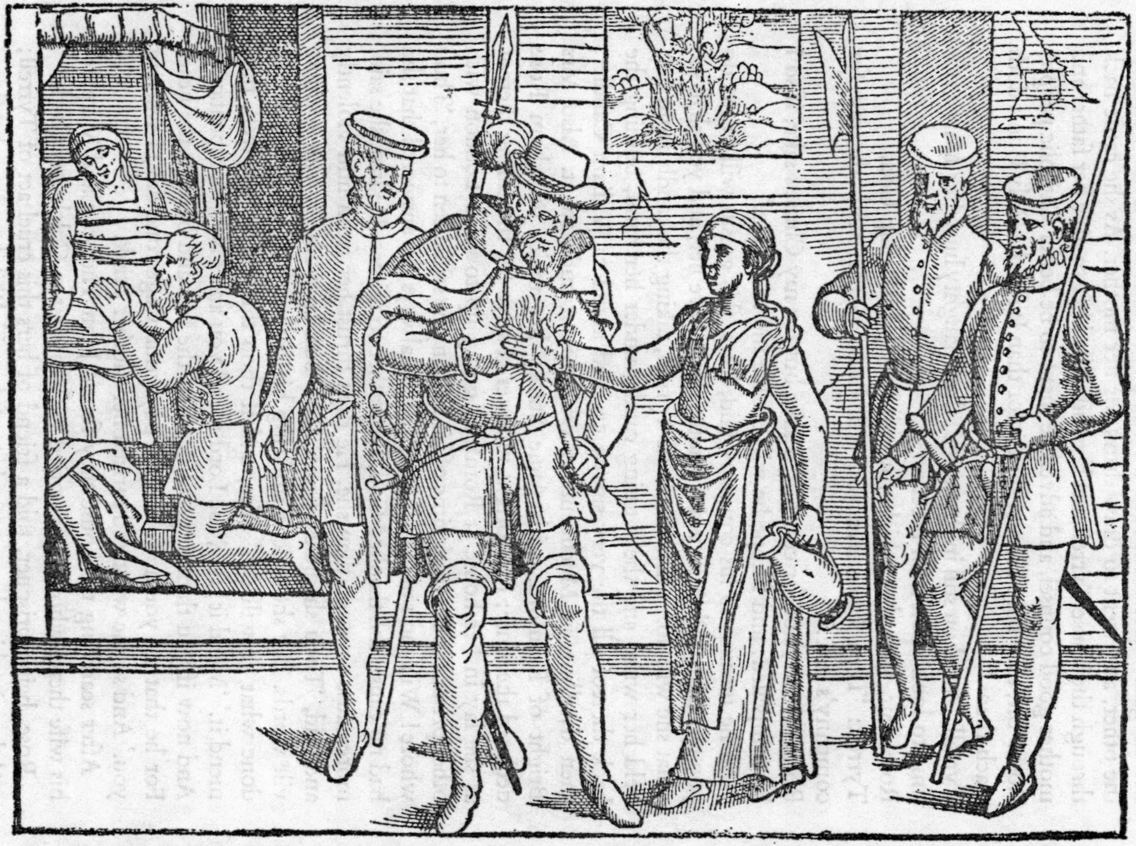

'The burning of Rose Allins hand, by Edmund Tyrrell, as she was going to fetch drinke for her mother, lying sicke in her bedde.'

might first fetch her some drink. He gave her leave and bade her go. So her daughter Rose Allin took a stone pot in one hand and a candle in the other, and went to draw drink for her mother. As she came back through the house Tyrrell met her and willed her to give her father and mother good counsel, and advertise them to be better Catholic people.

Rose: 'Sir, they have a better instructor than I; for the Holy Ghost doth teach them.'

Tyrrell: 'Art thou still in that mind, thou naughty huswife? Marry, it is time to look upon such heretics.'

Rose: 'Sir, with that which you call heresy I worship God.'

Tyrrell: 'Then I perceive you will burn, gossip, with the rest for company's sake.'

Rose: 'No sir, not for company's sake but for my Christ's sake, if so I be compelled; and I hope he will enable me to bear it.'

So he turning to his company said, 'Sirs, this gossip will burn; do you not think it?' 'Marry sir,' quoth one, 'prove her, and you shall see what she will do.' Then that cruel Tyrrell, taking the candle from her, held her wrist, and the burning candle under her hand, burning the back thereof till the very sinews cracked asunder. William Candler, then dwelling in Muchbentley, was present and saw it. Also Mrs Bright of Romford, with Anne Starky her maid, to whom Rose declared the same; Mrs Bright ministered salve for the curing thereof as she lay in her house at Romford going up towards London with other prisoners. In which time of his tyranny he said often to her, 'Thou whore! Wilt thou not cry?' Unto which always she answered that she had no cause, she thanked God, but rather to rejoice. He had, she said, more cause to weep than she. He then thrust her from him violently and said, 'Thou shameless beast! thou beastly whore!' with suchlike vile words. But she quietly suffering his rage at last said, 'Sir, have ye done what ye will do?' 'Yea, and if thou think it be not well, then mend it.' 'Mend it! nay, the Lord mend you and give you repentance. And now if you think it good begin at the feet and burn to the head. For he that set you a work shall pay your wages one day, I warrant you.' And so she went and carried her mother drink.

After searching the house they found John Thurston and Margaret his wife there, whom they carried with the rest to Colchester Castle.

Rose, being prisoner, told a friend of hers this cruel act of Tyrrell; and showing him the manner thereof she said, 'While my one hand was a burning, I having a pot in the other hand might have laid him on the face with it if I had would. But I thank God with all my heart I did it not.'

And because Tyrrell shall not go alone in this kind of cruelty, you shall hear a like example of a blind harper's hand burnt by Boner, as is testified by Valentine Dingley, gentleman to the said bishop, who declared how Boner having this blind harper before him spake thus unto him: that such blind abjects which follow heretical preachers, when they come to the feeling of the fire, will be the first that will fly from it. The blind man said that if every joint of him were burnt he trusted in the Lord not to fly. Then Boner signifying privily to certain of his men what they should do, they brought him a burning coal; which being put into the poor man's hand, they closed it fast; so was his hand piteously burned. Amongst the doers whereof was Valentine Dingley, witness and reporter hereof.

But to return to our Colchester martyrs again: as touching William Mount and his wife, and burning of their daughter Rose Allin's hand, sufficient hath been declared. With William and his family was joined also in the same prison at Colchester another faithful brother named John Johnson, of Thorpe in Essex, labourer, of the age of thirty-four, years, having no wife alive but three young children, who also was indicted of heresy; and so all these four lay together in Colchester Castle. The other five prisoners lay in Mote Hall, whose names were William Bongeor of Colchester, glazier, of the age of sixty years; Tho. Benold of Colchester, tallow-chandler; W. Purcas of Bocking, fuller, a young man of twenty years; Agnes Silverside, dwelling in Colchester, widow, of the age of sixty years; Helene Ewring, wife of John Ewring, miller, dwelling in Colchester, of the age of five and forty years; who was one of the two and twenty prisoners mentioned before, sent up from Colchester to London, and after being delivered with the rest repaired home to her husband. Notwithstanding she enjoyed her liberty not very long; for shortly after her return met with her Robert Maynard, Bailiff of Colchester, who spying her came to her and kissed her, and bade her welcome home. She said that it was but a Judas kiss. 'For,' quoth she, 'I know you will betray me.' As indeed it came to pass, for immediately after that talk she was apprehended by him again and lodged with the rest in the Mote Hall. The sixth of the company was Elizabeth Folkes, a servant in Colchester of the age of twenty years.

Divers examinations these good men had at sundry times before divers justices, priests, and officers, whereof John Boswell, priest, made relation to Bishop Boner, as is to be read in our first book of *Acts and Monuments.* Last of all they were examined in Mote Hall the 23rd of July by Dr Chadsey in the presence of the two bailiffs, Robert Browne and Robert Maynard, with other justices and gentlemen a great sort. Before the said persons they had sentence of condemnation read against them. Dr Chadsey wept, that the tears trickled down his cheeks. Maynard the bailiff commonly when he sat in judgment upon life and death would sit sleeping on the bench: so careful was his mind on his office. Thus these poor lambs being delivered into the hands of the secular power were committed again into the prison from whence they came, where they remained with much joy, ever looking and expecting the happy day of their dissolution.

The 2nd of August 1557 was brought from Mote Hall unto a plot of ground hard by the town wall of Colchester William Bongeor, William Purcas, Thomas Benold, Agnes Silverside, Helene Ewring, and Elizabeth Folkes; which being there and all things prepared for their martyrdom, these constant martyrs kneeled down and made their humble prayers to God. When they had made their prayers they rose and made them ready to the fire. When all six were nailed at their stakes and the fire about them, they clapped their hands for joy in the fire, that the standersby, by estimation thousands, cried, 'The Lord strengthen them; the Lord comfort them; the Lord pour his mercies on them'; with suchlike words, as was wonderful to hear. Thus yielded they up their souls and bodies into the Lord's hands for the testimony of his truth.

In the afternoon was brought forth into the castle yard William Mount, John Johnson, Alice Mount, and Rose Allin; which after they had made their prayers and were joyfully tied to the stakes, calling upon God and exhorting the people earnestly to flee from idolatry, suffered their martyrdom with such triumph and joy that the people did no less shout to see it than at the other that were burnt the same day in the morning.

Thus ended all these glorious ten souls that day their happy lives unto the Lord.

The death of Joyce Lewes at Lichfield

Mrs Joyce Lewes, a gentlewoman born, was delicately brought up in the pleasures of the world, having delight in gay apparel and suchlike foolishness, with which follies the most part of the gentlefolk of

England were then and are yet infected; who was married first to one Appleby and afterward to Thomas Lewes of Manceter. In the beginning of Queen Mary's time she went to church and heard mass as others did; but when she heard of the burning of Laurence Sanders, who suffered in Coventry, she began to take more heed to the matter, and enquired earnestly of such as she knew feared God the cause of his death. When she perceived it was because he refused to receive the mass, she began to be troubled in conscience and waxed very unquiet. And because her house was hard by John Glover's, of whom mention was made before, she did oftentimes resort to him, and desired him to tell her the faults that were in the mass and other things urged as necessary to salvation. He perceiving her unquiet mind and the desire she had to know the truth did most diligently instruct her in the ways of the Lord, approving unto her out of God's holy word that the mass with all other Papistical inventions was odious in God's sight; and besides this reproved her for that she delighted in the vanities of the world so much. By which counsel it happened that she began to wax weary of the world, sorrowful for her sins, inflamed with the love of God, desirous to serve him according to his word, purposing also to be free from those things which did displease the Lord. And because she had learned the mass to be evil, she began to hate it. When she was compelled by the furiousness of her husband to come to church, at the time when the holy water was cast she turned her back towards it and showed herself displeased with their blasphemous holy water, injurious to the blood of Christ. Whereupon she was accused before the bishop for the despising of their sacramentals.

Immediately a citation was sent for her to her husband's house, to appear before the bishop incontinently. The sumner that brought the citation delivered it to her husband, who looking upon it and perceiving what it was was moved with anger, willing the sumner to take the citation with him again or he would make him eat it. The sumner refused to take it, for he thought no man durst have been so bold to trouble him; but in the end Lewes compelled the sumner to eat the citation indeed, by setting a dagger to his heart; and when he had eaten it he caused him to drink to it and so sent him away. But immediately after Lewes with his wife were commanded to appear before the bishop, where Lewes by and by submitted himself, and desiring the bishop to be good to him excused himself after the best fashion he could. The bishop was content, with condition that his wife should submit herself also. But she stoutly told the bishop that by refusing the holy water she had neither offended God not any part of his laws. The bishop, grievously offended, because she was a gentlewoman gave her one month's respite, binding her husband in an hundred pound to bring her again unto him at the month's end; and so they were both let go.

When the month was now almost expired, her husband, being advertised by Glover and others not to carry her to the bishop but to seek some ways to save her, or if the worst should come to forfeit so much money rather than cast his own wife into the fire, answered he would not forfeit anything for her sake. And so, like a murderer of his own wife, he carried her to the bloody bishop, where she was examined and found more stout than she was before death was threatened. To begin withal, she was sent to such a stinking prison that a maid appointed to keep her company did swoon in the prison. Being oftentimes examined and ever found stout, at length she was brought in judgment and pronounced an heretic worthy to be burnt. When the bishop reasoned with her why she would not come to mass and receive the sacraments and sacramentals of Holy Church, she answered, 'Because I find not these things in God's word.' The bishop answered, 'If thou wilt believe no more than is in the Scripture concerning matters of religion thou art in a damnable case.' At the which words she was wonderfully amazed, and moved by the Spirit of God told the bishop that his words were ungodly and wicked.

After her condemnation she continued a whole twelvemonth in prison, because she was committed to the sheriff that was of late chosen, who could not be compelled to put her to death in his time; for which after her death he was in danger of his life. All that time she was in prison, her behaviour was such both in words and deeds that all they that had a spark of godliness or civil honesty did greatly lament that she should be put to death.

In the evening before the day of her suffering two of the priests of the Close of Lichfield came to the undersheriff's house where she lay, and sent word that they were come to hear her confession; for they would be sorry she should die without. She sent them word again she had made her confession to Christ her Saviour, at whose hands she was sure to have forgiveness of her sins. Concerning the cause for which she should die, she had no cause to confess that, but rather to give God most humble praise that he did make her worthy to suffer death for his word: concerning that absolution that they were able to give unto her, being authorized by the Pope, she did defy the same from the bottom of her heart. Which when the priests heard, they said to the sheriff, 'Well, tomorrow her stoutness will be proved and tried; for although perhaps she hath now some friends that whisper in her ears, tomorrow we will see who dare be so hardy as to come near her.' So they went their ways with anger that their absolution was nought set by.

All that night she was wonderfully cheerful and merry, with a certain gravity, insomuch that the majesty of the Spirit of God did manifestly appear in her, who did expel the fear of death out of her heart; spending the time in prayer, reading, and talking with them that were come unto her to comfort her. About three o'clock in the morning Satan (who never sleepeth, especially when death is at hand) began to stir himself busily, shooting at her that fiery dart which he is wont to do against all that are at defiance with him, questioning how she could tell that she was chosen to eternal life and that Christ died for her: 'I grant that he died; but that he died for thee how canst thou tell?' With this suggestion when she was troubled, they that were about her did counsel her to follow the example of Paul, where he saith, 'which hath loved me and given himself for me.' Also that her calling to the knowledge of God's word was a manifest token of God's love towards her, especially that Holy Spirit working in her heart, that love and desire towards God to please him and to be justified by him through Christ. By these and like persuasions Satan was put to flight, and she comforted in Christ.

About eight o'clock Mr Sheriff came into her chamber saying these words: 'Mrs Lewes, I am come to bring you tidings of the queen's pleasure, which is that you shall live but one hour longer; therefore prepare yourself thereunto.' At which words, so grossly uttered and so suddenly by such an officer, she was somewhat abashed. Wherefore one of her friends standing by said, 'Mrs Lewes, you have great cause to praise God, who wil vouchsafe so speedily to take you out of this world and make you a witness of his truth.' After which she said, 'Mr Sheriff, your message is welcome: I thank God he will make me worthy to adventure my life in his quarrel.' Thus Mr Sheriff departed, and within one hour he came again *cum gladiis & fustibus*.

She was brought through the town with a number of billmen, a great multitude of people being present, she being led by two of her friends, Mr Michael Reniger and Mr Augustine Bernher, to the place of execution. And because the place was far off and the throng of people great, and she not acquainted with fresh air, being so long in prison, one of her friends sent to the sheriff's house for some drink. She prayed there several times, in which prayer she desired God to abolish the idolatrous mass and deliver the realm from Papistry—at which most of the people cried Amen; yea, even the sheriff that stood hard by her, ready to cast her in the fire for not allowing the mass, said Amen. When she had thus prayed she took the cup into her hands saying, 'I drink to all them that love the gospel of Jesus Christ and wish for the abolishment of Papistry.' When she had drunk, her friends drank also. After that a great number, specially women, did drink with her; which afterward were put to open penance by the cruel Papists.

When she was tied to the stake she showed such cheerfulness that it passed men's reason, being so well coloured in her face and so patient that most of them that had honest hearts did lament, and with tears bewail the tyranny of the Papists. When the fire was set upon her she neither struggled nor stirred, but only lifted up her hands towards heaven, being dead very speedily; for the undersheriff at the request of her friends had provided such stuff by which she was suddenly dispatched out of this miserable world. The Papists had appointed some to revile her as she went to the place of execution and when she was at the stake. There was an old priest which had a pair of writing tables, to note the names of the women that drank of her cup, and also described her friends by their apparel and afterwards enquired for their names. So immediately after process was sent out for them to Coventry and other places. But God did defend them from the hands of these cruel tyrants.

Cicely Ormes burnt at Norwich

About the 23rd of September suffered at Norwich Cicely, wife of Edmund Ormes, worsted-weaver, dwelling in St Laurence parish in Norwich. She being of the age of thirty-two years or more was taken at the death of Simon Miller and Elizabeth Cooper in Lollards' Pit without Bishop's Gate, for that she said she would pledge them of the same cup that they drank on. For so saying one Corbet of Sprowston by Norwich took her and sent her to Chancellor Dunning. When she came before him he asked her what she said unto the sacrament of Christ's body: she said she did believe it was the sacrament of the body of Christ. 'Yea,' said the chancellor, 'but what is it that the priest holdeth over his head?' She answered, 'It is bread; and if you make it any better it is worse.' At which words the chancellor sent her to the bishop's prison, to the keeper called Fellow, with many threatening words, as a man in a great chafe.

The 23rd of July she was called before the chancellor again, who offered her, if she would go to church and keep her tongue, she should be at liberty and believe as she would. But she told him she would not consent to his wicked desire, do with her what he would: if she should, God would surely plague her. The chancellor told her he had showed more favour to her than ever he did to any, and that he was loth to condemn her, considering that she was an ignorant and foolish woman. But she, not weighing his words, told him if he did he should not be so desirous of her sinful flesh as she would be content to give it in so good a quarrel. Then rose he and read the bloody sentence of condemnation against her, and delivered her to the sheriffs of the city, Thomas and Leonard Sutherton, brethren, who immediately carried her to the Guild Hall, where she remained until her death.

Cicely was a very simple woman, but zealous in the Lord's cause, born in East Deram, the daughter of Thomas Haund, tailor. She was taken the 5th of July, and did for a twelvemonth before she was taken recant; but never after was she quiet in conscience until she was utterly driven from all their popery. Between the time that she recanted and that she was taken, she had gotten a letter made to give to the chancellor, to let him know that she repented her recantation from the bottom of her heart, and would never do the like again while she lived; but before she exhibited her bill she was taken and sent to prison, as is before said. She was burnt the 23rd of September between seven and eight o'clock in the morning, the two sheriffs being there, and people to the number of two hundred. When she came to the stake, she kneeled down and made her prayers to God. Then she laid her hand on the stake and said, 'Welcome the cross of Christ.' Which done, she, looking on her hand and seeing it blacked with the stake, wiped it upon her smock, for she was burnt at the same stake that Simon Miller and Elizabeth Cooper was burnt at. Then she kissed it and gave herself to be bound thereto. After the tormentors had kindled the fire, she said, 'My soul doth magnify the Lord, and my spirit rejoiceth in God my Saviour.' So saying she set her hands together against her breast, casting eyes and head upward; and so stood, heaving up her hands by little and little, till the sinews of her arms did brast asunder, and then they fell.

But she yielded her life unto the Lord as quietly as she had been in a slumber, or as one feeling no pain; so wonderfully did the Lord work with her: his name be praised for evermore.

Three constant witnesses of Christ

Not long after were three faithful witnesses of the Lord's Testament put to death in Smithfield, the 18th of November in the year aforesaid, whose names hereafter follow—John Hallingdale, William Sparrow, Richard Gibson. Which three were produced before Boner the 5th of November 1557, and had certain articles ministered unto them, unto all which articles John Hallingdale made answer, confessing them all. After which examination John was sent unto prison again. The next day he was called before the bishop again, who persuading him with some wrested sentences of the Scripture, John answered, 'Because I will not come to your Babylonical church, therefore you go about to condemn me.' And being of Boner further demanded whether he would stand in his opinions or no, he made answer that he would persist in them unto the death. Then Boner read the bloody sentence of condemnation; at which John affirmed openly that (thanking God) he never came into the church since the abomination came into it. So he was sent to prison again.

The same day also was produced before the bishop William Sparrow; and being charged with his submission made the year before unto the bishop he answered, 'I am sorry that ever I made it: it was the worst deed that ever I did.' Then being demanded what ground of learning he had to cleave to his opinions, he said that all the laws now used (meaning ecclesiastical laws) are naught and abominable; and the mass naught and abominable. Which words being spoken, the bishop immediately read sentence of condemnation upon him and delivered him to the secular power, by whom he was sent to prison again.

With the other two suffered also Richard Gibson, who first was cast into the Counter in the Poultry, where he had been prisoner two years for suretyship in a matter of debt, and then stood upon his deliverance, then upon suspicion was accused to Boner, for that in prison he was never confessed nor received at the popish altar; by reason whereof he was called for, and sustained divers conflicts and examinations in the cause of his religion. Notwithstanding he continued in the Counter from May to November, at what time he was again produced unto the final examination judiciary. Where is to be noted that Gibson, being a very big and tall man of a personable and heroical stature, was sent for of Boner by a little and short person, a promoter, like Robin Papist, called Robin Caley, if it were not he himself.

This Robin Caley, having the conducting of the said gentleman from the Poultry, would needs hale him through Cheapside, the gentleman desiring him to turn some other way. But the more the gentleman entreated, the more fierce was this silly jack upon him; and holding him by the arm would needs hale him through the high street, that all the world might see what he could do in his office. Gibson desirous to be led without holding entreated him to let his arm loose: he would go quietly with him whither he would, only craving that he might go freely without noting of the people. The saucy and impotent miser the promoter, scarce able to reach unto his shoulders, 'Nay,' saith he, 'thou shalt not escape me so; come on thy ways; thou shalt not choose but come'; and so reaching at his arm would needs drag him unto the bishop. The gentleman gently requested again and again that refraining his hold he would suffer him to go of his own free will: he should not need to fear him, for he would not start from him. The caitiff looking up to his face, 'Come on thy way,' saith he; 'I will hold thee fast, spite of thy beard and whether thou wilt or no.' Gibson seeing the intolerable bragging of the wretched miser could bear no longer, but said, 'Wilt thou?' and added that if he did not incontinently pluck away his hand, he would wring his neck from his body. Whereupon Robin Papist was fain to pluck away his hold, and so proceeded they unto the bishop, there to be examined again before him.

He was assigned the Saturday following to be present in the consistory court to hear his final sentence. The examinate appearing as he was commanded, the bishop asked him if he knew any cause why the sentence should not be read against him. Gibson answered that the bishop had nothing whereof justly to condemn him. The bishop again objected to him that men said he was an evil man. To whom Gibson replying, 'Yea,' saith he, 'and so may I say of you also.' After this and such other talk the bishop hasted unto the sentence; which being read, Gibson, again admonished to remember himself and save his soul, said that he would not hear the bishop's babbling. 'Blessed,' said he, 'am I that am cursed at your hands.' Thus this valiant soldier, fighting for Christ's truth and religion against falsehood and error, was committed to the secular power.

And so these three men, Hallingdale, Sparrow, and Gibson, were the day after their condemnation (the 18th of November) burnt in Smithfield. Being brought to the stake, after their prayer made they were bound thereunto with chains, and wood set unto them; and after wood, fire; in which they compassed about, and the flames consuming their flesh, at last they yielded gloriously and joyfully their souls and lives into the holy hands of the Lord.

John Rough and Margaret Mearing burned at London

In this furious time of persecution were also burned these two martyrs, John Rough, a minister, and Margaret Mearing. Rough was born in Scotland, who because some of his kinsfolk would have kept him from his right of inheritance to certain lands, did at seventeen years in despite profess himself into the order of Black Friars at Sterling, where he remained sixteen years until Lord Hamilton, Earl of Arren and governor of the realm of Scotland, casting a favour unto him, did sue unto the Archbishop of St Andrew's to have him out of his professed order, that as a secular priest he might serve him for his chaplain. At which request the archbishop caused the provincial of that house to dispense with him for his habit and order. This suit being thus by the earl obtained, Rough remained in his service one whole year, during which it pleased God to open his eyes and give him some knowledge of the truth; and thereupon was sent by the governor to preach in the freedom of Ayre, where he continued four years. Then after the death of the cardinal of Scotland he was appointed to abide at St Andrew's, and had assigned unto him a yearly pension of twenty pound from Henry the Eighth of England. Howbeit at last, weighing his own danger and abhorring the idolatry of his country, and hearing of the freedom of the gospel within this realm of England, he determined not to tarry any longer there; and soon after the battle of Musselburgh he came first unto Carlile, and from thence unto the Duke of Somerset, the Lord Protector of England; and by his assignment had appointed unto him out of the king's treasury twenty pounds of yearly stipend, and was sent as a preacher to serve at Carlile, Barwicke, and Newcastle; from whence, after he had there according to the laws of this realm taken a countrywoman of his to wife, he was called by the Archbishop of York unto a benefice in Hull, where he continued until the death of King Edward.

But in the beginning of the reign of Queen Mary he fled with his wife into Frieseland and dwelt at a place called Norden, labouring for his living in knitting of caps, hose, and suchlike things till the end of October before his death. Lacking yarn and other necessary provision for the maintenance of his occupation he came over into England to provide for the same, and the 10th of November arrived at London; where hearing of the secret society and holy congregation of God's children there assembled he joined himself unto them, and afterwards being elected their minister did continue in that godly fellowship, confirming them in the truth of the gospel. But the 12th of December he with Cutbert Simson and others, through the traitorous suggestion of a false hypocrite and dissembling brother called Roger Sergeant, a tailor, was apprehended by the vice-chamberlain of the queen's house at the Saracen's Head in Islington, where the congregation had then purposed to assemble themselves to their accustomable exercises of prayer and hearing the word of God: which pretence for the safeguard of all the rest they at their examinations covered and excused by hearing of a play that was then appointed to be at that place. The vice-chamberlain after he had apprehended them carried Rough and Simson unto the Council, who charged them to have assembled together to celebrate the Communion or Supper of the Lord. After sundry examinations and answers they sent Rough unto Newgate; but his examinations they sent unto the Bishop of London with a letter signed with their hands.

Boner minding to make quick dispatch did three days after the receipt of the letter (the 18th of December) send for Rough, and in his palace ministered unto him twelve articles. The next day he was again brought before the bishop and others, who when they perceived his constantness determined the next day to bring him openly into the consistory, there to condemn him as an heretic. Which purpose they accomplished; for the 20th at afternoon, in the presence of the Bishops of London and St David's, with Fecknam Abbot of Westminster and others, he was there produced. After many persuasions Boner read unto him the articles before mentioned, in which they charged him to have received the orders of the Church, and therefore might not marry, and that he had refused to consent unto the Latin service then used in the Church. He answered that their orders were nothing at all, and that he being a priest might lawfully marry, and that his children were lawful. As touching the service then used, he detested it: if he should live as long as Methuselah, he would never come to church to hear the abominable mass as it was then. Upon which the bishop proceeded to the actual degradation of Rough, exempting him from all benefits and privileges of their church; and after condemning him as an heretic committed his body to the secular power, who carried him unto Newgate.

Moreover as touching Mr Rough this is further to be noted, that being before Boner he affirmed that he had been twice at Rome, and had seen plainly with his eyes that the Pope was the very Antichrist; for he saw him carried on men's shoulders and the false-named sacrament borne before him; yet was there more reverence given to him than to that which they counted to be their god. When Boner heard this, rising up and making as though he would have torn his garments, 'Hast thou,' said he, 'been at Rome and seen our Holy Father, and dost thou blaspheme him after this sort?' And with that flying upon him he plucked off a piece of his beard; and after, making speedy haste to his death, he burnt him half an hour before six in the morning, because the day, belike, should not be far spent before he had done a mischievous deed.

In the company of John Rough was burnt Margaret Mearing, who, as the register maketh mention, was at one time and day brought with Rough to examination; where the bishop, having no private matters to charge her withal, did the 18th of December object against her those accustomable answers mentioned before. They were again propounded against her the 20th of December; and being demanded if she would stand unto her answers, she said, 'I will stand to them unto the death, for the very angels of heaven laugh you to scorn, to see your abomination that you use in church.' After which words the bishop pronounced sentence against her; and delivering her unto the sheriffs, she was with Rough carried unto Newgate; whence they were together led into Smithfield, and there most joyfully gave their lives for Christ's gospel.

Anno 1558

The cruel torments of Cutbert Simson

Next after the martyrdom of Mr Rough, minister of the congregation, succeeded in like martyrdom the deacon of that godly company, Cutbert Simson, committed to the fire the year of our Lord 1558, the 28th of March. Cutbert was a man of a faithful and zealous heart to Christ and his flock, insomuch that he never ceased labouring and studying, not only how to preserve them without corruption of the

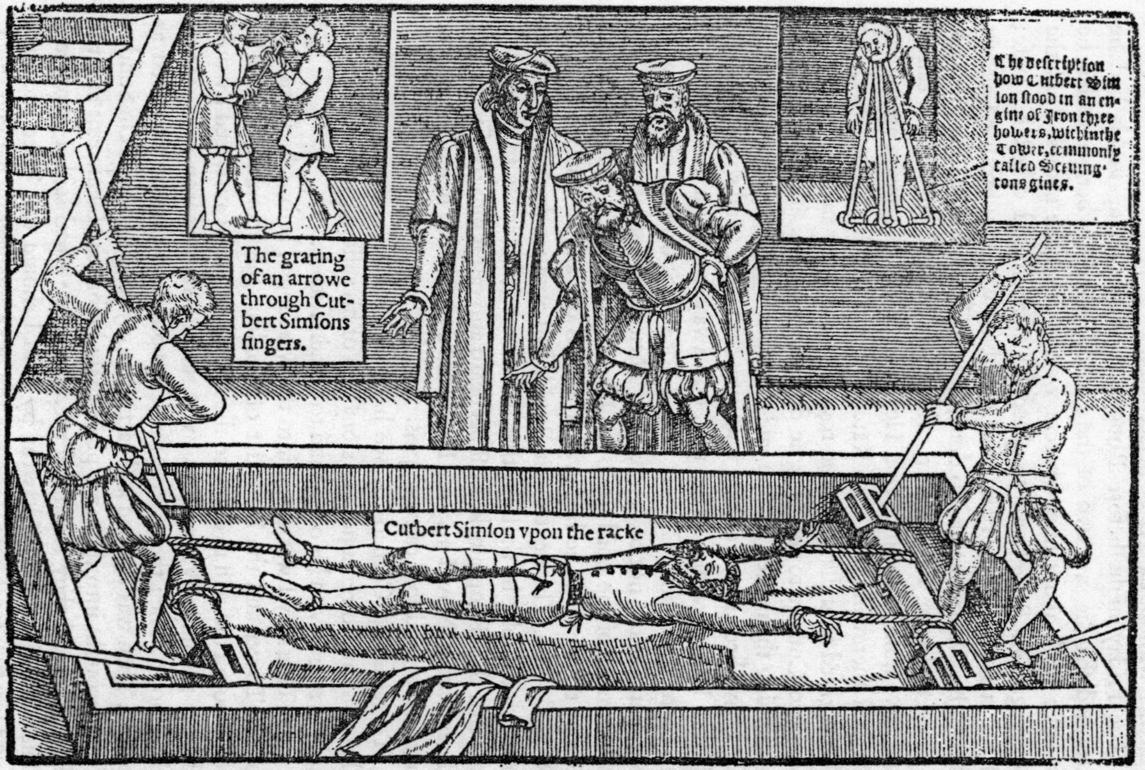

‘A true description of the racking and cruell handeling of Cutbert Simson in the Tower.’

popish religion; but also his care was ever vigilant to keep them together without danger of persecution.

The Friday night before Rough was taken, being in his bed he dreamed that he saw two of the guard leading Cutbert, and that he had the book about him wherein were written the names of all the congregation. Being sore troubled he awaked and called his wife: 'Kate, strike light, for I am much troubled with my brother Cutbert this night.' When she had so done, he gave himself to read in his book awhile, and then, feeling sleep come upon him, he put out the candle and gave himself again to rest. He dreamed the like dream again, and awaked therewith said, 'Oh Kate, my brother Cutbert is gone!' So they lighted a candle again and rose. As Rough was making him ready to go to Cutbert to see how he did, Cutbert came in with the book containing the names. Rough said, 'Brother Cutbert, ye are welcome; for I have been sore troubled with you this night'; and so told him his dream. He willed him to lay the book away from him and to carry it no more about him. Cutbert would not so do: dreams, he said, were but fantasies and not to be credited. Then Rough straitly charged him in the name of the Lord to do it. Whereupon Cutbert took such notes out of the book as he had willed him to do, and left the book with Rough's wife. The next night Rough had another dream concerning his own trouble; he thought that he was carried forcibly to the bishop and that the bishop plucked off his beard and cast it into the fire, saying these words: 'Now I may say I have had a piece of an heretic burned in my house'; and so it came to pass.

To return to Cutbert: as we have touched something concerning these visions, so remaineth to story also of his sufferings upon the rack, as he wrote it with his own hand to certain friends.

'On Thursday I was called into the warehouse, before the Constable of the Tower and the Recorder of London: they commanded me to tell whom I did will to come to the English service. I answered I would declare nothing. Whereupon I was set in a rack of iron the space of three hours. Then they asked me if I would tell them. I answered as before. Then was I loosed and carried to my lodging again. On Sunday I was brought into the same place again before the Lieutenant and the Recorder, and they examined me. As before I had said, I answered. Then the Lieutenant did swear by God I should tell. Then did they bind my two forefingers together and put a small arrow betwixt them, and drew it through so fast that the blood followed and the arrow brake. Then they racked me twice. Then was I carried to my lodging again, and ten days after the Lieutenant asked me if I would not confess that which they had asked me. I said I had said as much as I would. Five weeks after he sent me unto the High Priest, where I was greatly assaulted, and at whose hand I received the Pope's curse for bearing witness of the resurrection of Jesus Christ. And thus I commend you unto God. I praise God for his great mercy. Sing "Osanna unto the Highest" with me Cutbert Simson.'

The day before Simson, after his racking, should go before Boner to be burned, being in the bishop's coalhouse in the stocks, he had a vision very strange, which he himself declared to Mr Austen, to his own wife and Thomas Simson, and to others besides, in Newgate a little before his death; the relation whereof I stand in doubt whether to report, considering the diversity of men's judgments in the reading of histories. Some will not believe it; some will deride the same. Albeit it is no good argument, proceeding from the particular to the universal, to say that visions be not true in some, *ergo* they be true in none. This only which hath out of the man's own mouth been received, as I received it of the parties, I thought here to communicate to the reader, for him to judge thereof as God shall rule his mind.

The day before Simson was condemned, he being in the stocks, Cloney his keeper cometh in with the keys about nine o'clock at night to see whether all were present; who when he espied Cutbert departed, locking the doors after him. About eleven o'clock Cutbert (whether in a slumber or awake I cannot say) heard one coming in, first opening the outward door, then the second, after the third, and looking in to Cutbert, having no candle or torch that he could see, but giving a brightness and light most comfortable to his heart, saying, 'Ah,' and departed again. This that he saw he himself declared four or five times to Austen and other; at the sight whereof he received such joyful comfort that he also expressed no little solace in telling the same.

With Cutbert likewise were apprehended Hugh Foxe and John Devenish; who being brought before Boner the 19th of March had articles and interrogatories to them ministered. First to Cutbert several articles were propounded; then other articles in general were ministered to them altogether. These three, Cutbert, Foxe, and Devenish, as they were together apprehended at Islington, so all three together suffered in Smithfield, about the 28th of March, in whose perfect constancy the same Lord in whose cause they suffered be exalted for ever.

William Seaman, Thomas Carman, and Thomas Hudson

Three men at Norwich in Norfolk were cruelly put to death for the testimony of Jesus Christ the 19th of May 1558.

William Seaman was an husbandman of thirty-six years, dwelling in Mendlesham in Suffolk, who was sundry times sought for by commandment of Sir John Tyrrell: at last he himself in the night searched his house and other places for him; notwithstanding he missed of his purpose. Then he gave charge to his servants, Robert Baulding and James Clarke, to seek him; who went in the evening to his house, where he being at home, they took him and carried him to their master. Baulding, being Seaman's nigh neighbour and special friend, to do his master a favour became enemy to his chief friend and was one of the busiest in the taking of him. Now as they were going to carry him to their master, it is reported that there fell a light between them out of the element and parted them. Baulding, being in company with the rest, and albeit he was then in his best age, yet after that time never enjoyed good day, but pined away even to death.

Well, for all that strange sight they carried him to their master, who asked him why he would not go to mass, and receive the sacrament and worship it. William said it was an idol, and therefore would not receive it. Tyrrell sent him to Norwich to Hopton, and there, after examination had the bishop read his bloody sentence of condemnation and delivered him to the secular power, who kept him unto the day of martyrdom. Seaman left behind him a wife, and three children very young; with the children his wife was persecuted out of Mendlesham because she would not go to hear mass; and all her corn and goods were seized by Christopher Cole's officers, he being Lord of the town.

Thomas Carman (who pledged Richard Crashfield at his burning and thereupon was apprehended) being prisoner in Norwich was examined and brought before the bishop; who answered no less in his Master's cause than the other, and had the like reward, the bishop's bloody blessing of condemnation; and delivered also to the secular power, who kept him with the other until the day of slaughter, which was not long after.

Thomas Hudson was of Aylesham in Norfolk, a glover, a very honest poor man, having a wife and three children, and laboured diligently in his vocation, being of thirty years of age; and bearing so good a will to the gospel that he, two years before Mary's reign, learned to read English, wherein he greatly profited about the time of alteration of religion. For when Queen Mary had changed the service in church, putting in for wheat draff and darnel, and for good preaching blasphemous crying out against truth and godliness, he, avoiding their ceremonies of superstition, absented himself from his house and went into Suffolk a long time, travelling from one place to another as occasion was offered. At last he returned to his house at Aylesham to comfort his wife and children, being heavy and troubled with his absence. When he came home and perceived his continuance there would be dangerous, he and his wife devised to make him a place among his faggots to hide himself in, where he remained all day reading and praying for half a year, and his wife like an honest woman used herself faithfully and diligently towards him.

In the meantime came the vicar of the town, one of the bishop's commissioners named Berry, a very evil man, and enquired of Thomas's wife for her husband; unto whom she answered as not knowing where he was. Berry rated her and threatened to burn her for that she would not bewray her husband. When Hudson understood it, he waxed every day more zealous, and continually read and sang psalms, to the wonder of many, the people openly resorting to him to hear his exhortations and vehement prayers. At last he walked abroad for certain days openly in the town, crying out against the mass and all their trumpery. Then John Crouch, his next neighbour, went to the constables in the night to certify them thereof; for Berry commanded to watch for him; and the constables went to catch him in the break of day, the 22nd of April 1558. When Hudson saw them, he said, 'Welcome, friends. You be they that shall lead me to life in Christ. The Lord enable me thereto for his mercy's sake.' For ever he prayed that he might suffer for the gospel of Christ.

They led him to Berry, which asked him first where he kept his church for four years before: Hudson answered thus—wheresoever he was, there was the Church.

'The sacrament of the altar: what is it?'

'It is worm's meat: my belief is Christ crucified.'

'Dost thou not believe the mass to put away sins?'

'God forbid. It is a patched monster and a disguised puppet.'

'Thou villain, thou! I will write to the bishop my Lord and thou shalt be handled according to thy deserts.'

'Sir, there is no Lord but God.'

With that Berry thrust him back with his hand. One Richard Cliffar, standing by, said, 'I pray you, sir, be good to the poor man.' At which Berry was more mad than before, and would have had Cliffar bound in a recognizance of forty pounds for his good abearing. Then he asked Hudson whether he would recant. Hudson said, 'The Lord forbid. I had rather die many deaths than do so.' After long talk Berry, seeing it booted not to persuade with him, took pen and ink and wrote to the bishop, and sent Hudson to Norwich bound like a thief to him, which was eight miles from thence, who with joy and singing-cheer went thither, as merry as ever he were before. In prison he was a month, where he did continually read and invocate God.

These three, Seaman, Carman, and Hudson, after they were condemned, the 19th of May were carried out of prison to the place without Bishop's Gate in Norwich called Lollards' Pit, and there made their humble petitions unto the Lord. That done, they rose and went to the stake; and standing there with their chains about them, Hudson cometh forth from them under the chain, to the wonder of many: divers feared and doubted of him. Some thought he would have recanted; others judged that he went to ask further day; some thought he came forth to ask his parents' blessing. His two companions at the stake cried out to comfort him, exhorting him in the bowels of Christ to be of good cheer. But Hudson felt more in his heart and conscience than they could conceive in him; for alas, good soul! he was compassed with grief, not for his death, but for lack of feeling of his Christ; and therefore he fell upon his knees, and prayed earnestly unto the Lord, who at the last sent him comfort; then rose he with great joy, as a man new changed from death to life, and said, 'Now, I thank God, I am strong, and pass not what man can do unto me.' So going to the stake to his fellows again, they all suffered most joyfully and manfully together and were consumed in fire, to the terror of the wicked, the comfort of God's children, and the magnifying of the Lord's name.

After this Berry made great stir about other which were suspected within Aylesham, and caused two hundred to creep to the cross at Pentecost, besides the punishments which they sustained. On a time Berry gave a poor man of his parish of Marsham a blow with the swingle of a flail, that presently thereon he died; and Berry held up his hand at the bar therefore. In his parish of Aylesham also, *anno* 1557, one Alice Oxes came to his house, and going into the hall, he meeting her smote her with his fist, whereby she was fain to be carried home, and the next day was found dead in her chamber. To write how many concubines and whores he had, none would believe it but such as knew him in the country where he dwelt. He was rich and of great authority, a great swearer, altogether given to women.

When he heard that Queen Mary was dead, the Sunday after, the 19th of November 1558, he made a great feast, and had one of his concubines there, with whom he was in his chamber after dinner until evensong. Then went he to church, where he ministered baptism, and in going homeward, between the churchyard and his house he fell down suddenly to the ground with a heavy groan, and never stirred after, neither showed one token of repentance.

Three burnt at Colchester

Thou hast heard, good reader, of the three that were burnt at Norwich; whose blood quenched not the thirst of the Papists; for the same month, upon the 26th, was seen the like murder at Colchester of two men and a woman lying there in prison; who were brought forth the same day and gave their lives for the testimony of the truth, whose names followeth—William Harries, Richard Day, Christian George. These three good souls were brought unto the stake, and there joyfully made their prayers unto the Lord. Being settled in their places and chained unto their posts, with the fire flaming fiercely about them they triumphantly praised God, and offered up their bodies a lively sacrifice unto his holy Majesty; in whose house they now have their everlasting tabernacles.

Christian George's husband had another wife burnt before, Agnes, which suffered as you heard with the thirteen at Stratford the Bowe. After the death of Christian, he married again; and both Richard George and his last wife in the end were taken also and laid in prison, where they remained till the death of Queen Mary, and at last were delivered by our most gracious sovereign Lady, Queen Elizabeth, whom the Lord grant long to reign among us for his mercies' sake.

Thirteen condemned by Boner

Secretly in a back close in the field by the town of Islington were assembled a company of innocent persons to the number of forty, men and women, who there sitting together at prayer and occupied in the meditation of God's word, first cometh a certain man to them unknown; who looking over unto them stayed and saluted them, saying that they looked like men that meant no hurt. One of the company asked the man if he could tell whose close that was, and whether they might be so bold there to sit. 'Yea,' said he, and so departed. Within a quarter of an hour cometh the constable of Islington named King, warded with six or seven other accompanying him in the same business, one with a bow, another with a bill, and other with their weapons likewise. The which persons the constable left a little behind him in a close place, there to be ready if need should be, while he with one with him should go and view them before. Who so doing came through them, looking what they were doing and what books they had; and going a little forward and returning back bade them deliver their books. They understanding that he was the constable refused not so to do. With that cometh forth the residue of his fellows, who bade them stand and not depart. They answered they would go whithersoever they would have them; so were they carried to a brewhouse but a little way off, while some of the soldiers ran to the justice next at hand. The justice was not at home; whereupon they were had to Sir Roger Cholmley. Meantime some of the women escaped, some in the close, some before they came to the brewhouse. For so they were carried, ten with one man, eight with another, in such sort as it was not hard for them to escape that would. In fine, they that were carried to Sir Roger were twenty-seven; Sir Roger and the recorder taking their names in a bill and calling them one by one, so many as answered to their names they sent to Newgate. The number of them that were sent was twenty-two. These were in Newgate seven weeks before they were examined, to whom word was sent by Alexander the keeper that if they would hear a mass they should all be delivered. Of these twenty-two were burnt thirteen; in Smithfield seven, at Brainford six. In prison two died in Whitsun week; seven escaped with their lives although not without much trouble.

The first seven were produced before Boner the 14th of June, to answer such articles and interrogatories as should be ministered unto them. The bishop, dissevering them apart from one another, proceeded with them severally, beginning with Reinald Eastland, who being required to reconcile himself to the Catholic Faith and go from his opinions said that he knew nothing why he should recant, and would not conform himself. So sentence was read, and he given to the secular power. After him was called in John Holiday, who, likewise being advertised to renounce his heresies and return to the unity of their church, said that he was no heretic. Whereupon sentence was pronounced, condemning him to be burnt. Next was condemned with a like sentence Henry Pond, because he would not submit to the Romish Church, saying to Boner that he had done or spoken nothing whereof he was or would be sorry. Next followed John Floyd, who likewise denied to be of the Pope's church and said his mind of the Latin service, that the prayers made to saints is idolatry, and that the service in Latin is profitable to none but such as understand Latin. Being charged by Boner of heresy he was condemned with the same butcherly sentence, and so by the secular power was sent away. Then Robert Southam, after him Mathew Ricarby, last of all Roger Holland, were produced. Roger with his fellows standing to their answers and refusing to acknowledge the doctrine of the Romish Church, were altogether condemned; and all seven, sent to Newgate the 17th of June, about the 27th were had to Smithfield and there ended their lives in the glorious cause of Christ's gospel.

After this day there was never none that suffered in Smithfield for the testimony of the gospel, God be thanked.

The martyrdom of six at Brainford

Not long after the death of the forenamed seven that suffered in Smithfield, were six other witnesses of the Lord's Testament martyred at Brainford, seven miles from London, the 14th of July; which six were of that company that were apprehended in a close hard by Islington and sent to prison, whose names followeth—Robert Milles, Stephen Cotton, Robert Dymes, Stephen Wight, John Slade, William Pikes, a tanner. These had their articles ministered to them by Thomas Darbyshire, Boner's chancellor, at sundry times. In the end the chancellor commanded them to appear before them again the 11th of July at Paul's. When they came he required of them whether they would turn from their opinions to Holy Church: if not, whether there were any cause to the contrary, but that they might proceed with the sentence of condemnation. They all answered that they would not go from the truth while they lived. Then he charged them to appear before him again the next afternoon between one and two o'clock to hear the definitive sentence read. At which time he sitting in judgment, talking with these men, at last came Sir Edward Hastings and Sir Thomas

Cornewales, two of Queen Mary's officers of her house, and sat them down over against the chancellor, in whose presence the chancellor condemned those poor men and delivered them to the secular power, who carried them to prison and kept them there till the day of their death.

Meantime this naughty chancellor slept not, I warrant you, but that day in which they were condemned made certificate unto the Lord Chancellor's office, from whence the next day was sent a writ to burn them at Brainford, which was accomplished the 14th of July; whereunto they being brought made their humble prayers unto the Lord Jesus, undressed themselves, went joyfully to the stake, and fire flaming about them they yielded their souls, bodies, and lives into the hands of the omnipotent Lord, to whose protection I commend thee, gentle reader. Amen.

Carnificis nomen debetur iure Bonero,
Qui sine Christicolas crimine mactat oves.
Certe carnificis immiti nomine gaudet,
Sique isto peius nomine nomen, amat.
Carnificem vocitas? ridet. Crudelia facta
Narras? rem gratam non facit ipse magis.
Det Deus ut sapias meliora, Bonere, vel istis
Te feriant meritis munera digna precor.

The scourging of Thomas Hinshaw

In the number above mentioned which were apprehended at Islington, there congregated together for their exercise of prayer and reading, was this Thomas Hinshaw above named, a young man of the age of nineteen or twenty years, prentice in Paul's Churchyard, who with the rest was carried to the constables of Islington, and there every one of them searched and led forthwith to Chief Justice Cholmley, dwelling in the Old Baily. By him Thomas was sent to Newgate, and there remaining prisoner without conference with any about eight weeks at last was sent to Boner, and by him, Harpsfield, and Cole, examined. After which he was sent to Newgate again, where he remained three weeks. Which time being overpassed, he was sent for again before the bishop and with him had much talk to little purpose. The next day, Sunday, they persuaded with him very much in like manner, and perceiving they could not bend him unto their bow, the bishop going unto Fulham

'The right picture and true counterfeit of Boner, and his crueltie, in scourging of Gods saints, in his Orchard at Fulham.'

took him with him, where he was set in the stocks, remaining there all the first night with bread and water. The next morning the bishop came and examined him, and perceiving no yielding sent Harpsfield to talk with him; who after long talk fell to raging words, calling Thomas 'peevish boy', and asked him whether he thought he went about to damn his soul. Thomas answered that he was persuaded that they laboured to maintain their dark and devilish kingdom, and not for any love to truth. Then Harpsfield in a mighty rage told the bishop thereof; whereat the bishop fumed and fretted, that scant for anger being able to speak he said, 'Dost thou answer my archdeacon so, thou naughty boy? I shall handle thee well enough, be assured.' So he sent for a couple of rods and caused him to kneel against a long bench in an arbour in his garden, where Thomas without any enforcement offered himself to the beating, and did abide the fury of Boner so long as the fat-paunched bishop could endure with breath, and till for weariness he was fain to cease, and give place to his shameful act. He had two willow rods, but he wasted but one and so left off.

After this scourging Hinshaw did sustain divers conflicts and examinations. At last being brought before the bishop in his chapel at Fulham, there he had procured witnesses and gathered articles against him, which the young man would not affirm, do what they could. Not long after this the foresaid examinate fell sick of a burning ague, whereby he was delivered upon entreaty unto his master Martin Pugson; for the bishop thought verily he was more like to die than to live. His sickness endured a twelvemonth or more, so that in the meantime Queen Mary died. He shortly after recovered health and escaped death, being at the writing of this yet alive, both witness and reporter of the same, the Lord be praised.

The scourging of John Milles by Bishop Boner

Besides the above named was scourged also by the hands of Boner one John Milles,[1] a capper, a right honest man in all his dealings, brother to R. Milles burnt before at Brainford; who also was apprehended with them at Islington, and being brought before Boner and examined was commanded to the coalhouse with Thomas Hinshaw, where they remained one night in the stocks. Thence he was sent to Fulham, where he with Hinshaw remained eight or ten days in the stocks, during which

[1] This name appears in some editions, though not consistently, as Willes. —Ed.

time he sustained divers conflicts with Boner, who had him oftentimes in examination, urging him, and with a stick oftentimes rapping him on the head, and flirting him under the chin and on the ears, saying he looked down like a thief. After he had assayed all ways to cause him to recant, and could not, at length having him to his orchard there within a little arbour with his own hands he beat him with a willow rod; and that being worn wellnigh to the stumps he called for a birchen rod, which a lad brought out of his chamber. The cause why he beat him was this. Boner asked him when he had crept to the cross. He answered, not since he came to the years of discretion, neither would to be torn with wild horses. Then Boner bade him make a cross in his forehead, which he refused to do. Whereupon he had him incontinently to his orchard, and there showeth his cruelty upon him as is above declared.

Shortly after this beating Boner sent to him in prison a certain old priest lately come from Rome, to conjure out the evil spirit from him; who laying his hand upon his head began with certain words pronounced over him to conjure as he had been wont before to do. Milles, marvelling what the priest was about to do, said he trusted no evil spirit to be within him, and laughed him to scorn.

As Milles was divers times and oft called before Boner, so much communication and talk passed between them, which to recite all, it were too long. Ofttimes he would say, 'They call me bloody Boner. A vengeance on you all! I would fain be rid of you, but you have a delight in burning. But if I might have my will, I would sew your mouths, and put you in sacks and drown you.'

Now somewhat to say concerning the deliverance of John Milles. The same day that he was delivered, Boner came unto the stocks where he lay and asked him how he liked his lodging. 'Well,' said Milles,' if it would please God I might have a little straw to lie or sit upon.' Then said Boner, 'Thou wilt show no token of a Christian man.' And upon this his wife came in unknowing unto him, being very great with child and looking every hour for her lying down, entreating the bishop for her husband and saying that she would not go out of the house, but there would lay her belly in the bishop's house unless she had her husband with her. 'How sayest thou,' quoth Boner, 'thou heretic? If thy wife miscarry or thy child should perish, the blood of them would be required at thy hands.' Then to this agreement he came, that she should hire a bed in the town of Fulham, and her husband should go home with her the morrow after, upon condition that his kinsman there present (one Rob. Rousse) should bring Milles unto his house at Paul's the next day. Milles said he would not agree except he might go home by and by. At length, seeing she would there remain unless she had her husband with her, the bishop, fearing belike the rumour which might come upon his house thereby, bade Milles make a cross and say, *In nomine Patris & Filii & Spiritus Sancti. Amen.* Then Milles began to say, 'In the name of the Father, and of the Son, and of the Holy Ghost. Amen' 'No, no,' saith Boner, 'Say it me in Latin, *In nomine Patris & Filii & Spiritus Sancti. Amen.*' Milles, understanding the matter of that Latin to be but good, said the same, and so went home with his wife, his kinsman being charged to bring him the next day unto Paul's; 'either else,' said Boner, 'if thou doest not bring him, thou art an heretic as well as he.' Notwithstanding this kinsman did not bring him; but he of his own voluntary accord came to the bishop a few days after, where the bishop put unto him a writing in Latin to subscribe unto, containing as it seemed to him no great matter that he needed greatly to stick at; albeit what the bill was he could not certainly tell; so subscribed he and returned home. And thus much concerning the twenty-two taken at Islington.

The scourging of Steven Cotton, James Harris, and Robert Williams

Steven Cotton, burnt at Brainford, testifieth himself to be twice beaten by Boner in a letter written to his brother: 'I pray you provide me with a long shirt against the day of our deliverance; for the shirt you gave me last I have given to one of my companions who had more need than I. As for the money and meat you sent us, the bishop's servants delivered none to us. There is none of them to trust to, for *qualis magister, talis servus.* I have been twice beaten, and threatened to be beaten again, by the bishop himself.'

In this society of the scourged professors of Christ was also James Harris of Billerica in Essex, a stripling of seventeen years; who being apprehended and sent up to Boner by Sir John Mordant and Edmund Tyrrell, was by Boner divers times straitly examined. He was charged not to have come to his parish church by the space of one year or more. Whereunto he granted, confessing therewithal that once for fear he had been at the church and had received the Popish sacrament; for the which he was heartily sorry. Boner, the better to try him, persuaded him to go to shrift. The lad consented; but when he came to the priest he stood still and said nothing. 'Why,' quoth the priest, 'sayest thou nothing?' 'What should I say?' 'Thou must confess thy sins.' 'My sins be so many that they cannot be numbered.' The priest told Boner what he had said; and he of his accustomed devotion took the poor lad into his garden, and there with a rod gathered out of a cherry tree did most cruelly whip him.

Besides these was one Robert Williams, who being apprehended in the same company was tormented after the like manner with rods in Boner's arbour; who yielding himself by promise to obey the laws, after being let go refused so to do; whereupon he was earnestly sought for, but could not be found, for that he went not abroad but by stealth. In the time of this persecution Robert departed this life and so escaped the hands of his enemies.

Boner causeth certain boys to be beaten

Forasmuch as I have begun to write of Boner's scourging, cometh to mind his beating of children. The story, although it touch no matter of religion, yet because it toucheth the nature and disposition of that man and may refresh the reader, wearied percase with doleful stories, I thought not to omit. Boner, passing from London to Fulham by barge, having Milles and Hinshaw above mentioned with him, both prisoners for religion, by the way as he went by water was saying evensong with Harpsfield his chaplain in the barge; and being about the middle of their orisons they espied a sort of young boys swimming and washing themselves in the Thames over against Lambeth. Unto whom he went, and gave very gentle language and fair speech until he had set his men a land. That done, his men ran after the boys to get them, as the bishop commanded them before, beating some with nettles, drawing some through bushes of nettles naked; and some they made leap into the Thames to save themselves, that it was marvel they were not drowned.

Now as the children for fear did cry, and as this skirmishing was between them, immediately came a greater lad thither to know what the matter meant, that the boys made such a noise; whom when the bishop espied, he asked him whether he would maintain them in their doings or no. The young fellow made answer stoutly, 'Yea.' Then the bishop commanded him to be taken also; but he ran away with speed, and avoided the bishop's blessing. When the bishop saw him flee, and another man sitting upon a rail in the way where he ran, he willed him to stop the boy; and because he would not, commanded his men to fetch that man to him. But he hearing that ran away as fast as he could, and by leaping over the ditch escaped the bishop in like manner. Then the bishop, seeing the success of his battle to prove no better, cried to a couple of ferry-boys to run and hold him that last ran away. And for that they said they could not (as indeed was true) he caused his men by and by to take and beat them. The boys, hearing that, leapt into the water to save themselves; notwithstanding they were caught, and in the water by the bishop's men were holden and beaten.

After the end of this great skirmish the men returned to their master into the barge, and he and Harpsfield went to their evensong where they left, and so said the rest of their service, as clean without malice as an egg without meat.

A lad eight years old scourged to death in Boner's house

If bloody torments and cruel death of a poor innocent, suffering for no cause of his own but in the truth of Christ, make a martyr, no less deserveth the child of one J. Fetty to be reputed in the catalogue of holy martyrs, who in the house of Bishop Boner unmercifully was scourged to death, as by the sequels of this story here following may appear.

Amongst those who were persecuted and imprisoned for the profession of Christ's gospel, and yet mercifully delivered by the providence of God, was John Fetty, a simple and godly poor man dwelling in the parish of Clerkenwell, a tailor of the age of forty-two years or thereabout, who was complained of to one Brokenbury, a priest and parson of the same parish, by his own wife, for that he would not come unto church and be partaker of their idolatry. Through the priest's procurement he was apprehended and carried unto Sir John Mordant, one of the queen's commissioners. He upon examination sent him by Cluny the bishop's sumner unto the Lollards' Tower, where he was put into the painful stocks, and had a dish of water set by him with a stone put into it: to what purpose God knoweth, except it were to show that he should look for little other sustenance.

After Fetty had lain in prison fifteen days, hanging in the stocks, sometime by one leg and one arm, sometime by the other, and otherwhiles by both, one of his children, a boy of eight or nine years, came unto the bishop's house to see if he could get leave to speak with his father. One of the bishop's chaplains met him and asked what he lacked and whom he would have. The child answered that he came to see his father. The chaplain asked who was his father. The boy told him, and pointing to the Lollards' Tower showed him that his father was there in prison. 'Why,' quoth the priest, 'thy father is an heretic.' The child being of a bold and quick spirit, and also instructed by his father in the knowledge of God, answered, 'My father is no heretic; you are an heretic, for you have Balam's mark!' With that the priest took the child by the hand and carried him into the bishop's house; and there amongst them they did most shamefully and without all pity so scourge being naked, this tender child that he was all in a gore blood; then, in a jolly brag of their Catholic tyranny, they caused Cluny to carry the child in his shirt unto his father in prison, the blood running down by his heels.

At his coming unto his father the child fell upon his knees and asked him blessing. The poor man, beholding his child and seeing him so cruelly arrayed, cried out for sorrow, 'Alas, Will! Who hath done this to thee?' The boy answered that as he was seeking to see his father a priest with Balam's mark took him into the bishop's house, and there was he so handled. Cluny therewith violently plucked the child out of his father's hands and carried him back into the bishop's house, where they kept him three days. At the three days' end Boner, to appease the poor man for this their horrible fact, determined to release him, and caused him early in a morning to be brought out of Lollards' Tower into his bedchamber, where he found the bishop basting himself against a great fire. Whilst Fetty was standing in the bishop's chamber, he espied a little crucifix. He asked the bishop what it was: he answered that it was Christ. 'Was he handled so cruelly as is here pictured?' 'Yes, that he was.' 'And even so cruelly will you handle such as come before you; you are unto God's people as Cayphas was to Christ.' The bishop in a great fury said, 'Thou vile heretic! I will burn thee, or else I will spend all that I have unto my gown.' 'Nay, my Lord,' said Fetty, 'ye were better to give it to some poor body that he may pray for you.'

Yet Boner, bethinking of the danger which the child was in by their whipping and what peril might ensue, thought better to discharge him, willing him to go home and carry his child with him; which he did with a heavy heart, to see his poor boy in such extreme pain. But within fourteen days the child died.

The story of John Alcocke

There was in Hadley a young man named John Alcocke, which came to Hadley seeking work, for he was a shearman by occupation. This young man after the martyrdom of Dr Taylor used in the church of Hadley to read the service in English, as is above touched.[1]

After the coming of Parson Newall, he, being in Hadley Church upon a Sunday, when the parson came by with procession, would not move his cap nor show any sign of reverence but stood behind the font. Newall, perceiving this, when he was almost out of the church door ran back and caught him, and called for the constable. Then came Robert Rolfe, with whom this young man wrought, and asked, 'Mr Parson, what hath he done that ye are in such a rage with him?' 'He is an heretic and a traitor,' quoth the parson, 'and despiseth the queen's proceedings. Wherefore I command you in the queen's name, have him to the stocks, and see he be forthcoming.' 'Well,' quoth Rolfe, 'he shall be forthcoming; proceed you in your business and be quiet.' 'Have him to the stocks,' quoth the parson, 'I am constable,' quoth Rolfe, 'and will bail him; he shall not come in the stocks but he shall be forthcoming.' So went the good parson forth with his holy procession, and so to mass.

At afternoon Rolfe said to this young man, 'I am sorry for thee; for the parson will seek thy destruction, if thou take not good heed what thou answerest him.' The young man answered, 'Sir, I am sorry that it is my luck to be a trouble to you. As for myself, I am not sorry, but I commit myself into God's hands, and I trust he will give me mouth and wisdom to answer according to right.' 'Well,' quoth Rolfe, 'beware of him; for he is malicious and a bloodsucker and beareth an old hatred against me; and he will handle you the more cruelly because of displeasure against me.' 'I fear not,' quoth the young man; 'he shall do no more to me than God will give him leave; and happy shall I be, if God will call me to die for his truth's sake.'

After this talk they went to the parson, who asked him, 'Fellow, what sayest thou to the sacrament of the altar?' 'I say,' quoth he, 'as ye use the matter ye make a shameful idol of it, and ye are false, idolatrous priests, all the sort of you.' 'I told you,' quoth the parson, 'he was a stout heretic.' So the parson committed him to ward, and the next day rode to London and carried the young man with him. So came the young man no more to Hadley, but after long imprisonment in Newgate—after many examinations and troubles, for that he would not ask forgiveness of the Pope and be reconciled to the Romish religion—he was cast into the lower dungeon, where with evil keeping and sickness

[1] Page 231

of the house he died in prison. Thus died he a martyr of Christ's verity which he heartily loved, and received the garland of a well foughten battle at the hand of the Lord. His body was cast out and buried in a dunghill; for the Papists would not so much as suffer the dead to have honest and convenient sepulture.

Three burned at Bury

Although our history hasteth apace (the Lord be praised) to the happy death of Queen Mary, yet she died not so soon but some were burnt before, and moe should have been burnt soon after them if God's provision had not prevented her with death. In the number of them which suffered in the month when Queen Mary died were three that were burned at Bury, whose names were these—Philip Humfrey, John David, Henry his brother. Concerning the burning of these three, here is to be noted that Sir Clement Higham, about a fortnight before the queen died, did sue out a writ for the burning of these blessed martyrs, notwithstanding that the queen was known to be past remedy.

Five Christians which suffered the last in the time of Queen Mary

The last that suffered in Queen Mary's time were five at Canturbury, burned about six days before the death of Queen Mary, whose names follow—John Corneford of Wortham, Christopher Browne of Maidstone, John Herst of Ashford, Alice Snoth, Katherine Knight, an aged woman. These five (to close up the final rage of Queen Mary's persecution) for the testimony of that word for which so many had died before, gave up their lives meekly and patiently, suffering the violent malice of the Papists; which Papists, although they then might have either spared them or else deferred their death, knowing of the sickness of Queen Mary; yet such was the implacable despite of that generation that some say the Archdeacon of Canturbury, being at London and understanding the danger of the queen, made all post haste home to dispatch those whom he had then in his cruel custody.

The matter why they were judged to the fire was this: for believing the body not to be in the sacrament of the altar unless it be received; that it is idolatry to creep to the cross; that we should not pray to our Lady and other saints. For these and other such articles of Christian doctrine were these five committed to the fire. Against whom when the sentence should be read and they excommunicate, one of them, John Corneford, stirred with a vehement spirit of the zeal of God, proceeding in a more true excommunication against the Papists, in the name of them all pronounced sentence against them in these words: 'In the name of our Lord Jesus Christ, the Son of the most mighty God, and by the power of the Holy Spirit, and the authority of his Holy Catholic and Apostolic Church, we do here give into the hands of Satan to be destroyed the bodies of all those blasphemers and heretics that do maintain any error against his most holy word, or do condemn his most holy truth for heresy, to the maintenance of any false church or feigned religion; so that by this thy most just judgment, O most mighty God, against thy adversaries, thy true religion may be known, to thy glory and our comfort and to the edifying of all our nation. Amen.'

This sentence of excommunication, openly pronounced and registered, took such effect against the enemy that six days after, Queen Mary died, and the tyranny of English Papists with her. Albeit notwithstanding the sickness of that queen, whereof they were not ignorant, the archdeacon, with others of Canturbury, thought to dispatch the martyrdom of these men before. In which fact the tyranny of this archdeacon seemeth to exceed the cruelty of Boner; who, notwithstanding he had certain the same time under his custody, yet was not so importune in haling them to the fire, as appeareth by Father Living and his wife, and divers others, who being under the custody of Boner, delivered by the death of Queen Mary, remain yet some of them alive.

These martyrs, in their prayers which they made before their martyrdom, desired God that their blood might be the last that should be shed, and so it was.

CHAPTER II

THE LADY ELIZABETH

The miraculous preservation of Lady Elizabeth

But when all hath been said and told, whatsoever can be recited touching the admirable working of God's hand in defending and delivering any one person out of thraldom, never was there any example wherein the Lord's mighty power hath more admirably and blessedly showed itself, to the glory of his own name, the comfort of all good hearts, and the felicity of this whole realm, than in the miraculous custody and outscape of this our sovereign Lady, now Queen, then Lady Elizabeth, in the strait time of Queen Mary her sister. We have first to consider in what extreme misery, sickness, fear, and peril her Highness was; into what care, what trouble of mind, and what danger of death she was brought, first with great routs and bands of armed men being fetched up as the greatest traitor in the world, clapped in the Tower, and again tossed from thence, and from house to house, from prison to prison, from post to pillar, and guarded with a sort of cut-throats which ever gaped for the spoil. Secondly to consider we have how strangely, or rather miraculously, from danger she was delivered, what favour she found with the Almighty; who, when all help of man and hope of delivery was past, stretched out his mighty protection and preserved her Highness, and placed her in this princely seat wherein now she sitteth; and long may she sit, the Lord of his glorious mercy grant, we beseech him.

If I should set forth at large all the particulars and circumstances as just occasion of the history requireth, beside the importunate length of the story peradventure it might move offence to some yet alive, and truth might get me hatred. Yet notwithstanding I intend by the grace of Christ therein to use such brevity and moderation as may be to the glory of God, the discharge of the story, the profit of the reader, and hurt to none; suppressing the names of some, whom although I could recite, I thought not to be more cruel in hurting their names than the queen hath been merciful in pardoning their lives.

Therefore, to enter into the discourse of this tragical matter, first is to be noted that Queen Mary, when she was first queen, would go no whither but would have her by the hand and send for her to dinner and supper; but after she was crowned she never dined or supped with her but kept her aloof from her. After this, immediately upon the rising of Sir Thomas Wyat, Lady Elizabeth and Lord Courtney were charged with false suspicion of Wyat's rising. Whereupon Queen Mary, whether for that surmise or for what other cause I know not, being offended with her sister, at that time lying in her house at Ashridge, the day after the rising sent three of her Councillors, Sir Richard Southwell, Sir Edward Hastings, Master of the Horse, and Sir Thomas Cornewalles, with their retinue and troop of horsemen, to the number of 250; who at their sudden coming found her sore sick in her bed and very weak. Whither when they came, ascending up to her privy chamber, they willed one of her ladies to declare unto her that there were certain come from Court, which had a message from the queen.

Her Grace, having knowledge thereof, was right glad of their coming; howbeit being very sick and the night far spent (which was ten o'clock) she requested by the messenger that they would resort thither in the morning. To this they answered and by the said messenger sent word again that they must needs see her, and would do so in what case soever she were. The lady, aghast, went to show her Grace their words; but they, hastily following her, came rushing into her Grace's chamber unbidden. Her Grace, not a little amazed, said, 'Is the haste such that it might not have pleased you to come tomorrow morning?' They made answer that they were right sorry to see her in that case. 'And I,' quoth she, 'am not glad to see you here at this time of night.' They answered that they came from the queen: the queen's pleasure was that she should be at London the 7th day of that month. Whereunto she said, 'Certes no creature more glad than I to come to her Majesty, being right sorry that I am not in case at this time to wait on her, as you yourselves can testify.' 'Indeed we see it true,' quoth they; 'for which we are very sorry. Albeit we let you to understand that our commission is such that we must needs bring you with us, quick or dead.' In conclusion, they willed her to prepare against the next morning at nine o'clock to go with them, declaring that they had brought the queen's litter for her. After much talk, the messengers, declaring how there was no prolonging of times and days, so departed to their chamber, being entertained as appertained to their worships.

The next morrow they had her forth as she was, very faint and feeble, and in such case that she was ready to swound. What should I speak here, that cannot well be expressed, what an heavy house there was to behold the unreverent and doleful dealing of these men, but especially the fear and captivity of their innocent mistress. From Ashridge, all sick in the litter, she came to Redborne, where she was guarded all night; thence to St Albon's, to Sir Rafe Rowlet's house, where she tarried that night both feeble in body and comfortless in mind. From that place they passed to Mr Dod's house at Mymmes, where they remained that night; and so she came to Highgate, where she, being very sick, tarried that night and the next day; during which time came many pursuivants and messengers from the Court, for what purpose I cannot tell. From that place she was conveyed to the Court, where by the way came to meet her many gentlemen, which were very sorry to see her in that case. A great multitude of people were standing by the way, who flocking about her litter lamented and bewailed her estate. When she came to the Court, her Grace was straightways shut up and kept as close prisoner a fortnight, seeing neither king nor queen, lord nor friend, all that time, but only the Lord Chamberlain, Sir John Gate, and the vice-chamberlain, which were attendant unto the doors.

The Friday before Palm Sunday, the Bishop of Winchester with nineteen other of the Council (who shall be nameless) came unto her Grace from the queen's Majesty and burdened her with Wyat's conspiracy, which she utterly denied. They, not contented with this, charged her Grace with business made by Sir Peter Carew, and the rest of the gentlemen of the west country; which also she utterly denying cleared her innocency therein. After long debating they declared unto her that it was the queen's pleasure that she should go unto the Tower, while the matter were further examined. She, aghast, said that she trusted the queen's Majesty would be more gracious lady unto her, and would not otherwise conceive of her but that she was a true woman, declaring furthermore that she was innocent in all those matters wherein they had burdened her, and desired them to be a mean to the queen her sister, that she, a true woman in thought, word, and deed towards her Majesty, might not be committed to so notorious a place; protesting that she would request no mercy at her hand, if she should prove to have consented unto any such kind of matter as they laid unto her charge; and, in fine, desired their Lordships to think of her what she was. The lords answered that there was no remedy, for that the queen was fully determined that she should go unto the Tower; wherewith the lords departed with their caps hanging over their eyes.

Within an hour came four of the lords, the Lord Treasurer, the Bishop of Winchester, the Lord Steward, the Earl of Sussex, with the guard; who warding the next chamber to her secluded all her gentlemen and yeomen, ladies and gentlewomen; saving that for one gentleman-usher, three gentlewomen, and two grooms of her chamber, were appointed in their rooms three men of the queen's, and three waiting women to give attendance upon her, that none should have access to her. At which time there were a hundred northern soldiers in white coats, watching and warding about the garden all that night, a great fire being made in the midst of the hall and two lords watching there also with their band.

Upon Saturday following two lords of the Council—one was the Earl of Sussex, the other shall be nameless—came and certified her Grace that forthwith she must go unto the Tower, the barge being prepared and the tide now ready, which tarrieth for nobody. In heavy mood her Grace requested the lords that she might tarry another tide, trusting that the next would be more comfortable. But one of the lords replied that neither time not tide was to be delayed. When her Grace requested that she might be suffered to write to the queen, he answered that he durst not permit that; adding that in his judgment it would rather hurt than profit her Grace. But the other lord, the Earl of Sussex, kneeling down told her that she should have liberty to write, and as he was a true man he would deliver it to the queen and bring an answer, whatsoever came thereof. Whereupon she wrote, albeit she could in no case be suffered to speak with the queen.

Thus time and tide passed away for that season, they privily appointing all things ready that she should go the next tide, which fell about midnight; but for fear she should be taken by the way they durst not. So they stayed till the next day, Palm Sunday, when about nine o'clock these two returned, declaring that it was time for her Grace to depart, she answering, 'If there be no remedy, I must be contented,' willing the lords to go on before. Being come forth into the garden she did cast her eyes towards the window, thinking to have seen the queen, which she could not; whereat she said she marvelled what the nobility meant, which in that sort would suffer her to be led into captivity, the Lord knew whither. Meantime commandment was given in all London that everyone should keep the church and carry their palms, while in the mean season she might be conveyed without recourse of people into the Tower.

After this she took her barge with the two lords, three of the queen's gentlewomen and three of her own, her gentleman-usher, and two of her grooms, hovering upon the water a space for that they could not shoot the bridge, the bargemen being very unwilling to shoot the same so soon as they bid because of the danger; for the stern of the boat stroke upon ground, the fall was so big; and the water was so shallow that the boat being under the bridge there stayed again. At landing she first stayed, and denied to land at those stairs where all traitors and offenders used to land; neither well could she unless she should go over her shoe. The lords were gone out of the boat before and asked why she came not. One of the lords went back again to her, and brought word she would not come. Then said one of the lords, which shall be nameless, that she should not choose; and because it did rain he offered her his cloak, which she, putting it back with her hand with a good dash, refused. So she coming out, having one foot upon the stair said, 'Here landeth as true a subject as ever landed at these stairs; before thee, O God, I speak it, having no friends but thee alone.' To whom the same lord answered that if it were so it was the better for her.

At her landing there was a great multitude of their servants and warders standing in their order. 'What needed all this?' said she. 'It is the use,' said some, 'so to be when any prisoner came thither.' 'And if it be,' quoth she, 'for my cause, I beseech you that they may be dismissed.' Whereat the poor men kneeled down and with one voice desired God to preserve her Grace—who the next day were released of their cold coats. Passing a little further she sat down upon a cold stone and rested herself. To whom the Lieutenant said, 'Madam, you were best to come out of the rain; for you sit unwholesomely.' She answered again, 'Better sitting here than in a worse place; for I know not whither you will bring me.' With that her gentleman-usher wept. But forth she went into the prison. The doors were locked and bolted upon her; which did not a little discomfort and dismay her Grace. At what time she called to her gentlewoman for her book, desiring God not to let her build her foundation upon the sands but upon the rock, whereby all blasts of blustering weather should have no power against her.

The doors being thus locked and she close shut up, the lords had great conference how to keep ward and watch, every man declaring his opinion in that behalf, agreeing straitly and circumspectly to keep her. Then one of them, which was Lord Sussex, swearing said, 'My lords, let us take heed and do no more than our commission will bear us, whatsoever shall happen hereafter. And further let us consider that she was the king our master's daughter, and therefore let us use such dealing that we may answer unto it hereafter, if it shall so happen; for just dealing is always answerable.' Whereunto the other lords agreed that it was well said of him, and thereupon departed.

Within two days commandment was that she should have mass within her house. One Mr Yong was then her chaplain; and because there was none of her men so well learned to help the priest to say mass, the mass stayed for that day. The next day two of her yeomen, who had gone long to school before and were learned, had two A B C's provided and delivered them, so that upon the A B C's they should help the priest. One of the said yeomen, holding the A B C in his hand, pretending ignorance at *Kyrie eleison*, set the priest, making as though he could answer that no farther.

It would make a pitiful and strange story to recite what examination and rackings of poor men there were, to find that knife that should cut her throat; what gaping among my lords of the clergy, to see the day wherein they might wash their white rochets in her innocent blood; especially the Bishop of Winchester, Stephen Gardiner, then Lord Chancellor, ruler of the roost, who five days after came unto her with other of the Council, and examined her of the talk that was at Ashridge betwixt her and Sir James Acroft concerning her removing thence to Dunnington Castle, requiring her to declare what she meant thereby. To enforce the matter they brought forth Sir James. Winchester demanded of her what she said to that man. She answered that she had little to say to him, or to the rest that were prisoners in the Tower. 'But, my Lords,' quoth she, 'you examine every mean prisoner of me, wherein you do me great injury. If they have offended the queen's Majesty, let them answer accordingly. I beseech you, join not me with any of these offenders. As concerning my going unto Dunnington Castle, I remember that Mr Hobby and Sir James Acroft had such talk; but what is that to the purpose, my Lords, but that I may go to mine own houses at all times?'

That day or thereabouts divers of her own officers, who had made provision for her diet, brought the same to the utter gate of the Tower, the common rascal soldiers receiving it; which was no small grief unto the gentlemen, the bringers thereof. Wherefore they required to speak with the Lord Chamberlain, then Constable of the Tower; who coming before his presence declared that they were afraid to bring her Grace's diet and deliver it unto such common and desperate persons as did receive it, beseeching his Honour to consider her Grace and give such order that her viands might at all times be brought in by them which were appointed thereunto. 'Yea, sirs,' saith he, 'who appointed you this office?' They answered, 'Her Grace's council.' 'Council?' quoth he; 'there is none of them which hath to do in that case or anything else within this place. And I assure you, for that she is a prisoner, she shall be served with the Lieutenant's men as other the prisoners are.' Whereat the gentlemen said they trusted for more favour at his hands, considering her personage: they mistrusted not but that the queen and her Council would be better to her Grace than so; and therewith showed themselves to be offended at the ungrateful words of the Lord Chamberlain towards their lady and mistress. At this he sware by God, striking himself upon the breast, that if they did frown or shrug at him he would set them where they should see neither sun nor moon. Thus taking their leave they desired God to bring him into a better mind.

Upon the occasion whereof her Grace's officers made great suit unto the queen's Council that some might be appointed to bring her diet unto her, and that it might no more be delivered unto common soldiers; which was by them granted. Thereupon were appointed one of her gentlemen, her clerk of the kitchen, and her two purveyors, to bring in her provision once a day; all which was done, the warders ever waiting upon the bringers therefore. The Lord Chamberlain himself watched and searched what they brought, and gave heed that they should have no talk with any of her Grace's waiting servants; and so warded them both in and out. At the suit of her officers were sent by commandment of the Council to wait upon her two yeomen of her chamber, one of her robes, two of her pantry and ewery, one of her buttery, another of her cellar, two of her kitchen and one of her larder; all which continued with her the time of her trouble.

The Constable, not well pleased with the coming in of such a company against his will, would have had his men still to have served with her Grace's men; which her servants at no hand would suffer, desiring his lordship to be contented, for that order was taken that no stranger should come within their offices. At which answer sore displeased he brake out into these threatening words, 'Well, I will handle you well enough.' Then went he into the kitchen, and there would needs have his meat roasted with her Grace's meat, and said that his cook should come thither and dress it. To that her Grace's cook answered, 'I will never suffer any stranger to come about her diet but her own sworn men so long as I live.' He said they should. But the cook said his Lordship should pardon him for that matter. Thus did he trouble her poor servants, though afterward he were otherwise advised and they more courteously used. And good cause why. For he had good cheer and fared of the best, and her Grace paid well for it. Wherefore he used himself afterward more reverently toward her Grace.

Having lien a whole month there in close prison and being very evil at ease therewithal, she sent for the Lord Chamberlain and Lord Shandoys to come and speak with her. Who coming, she requested them that she might have liberty to walk in some place, for that she felt herself not well. To the which they answered that they were right sorry that they could not satisfy her Grace's request, for that they had commandment to the contrary which they durst not break. Furthermore she desired of them if that could not be granted, that she might walk but into the queen's lodging. 'No, nor yet that,' they answered, 'could by any means be obtained without a further suit to the queen and her Council.' 'Well,' said she, 'if the matter be so hard that they must be sued unto for so small a thing and that friendship be so strict, God comfort me.' And so they departed, she remaining in her old dungeon still without any kind of comfort but only God.

The next day Lord Shandoys came again unto her Grace, declaring that he had sued unto the Council for further liberty. Some of them consented thereunto, divers others dissented, for that there were so many prisoners in the Tower. But in conclusion they did all agree that her Grace might walk into those lodgings, so that he and the Lord Chamberlain and three of the queen's gentlewomen did accompany her, the windows being shut and she not suffered to look out at any of them. Wherewith she contented herself, and gave him thanks for his good will in that behalf. Afterwards there was liberty granted unto her Grace to walk in a little garden, the doors and gates being shut up, which was as much discomfort unto her as the walk in the garden was pleasant and acceptable. At which times of her walking there the prisoners on that side straitly were commanded not to speak or look out of the windows into the garden till her Grace were gone out again, their keepers waiting upon them for that time.

During this time there used a little boy, a man's child in the Tower, to resort to their chambers and many times bring her Grace flowers, which likewise he did to the other prisoners that were there. Whereupon suspicious heads, thinking to wring out some matter thereof, called the child unto them, promising him figs and apples, and asked him when he had been with the Earl of Devonshire, not ignorant of the child's wonted frequenting unto him. The boy answered that he would go by and by thither. Further they demanded of him when he was with the Lady Elizabeth. He answered, 'Every day.' Furthermore they examined him what the Lord of Devonshire sent by him to her Grace. The child said, 'I will go know what he will give to carry to her.' Such was the discretion of the child, being yet but four years of age. 'This same is a crafty boy,' quoth the Lord Chamberlain; 'how say you, my Lord Shandoys?' 'I pray you, my Lord,' quoth the boy, 'give me the figs you promised me.' 'No, marry,' quoth he, 'thou shalt be whipped if thou come any more to the Lady Elizabeth or the Lord Courtney.' The boy answered, 'I will bring my lady my mistress more flowers.' Whereupon the child's father was commanded to permit the boy no more to come up into their chambers.

The next day, as her Grace was walking in the garden, the child peeping in at a hole in the door cried unto her, 'Mistress, I can bring you no more flowers.' She smiled but said nothing, understanding what they had done. Wherefore afterwards the Chamberlain rebuked highly his father, commanding him to put him out of the house. 'Alas, poor infant,' quoth the father. 'It is a crafty knave,' quoth the Lord Chamberlain; 'let me see him here no more.'

The 5th of May the Constable was discharged of his office of the Tower, and one Sir Henry Benifield placed in his room, a man unknown to her Grace and therefore the more feared; which so sudden mutation was unto her no little amaze. He brought with him an hundred soldiers in blue coats, wherewith she was marvellously discomforted; and demanded of such as were about her whether Lady Jane's scaffold were taken away or no; fearing lest she should have played her part. Answer was made that the scaffold was taken away, and her Grace needed not to doubt of any such tyranny; for God would not suffer any such treason against her person. Wherewith being contented but not altogether satisfied, she asked who Sir Henry Benifield was, and whether he was of that conscience that if her murdering were secretly committed to his charge he would see the execution thereof.

She was answered that they were ignorant what manner of man he was; howbeit they persuaded her that God would not suffer such wickedness to proceed. 'Well,' quoth she, 'God grant it be so.'

About which time it was spread abroad that her Grace should be carried thence by this new jolly captain and his soldiers; but whither, it could not be learned. Which was unto her a great grief, especially for that such a company was appointed to be her guard, requiring rather to continue there than to be led thence with such a sort of rascals. At last plain answer was made by Lord Shandoys that there was no remedy, but from thence she must needs depart to the Manor of Woodstock. Being demanded of her for what cause, 'For that,' quoth he, 'the Tower is like further to be furnished.'

On Trinity Sunday the 19th of May she was removed from the Tower, the Lord Treasurer being there for the lading of her carts. Sir Henry Benifield being appointed her gaoler did receive her, with a company of rake-hells to guard her, besides Lord Darby's band, waiting in the country about for the moonshine in the water. At length came Lord Tame, joined in commission with Sir Henry for the safe guiding of her to prison, and they together conveyed her to Woodstock, as hereafter followeth. The first day they conducted her to Richmond, where she continued all night, restrained of her own men, which were lodged in outchambers, and Sir Henry's soldiers appointed in their rooms to give attendance on her person. Whereat she being dismayed, thinking some secret mischief to be a working towards her, called her gentleman-usher and desired him with the rest of his company to pray for her; 'For this night,' quoth she, 'I think to die.' Wherewith he being stricken to the heart said, 'God forbid that any such wickedness should be pretended against your Grace.' So comforting her as well as he could, at last he brast into tears, and went from her down into the court, where were walking Lord Tame and Sir Henry.

Then he coming to Lord Tame, who had proffered him much friendship, desired to speak with him a word or two. Unto whom he said he should with all his heart. Which when Sir Henry, standing by, heard, he asked what the matter was. The gentleman-usher answered, 'No great matter, sir, but to speak with my Lord a word or two.' Then, when Lord Tame came to him, 'My Lord,' quoth he, 'you have been always my good lord, and so I beseech you to remain. I come to you at this time to desire your Honour unfeignedly to declare unto me whether any danger is meant towards my mistress this night; that I and my poor fellows may take such part as shall please God to appoint; for we will rather die than she should innocently miscarry.' 'Marry,' said Lord Tame, 'God forbid that any such wicked purpose should be wrought; and rather than it should be so, I with my men are ready to die at her foot also.' And so they passed that doleful night, with no little heaviness of heart.

Afterwards passing over the water at Richmond, going towards Windsor, her Grace espied certain of her poor servants standing on the other side, which were very desirous to see her. Whom when she beheld, turning to one of her men standing by she said, 'Yonder I see certain of my men: go to them and say these words from me: *tanquam ovis*.' So she passing forward to Windsor was lodged that night in the dean's house, a place more meet for a priest than a princess. From thence her Grace was brought the next night to Mr Dormer's house, where much people standing by the way, some presented to her one gift, some another, so that Sir Henry was greatly moved, and troubled the poor people very sore for showing their loving hearts in such a manner, calling them rebels and traitors. Besides, as she passed through the villages the townsmen rang the bells as being joyful of her coming, thinking it had been otherwise than it was, as the sequels proved to the poor men. For immediately Sir Henry sent his soldiers, who apprehended some of the ringers, setting them in the stocks, and otherwise misusing other some, for their good wills.

On the morrow her Grace, passing from Mr Dormer's, where was a strait watch kept, came to Lord Tame's house, where she lay all night, being very princely entertained of knights and ladies, gentlemen and gentlewomen. Whereat Sir Henry grunted and was highly offended, saying unto them that they could not tell what they did; letting them to understand that she was the queen's prisoner; advising them therefore to take heed and beware of after-claps. Lord Tame answered that he was well advised of his doings, being joined in commission as well as he, adding with warrant that her Grace might and should in his house be merry. The next day, as she should take her journey from Richmond towards Woodstock, Lord Tame with another gentleman being at tables, playing and dropping vie crowns, Lady Elizabeth passing by stayed and said she would see the game played out, which Sir Henry would scarce permit. The game running long about, 'Come on,' saith he. 'I will tarry,' saith she, 'and will see this game out.'

After this Sir Henry went up into a chamber where was appointed for her Grace a chair, two cushions, and a foot-carpet very fair and princelike; wherein presumptuously he sat, and called one Barwick, his man, to pull off his boots. Which as soon as it was known among the ladies and gentles, everyone mused thereat and laughed him to scorn, observing his undiscreet manners in that behalf, as they might very well.

The next day her Grace took her journey from thence to Woodstock, where she was enclosed, as before in the Tower of London, the soldiers warding both within and without the walls every day to the number of threescore, and in the night without the walls forty, during the time of her imprisonment there. At length she had gardens appointed for her walk; but always when she did recreate herself therein the doors were locked in as strait a manner as in the Tower, being at least five or six locks between her lodging and her walks; Sir Henry himself keeping the keys and trusting no man therewith. Whereupon she called him her gaoler, and he kneeling down desired her not to call him so, for he was appointed there to be one of her officers. 'From such officers,' quoth she, 'good Lord deliver me.'

Occasion here moveth me to touch briefly what happened in the same place and time by a certain merry-conceited man, being then about her Grace; who noting the strait keeping of his mistress by Sir Henry, with so many locks and doors, with such watch and ward about her as was strange and wonderful, spied a goat in the ward where her Grace was; and whether to refresh her oppressed mind, or to notify her strait handling by Sir Henry, or both, he took it upon his neck, and followed her Grace therewith as she was going into her lodging. Which when she saw, she asked him what he would do with it, willing him to let it alone. Unto whom the party answered, 'No, by St Mary (if it like your Grace) will I not; for I cannot tell whether he be one of the queen's friends or no. I will carry him to Sir Henry Benifield to know what he is.' So leaving her Grace he went with the goat on his neck and carried it to Sir Henry, who when he saw him coming with it asked him half angerly what he had there. 'Sir,' quoth he, 'I cannot tell what he is. I pray you examine him, for I found him in the place where my lady was walking, and what talk they have had I cannot tell; for I understand him not. He should seem to me to be some stranger, I think a Welchman, for he hath a white frieze coat on his back, And forsomuch as I, being the queen's subject, and perceiving the strait charge committed unto you, of her keeping, that no stranger should have access to her without sufficient licence, I have here found a stranger (what he is I cannot tell) in the place where her Grace was walking; and therefore, for the necessary discharge of my duty, I thought it good to bring the stranger to you, to examine as you see cause.' And so he set him down. At which words Sir Henry seemed much displeased.

About the 8th of June came Dr Owen and Dr Wendy, sent by the queen to her Grace, for that she was sickly; who, ministering to her and letting her blood, attended on her five or six days. Then, she being amended, they returned to the Court, making their good report to the queen and the Council of her Grace's behaviour and humbleness towards the queen's Highness; which her Majesty took very thankfully; but the bishops repined, looked black in the mouth, and told the queen they marvelled that she submitted not herself to her Majesty's mercy, considering that she had offended her Highness.

About this time her Grace was requested by a secret friend to submit herself unto the queen. She answered that she would never submit herself to them whom she never offended. 'For if I am guilty, I crave no mercy but the law; which I am certain I should have had ere this if it could be proved by me. For I know myself to be out of danger thereof, wishing that I were as clear out of the peril of my enemies; and then I am assured I should not be so locked and bolted up within walls and doors as I am. God give them a better mind when it pleaseth him.'

About this time there was a great consulting among the bishops and gentlemen touching a marriage for her Grace, which some of the Spaniards wished to be with some stranger, that she might go out of the realm with her portion. A lord who shall be nameless said that the king should never have any quiet commonwealth in England unless her head were stricken from her shoulders. The Spaniards answered, God forbid that their king should consent to such a mischief. From that day the Spaniards never left off their good persuasions to the king that the like honour he should never obtain as he should by delivering Lady Elizabeth out of prison; whereby at length she was happily released from the same. Here is a plain and evident example of the good clemency and nature of the king and his counsellors toward her Grace. She was sent for shortly after to come to Hampton Court.

But before her removing from Woodstock we will a little stay to declare what dangers her life was in during this time she there remained; first through fire, which began to kindle between the boards and ceiling under the chamber where she lay, whether by a spark gotten into a cranny, or whether of purpose by some that meant her no good, the Lord doth know. Nevertheless a knight of Oxfordshire, joined with Sir Henry in keeping that lady (who then took up the boards and quenched the fire) supposed it to be done of purpose. Furthermore it is affirmed of one Paul Peny, a keeper of Woodstock, a notorious ruffian, that he was appointed to kill Lady Elizabeth; who both saw the man and also knew thereof. Another time one of the privy chamber, a great man about the queen and chief darling of Stephen Gardiner, named James Bassett, came to Blandenbridge a mile from Woodstock, with twenty or thirty privy coats, and sent for Sir Henry to come and speak with him. But it happened that a little before Sir Henry was sent for by post to the Council, leaving strait word behind him with his brother that no man, whatsoever he were, though coming with a bill of the queen's hand or any other warrant, should have access to her before his return. By reason whereof it fell out that Benifield's brother, coming to him at the bridge, would suffer him in no case to approach in, who otherwise (as is supposed) was appointed to murder the innocent lady.

During the imprisonment of this princess one Edmund Tremaine was on the rack, and Mr Smithwike and divers other in the Tower were examined, and offers made to them to accuse the guiltless lady, being in her captivity. Howbeit no matter could be proved by all examinations, as she, lying at Woodstock, had certain intelligence by means of one John Gaier; who under colourable pretence of a letter to Mrs Cleve from her father was let in, and gave them secretly to understand of all this matter. Whereupon Lady Elizabeth, at her departing out of Woodstock, wrote these verses with her diamond in a glass window:

Much suspected by me:
Nothing proved can be.
Quoth Elizabeth, prisoner.

Thus much concerning the troubles of Lady Elizabeth at Woodstock. This is to be added, that during the same time Lord Tame had laboured to the queen, and became surety for her to have her from Woodstock to his house, and had obtained grant thereof. Preparation was made accordingly, and all things ready in expectation of her coming. But through the procurement either of Mr Benifield, or by the doing of Winchester her mortal enemy, letters came over night to the contrary; whereby her journey was stopped. Thus this worthy lady, oppressed with continual sorrow, could not be permitted to have recourse to any friends, but still in the hands of her enemies was left desolate, and destitute of all that might refresh a doleful heart, fraught full terror and thraldom. Whereupon no marvel if she, hearing upon a time out of her garden at Woodstock a milkmaid singing pleasantly, wished herself to be a milkmaid as she was; saying that her case was better, and life more merrier, than was hers.

Now to proceed further where we left before, Sir Henry Benifield and his soldiers with Lord Tame and Sir Rafe Chamberlaine guarding and waiting upon her, the first night from Woodstock she came to Ricot; in which journey such a mighty wind did blow that her servants were fain to hold down her clothes about her; insomuch that her hood was twice or thrice blown from her head. Whereupon she disirous to return to a gentleman's house there near could not be suffered by Sir Henry so to do, but was constrained under a hedge to trim her head as well as she could. The next night they journeyed to Mr Dormer's and so to Colbroke, where she lay all that night at the George, and by the way, coming to Colbroke, certain of her gentlemen and yeomen met her, to the number of threescore, much to all their comforts which had not seen her of long season before; notwithstanding they were commanded in the queen's name immediately to depart the town, to both their and her Grace's heaviness, who could not be suffered once to speak with them. That night all her men were taken from her, saving her gentleman-usher, three gentlewomen, two grooms, and one of her wardrobe, the soldiers watching about the house, and she close shut up within her prison.

The next day her Grace entered Hampton Court on the backside into the prince's lodging, the doors being shut to her; and she guarded with soldiers as before lay there a fortnight at least or ever any had recourse unto her. At length came Lord William Haward, who marvellous honourably used her Grace. Whereat she took much comfort, and requested him to be a mean that she might speak with some of the Council; to whom not long after came the Bishop of Winchester, Lord Arundel, Lord Shrewsbury, and Secretary Peter, who humbled themselves to her Grace. She likewise saluting them said, 'My Lords, I am glad to see you; for me think I have been kept a great while from you desolate alone. Wherefore I would desire you to be a mean to the King and Queen's Majesties, that I may be delivered from prison, wherein I have been kept a long space, as to you, my Lords, it is not unknown.'

When she had spoken, Gardiner kneeled down and requested that she would submit herself to the Queen's Grace, and in so doing he had no doubt but that Her Majesty would be good unto her; she making answer that rather than she would so do she would lie in prison all the days of her life, adding that she craved no mercy at Her Majesty's hand, but rather desired the law if ever she did offend Her Majesty in thought, word, or deed. 'And besides this, in yielding,' quoth she, 'I should speak against myself and confess myself to be an offender, which never was towards Her Majesty, by occasion whereof the king and the queen might ever hereafter conceive of me an evil opinion. And therefore I say, my Lords, it were better for me to lie in prison for the truth than to be abroad and suspected of my prince.' And so they departed, promising to declare her message to the queen.

On the next day the Bishop of Winchester came again unto her Grace, and kneeling down declared that the queen marvelled that she would so stoutly use herself, not confessing to have offended, so that it should seem the Queen's Majesty wrongfully to have imprisoned her Grace. 'Nay,' quoth the Lady Elizabeth, 'it please her to punish me as she thinketh good.' 'Well,' quoth Gardiner, 'her Majesty willeth me to tell you that you must tell another tale ere that you be set at liberty.' Her Grace answered that she had as lief be in prison with honesty and truth as to be abroad suspected of her Majesty; 'And this that I have said I will,' said she, 'stand unto, for I will never belie myself.' Winchester again kneeled down and said, 'Then your Grace hath the vantage of me and other the lords for your wrong and long imprisonment.' 'What vantage I have,' quoth she, 'you know; taking God to record I seek no vantage at your hands for your so dealing with me; but God forgive you and me also.' With that the rest kneeled, desiring her Grace that all might be forgotten, and so departed, she being fast locked up again.

A sevennight after the queen sent for her Grace at ten o'clock in the night to speak with her; for she had not seen her in two years before. She was amazed at the sudden sending for, thinking it had been worse than afterwards it proved, and desired her gentlemen and gentlewomen to pray for her; for she could not tell whether she should see them again. Coming in Sir Henry with Mrs Clarentius, her Grace was brought into the garden unto a stair's foot that went into the queen's lodging, her Grace's gentlewomen waiting upon her, her gentleman-usher and her grooms going before with torches; where her gentlemen and gentlewomen being commanded to stay all saving one woman,

Mrs Clarentius conducted her to the queen's bedchamber where her Majesty was. At the sight of whom her Grace kneeled down and desired God to preserve Her Majesty, not mistrusting but that she should try herself as true a subject as ever did any; and desired Her Majesty so to judge of her, and said that she should not find her to the contrary, whatsoever report had gone of her. The queen answered, 'You will not confess your offence but stand stoutly to your truth: I pray God it may so fall out.'

'If it doth not, I request neither favour nor pardon at your Majesty's hands.'

'Well, you stiffly still persever in your truth. Belike you will not confess but that you have been wrongfully punished.'

'I must not say so to you.'

'Why then, belike you will to others.'

'No, if it please your Majesty; I have borne the burden and must bear it. I humbly beseech your Majesty to have a good opinion of me, and to think me your true subject, not only from the beginning hitherto, but as long as life lasteth.'

So they departed, with very few comfortable words of the queen in English: what she said in Spanish, God knoweth. It is thought that King Philip was there behind a cloth and not seen, and that he showed himself a very friend in that matter. Thus her Grace departing went to her lodging again, and the sevennight after was released of Sir Henry her gaoler, as she termed him, and his soldiers. Her Grace being set at liberty went into the country, and had appointed to go with her Sir Thomas Pope, one of Queen Mary's Councillors, and one of her gentlemen-ushers, Mr Gage; and thus straitly was she looked to all Queen Mary's time.

Then there came to Lamheyre Mr Jerningham and Mr Norris, gentleman-usher, Queen Mary's men, who took away from her Grace Mrs Ashley to the Fleet, and three other of her gentle-women to the Tower; which was no little trouble to her Grace, saying that she thought they would fetch all away at the end. But God be praised, shortly after was fetched away Gardiner, by occasion of whose opportune decease the life of this excellent princess, the wealth of all England, was preserved. For this is to be supposed, that the wicked Gardiner had long laboured his wits and bent all his devices to bring this our dear sovereign out of the way, as both by his words and doings before notified may sufficiently appear.

After the death of Gardiner followed the death and dropping away of other her enemies, whereby by little and little her jeopardy decreased, fear diminished, and hope of comfort began to appear as out of a dark cloud; and albeit as yet her Grace had no assurance of safety, yet more gentle entertainment daily did grow unto her, till at length in the month of November and 17th day of the same, three years after the death of Gardiner, followed the death of Queen Mary, as hereafter shall be more declared. After whose decease succeeded her sister Elizabeth into the right of the crown of England; who after so long restrainment, so great dangers escaped, such blusterous storms overblown, so many injuries digested and wrongs sustained by the mighty protection of our merciful God, to our no small comfort and commodity hath been exalted and erected out of thrall to liberty, out of danger to peace and quietness, from dread to dignity, from misery to majesty, from mourning to ruling: briefly, of a prisoner made a princess and placed in her throne royal, proclaimed queen with as many glad hearts of her subjects as ever was any king or queen in this realm before her, or ever shall be, I dare say, hereafter. Touching whose flourishing state, princely reign, and peaceable government, forsomuch as the tractation hereof requireth another volume by itself, I shall defer the reader to the next section ensuing.

After these great afflictions falling upon this realm from the beginning of Queen Mary's reign, wherein so many men, women, and children were burnt, many imprisoned and in prisons starved, divers exiled, some spoiled of goods and possessions, great number driven from house and home, so many weeping eyes, so many sobbing hearts, so many children made fatherless, so many fathers bereft of their wives and children, so many vexed in conscience, and divers against conscience constrained to recant; and, in conclusion, never a good man almost in all the realm but suffered something during this bloody persecution; after all this, I say, we are come at length, the Lord be praised, to the 17th of November, which as it brought to the persecuted members of Christ rest from their careful mourning, so it easeth me somewhat of my labours in writing, by the death of Queen Mary; who, being long sick before, upon the 17th day of November in the year above said, about three or four o'clock in the morning, yielded life to nature and her kingdom to Elizabeth her sister.

Touching the manner of whose death, some say that she died of a tympany, some by her much sighing before her death supposed she died of thought and sorrow. Whereupon her Council, seeing her sighing and desirous to know the cause, to the end they might minister the more ready consolation unto her, feared as they said that she took that thought for the king her husband, which was gone from her. To whom she answering again, 'Indeed,' said she, 'that may be one cause, but that is not the greatest wound that pierceth my oppressed mind.' But what that was she would not express to them. Albeit afterward she opened the matter more plainly to Mr Rise and Mrs Clarentius, if it be true that they told me, which heard it of Mr Rise himself; who then, being most familiar with her and most bold about her, told her that they feared she took thought for King Philip's departing from her. 'Not that only,' said she; 'but when I am dead and opened, you shall find Calice lying in my heart.'

And here an end of Queen Mary; of which queen this truly may be affirmed, and left in story for a perpetual memorial or epitaph for all kings and queens that shall succeed her to be noted, that before her never was read in story of any king or queen of England since the time of King Lucius, under whom in time of peace, by hanging, heading, burning, and prisoning, so much Christian blood, so many Englishmen's lives, were spilled within this realm, as under Queen Mary for the space of four years was to be seen, and I beseech the Lord never may be seen hereafter.

The unprosperous success of Queen Mary

Now forsomuch as Queen Mary during all the time of her reign was such a vehement adversary and persecutor against the sincere professors of Christ Jesus and his gospel; for the which there be many which do highly approve her doings therein, reputing her religion to be sound and Catholic and her proceedings to be blessed of Almighty God: to the intent therefore that all may understand how the blessing of God did not only not proceed with her proceedings, but contrary how his manifest displeasure ever wrought against her in plaguing both her and her realm and in subverting all her counsels and attempts, whatsoever she took in hand, we will bestow a little time therein to survey the whole course of her doings and chievances and consider what success she had in the same. Which being well considered, we shall never find no reign of any prince in this land or any other which had ever to show in it, for the proportion of time, so many arguments of God's displeasure as was to be seen in the reign of Queen Mary, who seemed never to purpose anything that came luckily to pass, neither did anything frame to her purpose whatsoever she took in hand touching her own private affairs.

Of good kings we read in the Scripture, in showing mercy and pity, in seeking God's will in his word, and subverting the monuments of idolatry, how God blessed their ways, and prospered all their proceedings; as we see in King David, Salomon, Josaphath, Ezekias, with such other. Manasses made the streets of Hierusalem to swim with the blood of his subjects; but what came of it the text doth testify. Of Queen Elizabeth which now reigneth among us, this we must needs say which we see: that she, in sparing the blood, not only of God's servants but also of God's enemies, hath doubled now the reign of Mary her sister, with such abundance of peace and prosperity that it is hard to say whether the realm of England felt more of God's wrath in Queen Mary's time, or of God's favour and mercy in these blessed and peaceable days of Queen Elizabeth.

Gamaliell, speaking his mind in the Council of the Pharisees concerning Christ's religion, gave this reason, that if it were of God it should continue, whosoever said nay; if it were not, it could not stand. So may it be said of Queen Mary and her Romish religion; if it were so perfect and Catholic as they pretend, how cometh it that this so Catholic a queen, such a necessary pillar of the Church, continued no longer till she had utterly rooted out of the land this heretical generation? How chanced it rather that God, to spare these poor heretics, rooted out Queen Mary so soon from her throne, after she had reigned but five years and five months?

God blessed her ways and endeavours while[1] she persecuted the servants of God: when she first began to stand for the title of the crown, and yet had wrought no resistance against Christ and his gospel but had promised her faith to the Suffolk men, to maintain the religion left by King Edward her brother, so long God went with her, advanced her, and by means of the gospellers brought her to the possession of the realm. But after that she breaking her promise with God and man began to take part with Stephen Gardiner and had given over her supremacy unto the Pope, by and by God's blessing left her, neither did anything well thrive with her afterward during the whole time of her regiment.

First incontinently the fairest and greatest ship she had, called Great

[1] Reader, beware!—Ed.

Harry, was burned—such a vessel as in all these parts of Europe was not to be matched. Then would she needs bring in King Philip and by her marriage with him make the whole realm of England subject unto a stranger. And all that notwithstanding either that she did or was able to do, she could not bring to pass to set the crown of England upon his head. With King Philip also came in the pope and his popish mass; with whom also her purpose was to restore again the monks and nuns unto their places, neither lacked there all kind of attempts to the uttermost of her ability; and yet therein also God stopped her of her will, that it came not forward. After this what a dearth happened in her time here in her land! the like whereof hath not lightly in England been seen, insomuch that in sundry places her poor subjects were fain to feed off acorns for want of corn. Furthermore, where other kings are wont to be renowned by some worthy victory and prowess by them achieved, let us now see what valiant victory was gotten in this Queen Mary's days. King Edward the Sixth, her blessed brother, how many rebellions did he suppress in Devonshire, in Norfolk, in Oxfordshire, and elsewhere! What a famous victory in his time was gotten in Scotland, by the singular working of God's blessed hand rather than by any expectation of man! King Edward the Third, the eleventh king from the Conquest, by princely puissance purchased Calice unto England, which had been kept English ever since till at length came Queen Mary the eleventh likewise from the said King Edward, which lost Calice from England again; so that the winnings of this queen were very small: what the losses were let other men judge.

Hitherto the affairs of Queen Mary have had no great good success, as you have heard. But never worse success had any woman than had she in her childbirth. For seeing one of these two must needs be granted, that either she was with child or not with child: if she were with child and did travail, why was it not seen? if she were not, how was all the realm deluded? and in the meanwhile where were all the prayers, the solemn processions, the devout masses of the Catholic clergy? Why did they not prevail with God if their religion were so godly as they pretend? If their masses *ex opere operato* be able to fetch Christ from heaven and to reach down to purgatory, how chanced then they could not reach to the queen's chamber, to help her in her travail if she had been with child indeed? if not, how then came it to pass that all the Catholic Church of England did so err and was so deeply deceived?

Queen Mary after these manifold plagues and corrections, which might sufficiently admonish her of God's disfavour provoked against her, would not cease her persecution, but still continued more and more to revenge her Catholic zeal upon the Lord's faithful people, setting fire to their poor bodies by half dozens and dozens together. Whereupon God's wrathful indignation, increasing more and more against her, ceased not to touch her more near with private misfortunes and calamities. For after that he had taken from her the fruit of children, which above all things she desired, he bereft her of that which of all earthly things should have been her chief stay of honour and staff of comfort; that is, withdrew from her the affection and company even of her own husband, by whose marriage she had promised to herself whole heaps of joy and felicity; but now the omnipotent Governor of all things so turned the wheel of her own spinning against her that her high buildings of such joys and felicities came all to a castlecomedown, her hopes being confounded, her purposes disappointed, and she now brought to desolation; who seemed neither to have the favour of God, nor the hearts of her subjects, nor yet the love of her husband; who neither had fruit by him while she had him, neither could now enjoy him whom she had married, neither yet was in liberty to marry any other whom she might enjoy. Mark here, Christian reader, the woeful adversity of this queen, and learn withal what the Lord can do when man's wilfulness will needs resist him and will not be ruled.

At last, when all these fair admonitions would take no place with the queen, nor move her to revoke her bloody laws nor to stay the tyranny of her priests nor yet to spare her own subjects, but that the poor servants of God were drawn daily by heaps most pitifully as sheep to the slaughter, it so pleased the heavenly Majesty of Almighty God, when no other remedy would serve, by death to cut her off which in her life so little regarded the life of others, giving her throne, which she abused to the destruction of Christ's church and people, to another who more temperately and quietly could guide the same, after she had reigned five years and five months. The shortness of which reign unneth we find in any other king or queen, since the Conquest or before, save only in King Richard the Third.

The punishment of God upon the persecutors of his people

Leaving now Queen Mary I come to them which under her were the chief ministers and doers in this persecution, the bishops and priests to whom Queen Mary gave all the execution of her power, as did Queen

Alexandra to the Pharisees after the time of the Machabees. Of whom Josephus thus writeth:[1] *Ipsa solum nomen regium ferebat, caeterum omnem regni potestatem Pharisaei possidebant*; 'She only retained to herself the name and title of the kingdom, but all her power she gave to the Pharisees to possess.' Touching which prelates and priests here is to be noted in like sort the wonderful providence of God, which as he abridged the reign of their queen, so he suffered them not to escape unvisited; beginning with Stephen Gardiner the archpersecutor, whom he took away about the midst of the queen's reign. Of whose poisoned life and stinking end sufficient hath been touched before. After him dropped other away also, some before the death of Queen Mary and some after; as Morgan Bishop of St David's, who, sitting upon the condemnation of the blessed martyr Bishop Farrar and unjustly usurping his room, not long after was stricken after such a strange sort that his meat would not go down but rise and pick up again, sometimes at his mouth, sometimes blown out at his nose most horrible to behold and so he continued till his death. Note moreover that when Mr Leyson, sheriff at Farrar's burning, had fet away the cattle of the bishop from his servant's house called Mathew Harbottell into his own ground, divers of them would never eat meat but lay bellowing and roaring and so died. This Bishop Morgan bringeth me also in remembrance of Justice Morgan, who sat upon the death of Lady Jane and not long after fell mad and was bereft of his wits, and so died, having ever in his mouth, 'Lady Jane, Lady Jane.'

Before the death of Queen Mary died Dr Dunning, the bloody Chancellor of Norwich, who after he had most rigorously condemned and murdered so many faithful saints of the Lord continued not long himself, but in the midst of his rage died in Lincolnshire, being suddenly taken as some say sitting in his chair. Sudden death fell also upon Berry, commissary in Norfolk, who, as is showed in the story of Thomas Hudson, four days after Queen Mary's death, when he had made a great feast and had one of his concubines there, coming home from the church after evensong, where he had ministered baptism the same time, suddenly fell to the ground with a heavy groan and never stirred after, neither showed any one token of repentance.

What a stroke of God's hand was brought upon the cruel persecutor Bishop Thornton, suffragan of Dover, who after he had exercised his cruel tyranny upon so many godly men at Canturbury, at length

[1] De Antiquit. lib. 13

cometh upon a Saturday from the chapterhouse at Canturbury to Borne, and there upon Sunday following looking upon his men playing at the bowls fell suddenly in a palsy, and so had to bed was willed to remember God: 'Yea, so I do,' said he, 'and my Lord Cardinal too.' After him succeeded another bishop or suffragan ordained by the foresaid cardinal. It is reported that he had been suffragan before to Boner; who not long after was made Bishop or Suffragan of Dover, brake his neck, falling down a pair of stairs in the cardinal's chamber at Greenwich, as he had received the cardinal's blessing.

Not long before the death of Queen Mary died Dr Capon Bishop of Salisbury. About the which time also followed the unprepared death of Dr Geffrey, Chancellor of Salisbury, who, in the midst of his buildings being suddenly taken by the mighty hand of God, yielded his life, which had so little pity of other men's lives before. Here is to be noted that he departing upon a Saturday, the next day before the same he had appointed to call before him ninety persons to examine them by inquisition, had not the goodness of the Lord thus prevented him with death, providing for his poor servants in time.

And now to come from priests to laymen, we have to find in them also no less terrible demonstration of God's heavy judgment upon such as had been vexers and persecutors of his people.

In the story of Mr Bradford mention was made of Mr Woodrofe, who being then sheriff used much to rejoice at the death of the poor saints of Christ, and so hard he was in his office that when Mr Rogers was in the cart going toward Smithfield, and in the way his children were brought unto him, the people making a lane for them to come, Mr Woodrofe bade the carman's head should be broken for staying his cart. But what happened? He was not come out of his office the space of a week but he was stricken by the sudden hand of God, the one half of his body, in such sort that he lay benumbed and bedridden, not able to move himself but as he was lifted of others; and so continued in that infirmity seven or eight years till his dying day.

Of James Abbes, martyr, ye heard before. In the time of whose martyrdom what befel upon a wicked railer against him now you shall understand; whereby all such railing persecutors may learn to fear God's hand and to take heed what they speak against his servants. As Abbes was led by the sheriff toward his execution, divers people stood in the way and asked their alms. He, having no money to give them, and desirous yet to distribute something amongst them, did pull off all his apparel save his shirt and gave the same unto them, to some one thing, to some another; in the giving whereof he exhorted them to be strong in the Lord, and as faithful followers of Christ to stand steadfast unto the truth of the gospel, which he through God's help would in their sight seal with his blood. Whiles he was thus charitably occupied and zealously instructing the people, a servant of the sheriff's going by and hearing him cried out aloud unto them and blasphemously said, 'Believe him not, good people: he is an heretic and a madman, out of his wit: believe him not.' And as the other continued in his godly admonitions, so did this wicked wretch still blow forth his blasphemous exclamations until they came unto the stake where he should suffer; unto the which this constant martyr was tied, and in the end cruelly burnt, as in his story is already declared. But immediately after the fire was put unto him, such was the fearful stroke of God's justice upon this blasphemous railer that he was there presently in the sight of all the people stricken with a frenzy, wherewith he had charged that good martyr; who in this furious rage and madness casting off his shoes with all the rest of his clothes cried out unto the people, 'Thus did James Abbes, that true servant of God, who is saved; but I am damned.' And thus ran he round about the town of Bury, still crying out that Abbes was a good man and saved; but he was damned.

The sheriff, amazed, caused him to be taken and tied in a dark house, and by force compelled him again to put on his clothes, thinking thereby within a while to bring him to some quietness. But he, as soon as they were gone, continued his former raging, and casting off his clothes cried as he did before, 'James Abbes is the servant of God and is saved; but I am damned.' At length he was tied in a cart and brought home unto his master's house, and within half a year or thereabouts, he being at the point of death, the priest of the parish was sent for; who coming unto him brought with him the crucifix and their houseling host of the altar; which gear when the poor wretch saw, he cried out of the priest and defied all that baggage, saying that the priest with such other as he was were the cause of his damnation, and that James Abbes was a good man and saved. And so shortly after he died.

Clarke, an open enemy to the gospel in King Edward's days, hanged himself in the Tower of London. The notable Papist called Trolling Smith of late fell down suddenly in the street and died. Dale the promoter was eaten into his body with lice and so died, as is well known of many and confessed also by his fellow John Avales before credible witness. Coxe, an earnest Protestant in King Edward's days and in Queen Mary's time a Papist and a promoter, going well and in health to bed was dead before the morning. Testified by divers of the neighbours.

Alexander the keeper of Newgate, a cruel enemy of those that lay there for religion, died very miserably, being so swollen that he was more like a monster than a man, and so rotten within that no man could abide the smell of him. This cruel wretch, to hasten the poor lambs to the slaughter, would go to Boner, Story, Cholmley, and other, crying out, 'Rid my prison, rid my prison. I am too much pestered with these heretics.' The son of Alexander, called James, having left unto him by his father great substance, within three years wasted all to nought; and when some marvelled how he spent those goods so fast, 'Oh,' said he, 'evil gotten, evil spent'; and shortly after as he went in Newgate market fell down suddenly, and there wretchedly died. John Peter, son-in-law to this Alexander, and a horrible blasphemer of God, and no less cruel to the prisoners, rotted away and so most miserably died; who commonly when he would affirm anything, were it true or false, used to say, 'If it be not true, I pray God I rot ere I die.' Witness the printer hereof with divers others.

With these I might infer the death of Robert Baulding, stricken with lightning at the taking of William Seaman, whereupon he pined away and died; the story of which William Seaman see before. Likewise the wretched end of Beard the promoter. Pavier or Pavy, Town Clerk of London and a bitter enemy to the gospel, hanged himself.

John Fisher Bishop of Rochester and Sir Thomas More, in King Henry's time, after they had brought Frith, Bayfield, and Bainham, and divers others to their death, what great reward won they thereby with Almighty God? Did not the sword of God's vengeance light upon their own necks shortly after, and they themselves made a public spectacle at the Tower Hill of bloody death, which before had no compassion of the lives of others? Thus ye see the saying of the Lord to be true, 'He that smiteth with the sword shall perish with the sword.' So did Antiochus, Herod, Julian, Valerianus the emperor, Decius, Maxentius, with infinite others, after they had exercised their cruelty upon God's people, feel the like striking hand of God themselves also in revenging the blood of his servants.

And thus much concerning those persecutors which were stricken and died before the death of Queen Mary. With whom also are to be numbered in the race of persecuting bishops which died before Queen Mary these bishops following—Coates, Bishop of Westchester; Parfew, Bishop of Hereford; Glyn, Bishop of Bangor; Brookes, Bishop of Gloucester; King, Bishop of Tame; Peto, elect of Salisbury; Day, Bishop of Chichester; Holyman, Bishop of Bristow. After the queen immediately followed, or rather waited upon her, the death of Cardinal Poole, who the next day departed; of what disease although it be uncertain to many, yet by some it is suspected that he took some Italian physic which did him no good. Then followed these bishops in order—John Christopherson, Bishop of Chichester; Hopton, Bishop of Norwich; Morgan, Bishop of St David's; John White, Bishop of Winchester; Rafe Bane, Bishop of Lichfield and Coventry; Owen Oglethorpe, Bishop of Carlile; Cutbert Tonstall, Bishop of Durham; Thomas Rainolds, elect of Hereford. Besides these bishops above named, first died at the same time Dr Weston, Dean of Westminster, chief disputer against Cranmer, Ridley and Latimer; Mr Slethurst, Master of Trinity College in Oxford; Seth Holland, Dean of Worcester and Warden of All Soul College; William Copinger, who bare the Great Seal before Gardiner, made himself monk in the house of Westminster, and shortly after fell mad, and died in the Tower; Dr Steward, Dean of Winchester.

To behold the working of God's judgments, it is wondrous. When the disputation was in Oxford against Dr Cranmer, Ridley and Latimer, he that had seen then Dr Weston the prolocutor in his ruff, how highly he took upon him in the Schools, and how stoutly he stood in the Pope's quarrel against simple and naked truth, full little would have thought that his glory and lofty looks should have been brought down so soon by them of his own religion, whose part he so doughtily defended. But not long after the disputation God so wrought against Dr Weston that he fell in great displeasure with Cardinal Poole and other bishops, because he was unwilling to give up his deanery and house of Westminster unto the monks, whom indeed he favoured not although in other things he favoured the Church of Rome; who notwithstanding at last through importunate suit gave up Westminster and was Dean of Windsor; where not long after he was apprehended in adultery and for the same was by the cardinal put from all his spiritual livings. Wherefore he appealed to Rome and purposed to have fled out of the realm, but was taken by the way and committed to the Tower of London; and there remained until Queen Elizabeth was proclaimed queen, at which time he being delivered fell sick and died. The common talk was that if he had not so suddenly ended his life he would have revealed the purpose of the chief of the clergy (meaning the cardinal) which was to have taken up King Henry's body at Windsor and to have burned it.

The residue that remained of the persecuting clergy and escaped the stroke of death were deprived and committed to prisons; the catalogue of whose names here followeth—In the Tower: Nicholas Heath, Archbishop of York and Lord Chancellor; Thomas Thurlby, Bishop of Ely; Thomas Watson, Bishop of Lincoln; Gilbert Bourne, Bishop of Bath and Wells; Richard Pates, Bishop of Worcester; Troublefield, Bishop of Exeter; John Fecknam, Abbot of Westminster; John Boxall, Dean of Windsor and Peterborough.

Ran away: Goldwell, Bishop of St Asse; Maurice, elect of Bangor.

Edmund Boner, Bishop of London, in the Marshalsea; Thomas Wood, bishop elect, in the Marshalsea; Cutbert Scott, Bishop of Chester, was in the Fleet, from whence he escaped to Lovaine, and there died.

In the Fleet: Henry Cole, Dean of Paul's; John Harpsfield, Archdeacon of London and Dean of Norwich; Nicholas Harpsfield, Archdeacon of Canturbury; Anthony Draycot, Archdeacon of Huntington; William Chadsey, Archdeacon of Middlesex.

Edmund Boner, commonly called the bloody Bishop of London, after he had long feasted and banqueted in durance at the Marshalsea, died in his bed unrepentant. Yet was it so provided by God that as he had been a persecutor of the light and a child of darkness, so his carcase was tumbled into the earth in obscure darkness at midnight, contrary to the order of all other Christians; and as he had been a murderer, so was he laid among thieves and murderers, a place by God's judgment rightly appointed for him.

And now to re-enter again into the story of Queen Elizabeth where we left before. In whose advancement and this her princely governance, it cannot sufficiently be expressed what blessed happiness this realm hath received in receiving her at the Lord's gracious hand. For as there have been divers kings and rulers over this realm, and I have read of some, yet I could never find in English chronicle the like that may be written of this our noble and worthy queen, whose coming in not only was so calm, so joyful, and so peaceable, without shedding of any blood, but also her reign hitherto (reigning now twenty-four years and more) hath been so quiet that to this present day her sword is a virgin spotted and polluted with no drop of blood. In speaking whereof I take not upon me the part of the moral or divine philosopher, to judge of things done, but only keep me within the compass of an historiographer, declaring what hath been before and comparing things done with things now present, the like whereof, as I said, is not lightly to be found in chronicles before. And this as I speak truly, so I would to be taken without flattery, to be left to our posterity *ad sempiternam clementiae illius memoriam*. In commendation of which her clemency I might add here how mildly her Grace, after she was advanced to her kingdom, did forgive Sir Henry Benifield, without molestation suffering him to enjoy goods, life, lands, and liberty. But I let that pass.

And here also I let pass the coronation of our noble and Christian princess and the order of the same, which was the 15th of January 1559. To pass over also the triumphant passage and honourable entertainment of our most dread sovereign through the City of London, with such celebrity, prayers, wishes, welcomings, cries, tender words, pageants, interludes, declamations, and verses set up, as the like hath not commonly been seen, arguing and declaring a wonderful earnest affection of loving hearts towards their sovereign. Item, to pretermit in silence the letters gratulatory sent to her Majesty from divers and sundry foreign places, as from Zurick, Geneva, Basil, Berne, Wittemberg, Argentine, Frankford, etc. These I with many other things let pass.

THE CONCLUSION OF THE WORK

And thus to conclude, good Christian reader, this present tractation, not for lack of matter but to shorten rather the matter for largeness of the volume, I here stay for this present time with further addition of more discourse either to overweary thee with longer tediousness, or overcharge the book with longer prolixity; having hitherto set forth the acts and proceedings of the whole Church of Christ, namely of the Church of England, although not in such particular perfection that nothing hath overpast us; yet in such general sufficiency that I trust not very much hath escaped us, necessary to be known, touching the principal affairs, doings, and proceedings of the Church and churchmen. Wherein may be seen the whole state, order, descent, course, and continuance of the same, the increase and decrease of true religion, the creeping in of superstition, the horrible troubles of persecution, the wonderful assistance of the Almighty in maintaining his truth, the glorious constancy of Christ's martyrs, the rage of the enemies, the alteration of times, the travails and troubles of the Church, from the first primitive age of Christ's gospel to the end of Queen Mary and the beginning of this our gracious Queen Elizabeth. During the time of her happy reign, which hath hitherto continued (through the gracious protection of the Lord) the space now of twenty four years, as my wish is, so I would be glad the good will of the Lord were so, that no more matter of such lamentable stories may ever be offered hereafter to write upon. But so it is, I cannot tell how, the elder the world waxeth, the longer it continueth, the nearer it hasteneth to his end, the more Satan rageth, giving still new matter of writing books and volumes; insomuch that if all were recorded and committed to history, that within the said compass of this queen's reign hitherto hath happened in Scotland, Flanders, France, Spain, Germany, besides this our own country of England and Ireland, with other countries moe, I verily suppose one Eusebius, or Polyhistor which Pliny writeth of, would not suffice thereunto.

But of these incidents and occurrents hereafter more, as it shall please the Lord to give grace and space. In the meantime, the grace of the Lord Jesus work with thee, gentle reader, in all thy studious readings. And while thou hast space, so employ thyself to read that by reading thou mayest learn daily to know that may profit thy soul, may teach thee experience, may arm thee with patience, and instruct thee in all spiritual knowledge more and more, to thy perpetual comfort and salvation in Christ Jesu our Lord; to whom be all glory *in secula seculorum*. Amen.

FINIS

GLOSSARY

IMPORTANT: Words most likely to be misunderstood are printed in SMALL CAPITALS

abearing: behaviour
ABROAD: away from home
accidents: non-essential qualities, material attributes
actuary: recorder of court proceedings
admiration: astonishment
advertise: urge
advoutry: adultery
after: afterwards
afterclaps: unpleasant consequences
ale-brew: bread, sugar, and spice boiled in ale
all to: actually
allege: assert
altogether: all together
amaze: dumbfound
amice: linen vestment
amner: almoner
answerer: defendant
antics: tricks, grotesque figures
apert: open
apostle: *see* dimissorial
apparent: unmistakable
appellation: appeal
apply: study
apposed of: confronted with
approve: prove
argument: indication
as: as soon as
as well . . . as: both . . . and
assoil: solve, absolve, rebuff
avoid: go away, excrete

bailey errant: sheriff's officer
baiting place: place where animals were tormented
ballet: ballad
battle: armed force
bill: document, long-handled axe
blasphemous: abusive
book: copy
brabling: wrangling
brag: proudly
braid: assault
brickle: brittle
bruited: noised
buskle: bustle, prepare
BY: against
BY AND BY: immediately
by that: by the time that
by the way: en route

carceral: in a gaol
careful: anxious
carriage: baggage
carry: conduct
castlecomedown: complete collapse
catchpole: bailiff's officer
cautel: stratagem, cunning, caution
cavillation: frivolous objection
certes: certainly
chafe: rage
chievance: achievement
civilian: professor of civil law
CLERK: learned man, cleric
close: secret
coact: compel
collation: short sermon

comfort: strength, strengthen
commissary: chancellor
commodity: advantage
compatient: sympathetic
con: learn by heart
conduct: college chaplain
conspire: agree
constant: patient
contentation: contenting, contentment
CONTINUE: adjourn
contrary: contradict, oppose
CONVENIENT: proper, desirable, suitable
CONVERSATION: manner of life
CONVINCE: convict
counter: law-court, prison
COUNTRY: district
courage: initiative
covent: assembly, congregation
croysie: levy
cry: shout

DARE SAY: be certain
decay: ruin, remains; (verb) damage
delude: defraud, mock, elude, frustrate
denounce: announce
detract: malign
dial: clock, watch
dimissorial: short statement of a case sent to court of appeal
dimitted: dismissed
dirige: matins of the dead
discourse: course of life
discover: reveal
discuss: judge
distain: dye, defile, dim
doctors: early Fathers
Dolphin: Dauphin
DOUBT: fear
doubtless: undoubtedly
draff: chaff
drop vie: wager
Dutch: Flemish, German

enmious: hostile
entreat: treat
ewery: room for ewers and towels
excerp: pick out
experiment: proof
eyne: eyes

fact: deed
fantasy (noun and verb): fancy
FATHER: old man
fautor: abettor
feared: frightened
fet: fetch, fetched
fetch a compass: make a detour
fetches: tricks
flirt: strike
foins: polecat fur
folded: matted
fond: foolish
forbar: obstruct, shut out
forshield: forbid
forslack: neglect, be negligent
frequent: thronging
frit: stock
from: away from
frowes (= frounce?): ruff

gainstand: withstand
Gang Monday: Monday before Ascension
gardeviance: outfit
gaud: bauble
glaive: lance
glavering: flattering
gloze: comment, flatter, pretend
groundsel: threshold
grudge: hostility, be hostile

halberd: combined spear and battle-axe
harborous: hospitable
harish: like a mad hare
harness: armour
harquebusiers: musketeers
HAVE TO: be able to
HIS: its
honest: respectable
house: college, monastery
HURRY: tumult
hypocras: spiced wine

IMBECILITY: weakness
immanity: atrocious savagery
imp: lad
improve: disprove
incontinent(ly): immediately
indifferent: fair
indurance: imprisonment
infer: introduce, mention
inquest: jury
instantly: vehemently
instrument: document, record
intermeddle: intermix
inveigh: attack

jolly: arrogant
journey: a day's doings
jurat: Channel Island magistrate

LET: hinder, hesitate
letters: a letter
lewd: ignorant, vulgar, evil
lightly: commonly, easily
Limbo: prison
list: desire
lively: living
lordship: estate, manor
lusty: merry

macerate: starve
manchet: small loaf
mansuetude: gentleness
maugre: despite
maumetry: image-worship
mean: (noun) go-between; (adjective) humble, low
meat: food
merry: cheerful
mess: group dining together
milner: miller
miser: wretch
moe: more
monument: record
mortuary: gift claimed by incumbent from dead parishioner's estate
move: induce, anger
mute: mutter
mystery: craft, occupation

NAMELY: especially
naughty: wicked
nasturtium: watercress
ne, ne: neither, nor
neatherd: cowman
next: nearest
no doubt: undoubtedly
notary: *see* actuary
nott: shear

object: allege, present, adduce
of: by, from
once: some day
or, or ever: before
order: deal with, manage
ordinary: diocesan bishop, daily fare
original: beginning
ought: owed
outscape: escape

packing: plotting
pain: trouble

palsgrave: count palatine, palace superintendent
parcel: portion
partially: like a partisan
pash: strike
paste: ornamental border of headdress mounted on pasteboard
percase: perchance
petticoat: under-jacket
pillar: whipping-post
pinfold: place of confinement
polling: extortion
portuaries, portues: breviaries
portused: canonized
postil: comment
posy: short quotation
power: army
premises: statements already made
premonition: warning
PRESENTLY: immediately
PREVENT: forestall
prince: king, queen
probations: proofs
proctor: proxy, advocate
PROLONG: postpone
promoter: informer
PROTRACT: postpone
puissance: power
pursuer: persecutor

quarrel: argument
quest: jury
quiddity: subtlety
quirk: quibble

rabbin: learned person
rase: root
recite: read aloud
reclaim: claim
refricate: reopen
refuse: object
regiment: governance
register: register, registrar
relation: bidding-prayer
replication duplic: counter-arguments
restrain: deprive
right: straight, erect
rip up: tear open, make known
rochet: bishop's surplice
room: place
rub out: manage, keep going
ruddish: ruddy
ruffle: make a commotion

salt-house: salt store
secret: private
semblable: similar
sentence: opinion
several: separate
shift: reclothe
shog: shake
should be: was
should say: said, had said
shroud: garment
side: partisan group
SILLY: simple
simplicity: honesty, trustfulness
sithence: since
syze: assize
sleightly: cleverly, cunningly
slipt: disregarded
slubber up: concoct
snuffing: contemptuous
so: so long as
sort: set, way
spiritual: in holy orders
stand upon: be on the verge of
starken: stiffen
stocks and stones: images of wood and stone
stout: strong, active
strait: narrow, strict
stranger: foreigner
subamner: subalmoner

subordinate: suborn
sudden: not prepared for
sumner: summoner
swinge: sway
swingle: striking part
swound: swoon
sycophant: cynic, sceptical critic

take: hand over
take advice: give advice
take one's original: make a beginning
take orders: give orders
take thought: worry oneself
tall: impulsive, valiant
tell: count
that: so that, that which
thinketh: seems, seems good
TICKLE: infuriate
tippet: something worn round the neck
tipstaff: staff with metal tip
touch: mention, wound
tractation: account, handling, carrying out
trade: manner (of life)
trecenary: mass of 300 days
trental: mass of 30 days
trial: vindication
truss: close-fitting jacket
try: vindicate
tutor: governor
tympany: hard swelling in the womb

unbolted: unsifted, untested
understand: ascertain
unneth: scarcely
unwieldy: unable
utter: outer

vail: doff
vie: *see* drop
vizor: features, mask
void: flee from
voyage: journey

wainables: agricultural land
warrant: authority
waster: cudgel
whether: which of two
WHILE: until
will: instruct
wit: intelligence
would: willed, instructed
would he or nild he: willy-nilly

INDEX OF PLACES

(Modern spelling in brackets)

INDEX OF PERSONS